Public Prosecutors in the United States and Europe

Gwladys Gilliéron

Public Prosecutors in the United States and Europe

A Comparative Analysis with Special Focus on Switzerland, France, and Germany

Springer

Gwladys Gilliéron
Rechtswissenschaftliche Fakultät
Universitäre Fernstudien Schweiz
Brig, Switzerland

Habilitation Thesis of the Faculty of Law of the University of Zurich 2013

ISBN 978-3-319-04503-0 ISBN 978-3-319-04504-7 (eBook)
DOI 10.1007/978-3-319-04504-7
Springer Cham Heidelberg New York Dordrecht London

Library of Congress Control Number: 2014936853

Printed on acid-free paper

Springer is part of Springer Science+Business Media (www.springer.com)

C'est une expérience éternelle, que tout homme qui a du pouvoir est porté à en abuser; il va jusqu'à ce qu'il trouve des limites. [...] *Pour qu'on ne puisse abuser du pouvoir, il faut que par la disposition des choses, le pouvoir arrête le pouvoir.*
Montesquieu, De l'esprit des lois (1748)

Preface and Acknowledgements

This monograph is devoted to enriching the understanding of European and American prosecutors and to furthering the comparative dialogue on the prosecutorial function. Prosecutors, whose traditional legal duty lies in determining whether or not a criminal case should enter the criminal justice process, turn out to be the centerpiece of the process. This key position of the prosecutor in the criminal justice system is strengthened by the fact that in some instances, he acts as the sole adjudicator of the criminal case. The practice of plea bargaining in the United States and the penal order procedure in Europe best illustrate the power of the de facto adjudication of prosecutors. Plea proposals are only rarely rejected by the judge. The same is true for penal orders in those criminal justice systems where the approval of the court is required. The Swiss penal order, for its part, is an excellent example of a de jure power of the prosecutor to adjudicate cases. In the last years, some criminal justice systems in Europe have undergone a clear change by introducing the possibility of informal negotiations between the prosecution and the defense; this is in response to the pressure for greater efficiency in criminal justice systems. Thus, several continental European jurisdictions have adopted adversarial elements. It follows that the European prosecutor has become more like his American counterpart than inversely. Given the broad power of American and European prosecutors, it is essential that they exercise this power in the most responsible fashion. However, since there is an unavoidable risk that prosecutors abuse this power, every criminal justice system should have a system that holds prosecutors accountable.

This research provides a comparative analysis of the prosecution service in Switzerland and in the United States and is completed by an overview of the prosecution institutions in France and Germany. The position, powers, and accountability of public prosecutors are examined within their respective judicial systems. Several factors influenced my decision to analyze public prosecution services in Switzerland, the United States, Germany, and France. In recent years, significant changes in criminal procedure and in public prosecution have occurred in many parts of the world, including Switzerland, as a result of rationalization of criminal justice systems. On January 1, 2011, the first Swiss Criminal Procedure Code came into force and replaced the 26 cantonal criminal procedure codes and the Federal Act on the Administration of Federal Criminal Justice. Prior to 2011, the inquiry models could basically be differentiated between those cantons following the system of an investigating judge, inspired by the French legal system and those that have adopted the German system of the prosecutor with one or more district prosecutors. The unified Swiss Code of Criminal Procedure has opted for the German system and thus the examining magistrate, previously known in some cantons, has been abolished. In contrast to other European criminal justice systems, the Swiss legal system is only rarely considered in comparative research. This contribution closes that gap. Because the Swiss legal system was influenced by the French and German criminal justice systems, this research could not have been done without taking a look at the evolution and current situation of the prosecutorial role in those countries. The increasing workload of criminal justice systems will make prosecutorial discretion more and more of a necessity. However, before modifying a current system, it is important to know all the advantages and disadvantages related to a prosecutor having broad discretionary power. Absolute prosecutorial discretionary power having a long history in the U.S. system, it was an obvious choice to include American prosecutors in this research. Comparison of different legal and prosecutorial systems aims to improve the systems currently in place.

This research has been accepted as habilitation thesis by the Faculty of Law of the University of Zurich in March 2013 under a slightly different title. For the present publication, the original presentation of the manuscript has been adapted to meet the publisher's guidelines.

This book could not have been written without the help and support of a number of people and institutions. First of all, I would like to express my sincere gratitude to Prof. Dr. Martin Killias for his advice, guidance, and encouragement throughout the course of this work. I am grateful to the Max Planck Institute for Foreign and International Criminal Law in Freiburg im Breisgau, in particular Prof. Dr. Dr. h.c. Hans-Jörg Albrecht, for the hospitality and excellent working environment. I also want to thank the Institute on Crime and Public Policy at the University of Minnesota, in particular Prof. Michael Tonry, for hosting me. For their advice and support, I thank Prof. Richard S. Frase and Prof. Kevin R. Reitz. I especially want to thank Robert M.A. Johnson, former County Attorney in Anoka, Minnesota, as well as Bryan Lindberg and Paul Young, for all the interesting and informative discussions on the position of the public prosecutor in the United States, for providing useful materials, and for having given me the opportunity to gain insight into the daily work of prosecutors. Thanks are due to Patrick Diamond, Jennifer M. Inz, Marlene Senechal, Paul Scoggin, John Sommerville, Lolita Ulloa, and Susan E. Gärtner for their helpful discussions. I would like to express further greatest thanks to Effie Saxe, Kathy Holland, Mary Kiley, Jill Gerber, Jodie Wierimaa, and Mary Podkopacz for giving me the necessary statistical data. I am grateful to Dr. Andreas Brunner, Alberto Fabbri, Dr. Ursula Frauenfelder Nohl, Jürg Vollenweider, Christian Triet, and Helena Götte-Kreyenbühl for answering my questions and for providing all requested documents necessary to enhance the quality of the Swiss part of this research. I want to express my sincere gratitude to Oliv Brunner and Dr. Andreas Galli for their careful reading of the book and for their helpful comments. I would like to thank Zhao Shuhong for his assistance in the last phase of the work and Ulrike Anderson for the excellent proofreading. I want to thank the Swiss National Science Foundation for the generous fellowship that made the research for this book possible. I am very grateful to my sister, my brother, and closest friends, whose friendship and support means a lot to me. Finally, my parents have my deepest thanks.

Riehen
November 2013

Gwladys Gilliéron

Abbreviations

ABA	American Bar Association
ABA Pleas of Guilty	ABA Standards Relating to Pleas of Guilty (3rd edn 1999)
ABA Prosecutorial Investigations Standard	ABA Standards for Criminal Justice Relating to Prosecutorial Investigations (2008)
ABA Prosecution Standard	ABA Standards for Criminal Justice: Prosecution Function and Defense Function (3rd edn 1993)
AB N	Amtliches Bulletin Nationalrat [Official Bulletin of the National Council]
AB S	Amtliches Bulletin Ständerat [Official Bulletin of the Council of States]
AG	Aargau [Swiss canton]
AI	Appenzell Inner Rhodes [Swiss canton]
AR	Appenzell Outer Rhodes [Swiss canton]
Art.	Article
BE	Berne [Swiss canton]
BGE	Bundesgerichtsentscheid [Decision of the Federal Court]
BGHSt	Bundesgerichtshof in Strafsachen [Federal Supreme Court]
BL	Basel-Land [Swiss canton]
BS	Basel-City [Swiss canton]
BSK	Basler Kommentar
[canton]-COA	Cantonal Court Organization Act [Kantonales Gerichtsorganisationsgesetz]
[canton]-Courts Act	Cantonal Courts Act [Kantonales Justizgesetz]
[canton]-Law on Courts	Cantonal Law on Courts [Kantonales Gerichtsgesetz]
CCC	Constitutio Criminalis Carolina
CCrP	Swiss Criminal Procedure Code [Schweizerisches Strafprozessrecht StPO]

CDAA Association	California District Attorneys Association
CFR	Code of Federal Regulations
CHF	Swiss Franc
Chap./Chaps.	Chapter/s
CIC	*Code d'Instruction Criminelle* [Code of Criminal Instruction]
CISA	Convention Implementing the Schengen Agreement
cmt.	Commentary
COA	Court Organization Act
DCC	German Criminal Code
D-CCP	German Criminal Code of Procedure
DOJ	Department of Justice
ECHR	European Convention on Human Rights
e.g.	*exempli gratia*, for example
EG StPO [canton]	Cantonal Implementation Law of the Swiss Code of Criminal Procedure [kantonales Einführungsgesetz zur Schweizerischen Strafprozessordnung]
et al.	*et alii* or *et alia*, and others
etc.	*et cetera*, and so forth
et seq.	*et sequentes*, and the following
FBI	Federal Bureau of Investigation
FCC	French Criminal Code
F-CCP	French Code of Criminal Procedure
FR	Fribourg [Swiss canton]
FRCrP	Federal Rules of Criminal Procedure
FSCA	Federal Supreme Court Act [Bundesgerichtsgesetz BGG]
GE	Geneva [Swiss canton]
GL	Glarus [Swiss canton]
GR	Grisons [Swiss canton]
IAP	International Association of Prosecutor
IAPS	IAP Standards of Professional Responsibility and Statement of the Essential Duties and Rights of Prosecutors (1999)
ICCPR	International Covenant on Civil and Political Rights
i.e.	*id est*, that is
JU	Jura [Swiss canton]
KK	Karlsruher Kommentar
let.	letter
LU	Lucerne [canton]
Minn. Stat.	Minnesota Statutes (2010)
MN	Minnesota [state]
NDAA	National District Attorneys Association
NDAA Standards	National Prosecution Standards (3rd edn 2009)

NE	Neuchâtel [Swiss canton]
No.	Number [Ziffer]
NW	Nidwalden [Swiss canton]
OHG-Kommentar	Kommentar zum Opferhilfegesetz
OW	Obwalden [Swiss canton]
para.	Paragraph [Absatz]
R.	Rule
RCW	State of Washington Criminal Code
SCC	Swiss Criminal Code [Schweizerisches Strafgesetzbuch StGB]
SG	St. Gallen [Swiss canton]
SH	Schaffhausen [Swiss canton]
SO	Solothurn [Swiss canton]
SR	Systematische Rechtssammlung [Classified Compilation of Federal Legislation]
subs.	Subsection
s.v.	*sub verbo*, *sub voce*, under the word
SZ	Schwyz [Swiss canton]
TG	Thurgau [Swiss canton]
TI	Ticino [Swiss canton]
UR	Uri [Swiss canton]
U.S.	United States
USAM	United States Attorneys' Manual (1997)
U.S. attorney	United States attorney
USC	Code of Laws of the United States of America
USCA	United States Code Annotated (2010)
USSG	Federal Sentencing Guidelines (2012)
VCA	Victims of Crime Act [Opferhilfegesetz OHG]
VD	Vaud [Swiss canton]
VS	Valais [Swiss canton]
VSKC	Vereinigung der Schweizerischen Kriminal-polizeichefs
WOSTA	Guidelines of the Senior Public Prosecutor's Office of Zurich on the Preliminary Investigation [Weisungen der Zürcher Oberstaatsanwaltschaft für das Vorverfahren] (2012)
ZG	Zug [Swiss canton]
ZU	Zurich [Swiss canton]
§/§§	Section/sections

Contents

List of Figures

List of Tables

Chapter 1
Aim, Approach, and Methodology of the Study

1.1 Introduction

Public prosecutors have become of decisive importance due to the overloading of criminal justice systems. In fact, now prosecutors are responsible for making crucial decisions and in some cases—what was previously the responsibility of judges—even case-concluding decisions. The work of prosecutors is of significant importance in the way criminal proceedings are dealt with. This, in turn, can have an impact on the position of the individual in the criminal process and the fundamental principles of the states. By means of comparative analysis, lessons about the most effective practice for prosecutors can be identified.

Today, the comparative dialogue on the prosecutorial function is extremely topical on both sides of the Atlantic. Recently, a study that compares the powerful role of the American prosecutor with the role of European prosecutors has demonstrated that valuable lessons can be learned from a transnational examination of prosecutorial authority.[1] Another study funded by the Open Society Institute, Sofia, and Open Society Justice Initiative, New York has examined the prosecution services in nine countries[2] with a focus on prosecutorial accountability and independence with the purpose of enriching national debates in countries where the prosecution needs to be reformed.[3] The most recent and comprehensive study examining prosecution services across Europe was first published in 2006.[4] An extended follow-up version of this study was subsequently published in 2008 in a double issue of the European Journal on Crime and Criminal Policy Research.[5] This

[1] Luna and Wade (2012).

[2] Bulgaria, Chile, England and Wales, France, Germany, Hungary, Italy, South Africa, United States.

[3] Open Society Institute Sofia (2008).

[4] Jehle and Wade (2006).

[5] Wade and Jehle (2008).

G. Gilliéron, *Public Prosecutors in the United States and Europe*,

DOI 10.1007/978-3-319-04504-7_1,

research describes the results of an 11-nation study[6] of how criminal justice systems have reacted to high crime rates. This study was the first to reveal the strong shift in power toward prosecutorial decision-making in the criminal process in Europe. Prior to this study, the few comparative studies on the public prosecution service generally fell short of explaining working practice, and statistical data were only rarely considered.[7]

In contrast to other European criminal justice systems, the Swiss legal system has only rarely been considered in comparative research. This may be due to the fact that, until 2011, every canton had its own code of criminal procedure and its own inquiry model, so that a detailed comparison of the Swiss criminal justice system with other legal systems was not always an easy task. One solution was to focus on a single canton.[8] This situation now lies in the past. The first unified Swiss Criminal Procedure Code (CCrP)[9] became legally effective on January 1, 2011 and resulted in the cantons' differing regulations being abolished. By examining the prosecutor's discretionary power between civil law and common law systems, the Swiss criminal justice system can provide new approaches to the discussion at the international level.

The present research aims to analyze the public prosecution service in the United States (U.S.) and in Switzerland from a comparative perspective and seeks to enrich the American understanding of Swiss prosecutors and vice versa. My focus will lie on the position, powers, and accountability of both prosecution services within their respective criminal justice systems. In particular, the organizational structure of the prosecution services and their relationship with the police are highlighted, the prosecutor's role within the criminal justice systems extensively discussed, and the way prosecutors are controlled respectively held accountable presented. This last point deals with external and internal supervision as well as civil, criminal and disciplinary liability of prosecutors. In this research, common features and differences between both systems will be highlighted. In Switzerland, until 2011, the inquiry models could basically be differentiated between those cantons following the system of an investigating judge (*Untersuchungsrichter*), inspired by the French legal system and those that have adopted the German system of the prosecutor (*Staatsanwalt*) with one or more district prosecutors. These prosecutors are in many respects comparable to U.S. district attorneys. The CCrP has opted for the German prosecutor model. Switzerland has largely been influenced by the French and the German legal systems, so that this research could not have been done without taking a look at the evolution and current situation of the prosecutorial role in those

---

[6] The first wave included England and Wales, France, Germany, the Netherlands, Poland, and Sweden. The second wave extended the research to Croatia, Hungary, Spain, Switzerland, and Turkey.

[7] See e.g. Arbour et al. (2000), Jescheck and Leibinger (1979), Marguery (2008), Tak (2005), and Vander Beken and Kilchling (2000).

[8] See e.g. Gilliéron and Killias (2008).

[9] Swiss Criminal Procedure Code of October 5, 2007 (Criminal Procedure Code, CCrP) (Status as of July, 1 2011); *Schweizerische Strafprozessordnung vom 5. Oktober 2007* (*Strafprozessordnung, StPO*) (*Stand am 1. Juli 2011*); SR 312.0.

countries. Thus, this study is completed by an overview of the prosecution institutions in France and Germany.

Legal comparison and empirical data reflecting actual working practice are the methods used in this research. In addition, comparative tables intend to provide a brief overview of key issues.

This research is divided into 11 chapters. This chapter describes the aim, approach and methodology of the study. Chapter 2 deals with the available methods to cope with overloaded criminal justice systems. In order to understand the legal environment in which the prosecutor operates, Chap. 3 is devoted to a description of the U.S. and Swiss criminal justice systems. Chapter 4 of this book outlines the origins of the public prosecutor in both countries. This comparative analysis shall identify and explain the differences of the public prosecutor's position in both criminal justice systems. The chapter ends with a brief description of the different inquiry models in place in Switzerland prior to the introduction of the CCrP and explains the current situation. The next two chapters constitute the core of this research. An entire chapter is devoted to public prosecutors in the United States and exhaustively describes their position, powers, and accountability. After a description of the structure and organization of the prosecution service at federal and state levels and an examination of the relationship between the prosecution service and the police, a special focus is put on the broad discretionary power of prosecutors. The prosecutor's charging decision being the heart of the prosecution function, the decision to charge, what charges to file, when to drop the charges, and whether or not to plea bargain, receive particular attention in this research.[10] Because prosecutorial misconduct is a subject of scholarly concern, it deserves to be discussed. In line with this research, abuse of the charging function, misconduct in the plea bargaining process and in the grand jury are considered in greater detail. Reasons for misconduct, the frequency of prosecutorial misconduct, and available sanctions are outlined. This chapter ends by describing the mechanisms in place to control public prosecutors and the way they can be held accountable. The public prosecutor being an elected position in the United States, the effectiveness of the electoral process is particularly scrutinized. The next chapter is entirely devoted to the position, powers, and accountability of public prosecutors in Switzerland. The first section of this chapter describes the structure and organization of the prosecution service at federal and cantonal levels. The quality of cooperation between the police and prosecution being crucial for the success of criminal proceedings, the second section explains the relationship between the prosecution service and the police. Because the principle of legality was recently relaxed in favor of a moderate principle of opportunity, one section closely examines this new situation and evaluates the impact on the Swiss criminal justice system. A subsequent section is dedicated to prosecutorial decision-making, which includes the prosecutor's decision not to open proceedings, to open an investigation, to suspend an

[10] In contrast to the other public prosecution systems analyzed in this research, prosecutorial decision-making is discussed in the section addressing prosecutorial discretion and not in a separate section.

investigation, to discontinue proceedings, and to charge. The Swiss criminal justice system has a number of alternative proceedings to relieve heavy caseloads. One section discusses the penal order proceedings and some critical points related to this summary proceeding. It also presents the abridged proceedings, a procedure largely inspired by American plea bargaining. The chapter ends with an analysis of how prosecutors are controlled and in how far they are held accountable. Chapters 7 and 8 offer an overview of the position, powers, and accountability of public prosecutors in Germany and France. Chapter 9 gives a summary overview of the main findings of the research. Chapter 10 addresses some specific problems identified in the U.S. criminal justice system and proposes solutions. Furthermore, it discusses the problems related to the increase of prosecutorial power and the lessons the Swiss legal system can learn from U.S. experience. The research ends with some concluding remarks.

1.2 Aim of the Study

Criminal justice systems are confronted with growing caseload numbers. As a consequence, it is not possible to give every defendant a trial. Methods must be found to reserve full trials to those cases that deserve to go that route and treat the vast majority of other cases in another way. Decriminalization and selective enforcement and prosecution are the main methods for coping with the caseload problem. Hence, in this context, the position of public prosecutors has changed dramatically. This study aims to examine and compare the national role and function of public prosecutors in the United States and Switzerland. The structure and organization of the public prosecution service, the relationship of the public prosecution service to the police, independence, and accountability of public prosecutors are important aspects that will be examined.

The selection of Switzerland and the United States for this research on public prosecutors is interesting for a multitude of reasons. Both countries share some common features, such as the federalist structure. Decentralization—inherent in a federal state—produces diversity. In the United States, state jurisdiction comprises 50 states. Within each state, each county or district has its own prosecutor's office with its own organization. Although, since January 1, 2011, Switzerland has a unified Criminal Code of Procedure (CCrP), each canton remains responsible for its organization. Democracy is an essential part of political life in both countries. In the United States, the prosecutor is an elected position at the state level and is therefore a highly political one. In Switzerland, the appointment methods vary between the cantons. Nomination of the chief prosecutor occurs either by executive power, parliament, or by another official authority.[11] Beside these similarities,

[11] See Sect. 6.1.2.2, paras 1–3 for nomination respectively appointment methods of the chief prosecutor.

Switzerland and the United States follow different approaches regarding the organization of the criminal procedure. The United States has an adversarial system, whereas Switzerland follows the inquisitorial system. The U.S. criminal procedure adheres to the opportunity principle, the Swiss criminal procedure basically works with the legality principle.

It can be assumed that, although theoretically the criminal justice systems of both countries seem to have an entirely opposite approach, in reality they are similar. This is mostly due to the fact that the overwhelming majority of cases are dealt with by way of alternative procedures. Today, Switzerland and the United States have an administrative criminal justice system.

The increasing workload of criminal justice systems will make prosecutorial discretion more and more necessary. Since the prosecutor's broad charging discretion has a long history in the U.S. criminal justice system, the Swiss criminal justice system can learn from the positive as well as from the negative aspects of the U.S. system. On the other hand, the U.S. criminal justice system can draw on positive experiences from the Swiss criminal justice system.

1.3 Approach

In order to understand how both criminal justice systems deal with an increasing caseload, this research on public prosecutors is done from a criminological and a legal point of view.[12]

From a criminological point of view, the prosecution service is considered an integral part of the criminal justice system. Under increasing pressure of having to deal with a growing number of criminal cases, prosecutors have become of crucial importance over the years. They have been given more and more power, mainly through the use of simplified proceedings. In some cases, they are even responsible for making case-concluding decisions, a function that was traditionally exclusively reserved for judges.

From a legal point of view, the shift of powers to public prosecutors raises questions with respect to the fundamental principles of the states. How are the accused person's legal rights guaranteed? What impact does such a shift have on procedural guarantees? What does this mean for the principles of legality and opportunity?

[12] In this research I will take the same approach as the one already used in the research carried out by Jehle and Wade (see Jehle 2006, p. 3).

1.4 Methodology of the Study

In contrast to the Swiss prosecution service, the U.S. prosecution service, depending on jurisdiction, is not only responsible for the prosecution of criminal cases, but also handles civil matters. Hence, prosecution services in the United States are generally divided into criminal and civil divisions. However, in this study, I will only consider the criminal division.

In the Swiss as well as in the U.S. legal system, the vast majority of criminal prosecutions are handled in the cantonal respectively the state court systems. Therefore, in order to understand the structure and organization of the public prosecution services in both criminal justice systems, my focus will lie on cantonal and state level prosecutions. For illustration purpose, the state of Minnesota (MN) in the United States and the cantons of Basel-City (BS), Zug (ZG), and Zurich (ZH) in Switzerland will be more closely presented. In these cantons, the inquiry model chosen by the CCrP was already in place, so that the statistical data of these cantons will be used in this research. For the sake of completeness, prosecutions at the federal level will be described succinctly.

In this comparative research on public prosecutors, the current state of literature in both countries is reviewed. In addition, actual statistical data reflecting the prosecutor's work and practice are included. This methodology allows identification of similarities and differences in the criminal justice systems being analyzed. It also helps to identify whether one legal tradition is moving toward another and to what extent.

The scientific literature consulted on public prosecution service in Switzerland includes in particular German-language books and papers. French-language literature is included as far as the opinions differ from those expressed in the German literature. The reader will not find many references to English language literature about the Swiss criminal justice system and the prosecution service since so far very little has been written in English about these topics.

Statistical data used in this research report on the number of cases received by prosecution services, the number of prosecutorial dispositions, and the number of proceedings that are dealt with by way of alternative procedures. In this way, common and divergent trends can be identified. However, the comparison of statistical data between both countries is subject to some limitations. In both nations, statistical data on the prosecutors' activities from the states respectively cantons are not annually published in a nationwide report, so that statistical information presented in this research may not always be representative of the whole country but may be the expression of local practices. This is the case in the United States, for instance, concerning the number of cases rejected at screening, which varies among the states. However, keeping this in mind, the presented data can still allow the detection of trends. While prosecution services in Switzerland always deal with felonies and misdemeanors, in the United States it may happen that, in some municipalities or cities, misdemeanors and petty offenses are not prosecuted by district prosecutors but by city attorneys.[13] This is the case in the state of Minnesota, for instance, the state more closely examined in this research. In this study, the data presented for the United States refer to felonies, those from Switzerland to felonies and misdemeanors. The decision to focus more on felonies in the United States than on low-level offenses is connected to the fact that academic literature tends to overwhelmingly focus on serious crimes and thus the data presented in this research presents the advantage of being compared to prior empirical research. Another reason for focusing on serious crimes has to do with the fact that obtaining detailed statistical data from the prosecutors' activities turned out to be more difficult than originally expected. The challenge was finding prosecution offices willing to provide information not necessarily accessible to the public. Especially Robert M.A. Johnson, former Anoka County Attorney was very open-minded and gave me access to all information I needed for the completion of this study. In contrast to the Swiss legal system, where alternatives are limited to certain minor offenses, plea bargaining in the United States is applied equally to felonies and misdemeanors. Thus, the exclusion of misdemeanors does not lessen the quality of the study.

In order to complete the picture of the position and power of European prosecutors and to show that strong powers of prosecutors in adjudicating criminal cases is not a uniquely U.S. problem anymore, this comparative research concludes with an overview of the prosecution institutions in Germany and France. In contrast to the United States and Switzerland, Germany and France have nationwide statistical data about the prosecutors' activities, which are accessible to the public and are published on an annual basis. This is an undeniable advantage in comparative research. The academic literature consulted includes English, German, and French-language books and papers.

References

Arbour L, Eser A, Ambos K, Sanders A (eds) (2000) The Prosecutor of a permanent International Criminal Court. In: International workshop in co-operation with the office of the Prosecutor of the International Criminal Tribunals (ICTY and ICTR), Freiburg im Breisgau, May 1998 = Le procureur d'une cour pénale internationale permanente = El fiscal de una Corte Penal Internacional Permanente. Edition Iuscrim, Freiburg i. Br

Gilliéron G, Killias M (2008) The prosecution service function within the Swiss criminal justice system. Eur J Crim Policy Res 14(2–3):333–352

Jehle J (2006) The function of public prosecution within the criminal justice system. Aim, approach and outcome of a European comparative study. In: Jehle J, Wade M (eds) Coping with overloaded criminal justice systems. The rise of prosecutorial power across Europe. Springer, Berlin, pp 3–25

Jehle J, Wade M (eds) (2006) Coping with overloaded criminal justice systems. The rise of prosecutorial power across Europe. Springer, Berlin

[13] For the classification of criminal actions, see Appendix I.

Jescheck H, Leibinger R (eds) (1979) Funktion und Tätigkeit der Anklagebehörde im ausländischen Recht (Rechtsvergleichende Untersuchungen zur gesamten Strafrechtswissenschaft, Folge 3, 6). Nomos, Baden-Baden

Luna E, Wade M (2012) The prosecutor in transnational perspective. Oxford University Press, New York

Marguery TP (2008) Unity and diversity of the public prosecution services in Europe. A study of the Czech, Dutch, French and Polish systems. Dissertation, Groningen

Open Society Institute Sofia (ed) (2008) Promoting prosecutorial accountability, independence and effectiveness. Comparative research. Open Society Institute Sofia, Bulgaria

Tak PJP (ed) (2005) Tasks and powers of the prosecution services in the EU Member States, 2 vols. Wolf Legal Publisher, Nijmegen

Vander Beken T, Kilchling M (eds) (2000) The role of the public prosecutor in the European criminal justice systems. Vlaams Kennis- en Cultuurforum, Brussels

Wade M, Jehle J (eds) (2008) Prosecution and diversion within criminal justice systems in Europe. Eur J Crim Policy Res 14(2–3):91–368

Chapter 2
Methods for Coping with Overloaded Criminal Justice Systems

2.1 Overview

Basically, there are three different methods for coping with the caseload problem in criminal justice systems: (1) decriminalization of material law, (2) discretionary powers on the police and prosecution service level, and (3) summary or alternative proceedings. A fourth option—in accordance with the principle of legality—would consist of continuing to bring all cases to court. This, however, would mean a considerable increase in personnel at the prosecution and the court levels, which in turn would create additional costs. For this reason, such an option is not really envisaged by any criminal justice system.[1]

2.2 Decriminalization of Material Law

There are two types of decriminalization: (1) material decriminalization, where administrative offenses are dealt with by administrative procedures, and (2) procedural decriminalization, where administrative fines are imposed for criminal offenses by administrative agencies.[2]

Decriminalization often happens in relation to minor traffic offenses. Such minor illegal acts, which provide for the imposition of an administrative fine, are known as offenses against the order (*Ordnungswidrigkeiten*) in Germany.[3] In Switzerland,

---

[1] Jehle (2006), pp. 5–6.

[2] Wade (2006), p. 33.

[3] See Elsner and Peters (2006), pp. 225–226.

G. Gilliéron, *Public Prosecutors in the United States and Europe*,
DOI 10.1007/978-3-319-04504-7_2,

the Road Traffic Act[4] and the regulatory statutes belonging to it[5] provide for a direct imposition and collection of fines by the cantonal police that may not exceed CHF 300.00. (*Ordnungsbusse*).[6] If the payment is not made within the prescribed timeline of 30 days, the police assume that the concerned person does not agree with the sanction and initiate the ordinary proceedings respectively penal order proceedings.[7] Cantons may also provide for the imposition of on-the-spot fines for petty violations of cantonal law.[8] In other European countries similar approaches to those just described exist.[9]

Minor traffic violations have also been decriminalized in the U.S. criminal justice system. The Traffic Violations Bureau—an administrative agency that is implemented in every state throughout the nation—is responsible for processing the citations issued by various law enforcement agencies for the violation of local ordinances and state motor vehicle codes. Collecting all fines and fees are among several of the various duties and functions of the office. Payment of the traffic ticket (citation) prior to the court date is deemed a waiver of the court hearing and an entry of a guilty plea. Ordinance violations in the United States are usually prosecuted by a municipal attorney, whereas the more severe offenses are reserved for the district attorney. For many years, ordinance violations were considered as "quasi-criminal". Today, depending on the jurisdiction, some ordinance violations are procedurally treated in the same way as misdemeanors. However, some states view an ordinance violation punishable only by a fine as non-criminal.[10] In the state of Minnesota for instance, petty misdemeanors are not viewed as criminal.[11]

Police involved in this kind of administrative procedures do not act as part of the criminal justice system and are therefore generally not controlled by the prosecutor when acting in this capacity.

---

[4] *Strassenverkehrsgesetz vom 19. Dezember 1958*; SR 741.01.

[5] *Ordnungsbussengesetz vom 24. Juni 1970*; SR 741.03.

[6] On this administrative proceeding, see Riedo et al. (2010), Margin Nos. 2619–2638.

[7] See Sect. 6.5.1.

[8] See e.g. the Ordinance of December 6, 2005 on the tickets to be handed out on the spot by police officers of the canton of Basel-City; *Verordnung über die direkte Erhebung von Bussen für Übertretungen des baselstädtischen Rechts vom 6. Dezember 2005*.

[9] Jehle (2006), p. 19.

[10] On ordinance violations, see LaFave et al. (2007), Section 1.8 (d).

[11] See Appendix I.

2.3 Discretionary Powers

Use of discretionary powers[12] on police and prosecution levels[13] is a simple and very effective method for dealing with large caseloads.

Criminal justice systems adhering to the principle of opportunity may use discretion at different stages of the criminal proceeding. In the United States for instance, the police are not required by law to pass every case to the prosecutor but instead are allowed to make a discretionary decision as to whether to hand over a case to the prosecutor or not.[14] To a certain extent, because police officers are almost always at the front line of the criminal process, the discretion exercised by them may be more important than the one exercised by the prosecutor. In contrast, the latter rarely has the occasion to consider a case unless it's brought to his attention by the police.[15] Police discretion has only rarely come under judicial review.[16] Once the police report the incident to the prosecutor, the prosecutor for his part decides whether he wants to go forward with a case or not. His decision is led by various public interest considerations such as the gravity of the offense and the availability of resources.

Police operating in a criminal justice system that follows the principle of legality are required to hand over every case to the prosecutor with the exception of those minor offenses that fall within the responsibility of the police.[17] The only grounds for not passing a case on to the prosecutor is lack of evidence that a punishable action has been committed, or if the preliminary proceeding proves the innocence of the accused.[18] The prosecutor, bound by the principle of legality, cannot exercise any discretion in deciding whether to prosecute or not. As soon as there is enough

---

[12] Under "discretion" one refers to "the power to act within general guidelines, rules, or laws, but without either specific rules to follow or the need to completely explain or justify each decision or action" (Oran's Dictionary of the Law, 4th ed., s.v. "discretion"). "Discretion" is a "legally recognized prerogative granted to public functionaries, [. . .], to make their own judgments and to act in an official capacity in situations or under conditions that are ambiguous requiring a decision that is proper and just under the totality of the circumstances" (Prentice Hall's Dictionary of American Criminal Justice, Criminology, and Criminal Law, 2nd ed., s.v. "discretion"; see also the Black's Law Dictionary, 8th ed., s.v. "discretion").

[13] According to various legal dictionaries, "prosecutorial discretion" is a "prosecutor's power to choose from the options available in a criminal case, such as filing charges, prosecuting, not prosecuting, plea-bargaining, and recommending a sentence to the court" (Black's Law Dictionary, 8th ed., s.v. "prosecutorial discretion"; see also the definition given in Oran's Dictionary of the Law, 4th ed.).

[14] In contrast, French law does theoretically not allow judicial police officers to decide on the route a criminal offense has to follow once the case has been reported (Aubusson de Cavarlay 2006, pp. 198–199). See Sect. 8.2 for the relationship between the prosecution service and the police in France.

[15] Davis (1998), p. 25. See Lawless (2008), Section 1.15.

[16] See, e.g. Davis v. Mississippi, 394 U.S. 721 (1969).

[17] See Sect. 2.2, para 2.

[18] Jehle (2006), p. 20. On the possibility to give the police more power, see Elsner (2008).

evidence to believe that a crime has been committed, the case has to be prosecuted and brought to the court. However, today, criminal justice systems that strictly adhere to the principle of legality are virtually nonexistent. Exceptions to this principle have been developed and implemented. The German and Swiss criminal justice systems are illustrative examples for such an evolution.[19]

2.4 Alternative Proceedings

Alternative proceedings are another simple method for relieving courts' heavy caseload. In this context, the prosecutor plays a crucial role. Although the court may be involved in the final stage to impose a sanction, it is the prosecutor who plays the central role.[20] The German penal order (*Strafbefehl*) and the French penal order (*ordonnance pénale*) are examples of such proceedings.[21] In both proceedings, it is the prosecutor who does the preparatory work and formulates a written recommendation to the judge. The court only rarely refuses to follow the prosecutor's advice. Hence, in reality, the penal order is a decision issued by the prosecution, which is checked and usually approved by the court.[22] There are even proceedings in which the court is no longer involved, but where the prosecutor is responsible for imposing a sanction and therefore makes a case-ending decision. An excellent example of such a procedure is the Swiss penal order (*Strafbefehl*).[23] Another observable trend is the implementation of criminal procedures that are similar to American plea bargaining. The Swiss criminal procedure with its abridged proceedings[24] and the French criminal procedure with its "guilty plea" proceedings[25] took a step in this direction. The advantage of these types of proceedings is that, through negotiations between the prosecutor and the defendant prior to trial, the procedure before the court is accelerated. In the vast majority of cases, the judges accept the agreement between the prosecutor and the defendant so that in reality the prosecutor makes a decision that is to a large extent adjudicatory.

---

[19] See Sect. 6.3 for a description of the moderate principle of opportunity in the Swiss legal system and Sect. 7.3.3 for a discussion of the different possibilities to dismiss a case on discretionary grounds in the German legal system.

[20] For an overview over the prosecutor's influence on court level in European criminal justice systems, see Jehle (2006), pp. 22–23.

[21] See Sect. 7.5.2 for the German penal order and Sect. 8.4.3.3.1 for the French penal order.

[22] See Jehle (2006), p. 23.

[23] See Sect. 6.5.1.

[24] See Sect. 6.5.2.

[25] See Sect. 8.4.2.3 for the transaction (*composition pénale*) and Sect. 8.4.3.3.2 for the procedure of plea negotiation (*plaider coupable*).

It is certainly true that these alternative proceedings increase the efficiency of criminal justice systems. However, it must not be forgotten that simplifications of proceedings usually go along with restrictions on criminal defendant's rights, such as the right to be heard. This in turn may reinforce the risk of wrongful convictions.

References

Aubusson de Cavarlay B (2006) The prosecution service function within the French criminal justice system. In: Jehle J, Wade M (eds) Coping with overloaded criminal justice systems. The rise of prosecutorial power across Europe. Springer, Berlin, pp 185–205

Davis AJ (1998) Prosecution and race: the power and privilege of discretion. Fordham Law Rev 67:13–67

Elsner B (2008) Entlastung der Staatsanwaltschaft durch mehr Kompetenzen für die Polizei? Eine deutsch-niederländisch vergleichende Analyse in rechtlicher und rechtstatsächlicher Hinsicht. Diss. Göttingen, Göttinger Studien zu den Kriminalwissenschaften, vol 5. Universitätsverlag Göttingen, Göttingen

Elsner B, Peters J (2006) The prosecution service function within the German criminal justice system. In: Jehle J, Wade M (eds) Coping with overloaded criminal justice systems. The rise of prosecutorial power across Europe. Springer, Berlin, pp 207–236

Jehle J (2006) The function of public prosecution within the criminal justice system. Aim, approach and outcome of a European comparative study. In: Jehle J, Wade M (eds) Coping with overloaded criminal justice systems. The rise of prosecutorial power across Europe. Springer, Berlin, pp 3–25

LaFave WR, Israel JH, King NJ, Kerr OS (2007) Criminal procedure, 3rd edn. 7 vols. Criminal practice series. Thomson/West, St. Paul

Lawless JF (2008) Prosecutorial misconduct. Law, procedure, forms, 4th edn. LexisNexis, Newark

Riedo C, Fiolka G, Niggli MA (2010) Schweizerisches Strafprozessrecht. Eine Einführung. Helbing & Lichtenhahn, Basel

Wade M (2006) The power to decide – prosecutorial control, diversion and punishment in European criminal justice systems today. In: Jehle J, Wade M (eds) Coping with overloaded criminal justice systems. The rise of prosecutorial power across Europe. Springer, Berlin, pp 27–126

Chapter 3
The Criminal Justice Systems Studied

3.1 The United States Criminal Justice System

3.1.1 Overview

The United Sates is a federalist system. It consists of 50 sovereign states.[1] The Federal Government and each state government are divided into executive, legislate, and judicial branches. The Federal Government has specific powers that are enumerated in the U.S. Constitution. Hence, the 50 states retain substantial autonomy, since any powers not delegated to the Federal Government and not prohibited to the states by the Constitution are reserved to the states.[2] Title 18 of the United States Code (USC) is the criminal code for federal crimes. All 50 states have their own criminal codes. In addition, the Congress has created a separate criminal code for the District of Columbia.[3] By far the vast majority of criminal cases are prosecuted at the state level.[4] Criminal actions are classified as "felony" and "misdemeanor".[5] The Federal Rules of Criminal Procedure (FRCrP) are the procedural rules that govern how federal criminal prosecutions are conducted in U.S. district courts.[6] They were first promulgated by the Supreme Court in 1944 and

---

[1] Alabama, Alaska, Arizona, Arkansas, California, Colorado, Connecticut, Delaware, Florida, Georgia, Hawaii, Idaho, Illinois, Indiana, Iowa, Kansas, Kentucky, Louisiana, Maine, Maryland, Massachusetts, Michigan, Minnesota, Mississippi, Missouri, Montana, Nebraska, Nevada, New Hampshire, New Jersey, New Mexico, New York, North Carolina, North Dakota, Ohio, Oklahoma, Oregon, Pennsylvania, Rhode Island, South Carolina, South Dakota, Tennessee, Texas, Utah, Vermont, Virginia, Washington, West Virginia, Wisconsin, Wyoming.

[2] Amendment X to the U.S. Constitution.

[3] LaFave et al. (2007), Section 1.2 (a).

[4] LaFave et al. (2007), Section 1.2 (e).

[5] For a definition of criminal actions in the United States, see Appendix I.

[6] LaFave et al. (2007), Section 1.7 (f).

G. Gilliéron, *Public Prosecutors in the United States and Europe*,
DOI 10.1007/978-3-319-04504-7_3, © Springer International Publishing Switzerland 2014

became effective on March 21, 1946. Like substantive criminal law, each state and the District of Columbia has its own criminal procedure.[7]

In the United States, prosecutions are carried out through U.S. attorneys at the federal level and by district attorneys at county level. There is no examining magistrate.[8]

3.1.2 *Main Features of the United States Criminal Procedure*

3.1.2.1 The *Ex Officio* Principle

The state has a monopoly on criminal prosecution. Whether or not to initiate criminal proceedings is a matter for the discretion of the public prosecutor.

3.1.2.2 Principle of Opportunity

The principle of opportunity—as opposed to the principle of legality—leaves the prosecutor broad discretion to decide whether to prosecute or not. Prosecution systems adhering to the opportunity principle allow prosecutors to take into account various factors not limited to evidence in making their decisions. Hence, prosecutors are not obliged to prosecute every case where there is sufficient evidence to believe that a crime has been committed. Reasons for not prosecuting are commonly known as public interest factors. Such factors include for example the gravity of the offense, the availability of resources, and the victim.

3.1.2.3 The Adversarial and Accusatorial Nature of Criminal Proceedings

The U.S. criminal process is designed to be accusatorial as well as adversarial. The adversary model gives the parties the responsibility of investigating the case and presenting their evidence before a passive and neutral judge or jury who will determine guilt. The duty of the judge is to ensure fair play of due process, whereas the responsibility to seek the truth of the case relies on the defense and prosecution.[9]

The accusatorial character of the criminal justice process is reflected in various elements of the process. The most important of these elements is that the burden of establishing the guilt of the accused is upon the prosecution. The prosecutor has to

[7] LaFave et al. (2007), Section 1.2 (a).

[8] An examining magistrate is an officer charged with the investigation in a criminal law case.

[9] LaFave et al. (2007), Section 1.5 (c).

prove guilt "beyond a reasonable doubt".[10] Other elements of the accusatorial process include the presumption of innocence and the defendant's privilege against self-incrimination.[11]

3.1.2.4 Legal Rights of the Accused: The Bill of Rights

The Bill of Rights ratified in 1791 constitutes the first ten amendments of the U.S. Constitution. These constitutional rights are the minimum rights of individuals facing criminal prosecution. Therefore, each state is free to provide more protection for its people in its own state constitution or state law.[12]

Prior to the adoption of the 14th Amendment in 1868 the Bill of Rights applied only to the Federal Government. With the adoption of the 14th Amendment, the question of whether and to what extent the guarantees found in the Bill of Rights apply to state criminal proceedings arose. The second sentence of section one of the 14th Amendment states that "[n]o State shall make or enforce any law which shall abridge the privileges or immunities of citizens of the United States; nor shall any State deprive any person of life, liberty, or property, without due process of law; nor deny to any person within its jurisdiction the equal protection of the laws."

Over the years, three different positions have emerged to answer the question of what constitutional rights are to be incorporated into the Due Process Clause of the 14th Amendment: (1) the "total incorporation" position,[13] (2) the "fundamental fairness" position,[14] and (3) the "selective incorporation" position.[15] Selective incorporation has been the predominant approach since the mid-1960s. This approach assumes that only those rights considered fundamental should be incorporated under the Due Process Clause of the 14th Amendment and hence be applicable to the states.[16] Applying this approach, the Supreme Court has held the following provisions as fundamental: (1) the Fourth Amendment's protection against unreasonable searches; (2) the Fourth Amendment's warrant clause; (3) the Fifth Amendment's protection against self-incrimination; (4) the Fifth Amendment's prohibition against double jeopardy; (5) the Sixth Amendment's right to counsel; (6) the Sixth Amendment's right to a speedy trial; (7) the Sixth Amendment's right to a public trial; (8) the Sixth Amendment's right to be informed of the

---

[10] LaFave et al. (2007), Section 1.5 (d).

[11] LaFave et al. (2007), Section 1.5 (d).

[12] Del Carmen (2007), p. 20.

[13] According to this approach, the 14th Amendment's Due Process Clause embraces all the guarantees in the Bill of Rights and applies them to cases under state law.

[14] In this approach, those rights that are fundamental and essential to an ordered liberty are incorporated. The fundamental fairness doctrine held that no relationship existed between the Bill of Rights and those deemed fundamental, although the rights recognized under the fundamental fairness doctrine may parallel rights recognized by the Bill of Rights.

[15] See LaFave et al. (2007), Sections 2.3–2.6 for a detailed discussion on these approaches.

[16] LaFave et al. (2007), Section 2.5 (a).

nature and cause of the accusation; (9) the Sixth Amendment's right to confrontation of opposing witnesses; (10) the Sixth Amendment's right to an impartial jury; (11) the Sixth Amendment's right to a compulsory process for obtaining witnesses; (12) the Eight Amendment's prohibition against cruel and unusual punishment.[17] The Fifth Amendment right to indictment by grand jury, however, was not considered fundamental by the Supreme Court, so that the states are not required to grant this right.[18] In sum, with the exception of the right to grand jury indictment, individuals facing federal or state criminal charges have exactly the same rights.

In a criminal prosecution, the Fifth, Sixth, and Eighth Amendments are of particular importance. The content of each amendment is briefly described in the following.

3.1.2.4.1 The Fifth Amendment

The Fifth Amendment protects defendants against double jeopardy[19] and against being required to testify against themselves in criminal cases.[20] It also guarantees the right to a grand jury indictment for a capital or other serious crime,[21] and the defendants' rights to due process.[22]

3.1.2.4.2 The Sixth Amendment

The Sixth Amendment guarantees the right to a speedy[23] and public trial,[24] the right to an impartial jury,[25] the right to be informed of the nature and cause of accusation, the right to confront witnesses, the right to summon witnesses, and the right to the assistance of counsel.[26]

[17] Del Carmen (2007), pp. 25–26; LaFave et al. (2007), Section 2.6 (a).

[18] Del Carmen (2007), p. 26. The Supreme Court has still to rule on the following safeguards: The Eight Amendment prohibition against excessive bail, the Eight Amendment prohibition against excessive fines, and the vicintage requirement of the Sixth Amendment. The first two are considered as fundamental by lower courts [see LaFave et al. (2007), Section 2.6 (b)].

[19] Double jeopardy is a constitutional protection against being subject to liability for the same offense more than one time. On double jeopardy, see LaFave et al. (2007), Chap. 25.

[20] On the legal protection against self-incrimination, see LaFave et al. (2007), Sections 2.10, 6.5–6.10. See also Amar and Lettow (1995), pp. 857–928.

[21] On the grand jury review, seeLaFave et al. (2007), Chap. 15.

[22] On "due process", see LaFave et al. (2007), Chap. 2.

[23] On the right to speedy trial, see LaFave et al. (2007), Chap. 18.

[24] On the right to a public trial, see LaFave et al. (2007), Section 24.1.

[25] On the right to an impartial jury, see LaFave et al. (2007), Section 22.1.

[26] On the right to counsel, see LaFave et al. (2007), Chap. 11.

3.1.2.4.3 The Eight Amendment

Protection against excessive bail and cruel and unusual punishment are guaranteed under the Eight Amendment.[27]

3.1.2.5 Victims' Rights

3.1.2.5.1 The Emergence of Crime Victim Rights and Remedies

By the end of the eighteenth century, the concept of public prosecution was well established in the United States. The perception was that, in a system of public prosecution,—as opposed to a system of private prosecution—all criminal acts were against the state and hence, the victim was society as a whole. Victims of crimes had no right to participate in the criminal process at all. The responsibility for conducting criminal justice processes rested entirely in the hands of the prosecutor, and the victim just had the role of witness in the prosecution.[28] As a result, during many years, U.S. criminal justice system has paid little attention to victim concerns. It is with the rise of the victims' rights movement at the end of the twentieth century that interest in crime victims increased.[29] This movement emerged from the belief that crime victims in a criminal process were not fairly treated. Since then, victims have progressively won the right to participate in the criminal process.[30]

The first federal victims' rights legislation was the Victim and Witness Protection Act of 1982. Since then, U.S. Congress has subsequently amended and expanded the provisions of the 1982 Act with the Victims of Crime Act of 1984, the Victims' Rights and Restitution Act of 1990, the Violent Crime Control and Law Enforcement Act of 1994, the Antiterrorism and Effective Death Penalty Act of 1996, the Victim Rights Clarification Act of 1997, and finally with the Justice for All Act of 2004 that contains four major sections related to crime victims and the criminal justice process.[31]

The Crime Victim's Rights Act that is part of the Justice for All Act of 2004 has strengthened the rights of victims of federal crimes and has implemented additional

---

[27] See LaFave et al. (2007), Sections 12.2–12.3.

[28] Cardenas (1986), pp. 366–372; Gittler (1984), pp. 120–121; McDonald (1976), pp. 654–668; O'Hara (2005), pp. 235–236; Tobolowsky et al. (2010), pp. 5–6. On the shift from private to public prosecution, see Sect. 4.1.4.1.

[29] For more information on the Victims' Rights Movement, see Cassell (2007), pp. 865–869; Karmen (1992).

[30] Gittler (1984), pp. 121–125; Tobolowsky et al. (2010), pp. 8–9.

[31] On international instruments that provide guidance on how best to protect and promote victims' rights and that are legally binding on the U.S. federal and state governments, see Parker (2008).

enforcement mechanisms and remedies for violations of victims' rights.[32] In 2008, key applicable provisions of the Crime Victim's Rights Act were incorporated into the Federal Rules of Criminal Procedure.[33]

3.1.2.5.2 Crime Victim Rights and Remedies

Section 3771 of Title 18 of the USC provides the following rights: (1) the right to be reasonably protected from the accused,[34] (2) the right to notification of public court and parole proceedings and of any release of the accused,[35] (3) the right not to be excluded from public court proceedings under most circumstances,[36] (4) the right to be heard in public court proceedings relating to bail, the acceptance of a plea bargain,[37] sentencing, or parole,[38] (5) the right to confer with the prosecutor,[39] (6) the right to restitution under the law,[40] (7) the right to proceedings free from unwarranted delays,[41] and (8) the right to be treated fairly and with respect to one's dignity and privacy.[42]

Today, over 30 states have added a crime victim "bills of rights" or other victim-related provisions to their state constitution.[43] Each of the states has a general statutory declaration of victims' rights.[44] The state of Minnesota, for example, requires victim notification of important events and actions in the criminal justice process. Furthermore, it allows crime victim presence and hearing at various stages of the criminal justice process.[45]

The Federal Government and all of the states recognize compensation programs[46] and restitution provisions.[47]

---

[32] See Appendix II for an overview over the rights conferred by the Crime Victims' Rights Act 2004.

[33] See 18 USCA Section 3771 (West Supp. 2010); FRCrP 1, 12.1, 17, 18, 32, 60; See also Tobolowsky et al. (2010), p. 12.

[34] See Beloof et al. (2006), pp. 127–162; Doyle (2008), pp. 9–10.

[35] See Doyle (2008), pp. 10–16; Tobolowsky et al. (2010), pp. 23–47.

[36] See Doyle (2008), pp. 16–18; Tobolowsky et al. (2010), pp. 49–64. See also Beloof et al. (2006), pp. 521–570.

[37] Doyle (2008), pp. 18–23; Tobolowsky et al. (2010), pp. 65–89. On victims' participation in plea bargains, see Beloof et al. (2006), pp. 476–497. On the victims' rights in plea bargains in the state of Minnesota, see Appendix III.

[38] Doyle (2008), pp. 23–24; Tobolowsky et al. (2010), pp. 91–129.

[39] See Doyle (2008), pp. 24–25.

[40] Doyle (2008), pp. 25–27; Tobolowsky et al. (2010), pp. 151–181.

[41] Doyle (2008), pp. 27–30.

[42] Doyle (2008), p. 30.

[43] For an overview over these states, see Tobolowsky et al. (2010), p. 12, n 53; Doyle (2008), p. 3, n 7; Hammond (2006), pp. 17–18.

[44] See Doyle (2008), p. 3, n 8.

[45] An overview is given in Appendix II.

[46] Tobolowsky et al. (2010), pp. 183–204.

[47] Tobolowsky et al. (2010), pp. 151–181.

3.1.2.5.3 The Definition of a "Victim"

The definition of the term "victim" is important for determining the field of application of the victims' rights provisions.[48]

The Federal Crime Victims' Rights Act defines a "crime victim" as follows: "For the purposes of this chapter, the term "crime victim" means a person directly and proximately harmed as a result of the commission of a Federal offense or an offense in the District of Columbia. In the case of a crime victim who is under 18 years of age, incompetent, incapacitated, or deceased, the legal guardians of the crime victim or the representatives of the crime victim's estate, family members, or any other persons appointed as suitable by the court, may assume the crime victim's rights under this chapter, but in no event shall the defendant be named as such guardian or representative."[49] From this it follows that the prescribed rights are not limited only to direct crime victims, but extend to representatives of incompetent, incapacitated, minor, or deceased victims. Defendants are excluded.[50] In *United States v. Ekanem*,[51] the Court concluded that "person" also included the government so that restitution in favor of the government is possible.[52]

On the state level, crime victim rights provisions may cover only the direct victim,[53] or similar to the federal Crime Victims' Rights Act, extend to representatives of incapacitated, incompetent, deceased, or minor victims as well.[54] Some jurisdictions confer those rights, even to governmental entities and corporations.[55] Some states explicitly exclude the person charged with or alleged to have committed the crime.[56]

3.1.2.5.4 The Definition of a "Crime"

The Crime Victims' Rights Act does not limit or restrict the federal crimes to which it applies.[57] In contrast to this, most jurisdictions restrict the application of victims'

---

[48] For the definition of a "victim", see Beloof et al. (2006), pp. 49–126; Tobolowsky et al. (2010), pp. 16–19. For the definition of a "victim" in the states, see Hammond (2006), pp. 5–16.

[49] 18 USC Section 3771 (e).

[50] For the persons excluded from the definition of "victim" status, see Beloof et al. (2006), pp. 70–72.

[51] U.S. v. Ekanem, 383 F.3d 40 (2d Cir. 2004).

[52] On the question whether governmental entities deserve to be covered by victims' rights enactments, see Dubber (2002), pp. 211–231.

[53] See e.g. Kansas Statutes Annotated, Section 74-7333 (2009).

[54] See e.g. Minn. Stat., Section 611 A.01(b) (2010).

[55] See e.g. Minn. Stat., Section 611 A.01(b).

[56] See e.g. Minn. Stat., Section 611 A.01(b).

[57] See 18 USCA Section 3771 (2010).

rights to only certain crimes.[58] In some states, victims' rights constitutional provisions extend to victims suffering financial, psychological, or physical harm due to crime. In others, those rights cover only victims of felony offenses. Statutory provisions may limit victims' rights to victims of crimes involving physical or sexual violence or injury. Other states limit their rights provisions to victims of specifically enumerated offenses.[59] The state of Minnesota limits the victim rights provisions to individuals who have suffered bodily harm.[60]

3.2 The Swiss Criminal Justice System

3.2.1 Overview

Switzerland, like the United States, is a federal state.[61] It consists of 26 federated states called cantons[62] that enjoy some degree of autonomy. The Federal Government and each canton are divided into executive, legislate, and judicial branches.[63] Similar to the United States, all powers not specifically given to the Confederation belong to the cantons. A Swiss Criminal Code (SCC)[64] was adopted by the Federal Parliament in 1937 so that the substantive criminal law was codified on a national level. The SCC classifies criminal actions as *Verbrechen* (felony), *Vergehen* (misdemeanor), and *Übertretung* (petty offense).[65] Until 2010, procedural law was vested in the cantons. As a consequence, every canton had its own code of criminal procedure. The new Swiss Federal Constitution, which came into force on January 1, 2000, transferred the powers to unify the law of criminal procedure to the Confederation.[66] On January 1, 2011, the CCrP came into force and replaced the 26 cantonal codes of criminal procedure. Hence, criminal acts in Switzerland are

---

58 Tobolowsky et al. (2010), p. 19.

59 Tobolowsky et al. (2010), pp. 19–21.

60 Minn. Stat., Section 611 A.01(a) (2010).

61 On the Swiss federal system, see Fleiner et al. (2005), pp. 101–144.

62 Zurich (ZH), Berne (BE), Lucerne (LU), Uri (UR), Schwyz (SZ), Obwalden (OW) and Nidwalden (NW), Glarus (GL), Zug (ZG), Fribourg (FR), Solothurn (SO), Basel-City (BS) and Basel-Land (BL), Schaffhausen (SH), Appenzell Inner Rhodes (AI) and Appenzell Outer Rhodes (AR), St. Gallen (SG), Grisons (GR), Aargau (AG), Thurgau (TG), Ticino (TI), Vaud (VD), Valais (VS), Neuchâtel (NE), Geneva (GE) and Jura (JU) [see Article 1 Federal Constitution of the Swiss Confederation of April 18, 1999 (Status as of January, 1, 2011); *Bundesverfassung der Schweizerischen Eidgenossenschaft vom 18. April 1999* (*BV*) (*Stand am 1. Januar 2011*); SR 101].

63 On the state organization, see Fleiner et al. (2005), pp. 59–99.

64 Swiss Criminal Code of December 21, 1937 (SCC) (Status as of January 1, 2012); *Schweizerisches Strafgesetzbuch vom 21. Dezember 1937* (*StGB*) (*Stand am 1. Januar 2012*); SR 311.0.

65 For a definition, see Appendix I.

66 Article 123 para. 1 Swiss Federal Constitution.

now prosecuted and judged under the same procedural rules. For reasons of efficiency, the examining magistrate, previously existing in some cantons, has been abolished. This means that the prosecutor occupies a central position. He directs examination, charges, and prosecutes. Moreover, in order to deal with an increasing caseload, prosecutors have been given more power to divert cases. The immense power vested in the prosecution is compensated by the judge's responsibility for compulsory acts and extended defense powers.[67]

The public prosecutor in Switzerland has largely been influenced by the French and German prosecution systems. Until 2010, this was reflected in the different inquiry models in place in the cantons.[68]

3.2.2 *Main Features of the Swiss Criminal Procedure*

3.2.2.1 The *Ex Officio* Principle (Article 2 CCrP)

The state has a monopoly on criminal prosecution and it has a duty to proceed *ex officio* (*Offizialprinzip*).[69] This means that offenses will be prosecuted irrespective of the wishes of the victim.[70] The *ex officio* principle is restricted by the fact that certain offenses are prosecuted after a complaint by the victim or are dependent on the authorization of a non-judicial authority.[71]

Prior to the introduction of the CCrP, some cantons recognized the possibility of private prosecution (*Privatstrafklageverfahren*). This kind of prosecution was restricted to certain offenses such as offenses against personal honor (Article 173 et seq. SCC), acts of aggression (Article 126 para. 1 SCC), removal of property (Article 141 SCC), criminal damage (Article 144 para. 1 SCC), and unlawful entry (Article 186 SCC). The victim respectively the person entitled to file a complaint exercised the function of the public prosecutor but without being endowed with means of coercion and without having the authority to instruct the police.[72] The CCrP did not retain private prosecution.[73]

---

[67] See Sect. 4.2.3.4.

[68] See Sects. 4.2.3.1–4.2.3.4 for description of these models.

[69] Straub and Weltert. In: Niggli et al. (2011) BSK StPO, Art. 2, Margin Nos. 1–11; Wohlers. In: Donatsch et al. (2010) Kommentar StPO, Art. 2, Margin Nos. 1–4; Riedo et al. (2010), Margin Nos. 100–103 and 108.

[70] Pieth (2009), p. 37; Riedo et al. (2010), Margin No. 108; Schmid (2009a), Margin No. 85.

[71] See Sects. 3.2.2.3.2 and 3.2.2.3.3.

[72] Wohlers. In: Donatsch et al. (2010) Kommentar StPO, Art. 2, Margin No. 5; Riedo et al. (2010), Margin Nos. 114–116.

[73] Wohlers. In: Donatsch et al. (2010) Kommentar StPO, Art. 2, Margin No. 5; Pieth (2009), p. 37; Riedo et al. (2010), Margin No. 117; Schmid (2009a), Margin No. 1349; Federal Council (2006), pp. 1111–1112.

3.2.2.2 Principle of Legality (Article 7 CCrP)

Beyond the *ex officio* principle, which exclusively leaves the decision as to whether a criminal proceeding should be initiated with the criminal justice authorities, the Swiss criminal justice system basically adheres to the principle of legality or the principle of compulsory prosecution (*Verfolgungszwang*).[74] This rule is based on the absolute equality of all citizens before the law. Hence, the prosecutor is required by law to prosecute whenever there is enough evidence to believe that a criminal offense has been committed.[75] The prosecutor cannot exercise any discretion in deciding whether to prosecute or not. His role is limited to the assessment of the legal sufficiency of the evidence against the suspect. Thus, in contrast to prosecution systems adhering to the principle of opportunity, the prosecutor is not allowed to take public interest factors into account when making his decision. The prosecution only has the power to decide whether it is obvious from the start that for lack of sufficient clues a condemnation may never be made by court.

Today, the vast majority of cases are resolved by alternative proceedings[76] so that the traditional distinction between criminal justice systems that adhere to the principle of legality and those that adhere to the principle of opportunity gradually shrinks.

3.2.2.3 Exceptions to the Principle of Legality

3.2.2.3.1 Introduction of a Moderate Principle of Opportunity (Article 8 CCrP)

The CCrP has introduced a moderate principle of opportunity.[77] According to Article 8 para. 1 CCrP, the prosecution and the courts are required to refrain from conducting a prosecution if (1) the level of culpability and consequences of the offense are negligible (Article 52 SCC), or if (2) the offender has made reparation for the loss, damage, or injury or made every reasonable effort to right the wrong that he has caused (Article 53), or if (3) the accused is so stricken by the immediate

[74] On the relationship between the *ex officio* principle and the principle of legality, see Riedo and Fiolka. In: Niggli et al. (2011) BSK StPO, Art. 7, Margin Nos. 1 6.

[75] Article 7 para. 1 CCrP states: "The criminal justice authorities are required, within the scope of their competence, to institute and carry out criminal proceedings if they are aware, or have sufficient grounds to suspect, that a criminal offense has been committed."

[76] On the American plea bargaining, see Sect. 5.3.7. On the penal order proceedings and the abridged proceedings, see Sects. 6.5.1 and 6.5.2.

[77] Riedo and Fiolka. In: Niggli et al. (2011) BSK StPO, Art. 8, Margin No. 3; Wohlers. In: Donatsch et al. (2010) Kommentar StPO, Art. 8, Margin No. 3; Pieth (2009), p. 38; Riedo et al. (2010), Margin No. 172.

consequences of the offense that an additional penalty would be inadequate (Article 54).[78] Furthermore, Article 8 para. 2 CCrP provides for three situations in which the prosecutor and the courts are obliged to refrain from prosecution unless this does not conflict with the overriding interests of the private claimant, namely (1) if the offense is, in light of the other criminal offenses with which the accused is charged, of negligible importance to the determination of the sentence or measure, or (2) if an additional sentence, which is likely to be of little consequence, would be imposed in combination with a pre-existing sentence, or (3) if an equivalent sentence imposed abroad would have to be taken into account when imposing a sentence for the offense prosecuted.[79]

Finally, according to Article 8 para. 3 CCrP, the prosecution and the courts may waive prosecution if the criminal offense is already being prosecuted by a foreign authority or if the prosecution was relinquished in favor of such an authority and provided that this does not conflict with the private claimant's overriding interests.[80]

3.2.2.3.2 Offenses Prosecutable upon Victim's Request

Among the offenses that are prosecuted on the basis of a complaint by the victim (Article 30 SCC et seq.),[81] the Swiss criminal law makes the following two distinctions[82]:

- Certain offenses are only prosecuted after the victim has filed a valid complaint (*absolute Antragsdelikte*). They usually concern petty offenses against individual interests[83] or offenses where prosecution would create an additional distress for the victim.[84]
- Certain offenses normally prosecuted *ex officio*, require a complaint in the instance of a certain relationship between the perpetrator and the victim

[78] See Sects. 6.3.3 and 6.3.4.2 for more details.

[79] See Sect. 6.3.3, paras 4–6 for more details.

[80] See Sect. 6.3.3, paras 7–9 for more details.

[81] Riedo. In: Niggli and Wiprächtiger (2007) BSK StGB, Vor Art. 30, Margin No. 2. For a detailed discussion, see Riedo (2004), pp. 11–38.

[82] Riedo. In: Niggli and Wiprächtiger (2007) BSK StGB, Vor Art. 30, Margin No. 3 with further references.

[83] E.g. minor offenses against property (Article 172ter SCC).

[84] E.g. sexual harassment (Article 198 SCC).

(*relative Antragsdelikte*).[85] This aims to prevent the institution of a criminal proceedings against a relative or family member against the will of the victim.[86]

3.2.2.3.3 Other Exceptions

Article 7 para. 2 CCrP provides for further restrictions to the principle of mandatory prosecution. According to this provision, the cantons may stipulate that the criminal liability of members of their legislative and judicial authorities and of their governments be excluded or restricted in relation to statements made in the cantonal parliament. The cantons may also provide that the prosecution of felonies or misdemeanors committed by members of the prosecuting and judicial authorities while in office be made subject to the authorization of a non-judicial authority.[87]

Concerning officials on the federal level, the corresponding reservations are based on other federal laws.[88]

3.2.2.4 Principle of Instruction (Article 6 CCrP)

Following the principle of instruction (*Ermittlungsmaxime* or *Instruktionsmaxime*),—as opposed to the principle of negotiation (*Verhandlungsmaxime* or *Dispositionsmaxime*)[89]—all criminal justice authorities are required to *ex officio* search for the truth (Article 6 CCrP). The Swiss procedure is guided by the principle of the factual truth (*Prinzip der materiellen Wahrheit*).[90]

---

[85] To the contrary, since April 2004, various offenses normally prosecuted only on complaint are prosecuted *ex officio* in the presence of a certain offender-victim-relation. This rule applies on offenses committed in the intimate social environment (see Riedo. In: Niggli and Wiprächtiger (2007) BSK StGB, Vor Art. 30, Margin No. 3a; Riedo et al. 2010, Margin Nos. 118–119). However, according to Article 55a SCC, upon a victim's request, there is a possibility to discontinue a criminal proceeding that concerns such offenses (see Riedo and Saurer. In: Niggli and Wiprächtiger (2007) BSK StGB, Art. 55a; Fiolka and Riedo. In: Niggli et al. (2011) BSK StPO, Art. 8, Margin Nos. 57–59). The prosecution and the courts have wide discretion in deciding whether they want to accede to the victim's request (Riedo and Saurer. In: Niggli and Wiprächtiger (2007) BSK StGB, Art. 55a, Margin Nos. 114–125).

[86] E.g. theft to the detriment of a relative or family member (Article 139 no. 4 SCC).

[87] For more details on this provision see Riedo and Fiolka. In: Niggli et al. (2011) BSK StPO, Art. 7, Margin Nos. 37–117; Riedo et al. (2010), Margin Nos. 120–123; Schmid (2009b), Art. 7, Margin Nos. 8–15, Wohlers. In: Donatsch et al. (2010) Kommentar StPO, Art. 7, Margin Nos. 21–24.

[88] Riedo and Fiolka. In: Niggli et al. (2011) BSK StPO, Art. 7, Margin Nos. 122–134; Riedo et al. (2010), Margin Nos. 124–133; Wohlers. In: Donatsch et al. (2010) Kommentar StPO, Art. 7, Margin Nos. 12–20.

[89] Riedo and Fiolka. In: Niggli et al. (2011) BSK StPO, Art. 6, Margin No. 5; Riedo et al. (2010), Margin No. 167.

[90] Riedo and Fiolka. In: Niggli et al. (2011) BSK StPO, Art. 6, Margin Nos. 59–62; Riedo et al. (2010), Margin No. 166; Schmid (2009b), Art. 6, Margin No. 1; Wohlers. In: Donatsch et al. (2010) Kommentar StPO, Art. 6, Margin Nos. 1–3.

The goal of the prosecution is not to seek a conviction but to discover the truth and to apply the law. As a consequence of both principles, prosecutors are required to investigate exculpatory and incriminatory circumstances with equal care (Article 6 para. 2 CCrP)[91] and judges are not bound by the evidence brought before them by the parties.

Alternative proceedings such as the penal order and the abridged proceedings restrict the principle of instruction.[92]

3.2.2.5 Inquisitorial and Accusatorial Elements in the Swiss Criminal Procedure

The Swiss model of criminal procedure combines inquisitorial and accusatorial elements and thus, it is a mixed system of prosecution.[93] Preliminary proceedings mostly follow the inquisitorial system (non-adversarial, written, and secret) while the accusatorial system prevails at the trial stage (oral, adversarial, and public).[94]

The investigation is assigned to the prosecutor, whose duty is to collect all evidence, incriminating or exculpatory. The investigation is not public, the rationale being to uphold the presumption of innocence and to protect the suspect from the public eye. The written dossier prepared by the prosecutor is transmitted to the court if he believes that there are "sufficient grounds for suspicion" that the accused person has committed the criminal offense. Criminal trials take place in public and are oral. It is the judge who conducts the trial and asks questions in order to find the material truth. There is no cross-examination as such. However, parties may suggest to the judge additional questions to be asked (Article 341 CCrP).

3.2.2.6 Legal Rights of the Accused

3.2.2.6.1 The Right to Be Heard (Article 107 CCrP)

The right to be heard (*Rechtliches Gehör*) is one of the fundamental legal rights of Swiss law and continental law in general. It is explicitly guaranteed in Article 29 para. 2 of the Swiss Federal Constitution, in Article 107 of the CCrP, and is part of the fair trial standards set forth in Article 6 of the European Convention on

[91] Riedo and Fiolka. In: Niggli et al. (2011) BSK StPO, Art. 6, Margin Nos. 90–93; Riedo et al. (2010), Margin No. 165; Schmid (2009b), Art. 6, Margin No. 6; Wohlers. In: Donatsch et al. (2010) Kommentar StPO, Art. 6, Margin No. 7.

[92] Riedo and Fiolka. In: Niggli et al. (2011) BSK StPO, Art. 6, Margin Nos. 37–45; Wohlers. In: Donatsch et al. (2010) Kommentar StPO, Art. 6, Margin No. 5; Federal Council (2006), p. 1130.

[93] On the mixed system, see Piquerez et al. (2011), Margin Nos. 139–143.

[94] Piquerez et al. (2011), Margin No. 141; Trechsel and Killias (2004), p. 277.

Human Rights (ECHR).[95] In particular, this rule contains the right of the parties (a) to have access to the files,[96] (b) to take part in procedural activities,[97] (c) to appoint a legal adviser,[98] (d) to comment on the facts and proceedings,[99] and (e) to submit a claim that evidence be heard.[100] Another consequence of the right to be heard is the court's obligation to cite its rationale for the verdict and the sentence.[101] The aim of this duty is the protection of citizens against arbitrary state decisions. The right to be heard gives the parties the opportunity to present their case and, more specifically, to ensure that the point of view of the accused has been taken into account before a decision affecting him has been made.[102] Unlike the United States, since all authorities are obliged to fully disclose the files of the case to the parties, there are no specific rules of disclosure. The complete disclosure of the files may only be restricted under certain conditions. A restriction of the right to be heard may be necessary if there is reasonable suspicion that a party is misusing its rights,[103] to ensure the safety of people, or to guarantee public or private confidentiality interests (Article 108 CCrP).[104]

Certain aspects of the right to be heard also serve as self-control for the prosecution. This is, for instance, the case with Article 317 CCrP, which provides for a final examination hearing before the conclusion of the investigation. In large and complicated preliminary proceedings, the prosecutor should question the accused person again and ask him to comment on the findings. By conducting such an examination hearing, the prosecutor has the possibility to recognize whether all facts have been sufficiently investigated and if there are major gaps in his reasoning.[105] This provision is not mandatory, so that the prosecutor can

[95] Switzerland ratified the ECHR in 1974. This convention is like the ICCPR directly applicable by Swiss courts (see also Trechsel and Killias 2004, p. 271).

[96] Vest and Horber. In: Niggli et al. (2011) BSK StPO, Art. 107, Margin Nos. 10–18.

[97] Vest and Horber. In: Niggli et al. (2011) BSK StPO, Art. 107, Margin Nos. 19–23.

[98] Vest and Horber. In: Niggli et al. (2011) BSK StPO, Art. 107, Margin Nos. 24–26.

[99] Vest and Horber. In: Niggli et al. (2011) BSK StPO, Art. 107, Margin Nos. 27–32.

[100] Vest and Horber. In: Niggli et al. (2011) BSK StPO, Art. 107, Margin Nos. 33–35.

[101] Hauser et al. (2005), Section 55, Margin Nos. 22–24a; Lieber. In: Donatsch et al. (2010) Kommentar StPO, Art. 107, Margin No. 10; Pieth (2009), pp. 49–50.

[102] Vest and Horber. In: Niggli et al. (2011) BSK StPO, Art. 107, Margin Nos. 1–5.

[103] Federal Council (2006), p. 1164; Lieber. In: Donatsch et al. (2010) Kommentar StPO, Art. 108, Margin No. 4; Pieth (2009), p. 50; Riedo et al. (2010), Margin No. 809; Vest and Horber. In: Niggli et al. (2011) BSK StPO, Art. 108, Margin No. 5.

[104] Lieber. In: Donatsch et al. (2010) Kommentar StPO, Art. 108, Margin No. 6; Riedo et al. (2010), Margin No. 802; Schmid (2009a), Margin No. 114; Vest and Horber. In: Niggli et al. (2011) BSK StPO, Art. 108, Margin No. 6.

[105] Federal Council (2006), p. 1270; Landshut. In: Donatsch et al. (2010) Kommentar StPO, Art. 317, Margin No. 1; Schmid (2009a), Margin No. 1243; Schmid (2009b), Art. 317, Margin No. 1; Steiner. In: Niggli et al. (2011) BSK StPO, Art. 317, Margin No. 2.

exercise discretion in deciding whether to conduct such a hearing.[106] If the prosecutor intends to issue an order discontinuing a proceeding, then he may renounce conducting a final examination hearing.[107]

3.2.2.6.2 The Right to Remain Silent or the Right Against Self-Incrimination (Article 113 CCrP)

The CCrP guarantees the right to remain silent. The accused person is not required to incriminate himself.[108] He has the right to refuse any cooperation in the criminal proceedings,[109] but must submit to those coercive measure designated by law.[110] This right implies that no disadvantageous conclusions can be drawn from silence.[111] The right against self-incrimination is also explicitly established in Article 14 para. 3 (g) of the International Covenant on Civil and Political Rights (ICCPR)[112] and is part of the presumption of innocence guaranteed by Article 6 para. 2 ECHR.[113]

[106] Landshut. In: Donatsch et al. (2010) Kommentar StPO, Art. 317, Margin No. 4; Schmid (2009b), Art. 317, Margin No. 4; Steiner. In: Niggli et al. (2011) BSK StPO, Art. 317, Margin No. 5.

[107] Landshut. In: Donatsch et al. (2010) Kommentar StPO, Art. 317, Margin No. 2: Schmid (2009b), Art. 317, Margin No. 2.

[108] Engler. In: Niggli et al. (2011) BSK StPO, Art. 113, Margin No. 3; Hauser et al. (2005), Section 39, Margin Nos. 14–20d; Lieber. In: Donatsch et al. (2010) Kommentar StPO, Art. 113, Margin Nos. 1–3.

[109] Engler. In: Niggli et al. (2011) BSK StPO, Art. 113, Margin No. 2; Lieber. In: Donatsch et al. (2010) Kommentar StPO, Art. 113, Margin Nos. 19–22; Riedo et al. (2010), Margin No. 834.

[110] Engler. In: Niggli et al. (2011) BSK StPO, Art. 113, Margin No. 8; Lieber. In: Donatsch et al. (2010) Kommentar StPO, Art. 113, Margin Nos. 42–53; Riedo et al. (2010), Margin Nos. 838–839.

[111] Engler. In: Niggli et al. (2011) BSK StPO, Art. 113, Margin No. 4; Riedo et al. (2010), Margin No. 834.

[112] Switzerland ratified the ICCPR in 1992. Because Switzerland relies on the monistic system, this convention is directly applicable by Swiss courts (Fleiner et al. 2005, pp. 43–44). The United States also ratified this convention in 1992. The U.S. Senate has added a reservation to Article 7 ICCPR prohibiting torture or cruel, inhuman, or degrading treatment or punishment. An "understanding" with respect to Article 14 states that its "counsel" provisions "do not require the provision of a criminal defendant's counsel of choice when the defendant is provided with the court-appointed counsel on grounds of indigence, when the defendant is financially able to retain alternative counsel, or when imprisonment is not imposed." On treaty enforcement in the United States, see LaFave et al. (2007), Section 1.7 (c).

[113] Engler. In: Niggli et al. (2011) BSK StPO, Art. 113, Margin No. 3; Lieber. In: Donatsch et al. (2010) Kommentar StPO, Art. 113, Margin Nos. 5–11; Riedo et al. (2010), Margin Nos. 832–833.

3.2.2.6.3 Presumption of Innocence and the Principle *In Dubio Pro Reo* (Article 10 CCrP)

The presumption of innocence is stated explicitly in various laws and conventions.[114] Article 32 para. 1 of the Swiss Federal Constitution says: "Everyone is presumed innocent until they have been found guilty by a legally enforceable judgment." The presumption of innocence is similarly guaranteed in Article 10 para. 1 CCrP.[115] Article 6 para. 2 ECHR says: "Everyone charged with a criminal offense shall be presumed innocent until proved guilty according to law." The presumption of innocence is also established in Article 14 para. 2 ICCPR.

In connection with this principle, the maxim *in dubio pro reo* must be respected (Article 10 para. 3 CCrP), according to which the accused can only be convicted if the court has found sufficient evidence for his guilt. In criminal trials, doubt must be resolved in favor of the accused.[116]

3.2.2.6.4 *Ne Bis In Idem* (Article 11 CCrP)

The *ne bis in idem* principle (prohibition of double jeopardy) is guaranteed in Article 11 CCrP and states that "[a] person who has been convicted or acquitted in Switzerland shall not be prosecuted again for the same criminal offense." Thus, the Swiss criminal justice system recognizes this principle only within its own domestic legal order. As a consequence, if a case has been disposed in a foreign country, Article 11 CCrP does not preclude another prosecution for the same offense in Switzerland. Article 4 of Protocol No. 7 to the Convention for the Protection of Human Rights and Fundamental Freedoms and Article 14 para. 7 ICCPR also only guarantee a national *ne bis in idem* principle. The validity of foreign judgments in criminal matters can only be recognized if there is a treaty basis. Article 54 of the Convention Implementing the Schengen Agreement (CISA) provides such a basis, which is applicable in Switzerland.[117]

According to Article 11 para. 2 CCrP, the *ne bis in idem* principle "applies subject to the provisions on the re-opening of proceedings which were

[114] Tophinke. In: Niggli et al. (2011) BSK StPO, Art. 10, Margin No. 4; Wohlers. In: Donatsch et al. (2010) Kommentar StPO, Art. 10, Margin No. 1.

[115] See Riedo et al. (2010), Margin No. 229; Tophinke. In: Niggli et al. (2011) BSK StPO, Art. 10, Margin Nos. 1–40; Wohlers. In: Donatsch et al. (2010) Kommentar StPO, Art. 10, Margin Nos. 2–10.

[116] Riedo et al. (2010), Margin No. 230; Tophinke. In: Niggli et al. (2011) BSK StPO, Art. 10, Margin Nos. 75–87; Wohlers. In: Donatsch et al. (2010) Kommentar StPO, Art. 10, Margin Nos. 11–15.

[117] Article 54 CISA reads as follows: "A person whose trial has been finally disposed of in one Contracting Party may not be prosecuted in another Contracting Party for the same acts provided that, if a penalty has been imposed, it has been enforced, is actually in the process of being enforced or can no longer be enforced under the laws of the sentencing Contracting Party."

discontinued, to those on proceedings which were not opened, and to those regulating the retrial."

3.2.2.6.5 Equality Before the Law and Requirement of Fairness (Article 3 CCrP)

Equality before the law is guaranteed in Article 8 of the Swiss Federal Constitution,[118] Article 3 para. 2 (c) CCrP[119] and Article 14 ECHR and states that no one may be discriminated against, on grounds of origin, race, gender, age, language, social status, religious, or political convictions. All persons involved in a criminal proceedings shall be treated equally.

Furthermore, Article 3 para. 2 (c) CCrP states that all persons involved in a criminal proceedings should be treated fairly. Thus, this right is not limited to the accused. Important aspects of the right to be treated fairly include: the right of the accused to be judged by an independent and impartial tribunal (Article 4 CCrP, Article 30 para. 1 Swiss Federal Constitution, Article 6 ECHR), the right to be heard (Article 107 CCrP, Article 6 ECHR),[120] the right to a public hearing and public pronouncement of judgments (Article 30 para. 3 Swiss Federal Constitution, Article 6 para. 1 ECHR), the right of having the charge determined within a reasonable time (Article 5 CCrP; Article 29 para. 1 Swiss Federal Constitution, Article 6 para. 1 ECHR), the right against self-incrimination (Article 3 CCrP),[121] the guarantee of participation rights and the rights of the defense (Article 3 and 147 CCrP, Article 6 para. 3 ECHR), and the prohibition of torture and any other form of cruel, inhuman or degrading treatment (Article 10 para. 3 Swiss Federal Constitution, Article 3 ECHR, see also Article 140 CCrP).

3.2.2.7 Victims' Rights

3.2.2.7.1 The Emergence of Crime Victim Rights and Remedies

For centuries, the role of the victim in criminal prosecution was essential, namely when all offenses were considered private.[122] By the fourteenth century, with the involvement of the state in criminal prosecution, the victim was not longer the center of attention and thus victims' rights were not considered to be of great

[118] On the Equal Protection Clause in Article 8 of the Swiss Federal Constitution, see Fleiner et al. (2005), pp. 162–166.

[119] Wohlers. In: Donatsch et al. (2010) Kommentar StPO, Art. 3, Margin No. 19.

[120] On the right to be heard, see Sect. 3.2.2.6.1.

[121] On the right against self-incrimination, see Sect. 3.2.2.6.2.

[122] A historical overview on the victim's participation in the criminal procedure is given in Jabornigg (2001), pp. 178–302.

importance. Hence, it is mainly due to the rise of the inquisitorial criminal process that for many years, Swiss criminal justice has paid little attention to victim concerns.[123] It is only since the nineteenth century that victims' rights have progressively been implemented in the criminal procedure.[124] The development of victimology—a branch of criminology—in the 1940s, has shown that the interests of crime victims are not limited to the punishment of the offender.[125] Rehabilitation, reparation, and protection against the accused during a criminal proceeding to avoid secondary victimization are the victim's main needs.[126]

In most European countries, victims' rights movements emerged around 1985, since at that time one convention[127] and two recommendations from the Council of Europe[128] were passed.[129]

The first federal victims' rights legislation was the Victims of Crime Act of October 4, 1991 (VCA). Provisions of this act have subsequently been amended and expanded.[130] The completely revised VCA from March 27, 2007[131] became legally effective on January 1, 2009. It regulates and improves the position of the injured party and their relatives relating to offenses against the physical, sexual, or psychical integrity. The three-pillars concept introduced in the first Victim Aid Code was retained. It consists of advice, preservation of rights during criminal proceedings, as well as claims for reparation and satisfaction against the state. However, regulations regarding the protection of the victim within criminal proceedings were incorporated into the CCrP.

3.2.2.7.2 Victim's Rights Within Criminal Proceedings According to the Swiss Code of Criminal Procedure

According to Article 117 CCrP, the victim has special rights, in particular: (1) the right to the protection of his privacy (Article 70 para. 1 letter a, 74 para. 4, and 152 para. 1); (2) the right to be accompanied by a confidant (Article 70 para. 2 and 152 para. 2); (3) the right to benefit from protective measures (Article 152 et seq.);

---

[123] Jabornigg (2001), pp. 253–256.

[124] Jabornigg (2001), pp. 279–286.

[125] Jabornigg (2001), pp. 287–292.

[126] Zehntner. In: Gomm and Zehntner (2009) OHG Kommentar, Einleitung, Margin No. 4.

[127] European Convention on the Compensation of Victims of Violent Crime (1983). This convention has been ratified by Switzerland on June 20, 1991 (entry into force January 1, 1993).

[128] Recommendation R(85) 11 on the Position of the Victim in the Framework of Criminal Law and Procedure; Recommendation R(87) 21 on the Assistance to Victims and the Prevention of Victimization.

[129] See Jabornigg (2001), pp. 300–301.

[130] Zehntner. In: Gomm and Zehntner (2009) OHG Kommentar, Einleitung, Margin No. 7.

[131] Victims of Crime Act of March 23, 2007 (VCA) (Status as of January 1, 2011); *Bundesgesetz vom 23. März 2007 über die Hilfe an Opfer von Straftaten* (*Opferhilfegesetz, OHG*) (*Stand am 1. Januar 2011*); SR 312.5.

(4) the right to refuse to make statements (Article 169 para. 4); (5) the right to be informed of his rights (Article 305 and 330 para. 3); (6) the right to a special composition of the court (Article 335 para. 4). Additional provisions aim to protect the privacy of victims under the age of 18.[132]

This enumeration is not conclusive. Article 117 CCrP aims to provide an overview of the special procedural rights that are dispersed in the law. On the one hand, these rights intend to protect the victim against a secondary victimization and on the other hand, participatory rights shall facilitate civil claims.[133]

Article 305 CCrP concerns the victim's rights to information during the preliminary proceedings. Hence, the police or prosecutor shall inform the victim at the first hearing about his rights and duties in the criminal proceedings.[134] At the same time, the same authority shall inform the victim about (1) the address and role of the Victims Advice Service; (2) the opportunity for victims to claim various benefits; (3) the time limit for submitting an application for compensation and non-pecuniary loss.[135]

The victim has to be notified about the imposition and revocation of detention on remand or security detention and of the fact that an accused has escaped (Article 214 para. 4 CCrP). Furthermore, the prosecution informs the victim of the suspension (Article 314 para. 4 CCrP) and the discontinuation (Article 321 para. 1 CCrP) of the criminal proceedings.

Finally, victims shall be informed of possible party's rights as well as the possibility to participate as a civil claimant and exercise the corresponding rights.[136] In particular, the victim as civil claimant has the right to be heard[137] and the right to be present and to put questions to the person who is being examined in the context of the taking of evidence by the prosecution and the courts (Article 147 CCrP). He may also have recourse to legal remedy (Article 379 et seq. CCrP). However, he may not challenge a decision in relation to the sentence imposed (Article 382 para. 2 CCrP).

In sum, whereas rights to information and protection can be claimed regardless of whether or not the victim acts as a private claimant, rights to participation depend on the victim acting as a party to the procedure.

---

[132] In particular, these concern (1) restrictions in the context of the confrontation hearings with the accused (Art. 154 para. 4 CCrP); (2) particular protective measures in respect of examination hearings (Art. 154 para. 2–4 CCrP); (3) the discontinuation of the proceedings (Art. 319 para. 2 CCrP).

[133] Schaffner and Vogt. In: Gomm and Zehntner (2009) OHG Kommentar, Art. 117, Margin No. 1; Lieber. In: Donatsch et al. (2010) Kommentar StPO, Art. 117, Margin No. 2.

[134] See Landshut. In: Donatsch et al. (2010) Kommentar StPO, Art. 305, Margin Nos. 5–9 for more information.

[135] See Landshut. In: Donatsch et al. (2010) Kommentar StPO, Art. 305, Margin Nos. 10–13 for more information.

[136] Article 104–108 CCrP; Article 118–121 CCrP; Article 136–138 CCrP.

[137] On the right to be heard, see Sect. 3.2.2.6.1.

3.2.2.7.3 Victim's Rights According to the Victims of Crime Act

The right to obtain advice exists independently whether the victim has reported the criminal offense to the police or not.[138] The staff of the Victims' Counseling Center have the duty of discretion against authorities and private persons (Article 11 para. 1 VCA).[139]

The law makes a distinction between immediate assistance and longer-term assistance (Article 13 VCA).[140] The Victims' Counseling Centers provide the victim and his family with the appropriate medical, psychological, social, material, and legal assistance (Article 14 VCA).[141] Immediate assistance for the most urgent needs after a crime is free of charge for the victim (Article 5 VCA).[142] Victim's Help can contribute to the costs of longer-term assistance, based on the financial situation of the victim or his family (Article 16 VCA).[143]

Persons affected by violence have a claim to compensation regarding the costs arisen directly from the crime (Article 19 VCA).[144] The help is subsidiary, so that this financial help will be paid only if neither the offender nor an insurance company bears the costs. Furthermore, compensation is granted only to those victims whose countable income is under a set limit (Article 20 VCA).[145] Reparation is compensation provided for pain and suffering. This payment is awarded to someone who has experienced serious physical and mental harm as a result of an injury. Reparation payments are due without taking the victim's financial situation into account (Article 22 VCA).[146] The application for compensation and for reparation has to be made within 5 years after the offense (Article 25 VCA).[147]

3.2.2.7.4 The Definition of "Victim"

According to the VCA as well as the CCrP, a victim is an aggrieved person whose physical, sexual, or psychological integrity was directly affected by the criminal offense (Article 1 para. 1 VCA; Article 116 para. 1 CCrP). The prescribed rights are not limited to direct crime victims but extend to relatives. People considered relatives of the victim are his spouse, children, parents, and any people who are similarly close to him (Article 1 para. 2 VCA; Article 116 para. 2 CCrP). Hence, the

---

[138] Zehntner. In: Gomm and Zehntner (2009) OHG Kommentar, Art. 1, Margin No. 13.

[139] Vogt. In: Gomm and Zehntner (2009) OHG Kommentar, Art. 11.

[140] Zehntner. In: Gomm and Zehntner (2009) OHG Kommentar, Art. 13.

[141] Zehntner. In: Gomm and Zehntner (2009) OHG Kommentar, Art. 14.

[142] Zehntner. In: Gomm and Zehntner (2009) OHG Kommentar, Art. 5.

[143] Zehntner. In: Gomm and Zehntner (2009) OHG Kommentar, Art. 16.

[144] Gomm. In: Gomm and Zehntner (2009) OHG Kommentar, Art. 19.

[145] Gomm. In: Gomm and Zehntner (2009) OHG Kommentar, Art. 20.

[146] An overview of the amount of reparation awarded by courts for various kinds of offenses can be found in Gomm. In: Gomm and Zehntner (2009) OHG Kommentar, Art. 23, Margin Nos. 7–14.

[147] Gomm. In: Gomm and Zehntner (2009) OHG Kommentar, Art. 25.

law makes a distinction between direct and indirect victims. Corporate bodies are not entitled to claim.[148]

Victims within criminal proceedings have the same rights as the ones granted to the aggrieved person (Article 115 CCrP) and the private claimant.[149] The latter have to expressly declare their participation in the criminal proceedings as a criminal or civil claimant (Article 118 para. 1 CCrP). As a civil party, the victim can attach his claim to the criminal prosecution and hence participate as a party with legal representation (Article 122 CCrP). Beside compensation, the adhesion procedure entitles the victim to exercise several rights, such as the right to be heard in court.[150]

3.2.2.7.5 The Definition of a "Crime"

Victim's rights are only conferred to those persons whose physical, sexual, or psychological integrity was directly affected by the criminal offense. Hence, the mere endangerment of the victim is usually not sufficient to grant him these rights.[151] However, help according to the VCA is available regardless of whether the offender is sentenced or not, or whether the offender is culpable or not.[152]

The VCA does not provide a list of criminal offenses. Criminal acts recognized by courts include cases of violence (e.g. murder, physical injury, or robbery), sexual offenses (e.g. rape or sexual assault), domestic violence (e.g. physical injury, grievous bodily harm, or threat), and road accidents involving physical injury.[153] Thus, in particular, offenses against life and limb (Article 111 et seq. SCC), against liberty (Article 180 et seq. SCC), and against sexual integrity (Article 187 et seq. SCC) lead to the application of the VCA.

3.3 Comparison of U.S. and Swiss Prosecution Systems

Figure 3.1 provides a simplified comparative overview on the steps in the U.S. and Swiss criminal procedures, whereby the main actors involved are mentioned. In both countries, cases are investigated by the police, sent to the prosecutor, and

[148] Zehntner. In: Gomm and Zehntner (2009) OHG Kommentar, Einleitung, Margin No. 26.

[149] Lieber. In: Donatsch et al. (2010) Kommentar StPO, Art. 116, Margin No. 3.

[150] See Sect. 3.2.2.7.2, para 5 on this topic.

[151] Zehntner. In: Gomm and Zehntner (2009) OHG Kommentar, Art. 1, Margin No. 9. The threatened is considered as "victim" according to the VCA, although threatening behavior (Article 180 SCC) is an offense of endangerment (Jabornigg 2001, p. 19).

[152] Zehntner. In: Gomm and Zehntner (2009) OHG Kommentar, Art. 1, Margin Nos. 11–25.

[153] See Mizel (2003), pp. 44–45 and 55–72 for a list of accepted and refused criminal acts by the courts.

Fig. 3.1 Simplified comparison of U.S. and Swiss prosecution systems

finally taken to the court. In addition to the normal proceedings, alternative and summary proceedings are available in both prosecution systems. In the U.S. system, this is the plea bargain. In the Swiss legal system, these are the penal order and the abridged proceedings.

Apart from a few differences, the sequences of the normal procedures in both prosecution systems look quite similar.

References

Amar AR, Lettow RB (1995) Fifth Amendment first principles: the self-incrimination clause. Mich Law Rev 93:857–928

Beloof DE, Cassell PG, Twist SJ (2006) Victims in criminal procedure, 2nd edn. Carolina Academic Press, Durham

Cardenas J (1986) The crime victim in the prosecutorial process. Harv J Law Public Policy 9:357–398

Cassell PG (2007) Treating crime victims fairly: integrating victims into the federal rules of criminal procedure. Utah Law Rev 2007(4):861–970

Del Carmen RV (2007) Criminal procedure. Law and practice, 7th edn. Thomson/Wadsworth, Belmont

Donatsch A, Hansjakob T, Lieber V (eds) (2010) Kommentar zur Schweizerischen Strafprozessordnung (StPO) (Kommentar StPO). Schulthess, Zurich

Doyle C (2008) Crime victims' rights act. Novinka Books, New York

Dubber MD (2002) Victims in the war on crime. The use and abuse of victims' rights. New York University Press, New York

Federal Council (2006) Message from the Federal Council of December 21, 2005 on the unification of criminal procedure [Botschaft des Bundesrates zur Vereinheitlichung des Strafprozessrechts vom 21. Dezember 2005]. Federal Chancellery, Berne

Fleiner T, Misic A, Töpperwien N (2005) Swiss constitutional law. Kluwer Law International, The Hague

Gittler J (1984) Expanding the role of the victim in a criminal action: an overview of issues and problems. Pepperdine Law Rev 11:117–182

Gomm P, Zehntner D (eds) (2009) Kommentar zum Opferhilfegesetz (OHG-Kommentar). Bundesgesetz vom 23. März 2007 über die Hilfe an Opfer von Straftaten, 3rd edn. Stämpfli, Berne

Hammond SB (2006) Victims' rights laws in the states. National Conference of State Legislatures, Denver

Hauser R, Schweri E, Hartmann K (2005) Schweizerisches Strafprozessrecht, 6th edn. Helbing & Lichtenhahn, Basel

Jabornigg DV (2001) Die Stellung des Verletzten in den schweizerischen Strafprozessordnungen zwischen Beweismittel und Partei. Helbing & Lichtenhahn, Basel

Karmen AJ (1992) Who's against victims' rights? The nature of the opposition to pro-victim initiatives in criminal justice. St Johns J Leg Comment 8:157–175

LaFave WR, Israel JH, King NJ, Kerr OS (2007) Criminal procedure, 3rd edn, 7 vols. Criminal practice series. Thomson/West, St. Paul

McDonald WF (1976) Towards a bicentennial revolution in criminal justice: the return of the victim. Am Crim Law Rev 13:649–673

Mizel C (2003) La qualité de la victime LAVI et la mesure actuelle des droits qui en découlent. Journal des Tribunaux 2003(2):38–100

Niggli MA, Wiprächtiger H (eds) (2007) Basler Kommentar zum Strafrecht I (Art. 1-110 StGB) (BSK StGB), 2nd edn. Helbing & Lichtenhahn, Basel

Niggli MA, Heer M, Wiprächtiger H (eds) (2011) Basler Kommentar zur Schweizerischen Strafprozessordnung – Jugendstrafprozessordnung (BSK StPO). Helbing & Lichtenhahn, Basel

O'Hara EA (2005) Victim participation in the criminal process. J Law Policy 13:229–247

Parker A (2008) Mixed results. US Policy and International Standards on the rights and interests of victims of crime. Human Rights Watch, New York

Pieth M (2009) Schweizerisches Strafprozessrecht. Grundriss für Studium und Praxis. Helbing & Lichtenhahn, Basel

Piquerez G, Macaluso A, Piquerez L (2011) Procédure pénale suisse, 3rd edn. Schulthess, Geneva

Riedo C (2004) Der Strafantrag. Helbing & Lichtenhahn, Basel

Riedo C, Fiolka G, Niggli MA (2010) Schweizerisches Strafprozessrecht. Eine Einführung. Helbing & Lichtenhahn, Basel

Schmid N (2009a) Handbuch des schweizerischen Strafprozessrechts. Dike, Zurich

Schmid N (2009b) Schweizerische Strafprozessordnung (StPO): Praxiskommentar. Dike, Zurich

Tobolowsky PM, Gaboury MT, Jackson AL, Blackburn AG (2010) Crime victim rights and remedies, 2nd edn. Carolina Academic Press, Durham

Trechsel S, Killias M (2004) Law of criminal procedure. In: Dessemontet F, Ansay T (eds) Introduction to Swiss law, 3rd edn. Kluwer Law International (sold and distributed in North Central and South America by Aspen Publishers), Frederick, pp 269–286

Chapter 4
History of the Public Prosecutor

Before discussing the role of American and Swiss prosecutors, this chapter outlines the origins of the public prosecutor in both countries. The understanding of their current position begins with their historical origins. A comparative analysis of the evolution of the U.S. prosecutorial system with the Swiss system also helps to identify and understand the differences between both systems.

4.1 Historical Background of the American Public Prosecutor

The precise antecedent of the present American public prosecutor is enigmatic.[1] In fact, the historical developments leading to the creation of the public prosecution have been largely unexamined and archival research still remains to be done.[2] Most legal scholars assume that it descended from one of three European predecessors: either the English attorney general, the French *procureur publique*, or the Dutch *schout*.[3] The American public prosecutor has the power to terminate all criminal prosecutions, like the English attorney general. Like the French *procureur publique,* he has the power to initiate all public prosecutions.[4] Like the Dutch *schout*, he is a local official of regional government.[5] In addition to these similarities, there are also important differences between the American prosecutor in his current state and his antecedents. None of them was the primary law enforcement

---

[1] The birth of the American public prosecutor is sometimes seen as a "historical puzzle" (see van Alstyne 1952, p. 125; Shoemaker 2005, p. 339; Gittler 1984, p. 127; Kress 1976, p. 100).

[2] Shoemaker (2005), pp. 341 and 355; Jacoby (1980), p. 3; see also Langbein (1973), pp. 313 and 315. The same conclusion is drawn for England (see Kurland and Waters 1959, p. 493).

[3] Jacoby (1980), pp. 11–16; Worrall (2008), pp. 4–5.

[4] Jacoby (1980), p. 3.

[5] Jacoby (1980), p. 3.

G. Gilliéron, *Public Prosecutors in the United States and Europe*,
DOI 10.1007/978-3-319-04504-7_4, © Springer International Publishing Switzerland 2014

official within a specific jurisdiction but instead worked under a national central authority. Whereas the American prosecutor is generally elected, the European officials were appointed. Finally, the American prosecutor enjoys wide unreviewable discretion.[6]

Convincing arguments for and against the influence of all three figures can be made. However, none of these actors can claim to be the direct predecessor of the American public prosecutor. The development of the American public prosecutor is a product of long evolution. As Jacoby states, "the prosecuting attorney is a distinctly American figure, and for distinctly American reasons."[7] Before tracing the evolution of the public prosecutor throughout American history, the following section describes the predecessors from whom the American public prosecutor appears to have descended and who impacted the mode of prosecution in colonial America.

4.1.1 The English Attorney General

It has been asserted that the attorney general was the predecessor of the American public prosecutor.

The criminal justice system in colonial America reflected the English common law tradition.[8] In common law, a crime was viewed as a wrong against an individual rather than against the state.[9] As a result, the English system of criminal prosecution was primarily a system of private prosecution.[10] The victim of a crime or an interested individual had the right to bring and prosecute the case against a criminal offender.[11] Although private prosecution was predominant in England from the thirteenth century until the late twentieth century, there had always been an element of official prosecution. The parish constable, a chief law enforcement officer, appeared in the thirteenth century. His duty was to maintain law and order at the local level. He had the power to arrest when the offender was caught red-handed. Nevertheless, the burden of investigating crime was assumed by the justices of the

---

[6] Jacoby (1980), p. 5.

[7] Jacoby (1980), p. 6. See also Miller (1970), p. 54, n 22 ("The very institution of public prosecution is largely an American invention").

[8] Because of the Dutch influence, the legal system of England was not adopted wholesale (see below Sect. 4.1.2).

[9] Kress (1976), p. 100; National Commission on Law Observance and Enforcement (1931), p. 6.

[10] Cardenas (1986), p. 366; Reiss (1975), p. 4. Although a crime was predominantly seen as a private matter, it was also considered as an offense against the peace of the state (Ma 2008, pp. 191–192).

[11] Friedman (1993), p. 29. National Commission on Law Observance and Enforcement (1931), p. 6. See generally Sidman (1976).

peace.[12] Justices of the peace[13] were introduced during the fourteenth century.[14] The Marian Statutes of 1554 and 1555 empowered them to perform some investigative functions similar to those of the modern public prosecutor.[15] Justices of the peace had the power to interrogate the accused and witnesses, had the authority to commit relevant parties to trial, and could decide to continue prosecuting in spite of the complaining citizen's desire to withdraw from the case.[16] Prosecutions conducted by the constable and the justices of the peace were not public in nature. In a system of private prosecution, the right to prosecution was not restricted to the victim and his relatives but was extended to the public because it was the duty of all citizens to preserve the king's peace.[17]

During the Middle Ages, a number of king's attorneys represented the Crown in various courts. The duty of a king's attorney was to protect the king's interest. Therefore he restricted his prosecutions to those cases of special importance to the Crown.[18] The victim handled all violations of individual rights privately. In the fifteenth century, the kings' attorneys were replaced by a single attorney, the attorney general. He was the only figure that could be described as the public prosecutor.[19] He had the power to commence a prosecution and to file a writ of *nolle prosequi*,[20] meaning that he was unwilling to prosecute. The decision to dismiss a case was entirely within his discretion.[21] The power to terminate criminal prosecutions served as a check against abuse of private prosecution.[22] It was not until 1879 that the English Director of Public Prosecutions was created, which is the

---

[12] Devlin (1958), p. 5.

[13] John Langbein traces the origins of public prosecution in England to the Marian Statutes of 1554 and 1555. (Langbein 1973, p. 318; see also Langbein 1974, pp. 34–45). Jack Kress has suggested that the justices of the peace were "firmly established by the time of the American colonization," and that "the appearance of a separate public prosecutor in the colonies might be explained as a fairly logical next step, that is, a pragmatic division of the separate magisterial and prosecutorial functions" (Kress 1976, p. 102). In fact, in Maryland, for instance, the district attorney seems to have evolved from the "clerk of indictments". This position was created in Maryland in 1683 (Carr 1987, pp. 281–285; see Rice 1996, p. 467). For a more detailed discussion on the influence of the clerk of indictments might have had on the American public prosecutor, see Shoemaker (2005), pp. 351–352.

[14] Devlin (1958), p. 5.

[15] Langbein (1973), pp. 317–324.

[16] Langbein (1974), p. 35; Devlin (1958), p. 6.

[17] In the same sense, police prosecutions are private prosecutions as well (Cardenas 1986, p. 364; Devlin 1958, p. 20).

[18] Cardenas (1986), pp. 359–360; National Commission on Law Observance and Enforcement (1931), p. 6; Jacoby (1980), p. 8; Goldstein (2002), p. 1242.

[19] Devlin (1958), p. 20.

[20] *Nolle prosequi* is a Latin legal phrase meaning "be unwilling to pursue" and had existed in England since the sixteenth century (Goldstein 1981, p. 12).

[21] Goldstein (2002), p. 1242; Goldstein (1981), pp. 12–15; National Commission on Law Observance and Enforcement (1931), p. 6.

[22] Devlin (1958), p. 21; Goldstein (2002), p. 1242; Goldstein (1981), p. 12.

closest analog to the American public prosecutor.[23] Nearly two centuries before, the public prosecutor had already made his appearance in the American colonies. In 1704, Connecticut was the first colony to create a decentralized prosecutorial system by statute: "Henceforth there shall be in every county a sober, discreet and religious person appointed by the county court, to be attorney for the Queen to prosecute and implead in the law all criminals and to do all other things necessary or convenient as an attorney to suppress vice and immorality."[24] This leads some scholars to argue that the system of public prosecution could not be traced to England.[25]

4.1.2 The Dutch Schout

A possible origin of the American public prosecutor is the Dutch *schout*.[26] The *schout* was a Dutch public official[27] who combined the powers and duties of a sheriff and public prosecutor.[28]

In the seventeenth century, the Dutch brought their legal institutions, including the office of the *schout*, to the American colony of New Netherland.[29] In 1653, New Amsterdam became the first Dutch settlement to establish the *schout*.[30] In 1664, the English captured New Amsterdam (now Manhattan) and took over the New Netherlands colony. The Dutch retook the colony in 1673, but ceded it to England by treaty in 1674.[31] English common law was established in the former Dutch settlements. When the English seized New Netherland in 1664 and 1674, records of the New Amsterdam courts indicate that the *schout* continued to bring cases but that he

[23] Kress (1976), p. 100; Carr (1987), p. 285. For the history of the Prosecution of Offences Act that has established the English Director of Public Prosecutions, see Kurland and Waters (1959).

[24] See *Records of the States of the United States of America 1650–1715,* reel I (Connecticut, B) 195–196; National Commission on Law Observance and Enforcement (1931), p. 7. Van Alstyne suggests that the Dutch tradition and practice might have influenced the creation of the public prosecutor in Connecticut (van Alstyne 1952, p. 136). However, it seems that the statute reflects the views of English Puritans rather than the civilian jurists (see Shoemaker 2005, pp. 344–346).

[25] See e.g. Reiss (1975), p. 5; Lois Carr stated that "the creation of this office was a departure from contemporary English precedent" (Carr 1987, p. 285).

[26] W. Scott Van Alstyne, Jr. pioneered this thesis. For a discussion on the actual position of the Public Prosecution Service in the Netherlands, see Blom and Smit (2006).

[27] The *schout* corresponds to the *Schultheiss* in medieval Germany. As executive official of the ruler, it was his duty to order his assigned village to pay the taxes.

[28] Jacoby (1980), p. 14; van Alstyne (1952), pp. 129–131 and 133–135; Kress (1976), p. 104.

[29] Goldstein (2002), p. 1243; van Alstyne (1952), pp. 129–130; Kress (1976), p. 104; Jacoby (1980), pp. 12–14. New Netherland covered an area which today is Connecticut, New York, New Jersey, Pennsylvania, and Delaware. For more information on New Netherland, see Jacobs (2005).

[30] The first *schout* to appear as prosecutor in a criminal trial was Cornelius Van Tienhoven (van Alstyne 1952, p. 131).

[31] van Alstyne (1952), p. 133.

bore the title of sheriff.[32] Colonial records suggest that the office of the *schout* was also established in New Jersey, Delaware, and Pennsylvania, and that it underwent a similar process.[33] The separation of the function of law enforcement from that of prosecution occurred at the beginning of the eighteenth century.

For different reasons, it is questionable whether it was the Dutch criminal prosecution that was predominant in producing the American public prosecutor. The Dutch population outside of New Amsterdam was small, and the Dutch control over its colonies was quite brief. It lasted from 1653 until 1664 and from 1673 until 1674.[34] It is not known how long the office of the sheriff continued to be in place after the Dutch gave over control. In New York, for example, it was only in 1801 that a district attorney's office was created. The extent to which the Dutch *schout* had an influence at this time is more than questionable. Scholars analyzing the legal history of New York attribute the district attorney to the English attorney general rather than to the Dutch *schout*.[35] Further, in former Dutch settlements, evidence suggests the implementation of the attorney general. In Pennsylvania, this position was introduced in 1686.[36]

4.1.3 The French Procureur Publique

It is argued that the American public prosecutor is descended from the French *procureur publique*.[37]

The French system of a public prosecutor's office, that of the *procureur du roi* (the king's prosecutor), can be traced back in the late Middle Ages. His duties were limited to protecting the king's interests, enforcing penalties, and collecting fines.[38] Originally, the king's prosecutor could also bring prosecution in cases where there were no private complainants.[39] As the *procureur* gained more power in prosecution, his title changed from *procureur du roi* to *ministère public* (public prosecutor).[40] At this time, the prosecutor took the responsibility of investigating offenses and instituting criminal prosecutions regardless of whether there was a private

---

[32] van Alstyne (1952), pp. 132–137; Goldstein (2002), p. 1243.

[33] van Alstyne (1952), pp. 132–137; Jacoby (1980), p. 14.

[34] Kress (1976), p. 104.

[35] Julis Goebel and Thomas Raymond Naughton state that there are other possible models for the American public prosecutor than the Dutch *schout* (Goebel and Naughton 1970, p. 332). The New York legislature sees the district attorney as well as extension of the English Attorney General [see e.g. Spielman Motor Sales Co, Inc., v. Dodge, 295 U.S. 89, 92 (1935)].

[36] See Poserina (1959), p. 83.

[37] For a discussion of the French Public Prosecution Service in its current state, see Sects. 8.1 and 8.2. See also the contribution of Verrest (2000) and of Aubusson de Cavarlay (2006).

[38] Esmein (1882), p. 101; Esmein (1913), p. 115; Sheehan (1975), p. 15.

[39] Langbein (1974), p. 217.

[40] Sheehan (1975), p. 15.

complaint. During the fifteenth century, the inquisitorial system replaced the accusatorial.[41] The French did, however, retain private prosecution, which may be pursued in the event of neglect, inertia, or corruption of the public authorities.[42] By the sixteenth century, the public prosecutor had the exclusive power to seek criminal sanctions. The aggrieved victim was limited to claiming civil damages in his own right. This development was connected to the fact that an offense was seen as being against the public.[43] However, the French *ministère public* in its current state was not created until 1808. It was at that time of the *Code d'Instruction Criminelle* (CIC, Code of Criminal Instruction) that the French public prosecutor received his main characteristics.[44]

In Louisiana (New France),[45] the mode of prosecution was influenced by the French system of prosecution. Louisiana was under French control from 1682 until 1763 and from 1800 until 1803. The area was named in honor of Louis XIV.[46] It was not until 1714 that the first permanent settlement, Natchitoches, was established. The legal history of Louisiana begins in 1712. Before this date, there was little or no law in Louisiana.[47] The colony's first court, the Superior Council, was founded in 1716 following the French model.[48] It embodied Louis XIV's authority to act as a legislature and court of last resort in all criminal and civil cases. All of the courts in the region applied the major French statutes and the French procedural rules.[49] Louis XV ceded western Louisiana and New Orleans to Spain in the secret treaty of Fontainebleau on November 3, 1762.[50] Under the Treaty of Paris, signed in 1763, the French king agreed to grant eastern Louisiana and Illinois to England. The Spanish did not assume the control of the territory until 1766.[51] In order to establish Spanish authority over the colony, all French laws, with the exception of the *Code Noir*, were abrogated in 1769 and Spanish civil and criminal law were introduced in their stead.[52] The Superior Council was also abolished and replaced with the *Cabildo*, a city council that existed "for the

---

[41] Wright (1928), pp. 329–330; Sheehan (1975), p. 15. See also Robinson (1968), p. 310. The inquisitorial system was confirmed in a ordinance of 1670 (Esmein 1882, pp. 177–283).

[42] Wright (1928), p. 329.

[43] Langbein (1974), p. 225. See Esmein (1882), pp. 136–174.

[44] Verrest (2000), p. 211.

[45] French Louisiana originally covered an expansive territory that included most of the drainage basin of the Mississippi River and stretched from the Great Lakes to the Gulf of Mexico and from the Appalachian Mountains to the Rocky Mountains. For a detailed history of Louisiana, see Martin (1827).

[46] Howard (1902), p. 19.

[47] Batiza (1958), p. 29; Fernandez (2001), p. 1.

[48] A brief description of the Superior Council may be found in Plauché Dart (1919).

[49] Levasseur (1996), p. 586. See also Goulka (2002), p. 170.

[50] Levasseur (1996), p. 587; Goulka (2002), p. 171.

[51] Howard (1902), p. 28; Fernandez (2001), pp. 4–5; Martin (1827), pp. 193–205.

[52] Batiza (1958), p. 30; Fernandez (2001), p. 13.

administration of justice and preservation of order."[53] Spain ceded Louisiana back to France in the secret treaty of San Ildefonso on October 1, 1800. Formal transfer occurred in November of 1803. In the same year, Napoleon Bonaparte sold Louisiana to the United States. France transferred the province to the United States on December 20, 1803.[54] The return of Louisiana to France did not affect the Spanish laws. The French abolished the Spanish courts and replaced them with a form of French court. However, the French law that had been repealed by the Spanish in 1769 never reappeared in Louisiana.[55] When the United States bought Louisiana, it purchased a territory with a civil law tradition.[56] Nonetheless, Anglo-American common law influenced the criminal procedure in the territory as early as 1805. Section 33 of chapter 50 of the Crimes Act of 1805 stated that "[a]ll the crimes, offenses and misdemeanors herein before named, shall be taken, intended and construed according to and in conformity with the common law of England; and the forms of indictment (divested however of unnecessary prolixity), the method of trial, the rules of evidence and all other proceedings whatsoever in the prosecution of the said crime, offenses and misdemeanors, changing what ought to be changed, shall be, except as is by this act otherwise provided for, according to the said common law."[57] Civil law triumphed only in the area of private law. The Louisiana Civil Code promulgated in 1808 was influenced by the Civil Code of Napoleon.[58] Common law institutions prevailed in the procedural, commercial, and public law realms.[59] In Louisiana, the court structure was American. Some aspects of the common law, such as trial by jury, the post of attorney general, and the district attorney, were introduced soon after the United States had bought the territory.[60] After the province of Louisiana came under American control, the French *ministère publique* had no direct impact on the development of public prosecution in the United States.[61]

However, beside French legal historians who have assumed that the French *procureur publique* is the direct predecessor of the American public prosecutor,[62]

---

[53] Levasseur (1996), p. 590; Fernandez (2001), p. 13; Martin (1827), pp. 205–215.

[54] Martin (1827), pp. 287–298.

[55] Levasseur (1996), pp. 593–609.

[56] Friedman (2005), p. 116; Goulka (2002), p. 173; Lambert (1992), p. 248.

[57] Hubert (1959), p. 740 (quoting the Crimes Act of 1805). For a discussion of the meaning of the term "common law of England", see Hubert (1959), pp. 740–741; Fernandez (2001), p. 32; Goulka (2002), pp. 165–166.

[58] Friedman (2005), p. 117; Lambert (1992), p. 248; see also Levasseur (1996), pp. 610–628. For the influence of Spanish law of the Louisiana Civil Code, see Batiza (1958).

[59] Lambert (1992), p. 248.

[60] Friedman (2005), p. 118; Ma (2008), p. 201; Fernandez (2001), p. 39; On the grand jury in Louisiana's criminal justice system, see Coffey and Norman (1978).

[61] Ma (2008), p. 201.

[62] See Esmein (1913), p. 594, n 2. See also Pound (1908), p. 357.

the Wickersham Commission[63] in 1931 concluded in their report on Prosecution that France was the primary origin of the public prosecutor, since after the American Revolution English institutions were rejected and French institutions were regarded with enthusiasm.[64] Nevertheless, this theory overlooks the fact that the American public prosecutor appears during the colonial period, well before the French influenced the young American republic.[65] Furthermore, it was not English law but English law enforcement that was rejected.[66] Finally, whereas the American public prosecutor was already an independent and local officer at that time, the French *procureur publique* was part of a national service hierarchy and enjoyed little freedom.[67] For these reasons, locating the roots of the American public prosecutor exclusively in French traditions is problematic.

4.1.4 American Public Prosecutor as a Result of His Environment

In addition to the aforementioned possible antecedents of the American public prosecutor, there is another explanation for his origin. The office of the American public prosecutor may be the result of legal, social, and political evolution occurring in the United States since the colonial era. Jacoby has identified four such factors: Americans adopted a system of public instead of private prosecution; Americans' pursuit of democracy resulted in the emergence of local government systems; prosecutors became elected officials instead of being appointed; public prosecutors became members of the executive branch of government.[68]

4.1.4.1 From Private to Public Prosecution

The American public prosecutor is not part of British common law heritage. In 1976, Jack M. Kress stated that the "district attorney is a distinctive and uniquely American contribution to common law jurisprudence. Whereas Americans typically describe their legal system as based upon the English common law, in terms of both its procedural attributes and substantive state penal codes, the public prosecutor is a figure virtually unknown to the English system, which is primarily one of

[63] The Wickersham Commission is the popular name for the National Commission on Law Observance and Enforcement.

[64] National Commission on Law Observance and Enforcement (1931), p. 7.

[65] Shoemaker (2005), p. 347; Kress (1976), p. 103; Jacoby (1980), p. 4.

[66] Shoemaker (2005), p. 347; Kress (1976), p. 103.

[67] Jacoby (1980), p. 4.

[68] Jacoby (1980), pp. 6–7. See also Worrall (2008), p. 5.

private prosecution to this day."[69] It was only in 1879 that England established a Director of Public Prosecutions. His function was limited to making prosecution decisions in very serious cases, such as homicide.[70] At the beginning of the eighteenth century, the colonies had already begun to introduce a system of public prosecution.

Joan E. Jacoby has suggested that private prosecution provided unsatisfactory remedies to colonial society and that "[f]or the colonists, bound together by the overriding need to conquer a foreign and alien environment, the focus on the survival of the colony may have given rise to the concept of public protection."[71] A system of private prosecution might also have been perceived as inconsistent with the American concept of democratic process.[72] The danger in a system of private prosecution is the failure of the victim or other interested individuals to bring prosecutions.[73] This is even truer for the poor and the powerless, particularly in view of the fact that the English justice system was intended to protect property in a society based on property.[74] The old English system of private prosecution was a system favoring people of means. In a system of private prosecution, an individual needed to avenge himself and bear the cost of prosecution. Hence, an individual could not expect protection from the state. In addition, private prosecution produced some abuses. It was not uncommon for the accused and the accuser to meet each other in a pretrial collaboration and agree that, in exchange for payment of a percentage of the anticipated penalty by the offender to the accuser, the accuser would not prosecute the offense. As a consequence, this practice threatened the financial solvency of the courts.[75] The public prosecutor was also seen as protection against an unfettered grand jury.[76] In 1704, Connecticut became the first colony to eliminate the system of private prosecution entirely, and other colonies soon

---

[69] Kress (1976), p. 100.

[70] The Crown Prosecution Service (CPS), which is the public prosecution service in England and Wales, was created by the Prosecution of Offences Act 1985 and began to operate in 1986. Its head is the Director of Public Prosecutions. Until 2002, the police retained considerable power over prosecutions in England and Wales since the role of the Crown Prosecution Service began only after the police had investigated the case and had decided whether or not to charge a suspect with an offense. The principal duty of the Crown Prosecution Service was to review the files of cases in which it has been decided to prosecute. Following the Criminal Justice Act 2003, the decision to charge an individual with an offense has become a matter for the Crown Prosecution Service in all but minor cases. However, about 60 % of charging decisions remain with the police (see House of Commons Justice Committee 2009, p. 10). See generally Lewis (2006).

[71] Jacoby (1980), p. 17.

[72] Jacoby (1980), p. 10.

[73] Wright (1928), p. 329; Jacoby (1980), p. 10. See also Shoemaker (2005), p. 345.

[74] Jacoby (1980), p. 8.

[75] See Chitwood (1905), pp. 120–121.

[76] Jacoby (1980), p. 8. On the Grand Jury, see Sect. 5.5.1.3.2.2, paras 2–8.

followed.[77] By the end of the eighteenth century, a system of public prosecution was established in nearly every state of the union.[78]

In America, the concept of public prosecution is well established. In opposition to private prosecution, where a crime is primarily a private matter between the offender and the victim, in a system of public prosecution all criminal acts are considered against the state. The victim is the society as a whole. A decision in 1921 from a Connecticut court expressed this view: "In all criminal cases in Connecticut, the state is the prosecutor. The offenses are against the state. The victim of the offense is not a party to the prosecution, nor does he occupy any relation to it other than that of a witness, an interested witness mayhaps, but none the less, only a witness.... It is not necessary for the injured party to make complaint nor is he required to give bond to prosecute. He is in no sense a relator. He cannot in any way control the prosecution and whether reluctant or not, he can be compelled like any other witness to appear and testify."[79]

Nowadays, private individuals have no right to commence a criminal proceeding in America. Victims are seen as complainants and witnesses and have no power to initiate or conduct prosecution. However, in the last years, victims of crimes have increasingly won the right to participate in the criminal process.[80]

4.1.4.2 From Centralized to Decentralized Prosecution

Most of the colonists were of English decent.[81] Therefore, criminal prosecutions in colonial America were highly influenced by the English common law tradition.[82] But given the great distances between towns in the colonies and their isolation from direct British control, the British influence on the colonies was weakened. In addition, the British government's neglect of the colonies[83] gave them the

[77] Jacoby (1980), pp. 10 and 16.

[78] Jacoby (1980), p. 19.

[79] Mallery v. Lane, 1921, 138.

[80] See Sect. 3.1.2.5.2 for crime victims' rights.

[81] See Aumann (1940), p. 3.

[82] On the legal system in colonial America, see Aumann (1940), pp. 3–18 and 43–63 as well as Chapin (1983). Criminal prosecutions in colonial America were also influenced by the Dutch, the French, and the Scottish legal system. Scottish influence was considerable in some areas of southern colonial America, with the large settlements of immigrants of Scottish origin. Because Scotland in 1587 gave a public prosecutor the authority to prosecute all crimes, it is possible that some colonies may have been influenced by the Scottish system of prosecution when they created public prosecutors (see Robinson 1968, pp. 309–310). For Dutch and French influence, see Sects. 4.1.2 and 4.1.3.

[83] British North American colonies experienced a period of "salutary neglect" (1720–1748) during Walpole's administration. See Speck (1985), pp. 398–401.

opportunity to start their own legislature.[84] This situation favored the creation and maintenance of self-government in the colonies. Hence, the desire for more local autonomy in the colonies, the geographical isolation of the colonies, and their neglect from the mother country laid the ground for the formation of the local prosecutorial structure.[85]

In 1662, Connecticut became the first colony to use county attorneys as prosecutors.[86] In 1686, the communities of Burlington, New Jersey, and Philadelphia, Pennsylvania established the position of county attorneys.[87] By 1687, the attorney general of Virginia had appointed deputy attorneys general to handle cases in the outlying counties,[88] and by 1711, the attorney general and deputy attorneys general handled all prosecutions and trials involving serious offenses.[89] In the Carolinas, the offices of attorney general and deputy attorneys general were created in 1738.[90] After the American Revolution, the progression from private to public prosecution expanded rapidly. The institution of local public officers who were charged with the prosecution of criminal matters was established by 1789.[91]

4.1.4.3 From Appointed to Elected Status

Originally, public prosecutors were appointed officials in almost all states. This continued to be the case after the revolution when the first Congress created the federal system of prosecution.[92] The Judiciary Act of 1789 established the office of the U.S. attorney general and the U.S. attorneys. They were appointed by the President of the United States with the advice and consent of the Senate.[93] The role of the attorney general was to represent the United States in cases before the Supreme Court and to give legal advice to the President and other officials of the executive departments. The duty of the U.S. attorneys was to prosecute criminal matters for the United States in the district courts.[94] The U.S. attorney general was

[84] "The British Government claimed the sole right to create courts, and the early courts except in the charter and proprietary colonies, were created by executive action. However, after the initial settlement, the judiciary received little attention from the King, and colonial courts were left to evolve without much thought, or consideration. England never tried to make the judicial system in the colonies uniform" (Surrency 1967, p. 253).

[85] Jacoby (1980), pp. 11–13.

[86] Jacoby (1980), p. 16.

[87] Jacoby (1980), p. 15. It must be noted that both towns were situated near former Dutch settlements.

[88] Jacoby (1980), p. 15.

[89] Chitwood (1905), pp. 120–121.

[90] McCain (1954), p. 18.

[91] Jacoby (1980), pp. 19–20.

[92] For the history of the office of the U.S. attorney, see Beale (2009), pp. 391–413.

[93] Beale (2009), p. 392.

[94] Judiciary Act of 1789, Section 35 (providing for appointment in each district of an attorney for the United States as well as "attorney general for the United States").

at the top of the federal prosecutorial hierarchy. Initially, he played a limited role in supervising the actions of the U.S. attorneys.[95] Until the Civil War, U.S. attorneys enjoyed great independence in the conduct of their office.[96] In 1861, the U.S. attorney general was given the responsibility of superintendence for the first time.[97] The establishment of the Department of Justice in 1870 further strengthened the authority of the U.S. attorney general. However, it was not until 1910 that, through the creation of a new internal organizational structure, the control of federal prosecutions became entirely established.[98] Nevertheless, prosecution remained primarily in the hand of state and local prosecutors.[99]

After the revolution, the state prosecuting system continued in the same way. Prosecutors' independence and autonomy were limited because of their appointive status. Their decisions were influenced by the opinions and wishes of the actors who had appointed them.[100] One of the most important changes that occurred during the progression of the public prosecutor was his shift from an appointed officer to an elected one.[101] This shift was influenced by the increased democratization of the American political process, which began in the 1820s, was highlighted by the election of Andrew Jackson, and culminated before the Civil War.[102] In 1832, Mississippi became the first state to adopt a constitutional provision for the popular election of local prosecuting attorneys.[103] In 1846, Iowa as well as New York provided for the election of the prosecuting attorney.[104] In 1850, Pennsylvania subjected the post of district attorney to the popular vote.[105] The states entering the Union after 1850 generally had an elective system of prosecutorial selection provided either through the state constitution or through state statutes.[106] Today, only the District of Columbia[107] and three states—Alaska, New Jersey, and Connecticut—have conserved the appointive system of selecting prosecutors.[108]

---

[95] Low Bloch (1989), pp. 585–589.

[96] National Commission on Law Observance and Enforcement (1931), p. 8.

[97] Act of August 2, 1861, Chapter 37, 12 Stat. 285.

[98] National Commission on Law Observance and Enforcement (1931), p. 8; Beale (2009), pp. 396–397.

[99] Jacoby (1980), p. 21.

[100] Jacoby (1980), p. 23.

[101] Jacoby (1980), pp. 22–25. Regarding the popular election of judges, see Friedman (2005), pp. 79–91.

[102] Jacoby (1980), p. 22.

[103] Jacoby (1980), p. 25.

[104] Ramsey (2002), p. 1327; Ma (2008), p. 202; Galie (1996), pp. 110–112.

[105] Poserina (1959), pp. 83–84.

[106] Jacoby (1980), p. 26.

[107] In the District of Columbia the U.S. attorney is responsible for the prosecution of both federal and common law offenses.

[108] See Appendix IV.

Popular election is one of the most significant events in the development of the American public prosecutor. The change from appointed to elected status allowed him to expand his power. Only directly answerable to the people,[109] he is no longer beholden by the opinions of those who had appointed him. Because the prosecutor, as an elected official, is given discretionary power by the constitution or by state statutes, his decisions are virtually unreviewable. The prosecutor also has absolute discretion in deciding which laws to enforce and which laws to ignore.[110]

As Professor Caldwell stated in 1932, the popular election can have negative aspects: "Most of the reasons that militate against the popular election of judges also stand opposed to the popular election of the administrative officers of our prosecutive system. Every thinking person knows that election by popular vote is determined not by merit or by ability but by popularity and that popularity is not always based on merit."[111] Unfortunately, there is a risk that the winner of the election may be more of a politician than a prosecutor.

4.1.4.4 From the Judicial to the Executive Branch

In the early republic, the public prosecutor was defined as a judicial figure. In fact, in many states, the prosecuting attorney was mentioned in the judicial articles of their constitutions. While at first the public prosecutor was seen as a minor actor in the court, the county sheriff and the county coroner enjoyed much more attention.[112] Their importance is attested by the fact that these figures were the first to gain independence and to be locally elected. Following the Civil War, the public prosecutor became a member of the executive branch. Hence, judicial and prosecutorial functions were clearly separated. The shift from the judicial to the executive branch of government was influenced by Montesquieu who promulgated the idea of full and complete separation between the branches of government.[113]

The local public prosecutor, as a member of the executive branch of the government, together with his elective status, increased prosecutorial power. He evolved from a figure with very little power to one with almost limitless power.

---

[109] On the direct accountability of the public prosecutor to the people as possible control over prosecutorial power, see Sect. 5.5.2.5.

[110] Jacoby (1980), p. 29.

[111] DeLong and Baker (1933), p. 962, n 147 (quoting Professor Caldwell).

[112] Jacoby (1980), pp. 23–24.

[113] Jacoby (1980), pp. 25–26. Montesquieu's ideas about separation of powers became the basis for the U.S. Constitution.

4.2 Historical Background of the Swiss Public Prosecutors

4.2.1 Influence of the French Public Prosecution Service in Civil Law Jurisdictions

The origins of the public prosecution in most civil law jurisdictions can be traced back to the *Code d'Instruction Criminelle* of 1808 (CIC), promulgated by Napoleon.[114]

The CIC[115] organized the criminal process in two phases. The preliminary proceeding was characterized by its secret nature (inquisitorial system) and the trial stage by its public and oral hearing as well as its principle of contradiction (accusatorial system). The investigation was carried out by an examining magistrate and the indictment was carried out by a public prosecutor.[116] The public prosecutor was neither entitled to investigate nor did he have the right to decide whether or not a criminal case should be prosecuted. An exception to this rule was made in the case of capture in the act. In such a situation, the public prosecutor was vested with investigative powers he could exercise before informing the examining judge. The CIC made a distinction between pursuit, examination, and adjudication.[117]

Following the creation of the *ministère public* in France, the French system of public prosecution was brought to other countries by Napoleon's military expansion. Countries and regions that came under French influence at that time were, for instance, Belgium, the Netherlands, Luxembourg, Italy, Switzerland,[118] the western region of Germany,[119] and part of Poland. After regaining sovereignty, they either retained the French system of public prosecution or reformed their system based on the French model.

Among the public prosecution services in continental law systems that have been influenced by the French system, it is striking to see that the institute of the examining magistrate was either not transplanted or, if adopted, often disappeared over time.[120] Even in the French prosecution system, the role of the examining magistrate has been decreasing since the middle of the nineteenth century. The French examining magistrate—at the demand of the public prosecutor after

---

[114] Similar institutions have existed since the fourteenth century (see Mathias 1999, pp. 14–22). See Sect. 4.1.3 for more information on the history of the French public prosecutor.

[115] See generally Jung et al. (2010).

[116] For a discussion about which powers to grant to the public prosecutor and the examining magistrate, see Esmein (1913), pp. 500–504.

[117] Esmein (1913), pp. 503–504.

[118] On the influence of Napoleon in Switzerland, see Sect. 4.2.2.1.

[119] See Wohlers (1994), pp. 63–65.

[120] For an overview on the examining magistrate's function and involvement in investigative matters in European criminal justice systems, see Elsner et al. (2008).

preliminary investigations[121] conducted by the police—is designated to undertake the judicial inquiry (*information judiciaire*).[122] This investigation in the pretrial phase is mandatory in the case of serious offenses[123] and optional for other offenses.[124] The examining magistrate directs the judicial police. During the judicial inquiry, the public prosecutor only follows the investigations at distance and thus is not involved. However, the examining magistrate is strictly bound by the public prosecutor's formal request and thus he is not entitled to investigate offenses not included in that request.[125] At the end of the judicial inquiry, the examining magistrate—after having heard the advice of the public prosecutor—will decide whether to dismiss the charges on legal or technical grounds or to refer the suspect to the court.[126] Today, only about 3 % of cases[127] involving violent crime, serious fraud, conspiracy, or public figures, are referred to the examining magistrate, so that a large majority of cases are disposed of by the public prosecutor without any intervention of the examining magistrate. Furthermore, the Act on the presumption of innocence in 2000 established the judge of liberty and detention who decides on pretrial detention and hence has further limited the role of the examining magistrate.[128]

The German system of public prosecution (*Staatsanwaltschaft*) is relatively new.[129] The office of the public prosecutor was created in the middle of the nineteenth century by splitting prosecution from investigation and adjudication.[130] In the former situation it was an inquisitorial judge who carried the responsibility for the investigation, prosecution, and adjudication process. Nevertheless, as Thomas Weigend reports, "the separation between judge and prosecutor remained incomplete throughout the 19th and the greater part of the 20th century. In that period, the public prosecutor shared dominance of the pretrial process with the German version of the *juge d'instruction* (*Untersuchungsrichter*)."[131] However, gradually the investigating judge lost his powers until the office was finally abolished by the end of 1974.[132] Since then, the public prosecutor has had a

[121] There are two kinds of investigation—a preliminary inquiry (*enquête préliminaire*) and an inquiry directly following the commission of a crime (*enquête de flagrance*).

[122] On this stage of the proceedings, see Pradel (1993), pp. 125–126.

[123] See Article 79 F-CCP.

[124] For the other cases, if after the preliminary investigation the prosecutor decides to prosecute, he has the following options: he may apply for penal order (*ordonnance pénale*) or summon the suspect directly before the trial court (*citation directe*).

[125] Elsner et al. (2008), p. 232.

[126] Elsner et al. (2008), p. 230; Verrest (2000), pp. 213–215.

[127] Ministry of Justice (2012), p. 109.

[128] Elsner et al. (2008), pp. 230–232.

[129] On the implementation of the public prosecutor in Germany, see Wohlers (1994), pp. 43–207. See also Schulz (2005).

[130] Fionda (1995), p. 133.

[131] Weigend (2005), p. 205. See also Wohlers (1994), p. 63; Mathias (1999), pp. 23–24.

[132] Wohlers (1994), pp. 208–215; Mathias (1999), pp. 23–24.

monopoly over the prosecution process. He became the "undisputed master of the pretrial process."[133]

4.2.2 *Implementation of the Public Prosecution Service in Switzerland*

4.2.2.1 Helvetic Republic (1798–1803)

In Switzerland, the history of the public prosecutor begins shortly after the French Revolution.[134] On April 12, 1798, a constitution for a centralized Helvetic Republic, modeled on the 1795 French constitution, was adopted. Before the advent of the Helvetic Republic, each canton had exercised sovereignty over its own territory. The new republic was based on the separation of powers, freedom of the press, and equal political rights. The legislature was comprised of two Chambers, the Grand Council and the Senate. The executive branch consisted of a five-member Directory.[135]

The constitution of the Helvetic Republic provided for a public accuser (*öffentlicher Ankläger*)—the predecessor of the public prosecutor—at each cantonal court[136] and the Supreme Court[137] who was elected by the executive branch and whose function was to support accusation before the courts in criminal cases.[138] Furthermore, public accusers, although not responsible for the investigation, had to be present in the course of the preliminary investigation during the oral hearing before the competent court.[139] In this sense, public accusers exercised some supervision. Compared to the prosecutor of today, public accusers could fulfill their tasks only in a restricted manner, since they could not institute a criminal prosecution.[140]

Several ordinances and decrees tried to outline the rights and obligations of the public accuser since the powers and duties of the prosecutor were not clearly described in the law.[141] However, these ordinances and decrees did not provide a clear and sharp definition of those functions and hence were not always able to solve the remaining questions.[142]

---

[133] Weigend (2005), p. 205.

[134] See Mettler (2001), pp. 171–194 for a complete discussion on the history of the public prosecution service in Switzerland.

[135] Grab (2003), p. 115.

[136] Article 96 of the Helvetic Constitution. For more information, see Lüthi (1923), pp. 4–8.

[137] Article 87 of the Helvetic Constitution. For more information, see Lüthi (1923), pp. 8–11.

[138] Lüthi (1923), pp. 2–15; Mettler (2001), p. 172.

[139] Mettler (2001), pp. 177–178.

[140] Mettler (2001), p. 183.

[141] Articles 87 and 96 of the Helvetic Constitution.

[142] On the different edicts, see Mettler (2001), pp. 176–182.

In the Helvetic Republic, torture was abolished and a unified criminal code (*Peinliches Gesetzbuch der Helvetischen Republik*) was introduced.[143] The criminal code had significantly been influenced by the French Penal Code of 1791.[144] A code of criminal procedure was missing. So far, criminal procedure was entirely based on the inquisition process. The implementation of the public accuser introduced the idea of an adversarial proceeding.[145]

4.2.2.2 Mediation (1803–1814)

The constitution of the Helvetic Republic disregarded the nation's tradition of federalism, and was therefore bitterly resisted by a majority of the people. The government of the Republic was divided between the federalists, who opposed the new system, and the centralists, who favored it.[146] The struggle between the federalists and the centralists came to an end in 1803, when Napoleon withdrew French troops from Switzerland and granted a new constitution with Swiss approval. This constitution, known as the Act of Mediation, restored the federal system and expanded the Confederation from 13 to 19 cantons.[147]

As a consequence, the cantons regained jurisdiction over criminal justice.[148] Most cantons restored the proceedings that were in force prior to 1798.[149] In many places, the accusatorial process was replaced by the written and secret inquisition process. This change often meant the abolishment of the public accuser.[150] In the rare case of his maintenance, his role—compared to the French model—lost its importance.[151] For instance, the public accuser was not a permanent office anymore. Instead, it was left to the government's discretion to appoint a prosecuting counsel from the practicing attorneys for the cases where charges were pressed.[152]

4.2.2.3 Restauration (1814–1830)

In the majority of the cantons, the criminal justice organizations changed only slightly. Instead, existing circumstances were consolidated. Overall, the situation

143 Grab (2003), p. 115.

144 Bühler (2010), pp. 257–258; Trechsel and Killias (2004), p. 246.

145 Mettler (2001), pp. 172–173.

146 Grab (2003), pp. 116–117.

147 Grab (2003), pp. 117–119.

148 Bühler (2010), p. 258.

149 Lüthi (1923), p. 16.

150 So for example in the cantons of Schaffhausen, Schwyz, Basel, Graubünden, Uri, and Solothurn (see Mettler 2001, p. 185 with further references).

151 Mettler (2001), pp. 184–187.

152 Mettler (2001), p. 185.

prior to the French invasion in 1798 was restored. Insofar as the institution of the public accuser still existed, this evolution provoked an even greater loss of importance of the institution.[153]

However, the special situation of the canton of Geneva during this period is noteworthy. The Congress of Vienna in 1815 returned Geneva, which had been annexed by France in 1798, to the Confederation.[154] In regard to the evolution of the public prosecutor in Switzerland, this is interesting insofar as it is the first time that a fully developed public prosecutor emerged in the Swiss criminal procedure. In fact, Geneva, previously belonging to France, had incorporated the institute of the public prosecutor based on the CIC.[155]

4.2.2.4 Regeneration (1830–1848)

The French July Revolution of 1830 marked the beginning of the Regeneration movement in Switzerland. Many of the cantons changed their conservative constitutions into liberal ones. At the same time, the principle of separation of powers between the three governmental branches was introduced. This evolution also had an impact on the criminal justice system. In some cantons—in order to better establish the idea of the separation of powers—a specific prosecuting authority had been implemented. However, in comparison with today's public prosecutor, this authority was vested with considerably fewer competences.[156]

During the period of "regeneration", the question arose whether to uphold the secret and written process (inquisitorial system) or to introduce an oral and public process (accusatorial system). The discussion took place between 1831 and 1838 on a nationwide basis, in relation to the organization of the military criminal procedure.[157] The Code of Military Criminal Procedure of 1837 opted for the accusatorial system by introducing an oral and public trial.[158] The extensive debate between the two opposing systems remained not without consequences in the further development of the cantonal criminal procedures.[159] In fact, the change from the inquisition process to the accusatorial system was often used to introduce the public prosecutor.[160] The public prosecutor has been established in Schwyz in

[153] Mettler (2001), pp. 187–188.

[154] The Congress of Vienna further guaranteed the Swiss neutrality. Beside Geneva, the cantons of Valais and Neuchâtel were readmitted to the Confederation, so that Switzerland now consisted of 22 cantons (Grab 2003, p. 121).

[155] Mettler (2001), pp. 188–189.

[156] Mettler (2001), pp. 189–192.

[157] See Lüthi (1932), pp. 68–81.

[158] Lüthi (1932), p. 80.

[159] Lüthi (1932), pp. 80–81.

[160] Mettler (2001), pp. 192–193.

1848, in Thurgau in 1852, in Berne in 1854, in Basel-City in 1861, in St. Gallen in 1865, in Glarus in 1871, and in Solothurn in 1885.[161]

4.2.2.5 Summary

Two different attempts were needed to implement the public prosecutor in Switzerland. When Napoleon established the Helvetic Republic in 1798, its constitution implemented the institute of a public accuser. However, with the collapse of the Helvetic Republic and the reintroduction of a federal system, the cantons regained sovereignty over criminal justice. Most cantons restored the proceedings that were in force prior to 1798. Hence, this evolution signified the disappearance of the public accuser since this institution had some difficulty gaining acceptance throughout the nation. Influenced by the July Revolution in France (1830), the principle of the separation of powers between the three governmental branches was introduced, which had an impact on the criminal justice system. The improved protection of the accused against judicial arbitrariness called for a shift from the inquisition process to the accusatorial system. As a consequence, a second government authority beside the judge had to be established, which brought charges and pleaded in favor of the criminal charges independently from the judge. This authority was the public prosecutor.

4.2.3 Role of the Public Prosecution Service Prior and After the Introduction of the CCrP

Until the first unified Swiss Code of Criminal Procedure (CCrP) came into force on January 1, 2011, different inquiry models existed in Switzerland, which could basically be divided into the "examining magistrate models I and II" (*Untersuchungsrichtermodell*) and the "public prosecutor models I and II" (*Staatsanwaltschaftsmodell*). The position and power of the public prosecutor differed between the various inquiry models. The CCrP choose to adopt the "public prosecutor model II".[162] The four basic inquiry models are briefly described below.

4.2.3.1 Examining Magistrate Model I

According to the "examining magistrate model I", the investigation was lead by an independent examining magistrate. The judicial police were directed by the

161 Mettler (2001), p. 193.

162 On the choice of the "public prosecutor model II", see Keller. In: Donatsch et al. (2010) Kommentar StPO, Art. 12, Margin Nos. 4–7.

examining magistrate so that in the preliminary proceeding there was no distinction between police investigation and examining. Hence, both proceedings were pooled. Proceedings started at the initiative of the examining magistrate and the judicial police acted upon the instructions of the examining magistrate. Within the preliminary proceedings, the public prosecutor appeared only as a party. Thus, the public prosecutor was not entitled to issue directives to the examining magistrate. After completion of the preliminary proceedings, the public prosecutor had to press charges and represent the prosecution in court. Prior to the introduction of the CCrP, four cantons used this inquiry model, namely Fribourg, Glarus, Vaud, and Valais.[163]

4.2.3.2 Examining Magistrate Model II

Following the "examining magistrate model II", the examining magistrate and the public prosecutor together were in charge of the preliminary proceedings. In contrast to the "examining magistrate model I", the examining magistrate acted not independently but was bound by the public prosecutor's instructions. The extent of this subordination differed according to the cantonal law and practice. Furthermore, the manner of cooperation was different as well. Whereas some cantons granted the power to discontinue the proceedings and to charge to the examining magistrate, others allowed only examinations and, at most, the discontinuance of proceedings. In the majority of cantons, the public prosecutor was exclusively responsible for charging and prosecuting in court. Cantons that recognized this inquiry model were Appenzell Outer Rhodes, Berne, Basel-Land, Grisons, Lucerne, Nidwalden, Obwalden, Schaffhausen, Schwyz, and Thurgau.[164]

4.2.3.3 Public Prosecutor Model I

The "public prosecutor model I" followed the French prosecution system. The intervention of an independent examining magistrate and the dual-based proceedings were characteristic. At first, investigations were carried out by judicial police under the direction of the public prosecutor. Subsequently, the public prosecutor ordered the independent examining magistrate to conduct examinations. During this phase of the proceedings, the public prosecutor appeared as a party and thus was not allowed to issue instructions. After completion of examinations, the examining magistrate transferred the files to the public prosecutor who decided whether to charge or discontinue the case. This inquiry model was recognized in the

[163] Federal Council (2006), p. 1104. The canton of Zug recognized this inquiry model until 2008 and then changed to the "public prosecutor model II".

[164] Federal Council (2006), p. 1104.

federal criminal procedure and in the following five cantons: Aargau, Geneva, Jura, Neuchâtel, and Uri.[165]

4.2.3.4 Public Prosecutor Model II

The CCrP, which came into force on January 1, 2011, has adopted the "public prosecutor model II". In this inquiry model, the absence of an examining magistrate is typical. The public prosecutor is master of preliminary proceedings, directs examinations, charges, and prosecutes. He normally leads the judicial police or is entitled to issue instructions. The advantage of such an inquiry model is the achievement of a high grade of efficiency of prosecution by realizing homogenous investigation, examination, and charging. Moreover, the public prosecutor carrying out the investigation from the beginning to the charge avoids dual proceedings as conditioned by the alternate work of examining magistrate and prosecution. In this way, a considerable expenditure of time and personnel is avoided. The enormous power vested in the prosecution is compensated by the judge being responsible for compulsory acts and extended defense powers. Prior to the introduction of the CCrP, seven cantons recognized this inquiry model, namely Appenzell Inner Rhodes, Basel-City,[166] St. Gallen, Solothurn, Ticino, Zug, and Zurich.[167]

4.2.3.4.1 Abolition of the Examining Magistrate

As described above, the CCrP follows the "public prosecutor model II" inquiry model and thus the examining magistrate, previously found in some cantons, has been abolished. As a consequence, the prosecution now occupies a pivotal position. It conducts the preliminary proceedings, pursues criminal offenses within the scope of the investigation, brings charges, and pleads in favor of the criminal charge (Article 16 para. 2 CCrP).

The abolition of the examining magistrate in the Swiss criminal procedure is in line with today's trend of abolishing the examining magistrate or diminishing his powers in various continental criminal justice systems. In a study of 11 prosecution systems across Europe, only Spain, France, Croatia, the Netherlands, and England and Wales have such an investigative body. In all of these countries, the importance of the examining magistrate has diminished over time. The tendency is that he gets involved only in serious crimes or sensitive cases or that he shares responsibility with the public prosecutor.[168]

---

[165] Federal Council (2006), pp. 1104–1105.

[166] The canton of Basel-Land recognized this model for economic crimes only (Federal Council 2006, p. 1105).

[167] Federal Council (2006), p. 1105.

[168] See Elsner et al. (2008), pp. 226–233.

Prosecution systems in continental law systems that have been influenced by the French system and that have abolished the examining magistrate include Switzerland, Germany, and Italy. Even in the French legal system, where the examining magistrate is a pillar of French justice, the future of this judicial institution has been threatened. A judicial reform in 2009 provided for the elimination of the examining magistrate with the consequence that all criminal investigation would have been conferred to the public prosecutor, who reports directly to the Ministry of Justice. Such a judicial reform caused concern among French magistrates, who were worried about the political influence that the criminal justice system could be subject to and the planned reform was finally abandoned in 2011. The decision to get rid of the examining magistrate in the French system was, however, not related to a simplification of criminal proceedings due to an overloaded criminal justice system; it was the consequence of several wrongful convictions. Following the Outreau child abuse scandal of 2000, in which 17 people were wrongfully imprisoned after a flawed investigation by a young and inexperienced magistrate,[169] a parliamentary inquiry was created in January 2006 on this judicial disaster in order to prevent a recurrence of this situation through alterations in France's legal system.[170] Among others, the responsibility and the large powers of the examining magistrate were examined. This judicial reform, which provided for an abolition of the examining magistrate, would have been in line with the recommendations made by the parliament inquiry commission. As a consequence, such a reform would have brought the French legal system closer to those used in common law systems.

4.2.3.4.2 Introduction of an Investigative Judge

Whereas in the nineteenth century the novelist Honoré de Balzac described the examining magistrate as the "most powerful man in France" in view of his large investigative power,[171] his role has since seriously decreased. On the other hand, the power of the prosecutor has drastically increased. The consequence of the elimination of the examining magistrate is that the prosecutor runs all inquiries. To counterbalance the enormous power vested in the prosecution, the introduction of an independent and impartial judicial authority that checks the legitimacy and proportionality of certain measures was necessary.

Coercive measures are regulated in Article 196 et seq. CCrP. The imposition of coercive measures may be ordered by the public prosecutor, the courts, and in urgent cases by the person in charge of the proceedings, and the police in those

---

[169] In 2009, the *Conseil supérieur de la magistrature* sentenced the examining magistrate with a *ré primand avec inscription au dossier*, the lowest penalty in the French judiciary system. For more information about disciplinary liability of French prosecutors, see Sect. 8.5.2.2.

[170] A summary of this case can be found in Grometstein (2008), pp. 19–20.

[171] Steiner (2010), p. 239.

cases provided for by statute (Article 198 para. 1 CCrP). However, the majority of coercive measures fall within the responsibility of the prosecution, so, for instance, house search (Article 244 et seq. CCrP), seizure (Article 263 et seq. CCrP), the examination of a person (Article 251 et seq. CCrP), and DNA analysis (Article 255 et seq. CCrP). For the imposition of detention (Article 224 CCrP), the monitoring of postal and telecommunications (Article 269 para. 1 and 272 para. 1 of the CCrP), the use of technical surveillance equipment (Articles 280 and 281 para. 4 of the CCrP), and the order of an undercover operation (Article 286 para. 1 and 289 para. 1 CCrP), the public prosecutor is regularly involved without having the power to make the final decision. The initiative for these coercive measures usually comes from the prosecutor. However, a definitive ordering or an authorization of the court responsible for coercive measures is necessary. For coercive measures that strongly infringe on fundamental rights, the court responsible for coercive measures plays a crucial role. So, for instance, it is responsible for ordering detention on remand and security detention (Article 18 para. 1 CCrP). Various coercive measures are within the responsibility of the police, for example, arresting people (Article 217 CCrP) or observation (Article 282 para. 1 CCrP).

In sum, in view of the position of the prosecution in the criminal justice system, it is essential that certain measures, especially those that might interfere with fundamental rights, are not the responsibility of the public prosecutor but of an investigative judge. In this sense, it is absolutely necessary that certain prosecuting actions are kept under at least the control of a judicial authority.

References

Aubusson de Cavarlay B (2006) The prosecution service function within the French criminal justice system. In: Jehle J, Wade M (eds) Coping with overloaded criminal justice systems. The rise of prosecutorial power across Europe. Springer, Berlin, pp 185–205

Aumann FR (1940) The changing American legal system: some selected phrases. The Ohio State University, Columbus

Batiza R (1958) The influence of Spanish law in Louisiana. Tulane Law Rev 33:29–34

Beale SS (2009) Rethinking the identity and role of the United States Attorneys. Ohio State J Crim Law 6:369–440

Blom M, Smit P (2006) The prosecution service function within the Dutch criminal justice system. In: Jehle J, Wade M (eds) Coping with overloaded criminal justice systems. The rise of prosecutorial power across Europe. Springer, Berlin, pp 237–256

Bühler T (2010) Schweizerische Rechtsquellen und Schweizerische Verfassungsgeschichte nach einer Vorlesung von Ulrich Stutz (1868–1932). Dike, Zurich

Cardenas J (1986) The crime victim in the prosecutorial process. Harv J Law Public Policy 9:357–398

Carr LG (1987) County government in Maryland. 1689–1709. American legal and constitutional history. A Garland series of outstanding dissertations. Garland, New York

Chapin B (1983) Criminal justice in Colonial America, 1606–1660. University of Georgia Press, Athens

Chitwood OP (1905) Justice in Colonial Virginia. John Hopkins Press, Baltimore

Coffey MA, Norman JB (1978) Selected problems of the Louisiana grand jury. Tulane Law Rev 52:707–768
DeLong EH, Baker NF (1933) The prosecuting attorney – provisions of law organizing the office. J Crim Law Criminol 23:926–963
Devlin PB (1958) The criminal prosecution in England. Yale University Press, New Haven
Donatsch A, Hansjakob T, Lieber V (eds) (2010) Kommentar zur Schweizerischen Strafprozessordnung (StPO) (Kommentar StPO). Schulthess, Zurich
Elsner B, Aubusson de Cavarlay B, Smit P (2008) The examining magistrate's function and involvement in investigative matters. Eur J Crim Policy Res 14(2–3):225–235
Esmein A (1882) Histoire de la procédure criminelle en France: et spécialement de la procédure inquisitoire, depuis le XIII siècle à nos jours. L. Larose et Forcel, Paris
Esmein A (1913) A history of continental criminal procedure. With special reference to France. Little Brown, Boston
Federal Council (2006) Message from the Federal Council of December 21, 2005 on the unification of criminal procedure [Botschaft des Bundesrates zur Vereinheitlichung des Strafprozessrechts vom 21. Dezember 2005]. Federal Chancellery, Berne
Fernandez MF (2001) From chaos to continuity. The evolution of Louisiana's judicial system, 1712–1862. Louisiana State University Press, Baton Rouge
Fionda J (1995) Public prosecutors and discretion. A comparative study. Oxford University Press, Oxford
Friedman LM (1993) Crime and punishment in American history. Basic Books, New York
Friedman LM (2005) A history of American law, a Touchstone book, 3rd edn. Simon & Schuster, New York
Galie PJ (1996) Ordered liberty. A constitutional history of New York. Fordham University Press, New York
Gittler J (1984) Expanding the role of the victim in a criminal action: an overview of issues and problems. Pepperdine Law Rev 11:117–182
Goebel J, Naughton TR (1970) Law enforcement in Colonial New York. A study in criminal procedure (1664–1776). Patterson Smith reprint series in criminology, law enforcement, and social problems, publication no. 122. Patterson Smith, Montclair
Goldstein AS (1976) Prosecution: history of the public prosecutor. In: Encyclopedia of crime and justice, vol 3. The Free Press, New York, pp 1287–1290
Goldstein AS (1981) The passive judiciary. Prosecutorial discretion and the guilty plea. Louisiana State University Press, Baton Rouge
Goldstein AS (2002) Prosecution: history of the public prosecutor. In: Dressler J (ed) Encyclopedia of crime and justice, vol 3, 2nd edn. Macmillan Reference USA, New York, pp 1242–1246
Goulka JE (2002) The first constitutional right to criminal appeal. Louisiana's constitution of 1845 and the clash of the common law and natural law traditions. Tulane Eur Civ Law Forum 17:151–196
Grab AI (2003) Napoleon and the transformation of Europe. European history in perspective. Palgrave Macmillan, Basingstoke
Grometstein R (2008) Wrongful convictions and moral panic: national and international perspectives on organized child sexual abuse. In: Huff CR, Killias M (eds) Wrongful conviction. International perspectives on miscarriages of justice. Temple University Press, Philadelphia, pp 11–32
House of Commons Justice Committee (2009) The crown prosecution service. Gatekeeper of the criminal justice system: ninth report of session 2008–2009: report, together with formal minutes, oral and written evidence. Stationery Office, London
Howard JQ (1902) History of the Louisiana purchase. Callaghan & Company, Chicago
Hubert LD (1959) History of Louisiana criminal procedure. Tulane Law Rev 33:739–750
Jacobs JA (2005) New Netherland. A Dutch Colony in seventeenth-century America. Brill, Leiden
Jacoby JE (1980) The American prosecutor. A search for identity. Lexington Books, Lexington

Jung H, Leblois-Happe J, Witz C (eds) (2010) 200 Jahre Code d'Instruction Criminelle – Le Bicentenaire du Code d'Instruction Criminelle. Nomos, Baden-Baden
Kress JM (1976) Progress and prosecution. Ann Am Acad Polit Soc Sci 423:99–116
Kurland PB, Waters DWM (1959) Public prosecutions in England, 1854–1879: an essay in English legislative history. Duke Law J 8:493–562
Lambert KA (1992) The suffocation of a legal heritage. A comparative analysis of civil procedure in Louisiana and France; the corruption of Louisiana's civilian tradition. Tulane Law Rev 67:231–269
Langbein JH (1973) The origins of public prosecution at common law. Am J Leg Hist 17:313–335
Langbein JH (1974) Prosecuting crime in the renaissance. England, Germany, France. Harvard University Press, Cambridge
Levasseur AA (1996) The major periods of Louisiana legal history. Loyola Law Rev 41:585–628
Lewis C (2006) The prosecution service function within the English criminal justice system. In: Jehle J, Wade M (eds) Coping with overloaded criminal justice systems. The rise of prosecutorial power across Europe. Springer, Berlin, pp 151–184
Low Bloch S (1989) The early role of the attorney general in our constitutional scheme: in the beginning there was pragmatic. Duke Law J 38:561–653
Lüthi W (1923) Die schweizerische Bundesanwaltschaft. Diss, Berne
Lüthi W (1932) Regenerationsbewegung und eidgenössische Strafrechtspflege. Schweizerische Zeitschrift für Strafrecht 46:61–81
Ma Y (2008) Exploring the origins of public prosecution. Int Crim Justice Rev 18:190–211
Martin F (1827) The history of Louisiana from the earliest period. Lyman & Beardslee, New Orleans
Mathias E (1999) Les Procureurs du droit. De l'impartialité du ministère public en France et en Allemagne. CNRS, Paris
McCain PM (1954) The county court in North Carolina before 1750. Duke University Press, Durham
Mettler C (2001) Staatsanwaltschaft. Position innerhalb der Gewaltentrias, Funktion im Strafprozess und aufsichtsrechtliche Situation sowie ein Vorschlag zur Neuordnung. Grundlegendes Recht, vol 1. Helbing & Lichtenhahn, Basel
Miller FW (1970) Prosecution: the decision to charge a suspect with a crime. Little Brown, Boston
Ministry of Justice (2012) Statistical yearbook of the justice system 2011–2012 [Annuaire Statistique de la justice 2011–2012]. Ministry of Justice, Paris
National Commission on Law Observance and Enforcement (1931) Report on prosecution. U.S. Government Printing Office, Washington
Plauché Dart H (1919) The legal institutions of Louisiana. La Hist Q 2:72–103
Poserina JJ (1959) Appointed attorney general's power to supersede an elected district attorney. Temple Law Q 33:78–88
Pound R (1908) The influence of French law in America. Ill Law Rev 3:354–363
Pradel J (1993) France. In: van Wyngaert C (ed) Criminal procedure systems in the European community. Butterworths, London, pp 105–136
Ramsey CB (2002) The discretionary power of "Public" prosecutors in historical perspective. Am Crim Law Rev 39:1309–1393
Reiss AJ (1975) Public prosecutors and criminal prosecution in the United States of America. Juridical Rev New Ser 20:1–21
Rice JD (1996) The criminal trial before and after the lawyers. Am J Leg Hist 40:455–475
Robinson TJ (1968) Private prosecution in criminal cases. Wake Forest Law Rev 4:300–327
Schulz L (2005) Die Teilung der erkennenden Gewalt. Zur Einführung der Staatsanwaltschaft in Deutschland. In: Durand B et al (eds) Staatsanwaltschaft. Europäische und amerikanische Geschichten. Klostermann, Frankfurt am Main, pp 311–338
Sheehan AV (1975) Criminal procedure in Scotland and France. A comparative study, with particular emphasis on the role of the public prosecutor. Her Majesty's Stationary Office, Edinburgh

Shoemaker KB (2005) Reflections on the birth of official criminal prosecutions in American Law. In: Durand B et al (eds) Staatsanwaltschaft. Europäische und amerikanische Geschichten. Klostermann, Frankfurt am Main, pp 339–355
Sidman A (1976) The outmoded concept of private prosecution. Am Univ Law Rev 25:756–762
Speck W (1985) The international and imperial context. In: Greene JP, Pole JR (eds) Colonial British America. Essays in the new history of the early modern era [based on papers presented at a conference held at St. Catherine's College, Oxford, August 1–7. 1981], 2nd edn. Hopkins University Press, Baltimore, pp 384–407
Steiner E (2010) French law. A comparative approach. Oxford University Press, New York
Surrency EC (1967) The courts in the American colonies. Am J Leg Hist 11:253–276
Trechsel S, Killias M (2004) Criminal law. In: Dessemontet F, Ansay T (eds) Introduction to Swiss law, 3rd edn. Kluwer Law International [sold and distributed in North Central and South America by Aspen Publishers], Frederick, pp 245–268
van Alstyne WS (1952) The district attorney – a historical puzzle. Wis Law Rev 11:125–138
Verrest P (2000) The French public prosecution service. Eur J Crime Crim Law Crim Justice 8:210–244
Weigend T (2005) The prosecution service in the German administration of criminal justice. In: Tak PJP (ed) Tasks and powers of the prosecution services in the EU member states, vol 1. Wolf Legal Publishers, Nijmegen, pp 203–222
Wohlers W (1994) Entstehung und Funktion der Staatsanwaltschaft. Ein Beitrag zu den rechtshistorischen und strukturellen Grundlagen des reformierten Strafverfahrens. Duncker & Humblot, Berlin
Worrall JL (2008) Prosecution in America: a historical and comparative account. In: Worrall JL, Nugent-Borakove ME (eds) The changing role of the American prosecutor. State University of New York Press, Albany, pp 3–27
Wright AC (1928) French criminal procedure. Law Q Rev 44:324–343

Chapter 5
Public Prosecutors in the United States: Position, Powers, and Accountability

5.1 Structure and Organization of the Prosecution Service

Due to the federal structure of the United States, the prosecution service is organized on state and federal levels.

5.1.1 Federal Level

5.1.1.1 United States Attorneys

United States attorneys (U.S. attorneys) belong to the executive branch. They are part of the Department of Justice (DOJ). The Department of Justice is headed by the attorney general who is appointed by, and serves at the discretion of, the President of the United States, with the advice and consent of the Senate (28 USC Section 503).

U.S. attorneys serve as the federal government's chief law enforcement officers in their districts.[1] They prosecute federal crimes (Title 18 of the USC). The position of the U.S. attorney was established by the Judiciary Act of 1789. The President of the United States appoints the U.S. attorney for each of the country's 94 federal judicial districts for a 4 year term with the advice and consent of the Senate. At the expiration of this term, he generally continues in office until a successor is appointed (28 USC Section 541). One U.S. attorney is assigned to each of the judicial districts, with the exception of Guam and the Northern Mariana Islands where a single U.S. attorney serves in both districts.[2] Hence, 94 federal districts exist today with 93 U.S. attorneys. U.S. attorneys are subject to removal at the will of the President of the United States.[3] U.S. attorneys serve under the direction and

[1] U.S. Attorney's Manual (USAM), Section 3-2.100 (1997).

[2] Executive Office for the United States Attorneys (2011), p. 1.

[3] For U.S. attorneys having served less than 4 years, see the report of Scott (2007).

G. Gilliéron, *Public Prosecutors in the United States and Europe*,
DOI 10.1007/978-3-319-04504-7_5, © Springer International Publishing Switzerland 2014

supervision of the attorney general of the United States (28 CFR Section 0.5). The deputy attorney general assists the attorney general in providing overall supervision and direction to all organizational units of the Department of Justice, including the U.S. attorneys' offices (28 CFR Section 0.15). U.S. attorneys are not subject to discipline or removal by the Department of Justice without the President's approval.

U.S. attorneys generally act within guidelines promulgated by the Department of Justice.[4] In practice, however, the federal prosecutor retains considerable autonomy. The day-to-day work and prosecution priorities of each U.S. attorney's office are to a great extent under the U.S. attorney's control. Although theoretically the attorney general has the power to control every case falling within the jurisdiction of the U.S. attorney, in reality, the attorney general rarely makes use of this authority.[5] U.S. attorneys are explicitly vested with "plenary authority" over prosecutions in their districts and retain large freedom to establish their own priorities.[6]

Each U.S. attorney is allowed to hire and fire assistant U.S. attorneys, and the attorney general may appoint additional assistant U.S. attorneys when the public interest so requires (28 USC Section 542).[7] Assistant U.S. attorneys are responsible to the U.S. attorney for the performance of duties assigned by that official.[8]

U.S. attorney's offices across the country vary considerably in size and composition.[9] Caseload also varies to a large extent between districts. As just mentioned, each U.S. attorney exercises wide discretion in the use of his resources and in the determination of prosecution priorities.[10]

In 2010, the U.S. attorney's offices nationwide had a total of 6,075 full time attorneys and 5,799 support staff, the majority of them (79 %) focusing on criminal prosecutions.[11] Assistant U.S. attorneys constituted about 66 % of Department attorneys with prosecution responsibilities.[12]

As of the end of the 2010 fiscal year, the U.S. attorney system consisted of 94 headquarter offices and 138 staffed branch offices.[13] Generally, a U.S. attorney's office will have at least a criminal division, a civil division, and an administrative division.[14] Larger U.S. attorney's offices will also have an appellate division.

---

[4] See e.g. USAM.

[5] Gramckow (2008), pp. 396–397.

[6] USAM, Section 9-2.001.

[7] See also Sect. 5.1.1.3.2, para 1.

[8] USAM, Section 3-2.210.

[9] The 94 U.S. attorney's offices vary in size from 20 employees to over 800 employees. For a description of each office, see http://www.justice.gov/usao/about/offices.html (accessed June 23, 2012).

[10] http://www.justice.gov/usao/about/mission.html (accessed June 23, 2012).

[11] See Executive Office for the United States Attorneys (2011), p. 2.

[12] See Executive Office for the United States Attorneys (2011), p. 2.

[13] See Executive Office for the United States Attorneys (2011), Introduction. Staffed branch offices are smaller satellite offices maintained by many U.S. attorney's offices throughout their districts.

[14] Gramckow (2008), p. 392.

In large jurisdictions, each division may be divided into different sections. The Criminal Division of the U.S. Attorney's Office for the district of Minnesota, for example, has three sections: the Fraud and Public Corruption Section, the Major Crimes and Priority Prosecutions Section, and the Organized Crime Drug Enforcement Task Force (OCDETF) and Violent Crime Section.

Generally, the criminal division is significantly larger than the civil division. The criminal division prosecutes violations of the federal criminal law such as organized crime, drug trafficking, political corruption, tax evasion, fraud, and bank robbery.

Depending on the size of the U.S. attorney's office, cases are prosecuted either vertically or horizontally.[15] Vertical prosecution means that a single prosecutor is responsible for a case from start to finish. Under a horizontal prosecution model, different sections of the U.S. attorney's office handle the same case at different stages in the prosecuting process. Small and medium U.S. attorney's offices will more likely follow a horizontal prosecution, while larger offices consists of different specialized sections that handle specific types of crimes, such as drug offenses, white collar crimes, and violent crimes.[16]

5.1.1.2 Evaluation of U.S. Attorneys' Offices

U.S. attorneys receive oversight, supervision, and administrative support services through the Justice Department's Executive Office for U.S. Attorneys (EOUSA), which was created in 1953 (28 CFR Section 0.22). Periodic performance evaluations of U.S. attorneys' offices are conducted by the Executive Office for U.S. Attorneys's Evaluation and Review Staff (EARS). The Evaluation and Review Staff coordinates 1-week performance evaluations of the U.S. attorneys' offices. These evaluations are conducted by a team of experienced assistant U.S. attorneys and administrative and financial litigation personnel from other U.S. attorneys' offices. Each U.S. attorney's office is evaluated every 3 years.[17]

5.1.1.3 Selection of U.S. Attorneys and Assistant U.S. Attorneys

5.1.1.3.1 U.S. Attorneys

The President of the United States has the authority to appoint U.S. attorneys with the consent of the Senate for a term of 4 years (28 USC Section 541). In general, state Senators of the same party as the President in the appointee's state have major influence on the selection of candidates. Their recommendations for U.S. attorney

[15] See Abadinsky (1998), pp. 202–204.
[16] Gramckow (2008), p. 399.
[17] U.S. Department of Justice (2008), pp. 9–10.

candidates are submitted to the White House. Candidates are interviewed by Department and White House officials and then a candidate's name is recommended to the President.[18] If the President approves the recommendation, the Federal Bureau of Investigation (FBI) performs a background investigation of the candidate. If this is successful, the presidential nomination to the position of U.S. attorney is referred to the Senate.[19]

5.1.1.3.2 Assistant U.S. Attorneys

Assistant U.S. attorneys are appointed by the attorney general,[20] although in practice each U.S. attorney, or a committee under his direction, is responsible for hiring new assistant U.S. attorneys.[21] Applicants must possess a Juris Doctor (J.D.),[22] be an active member of the bar (any jurisdiction), and have at least 2 years of post-J.D. experience as an attorney.[23] Candidates are usually evaluated with respect to their litigation experience, academic record, writing skills, commitment to public service, personal recommendations, and interviews. In addition, each office may have specific requirements corresponding to the advertised job. Only U.S. citizens can be considered for these positions, and they generally must reside in the district of their appointment, or within 25 miles thereof.[24] Employment is contingent upon satisfactory completion of a background investigation by the FBI, including credit, arrest, reference, and drug inquiries.

Of the many aspects considered, trial experience is the most significant requirement. Successful applicants usually have between 3 and 6 years legal experience beyond law school.[25] Usually, assistant U.S. attorneys worked as clerkships, as assistant district attorneys, or in private practice before joining a U.S. attorney's office.[26]

U.S. attorney's offices are considered prestigious places to work, so that assistant U.S. attorneys' positions are very competitive. Each job vacancy results in hundreds of applications. As a consequence, even experienced attorneys with a strong background cannot be sure to be hired.[27] Competition is stronger in large cities such

---

[18] Gramckow (2008), p. 415.

[19] U.S. Department of Justice (2008), pp. 8–9.

[20] USAM, Section 3-2.200 (1997).

[21] Gramckow (2008), p. 404; Chiu (2008), p. 4.

[22] Law degree in the United States.

[23] The years of litigation experience needed to apply may vary between the vacant positions. Before joining a U.S. attorney's office, up to 5 years litigation experience may be required.

[24] USAM, Section, 3-2.200.

[25] Chiu (2008), p. 4.

[26] Chiu (2008), pp. 5–6.

[27] Chiu (2008), p. 7.

as New York and San Francisco than in smaller cities or cities in the Midwest, West, and South.[28]

5.1.1.4 Training of U.S. Attorneys and Assistant U.S. Attorneys

The aim of continuing legal education (CLE)[29] is to maintain the legal skills of licensed attorneys.[30] Training covers a wide range of topics and includes courses that examine new areas of law or that review basic practices and trial principles. Continuing legal education for U.S. attorneys and assistant U.S. attorneys is proposed at the National Advocacy Center (NAC) and is carried out through the Office of Legal Education (OLE).

5.1.2 *State Level*

5.1.2.1 District Attorneys

On the state level, the prosecution system in the United States is highly decentralized. Within each state, each district has its own prosecutor's office with its own organization.[31] They are completely independent from one another. As a result, in 2005, there were 2,344 independent prosecutor's offices on the local level that prosecuted felony cases.[32] The size and composition of the district attorney's offices may vary considerably depending on the size of the jurisdiction served.[33] The state of Minnesota, for example, divided into 87 counties, has 87 elected county attorneys. Offices in this state range in size from a single county attorney to 170 staff members.

In general, district attorney's offices have both criminal and civil jurisdiction. The majority has jurisdiction over misdemeanor and felony cases.[34] In some municipalities or cities, misdemeanors and petty offenses are prosecuted by city attorneys.[35]

Every district attorney's office is headed by a chief prosecutor who is either elected or appointed.[36] Elected district attorneys are only responsible to the voters

---

[28] Chiu (2008), p. 7.

[29] CLE is also known as MCLE (mandatory or minimum continuing legal education).

[30] See Black's Law Dictionary, 8th ed., s.v. "continuing legal education".

[31] Gramckow (2008), p. 390.

[32] Perry (2006), p. 1.

[33] Perry (2006), p. 2.

[34] Gramckow (2008), pp. 387–388.

[35] See for example the Los Angeles City Attorney's Office at http://atty.lacity.org/index.htm (accessed June 23, 2012).

[36] On the selection of the chief prosecutor, see Appendix IV.

and can only be removed from office through a state disciplinary procedure for violating the ethical rules.[37] A district attorney can serve in a full-time capacity or in a part-time capacity if serving a small jurisdiction. In 2005, almost three-quarters of all offices had a full-time chief prosecutor. Moreover, half of all prosecutors' offices served districts of 36,500 people or less.[38] Prosecutors' offices throughout the United States had a staff of approximately 78,000 in 2005.[39]

The internal organizational structure of the district attorney's offices is the responsibility of each chief prosecutor. There are no rules or laws regulating this matter. Prosecutors' offices are hierarchical agencies where the district attorney stands at the top. Each district attorney controls the performance of the assistant district attorneys.[40] Complaints about acts and decisions by assistant district attorneys may be directed to the district attorney and this will usually lead to a review of the incident.[41] Larger offices, such as the Hennepin County Attorney's Office in Minnesota, may have chief deputy county attorneys assigned to head specific divisions (e.g. criminal and civil division[42]) and managing attorneys assigned to head special crime divisions.[43]

Each district attorney establishes prosecution policies and assistant district attorneys must comply with these policy directives.[44] The district attorney enjoys wide discretion in setting prosecutorial policies. The district attorney is completely independent and does not report to any statewide hierarchy when setting such policies. As a consequence, such policies may vary among prosecutors' offices. However, the advantage of such broad discretion is that district attorneys can establish policies that best respond to the needs of their jurisdictions and their budgets. Therefore, a district attorney may have a policy of not prosecuting certain misdemeanor violations or have a policy of pursuing certain crimes leniently. On the contrary, he may have a policy of pursuing certain types of crimes

---

[37] Gramckow (2008), pp. 394–396.

[38] Perry (2006), p. 2.

[39] Perry (2006), p. 2.

[40] Gramckow (2008), pp. 390–391.

[41] Gramckow (2008), p. 396. See ABA Prosecutorial Investigations Standard 3.1 (2008). On the role of the prosecutor's office in sanctioning individual prosecutors for unethical behavior, see Kirchmeier et al. (2010), pp. 1373–1374.

[42] The County Attorney acts as legal advisor for the county officials and county departments [see Minn. Stat., Section 388.051 (2010)]. He may not provide legal advice or assistance to citizens. The County Attorney provides legal advice in areas involving waste management, defending challenges to property tax values, representing the Human Services Department on welfare appeals, enforcing state law and county ordinances concerning environmental and health matters. The County Attorney's Office also assists the county in defending actions brought in state and federal court, including the appellate courts.

[43] The Criminal Division of the Hennepin County Attorney's Office has the following divisions: Drugs, Property Crimes, Juvenile Prosecution, Adult Prosecution, Special Litigation, and Victim Services, http://www.hennepinattorney.org/Divisions/CriminalDivision.aspx (accessed June 23, 2012).

[44] Gramckow (2008), pp. 392–393.

aggressively.[45] In such cases, it may be the policy of the office to not allow plea bargaining. Also, to better respond to the needs of the community, district attorneys offices have begun to implement community oriented prosecution.[46] The NDAA Standards—which are not binding—can provide district attorneys with some guidance for establishing prosecution policies, including screening, charging, diversion, and plea bargaining.

To ensure that the district attorney's policies are followed, senior prosecutors advise junior prosecutors on the application of these office policies.[47] Moreover, to help prosecutors apply prosecutorial policies of the office consistently, the district attorney may issue more detailed guidelines.[48] The district attorney, or in larger offices, the deputy county attorney respectively the managing attorney, may advise an assistant district attorney on how to handle a specific case.[49] If prosecutors do not follow the district attorney's directives, a complaint may be launched. If they repeatedly break the district attorney's policies, they risk losing their job.[50]

District attorney's offices can follow a model of horizontal or vertical prosecution policy or have a mixed structure.[51] A horizontal system appears to be predominant in large jurisdictions, whereas a vertical prosecution is typically used in smaller jurisdictions. In a mixed system, a district attorney's office may handle misdemeanors or simple felonies horizontally, whereas other more serious and complex cases may be prosecuted vertically.[52] A case may be assigned to a single prosecutor or to a team, under the supervision of a senior attorney.[53]

5.1.2.2 Selection of District Attorneys and Assistant District Attorneys

5.1.2.2.1 District Attorneys

Every district attorney[54] must first become a lawyer, pass the bar exam, and then gain professional experience as an assistant district attorney. Depending on the jurisdiction, the district attorney is either appointed or elected. Elections are held in

---

45 Gramckow (2008), p. 393.

46 See, for example, the Hennepin County Attorney's Office at http://www.hennepinattorney.org/Communities.aspx (accessed June 23, 2012).

47 Gramckow (2008), pp. 397–398.

48 On such guidelines, see Sect. 5.3.7.3.2.3. See also ABA Prosecutorial Investigations Standard 2.15.

49 Gramckow (2008), p. 400.

50 Gramckow (2008), p. 400.

51 Abadinsky (1998), pp. 202–204.

52 Abadinsky (1998), p. 204.

53 Gramckow (2008), p. 399.

54 There are a variety of titles that define a chief prosecutor. Titles include District Attorney, County Attorney, Prosecuting Attorney, Commonwealth Attorney, and State's Attorney.

all but three states (Alaska, Connecticut, and New Jersey).[55] State law determines the number of district attorneys. In 2005, Texas had the largest number of district attorney (155), followed by Virginia (120), and Missouri (115).[56] Prosecutors are elected to 4–8 year terms.[57]

5.1.2.2.2 Assistant District Attorneys

Assistant district attorneys are hired directly by the county district attorney. In order to become an assistant district attorney, a law degree from an accredited law school and the state bar exam are required. Although it is possible to become an assistant district attorney right out of law school, in practice, most offices look for some prior litigation experience.[58] Candidates go through a rigorous interview process and background check. Only U.S. citizens will be considered for this position. Successful candidates make a commitment to the office for a period of time that is generally 2–4 years.

Depending on jurisdiction, assistant district attorneys serve under the direction and at the pleasure of the district attorney or are civil servants.[59]

5.1.2.3 Training of District Attorneys and Assistant District Attorneys

After being hired, prosecutors have no further training requirements other than continuing legal education requirements. Continuing legal education is mandatory in 40 states, whereas it is voluntary in the remaining 10 states.[60] In states with mandatory continuing legal education, participants receive credits for attending lectures and seminars. Programs for continuing legal education are sponsored by state bar associations, private legal education organizations, or state's prosecutors' associations.[61] Unfortunately, those programs do not distinguish prosecutors from other legal professions, although both groups have different needs for skills training. Since 1998, courses given at the National Advocacy Center (NAC) address the specific needs of prosecutors.[62]

---

[55] The District of Columbia is not mentioned here, since the prosecution of crimes is within the responsibility of the U.S. Attorney's Office.

[56] Perry (2006), p. 2.

[57] See Appendix IV.

[58] Gramckow (2008), p. 403.

[59] Gramckow (2008), pp. 399–400.

[60] http://legal-dictionary.thefreedictionary.com/Continuing+Legal+Education (accessed June 23, 2012).

[61] See e.g. the continuing legal education program of the Minnesota State Bar at http://www.minncle.org/index.aspx (accessed June 23, 2012). See also the Minnesota State Board of Continuing Legal Education at http://www.mbcle.state.mn.us/MBCLE/pages/home.asp (accessed June 23, 2012).

[62] See Sect. 5.1.1.4, para 1.

5.2 Relationship Between the Prosecution Service and the Police

Due to overloaded criminal justice systems, it is not possible to give every defendant a trial. Methods must be found to reserve full trials to those cases that need to be handled in this way and treat the vast majority of other cases in another way. Decriminalization[63] and selective enforcement and prosecution are the main methods for coping with the caseload problem. The two key actors in the latter method are the police and the prosecutors. In deciding which cases to investigate and hand over to the prosecution, police have the opportunity to control the prosecutor's caseload. For that reason, the important position the police occupy within the criminal justice system is obvious.

In the following part, I will focus on the relationship between the prosecution service and the police. The relationship of the prosecution service with other state structures, such as the legislature, the judiciary, and the defense bar, will not be discussed in this research.[64]

5.2.1 *Independently of Each Other*

On the federal level, while federal prosecutors and federal criminal investigative agencies are part of the executive branch, they are completely independent of each other. The FBI[65] has authority to investigate all federal crimes not assigned exclusively to another federal agency. The Drug Enforcement Administration (DEA), for example, has the responsibility to enforce the federal drug laws and has the task of consolidating and coordinating the government's drug control activities. The Bureau of Alcohol, Tobacco, Firearms and Explosives (ATF) has the responsibility of investigating and preventing federal offenses involving the unlawful use, manufacture, and possession of firearms and explosives, acts of arson and bombings, and illegal trafficking of alcohol and tobacco products. The various criminal investigative agencies within the Department of Justice report to the attorney general through the deputy attorney general.[66]

There is no national police force in the United States. Instead, police are organized on a state and local level. As of September 2004, there were 12,766 local police departments of various sizes.[67] However, most of them were small,

---

[63] On decriminalization, see Sect. 2.2.

[64] On this subject, see Gramckow (2008), pp. 414–423.

[65] On the history of the FBI, see http://www.fbi.gov/about-us/history (accessed July 23, 2012).

[66] See Richman (2003).

[67] See Reaves (2007), p. 1.

with the majority employing fewer than ten full-time officers.[68] In each state, in addition to these local police offices, there are a number of other agencies (e.g. sheriffs' offices) with investigative powers.[69] Today, there are more than 900,000 sworn law enforcement officers serving in the United States.[70]

Police and other investigative organs are part of the executive branch. Police offices are headed by appointed chiefs[71] who serve at the pleasure of the mayor and city council which means the mayor can fire them without cause.[72] Police departments are independent from one another. They operate in their own geographic location. The same is true for the relationship between prosecutors and police offices. Their relationship is characterized by independence.[73] The police are not accountable to the prosecutor.[74] Police and prosecutors' offices do not belong to the same government agency. They both work independently of each other at different stages of the criminal process.

In general, investigation and arrest decisions are controlled entirely by the police. The prosecutor plays no role in the investigative phase of the process and does not have any influence in setting police policies. Hence, decisions about what crimes are investigated and who is arrested rest entirely under the police discretion.[75] Complaints directly received from citizens by the prosecutor are referred to the police for further investigation.[76] Once the investigative phase is complete, the case moves into the hands of the prosecutor. As illustrated in the next section, the screening function of the police should not be underestimated.

Depending on state jurisdiction, even the decision to charge a suspect is left to the police, so that the prosecutor's office receives the case only after charges against the individual have already been filed. In other state jurisdictions, the charging decision is the sole responsibility of the prosecutor. He is the one who will decide which, if any, charges should be filed. There are also jurisdictions in which the prosecutor must first give his permission, if a felony is to be charged by the police, whereas for misdemeanors, prior consultation with the prosecutor is usually not required.[77] These various practices among the jurisdictions have to be taken into account when interpreting statistical data concerning case rejections from different prosecutor's offices.

---

[68] Reaves (2007), p. 4.

[69] For an overview over the law enforcement agencies in the U.S., see http://www.usacops.com/ (accessed July 23, 2012).

[70] http://www.nleomf.org/facts/enforcement/ (accessed July 10, 2011). In September 2004, there were 732,000 full-time sworn employees and 46,000 part-time sworn officers (Reaves 2007, pp. 1–2).

[71] One exception to this paradigm is the elected sheriff in each county.

[72] Harris (2011), p. 1.

[73] Weigend (1978), p. 112; Harris (2011), p. 2.

[74] One exception is the state of New Jersey (Gramckow 2008, p. 417, n 128).

[75] Harris (2011), pp. 1–2; McDonald et al. (1982), p. 46; Weigend (1978), pp. 111–113.

[76] McDonald et al. (1982), p. 46.

[77] Abadinsky (1998), pp. 201–202; see also McDonald et al. (1982), pp. 47–48.

5.2.2 *Mutual Dependence*

Although prosecutors and police may act independently, there are some factors that foster a certain degree of mutual dependence between both offices.[78] Good cooperation may be essential to achieve a conviction.[79] On the one hand, police want their cases to be prosecuted but they are not able to conclude them on their own. Instead, they have to rely on the prosecutor. Moreover, the increasing complexities of substantive and procedural law make the police dependent on the prosecutor for legal advice.[80] On the other hand, since prosecutors have neither the resources nor the expertise to do the investigations they need the police to accomplish this task. Prosecutors must be able to show reliable evidence to get a conviction. Hence, the police must be able to find witnesses and collect evidence that is strong enough to put on a convincing case.[81]

5.3 Discretion in the U.S. Criminal Justice

5.3.1 *Rule: Principle of Opportunity*

U.S. criminal justice follows the principle of opportunity and thus the case is fully within the discretion of the prosecutor.[82] The prosecutor has entire authority to accept or decline a case, choose which crimes to allege, decide the number of counts to charge, and offer a plea bargain.

Prosecutors are not the only officials who make discretionary decisions. The police, the judge, and the jury also exercise discretion. Police officers have considerable discretion in deciding whether to arrest a suspect or not, and whether to investigate or not. The judge, for instance, decides if a suspect should be detained before his trial and, if convicted, what sentence he will receive. The jury has the power to decide whether to convict a suspect or not. The jury can even decide to acquit an apparently guilty defendant. In such a situation, no rules exist that would require the jury to convict.

The following section will closely examine the discretionary power of prosecutors.

---

[78] See also ABA Prosecutorial Investigations Standard 1.3 (2008).

[79] Gramckow (2008), p. 417.

[80] On the prosecutor acting as legal advisor to the police, see Weigend (1978), pp. 113–114. See also ABA Prosecutorial Investigations Standard 1.3(a)(ii).

[81] Gramckow (2008), pp. 417–419; Harris (2011), pp. 2–3; Weigend (1978), pp. 114–116.

[82] See Sect. 3.1.2.2.

5.3.2 *Necessity of Prosecutorial Discretion*

Reasons put forward for the necessity of prosecutorial discretion include growing crime rate, limitations on available resources, and the need to individualize justice.[83]

All criminal justice systems have to deal with increasing caseloads. Resource limitations make the prosecution of every alleged offense impossible.[84] The prosecutor is forced to choose cases that deserve special attention.[85] One can assume that limited resources are used to prosecute serious cases. In so doing, the prosecutor best serves the public interest.

Discretion helps to individualize the application of the law and to avoid the injustice that would occur in the strict adherence to the literal criminal law in unusual cases.[86] In this way, it's possible to take into account all relevant factual variations in a given case.[87]

Furthermore, prosecutorial discretion helps to mitigate the effects of legislative overcriminalization.[88] In any jurisdiction, there is a trend to criminalize every behavior that people find objectionable. The problem with this proliferation of criminal statutes is that, in the majority of cases, they reflect a certain view of a specific time. With time, public opinion about certain behaviors may change. The result is that some laws become obsolete[89] but still stay on the books long after social mores about these behaviors have changed. Hence, prosecutorial discretion is desirable in order to avoid law enforcement of comportments that are incompatible with current social views or goals.

5.3.3 *Problems Connected with Prosecutorial Discretion*

Public prosecutors are the most powerful actors in the U.S. criminal justice system.[90] One crucial aspect of the prosecutor's power is his broad discretion. The prosecutor is responsible for deciding whether to charge an individual, what

---

[83] Friedman (1973), pp. 441–444; Dickerson Moore (2000), pp. 377–380; Griffin (2000), p. 263.

[84] See Miller (1970), pp. 159–165.

[85] See Rosett (1972), pp. 21–23; Breitel (1960), pp. 430–432; Dickerson Moore (2000), p. 378; LaFave (1970), pp. 533–534.

[86] Breitel (1960), p. 430; Pound (1960), p. 927; Vorenberg (1976), p. 662; Rosett (1972), p. 25; see also Bubany and Skillern (1976), p. 478; Miller (1970), p. 152; Davis (1969), pp. 17–19.

[87] Vorenberg (1976), p. 662; Davis (2007), p. 14.

[88] LaFave (1970), p. 533; Dickerson Moore (2000), pp. 377–378; see also Lynch (1998), pp. 2136–2139.

[89] E.g., gambling laws which bar all forms of gambling; adultery statutes; see Davis (2007), p. 13; LaFave (1970), p. 533; Dickerson Moore (2000), pp. 377–378.

[90] See e.g. Davis (2007), pp. 3–5; Davis (1969), pp. 17–18; Bubany and Skillern (1976), p. 477.

charges to bring, and what plea bargains and sentences a defendant will face. In an adversarial system, the prosecutor's decision making is largely uncontrolled[91] and therefore may be problematic. Not every decision the prosecutor makes evokes criticism, but only those that are more likely to result in unequal treatment among similarly situated individuals. Thus, the risk of disparity in treatment of the individual is a major concern.[92] In this context several questions arise:

- Under which circumstances will a prosecutor make the decision not to prosecute an individual even though there would be sufficient evidence for commencing prosecution?[93]
- How can uniformity in charging decision be reached? If a criminal behavior fulfils more than one offense, how will the prosecutor decide which charges to bring against the defendant?[94]
- How can uniformity and fairness be reached in the practice of plea bargaining?[95]

Decisions—especially the charging decision—of prosecutors have profound effects on defendants, victims, and the public.[96] The decision to charge transforms the accused from a suspect into a defendant. An arrest may irreparably damage the defendant's reputation. He can suffer financial[97] as well as psychological[98] consequences. If a prosecutor decides not to prosecute a case, the victim has no legal means that would allow the checking of the appropriateness of the prosecutor's decision.[99] Therefore, the answers to the questions raised are of particular interest.

The following section examines the discretion exercised by public prosecutors in fulfilling their duties. In particular, the charging decision is scrutinized. This involves the decision of whether or not to charge a person or to offer plea bargaining.[100] In this section, I review empirical studies treating these important decisions. Available statistical data are discussed. The actual situation at the state level in Minnesota is presented. Questions concerning bail offers or sentencing recommendation will not be addressed.

---

[91] Misner (1996), pp. 736–741; Griffin (2000), p. 266.

[92] See, e.g. Breitel (1960), p. 429; Rosett (1972), p. 16; Bubany and Skillern (1976), pp. 477–478.

[93] See Sect. 5.3.5.

[94] See Sect. 5.3.6.

[95] See Sect. 5.3.7.

[96] Miller (1970), p. 3; Gottfredson and Gottfredson (1989), p. 113.

[97] The defendant can be asked to provide money bail. It can cause the loss of a job.

[98] The defendant can be held in jail awaiting trial.

[99] Victims, as well as defendants, may bring federal civil right claims against prosecutors alleging racially selective prosecution in violation of the Equal Protection Clause. Such claims may be brought under 42 USC Sections 1981–1983, 1985 and under the U.S. Constitution (see Davis 1998, p. 40). See also Singer (2008), p. 31. In this research this question will not be further examined.

[100] The decision on the appropriateness of pre-trial diversion programs is not discussed in this research.

5.3.4 Prosecutorial Decision-Making

5.3.4.1 Importance

The prosecutor's initial decision to prosecute or not is one of the most important decisions in the criminal procedure.[101] As mentioned under Sect. 5.3.3, para 2, the charging decision can have profound effects on the defendant even if he is acquitted.[102] The defendant may face pretrial incarceration,[103] loss of employment,[104] loss of reputation,[105] the financial cost of a criminal defense,[106] and the emotional stress and anxiety incident to awaiting final disposition of the charges.[107] Conversely, the decision not to charge can also affect the victim. He has no legal means that would allow the checking of the appropriateness of the prosecutor's decision.[108] However, victims and the general public can expect that prosecution of a known offender will not be avoided on impermissible grounds, such as favoritism, bias, or prejudice.

The prosecutor enjoys wide discretion in making the charging decision.[109] Their decisions are ordinarily immune from judicial review.[110] Prosecutors therefore possess ultimate discretion with respect to declination decisions. The Supreme Court stated in *Bordenkircher v. Hayes* that "so long as the prosecutor has probable cause to believe that the accused committed an offense defined by statute, the decision whether or not to prosecute and what charge to file or bring before a grand jury, generally rests entirely in his discretion."[111] Hence, the prosecutor is not obliged to file criminal charges whenever there is sufficient evidence of guilt. In contrast, the continental systems of prosecuting, like the Swiss and German ones,

---

[101] Melilli (1992), p. 671.

[102] See also USAM, Section 9-27.001 (1997).

[103] Gottfredson and Gottfredson (1989), p. 115; Fisher (1988), p. 232, n 152.

[104] Freedman (1975), p. 84; Freedman and Smith (2004), p. 311; Fisher (1988), p. 232, n 152.

[105] Freedman (1975), p. 84; Freedman and Smith (2004), p. 311; Miller (1970), p. 3; Fisher (1988), p. 232, n 152; Vorenberg (1981), p. 1525.

[106] Freedman (1975), p. 84; Freedman and Smith (2004), p. 311; Miller (1970), p. 3; Fisher (1988), p. 232, n 152; Vorenberg (1981), p. 1525.

[107] Freedman (1975), p. 84; Freedman and Smith (2004), p. 311; Gifford (1981), p. 661. The prosecutor's broad discretion has been recognized on numerous occasions by the courts. See, e.g., Oyler v. Boles, 368 U.S. 448 (1962); Newman v. U.S., 382 F.2d 479 (D.C. Cir. 1967); Powell v. Katzenbach, 359 F.2d 234 (D.C. Cir. 1965), *cert. denied*, 384 U.S. 906 (1966).

[108] On the victim's position in the U.S. criminal justice system, see Sect. 3.1.2.5.

[109] Sarat and Clarke (2008), p. 389; Bubany and Skillern (1976), p. 476; Vorenberg (1981), pp. 1524–1532; Vorenberg (1976), p. 678; Krug (2002), p. 645; Griffin (2000), p. 268.

[110] As the Supreme Court noted in U.S. v. Nixon, "the Executive Branch has exclusive authority and absolute discretion to decide whether to prosecute a case" [U.S. v. Nixon, 418 U.S. 683, 693 (1974)]. See also Gifford (1981), p. 660; Griffin (2000), p. 278. See Sect. 5.5.2.1.

[111] Bordenkircher v. Hayes, 434 U.S. 357, 364 (1978).

are strongly bound by the principle of legality. Cases of opportunity are restricted and only acceptable within a certain legal framework.[112]

Factors considered when making charging decisions are: the seriousness of the offense, the defendant's prior criminal record, the victim's interest in prosecution, the strength of the evidence, the likelihood of conviction, the availability of alternative dispositions, and the prosecutor's caseload.[113] Although every case is unique and must be treated individually, there are general principles that prosecutors should consider when making the decision whether to prosecute or not.[114] A number of guidelines help the prosecutor in fulfilling this duty.[115]

5.3.4.2 Written Guidelines

In order to promote consistency and impartiality in the charging decision, various "rules" and "standards" have been developed.[116] Four categories of such guidelines can be differentiated between: internal standards adopted by prosecutorial offices, model standards, legislative guidelines, and ethical rules.

---

[112] See Sects. 6.3.2–6.3.4 for elements of opportunity in the Swiss legal system and Sect. 7.3.3 for cases of opportunity in the German legal system.

[113] See Miller (1970), Chaps. 9–18; Bubany and Skillern (1976), p. 479; Ely (2004), p. 242; Dickerson Moore (2000), p. 377; Gifford (1981), p. 666; Thomas and Fitch (1976), pp. 514–515; Singer (2008), p. 34.

[114] Mills (1966), p. 515.

[115] The arguments in favor of structuring the prosecutor's discretion through rulemaking are: "(1) rules aid in training of new assistant prosecutors and in the internal review of all prosecution decisions, so that office policy is consistently and efficiently carried out; (2) rules give greater substance to administrative or judicial appeal rights, since in the absence of such rules it is difficult for victims and defendants to discover and prove that they have been treated differently; (3) in some cases, it may also be appropriate for defendants or complainants to challenge prosecution policy itself (as opposed to failures to follow the policy) as being inconsistent with legislative intent or constitutional requirements; (4) rules permit the legislature to know exactly how much of the substantive criminal law is being actively enforced, against which types of offenders, and for what purposes, and this information permits more intelligent and realistic legislative action; (5) rules serve to reassure the public, complainants and defendants that the prosecutor is not above the law; and (6) in the rare cases in which nonprosecution represents de facto decriminalization (such as fornication and homosexuality offenses), potential offenders are entitled to know that their conduct will not be criminally punished, so they need not to fear blackmail or harassment" (Frase 1980, pp. 296–297). The question whether internal guidelines should be made public is controversial (see Thomas and Fitch 1976, pp. 524–526). On the one hand, openness is important for public accountability (Misner 1996, pp. 769–770). On the other hand, there are also good reasons not to publish them. The availability of such guidelines may be of benefit to potential offenders (Frase 1980, p. 297).

[116] See also newly the UN Guidelines on the Role of Prosecutors. The UN Guidelines require that, in countries where prosecutors are vested with discretionary functions, the law or published rules or regulations shall provide guidelines to enhance the fairness and consistency of approach in making decisions in the prosecution process including the institution or waiver of prosecution (Guideline 17).

5.3.4.2.1 Internal Standards

Federal Level

The most well-known internal standards are the Principles of Federal Prosecution of the Department of Justice. The Principles of Federal Prosecution are set forth in Section 9-27 of the U.S. Attorneys' Manual (USAM).

The U.S. Attorneys' Manual, promulgated by the Department of Justice,[117] contains general policies and some procedures relevant to the work of the U.S. attorneys and their assistants. The Manual does not create any enforceable rights. Its purpose is only to provide guidance within the Department of Justice.[118]

The Principles of Federal Prosecution "should promote the reasoned exercise of prosecutorial authority and contribute to the fair, evenhanded administration of the Federal criminal laws."[119] The policies are intended to "provid[e] guidance rather than to mandat[e] results"[120] and to ensure that the public and individual defendants are fully aware that prosecutors will make their decisions "rationally and objectively on the merits of each case".[121]

The guidelines are not intended to "require a particular prosecutorial decision in any given case," but rather they will help prosecutors determine "how best to exercise their authority in the performance of their duties."[122]

The purpose of the principles is to "promote consistency in the application of Federal criminal laws."[123] However, "they are not intended to produce rigid uniformity among Federal prosecutors in all areas of the country at the expense of the fair administration of justice."[124] Hence, it is possible that some offices deviate from the principles set forth in the U.S. Attorneys' Manual.

Probable cause[125] that the suspect committed the charged crime is an indispensable condition for initiating a federal prosecution.[126] A federal prosecutor should proceed with prosecution only when "the admissible evidence will probably be sufficient to obtain and sustain a conviction."[127] In addition, federal prosecutors should take into account several factors when deciding to commence or recommend a prosecution, namely whether a substantial federal interest is served by

---

[117] These principles were originally promulgated by Attorney General Benjamin R. Civiletti on July 28, 1980 [USAM, Section 9-27.001 (1997)].

[118] USAM, Sections 1-1.000 and 9-27.150.

[119] USAM, Section 9-27.001.

[120] USAM, Section 9-27.001.

[121] USAM, Section 9-27.001.

[122] USAM, Section 9-27.120.

[123] USAM, Section 9-27.140.

[124] USAM, Section 9-27.140.

[125] On the ways probable cause is defined, determined and established, see Del Carmen (2007), Chap. 3.

[126] USAM, Section 9-27.200.

[127] USAM, Section 9-27.220.

prosecuting, whether another jurisdiction would effectively prosecute, and whether an "adequate non-criminal alternative to prosecution" exists.[128]

Factors to be considered in determining whether a federal prosecution should be declined because no substantial federal interest would be served by prosecuting include: priorities of federal law enforcement; the nature and seriousness of the crime; the deterrent effect of prosecuting the accused; the person's criminal record[129]; his culpability and his willingness to cooperate in the investigation or prosecution, and "[t]he probable sentence or other consequences if the person is convicted."[130] These factors are not exclusive. When determining whether another jurisdiction can effectively prosecute the accused, a prosecutor should take into account whether the other jurisdiction has a strong interest in prosecuting, its ability and willingness to prosecute, and the probable sentence the accused will receive if he is convicted.[131] Here again, the factors are not exclusive but illustrative. The prosecutor has the possibility to consider other factors that appear to be relevant in a given case. The prosecutor may decline to file criminal charges if adequate, non-criminal alternatives to prosecution are available. In determining the appropriateness of such alternatives, the prosecutor should consider the severity of the sanctions that could be imposed, the likelihood that the sanction would be imposed, and "the effect of such non-criminal disposition on Federal law enforcement interests."[132]

The prosecutor should make the charging decision without being influenced by "[t]he person's race, religion, sex, national origin, or political association, activities or beliefs,"[133] except when these characteristics are pertinent to the charged offense.[134] Prosecutors cannot consider their personal feelings about the accused, the victim, or the associated of the accused, or the possible effects of prosecuting on the attorney's own personal or professional life.[135] Finally, in the event that federal prosecutors decide neither to commence nor to recommend a prosecution, they must record their reasons.

State Level

There is no source available that would provide indications regarding the number of local prosecutorial offices that have adopted written internal standards. It may reasonably be assumed that only a minority have adopted such guidelines. In 2005,

---

[128] USAM, Section 9-27.220.

[129] In contrast, in the Swiss criminal justice system, the person's criminal record is considered in the determination of the sentence.

[130] USAM, Section 9-27.230.

[131] USAM, Section 9-27.240.

[132] USAM, Section 9-27.250.

[133] USAM, Section 9-27.260.

[134] USAM, Section 9-27.260 cmt.

[135] USAM, Section 9-27.260.

according to a national survey of prosecutors, 13 % of all offices had written guidelines regarding the handling of juvenile cases in criminal court.[136]

There is at least one state in which prosecutors are required to adopt their own internal standards. In the state of Minnesota, each county attorney is required to adopt written guidelines "governing the county attorney's charging and plea negotiation policies and practices."[137] The guidelines should address the situations under which plea negotiation agreements are allowed, the extent to which comments from persons concerned with a prosecution are considered in plea negotiations, and the criteria that are considered in making charging decisions and plea agreements.[138] The guidelines are not limited to these matters. Written guidelines from the state of Minnesota (Anoka, Hennepin) concerning plea negotiation policies are presented later at Sect. 5.3.7.3.2.3 et seq.

5.3.4.2.2 Model Standards

Besides the American Bar Association[139] Standards for Criminal Justice Relating to the Prosecution Function respectively relating to Prosecutorial Investigations and the National Prosecution Standards[140] of the National District Attorneys Association, some state prosecutors' associations, such as the California District Attorneys Association, have adopted model standards for adoption by local prosecutors.[141]

ABA Standards for Criminal Justice Relating to the Prosecution Function

The Department of Justice has not adopted the American Bar Association Standards for Criminal Justice as official policy. However, since courts look at them to determine prosecutors' ethical obligations, the U.S. Attorneys' Manual recommends that federal prosecutors become familiar with them.[142] The ABA

[136] Perry (2006), p. 7.

[137] Minn. Stat., Section 388.051, Subdivision 3 (2010).

[138] Minn. Stat., Section 388.051, Subdivision 3(a) (1)–(3).

[139] The American Bar Association (ABA) was founded on August 21, 1878, in Saratoga Springs, New York, and is the largest voluntary professional association in the world. Its mission is "To serve equally our members, our profession and the public by defending liberty and delivering justice as the national representative of the legal profession," http://www.abanet.org/about/history.html (accessed June 23, 2012).

[140] The National District Attorneys Association (NDAA) was founded in 1950 by local prosecutors. It is the oldest and largest professional organization representing prosecutors in the world. One of its purposes is to foster and maintain the honor and integrity of the prosecuting attorneys of the United States, http://www.ndaa.org/ndaa/about/index.html (accessed June 23, 2012).

[141] See, for example, Section 4.2 ("Crime Charging") of the Ethics and Responsibility for the California Prosecutor, adopted by the California District Attorneys Association (presented in James 1995, p. 25).

[142] USAM, Section 9-2.101 (1997).

Prosecution Function Standards are currently under review.[143] In the following, the actual situation is presented.

Like the U.S. Attorneys' Manual, the ABA Prosecution Standards themselves are not enforceable as law. They are intended "to be used as a guide to professional conduct and performance."[144]

In order to achieve a "fair, efficient, and effective enforcement of the criminal law," prosecutors' offices should promulgate "general policies to guide the exercise of prosecutorial discretion."[145]

The prosecutor has the initial and primary responsibility to decide whether to institute criminal proceedings against a defendant.[146] Before deciding not to prosecute, to dismiss charges, or to offer an accused a plea agreement, the prosecutor should consult with victims.[147] The ABA Prosecution Standards suggests, that in particular, if the defendant is a first-time offender and the offense is minor, prosecutors should consider available noncriminal dispositions even if there is probable cause to press criminal charges.[148] A prosecutor should prosecute if there is sufficient admissible evidence available to support a verdict of guilt.[149] Like the ABA Model Rules of Professional Conduct, the Prosecution Standards only sanction charges known not to be supported by probable cause.[150]

Even when the prosecutor chooses to bring charges, he "is not obliged to present all charges which the evidence might support."[151] Although sufficient evidence would support a conviction, the prosecutor may decide not to prosecute "for good cause consistent with the public interest."[152] Factors the prosecutor should consider in exercising this discretion include the prosecutor's reasonable doubt that the accused is in fact guilty, the extent of the harm caused by the offense, the disproportion of the authorized punishment in relation to the particular offense or the offender, possible improper motives of a complainant, reluctance of the victim to testify, cooperation of the accused in the apprehension or conviction of others, and availability and likelihood of prosecution by another jurisdiction.[153] The prosecutor's decision to prosecute should not be guided by the desire to enhance his record of convictions.[154] Furthermore, when deciding whether or not to

[143] On the ABA's project to revise the criminal justice standards relating to the prosecution function, see Gershman (2011) and Little (2011).

[144] ABA Prosecution Standard 3-1.1 (3rd edn 1993).

[145] ABA Prosecution Standard 3-2.5 (a).

[146] ABA Prosecution Standard 3-34 (a).

[147] ABA Prosecution Standard 3-3.2 (h).

[148] ABA Prosecution Standard 3-3.8.

[149] ABA Prosecution Standard 3-3.9 (a).

[150] ABA Prosecution Standard 3-3.9 (a) cmt. See Sect. 5.3.4.2.4.1 for more information about the ABA Rules of Professional Conduct.

[151] ABA Prosecution Standard 3-3.9 (b).

[152] ABA Prosecution Standard 3-3.9 (b).

[153] ABA Prosecution Standard 3-3.9 (b).

[154] ABA Prosecution Standard 3-3.9 (d).

prosecute, a prosecutor should not discriminate "against or in favor of any person on the basis of race, religion, sex, sexual preference, or ethnicity."[155]

ABA Standards for Criminal Justice Relating to Prosecutorial Investigations

In February 2008, the American Bar Association approved the Standards on Prosecutorial Investigations.[156] These standards are intended to supplement the Prosecution Function Standards and not to supplant them.[157] They are an attempt to compile a comprehensive set of best practices for prosecutors conducting investigations. Detailed sets of factors that prosecutors should consider are given for every step of the investigation process.

Standard 2.1 provides a wide range of factors prosecutors should consider when deciding to initiate or to continue an investigation. In deciding whether a prosecution would be in the public interest, the prosecutor should take into account various elements such as a lack of police interest, a lack of identifiable victims, and fear or reluctance of witnesses to testify.[158] Factors the prosecutor should consider when deciding whether to initiate or continue an investigation include, among others, whether there is evidence of the existence of a criminal offense, the extent of harm caused by the criminal conduct, the costs and benefits of the investigation and its impact on other enforcement priorities and resources, the collateral effects an investigation causes on witnesses and targets such as financial damage and harm to reputation, "the probability of obtaining sufficient evidence for a successful prosecution of the matter in question, including, if there is a trial, the probability of obtaining a conviction and having the conviction upheld upon appellate review,"[159] whether the society's interest would be equally served by civil, regulatory, administrative, or private remedies.[160] When making the charging decision, the prosecutor should not be influenced by "partisan or other improper political or personal considerations, or by the race, ethnicity, religion, gender, sexual orientation, political beliefs or affiliations, age, or social or economic status of the potential subject or victim, unless they are elements of the crime or are relevant to the motive of the perpetrator,"[161] or any other improper motivation.[162] If the prosecutor decides not to pursue a criminal investigation, he should record his reasons.[163]

[155] ABA Prosecution Standard 3-3.1 (b).

[156] On the content and development of these standards, see Pope (2011) and Little (2010).

[157] ABA Prosecutorial Investigations Standard, Preamble (2008).

[158] See ABA Prosecutorial Investigations Standard 2.1(b).

[159] ABA Prosecutorial Investigations Standard 2.1(c)(viii).

[160] ABA Prosecutorial Investigations Standard 2.1(c).

[161] ABA Prosecutorial Investigations Standard 2.1(d)(i).

[162] ABA Prosecutorial Investigations Standard 2.1(d)(ii).

[163] ABA Prosecutorial Investigations Standard 2.1(e).

NDAA Prosecution Standards

The National District Attorneys Association states in its National Prosecution Standards that the prosecutor's decision to initiate a criminal prosecution should neither be motivated by the "prosecutors individual or the prosecutor's office rate of conviction" nor by "political advantages or disadvantages that a prosecution might bring to the prosecutor."[164] With regard to the charging decision, the NDAA has adopted the same standards as those found in the ABA Prosecution Standards. A prosecutor "should file charges that he or she believes adequately encompass the accused's criminal activity and which he or she reasonably believes can be substantiated by admissible evidence at trial."[165] It requires that prosecutors file only those charges which they consider to be "consistent with the interest of justice" and provide a list of 13 factors which may be considered in making this decision.[166]

State Prosecutors' Associations

At state level, the California District Attorneys Association, for example, has established standards that prosecutors should follow when making charging decisions. Depending on which requirements are fulfilled, a case is "legally sufficient" or "trial sufficient".[167] A case is "legally sufficient" if the following three conditions are satisfied: (a) the prosecutor is satisfied that the evidence shows the accused is guilty of the crime to be charged; (b) there is legally sufficient, admissible evidence of a corpus delicti; (c) there is legally sufficient, admissible evidence of the accused's identity as the perpetrator of the crime charged.[168] A case is considered to be "trial sufficient" if, in addition to the mentioned three conditions, there is a reasonable probability of conviction.[169] Charges should be filed only when the

164 NDAA Standards 4-1.4 (3rd edn 2009).

165 NDAA Standards 4-2.2.

166 The factors are: nature of the offense; probability of conviction; characteristics of the offender; possible deterrent value of prosecution to the offender and society in general; value to society of incapacitating the accused in the event of a conviction; willingness of the offender to cooperate with law enforcement; defendant's relative level of culpability in the criminal activity; the status of the victim, including the victim's age or special vulnerability; whether the accused held a position of trust at the time of the offense; excessive cost of prosecution in relation to the seriousness of the offense; recommendations of the involved law enforcement agency; impact of the crime on the community; any other aggravating or mitigating circumstances (NDAA Standards 4-2.4). The 17 factors to be considered in screening (decision to initiate or pursue criminal charges) are listed in 4-1.3 and are quite similar to those to be applied in the charging decision. The availability of suitable diversion and rehabilitative programs may already be considered at screening [NDAA Standards 4-1.3(e)].

167 James (1995), p. 25.

168 Standard 4.2 (Crime Charging) of the Ethics and Responsibility for the California Prosecutor, adopted by the California District Attorneys Association (CDAA), quoted in James (1995), p. 25.

169 "The prosecutor has considered the probability of conviction by an objective fact-finder hearing the admissible evidence. The admissible evidence should be of such convincing force that it would warrant conviction of the crime charged by a reasonable and objective fact-finder after hearing all

four requirements are satisfied. In addition, it must be determined if the case is "trial worthy".[170] This means that a prosecutor may decline to prosecute although there would be enough evidence that would probably result in a conviction if the case is taken to trial.[171]

5.3.4.2.3 Legislative Guidelines

The State of Washington Criminal Code (RCW) contains detailed prosecutorial guidelines.[172] These standards are not intended to create any enforceable rights.[173] The standard for decisions to prosecute distinguishes between crimes against "persons" and "crimes against property" or "other" crimes. "Crimes against persons will be filed if sufficient admissible evidence exists, which, when considered with the most plausible, reasonably foreseeable defense that could be raised under the evidence, would justify conviction by a reasonable and objective fact finder."[174] "Crimes against property/other crimes will be filed if the admissible evidence is of such convincing force as to make it probable that a reasonable and objective fact finder would convict after hearing all the admissible evidence and the most plausible defense that could be raised."[175] It appears that the threshold for making the decision to prosecute is higher than "probable cause". The guidelines state that the prosecutor "should not overcharge to obtain a guilty plea."[176] Overcharging includes "Charging a higher degree" and "Charging additional counts."[177]

5.3.4.2.4 Ethical Rules

ABA Model Rules of Professional Conduct

The Model Rules of Professional Conduct were promulgated by the American Bar Association in 1983. They replaced the Model Code of Professional Responsibility, which had been adopted in 1969.[178] The Model Rules is not enforceable as such.

---

the evidence available to the prosecutor at the time of charging and after hearing the most plausible, reasonably foreseeable defense that could be raised under the evidence presented to the prosecutor" (CDAA, Standard 4.2(A)(d) of the Ethics and Responsibility for the California Prosecutor, quoted in James 1995, p. 25).

[170] James (1995), p. 25.

[171] The factors considered in making this decision are the same as those mentioned in the ABA Prosecution Standards (see Sect. 5.3.4.2.2.1, para 5).

[172] Chapter 9.94A.

[173] RCW 9.94A.401.

[174] RCW 9.94A.411 (2)(a).

[175] RCW 9.94A.411 (2)(a).

[176] RCW 9.94A.411 (2)(a)(ii).

[177] RCW 9.94A.411 (2)(a)(ii)(A) and (B).

[178] Preceding the Model Code were the 1908 Canons of Ethics.

However, with the exception of California,[179] each jurisdiction has adopted all or significant portions of the Model Rules.[180]

The Model Rules prohibit prosecutors from instituting criminal charges that they know are not supported by probable cause.[181] It requires prosecutors to disclose all evidence negating the defendant's guilt or mitigating the offense and to provide all unprivileged mitigating information to the tribunal and the defense at sentencing.[182]

IAP Standards of Professional Responsibility and Statement of the Essential Duties and Rights of Prosecutors

The Standards of Professional Responsibility and Statement of the Essential Duties and Rights of Prosecutors were first promulgated by the International Association of Prosecutors[183] (IAP) in 1999.

The International Standards require the prosecutors to carry out functions impartially and to avoid discrimination.[184] In addition, the prosecutor's decisions should be fair and consistent.[185] In criminal proceedings, prosecutors should proceed "only when a case is well-founded upon evidence reasonably believed to be reliable and admissible, and will not continue with a prosecution in the absence of such evidence."[186] Prosecutors are also encouraged to use alternatives to prosecution.[187]

5.3.4.2.5 Summary

Table 5.1 compares and summarizes the presented guidelines.

---

[179] California has adopted neither the Model Code nor the Model Rules. California has its own code of professional responsibility. The Rules of Professional Conduct in California are currently being revised. See http://ethics.calbar.ca.gov/Committees/RulesCommission.aspx (accessed September 13, 2012).

[180] An overview of the dates of adoption of the Model Rules of Professional Conduct by jurisdiction is available at http://www.abanet.org/cpr/mrpc/alpha_states.html (accessed June 7, 2010).

[181] ABA Model Rules of Professional Conduct, R. 3.8 (a) (2010); Minnesota Rules of Professional Conduct, R. 3.8 (a) (2011). See also ABA Model Code of Professional Responsibility, DR 7-103 (A) (1983).

[182] ABA Model Rules of Professional Conduct, R. 3.8 (d); Minnesota Rules of Professional Conduct, R. 3.8 (d). See also ABA Model Code of Professional Responsibility, DR 7-103 (B).

[183] The International Association of Prosecutors (IAP) was established in 1995 and is a non-governmental and non-political organization. It is the only world organization of prosecutors. One of its objects is "to promote the effective, fair, impartial and efficient prosecution of criminal offences," http://www.iap-association.org/default.aspx (accessed June 23, 2012).

[184] IAPS 3 (1999).

[185] IAPS 1.

[186] IAPS 4.2.

[187] IAPS 4.3.

Table 5.1 Overview of available written guidelines for charging decision

	Internal standards (manual)	Model standards (ABA, NDAA)	Legislative guidelines (Washington Criminal Code)	Ethical rules (ABA, IAP)
Decision to charge	**Probable Cause** Evidentiary sufficiency	Evidentiary sufficiency Disciplinary rule: **probable cause**	Evidentiary sufficiency	**Probable Cause**[a]
Reasons for declining charges even though sufficient evidence exits	Federal interest Prosecution in another jurisdiction Non-criminal alternative to prosecution	Public interest	Public interest	
Considering alternative to prosecution	Yes	Yes	No	IAP: yes
Enforceable as law	No	No	No	No[b]

[a]IAP: well-founded case (reliable and admissible evidence)

[b]Depending on the jurisdiction, ethics opinions may be advisory, persuasive, or binding in nature [Joy 2002, p. 318. The violation of mandatory, but not discretionary, rules is subject to professional discipline (Griffin 2000, p. 283)]

5.3.4.2.6 Conclusion

When public prosecutors receive a file from the police, their first task is to review it. This review should focus on two questions. The first question is whether there is probable cause to believe that the suspect committed an offense and whether the available evidence is sufficient to support a conviction. The strength of the evidence is evaluated on the basis of the file. This task is particularly difficult when the prosecutor has not met the witnesses at all. Often the prosecutor relies on the judgment of the police. The second question is whether it would be in the public interest to prosecute the defendant. This reason for discontinuing a prosecution expresses the principle of opportunity.

A number of guidelines aim to ensure that defendants are properly charged. However, the presented documents are principally based on the "probable cause" standard and therefore offer little guidance concerning the prosecutor's decision whether to prosecute or not. In fact, a number of commentators have criticized this standard for its low threshold. This condition lacks specificity and fails to furnish any predictive value.[188] Probable cause is only a little more than heightened suspicion, and is not really able to separate the guilty from the innocent. The

[188] Griffin (2000), p. 268; Misner (1996), p. 744; Zacharias (2001), p. 735, n 57; Vorenberg (1981), p. 1544.

standard does not prohibit the prosecutor from filing charges although he knows that the evidence against an accused is insufficient to prove guilt "beyond a reasonable doubt" at trial.[189] Furthermore, the "probable cause" standard is the same as that already required for an arrest warrant or an indictment.[190] The court or the grand jury will have determined probable cause prior to the defendant's arrest or summons. Hence, the prosecutor may be inclined not to carry out a detailed evaluation of each case. Similarly, the recommended threshold of the National Prosecution Standard and the U.S. Attorneys' Manual[191]—sufficient admissible evidence to support a conviction[192]—is easily fulfilled and is not able to provide any real limitation.[193] Although the ABA's Prosecution Function Standards and the ABA's Prosecutorial Investigations Standards use the same test,[194] they adopts the lesser "probable cause" standard as their disciplinary rule.

The authors of the ABA Standards defend the probable cause standard by stating that: "By its very nature, however the exercise of discretion cannot be reduced to a formula. Nevertheless, guidelines for the exercise of discretion should be established."[195]

In sum, the standard applied when making the charging decision is not as high as "beyond a reasonable doubt" that is required for the conviction of a person. Although the ABA Model Code of Professional Responsibility does say that "in our system of criminal justice the accused is to be given the benefit of all reasonable doubts,"[196] charging decisions may be made on the basis of "probable cause". The policy of the prosecutor's office should be to file criminal charges only in those cases where there is a reasonable probability of conviction and that are trial worthy.

5.3.5 Decision Not to Charge

Even when evidence of guilt is strong, the prosecutor may decide not to file criminal charges.[197] Decisions not to prosecute are the result of predictions about success and from concerns about desirability and appropriateness. The first type of decision might take into account various evidentiary issues. The second type of decision

[189] Freedman and Smith (2004), p. 315; Melilli (1992), pp. 680–681.

[190] USAM, Section 9-27.200 cmt (1997).

[191] USAM, Section 9-27.220.

[192] In order to make the decision to proceed, the prosecutor has to apply a so called "prima facie" test. This means that the prosecutor evaluates if the evidence is sufficient to survive a motion for a judgment of acquittal at the end of the government's case (Freedman and Smith 2004, p. 315).

[193] Melilli (1992), p. 681.

[194] ABA Prosecution Standard 3-3.9 (a).

[195] ABA Prosecution Standard 3-3.9 cmt.

[196] ABA Model Code of Professional Responsibility, EC 7-13.

[197] Gifford (1981), p. 666; Davis (1998), p. 21.

relates to the question of whether a prosecutor believes that a suspect should be punished. He may decline prosecution because there are adequate alternatives to charging. It's also possible to decline prosecution for policy reasons or for no justified reason at all.[198]

5.3.5.1 Federal Level

5.3.5.1.1 Number of Declinations

During the 2009 fiscal year,[199] federal prosecutors filed charges in district courts in 48 % of the criminal matters referred to them for investigation or prosecution. They declined to prosecute 15 % of the matters and referred 37 % of the suspects to federal magistrates.[200]

Figure 5.1 provides an overview of the federal prosecutors' decision not to prosecute in criminal matters concluded from 1994 to 2009.

The number of suspects in matters declined decreased from 36 % of matters concluded in 1994 to 15 % in 2009.[201] This trend might be connected to the fact that crime overall has been declining.[202]

These numbers do not include minor matters that the prosecutor spent less than 1 h investigating.[203] If these cases were included, a much higher percentage of declination may reasonably be expected. A study conducted in 1980 by Richard Frase analyzed the extent of nonprosecution in the federal criminal system. He

---

[198] Sarat and Clarke (2008), p. 391; Thomas and Fitch (1976), pp. 515–517.

[199] The various U.S. Attorneys' Annual Statistical Reports provide information about the reasons for declination for federal prosecution, but it's not possible to know the proportion of cases declined from the matters concluded. Furthermore, they do not give detailed information about offenses that are more likely to be prosecuted than others. Hence, the following data are taken from the most recent Federal Justice Statistics (Motivans 2011). For a detailed discussion about federal prosecutorial declinations between 1994 and 2000, see O'Neill (2004).

[200] Motivans (2011), Table 2.2. A total of 193,234 criminal matters (suspects) were concluded during 2009.

[201] According to the U.S. Attorney's Annual Statistical Reports, the same trend may be observed. Whereas in 1999 federal prosecutors declined 35,671 criminal cases, in 2010 this number reached 26,479 (Executive Office for the United States Attorneys 2000, p. 11; Executive Office for the United States Attorneys 2011, p. 9). Since data for decisions not to prosecute are provided on a *per-case* basis and decisions for prosecution (U.S. district court and before U.S. magistrates) are calculated on a *per-defendant* basis, it is not possible to compute the percentage of criminal cases declined.

[202] See e.g. the annual Uniform Crime Reports, Crime in the United States published by the Federal Bureau of Investigation, available at http://www.fbi.gov/about-us/cjis/ucr/ucr#cius (accessed June 23, 2012). Another-but less probable-explanation for this decrease might be improvements in the quality of referrals made by government agencies (see O'Neill 2004, p. 1445).

[203] Matters in which prosecutors spend less than 1 h are mostly such cases in which the suspect is unknown (Informal discussion with Richard Frase on June 4, 2010).

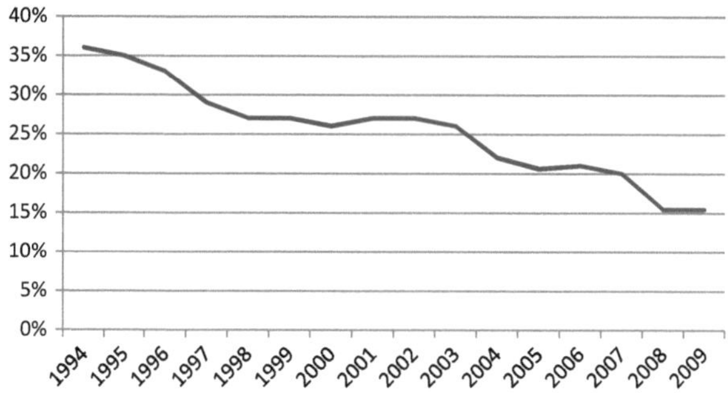

Fig. 5.1 Prosecution declined in criminal matters concluded at federal level in the United States (fiscal years 1994–2009). Source: Data from Smith and Scalia (1998a, b, c, 1999), Table 1.2; Smith and Scalia (2000, 2001), Table 2.2; Smith and Litras (2002), Table 2.2; Smith and Motivans (2003, 2004, 2005, 2006), Table 2.2; Motivans (2008, 2009, 2010a, b, 2011), Table 2.2

calculated that federal prosecutors nationwide filed criminal cases in less than one-fourth of the criminal matters received during 1974–1978.[204] In the Northern District of Illinois, the district most closely studied by Frase, prosecution occurred in 17 % of all matters received, and 21 % of the suspects were prosecuted.[205] His statements are still applicable today.[206]

Declination rates vary between the various offenses. During 2009, among matters declined, suspects were not prosecuted in 35.5 % of public-order offenses, 37 % of property offenses, 34 % of violent offenses, 28 % of weapon offenses, 15.5 % of drug offenses, and 1 % of immigration offenses.[207] The reason certain offenses are more likely to be prosecuted than others may be connected to the priorities of the U.S. attorneys. According to the U.S. Attorney's 2009 annual statistical report, beside the prevention of terrorist acts, the federal prosecutors also focused their attention on drug-trafficking, firearms enforcement, and corporate fraud.[208]

Figure 5.2 shows the way federal prosecutors disposed suspects in matters concluded between 1994 and 2009.

The percentage of suspects prosecuted in U.S. district courts for matters concluded by U.S. attorneys increased from 54 % in 1994 to 62 % in 2000, remained relatively stable at around 60 % until 2007 and decreased to 48 % in 2009. In contrast, while the percentage of suspects referred to U.S. magistrates was relatively stable at around 11 % between 1994 and 2003, this percentage increased to 20 % in 2004, remained stable until 2007 and continued to increase to 37 % in 2009.

[204] Frase (1980), p. 251.

[205] Frase (1980), pp. 256–257.

[206] Informal discussion with Richard Frase on June 4, 2010.

[207] Motivans (2011), Table 2.2.

[208] Executive Office for the United States Attorneys (2010), pp. 1 and 21–40.

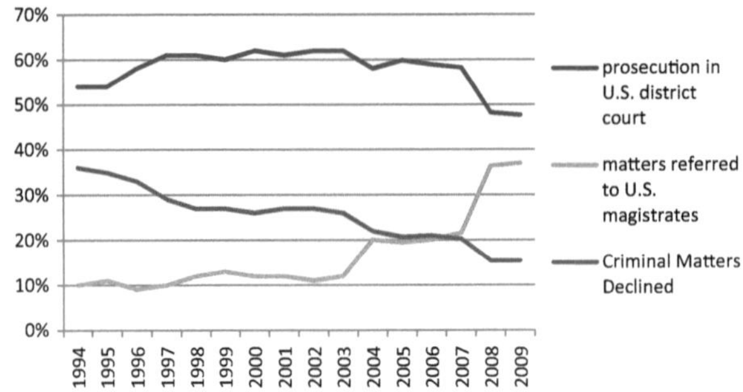

Fig. 5.2 Disposition of suspects in matters concluded at federal level in the United States (fiscal years 1994–2009). Source: Data from Smith and Scalia (1998a, b, c, 1999), Table 1.2; Smith and Scalia (2000, 2001), Table 2.2; Smith and Litras (2002), Table 2.2; Smith and Motivans (2003, 2004, 2005, 2006), Table 2.2; Motivans (2008, 2009, 2010a, b, 2011) Table 2.2

According to the figure it's possible to draw three conclusions:

- The percentage of suspects prosecuted in U.S. district courts was relatively stable at around 60 % between 1996 and 2007 and decreased to 48 % in 2009.
- The percentage of suspects referred to U.S. magistrates remained stable at around 11 % between 1994 and 2003 and increased to a high 37 % in 2009.
- The percentage of suspects in matters declined for federal prosecution decreased steadily from 36 to 27 % between 1994 and 1998, remained stable until 2003 and continued to decrease to a low 15 % in 2009. However, it must be kept in mind, that criminal matters in which federal prosecutors spend less than 1 h are not included. If these were also considered, the declination rate would be much higher, at around 80 %.

5.3.5.1.2 Reasons for Declinations

There are a variety of factors that influence the federal prosecutor to decline the prosecution of a case. The assistant U.S. attorney's self-selected reasons for declining prosecution offer some useful insights into the process of case management and criminal investigation.

During the 2009 fiscal year, 26.5 % of suspects in matters declined were not prosecuted due to the lack of a prosecutable offense. The majority of these were declined either because U.S. attorneys ascertained that no Federal law was violated (5 %) or because they found no proof of criminal intent (21.5 %). Another 23 % were not prosecuted because the evidence was too weak.[209]

[209] Motivans (2011), Table 2.3. These grounds (lack of evidence) are less likely to be questioned (Miller 1970, pp. 154–157; Bubany and Skillern 1976, p. 479, n 28).

22.5 % of all suspects were not prosecuted for other reasons, such as agency request (12 %), lack of resources (3.5 %), and minimal federal interest (3 %).[210]

The U.S. attorneys' decision not to prosecute does not automatically protect the suspect from other action. 19 % of the 29,780 suspects in matters declined during fiscal year 2009 were referred to another authority for prosecution. An additional 3 % were subject to some noncriminal proceedings.[211]

In sum, in 2009 the majority of declinations occurred because of case-related reasons or legal obstacles to prosecution. About one-fourth of the declinations involved the use of an alternative to federal prosecution and another one-fourth were based on policy considerations.

5.3.5.2 State Level

5.3.5.2.1 Number of Declinations

At state level, statistical data about the number of declinations are difficult to find and are hardly available. Beside the information I obtained from the Anoka County Attorney, the Hennepin County Attorney, and the Ramsey County Attorney, additional data can be found in older empirical research and very few official sources.

Number of Declinations According to Statistical Data in the State of Minnesota

Table 5.2 indicates the percentage of cases denied for prosecution in three counties in Minnesota.

The dismissal rate varies greatly between Anoka, Hennepin, and Ramsey counties. Anoka County has the lowest dismissal rate at initial screening. In Ramsey County, the prosecutor decides not to move forward in almost half of the criminal cases. In Hennepin County, the dismissal rate remains fairly constant across time. However, within each county there is a tendency to dismiss more criminal cases.

The variation in case disposition may reflect more than the prosecutor's workload. The court's workload and the availability of penal institutions may also influence the decision to reject the case.

As Fig. 5.3 shows, the dismissal rate varies depending on the crime type.

[210] Motivans (2011), Table 2.3.

[211] Motivans (2011), Table 2.3.

Table 5.2 Percentage of declination from the cases received in three counties of the state of Minnesota (2003–2009)[a]

	2003	2004	2005	2006	2007	2008	2009
Anoka	20	15	15.5	15.5	21	22	26.5
Hennepin[b]	27.3	29	29.5	29	30.7	31	31.5
Ramsey	–	–	–	–	41	45	50

[a]For the detailed data, see Appendix V

[b]Included are Adult Prosecution cases (Violent Crimes and Gang), Community Prosecution cases (Drug and Property), and Complex Crime cases (white collar crimes including mortgage fraud, identity theft, embezzlement, and financial exploitation of vulnerable adults)

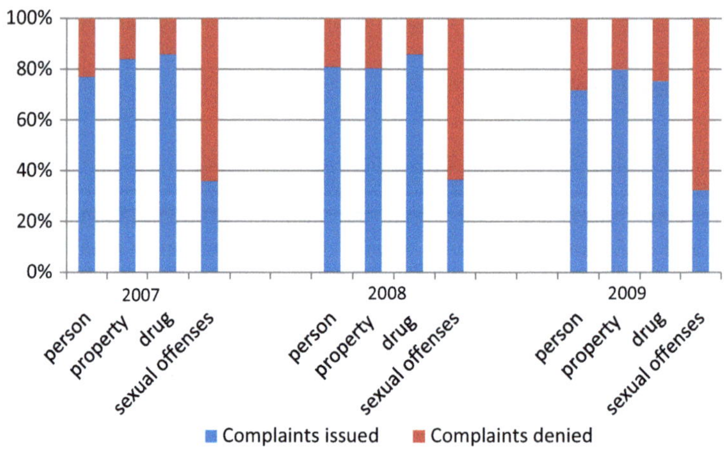

Fig. 5.3 Percentage of complaints denied respectively issued depending on crime type in Anoka County (2007–2009). Source: Data from Anoka County Attorney's Office (2008, 2009, 2010)

Cases involving offenses against the person[212] and property[213] as well as drug offenses[214] are almost always charged, whereas a very high percentage of cases

[212] Offenses against the person include the following: assault, att. murder, child neglect/child endangerment, domestic assault by strangulation, harassing, malicious punishment of a child, murder, manslaughter, and stalking. Offenses against the person are charged in about 77 % of the cases (3 year averages).

[213] Property offenses include burglary, damage to property, defrauding an insurer, financial transaction card fraud, identity theft, lottery fraud, mail theft, receiving stolen property, robbery, theft, welfare fraud, worthless checks, and unemployment compensation benefits fraud. Not included are: possession of stolen/counterfeit checks, possession of theft tools, and possession of stolen property. Property offenses are charged in about 81 % of the cases (3 year averages).

[214] Drug offenses include the following: controlled substance crimes (cocaine, heroin, mj., meth., psilocin). Drug offenses are charged in about 82 % of the cases (3 year averages).

involving sexual offenses[215] are not prosecuted.[216] The higher rate of dismissal in assault cases is connected with the fact that, in these cases, victim's testimonies are crucial to help achieve a conviction. If victims are reluctant to testify, the prosecutor will be more willing to drop the case, especially if he has no other evidence that would secure a conviction.

Number of Declinations According to Official Sources

The reports documenting the performance of the New Orleans criminal justice system, which are regularly issued since 2007 by the Metropolitan Crime Commission,[217] provide information about the outcomes of felony arrests. Its 2012 spring report offers a detailed analysis of outcomes of all 2012 felony arrests. At initial screening, charges were dismissed in 11 % of the cases. An additional 10 % of cases initially accepted were later dismissed. Furthermore, 23 % of felony arrests were prosecuted as misdemeanors, which include plea bargains and felony arrests that were charged as misdemeanors when they were accepted for prosecution.[218] Dismissal rates vary depending on the crime type. Violent felony arrests, which include homicide, rape/sex crime, robbery, and other violent crime, have a dismissal rate of 17 %, property felony arrests have a dismissal rate of 13 %, and drug felony arrests have a dismissal rate of 5 %.[219] This outcome is related to evidence problems inherent in the kind of offenses that are prosecuted.

Since 1988, the Bureau of Justice Statistics has sponsored a biennial collection of data on felony cases processed in state courts in the nation's 75 most populous counties. The most recent report analyzed cases filed during May 2006. Federal defendants and defendants originally charged with misdemeanors are not included. Among felony defendants in the 75 largest urban counties in 2006, charges against defendants initially charged with a felony were dismissed 23 % of the time.

---

[215] Offenses against sexual integrity include: crime sex conduct, sex conduct, solicitation of a child to engage in sexual conduct, use of minors in sexual performances. Offenses against sexual integrity are dismissed in about 65 % of the cases (3 year averages).

[216] For the exact data, see Appendix V.

[217] The Metropolitan Crime Commission (MCC) is a non-profit, citizen's organization dedicated to exposing and eliminating public corruption and to reducing the incidence of crime and improving the administration of justice in order to improve the quality of life for citizens in the Baton Rouge and New Orleans metropolitan areas and throughout Louisiana. Established in 1993, the Metropolitan Crime Commission's Research Program applies objective research and analysis to improve policy choices and decision-making in the criminal justice system. The research program has three underlying goals: "(1) Promote accountability and transparency in the criminal justice system and other governmental agencies; (2) Provide accurate information to decision-makers by identifying the strengths of existing practices and providing alternatives to improve governmental effectiveness and efficiency; (3) Educate the public through the dissemination of our research results," http://www.metropolitancrimecommission.org/html/research.html (accessed June 23, 2012).

[218] Metropolitan Crime Commission (2012a), p. 2.

[219] Metropolitan Crime Commission (2012b), pp. 1–4.

The report does not indicate in what proportion the prosecutor was responsible for this outcome. Defendants charged with assault (39 %) or rape (32 %) were more likely to have their case dismissed than those charged with a driving-related offense (11 %) or murder (13 %).[220] In 2002, the overall dismissal rate was 24 %,[221] in 2000 it was 26 %.[222] In 1998, charges were dismissed for 27 % of all defendants initially charged with a felony, whereas prosecutors accounted for two-fifths of the dismissals and courts for three-fifths.[223] However, the dismissal rate from these reports does not provide any indication as to the total number of arrests declined for prosecution.[224]

Number of Declinations According to Empirical Research

Empirical research conducted in the 1970s provide indications about the number of cases refused for prosecution in various jurisdictions across the country. A study from the Vera Institute on the prosecution and disposition of felony arrests in 1971 in New York City's Court estimated a dismissal rate of 43 %, while 40 % of all felony arrestees were ultimately charged with misdemeanors.[225] A second evaluation, in 1977, indicated a dismissal rate of 40 %.[226] Greenwood and his colleagues examined charging practices in Los Angeles during 1971. Overall, the district attorney refused to file felony charges against more than half of the defendants arrested by the police.[227] Furthermore, at preliminary hearings, 13 % of the felony cases filed were dismissed and 6 % were reduced to misdemeanors.[228] McIntyre and Lippmann estimated[229] a declination rate of 50 % of felony arrests in Los Angeles, 30 % in Detroit, and 25 % in Houston.[230] Forst, Lucianovic, and Cox analyzed felony processing in the District of Columbia in 1974.[231] The researchers found

220 Cohen and Kyckelhahn (2010), Table 11.

221 Cohen and Reaves (2006), Table 23.

222 Rainville and Reaves (2003), Table 23.

223 Reaves (2001), p. 24.

224 For the methodology of this survey, see Cohen and Kyckelhahn (2010), pp. 15–17.

225 Vera Institute of Justice (1977), pp. 6–8.

226 Vera Institute of Justice (1981), p. 143.

227 Greenwood et al. (1973), p. ix. During 1971, the District Attorney modified practices in the Office by prescribing the circumstances under which certain felonies should be filed as misdemeanor. Prior to the change, the dismissal rate was 45 %, whereas after the change it was 54 % (Greenwood et al. 1973, pp. ix and 61).

228 Greenwood et al. (1973), pp. xi and 72–73.

229 Estimations are calculated with available statistical information for the years 1965–1969 (McIntyre and Lippmann 1970, p. 1156).

230 In Chicago, Brooklyn, and Baltimore no declinations were reported. In these jurisdictions many cases were screened out at preliminary hearing, e.g. 80 % in Chicago (McIntyre and Lippmann 1970, p. 1156).

231 A replication analysis was conducted for seven jurisdictions but will not be presented here. Whereas all presented studies deal with felonies, the replication analysis considers felonies and misdemeanors and is therefore not comparable with the others (Forst et al. 1982, p. 8).

that, in 21 % of all arrests brought to the Superior Court Division of the U.S. Attorney's Office,[232] the prosecutor decided not to charge at initial screening.[233] 29 % of the arrests were dismissed after having been initially accepted.[234] In 1977, Brosi studied the attrition of felony cases in 13 jurisdictions. Data were available for five of these jurisdictions from the point of arrests. The rates of rejection at screening ranged from 18 % in Cobb County, Georgia to 40 % in New Orleans, Louisiana.[235] Brosi identified different rates of rejection depending on the crime type. Whereas accusations of assault and rape were more often rejected at screening than other felony cases, those involving property were less often rejected.[236]

Numbers of Misdemeanors Declined for Prosecution

Statistical data as well as empirical research do not provide any information about the number of misdemeanors declined for prosecution. Because felonies are the most serious crimes handled by the criminal justice system, the focus is always on felony arrests and convictions. The Metropolitan Crime Commission gives the following reason: "Only felony convictions can result in a sentence of incarceration in the Department of Corrections, with violent felony convictions having one of the highest incarceration rates. Felony convictions also offer the opportunity for enhanced sentencing if an offender has any future convictions. In contrast, most state misdemeanor, municipal and traffic convictions result in sentences of probation."[237]

5.3.5.2.2 Reasons for Declinations

Reasons for Declinations in the State of Minnesota

The County Attorney's Offices in Anoka (MN), Hennepin (MN), and Ramsey (MN) do not record the reasons for declinations. However, the prosecutor's decision to dismiss a case is usually due to evidence problems. Less than 1 % of cases submitted to a prosecutor are declined on policy reasons, i.e. when the elements of the crime may be proven.[238]

---

[232] In the District of Columbia, the U.S. attorney is responsible for the prosecution of both federal and common law offenses.

[233] Forst et al. (1977), p. 67.

[234] Forst et al. (1977), pp. 68–69.

[235] Brosi (1979), p. 7.

[236] Brosi (1979), p. 12.

[237] Metropolitan Crime Commission (2009), p. 3.

[238] Anoka County Attorney Robert Johnson, e-mail message to author, November 9, 2010.

Reasons for Declinations According to Empirical Research

A number of older empirical studies about the reasons given by prosecutors for the decision not to prosecute all arrive at the same conclusion: evidence and witness problems play a crucial role in the prosecutor's decision not to go forward with a case.

Greenwood et al. found in their study on charging practices among various counties in California and within offices in Los Angeles County that the major reasons for rejections of felony charges were based on lack of evidence and the district attorney's belief that the case was not serious enough to warrant felony processing.[239] A study conducted by the Vera Institute of Justice on felony disposition practices in New York City[240] identified two principal reasons for non-conviction and for reduction of charges, namely the prior relationship of the defendant and the victim and the defendant's criminal history.[241] The reason most frequently cited for dismissal in prior relationship cases was lack of cooperation by the complainant.[242] In their study on felony processing in the District of Columbia, Forst and his colleagues found that witness (25 %) and evidence problems (34 %) accounted for more than half of the cases for not charging.[243] Witness problems included failure to appear, refusal or reluctance to testify, and lack of credibility. Evidence problems included unavailable or insufficient scientific or physical evidence.[244] Brosi analyzed the reasons for rejections of felony cases at screening and post-filing dismissals in a number of jurisdictions. The major reasons for attrition were evidence insufficiencies and problems with witnesses.[245] Overall, these two reasons accounted for over half of the arrests that were rejected.[246] Witness problems appeared to be especially pronounced in cases of alleged assaults.[247] Insufficient testimonial evidence to corroborate the offense played an important role in burglary and larceny arrests.[248] Similar conclusions came from a study conducted by Feeney, Dill, and Weir, who gathered data in Jacksonville, Florida,

[239] Greenwood et al. (1973), pp. 73–75.

[240] Analyses of decision-making have been conducted for the following five offenses: felony assault (plus rape, murder, and attempted murder), robbery, burglary, grand larceny, and gun possession (Vera Institute of Justice 1977, p. 19; Vera Institute of Justice 1981, p. 19).

[241] Vera Institute of Justice (1977), p. 19; Vera Institute of Justice (1981), p. 19.

[242] Vera Institute of Justice (1977), p. 20; Vera Institute of Justice (1981), p. 20.

[243] Forst et al. (1977), p. 67. The replication analysis found the same results: Witness and evidence problems were the most commonly cited reasons for the rejections (Forst et al. 1982, pp. 9–10).

[244] Forst et al. (1977), p. 67.

[245] Some differences appeared between the analyzed cities. The frequency of evidence problems as reason for non-filing decisions ranged from 17 % in Cobb County, Georgia to 56 % in Salt Lake City, Utah. Witness problems were the reason for non-filing criminal charges in 6 % of the Los Angeles cases and 63 % of Cobb County cases rejected at screening (Brosi 1979, p. 16).

[246] Brosi (1979), p. 16.

[247] Brosi (1979), p. 17.

[248] Brosi (1979), p. 18.

and San Diego, California, and found that the vast majority of cases that resulted in non-convictions were based on insufficient evidence to convict and witness problems.[249] The unwillingness of the victim to prosecute appeared to present special problems in accusations of felony assaults.[250] The analysis was based on robbery, burglary, and felony assault cases.[251]

5.3.5.3 Conclusion

The case screening process is a critical point in the criminal justice system. The prosecutor decides what charges, if any, to bring against a defendant. An optimal cooperation between police and prosecutor is essential at this stage.

The empirical and statistical data presented support the proposition that the exercise of prosecutorial discretion has an important impact on the criminal justice system. A large number of criminal cases are disposed of at some early point in the criminal process. Federal prosecutors decline to file criminal charges in about 80 % of cases, and state prosecutors decline to file in 20 to 50 % of all felony cases. The variation in case disposition among the jurisdictions may reflect the prosecutor's workload, the court's workload, and the availability of penal institutions. Furthermore, procedural differences among the jurisdictions are to be considered.

A number of factors affect the rate at which cases are rejected at screening. The quality of the police report plays an important role. Deficiencies in arrest reports include: (1) poorly written reports that lack important descriptive details of the case; (2) lack of clear probable cause for making the arrest; (3) incomplete information on victims and witnesses; and (4) missing supporting documentation required for consideration by the county attorney's office.[252] The experience of the assistant prosecutors who review the files can also affect screening decisions.

Defendants charged with assaults and rapes are more likely to have their case dismissed than those charged with property offenses, such as robbery, burglary, and theft. The higher rate of dismissal in assault and rape cases is connected to the fact that in these cases, victim's testimonies are crucial for a conviction. If they are reluctant to testify, the prosecutor will be more willing to drop the case, especially if he has no other evidence that would secure a conviction.

The most common reason for declining prosecution is the prosecutor's decision that the evidence is not sufficient to convict. This expresses the evidentiary gap between what constitutes "probable cause" for an arrest and "beyond a reasonable doubt" for conviction. Of the cases that are prosecuted, most result in guilty pleas.[253]

---

[249] Feeney et al. (1983), pp. 202–206.

[250] Feeney et al. (1983), p. 204.

[251] Feeney et al. (1983), p. 53.

[252] See Metropolitan Crime Commission (2002), p. 8; Brosi (1979), p. 13.

[253] On plea bargaining, see Sect. 5.3.7.

5.3.6 Decision to Charge and What to Charge

5.3.6.1 Problem

Once the decision to charge a suspect has been made, the prosecutor then has to decide which specific charges to file. The prosecutor is not bound by the charge contained in the original police complaint but has to make a new evaluation based on possible information he might have learned from different sources.[254] In some situations, the prosecutor simply has to choose whether the charge should be for a greater or lesser crime. For example, he has to choose between felony burglary and misdemeanor breaking and entering. Other situations can be more complex. An apparently simple case of robbery can turn out to be more complicate than at first glance. The prosecutor may be confronted with the question of whether the suspect should be charged with more than one offense.[255] He may decide to file one or multiple charges, namely: robbery, armed robbery, possession of a gun, possession of a gun while committing a felony, possession of a gun by an ex-felon, theft of the getaway car, etc.[256] The defendant's criminal behavior violates more than one statute when, for example, the defendant appears to have committed a series of acts over a period of time, or when it appears that the defendant violated more than one statute during a single course of conduct.[257] The prosecutor's determination will be based upon the evidence, along with any other considerations—such as enforcement policy—that the prosecutor may properly take into account.[258] Nevertheless, in such a situation the risk exists that the prosecutor—in order to induce a guilty plea from the defendant—files the most serious crime although he knows that he is not able to prove it. This phenomenon is known as "overcharging". In anticipation of overcharging, the ABA Prosecution Standards advise the prosecutor not to file charges "greater in number than can reasonably be supported with evidence at trial or than are necessary to fairly reflect the gravity of the offense."[259] Finally, prosecutors often have the opportunity to choose between two statutes that punish the same offense but with different penalties.[260] It is within the prosecutor's discretion to determine the statute or statutes under which the prosecutor desires to proceed.[261]

---

[254] Singer (2008), p. 38.

[255] A survey among Wisconsin district attorneys confronted with exactly the same case found that charging decisions varied dramatically (see Mayer 1996, pp. 299–300).

[256] Singer (2008), pp. 38–39.

[257] LaFave et al. (2007), Section 13.1 (e). See also Singer (2008), p. 39.

[258] LaFave et al. (2007), Section 13.1 (e).

[259] ABA Prosecution Standard 3-3.9 (f) (3rd edn 1993). See also USAM, Section 9-27.300 (B) (1997) advising that "Charges should not be filed simply to exert leverage to induce a plea."

[260] Singer (2008), p. 39; Miller and Wright (2007), p. 939.

[261] See U.S. v. Batchelder, 442 U.S. 114 (1979); see also State v. Tanya Caskey, 539 N.W.2d 176 (Iowa 1995); State v. Watts, 601 S.W.2d 617, 620 (Mo. banc 1980).

5.3.6.2 Guidelines

Potential guidelines may be found in statements promulgated by prosecutorial offices themselves. The Principles of Federal Prosecution set forth in the U.S. Attorney's Manual is such an example. NDAA Prosecution Standards provides for some guiding principles.

5.3.6.2.1 Principles of Federal Prosecution

The Principles of Federal Prosecution promulgated 30 years ago by Attorney General Benjamin R. Civiletti contain specific guidance on how federal prosecutors should decide what charges to bring, what plea bargains to propose, and what sentences to recommend. These policies set forth in Section 9-27 of the U.S. Attorneys' Manual are subject to revision through "Bluesheets" issued by the respective attorney general, which become governing policy. Richard Thornburgh, Janet Reno, John Ashcroft and Eric H. Holder Jr. each issued their own interpretation of these policies.[262]

The Justice Department's charging policy has remained relatively consistent over time. It is a long-standing principle that federal prosecutors are supposed to charge a defendant with the most serious offense that is consistent with his criminal behavior and that is likely to lead to a conviction.[263] The notion of an "individualized assessment"[264] was introduced in 1993 by the Reno Memorandum and eliminated 10 years later by the Ashcroft Memorandum. Under the Ashcroft Memorandum federal prosecutors were required to charge—with limited exceptions[265]—the most serious, readily provable offense supported by the facts of the case.[266] As a consequence, prosecutorial discretion was completely eliminated.

[262] For a detailed analysis of the Thornburg Memorandum, the Reno Memorandum, and the Ashcroft Memorandum, see Federal Bar Council (2004).

[263] USAM, Section 9-27.300 (1997).

[264] The selection of charges should also be based on "an individualized assessment of the extent to which particular charges fit the specific circumstances of the case, are consistent with the purposes of the federal criminal code, and maximize the impact of federal resources on crime" (Reno 1993, p. 1).

[265] The Ashcroft Memorandum articulated the following six exceptions: (1) Sentence would not be affected; (2) "Fast-track" programs; (3) Post-indictment reassessment; (4) Substantial assistance; (5) Statutory enhancements, and (6) Other Exceptional Circumstances, with written supervisory approval (Ashcroft 2003, pp. 3–5). See Ely (2004), pp. 255–256.

[266] Regarding the prosecutor's decision to charge, the Ashcroft Memorandum stated that: "It is the policy of the Department of Justice that, in all federal criminal cases, federal prosecutors must charge and pursue the most serious, readily provable offense or offenses that are supported by the facts of the case.... The most serious offenses are those that generate the most substantial sentence" (Ashcroft 2003, p. 2).

This policy has been widely criticized[267] because such a mandatory charging scheme prevents federal prosecutors from fulfilling their quasi-judicial duties.[268] Under the Ashcroft Memorandum, federal prosecutors were obliged to file criminal charges, even though this might not have been in the interest of justice.[269] Such a policy certainly will increase uniformity, whereas fairness will not automatically be achieved.[270] In May of 2010, the Attorney General Eric H. Holder Jr., released a memo that resumed a more flexible standard. The Holder Memorandum states that a prosecutor "should ordinarily charge the most serious offense" and prescribes that this decision "must always be made in the context of an individualized assessment of the extent to which particular charges fit the specific circumstances of the case, are consistent with the purpose of the Federal criminal code, and maximize the impact of Federal resources on crime."[271] To ensure consistency, the Holder Memorandum provides for a review of all charging decisions by a supervisory attorney. Furthermore, written guidance describing the internal indictment review process shall be promulgated in each office.[272]

A legitimate question here is why should a prosecutor charge the most serious and not the least serious crime? A serious charge will certainly have an impact on the bail decision and will eventually lead to a denial of release. On the contrary, if prosecutors were required to file the lowest possible charge, the risk that a suspect would try to escape justice increases since he might expect that greater charges will occur at some time.[273]

5.3.6.2.2 NDAA Prosecution Standards

According to Standards promulgated by the National District Attorneys Association, the prosecutor will have to answer the following two questions when deciding to file charges:

- What possible charges are appropriate for the offense or offenses;
- What charge or charges would best serve the interest of justice?[274]

A prosecutor should file those charges he believes adequately reflect the suspect's criminal activity and which he reasonably believes can be proven.[275] In

[267] Critics of prosecutorial discretion also admit that the Ashcroft Memorandum was not a good solution (Osler 2005, pp. 634–635).

[268] Caves (2008), p. 7; Ely (2004), pp. 263–277.

[269] Before the Ashcroft Memorandum, federal prosecutors were free to decline prosecution for various reasons (e.g. suspect has already made restitution, suspect's culpability is minimal).

[270] Caves (2008), p. 18.

[271] Holder (2010), p. 2.

[272] Holder (2010), p. 2.

[273] Singer (2008), p. 39.

[274] NDAA Standards 4-2.2 and 4-2.4 (3rd edn 2009).

[275] NDAA Standards 4-2.2.

deciding whether the charges would be consistent with the interests of justice, the National Prosecution Standards contains a list of 13 factors that the prosecutor may consider, such as the nature of the offense, the probability of a conviction, whether the accused held a position of trust at the time of the offense, the impact of the crime on the community.[276]

5.3.6.3 Conclusion

The criteria mentioned in the U.S. Attorneys' Manual and in the NDAA Prosecution Standards are obviously and perhaps unavoidably vague.[277] In reality, those guidelines do not give any surprising direction to a prosecutor making a charging decision. In agreement with Osler, the U.S. Attorneys' Manual is neither directive[278] nor goal-oriented[279] nor amenable to consistent application.[280] Although the prosecutor should charge "the most serious offense that is consistent with the nature of the defendant's conduct and that is likely to result in a sustainable conviction,"[281] the Manual in the end allows that a prosecutor "may drop readily provable charges with the specific approval of the United States Attorney or designated supervisory level official for reasons set forth in the file of the case."[282] Reasons mentioned in the U.S. Attorneys' Manual for dropping charges are quite broad. Charges might be dropped "because the United States Attorney's office is particularly over-burdened," and "the case would be time-consuming to try."[283] In theory, the goal would be to prosecute all offenders to the fullest extent possible. However, this goal is undercut, on the one hand, by the possible exceptions for the decision to drop a case and, on the other hand, by the reasons mentioned in the U.S. Attorneys' Manual for declining prosecution.[284] At each step of prosecution, the

[276] "The nature of the offense, including whether the crime involves violence or bodily injury; the probability of conviction; the characteristics of the accused that are relevant to his or her blameworthiness or responsibility, including the accused's criminal history; potential deterrent value of a prosecution to the offender and to society at large; the value to society of incapacitating the accused in the event of a conviction; the willingness of the offender to cooperate with law enforcement; the defendant's relative level of culpability in the criminal activity; the status of the victim, including the victim's age or special vulnerability; whether the accused held a position of trust at the time of the offense; excessive costs of prosecution in relation to the seriousness of the offense; recommendation of the involved law enforcement personnel; the impact of the crime on the community; any other aggravating or mitigating circumstances" (NDAA Standards 4-2.4).

[277] Singer (2008), p. 39.

[278] See Osler (2005), pp. 636–637.

[279] See Osler (2005), pp. 637–638.

[280] See Osler (2005), pp. 638–640.

[281] USAM, Section 9-27.300 (1997).

[282] USAM, Section 9-27.400 (B).

[283] USAM, Section 9-27.400 (B). See also e.g. Ashcroft (2003), p. 5.

[284] USAM, Section 9-27.230 (B). See Sect. 5.3.4.2.1.1, paras 6–8 and Osler (2005), p. 638.

decision is left to the assistant U.S. attorney assigned to the case and his direct supervisor. The prosecutor assigned to the case, when deciding whether to initiate or decline prosecution, is advised to "weigh all relevant considerations" in order to determine if there is a substantial federal interest.[285] This practice allows some consistency at the local but not at the national level.[286]

5.3.7 Plea Bargaining

5.3.7.1 Background

In the U.S. criminal justice system, the overwhelming majority of criminal charges are resolved by pleas of guilty, and virtually all of those are the result of plea bargaining.[287] In 2009, about 97 % of cases in the federal system were settled by guilty pleas or nolo contendere.[288,289] On the state level, the situation is similar. In the nation's 75 largest counties, 98.2 % of felony charges were resolved through a guilty plea in 2006. Only murder charges produced trials in 48 % of the cases.[290] For misdemeanor charges, guilty pleas accounted for 91 % of convictions.[291] In Anoka County, from 2006 until 2009, 98 % of all felony criminal convictions were reached through a guilty plea.[292]

Plea bargain is an agreement between the defendant and the prosecutor in a criminal case.[293] In this agreement, the defendant agrees to plead guilty without a trial. In return, the prosecutor agrees to dismiss certain charges or to reduce the

---

285 USAM, Section 9-27.230 (A).

286 See Osler (2005), pp. 639–640. On the possibilities to guide discretion see Osler (2005), pp. 640–654.

287 For a historical overview of plea bargaining, see e.g. Fisher (2004), Alschuler (1979), Friedman (1979) and Langbein (1979).

288 A *plea of nolo contendere* (*I will not contest the charges*) allows the court to pronounce a sanction the same as if the defendant had pleaded guilty. The difference is that a plea of nolo contendere cannot be used against the defendant to prove wrongdoing in any civil litigation. A plea of nolo contendere may be entered after the court has agreed.

289 Bureau of Justice Statistics (2010), Table 5.22.2010.

290 In 2006, there were a total of 81 convictions for murder. 42 were resolved through guilty pleas and 39 through a trial.

291 Cohen and Kyckelhahn (2010), Table 11.

292 Anoka County Attorney's Office (2007, 2008, 2009, 2010) (for the exact data, see Appendix V). In Ramsey County, approximately 98 % of the convictions were the result of a guilty plea in 2009 (statistical information received by e-mail from Jill Gerber, 16 December, 2010). In Hennepin County, about 95 % of criminal cases are resolved through plea bargains (statistical information received by e-mail from Jodie Wierimaa, September 21, 2010).

293 According to the Black's Law Dictionary, "plea bargain" is "[a] negotiated agreement between a prosecutor and a criminal defendant whereby the defendant pleads guilty to a lesser offense or to one of multiple charges in exchange for some concession by the prosecutor, usually a more lenient

charge to something less serious than is supported by the evidence.[294] Or the prosecutor can make a specific sentence recommendation or refrain from making certain recommendations.[295] Prosecutors and defendants are allowed to bargain over a wide range of topics.[296] A relatively new and less common type of bargaining is "fact bargaining". This kind of negotiation occurs when prosecutors and defendants bargain over what circumstances of an event should be stipulated as true by the parties and presented to the court.[297] As a consequence, the prosecutor does not need to prove these facts. "Fact bargaining" emerged as a result of the introduction of sentencing guidelines on the federal level and in many states.[298] Sentencing guidelines provide for some structure and uniformity at the sentencing stage by defining offense and offender elements that should be considered in each case. Because the presence of certain facts may enhance the sentence, both parties now negotiate on these facts.[299] The plea may be the result of "implicit plea bargaining".[300] This means that the defendant pleads guilty without prior negotiation and any promise from the prosecutor because he expects to be treated more leniently than if he would exercise the right to trial.[301] The negotiated plea is subject to court approval. The accepted guilty plea is placed on the court records. Usually, plea bargaining occurs prior to a trial, but in some jurisdictions, it may occur any time before a verdict is reached. Under many victim rights statutes, victims have the right to have input in the plea bargaining process.[302]

On the federal level, the concept of plea bargaining is codified in Rule 11 of the Federal Rules of Criminal Procedure. On the state level, this legal practice is regulated by different state statutes.[303] Although defendants have no constitutional

---

sentence or a dismissal of the other charges" (Black's Law Dictionary, 8th ed., s.v "plea bargain"). On the different forms of plea bargaining see e.g. LaFave et al. (2007), Section 21.1 (a).

[294] This is called "charge bargaining". See FRCrP 11(e)(1)(A).

[295] This is called "sentence bargaining". See FRCrP 11(e)(1)(B).

[296] Legislatures, prosecutorial supervisors, and judges may impose some limits on plea bargaining. For example, it is not unusual for legislatures to instruct prosecutors not to dismiss or reduce charges for specific crimes (see e.g. Nev. Rev. Stat. Sections 483.560, 484.3792). On the categorical restrictions on plea bargaining, see Miller and Wright (2007), pp. 1117–1161.

[297] Singer (2008), p. 138.

[298] For an overview of state sentencing guidelines, see Kauder and Ostrom (2008).

[299] Singer (2008), p. 138.

[300] "Implicit plea bargaining" is generally contrasted with "express bargaining", which includes charge and sentence bargaining.

[301] LaFave et al. (2007), Section 21.1(a). See also Miller and Wright (2007), p. 1107.

[302] Miller and Wright (2007), pp. 1154–1161; see Tobolowsky et al. (2010), pp. 76–89; Beloof et al. (2006), pp. 476–497. For a comparison of U.S. and Swiss crime victims' rights in general, see Appendix II and for the crime victims' rights in the plea bargaining, see Appendix III.

[303] Plea bargaining is not a creature of law, but is one of legal practice. The Supreme Court recognized and accepted plea bargaining as legitimate in Santobello v. New York 404 U.S. 257 (1971). The court stated that plea bargaining had become "an essential component of the administration of justice" and that "[i]f every criminal charge were subject to a full-scale trial, the States and the Federal Government would need to multiply by many times the number of judges and court

right to a plea bargain, prosecutors must comply with equal protection[304] requirements.[305]

A guilty plea implies that the defendant waives their constitutional right to a jury trial, and the concomitant rights to cross-examination and confrontation, as well as the requirement that the government meet the burden of proving guilt beyond a reasonable doubt.[306] As part of the agreement, most state and federal courts have concluded that a defendant may explicitly waive the right to appeal.[307] In general a judge will accept a plea agreement if he is convinced that the defendant makes a voluntary[308] and knowing waiver of his trial rights. Furthermore, he must ascertain that there is a factual basis to support the charges to which the defendant pleads guilty.[309] Since the court rarely refuses to reject a guilty plea,[310] the court is not an efficient safeguard against wrongful confessions.[311] The reason for accepting guilty plea proposals is that the prosecutor knows all details about the case, whereas the judge has less background information on the alleged crime and the defendant. Moreover, if judges started calling the prosecutors' decisions into question, the caseload would become overwhelming.[312]

The practice of plea bargaining is a controversial issue[313] of the U.S. criminal justice system that benefits everyone through the criminal process. The defendant avoids uncertainties of a trial and gains a speedy disposition of the case. For the prosecutor, the negotiated plea allows him to save time and resources and to concentrate on high priority cases, and has the advantage of increasing the conviction rate. The court is able to dispose of a case quickly and will therefore conserve scarce resources. Furthermore, since jail time may have been suspended as a

facilities" (Santobello v. New York, 260). Furthermore, it held that plea bargaining should be "encouraged" (Santobello v. New York, 260).

304 The Equal Protection Clause is part of the 14th Amendment to the U.S. Constitution.

305 Lawless (2008), Section 6:06, n 55. On the problem of disparity, see Sect. 5.3.7.3.1.

306 Singer (2008), p. 120. See e.g. U.S. v. Mezzanatto, 513 U.S. 196, 201 (1995).

307 Miller and Wright (2007), pp. 1115–1116.

308 I will not discuss the problem of "Alford pleas" (defendant pleads guilty but at the same time insists that he did not commit the crime). See Miller and Wright (2007), pp. 1173–1179; Del Carmen (2007), p. 47.

309 On the prerequisites of a valid guilty plea, see Miller and Wright (2007), pp. 1161–1186; Singer (2008), pp. 120–127.

310 See Alschuler (1976), pp. 1065–1066.

311 Judge John Sommerville (Hennepin Court) sees no reason to refuse a plea bargain if the prosecutor and the defendant can reach an agreement. A guilty plea may be refused in cases involving guns (informal discussion with Judge John Sommerville on May 6, 2010).

312 Wright (2009), p. 587.

313 Some claim that without plea bargaining the criminal justice system would collapse due to the high amount of criminal cases (see Gershman 2007–2008, Section 7:1. Others consider this practice an abuse that should be abolished (see, e.g. Langbein 1978; Schulhofer 1992; Lawless 2008, Section 6.01). The following section will not discuss the risk of wrongful convictions related to the practice of plea bargaining.

condition of plea bargaining, the number of inmates entering the facilities can be reduced.[314]

5.3.7.2 Administrative System of Criminal Justice

The jury trial has traditionally been the normative procedure for determining criminal charges. As mentioned above, in modern criminal justice, the overwhelming majority of convictions are attributable to guilty pleas.[315] The difference between the two procedures is that, at trial, the guilty plea process is not protected by the same number of safeguards. A jury trial serves as a check on governmental excesses[316] and is intended to assure the accuracy of the verdict. The prosecutor, in order to accept a defendant's confession, is not required to be assured of guilt beyond a reasonable doubt.

In a system in which criminal trials become relatively infrequent, the determination of guilt is made by the prosecutor. Today, the United States has an administrative criminal justice system where the prosecutor combines the executive and judicial powers.[317] Even though, formally, the defendant's culpability occurs in court, the judge does not have enough information to be able to determine the defendant's guilt with certainty and this is not his role.[318] The charging document may be quite succinct and the explanation of the defendant's admission of guilt rather brief. The judicial inquiry is more limited to ascertaining that the defendant is of sound mind and understands the consequences of his actions rather than examining the accuracy of the facts to which he is attesting.[319] In fact, the judge is only required to assure that the conduct to which the defendant confess constitutes in fact

---

[314] Singer (2008), p. 133; Gershman (2007–2008), Section 7:1; Lawless (2008), Section 6.01.

[315] See Sect. 5.3.7.1, para 1.

[316] The Supreme Court has recognized the value of jury trials in stating that "providing an accused with the right to be tried by a jury of his peers gave him an inestimable safeguard against the corrupt or overzealous prosecutor and against the compliant, biased, or eccentric judge." Furthermore, the Court said that "the essential feature of a jury obviously lies in the interposition between the accused and his accuser of the commonsense judgment of a group of laymen and in the community participation and shared responsibility that results from that group's determination of guilt or innocence" [Williams v. Florida, 399 U.S. 78, 100 (1970), *quoting* Duncan v. Louisiana, 391 U.S. 145, 156 (1968)].

[317] Barkow (2006), p. 1048.

[318] The federal rules require the court to find that there is a "factual basis" for the plea, and not that the defendant is actually guilty. In U.S. v. Maher, 108 F.3d 1513, 1524 (2d Cir. 1997) the Court held that "Rule 11(f) does not require that the court be satisfied that a jury would return a verdict of guilty. Nor does it require the court to weigh evidence to assess whether it is even more likely than not that the defendant is guilty. Indeed, when the court considers a plea of guilty prior to trial, it often has no actual evidence to assess."

[319] Lynch (1998), p. 2122.

an offense under the statutory provision under which he is pleading guilty.[320] In reality, the assessment of the defendant's responsibility is made within the executive branch, in the office of the prosecutor, and does not occur in court at all.[321] In this process, the prosecutor acts largely as an administrative, quasi-judicial decision-maker.[322] He is a public official making a decision that is to a large extent adjudicatory.[323] This view does not fit an adversarial model. The prosecutor does not sit as a neutral fact finder between two opposing parties, nor does he act as a representative of one interested parties negotiating with another on an equal footing.[324] The prosecutor in deciding whether to punish the defendant is an "inquisitor seeking the 'correct' outcome."[325] Defendants have the possibility to influence the decision by submitting their arguments and evidence to the prosecutor,[326] who then decides on the importance he wants to give them.[327] Since defendants have the opportunity to be heard before the prosecutor makes any decision, the plea bargaining process is not unfair *per se*. The prosecutor is under no obligation to justify the rejection of the defendant's arguments. Thus, this can have some serious impacts on the equal treatment of similarly situated defendants.[328] In case the defendant contests the prosecutor's judgment, he can insist on a jury trial, which serves as a kind of judicial review in this system.[329]

From what has been said above, plea bargaining may be defined as an "informal, administrative, inquisitorial process of adjudication, internal to the prosecutor's office–in absolute distinction from a model of adversarial determination of fact and law before a neutral judicial decision maker."[330]

According to Barkow, plea bargaining "causes a systematic imbalance of power by allowing prosecutors to bypass the check of the judicial process."[331] In fact, the prosecutor faces extremely limited oversight over his decisions. Hence, abuse of discretion and arbitrariness might be a risk.[332] In the U.S. criminal justice

[320] The judge must determine "that the conduct which the defendant admits constitutes the offense charged in the indictment or information or an offense included therein to which the defendant has pleaded guilty" [U.S. v. Maher, 108 F.3d 1513, 1524 2d Cir. (1997)].

[321] Lynch (1998), p. 2123.

[322] Lynch (1998), p. 2135.

[323] Lynch (1998), p. 2127.

[324] Lynch (1998), p. 2128.

[325] Lynch (1998), p. 2135.

[326] The Rules of Criminal Procedure do not give a defendant the right to be heard by the prosecutor (Lynch 1998, p. 2124). Although the prosecutor is not obliged to listen to the defendant's arguments, it is almost always in the prosecutor's interest to do so (see Lynch 1998, p. 2125).

[327] Lynch (1998), p. 2135.

[328] Lynch (1998), pp. 2129, 2131–2132. See also Wright and Miller (2003), p. 1411. On the problem of disparity, see Sect. 5.3.7.3.1.

[329] Lynch (1998), p. 2135.

[330] Lynch (2003), p. 1404.

[331] Barkow (2006), p. 1050.

[332] See Sect. 5.4 for prosecutorial misconduct.

system prosecutors have almost unreviewable discretion over bargaining. They can decide to make or not to make a deal in any given case. It is exactly this kind of discretionary power that the separation of powers is supposed to prevent,[333] and it is obvious that an entity vested with prosecutorial and judicial functions is unlikely to engage in a self-checking exercise.[334] It is highly questionable how a system where the vast majority of cases are settled through plea bargains can fit within the separation of powers.

5.3.7.3 The Problem of Disparity

The problem of disparity has two aspects. Disparity may occur between the guilty plea and trial defendants and within defendants who plead guilty.

5.3.7.3.1 Disparity Between Guilty Plea and Trial Defendants

The disparity in treatment of guilty pleas and trial defendants[335] results from the inherent fact that plea agreements between prosecutors and defendants are grounded in the granting of concessions in exchange for guilty pleas. Such sentencing concessions are generally not considered improper by the courts.[336] In *United States v. Rodriguez*, the court stated that an "enormous sentencing disparity," one that "would strike many as unfair," is something that remains "within the government's discretion."[337]

Different approaches exist to explain the disparity. One commentator argues "that common good, particularly the principles and norms which justify and shape

---

[333] Barkow (2006), p. 1049.

[334] "Someone vested with both executive and judicial powers will undoubtedly decide whether someone has violated the laws. But she will make this decision only once and not twice. When it comes to law execution, the genius of the separation of powers is that, typically, two branches must independently conclude that some party has violated the law before anyone is punished. That benefit is clearly absent when the executive and judiciary are one and the same" (Prakash 2005, p. 545, n 147). Wright expresses a similar concern: "Sentencing discounts resting solely in the hands of prosecutors, such as substantial assistance departures create the greatest threat of trial distortion. The size of the trial penalty can remain reasonably small and relatively uncertain–as it should be–only if judges retain some authority to disagree with prosecutors about proposed discounts. Rules that designate judges as legitimate counterweights to prosecutors create a separation of powers for sentencing, a state of affairs that holds the best hope for reliable and accurate criminal justice" (Wright 2005, p. 139).

[335] See LaFave et al. (2007), Section 21.1 (e).

[336] E.g. Hitchcock v. Wainwright, 745 F.2d 1332 (11th Cir. 1984); U.S. v. Lippert, 740 F.2d 457 (6th Cir. 1984); Smith v. Wainwright, 664 F.2d 1194 (11th Cir. 1981); Wade v. State, 802 So.2d 1023 (Miss.2001); State v. Davis, 155 Vt. 417, 584 A.2d 1146 (1990); Drinkwater v. State, 73 Wis.2d 674, 245 N.W.2d 664 (1976).

[337] U.S. v. Rodriguez, 162 F.3d 135 (1st Cir. 1998).

punishment of criminals, not only allows, but requires favorable consideration of the pleading defendant. That is, a sound view of crime and punishment includes favorable consideration of the defendant who pleads guilty."[338] He considers a favorable sentencing as a right of the pleading defendant.[339] According to the ABA Standards relating to Pleas of Guilty, various factors calling for leniency may be considered if the courts are able to show substantial evidence that establish, for example, that: "the defendant is genuinely contrite and has shown a willingness to assume responsibility for his or her conduct; the concessions will make possible alternative correctional measures which are better adapted to achieving protective, deterrent, or other purposes of correctional treatment, or will prevent undue harm to the defendant from the form of conviction; the defendant, by making public trial unnecessary, has demonstrated genuine remorse or consideration for the victims of his or her criminal activity; or the defendant has given or agreed to give cooperation."[340]

These factors are partially controversial. For example, it is highly questionable if guilty pleas demonstrate repentance. In fact, it is rather difficult if not impossible to distinguish between those defendants pleading guilty because they are truly repentant and those who expect a less severe sentence and only plead for strategic reasons.[341]

The Federal Sentencing Guidelines provide for a two-count reduction if the defendant clearly demonstrates acceptance of responsibility for his offense.[342] In addition, if the defendant has assisted authorities in the investigation or prosecution of his own misconduct by notifying authorities of his intention to enter a plea of guilty in a timely manner, a third level of reduction may be obtained.[343] Pleading guilty does not ensure this adjustment[344] but will serve as a basis for it.[345] The reduction for acceptance of responsibility is determined by reference to the offense of conviction. The defendant is not required to admit relevant conduct.[346] Under the Federal Sentencing Guidelines, defendants pleading guilty and therefore waiving the right to a trial by jury often receive significantly lower sentences.[347] On average,

---

338 Bradley (1999), p. 66. In contrast, see Greene Burnett (1999).

339 Bradley (1999), p. 65.

340 ABA Pleas of Guilty, Standard 14-1.8 (a) (3rd edn 1999).

341 See LaFave et al. (2007), Section 21.1 (e).

342 USSG Section 3E1.1 (a) (2012).

343 USSG Section 5K3.1 allows up to a four level deduction for defendants pleading guilty in fast-track jurisdictions.

344 See e.g. U.S. v. Tellez, 882 F.2d 141 (5th Cir. 1989); U.S. v. Guarin, 898 F.2d 1120 (6th Cir. 1990); U.S. v. Harris, 882 F.2d 902 (4th Cir. 1989).

345 See Bemporad (2011), p. 14.

346 USSG Section 3E1.1 cmt; see also Bemporad (2011), p. 14.

347 For 2004, the Bureau of Justice Statistics reports that "the average prison term imposed on defendants convicted at trial was almost three times longer than the term imposed on defendants convicted by plea. Defendants convicted at trial received 148.2 months on average, while those convicted by plea received an average of 56.2 months" (Smith and Motivans 2006, pp. 70–71).

defendants receive a sentence that is 250 % lower than similarly situated defendants who insist on a jury trial.[348]

On the state level, it is the prosecutor's office policy that determines how to proceed when making a plea offer and what kind of discount may be offered.[349]

5.3.7.3.2 Disparity Within Defendants Who Plead Guilty

It is desirable that similarly situated defendants receive similar offers. This means that the prosecutor's offer should be fair, impartial, just, and equitable and should not take into account improper considerations like race, class, and gender. Prosecutorial guidelines[350] may help achieve this goal.

Federal Level: Principles of Federal Prosecution

If a federal prosecutor decides to conclude a prosecution pursuant to a plea agreement,[351] according to the U.S. Attorneys' Manual he has to take various considerations into account when determining the charges to which a defendant should be allowed to plead guilty. In principle, the prosecutor should charge the most readily provable charge that is consistent with the defendant's criminal conduct. The federal prosecutor should be sure that there is a factual basis for the charge(s) to which a guilty plea is entered. Furthermore, the plea agreement should provide for adequate scope for sentencing under all the circumstances of the case. Finally, in a case involving several defendants, care must be taken that the disposition of the charges against one defendant does not adversely affect the investigation or prosecution of co-defendants.[352] In addition to the written plea bargaining policies set forth in the U.S. Attorneys' Manual, many of the U.S. attorneys' offices in the 94 federal districts have developed their own

Judge Heaney reported that, under the sentencing guidelines, defendants who went to trial were sentenced to two-and-a-half more years than defendants who pleaded guilty, whereas, under pre-guidelines law, the sentencing difference was on average 1 year and 2 months (Heany 1991, pp. 176–179).

[348] In 2004, for instance, drug offenders convicted at trial received an average of 195.9 months compared to the 79.5 months for drug offenders convicted by guilty plea (Smith and Motivans 2006, pp. 70–71).

[349] Due to certain restrictions on plea bargaining, the prosecutor may not always be able to propose an offer. Limits may be placed by legislatures, prosecutorial supervisors, and judges. On the limits to plea bargaining, see Miller and Wright (2007), pp. 1117–1161.

[350] For the federal plea bargaining policies, see USAM, Section 9-27.400–450 (1997).

[351] Federal prosecutors take the following considerations into account when deciding whether to enter into a plea agreement with the defendant: defendant's cooperation; defendant's criminal history; nature and seriousness of offense charged; defendant's attitude; prompt disposition; likelihood of conviction; effect on witnesses; probable sentence; trial rather than plea; expense of trial and appeal; prompt disposition of other cases (USAM, Section 9-27.420).

[352] USAM, Section 9-27.430.

guidelines for taking into account caseloads, resources, and other factors in each district.[353]

The Holder Memorandum's[354] plea bargaining policy provides that a plea agreement "should reflect the totality of a defendant's conduct."[355] This means that while a prosecutor "should seek a plea to the most serious offense that is consistent with the defendant's conduct,"[356] that decision should be "informed by an individualized assessment of the specific facts and circumstances of each particular case."[357] The memo prohibits overcharging to induce a plea as well as the dropping of certain charges in order "to arrive at a plea bargain that does not reflect the seriousness of the defendant's conduct."[358] Furthermore, it requires the review of all plea agreements by a supervisory attorney, and the promulgation in each office of written guidance concerning "the standard elements required in its plea agreements, including the waivers of a defendant's rights."[359]

The notion of individualized assessment, initially introduced by the Reno Memorandum, was eliminated by the Ashcroft Memorandum. Under the Ashcroft Memorandum, prosecutors were permitted to negotiate a plea for less than the most serious, readily provable charge only under constrained conditions.[360] A federal prosecutor might depart under the same exceptions as set forth under the charging policy.[361] In this sense, the Ashcroft Memorandum represented a movement away from the individual case-by-case determination of a defendant's culpability. As with the charging policy, the Holder Memorandum reintroduced the notion of individualized assessment.

State Level: Overview

Plea policies in many state systems pursue goals similar to those of the Department of Justice. However, whereas plea bargaining policies in the federal system are written, such policies are rarely written within the state systems.[362] Plea bargaining

---

[353] Miller and Wright (2007), p. 1129.

[354] On the different memos issued by the Federal Attorney Generals, see Sect. 5.3.6.2.1.

[355] Holder (2010), p. 2.

[356] Holder (2010), p. 2.

[357] Holder (2010), p. 2.

[358] Holder (2010), p. 2.

[359] Holder (2010), p. 2.

[360] For a detailed discussion of how the Ashcroft Memorandum has limited discretion with regard to plea bargaining, see Ely (2004).

[361] Ashcroft (2003), p. 6. In case of sentence bargaining, the federal prosecutor with approval of an assistant attorney general, U.S. attorney, or designated supervisory attorney, might depart only in the following circumstances: (1) the defendant has provided "substantial" assistance; (2) the office has a "fast-track" program for the offense; (3) in "rare occurrences" prosecutors may acquiesce in other downward departures, but they must "affirmatively oppose downward departures that are not supported by the facts and the law, and cannot agree to "stand silent" with respect to such departures" (Ashcroft 2003, p. 7).

[362] Miller and Wright (2007), pp. 1143–1144.

policies vary greatly in their level of detail. Particularly in smaller prosecutor's offices, it is usual that prosecutors follow unwritten[363] but explicit guidelines. Prosecutors may elaborate formal plea review standards, describing the types of plea bargains that are admissible. It is also possible that they create procedural review mechanisms, so that settlement offers are reviewed by a superior such as a senior or managing attorney. These guidelines or procedures might be restricted to some types of offenses.[364] How a prosecutor decides to run an office depends on different factors, such as the size of the office, the volume of criminal cases, and the level of experience of the assistants in that office. Hence, there is no single solution for determining the administrative structure of a high quality prosecutor's office.[365] The extent of discretion allocated to assistant prosecutors may vary between different prosecutor's offices. In some offices, assistant prosecutors will have considerable discretion in dealing with minor offenses, while in others—in order to control the handling of cases—they will have to follow internal guidelines[366] or policies. However, no matter which policy is implemented, in general each office will have some informal system of internal controls. In this way, it may be guaranteed that less experienced prosecutors are supervised to a certain extent by more experienced prosecutors either through a system of written guidelines or internal policies or through a system of direct review of charging decisions.[367]

State Level: Minnesota

The following section describes the situation in the state of Minnesota, a state where each county attorney is required to adopt written guidelines "governing the county attorney's charging and plea negotiation policies and practices."[368] The guidelines should address the situations under which plea negotiation agreements are allowed, the extent to which comments from persons concerned with a prosecution are considered in plea negotiations, and the criteria that are considered in making charging decisions and plea agreements.[369] The following examples describe two

[363] The reasons why offices want to keep their plea bargaining policies informal and unwritten include: ill effects on deterrent value of criminal law, unfavorable public impressions of perceived lenient policies, need for flexibility in unusual cases, need to avoid judicial review of prosecutorial decisions (see Pizzi 1993, pp. 1364–1367). For advantages of written guidelines, see Mayer (1996), pp. 304–306. Benefits of guidelines made public include: leads to effective use of resources, helps to set priorities and allocating resources accordingly, greater understanding of decision-making process, inform the public of its elected officials' policies (Mayer 1996, pp. 304–306).

[364] Miller and Wright (2007), p. 1129.

[365] Pizzi (1993), p. 1344.

[366] For a detailed discussion of written guidelines that were in place in the Manhattan District Attorney's Office while Richard Kuh was the District Attorney, see Kuh (1975).

[367] Pizzi (1993), pp. 1344–1345.

[368] Minn. Stat., Section 388.051, Subdivision 3 (2010). The American Bar Association suggests that every prosecutor's office adopt written policies that guide prosecutorial discretion [ABA Prosecution Standard 3-2.5 (3rd edn. 1993)].

[369] Minn. Stat., Section 388.051, Subdivision 3(a) (1)–(3).

different approaches to developing and using written guidelines. The guidelines from both prosecutor's offices are not accessible to the public,[370] so that the description will not go into every detail, but rather will remain more general.

The policy of the Hennepin County Attorney's Office is that similarly situated defendants receive similar offers. This means that all offers must be fair, impartial, just, and equitable, as well as race, class, and gender neutral. The case disposition policies of the Hennepin County Attorney's office[371]—like the Holder Memorandum—follow the notion of an "individualized assessment" of the facts of each case. Hence, prosecutors should not merely apply the predetermined "Hennepin County Discount" when making settlement offers. Factors they should consider when making an offer include:

- (1) presence of aggravating factors[372]
- (2) presence of mitigating factors[373]

---

[370] For an example of published guidelines in the state of Minnesota, see the Rice County Attorney's Office. Their office policies and procedures can be found at http://www.co.rice.mn.us/attorney/ (accessed June 24, 2012).

[371] Case disposition policies from 08/11/09.

[372] Section II.D.2.b. of the Minnesota Sentencing Guidelines sets out a nonexclusive list of aggravating factors: (1) The victim was particularly vulnerable due to age, infirmity, or reduced physical or mental capacity, which was known or should have been known to the offender, (2) The victim was treated with particular cruelty for which the offender should be held responsible; (3) The current conviction is for a Criminal Sexual Conduct offense or an offense in which the victim was otherwise injured and there is a prior felony conviction for a Criminal Sexual Conduct offense or an offense in which the victim was otherwise injured; (4) The offense was a major economic offense; (5) The offense was a major controlled substance offense; (6) The offender committed, for hire, a crime against the person; (7) Offender is sentenced according to Minn. Stat., Section 609.3455, Subdivision 3a; (8) Offender is a "dangerous offender who commits a third violent crime" (see Minn. Stat., Section 609.1095, Subdivision 2); (9) Offender is a "career offender" (see Minn. Stat., Section 609.1095, Subdivision 4); (10) The offender committed the crime as part of a group of three or more persons who all actively participated in the crime; (11) The offender intentionally selects the victim or the property against which the offense is committed, in whole or in part, because of the victim's, the property owner's or another's actual or perceived race, color, religion, sex, sexual orientation, disability, age or national origin; (12) The offender's use of another's identity without authorization to commit a crime. This aggravating factor may not be used when the use of another's identity is an element of the offense.

[373] Section II.D.2.a of the Minnesota Sentencing Guidelines sets out a non-exclusive list of mitigating factors: (1) The victim was an aggressor in the incident; (2) The offender played a minor role in the crime or participated under circumstances of coercion or duress; (3) The offender, because of physical or mental impairment, lacked substantial capacity for judgment when the offense was committed. The voluntary use of intoxicants (drugs or alcohol) does not fall within the purview of this factor; (4) The offender's presumptive sentence is a commitment to the commissioner but not a mandatory minimum sentence, and either of the following exist: (a) The current conviction offense is at severity level I or II and the offender received all of his or her prior felony sentences during less than three separate court appearances; or (b) The current conviction offense is at severity level III or IV and the offender received all of his or her prior felony sentences during one court appearance; (5) Other substantial grounds exist which tend to excuse or mitigate the offender's culpability, although not amounting to a defense; (6) Alternative placement for offender with serious and persistent mental illness (See Minn. Stat., Section 609.1055).

- (3) strength of the evidence
- (4) input from the victim(s), in compliance with the Victims' Rights Act
- (5) number of victims
- (6) mandatory sentencing provisions
- (7) consecutive sentencing procedures

The prosecutor, before making a settlement offer, should estimate the strength of the case. He must be fully aware of the strengths and weaknesses of witnesses. Hence, in a serious crime against person case, it may be necessary to interview the victim and key witnesses, whereas in other cases it may be appropriate to consult with the investigator on the case.[374] Pursuant to Section 611 A.03 of the Minnesota Statutes (2010), it is essential that the prosecutor contact the victim advocate in advance of making a settlement offer in order to allow adequate time for the advocate to contact the victim and obtain his input.[375] The prosecutor should be mindful of the statutes that establish mandatory sentencing provisions.[376]

To ensure that similarly situated defendants receive similar offers, individual prosecutors have discretion to make offers within certain parameters.[377] The prosecutor's discretion varies depending on the type of offense the suspect is accused of respectively is charged with. Settlement offers for presumptive stayed (non-prison) crimes[378] can be made—with the exception of assistant attorneys who have been in the office for less than 1 year—without prior agreement from the senior attorney. However, a dismissal must always have the permission of a senior attorney. In other cases, if a prosecutor believes that it is appropriate or necessary to depart from those parameters, the prosecutor must consult with a senior attorney or division manager and obtain permission prior to making the offer.

Prosecutors must always record the reasons for negotiation. If a deviation from the guidelines occurs, the prosecuting attorney should articulate the reasons for variance.

The case disposition policies of the Hennepin County Attorney's Office provide further guidance in a variety of areas, such as what to do in the event of multiple charges, Alford plea,[379] and dismissals.

---

[374] Case disposition policies of the Office of the Hennepin County Attorney.

[375] On the Victims Rights in Minnesota, see Appendix II.

[376] E.g. Heinous crimes (Minn. Stat., Section 609.106), certain murders (Minn. Stat., Section 609.107), repeat sex offenders (Minn. Stat., Section 609.109), dangerous and repeat felony offenders (Minn. Stat., Section 609.1095), gun crimes and felon in possession crimes (Minn. Stat., Section 609.11), DWI (Minn. Stat., Section 169A.275), certain burglaries (Minn. Stat., Section 609.582, 609.583), assault on peace officers (Minn. Stat., Section 609.221), repeat domestic assaults (Minn. Stat., Section 609.2243).

[377] These parameters are explained in the case disposition policies of the Hennepin County Attorney's Office and vary depending on the charge(s) the defendant is accused of.

[378] Level I–IV and F and G Offenses.

[379] Defendant pleads guilty but at the same time insists that he did not commit the crime.

The Anoka County Attorney's Office guidelines for negotiated guilty pleas[380] are quite similar to those of the Hennepin County Attorney's Office. Following these guidelines, the individual prosecutor, if he wants to depart from the guidelines because aggravating or mitigating factors may require it, must always have the prior approval from a superior.[381]

The guidelines make a distinction between presumptive stayed (non-prison) crimes and presumptive executed (prison) sentence crimes. Settlement offers for any presumptive stayed (non-prison) crime are made according to a table. A certain amount of jail cap is determined for each severity level of an offense (I–VII). Jail caps are correspondingly higher in each severity level for defendants with a criminal history score of one or more. For each additional criminal history, a determined amount of days are added. The plea negotiation jail cap is reduced by a certain percentage if the defendant pleads guilty at or before the pretrial hearing. If the prosecutor establishes aggravating or mitigating factors that cause exceptions to these guidelines, he must have a supervisor's approval. The guidelines for negotiated pleas enumerate a number of reasons that may justify an exception to these guidelines. This list is not exhaustive. Reasons mentioned are, e.g. age or vulnerability of the victim, sufficiency of admissible evidence to support a verdict, possible deterrent value of prosecution, a consideration of the feelings, attitude, and opinion of the victim, the extent of injury to the victim, and any potential evidentiary concerns. Settlement offers for all presumptive executed (prison) sentence crimes and for all severity level VIII through XI crimes and for all severity level A, B, C, and H crimes (including any mandatory minimum sentence crime) should be a Minnesota Sentencing Guidelines disposition. With the exception of dangerous or career offenders, where the policy is "plead as charged", a presumptive prison sentence may be agreed to that is less than the high end of the presumptive guidelines cell range.

If a defendant has committed multiple crimes (not same course of conduct), consideration will be given to permitting the defendant to plead guilty to less than all crimes he may be charged with in an effort to obtain a result in conviction and sentence that is appropriate for the conduct. A matrix helps the prosecutor decide how many charges he should file in such situations.

In sum, the policy of the Anoka County Attorney's Office guidelines is that equal reductions are usually automatically applied in settlement offers concerning presumptive stayed crimes. Any deviation from these guidelines requires prior approval of a superior. The policy of the Hennepin County Attorney's Office is that identical reductions are not merely applied but that each case is individually assessed. Assistant prosecutors from the Hennepin County Attorney's Office, in

[380] The guidelines from the Rice County Attorney's Office (MN) are very similar and can be found at http://www.co.rice.mn.us/uploadedcontent/forms/negotiations.pdf (accessed June 23, 2012).

[381] The five approval authorities are: the weekly Criminal Division meeting, the Property Crimes Unit's Managing Attorney, the Violent Crimes Unit Managing Attorney, the Chief Deputy County Attorney, the County Attorney.

contrast to those from the Anoka County Attorney's office, have the liberty to consider aggravating and mitigating factors when making a settlement offers concerning presumptive stayed crimes[382] without prior approval of a superior.[383] If the negotiation falls into a presumptive executed (prison) sentence crimes and some factors call for a deviation from the guidelines, the approval of a superior is required in both county attorney's offices.

Although the presented guidelines diverge to some extent from the allocated discretion, both have the following common features: (1) The presented guidelines provide a list of possible reasons for deviation from the general rule. Rather than being exhaustive, they are illustrative and may serve as guidance for the prosecutor. (2) Possible deviations should be approved by a superior, this in order to ensure consistency. In sum, both presented guidelines permit controlled discretion on the part of assistants, but at the same time permit assistants to depart from the guidelines with approval of a superior.

These guidelines are completely realistic in light of what guidelines can and cannot achieve. Such guidelines do not completely eliminate prosecutorial discretion but are helpful to assistant prosecutors in the sense that they help them to understand the general office expectations.

5.4 Prosecutorial Misconduct

5.4.1 Definition

Prosecutorial misconduct is defined as "a prosecutor's improper or illegal act (or failure to act), especially involving an attempt to avoid required disclosure or to persuade the jury to wrongly convict a defendant or assess an unjustified punishment."[384] Prosecutorial misconduct is "conduct which violates the law and/or ethical standards of law practice."[385] The term implies willful and dishonest behavior.[386]

[382] Level of offense: I–IV; F and G Offenses.

[383] Approval is only required if the assistant prosecutor is in the office for less than 1 year.

[384] Black's Law Dictionary, 8th ed., s.v. "prosecutorial misconduct."

[385] Fisher (1989), p. 9.

[386] See Diepraam (2006), p. 776; Jonakait (1987), p. 560, n 23.

5.4.2 Types of Misconduct

Prosecutorial misconduct can happen at any stage of the criminal procedure, from investigation and grand jury indictment to trial and sentencing.

Gershman[387] as well as Lawless[388] divide prosecutorial infractions into 13 categories. Types of prosecutorial misconduct include: abuse of charging function, nondisclosure of evidence, misuse of media, misconduct in plea bargaining process, delay, jury selection, misconduct in presence of evidence, forensic misconduct (jury argument), misconduct at sentencing, misconduct in grand jury, abuse of process, and mistrials, convictions, and double jeopardy.

Scholars mostly center the prosecutorial misconduct discussion on forensic misconduct,[389] the misconduct that happens in court.[390] Methods used by some prosecutors to prejudice a defendant's fair trial rights include making inflammatory remarks, eliciting inadmissible and prejudicial evidence, and violating the defendant's constitutional rights.[391]

The failure to provide the defense with possibly exculpatory evidence is a frequent basis for overturning convictions.[392] Such lack of disclosure is known as a "Brady violation".[393] This is also the most difficult type of misconduct to uncover.[394] It is impossible to know exactly how often this occurs. Brady violations only become apparent when the hidden material is revealed in other ways. Withheld material may appear by chance. However, it is suggested that Brady violations are among the most pervasive forms of prosecutorial misconduct.[395]

It is not possible to discuss every type of prosecutorial misconduct in light of the extent of the problem and this would be beyond the scope of my research. In the

---

[387] Gershman (2007–2008).

[388] Lawless (2008).

[389] "When courts and commentators talk about prosecutorial misconduct, they often are referring to the prosecutor's argument to the jury" Gershman (2007–2008), Section 11:1. "When one thinks of 'prosecutorial misconduct' one immediately envisions the prosecutor railing before the jury, spewing invectives, and verbally abusing the defendant, defense counsel, and those laws which protect and coddle criminals" (Lawless 2008, Section 9:01).

[390] See e.g. Gershman (1995), Singer (1968), Celebrezze (1987), and Alschuler (1972). For a discussion about the prosecutor's trial (mis-) conduct, see Gershman (2007a), Sections 2-1–2-10.

[391] For a detailed discussion, see Gershman (2007–2008), Chap. 11 and Lawless (2008), Chap. 9.

[392] For an overview of overturned convictions see Gershman (2007a), Section 2-2(b)(1). Studies that primarily identified prosecutorial misconduct through the analysis of appellate rulings arrive at the same conclusion (see Ridolfi and Possley 2010, pp. 36–38; Armstrong and Possley 1999). See also Pollock (2010), p. 290.

[393] On the development of the Brady doctrine and its significance, see Gershman (2007–2008), Chap. 5.

[394] Ridolfi and Possley (2010), pp. 36–37.

[395] See Gershman (2007b), p. 533. See also Ridolfi and Possley (2010), pp. 36–38; Armstrong and Possley (1999). For examples of capital cases where exculpatory evidence was withheld, see Kirchmeier et al. (2010), pp. 1337–1342.

following, my focus will lie on prosecutorial misconduct that occurs behind closed doors and that is closely related to the topic of my research: the abuse of charging function, misconduct in the plea bargaining process, and misconduct in Grand Jury.

5.4.2.1 Abuse of Charging Function

The prosecutor's discretion, which is largely unchecked, unstructured, and hidden from the public view, creates the danger that some charging decisions may be the result from improper considerations, such as racial prejudice,[396] political favoritism, or personal animosity. Another abuse of the prosecutor's discretionary power is prosecutorial vindictiveness.

5.4.2.1.1 Selective Prosecution

Arbitrary selection of a defendant may violate the Equal Protection Clause of the 14th Amendment. Claims of selective prosecution are extremely difficult to prove, so that such claims have rarely been successful.[397]

In 1886, in *Yick Wo v. Hopkins*[398] the Supreme Court held for the first time that a law that is fair on the surface and impartial in appearance, but is administered in a discriminatory fashion, is an infringement of the Equal Protection Clause guaranteed by the 14th Amendment. *Yick Wo*, a Chinese alien, was arrested and convicted of violating a San Francisco ordinance prohibiting the maintenance of laundries located in wooden buildings without a license. The Board of Supervisors granted permission to operate laundries in wooden buildings to all but one of the non-Chinese operators, but none of the 200 Chinese applicants.

Under the two-pronged analysis outlined by the Second Circuit in *United States v. Berrios*,[399] the defendant claiming selective or discriminatory prosecution must establish: (1) that those similarly situated have not been prosecuted, and (2) that the decision to prosecute him was discriminatory and made invidiously or in bad faith, i.e., based upon constitutionally impermissible considerations such as race, religion, or a desire to prevent the exercise of constitutional rights.[400] Thus, the

[396] For an excellent review of empirical research and discussion on racial disparity in charging decisions, see Free (2002). In his paper, he arrived at the conclusion that, in the majority of studies in which the impact of defendant race on prosecute/dismiss decisions was examined, no significant relationship between defendant race and prosecute/dismiss decisions was disclosed. However, studies of prosecutorial discretion in capital charging provided evidence of unwarranted racial disparity. Furthermore, empirical research supports the assumption that prosecutors are more likely to charge defendants with capital offenses when their victims are white.

[397] Singer (2008), p. 41; Lawless (2008), Section 3.23; Gershman (2007–2008), Section 4:9.

[398] Yick Wo v. Hopkins, 118 U.S. 356 (1886).

[399] U.S. v. Berrios, 501 F.2d 1207 (2d Cir. 1974).

[400] U.S. v. Berrios, 1211.

defendant is required to prove that the prosecution has a discriminatory impact as well as a discriminatory intent.

In 1985, in *Wayte v. United States*,[401] the Supreme Court applied the strict intent standard to a claim of selective prosecution. The Court made it clear that showing of discriminatory effect was not sufficient to infer a discriminatory motive.[402] Since *Wayte*, defendants must make a prima facie showing a discriminatory effect and purpose to obtain an evidentiary hearing.

The burden established by *Wayte* for selecting prosecution was high but not insurmountable. The standard adopted in 1996 by the Court in *United States v. Armstrong*[403] created a significant barrier: "In order to dispel the presumption that a prosecutor has not violated equal protection, a criminal defendant must present 'clear evidence to the contrary'."[404]

Discriminatory Impact

The defendant must show that other persons who are similarly situated have not been prosecuted.[405] Thus, the defendant must first establish the existence of a class of persons engaging in the same criminal behavior and that are equally subject to penal prohibitions.[406]

In addition to showing the existence of a class of similarly situated offenders, a defendant must show that these members of this class were not prosecuted. A bare allegation is not sufficient.[407]

Statistical evidence is helpful when proving disparity treatment and has often been used, particularly in claims of selective prosecution based on race. However, statistics may not always be sufficient to prove a discriminatory impact. In *United States v. Armstrong*,[408] the Court rejected statistics showing that the overwhelming majority of the persons sentenced in Federal Court for crack cocaine trafficking were black as insufficient to prove that other similarly situated persons are not

[401] Wayte v. U.S., 470 U.S. 598 (1985).

[402] Wayte v. U.S., 608.

[403] U.S. v. Armstrong, 517 U.S. 456 (1996).

[404] U.S. v. Armstrong, 465 [quoting U.S. v. Chemical Foundation, 272 U.S. 1, 14–15 (1926)]. For further details, see Sects. 5.4.2.1.1.1–5.4.2.1.1.3.

[405] U.S. v. Berrios, 501 F.2d 1207, 1211 (2d Cir. 1974).

[406] See e.g. U.S. v. Jones, 159 F.3d 969, 977 (6th Cir. 1998); U.S. v. Graham, 146 F.3d 6, 9 (1st Cir. 1998); U.S. v. Nelson, 137 F.3d 1094, 1105 (9th Cir. 1998).

[407] See e.g. U.S. v. Jennings, 724 F.2d 436, 446 (5th Cir. 1984); U.S. v. Greene, 697 F.2d 1229, 1234 (5th Cir.). *cert. denied*, 463 U.S. 1210, 103 S. Ct. 3542, 77 L. Ed. 2d 1391 (1983).

[408] U.S. v. Armstrong, 517 U.S. 456 (1996).

prosecuted.[409] The sample, containing 24 defendants, was too small to demonstrate statistically reliable racial differences.[410]

In the same decision, the Supreme Court created a significant barrier in selective prosecution claims. It held, that "to establish a discriminatory effect in a race case, the claimant must show that similarly situated individuals of a different race were not prosecuted."[411] The defendant had identified those of the same race who were prosecuted, but failed to identify similarly situated individuals who were not black, who could have been prosecuted under the same charges, but were not.[412]

It is not easy for the defendant to show how many more individuals are committing the offenses than are arrested and charged, since crimes are not all systematically reported.

Discriminatory Intent

The second requirement of the selective prosecution defense—that the defendant was singled out for prosecution upon an impermissible classification, such as race, religion, sex, national origin, the desire to exercise constitutional rights, or other arbitrary consideration,[413]—is extremely difficult to prove. If there is no overt discriminatory classification present, the defendant is required to look into a prosecutor's subjective motivation. Showing evidence of discriminatory intent often requires data about the prosecutor's office's thought process. However, in order to attain discovery, discriminatory intent has to be shown and it is very difficult to present evidence of discriminatory intent without discovery.

In *United States v. Armstrong*, the defendant presented evidence obtained from the Federal Public Defender's Office that showed that, of the 24 crack firearms cases the Office had closed in 1991, all 24 were black.[414] While the Ninth Circuit, sitting en banc, ruled that these data provided a "colorable basis" tending to show that discriminatory prosecution had occurred, and ordered discovery, the Supreme

---

[409] See also U.S. v. Jones, 287 F.3d 325 (5th Cir. 2002); U.S. v. Gutierrez, 990 F.2d 472, 476 (9th Cir. 1993); U.S. v. Kearney, 436 F. Supp. 1108 (S.D. N.Y. 1977); U.S. v. Bass, 536 U.S. 862, 122 S. Ct. 2389, 153 L. Ed. 2d 769 (2003) ("raw statistics regarding overall charges say nothing about charges brought against similarly situated defendants").

[410] But see U.S. v. Jones, 159 F.3d 969, 978, 1998 FED App. 0331 (6th Cir. 1998).

[411] U.S. v. Armstrong, 465. Other language in the opinion differentiated the standard only slightly. The Court held that to obtain discovery, a defendant must produce "some evidence that similarly situated defendants could have been prosecuted, but were not" (U.S. v. Armstrong, 469). It also held that the defendant must make a "credible showing of different treatment of similarly situated persons" (U.S. v. Armstrong, 470).

[412] U.S. v. Armstrong, 470.

[413] See e.g. Oyler v. Boles, 368 U.S. 448 (1962); U.S. v. Lawrence, 179 F.3d 343, 30 (5th Cir. 1999); U.S. v. Perry, 152 F.3d 900, 903 (8th Cir. 1998); U.S. v. Jones, 159 F.3d 969, 977 (6th Cir. 1998).

[414] U.S. v. Armstrong, 517 U.S. 456, 480 (1996).

Court reversed the decision, holding that race statistics alone do not support a claim of selective prosecution.

The courts presume that each prosecution is initiated in good faith.[415] As a result, the defendant carries a heavy burden of overcoming this presumption. In addition, in *Oyler v. Boles*, the court recognized that "the conscious exercise of some selectivity in enforcement is not in itself a federal constitutional violation."[416]

Procedure and Proof in Discriminatory Prosecution Cases

A claim of selective prosecution is often raised in a pretrial motion to dismiss the charges.[417] To be successful, several conditions have to be fulfilled.

As noted, a prosecutor is presumed to have acted in good faith. To overcome this presumption, a defendant must establish a prima facie case that he has been intentionally singled out for prosecution while others similarly situated have not been prosecuted, and that the selection was based on constitutionally impermissible considerations.[418] Since *Armstrong*, it is crucial that the defendant show both elements of this defense or the motion to dismiss will fail. If the defendant is successful in establishing a prima facie case, the burden of proof is shifted to the government[419] and the court will conduct an evidentiary hearing. The defendant then has the opportunity to gain access to the government's files and to question the prosecutor.[420]

The standard of proof adopted by the Supreme Court in *Armstrong*, however, makes it extremely difficult for the defendant to obtain discovery of the prosecutor's record. The defendant is required to prove an equal protection violation before a court can allow discovery of the prosecutor's motive. In return, such discovery will be used to establish the selective prosecution claim.[421] In determining the threshold for discovery, the Supreme Court found that "the vast majority of the Courts of Appeals require a defendant to produce some evidence that similarly situated defendants of other races could have been prosecuted, but were not, and this requirement is consistent with our equal protection law."[422] The Court held that "the required threshold—a credible showing of different treatment of similarly

[415] U.S. v. Serafino, 281 F.3d 327, 331 (1st Cir. 2002); U.S. v. Parham, 16 F.3d 844 (8th Cir. 1994); U.S. v. Saade, 652 F.2d 1126, 1135 (1st Cir. 1981).

[416] Oyler v. Boles, 368 U.S. 448, 456 (1962).

[417] FRCrP 12(b).

[418] U.S. v. Berrios, 501 F.2d 1207, 1211 (2d Cir. 1974).

[419] U.S. v. Falk, 479 F.2d 616, 624 (7th Cir. 1973).

[420] On the cross-examination of the prosecutor, see Gershman (2007–2008), Section 4:31.

[421] Gershman (2007–2008), Section 4:32.

[422] U.S. v. Armstrong, 517 U.S. 456, 469 (1996). Before *Armstrong*, different tests have been adopted to determine the standard of the initial showing to warrant an evidentiary hearing. The defendant may be required (1) to show "facts sufficient to raise a reasonable doubt", (2) to establish "a colorable basis", or (3) to constitute "a prima facie case" (see U.S. v. Armstrong, 468).

situated persons—adequately balances the Government's interest in vigorous prosecution and the defendant's interest in avoiding selective prosecution."[423]

The purpose of the evidentiary hearing is to give the defendant a chance to prove the prima facie case of discriminatory prosecution. A prima facie showing does not necessarily mean a dismissal of the charges. The burden of proof is shifted to the prosecutor and he has to justify or explain the reasons for the prosecution.

5.4.2.1.2 Prosecutorial Vindictiveness

Constitutional guarantee of due process[424] protects defendants against prosecutorial vindictiveness. Prosecutorial vindictiveness is defined by the courts as the forbidden practice of penalizing criminal defendants in response to defendants' exercise of constitutional rights.[425] Punishing a defendant, either by increasing the sentence or by filing excessive or severe charges, usually occurs after a defendant refuses to plead guilty or after a successful appeal of a conviction by a defendant.[426]

The Doctrine of Prosecutorial Vindictiveness

The doctrine prohibiting vindictiveness was first discussed by the Supreme Court in 1969 in *North Carolina v. Pearce*[427] and addressed the issue of judicial vindictiveness. In this case, the defendant, after having successfully appealed his conviction, was retried, reconvicted, and resentenced.[428] However, this time, the judge gave him a harsher sentence than that originally imposed.[429] The Supreme Court vacated the conviction holding that the right to due process was violated. It stated that "vindictiveness against a defendant for having successfully attacked his first conviction must play no part in the sentence he receives after a new trial. And since the fear of such vindictiveness may unconstitutionally deter a defendant's exercise of the right to appeal or collaterally attack his first conviction, due process also requires that a defendant be freed of apprehension of such a retaliatory motivation on the part of the sentencing judge."[430] The judge's imposition of a more severe sentence upon a defendant after a new trial is constitutional only when based upon

[423] U.S. v. Armstrong, 470.

[424] Due Process is guaranteed by the 5th and the 14th Amendment.

[425] North Carolina v. Pearce, 395 U.S. 711 (1969); Colten v. Kentucky, 407 U.S. 104 (1972); Chaffin v. Stynchcombe, 412 U.S. 17 (1973); Blackledge v. Perry, 417 U.S. 21 (1974).

[426] Gershman (2007–2008), Section 4:33; Lawless (2008), Section 3.33.

[427] North Carolina v. Pearce, 395 U.S. 711 (1969).

[428] It is not completely clear if Pearce was sentenced both times by the same judge (see Schwartz 1983, p. 129, n 21).

[429] North Carolina v. Pearce, 713.

[430] North Carolina v. Pearce, 725.

"objective information concerning identifiable conduct on the part of the defendant occurring after the time of the original sentencing proceeding."[431]

In 1974, the Supreme Court extended the doctrine of vindictiveness to prosecutors in *Blackledge v. Perry*.[432] In that case, the prosecutor increased charges against the defendant after he appealed to a higher court for a trial de novo. The Court ruled that, the lack of evidence notwithstanding, the prosecutor acted in bad faith or maliciously in seeking a felony indictment against the defendant, "the opportunities for vindictiveness in this situation are such as to impel the conclusion that due process of law requires a rule analogous to that of the Pearce case."[433] The Court concluded that "the Due Process Clause is not offended by all possibilities of increased punishment upon retrial after appeal, but only by those that pose a realistic likelihood of 'vindictiveness.'"[434]

In *Bordenkircher v. Hayes*,[435] the Supreme Court addressed the applicability of prosecutorial vindictiveness to the practice of plea bargaining. It held that the threat of seeking more serious charges if the defendant did not plead guilty to the initial indictment but insisted on a jury trial was constitutionally acceptable in the context of plea bargaining.[436] The Supreme Court stated that "in the 'give-and-take' of plea bargaining, there is no such element of punishment or retaliation as long as the accused is free to accept or reject the prosecution's offer."[437] Furthermore, it noticed that the prosecutor's intention to increase the charges "was clearly expressed at the outset of the plea negotiations. Hayes was thus fully informed of the true terms of the offer when he made his decision to plead not guilty."[438]

In *United States v. Goodwin*,[439] the Supreme Court underlined the importance of making a distinction between pretrial and post trial rights. It stated that, at the pretrial stage of the proceedings, "the prosecutor's assessment of the proper extent of prosecution may not have crystallized."[440] Moreover, a defendant before trial routinely files a variety of pretrial motions that burden the prosecution but which are an integral part of the adversary process. It would be unrealistic to assume that "a prosecutor's probable response to such motions is to seek to penalize and to deter."[441] Thus, the Court declined to apply the presumption of vindictiveness, arguing that there was "good reason to be cautious before adopting an inflexible presumption of prosecutorial vindictiveness in a pretrial setting."[442]

[431] North Carolina v. Pearce, 726.

[432] Blackledge v. Perry, 417 U.S. 21, 94 S. Ct. 2098, 40 L. Ed. 2d 628 (1974).

[433] Blackledge v. Perry, 27.

[434] Blackledge v. Perry, 27.

[435] Bordenkircher v. Hayes, 434 U.S. 357 (1978).

[436] Bordenkircher v. Hayes, 358–359.

[437] Bordenkircher v. Hayes, 363.

[438] Bordenkircher v. Hayes, 360.

[439] U.S. v. Goodwin, 457 U.S. 368 (1982).

[440] U.S. v. Goodwin, 381.

[441] U.S. v. Goodwin, 381.

[442] U.S. v. Goodwin, 381.

In sum, the actual doctrine of prosecutorial vindictiveness provides little protection for defendants. *Bordenkircher* and *Goodwin* support the proposition that prosecutorial vindictiveness in criminal proceedings is acceptable to a certain extent.[443] Bringing increased charges after a defendant refuses to plead guilty or withdraws his guilty plea, does not invoke a presumption of vindictiveness. Thus, since *Goodwin*, claims of prosecutorial vindictiveness in the pretrial setting have rarely been successful.[444]

Procedure and Proof in Cases of Prosecutorial Vindictiveness

A claim of prosecutorial vindictiveness is usually raised by a pretrial motion to dismiss the indictment.[445]

Courts have applied different tests for judging claims of prosecutorial vindictiveness. One is the "appearance of vindictiveness" test and the other standard is "a reasonable likelihood of vindictiveness".[446]

The "appearance of vindictiveness" test has been applied by the majority of federal and state courts.[447] Under this test, once a defendant is able to show that there was an increase in the severity of the charges after he had exercised a statutory or constitutional right, a presumption of vindictiveness is established. The burden then shifts upon the prosecutor to show that any increase was motivated by independent reasons or intervening circumstances.[448] The other standard used by the courts employ an objective test based on a showing of a realistic likelihood of vindictiveness.[449] The question here is "whether a reasonable person would think there existed a realistic likelihood of vindictiveness."[450] Hence, this test does not depend on a defendant's subjective impressions.[451] Once the determination of a realistic likelihood of vindictiveness is made, the burden of disproving it rests on the government. "[O]nly objective, on-the-record explanations can suffice to rebut a finding of realistic likelihood of vindictiveness."[452]

---

[443] Henning (1999a), pp. 742–743.

[444] See Gershman (2007–2008), Section 4:42, Note (2001), pp. 2078–2080.

[445] See, e.g., FRCrP 12(b).

[446] On both tests, see Krimmel (1994), pp. 22–25.

[447] See, e.g., U.S. v. Shaw, 655 F.2d 168, 171 (9th Cir. 1981); U.S. v. Jamison, 505 F.2d 407 (D.C. Cir. 1974); Wilson v. State, 633 S.W.2d 952 (Tex. App. El Paso 1982). See Gershman (2007–2008), Section 4:64; Lawless (2008), Section 3.34.

[448] See, e.g. U.S. v. Johnson, 171 F.3d 139 (2d Cir. 1999); U.S. v. Shaw, 655 F.2d 168, 171 (9th Cir. 1981); Gershman (2007–2008), Section 4:64.

[449] Krimmel (1994), pp. 22–23. On the advantages of such a test, see LaFave et al. (2007), Section 13.7 (c).

[450] U.S. v. Andrews, 633 F.2d 449 (6th Cir. 1980).

[451] Gershman (2007–2008), Section 4:66.

[452] U.S. v. Andrews, 633 F.2d 449, 456 (6th Cir. 1980).

A wide range of excuses will suffice to rebut a presumption of vindictiveness: prosecutorial inexperience, continuation of an investigation, protection of an informant, desire to retain an option to bring less serious or fewer charges later.[453]

5.4.2.2 Misconduct in the Plea Bargaining Process

As previously stated,[454] plea bargaining in the U.S. criminal justice system is an extremely important tool. However, the prosecutor's tremendous power in the plea bargaining process creates a potential risk for abuses. Since the defendant is required to waive fundamental constitutional rights,[455] it is all the more important that the prosecutor behave properly. Various ethical standards[456] aim to regulate the prosecutor's conduct during the negotiation process. Although these standards are not binding upon the prosecutor, they certainly provide a basis for proper prosecutorial conduct during plea negotiations and may serve as guidance for the trial judge when evaluating a claim of prosecutorial misconduct. For a guilty plea to be valid, it is essential that it was entered intelligently and voluntarily.[457]

A guilty plea is involuntary if it is induced by false promises, fraud, mistake, or misapprehension of the conditions.[458] Furthermore, a prosecutor is not allowed to use meaningless or illusory promise to induce a plea.[459] A guilty plea that is reached in the absence of defense counsel renders the plea invalid and involuntary. An exception to this is made when the defendant specifically waives his Sixth Amendment right to counsel.[460] A prosecutor's failure to disclose exculpatory evidences may result in vacating the guilty plea for the reason that such information is crucial to enabling the defendant to decide whether to plead guilty.[461] A prosecutor's decision to treat a similarly situated defendant differently may lead to the invalidity of the plea under the condition that the defendant can show that the prosecutor's

---

453 Gershman (2007–2008), Section 4:60; Lawless (2008), Section 3.35.

454 See Sects. 5.3.7.1 and 5.3.7.2.

455 Such waiver includes the privilege against self-incrimination, right to trial by jury, and right to confront one's accusers (see Gershman 2007–2008, Section 7:13). Some constitutional rights are not waived, such as the right to effective assistance of counsel, the right to be tried in a court with proper jurisdiction, the right to conflict-free representation, the right to nonracially discriminatory sentencing, the right not to be subject to a statutorily excessive sentence, the right against double jeopardy (see Singer 2008, p. 141).

456 See ABA Model Rules of Professional Conduct, R. 3-1–3.9 (2010); ABA Prosecution Standards 3-4.1–3-4.2 (3rd edn 1993); ABA Pleas of Guilty Standard 14-3.1 (3rd edn 1999); NDAA Standards 66.1–71.1 (3rd edn 2009); USAM, Sections 9-27.330–9-27.641 (1997); FRCrP 11.

457 See e.g. ABA Prosecution Standard 3-4.1.

458 Gershman (2007–2008), Section 7:3.

459 Gershman (2007–2008), Section 7:4.

460 See e.g. ABA Prosecution Standard 3-4.1 (b); ABA Pleas of Guilty Standard 14-3.1.

461 ABA Model Rules of Professional Conduct, R. 3.8; see also Gershman (2007–2008), Section 7:19; Lawless (2008), Section 6:06.

conduct was arbitrary or irrational.[462] The use of threats and promises intended to deprive the defendant of his freedom of choice constitutes a denial of procedural fairness.[463] It is, however, difficult to define under which circumstances promises and threats are considered coercive. There is strong support that the threat of additional charges made during plea negotiations is not a denial of due process but is legitimate to induce a plea.[464] However, in some situations courts have recognized that a threat to prosecute a defendant under a habitual offender statute might be coercive.[465] From those cases it emerges that the timing of the indictment under a recidivist statute, and the way in which a prosecutor uses the threat during the plea bargaining process, will have an influence on the decision regarding whether his actions are considered as impermissibly coercive.

In contrast to the aforementioned behaviors, the prosecutor's offer of a more lenient sentence does not constitute coercion. In fact, a guilty plea is often induced by the prosecutor through the offer of a plea to a lesser charge, the dismissal of other charges, or the recommendation of a specific sentence.[466] In the same way, threats of higher charges are usually upheld, unless the defendant pleads guilty and cooperates with the government.[467] Courts normally consider a defendant's plea un-coerced if he pleads guilty to avoid a possible death sentence after trial.[468]

In the event that the prosecutor fails to perform his part of the bargain,[469] alternative remedies are available to the defendant such as vacating the plea, specific performance of the agreement, or withdrawal of the plea.[470,471] The burden of proving the breach of the bargain rests upon the defendant.[472]

---

[462] Gershman (2007–2008), Sections 7:20–7:24. "Equal protection does not require identity of treatment. It only requires that classification rest on real and not feigned differences, that the distinction have some relevance to the purpose for which the classification is made, and that the different treatments be not so disparate, relative to the difference in classification, as to be wholly arbitrary" [U.S. v. Bell, 506 F.2d 207, 222 (D.C. Cir. 1974), *quoting* Walters v. City of St. Louis, Mo., 347 U.S. 231 (1954)].

[463] Gershman (2007–2008), Section 7:17.

[464] See e.g. Bordenkircher v. Hayes, 434 U.S. 357 (1978).

[465] See e.g., McClure v. Boles, 233 F. Supp. 928 (N.D.W.Va. 1964); State v. Sather, 172 Mont. 428, 564 P.2d 1306 (1977).

[466] Gershman (2007–2008), Section 7:7. Brady v. U.S., 397 U.S. 742 (1970); Jeffers v. Lewis, 38 F.3d 411 (9th Cir. 1994).

[467] Gershman (2007–2008), Section 7:12; U.S. v. Williams, 47 F.3d 658 (4th Cir. 1995).

[468] Gershman (2007–2008), Section 7:18. See, e.g. Brady v. U.S., 397 U.S. 742 (1970); Parker v. North Carolina, 397 U.S. 790 (1970); North Carolina v. Alford, 400 U.S. 25 (1970).

[469] On the various ways a prosecutor may breach the bargain, see Gershman (2007–2008), Sections 7:30–7:36.

[470] See e.g. FRCrP 32(e); ABA Pleas of Guilty Standard 14-2.

[471] In Santobello v. New York [404 U.S. 257 (1971)], a seminal case, the court left the choice of remedies for a prosecutor's breach of a plea agreement to the lower court. As a consequence, various policies have emerged. See Gershman (2007–2008), Sections 7:27–7:29; Lawless (2008), Sections 6.14-22; Singer (2008), p. 144.

[472] Gershman (2007–2008), Section 7:37; Lawless (2008), Sections 6:15 and 6:20.

5.4.2.3 Misconduct in Grand Jury

Today it is widely acknowledged that the grand jury,[473] originally set up to protect the citizen from unjust prosecution, has become the prosecutor's tool.[474] Recognizing the reality of the grand jury, William O. Douglas observed that, "[a]ny experienced prosecutor will admit that he can indict anybody at any time for almost anything before any grand jury."[475] In a grand jury process the prosecutor occupies a central role. Among others, he serves as a legal advisor to the grand jury and presents evidence for its consideration. The prosecutor, in fulfilling these duties, "must be scrupulously fair to all witnesses and must do nothing to inflame or otherwise improperly influence the grand jurors."[476] However, this standard is often ignored.[477] Grand jury proceedings are secret[478] and nonadversarial. There is no judge who oversees the proceedings, nor is a lawyer present to protect the witness rights.[479] Rather, prosecutors have considerable freedom in deciding which witness to summon and to force that person to testify under oath on everything he knows about the case under investigation.[480] In fact, there is no right to remain silent.[481] Furthermore, the prosecutor is also allowed to present hearsay evidence and other evidence that is normally inadmissible in court.[482] The absence of judge and witness counsel, the rules of secrecy, and the wide discretion granted to the prosecutor, make the grand jury fertile ground for misconduct. Prosecutorial abuses in grand jury processes include prejudicial comments and information, misleading instructions to grand jury witnesses, improper statements by prosecutor to the grand jury, failure to disclose exculpatory evidence, using unreliable evidence, and presence of unauthorized persons before the grand jury.[483]

5.4.2.3.1 Prejudicial Comments and Information

According to the ABA Prosecution Standards, "[t]he prosecutor should not make statements or arguments in an effort to influence grand jury action in a manner

[473] On the grand jury, see also Sect. 5.5.1.3.2.2.

[474] See e.g. Leipold (1995).

[475] U.S. v. Dionisio, 410 U.S. 1, 23 (1973) (Douglas, J., dissenting).

[476] USAM, Section 9-11.010 (1997).

[477] Lawless (2008), Section 2.21.

[478] On the secrecy of grand jury proceedings, see LaFave et al. (2007), Section 8.5; Singer (2008), pp. 58–59.

[479] FRCrP 6(d).

[480] Gershman (2007–2008), Section 2:2.

[481] Gershman (2007–2008), Section 2:1.

[482] See e.g. U.S. v. Costello, 350 U.S. 359 (1966).

[483] For a detailed discussion on prosecutorial misconduct in grand jury, see Gershman (2007–2008), Chap. 2; Lawless (2008), Chap. 2.

which would be impermissible at trial before a petit jury."[484] Improper prosecutorial statements can occur in different ways. Prosecutors are not permitted to impugn the defendant's character. In this sense, courts for example have condemned questions that imply that the person under investigation is connected to organized crime,[485] or hired a lawyer with the aim of hindering other witnesses from testifying against him.[486] The prosecutor acting as legal advisor to the grand jury may express his "opinion on the legal significance of the evidence,"[487] but is not permitted to make comments with the intention of prejudicing the jury. The line between legitimate and illegitimate comments can sometimes be difficult to delineate.[488] The prosecutor is not allowed to make misleading remarks which may have negative consequences on the independent evaluation of evidence by the grand jury.[489] Furthermore, the prosecutor is prohibited from making inflammatory and abusive remarks since this can have an influence on the credibility of the witness and prejudice the jury.[490] The fact that the prosecutor in the grand jury proceeding takes on an additional role, namely that of legal advisor, must be taken into consideration when determining what constitutes misconduct. As legal advisor, he may be permitted to make comments that would not be allowed during a trial, where he only acts as an advocate and where the trial judge is responsible for giving legal advice.[491] Moreover, since the grand jury has the responsibility of investigating all possible crimes, the prosecutor, through adequate background information related to the case, may help the grand jury in this duty by providing such information that would not have been admissible at trial.[492]

5.4.2.3.2 Undermining a Witness' Legal Safeguard

A prosecutor in a grand jury proceeding has different tactics to undermine the witness's legal safeguards. Although a grand jury witness does not have the right to remain silent, he has the right to refuse to answer questions which could incriminate him based on his Fifth Amendment privilege. However, if the claim is legitimate, a grand jury witness may be granted immunity and compelled to give testimony under oath.[493] It is an abuse, for example, if the prosecutor tricks the witness into

[484] ABA Prosecution Standard 3-3.5 (b).

[485] U.S. v. Serubo, 604 F.2d 807 (3d Cir. 1979).

[486] U.S. v. DiGregorio, 605 F.2d 1184 (1st Cir. 1979). See also Gershman (2007–2008), Section 2:3.

[487] ABA Prosecution Standard 3-3.5 (a).

[488] For examples of illegitimate comments, see Gershman (2007–2008), Section 2.4.

[489] Gershman (2007–2008), Section 2:5.

[490] Gershman (2007–2008), Section 2:6.

[491] LaFave et al. (2007), Section 15.7 (b). On the prosecutor's dual role, see Sect. 5.4.3.1.

[492] LaFave et al. (2007), Section 15.7 (b).

[493] Singer (2008), pp. 60–61.

believing that he does not have the right to refuse to answer questions.[494] Inside the grand jury room, a witness does not have the right to counsel. But this does not mean that a witness cannot leave the grand jury room to consult with counsel prior to answering a question. Therefore, it is improper to prevent a witness from seeking legal advice.[495] In general, a jury witness has no right to be informed of his status as a prospective defendant. It is the policy of the Department of Justice, however, to warn witnesses of their statutes as targets.[496] A failure to comply with this guideline might not quash an indictment but may result in disciplinary action by the Justice Department's Office of Professional Responsibility.[497] A grant of immunity to a witness completely rests within the discretion of the prosecutor and serves as protection for the witness from having his testimony used against him. If the prosecutor intends to indict a witness who has testified under immunity, he has a heavy burden of proving that the evidence used for the indictment came from a different source than that for the compelled testimony. The potential for this kind of prosecutorial abuse of witness' rights is obvious and may be the most well-established. An immunized testimony used for conviction is subject to "harmless error" review.[498] The prosecutor may attempt to circumvent the statutory immunity laws[499] by granting informal immunity through an agreement with the witness.[500] This practice is known as "pocket immunity" or "letter immunity" and has been condemned by a number of courts, since this kind of deal between the prosecutor and the witness is subject to abuse.[501] Whereas statutory immunity is binding for every prosecutor at the state and federal level, informal immunity only binds the individual prosecutor's office.[502] A prosecutor in a grand jury proceeding has to respect privileged relationships and is therefore not permitted to infringe upon attorney–client privilege,[503] marital privilege,[504] physician–patient privilege,[505] and clergyman–communicant privilege.[506] Two different views exist regarding the consequence of a prosecutor's violation of the witness's rights. Some courts have considered a dismissal of the subsequent indictment as appropriate; others have seen the suppression of the testimony in question as legitimate.[507]

[494] Gershman (2007–2008), Section 2:10.

[495] Gershman (2007–2008), Section 2:10.

[496] USAM, Section 9-11.151 (1997).

[497] Gershman (2007–2008), Section 2:11.

[498] Gershman (2007–2008), Section 2:12.

[499] For the federal immunity statute, see 18 USC Sections 6002 and 6003.

[500] U.S. v. Kilpatrick, 594 F. Supp. 1324, 1336 (D. Colo. 1984).

[501] See Gershman (2007–2008), Section 2:13; Lawless (2008), Section 2.28.

[502] Singer (2008), pp. 60–61; Lawless (2008), Section 2.28.

[503] Gershman (2007–2008), Section 2:15.

[504] Gershman (2007–2008), Section 2:17.

[505] Gershman (2007–2008), Section 2:18.

[506] Gershman (2007–2008), Section 2:19.

[507] LaFave et al. (2007), Section 15.7 (b).

5.4.2.3.3 Failure to Disclose Exculpatory Evidence

The extent to which a prosecutor is required to disclose exculpatory evidence to a grand jury is a matter of debate. Basically, there are two views. On the one hand, the grand jury's function is to bring to trial those who may be guilty and to serve as protection for the ordinary citizen against an overzealous prosecutor.[508] Since a grand jury proceeding is ex parte and nonadversarial,[509] the only way the grand jury can learn about the presence of exculpatory evidence is from the prosecutor.[510] On the other hand, the grand jury does not have to determine the guilt or innocence of a defendant, but is only required to establish whether the prosecutor's accusations are supported by probable cause. Furthermore, at this preliminary stage of the proceeding it may be difficult for the prosecutor to decide what evidence might be exculpatory.[511]

It is the policy of the Department of Justice that when the prosecutor presenting the case to the grand jury personally knows of substantial evidence that directly negates guilt of the person under investigation, the prosecutor must disclose such evidence to the grand jury before seeking an indictment.[512] Similarly, the ABA Prosecution Standards takes the position that "no prosecutor should knowingly fail to disclose to the grand jury evidence which tends to negate guilt or mitigate the offense."[513]

Approximately a third of the states have recognized a prosecutorial obligation to disclose exculpatory evidence.[514] The Supreme Court in *United States v. Williams*,[515] however, found no prosecutorial duty to disclose known exculpatory information to the grand jury. As a consequence, the Brady doctrine,[516] requiring the prosecution to disclose exculpatory material at trial, has no application in the grand jury proceeding at the federal level. The Court held that requiring a prosecutor to present exculpatory evidence would "alter the grand jury's historical role, transforming it from an accusatory body that sits to assess whether there is adequate basis for bringing a criminal charge into an adjudicatory body that sits to determine guilt or innocence."[517]

---

[508] U.S. v. Dionisio, 410 U.S. 1 (1973). On the history of the Grand Jury, see Sect. 5.5.1.3.2.2, para 2.

[509] See U.S. v. Calandra, 414 U.S. 338, 343–344 (1974).

[510] On the feasibility and desirability of an obligation of the prosecutor to present exculpatory evidence to the grand jury, see Note (1977).

[511] U.S. v. Mandel, 415 F. Supp. 1033 (D. Md. 1976).

[512] USAM, Section 9.11.223 (1997).

[513] ABA Prosecution Standard 3-3.6 (b).

[514] See LaFave et al. (2007), Section 15.7 (f).

[515] U.S. v. Williams, 504 U.S. 36, 112 S. Ct. 1735, 118 L. Ed. 2d 352 (1992).

[516] On this doctrine, see e.g. Gershman (2007–2008), Chap. 5.

[517] U.S. v. Williams, 504 U.S. 36, 37 (1992).

5.4.2.3.4 Using Unreliable Evidence

In general, prosecutors are permitted to present to grand juries hearsay evidence. In *Costello v. United States*,[518] the Supreme Court held that if a grand jury is legally constituted and unbiased, an indictment will not be subject to challenge even when based on unconstitutionally obtained evidence.[519] With *Costello*, prosecutors were therefore encouraged to rely heavily on inadequate or incompetent evidence. Because the *Costello* rule created the danger of excessive use of hearsay, courts intended to introduce some limits. In *United States v. Estepa*,[520] the Court dismissed an indictment that was based on hearsay testimony. In this case, the grand jury was misled into believing that the witness, a federal narcotics agent, gave eyewitness testimony, whereas in reality he recounted from reports the actions of other agents who investigated the case.[521] This means that as long as the grand jury is advised when hearsay is presented, there is no reason to dismiss an indictment. However, in general, the *Costello* principle has been upheld by the Supreme Court, so that indictments based excessively on hearsay evidence have not been dismissed.[522]

At the state level, several states have passed legislation that governs the use of hearsay evidence in a grand jury. In general, only evidence that would be admissible at trial can be presented to a grand jury, whereas the use of hearsay evidence is only allowed under some exceptions.[523]

5.4.2.3.5 Presence of Unauthorized Persons Before the Grand Jury

The secrecy of grand jury proceedings is essential to ensuring the effectiveness of the grand jury in performing its investigative and screening functions. It is said that secrecy contributes to: (1) encouraging witnesses to testify freely without fear of retaliation; (2) preventing the escape of those under investigation; (3) preventing those under investigation from attempting to importune the grand jurors; and (4) protecting the reputation of those investigated by the grand jury but not indicted.[524] Grand jury secrecy provisions usually provide that, during deliberations and voting, no persons other than the grand jurors are allowed to be present inside the chambers, while only the jurors, attorneys for the government, the witness under examination, and, if needed, supporting personnel (e.g. stenographers) may be present during other phases of the proceedings.[525] The presence of unauthorized

---

[518] Costello v. U.S., 350 U.S. 359 (1956).

[519] Costello v. U.S., 362–363. See also LaFave et al. (2007), Section 15.5 (a).

[520] U.S. v. Estepa, 471 F.2d 1132 (2d Cir. 1972).

[521] U.S. v. Estepa, 1136.

[522] LaFave et al. (2007), Section 15.5 (a).

[523] Gershman (2007–2008), Section 2:44.

[524] See e.g. U.S. v. Procter & Gamble Company, 356 U.S. 677 (1958).

[525] See e.g. FRCrP 6(d).

persons in the grand jury room may justify a pretrial dismissal of an indictment. This was the case prior to *United States v. Mechanik*.[526] As a consequence of an unauthorized appearance of persons before a grand jury, the indictment was declared void without the need to show prejudice. In *Mechanik*, two law enforcement agents testified in tandem before the grand jury. The Supreme Court held that the attendance of unauthorized persons before a grand jury does not necessarily lead to reversal but is subject to harmless error review to establish whether the defendant was prejudiced. In view of this, dismissal is based on a case specific showing of likely prejudice. In light of this, it is possible to distinguish between two different approaches: a per se and a case-by-case approach. Today, in contrast to federal courts,[527] the majority of state courts follow the first approach and treat unauthorized presence before the grand jury as per se ground for dismissal.[528]

5.4.2.3.6 Remedies for Misconduct

Remedies for prosecutorial misconduct in the grand jury include dismissal of indictments, reversal of convictions, suppressing grand jury testimony, quashing subpoenas, recommending disciplinary action against the prosecutor, and the imposition of other similar sanctions.[529]

Dismissal or reversal can either occur on constitutional grounds or under the supervisory power doctrine.[530] Courts have ordered the dismissal of an indictment or the reversal of a conviction under the Due Process Clause. The knowing use of perjured testimony, the prosecutor's failure to inform the grand jury of the existence of substantial evidence negating guilt, and the extensive improper use of hearsay evidence have been considered by some courts as a violation of due process.[531] In *Bank of Nova Scotia v. United States*[532] and *United States v. Williams*,[533] the Supreme Court seriously limited the scope of supervisory power to dismiss indictments for prosecutorial misconduct in grand jury. In *Bank of Nova Scotia v. United States*, the Court held that as a general matter an indictment may not be dismissed for misconduct in grand jury proceedings unless such misconduct prejudiced the defendants. Such prejudice exists only if "the violations substantially influenced the grand jury's decision to indict," or if there is "grave doubt" that the decision to

[526] U.S. v. Mechanik, 475 U.S. 66 (1986).

[527] U.S. v. Mechanik; Bank of Nova Scotia v. U.S., 487 U.S. 250 (1988).

[528] LaFave et al. (2007), Section 15.7 (h).

[529] Gershman (2007–2008), Sections 2:53–2:57.

[530] Supervisory power is a court's power to supervise the administration of justice by establishing and maintaining standards of procedure and evidence [see McNabb v. U.S., 318 U.S. 332, 340 (1943)].

[531] Gershman (2007–2008), Section 2:53; Lawless (2008), Section 2.21.

[532] Bank of Nova Scotia v. U.S., 487 U.S. 250 (1988).

[533] U.S. v. Williams, 504 U.S. 36 (1992).

indict was free from the substantial influence of such violations.[534] In *United States v. Williams*, the Supreme Court further narrowed its holding. In *Williams*, the court stated that the grand jury "belongs to no branch of the institutional government" and that this precluded the courts from exercising its supervisory power over what happened inside the room.[535]

In general, a dismissal for prosecutorial misconduct does not bar the prosecutor from re-indicting.[536]

5.4.3 *Reasons for Misconduct*

Various reasons have been advanced to explain the causes of prosecutorial misconduct: the adversary system, the nature of the office, and the system for enforcing professional ethics.

5.4.3.1 Conflict of Prosecutor's Dual Role in the Criminal Justice System

Public prosecutors occupy a difficult dual role.[537] On the one hand, prosecutors are key participants in a criminal justice system that is adversarial in nature. In this role, they function as an advocate for the state and against the defendant. As an advocate[538] for the state, the prosecutor's aim is to win the case by obtaining convictions.[539] On the other hand, prosecutors are ministers of justice. In this regard, they act impartially and their orientation to the factual contest is neutral. The prosecutor's responsibility is to see that justice is done. He should protect the innocent, only prosecute those he believes are guilty, guard the rights of the accused, and enforce the rights of the public.[540] When prosecuting, he should only use fair methods.

---

[534] Bank of Nova Scotia v. U.S., 251.

[535] U.S. v. Williams, 47.

[536] Gershman (2007–2008), Section 2:56.

[537] "A prosecutor has the responsibility of a minister of justice and not simply that of an advocate" (ABA Model Rules of Professional Conduct, R. 3.8 cmt. 1 (2010)). For a detailed discussion on the dual role, see Fisher (1988), pp. 9–23.

[538] In this position, the public prosecutor is confronted with pressures that the defense attorney not faces. For a discussion, see Jonakait (1987), pp. 550–556. Dissenting opinion, Green (1988).

[539] As advocate, the prosecutor tries to "maximize both the number of convictions and the severity of the sentences that are imposed after conviction" (Alschuler 1968, p. 52).

[540] ABA Prosecution Standard 3-3.9 cmt (3rd edn 1993). In addition, the prosecutor may also be seen as an "administrator of justice". He is the one who will decide whether to bring charges, and if so, what charges to bring against the accused, whether to prosecute or dismiss charges (American Bar Association, 5). In this function he manages limited resources (see Fisher 1988, p. 14).

In its ethical rules the American Bar Association recognizes the special place of prosecutors in the criminal justice system: "The responsibility of a public prosecutor differs from that of the usual advocate; his duty is to seek justice, not merely to convict."[541]

The tension between doing justice and the prosecutor's role as the government's advocate[542] in the criminal justice system may result in prosecutorial misconduct.[543] It is in the adversarial role that the prosecutor can be tempted by a variety of improper tactics, such as failure to disclose exculpatory evidence and presenting false evidence.[544]

5.4.3.2 Nature of the Office

Decades ago, George Felkenes observed that the prosecutor's office is exposed to external as well as internal pressures and that both may contribute to a "conviction psychology".[545] Over the years, there has been nothing that would indicate that this phenomenon has disappeared.[546]

---

[541] ABA Model Code of Professional Responsibility, EC 7-13 (1983); ABA Prosecutorial Investigations Standard 1.2 (a) (2008). See also NDAA Standards 1-1.1 (3rd edn 2009). In Berger v. U.S. (1935), Justice Sutherland delivered the prosecutor's duty of fairness: "The U.S. Attorney is the representative not of an ordinary party to a controversy, but of a sovereignty whose obligation to govern impartially is as compelling as its obligation to govern at all; and whose interest, therefore, in a criminal prosecution is not that it shall win a case, but that justice shall be done. As such, he is in a peculiar and very definite sense the servant of the law, the twofold aim of which is that guilt shall not escape or innocence suffer. He may prosecute with earnestness and vigor—indeed, he should do so. But, while he may strike hard blows, he is not at liberty to strike foul ones. It is as much his duty to refrain from improper methods calculated to produce a wrongful conviction as it is to use every legitimate means to bring about a just one" [Berger v. U.S., 295 U.S. 78, 79 (1935)]. On the Berger doctrine, see Singer (1968), pp. 229–230.

[542] The "surrogate client" model (the prosecutor has no individual client, but instead has to decide which decision is in the best interest of the public. Because the public is neutral, the prosecutor will act in his quasi-judicial role when making the charging decision) and the "adversary stage" theory (depending on the task the prosecutor fulfils, he will act either as minister of justice or lawyer) attempt to clarify the prosecutor's dual role. Both suggest that the quasi-judicial role applies only to certain prosecutorial tasks. In general, in stages that lack the adversary system's safeguards against abuse, the prosecutor's role as minister of justice is most appropriate. However, both models fail (see Fisher 1988, pp. 15–17).

[543] "He is torn between his image as a powerful, callous attorney and a crusader for justice" (Felkenes 1975, p. 118). "The anomie resulting from this conflict may cause the prosecutor to ignore his quasi-judicial role, or he may play this role only in making the initial decision to charge. If he is forced to choose only one of the roles, it is likely that he will choose the advocate role because ... the criterion by which his efficiency is judged is quite likely to be his conviction record" (Felkenes 1975, p. 119).

[544] For a discussion about the prosecutor's dual role see Fisher (1988), pp. 9–23. See also Pollock (2010), pp. 271–273.

[545] On the "conviction psychology", see Felkenes (1975), pp. 110–112.

[546] Medwed (2009), p. 46.

5.4.3.2.1 External Pressures

The political character of any prosecution office may contribute to prosecutorial misconduct.[547] The position of prosecutor is often viewed as a stepping stone to a higher political office.[548] To demonstrate the effectiveness of his work, the prosecutor can point to conviction statistics. A record of many convictions helps the prosecutor who wishes to further his political ambitions. Therefore, the emphasis may focus on the achievement of a high conviction rate rather than a high rate of justice.[549] However, in reality, the conviction rate by itself is a very poor measure of prosecutor performance.[550]

The community demands that the criminal laws are enforced, but rarely realizes that the prosecutor is also responsible for the protection of the accused's rights.[551] In cases receiving high media attention, the community wants to see the cases resolved as quickly as possible. The prosecutor's concern is to win approval from the public. As a result, he may be inclined to neglect the safeguard of the accused rights.

5.4.3.2.2 Internal Pressures

At the beginning of their careers, assistant prosecutors are young and inexperienced.[552] These characteristics render them particularly vulnerable to influence by their more experienced peers. Assistant prosecutors tend to conform to the expectations of their superiors. If the prosecution office shares conviction-oriented values, the young prosecutor will assimilate these attitudes.[553] Therefore, initiation into work as a prosecutor is of great importance. It determines how he will fulfill his duties.

5.4.3.3 System for Enforcing Professional Responsibility

The available remedies for misconduct, such as appellate review of claims of misconduct, judicial reporting of prosecutor's acts of misconduct, state bar disciplinary action, and internal systems of accountability within prosecutors' offices, are all ineffective in preventing misconduct. Prosecutors are rarely disciplined for

---

[547] Note (1959). ABA Standards on Prosecutorial Investigations provide some guidance about the way prosecutors should react to political pressure (Standard. 3.6).

[548] Pollock (2010), p. 261; Note (1959), p. 483.

[549] On the problem with the adversary system, see Lawless (2008), Section 1.06.

[550] See Gordon and Huber (2002), p. 335.

[551] Note (1959), p. 483.

[552] On the selection of assistant district attorneys, see Sect. 5.1.2.2.2.

[553] Singer (1968), pp. 227–228; Felkenes (1975), pp. 111–112.

abuses of power. The failure to sanction prosecutorial misconduct encourages prosecutors to continue to commit misconduct.[554]

5.4.3.4 Other Reasons

Other reasons that are advanced as causes of prosecutorial misconduct include the desire to hide a weak case, and "prosecutor's bias",[555] which leads the prosecutor to believe those charged are guilty.[556]

5.4.4 Frequency of Prosecutorial Misconduct

5.4.4.1 Statistics

Official statistics about the extent of prosecutorial misconduct and the frequency of sanctions are nonexistent. While prosecutors say that misconduct occurs infrequently, scholars assume that abuses of power are more common than acknowledged by prosecutors.[557] According to Gershman, acts of misconduct by prosecutors are "pervasive."[558] It is assumed that most of the time prosecutorial misconduct is committed unintentionally or unconsciously.[559]

5.4.4.2 Studies

Different studies have been conducted to measure the extent of prosecutorial misconduct.

The first study of this kind was undertaken by Chicago Tribune staff reporters Ken Armstrong and Maurice Possley and published in a five-part series in the *Chicago Tribune* in 1999.[560] To determine the number of convictions overturned because of prosecutorial misconduct in homicide cases, they reviewed court record and appeals on a nationwide basis between 1963 and 1999. The investigation found

---

[554] For a discussion on the ineffectiveness of available sanctions, see Sect. 5.4.5.

[555] Hobbs (1949).

[556] Singer (1968), p. 228.

[557] See Jost (2007), p. 943.

[558] "[A]cts of misconduct by prosecutors are recurrent, pervasive, and very serious. Case reports do not adequately describe the extent of such misconduct because so much of the prosecutor's work is conducted secretly and without supervision. One example is the suppression of evidence. Only when information is subsequently revealed can the prosecutor be charged with misconduct" (Gershman 2007–2008, p. vi).

[559] Jonakait (1987), p. 563; Diepraam (2006), p. 776; Terzano et al. (2009), p. 2.

[560] Armstrong and Possley (1999).

at least 381 homicide convictions reversed because prosecutors withheld evidence favorable to the defense or knowingly used false evidence.

In 2003, a study conducted by the Center for Public Integrity found that prosecutorial misconduct was a factor in dismissed charges, reversed convictions, or reduced sentences in at least 2,012 cases since 1970. The Center's researchers analyzed every accessible state court appellate opinion, trial court ruling, and state bar disciplinary finding between 1970 and 2003. In addition, the researchers supplemented these findings with media sources, inmates, defense lawyers, state bar disciplinary counsels, judges, and other sources. The Center included any case found in the Lexis and Westlaw legal databases containing the words "prosecutorial misconduct".[561] The findings of misconduct were made by appellate court judges and not by Center researchers.[562]

The study found that prosecutorial misconduct led to the wrongful conviction of 32 defendants. But guilty defendants have also seen their convictions overturned and sometimes they couldn't be retried because of double jeopardy rules.[563]

The Center also found some prosecutors to be responsible for more than one conviction of innocent individuals. Furthermore, some of these prosecutors were mentioned more than one time for prosecutorial misconduct.[564]

The Center for Public Integrity studied all states, including Minnesota. According to the Center, in Minnesota, from 1970 to 2003, there were 240 cases where a party claimed prosecutorial error or misconduct. In 32 of those cases there was a finding of misconduct requiring a reversal.[565] Of those cases, 24 involved improper trial arguments, two involved improper tactics, and six involved withholding evidence. Out of the 240 cases in which a defendant alleged prosecutorial misconduct, the Hennepin County District Attorney's Office was responsible for 88 cases. In 12 of those cases there was a finding of prosecutorial misconduct requiring a reversal.[566]

Professor Kathleen Ridolfi and Maurice Possley engaged in a comprehensive analysis of publicly available cases of prosecutorial misconduct in California, reviewing more than 4,000 state and federal appellate rulings, as well as media reports and trial court decisions, from 1997 through 2009.[567] The study identified 707 cases of admitted prosecutorial misconduct. In about 3,000 of the 4,000 cases the courts rejected the misconduct allegations.[568] In another 282 cases, courts did

---

[561] Therefore, it must be kept in mind that the Center's findings of "prosecutorial misconduct" are not complete. Legal databases like Lexis and Westlaw contain only published opinions.

[562] The Center for Public Integrity (2011a).

[563] Gordon (2011a).

[564] Gordon (2011b).

[565] The Center for Public Integrity (2011b).

[566] http://projects.publicintegrity.org/pm/states.aspx?st=MN (accessed October 10, 2011).

[567] Ridolfi and Possley (2010), p. 10.

[568] Ridolfi and Possley (2010), p. 10.

not address the issue, holding that any error would have been harmless or that the issue was waived because the defense failed to make a proper objection.[569]

Out of the 707 cases in which courts explicitly found that prosecutors had committed misconduct, the misconduct was found to be harmless[570] in nearly 80 % of the cases and to be harmful[571] in about 20 % of the cases.[572]

The most common forms of misconduct were improper argument, improper examination, and failing to disclose exculpatory evidence.[573]

Out of the 600 identified prosecutors, the study uncovered 67 repeat offenders, including three prosecutors who committed misconduct in four different trials, and two prosecutors who did so in five.[574]

5.4.4.3 Limits of the Studies

In order to determine the frequency of prosecutorial misconduct, these studies applied all the same methodology. Primarily through online legal database searches using Westlaw and Lexis, state and federal appellate rulings that raise prosecutorial misconduct allegations were identified. These findings were supplemented with different sources such as court records, reports and interviews with attorneys, inmates, and judges.

The number of cases in which prosecutorial misconduct was found, does not reflect the whole extent of the problem. Identified cases of misconduct are principally ones reviewed by appellate courts. However, the overwhelming majority of cases are resolved without trial. In most jurisdictions, cases end with a guilty plea in over 95 %.[575] Cases that do not go to trial cannot generate appellate opinions and thus are beyond the scope of the studies. It is suggested that prosecutorial misconduct that occurs away from the public might be more prevalent than in cases that go to trial.[576] Moreover, findings of misconduct at the trial court level, if not reflected in appellate opinions, are not captured by the studies. The number of cases not appealed due to prosecutorial misconduct is not known.

---

[569] Ridolfi and Possley (2010), pp. 38–40.

[570] "The harmless category is defined as cases where misconduct was found, but the courts nevertheless upheld the convictions, ruling that the misconduct did not alter the fundamental fairness of the trial" (Ridolfi and Possley 2010, p. 13).

[571] "The harmful error category is defined as cases where misconduct was found and where the finding resulted in courts setting aside convictions or sentences, declaring mistrials or barring evidence" (Ridolfi and Possley 2010, p. 13).

[572] In 548 of the 707 cases the misconduct was found to be harmless. In only 159 of the 707 cases the misconduct was found to be harmful (Ridolfi and Possley 2010, p. 12).

[573] Ridolfi and Possley (2010), pp. 24–38.

[574] Ridolfi and Possley (2010), p. 57.

[575] See Sect. 5.3.7.1, para 1.

[576] See declaration made by Katherine Goldwasser to the Center for Public Integrity and reproduced in the article of Weinberg (2011).

The difficulty to evaluate the frequency of misconduct is reinforced by the fact that since every case is different it is not unusual that exactly the same prosecutorial conduct may constitute harmless error in one case and be a reversible error in another.[577]

5.4.5 Sanctions

5.4.5.1 Overview

Sanctions for prosecutorial misconduct include appellate reversal of convictions,[578] holding the prosecutor in contempt,[579] referring the prosecutor to a bar association grievance committee, and removing or disqualifying the prosecutor from office.[580] Further judicial sanctions to enforce discipline are the prosecutor's suspension from practice, the imposition of fines and costs of proceedings upon the prosecutor, and the reprimand of the prosecutor in a published opinion that identifies the prosecutor by name.[581] Bar associations and grievance committees have the responsibility of investigating complaints of attorney misconduct and prescribing appropriate discipline. The sanctions imposed for prosecutorial misconduct include censure, suspension from practice, and disbarment.[582] In addition, prosecutorial misconduct can be the basis for civil damage actions under 42 USC Section 1983.[583] However, the doctrine of prosecutorial immunity[584] is a major obstacle to the civil liability of the prosecutor.[585]

5.4.5.2 Frequency

Statistics on the frequency of sanctions due to prosecutorial misconduct are nonexistent.

[577] Jost (2007), p. 943; Gershman (1986), p. 138; Kirchmeier et al. (2010), p. 1370. On the "harmless doctrine", see Sect. 5.4.5.3.

[578] See Gershman (2007–2008), Section 14:2.

[579] See Gershman (2007–2008), Section 14:9; Lawless (2008), Section 13.38.

[580] See Gershman (2007–2008), Section 14:11; Lawless (2008), Sections 13.33–13.37.

[581] See Gershman (2007–2008), Section 14:10.

[582] See Gershman (2007–2008), Section 14:12.

[583] Lawless (2008), Section 13:02.

[584] The prosecutor enjoys absolute immunity for advocacy activities and qualified immunity for investigative or administrative activities (see Gershman 2007–2008, Sections 14:14–14:20; see also Lawless 2008, Sections 13.03–13.12).

[585] See Gershman (2007–2008), Section 14:13.

The studies identifying prosecutorial misconduct primarily through the analysis of appellate rulings[586] also looked at the consequences for the prosecutors found to have committed misconduct in these cases. The researchers were confronted with the problem of identifying those prosecutors, since most of the time their names are not mentioned in the opinions. Through the examination of court dockets, and by contacting district attorneys' and public defenders' offices the prosecutor's identity could be determined in some cases.[587] Another way to find out the amount of punishment for such misconduct was the survey of all 59 lawyer disciplinary agencies nationwide as well as the examination of databases that publish sanctions, issued by courts.[588]

The research by journalists Ken Armstrong and Maurice Possley, which examined 381 murder cases reversed on prosecutorial misconduct from 1963 to 1999, found that from the prosecutors involved in those cases, one was fired but appealed and was reinstated with back pay, another received an in-house suspension of 30 days, and a third prosecutor had his law license suspended for 59 days, but because of other misconduct in the case. Not a single prosecutor has been disciplined by a state lawyer disciplinary agency or convicted of any crime for hiding or presenting false evidence.[589]

The study conducted by the Center for Public Integrity[590] analyzed only those cases in which prosecutorial misconduct affected the fundamental fairness of criminal proceedings or harmed the criminal defendants' constitutional rights.[591] Out of 44 disciplinary cases, the prosecutor was disbarred in only two cases. In 20 cases, the court imposed a reprimand or censure, 19 of which were public. In 24 cases, the costs of the disciplinary proceedings were imposed to the prosecutor. The amounts ranged from $272.20 to $12,156.00. The prosecutor's license to practice law was suspended in 12 cases. The suspensions generally ranged from 30 days to 6 months. In seven cases, the court dismissed the complaint or did not impose a sanction. In one case a period of probation was imposed and in three cases the court remanded the case for further proceedings.[592]

The study by the Northern California Innocence Project at Santa Clara University law school, which surveyed 707 cases of identified prosecutorial misconduct from 1997 to 2009, found that in only six cases were prosecutors disciplined by the State Bar of California.[593] It is worth mentioning that, prior to 2005, not a single

[586] On these studies, see Sects. 5.4.4.2 and 5.4.4.3.

[587] The Center for Public Integrity (2011a); Ridolfi and Possley (2010), p. 13.

[588] Armstrong and Possley (1999).

[589] Armstrong and Possley (1999).

[590] For the methodology of this research, see Sect. 5.4.4.2, para 3.

[591] Such misconduct include for example: discovery violations; improper contact with witnesses, defendants, judges or jurors; improper behavior during hearings or trials; prosecuting cases not supported by probable cause; using improper, false or misleading evidence.

[592] Gordon (2011b).

[593] Ridolfi and Possley (2010), pp. 54–61.

prosecutor was disciplined for misconduct in a criminal case, and until 2010, no prosecutor has been disbarred for misconduct in the state of California.[594]

In sum, all studies highlight the fact that prosecutorial misconduct is rarely followed by disciplinary sanctions. The infrequency of reversal for prosecutorial misconduct may be attributed to the harmless error rule.

5.4.5.3 Harmless Error Doctrine

Under the harmless error rule, an appellate court may ignore claims of prosecutorial misconduct, if it believes that the error did not affect the outcome of the case.[595]

In 1967, the United States Supreme Court enunciated the federal standard in the landmark case *Chapman v. California*, holding that "there may be some constitutional errors which, in the setting of a particular case, are so unimportant and insignificant that they may, consistent with the Federal Constitution, be deemed harmless, not requiring the automatic reversal of the conviction."[596] When a Constitutional error is committed, a reviewing court may affirm a conviction only if it is convinced beyond a reasonable doubt that the error did not contribute to the conviction. The prosecutor has the burden of proving, beyond a reasonable doubt, that the Constitutional error complained of was harmless.[597] In the event of a nonconstitutional error, reversal is only required if the error "probably" or substantially affected the jury's verdict.[598]

When determining whether an error is harmless, courts generally consider the strength of the evidence against the defendant and the fairness of the initial trial process, not the egregiousness of the prosecutor's misconduct.[599] As a consequence, identical misconduct may be deemed a harmful error in one case and a harmless error in another.[600]

An error that is deemed harmful results in a modification or reversal of the original conviction.

If states require appellate courts to only report cases of harmful error, the majority of prosecutorial misconduct will remain unnoticed.

---

[594] Ridolfi and Possley (2010), p. 57.

[595] The harmless error rule is currently codified at 28 USC Section 2111 and at FRCrP 52(a) which states: "Any error, defect, irregularity or variance which does not affect substantial rights shall be disregarded." All 50 States have harmless error statutes or rules. In Minnesota, the harmless error rule is rooted in Rule 31.01 of the Minnesota Rules of Criminal Procedure which states: "Any error that does not affect substantial rights must be disregarded." For more details about the harmless error rule, see Cooper (2002); Landes and Posner (2001); Mitchell (1994).

[596] Chapman v. California, 386 U.S. 18, 22 (1967).

[597] Chapman v. California, 23–24.

[598] See e.g., Hovis v. State, 455 N.E.2.d 577, 583 (Ind. 1983).

[599] Gershman (2007–2008), Section 14:5.

[600] Terzano et al. (2009), p. 11; see also Ridolfi and Possley (2010), pp. 18–24.

5.5 Prosecutorial Control and Accountability

5.5.1 *Control of Public Prosecutors*

The following section outlines the supervisory authority over prosecutors and the scope of supervision. It also briefly describes the extent to which the kind of procedure chosen may have an influence on prosecutorial discretion. Finally, this section examines to what degree the prosecutor's charging decision is externally controlled. Several mechanisms may be available for reviewing the prosecutor's discretionary decisions, such as preliminary hearings and the grand jury.

5.5.1.1 External Supervisory Structures

U.S. attorneys are part of the Department of Justice and thus belong to the executive branch.[601] U.S. attorneys are appointed by the President for a term of 4 years, with appointments subject to approval by the Senate. They serve under the supervision of the attorney general of the United States who is the head of the Department of Justice. Federal prosecutors are lead by guidelines promulgated by the Department of Justice when applying discretion in their decision-making process. These guidelines largely reflect the President's crime policies.[602] In addition, the attorney general may have priorities he wants to see enforced through the U.S. attorney's offices.[603] For this purpose, the Justice Department's Executive Office for U.S. Attorneys[604] provides support to the attorney general by formulating guidelines, assisting in their implementation, and providing related training.[605] In practice, however, the decision of which individual cases to charge remains to a large extent with the U.S. attorney's office. The attorney general is only involved in certain types of cases. In capital cases for instance, the attorney general will make the final decision about whether to seek the death penalty.[606] In other cases, U.S. attorneys need to obtain prior authorization to indict from special Department of Justice divisions. In criminal civil rights cases, the Civil Rights Division is responsible for approving prosecution.[607] In tax cases, the Tax Division must approve any criminal charges that a U.S. attorney intends to bring against a defendant.[608]

[601] On the structure and organization of the U.S. prosecution service, see Sect. 5.1.1.
[602] Gramckow (2008), p. 396.
[603] On the Executive Office for U.S. Attorneys, see Sect. 5.1.1.2.
[604] 28 CFR Section 022.
[605] Gramckow (2008), p. 396.
[606] USAM, Section 9-10.040 (1997).
[607] USAM, Section 8-3.140.
[608] USAM, Section 6-4.210.

In practice, federal prosecutors retain considerable autonomy in setting prosecution priorities and policies in their own judicial district. The U.S. Attorneys' Manual also holds that U.S. attorneys are vested with "plenary authority" over prosecutions in their districts.[609] Priorities between districts may vary due to different needs of the particular jurisdiction and vision of the U.S. attorney for his office.[610] The political interest in prosecuting certain crimes and the resources available can influence the priority setting.[611] As a consequence, each office has a unique identity and local office cultures vary greatly.

U.S. attorneys must report their activities to the attorney general. For that purpose, the Executive Office for U.S. Attorneys maintains a database that collects information from the 94 U.S. attorney's offices regarding criminal and civil matters, cases and appeals, and personnel resources. This case management system is used primarily to produce management reports and to justify budget requests. This information is also used to produce the U.S. Attorneys' Annual Statistical Report at the end of each fiscal year.[612] All U.S. attorney's offices compile a Monthly Resource Summary Report that documents the use of personnel resources allocated to the office. The information from this report is also used to formulate and justify budgets, and to monitor resource allocation.[613]

U.S. attorneys receive oversight, supervision, and administrative support services through the Executive Office for U.S. Attorneys. Periodic performance evaluations of the U.S. attorneys offices are conducted by the Executive Office for U.S. Attorneys's Evaluation and Review Staff. The Evaluation and Review Staff coordinates 1-week evaluations of the performance of the U.S. attorneys' offices. These evaluations are conducted by a team of experienced assistant U.S. attorneys and administrative and financial litigation personnel from other U.S. attorneys' offices. Each U.S. attorneys' office is evaluated every 3 years.[614]

Supervision of public prosecutors at the state level is different from supervision at the federal level. The public prosecutor's office at the state level is completely independent and does not report to any statewide hierarchy. Prosecutors are most often chosen through local elections. Once elected, a prosecutor is not responsible to anyone but the voters. Thus, in theory, the electorate should hold prosecutors responsible for their actions. Whether this democratic check works on prosecutors will be discussed later.[615]

Prosecutors' offices are hierarchical institutions headed by chief prosecutors who are either elected or appointed in a democratic process.[616] The internal

[609] USAM, Section 9-2.001.

[610] Gramckow (2008), p. 396.

[611] Gramckow (2008), p. 397.

[612] USAM, Section 3-16.110.

[613] USAM, Section 3-16.120.

[614] U.S. Department of Justice (2008), pp. 9–10.

[615] See Sect. 5.5.2.5.

[616] On the organization of the prosecution service at state level, see Sect. 5.1.2.

organizational structure of the prosecutors' offices is the responsibility of each chief prosecutor. They establish prosecution policies and prosecutors must comply with these policy directives. It is evident that prosecutorial policies may vary among prosecutors' offices. However, the advantage of this situation is that chief prosecutors can issue policy directives that best fit the needs of their jurisdictions and their budgets. In order to respond to particular crime trends, prosecution policies may vary over time. As a consequence, the policy of a prosecutor's office may be to renounce from prosecuting certain misdemeanors, such as prostitution. A prosecutor's office may have a policy of pursuing certain crimes leniently or, to the contrary, aggressively. Under such circumstances, the chief prosecutor's policy may be to prohibit plea bargaining for certain types of serious offenses, such as crimes against sexual integrity.[617] Offices' resources may influence the way criminal cases are prosecuted. Scarce resources mean that processing priorities must be set or that the range of cases to be pursued may be limited. This has the consequence that prosecutors will not proceed with all cases fulfilling the evidentiary requirements.[618]

Various sources are available to chief prosecutors to help them to establish prosecution guidelines. The NDAA Standards, although not binding, can provide some guidance. In addition, district attorneys associations may be of assistance. The only limits prosecution policies have to respect are the margins of discretion allowed by law and the state's professional ethics rules.

The degree of concretization of prosecution policies varies depending on the size of the prosecutor's office. In small offices, chief prosecutors may believe that there is no need to have detailed, formalized policies. Rather, they will communicate them in an informal way. Inversely, larger offices prefer to implement comprehensive policy manuals that outline policies and the way they should be applied to prosecutorial decisions.[619]

There are no formal reporting requirements concerning the office and individual prosecutor performance.[620] For reasons of transparency, many larger prosecution offices publish an annual report. This report has the purpose of informing the public respectively the voters about the prosecutors' activity.[621] In general, prosecutors' offices provide the public with access to information and decisions from within the office.[622]

---

617 Gramckow (2008), p. 393.

618 Gramckow (2008), p. 393.

619 Gramckow (2008), p. 394.

620 Gramckow (2008), p. 395.

621 Gramckow (2008), p. 394.

622 The Hennepin County Attorney's Office for instance provides the community with information on cases that are high profile cases or have generated community interest. In addition, information about a specific case can be found by using the public version of Minnesota Court Information System; see http://www.hennepinattorney.org/CaseInformation.aspx (accessed June 25, 2012).

5.5.1.2 Internal Supervisory Structures

U.S. attorney's offices and district attorney's offices are organized hierarchically and thus, the lower-ranking prosecutors have to carry out the instructions of their superiors. Assistant U.S. attorneys and assistant district attorneys must comply with the prosecution policies of their offices, as long as they are within the scope and meaning of the laws the policies aim to enforce.[623] The chief prosecutor or, in larger offices, supervisory prosecutors may advise an assistant district attorney on how to handle a specific case.[624]

To ensure good functioning of the office, chief prosecutors will issue policy and procedures manuals to all staff and train them on it. Usually, senior prosecutors advise junior prosecutors on applying these office policies. Supervising prosecutors may control whether individual prosecutors' decisions comply with existing policies and they may intervene to guarantee that criminal cases are handled within the scope of the guidelines issued by the office.[625] In small offices, supervision of and communication on cases happens informally through regularly scheduled meetings.[626] In larger structures, such a procedure is virtually impossible. In such circumstances, a formal structure of communication is needed.[627] In larger offices, a "screening unit" is usually responsible for deciding whether to or not prosecute and which prosecutor to assign to the case. Given the impact of the prosecutor's decision at this stage of the proceeding,[628] it is recommended that the more experienced prosecutors are responsible for this task. In fact, it is of great importance that sufficient evidence supports the charges.[629] After screening, the case will be assigned to special divisions (i.e. drugs and property crimes, juvenile prosecution, adult prosecution).[630] In smaller offices, specialized units do usually not exist. The chief prosecutor retains the discretion to reassign tasks.[631]

---

[623] Gramckow (2008), pp. 393 and 401.

[624] Gramckow (2008), p. 400.

[625] Gramckow (2008), p. 398.

[626] E.g. meetings take place once every week at the District Attorney's Office of Anoka County.

[627] Gramckow (2008), p. 398.

[628] On the impact such a decision may have, see Sect. 5.3.3, para 2; Sect. 5.3.4.1, para 1.

[629] Gramckow (2008), p. 398.

[630] See for instance the different units within the criminal division of the Hennepin County Attorney's Office, http://www.hennepinattorney.org/Divisions/CriminalDivision.aspx (accessed June 25, 2012).

[631] Gramckow (2008), pp. 398–399.

5.5.1.3 Control Over Prosecutorial Decision-Making

5.5.1.3.1 Type of Decision: Full Trial and Plea Bargaining

The extent to which public prosecutors' decisions are subject to legal barriers varies with the type of decision made and the point in the criminal process at which it was made.

A full trial is a significant restriction on prosecutorial discretion because all procedural rules applicable to the trial of criminal cases operate as checks on the prosecutor. The prosecutor must be able to prove "guilt beyond a reasonable doubt". A simplified procedure, such as plea bargaining, still requires a decision by the judge. However, the court hearing in this kind of procedure provides restriction to a much lesser degree.[632] Courts refuse to reject a guilty plea in the rarest cases. The duties of a judge are to ensure the voluntary and knowing waiver of the defendant's trial rights and to ascertain that there is a factual basis to support the charges to which the defendant pleads guilty. The determination of the defendant's responsibility is in reality made within the prosecutor's office and does not occur in court at all. In fact, the judge is only required to assure that the conduct to which the defendant confesses in fact constitutes an offense under the statutory provision under which he is pleading guilty.[633]

5.5.1.3.2 Review of the Prosecutor's Charging Decision in the Pretrial Phases

A citizen suspected of having committed a felony has a right to a probable cause hearing. To determine whether there is sufficient evidence to bind a defendant over to trial, the U.S. criminal justice system uses two legal procedures, namely the preliminary hearing and the grand jury. Although decisions to charge are theoretically subject to review in the pretrial phases, in practice, neither the preliminary hearing nor the grand jury are effective checks against prosecutors' decisions to charge a crime.[634]

Preliminary Hearing

The primary function of a preliminary hearing is to provide a judge or a magistrate an opportunity to determine whether there is sufficient evidence to support the charge(s) to bind a defendant over to the trial for further proceedings.[635]

---

[632] On plea bargaining, see Sect. 5.3.7.

[633] On the problematic practice of plea bargaining in the U.S. system, see Sects. 5.3.7.2 and 5.3.7.3.

[634] See Vorenberg (1981), pp. 1537–1538; Gifford (1981), p. 670.

[635] Del Carmen (2007), pp. 41–43; LaFave et al. (2007), Section 14.1 (a).

A defendant may waive the preliminary hearing. Waiver rates can reach 50 %.[636] In contrast to a procedure before a grand jury, in a preliminary hearing, an accused enjoys due process rights to ensure that the proceeding is a fair one.[637] In reality, many procedural aspects of a preliminary hearing are similar to a trial. The defendant has a right to be present throughout the proceedings, to be represented by counsel,[638] and to cross-examine those witnesses presented by the prosecution.[639] In most jurisdictions, hearsay evidence is permitted in preliminary hearings, whereas this would not be allowed at a trial.[640]

The purpose of the preliminary hearing is "to prevent hasty, malicious, improvident, and oppressive prosecutions, to protect the person charged from open and public accusations of crime, to avoid both for the defendant and the public the expense of a public trial, and to save the defendant from the humiliation and anxiety involved in public prosecution, and to discover whether or not there are substantial grounds upon which a prosecution may be based."[641]

The effectiveness of the preliminary hearing screening in achieving these aims is questionable. In reality, it is very rare that the judge determines that probable cause does not exist. Hence, defense counsel rarely expects to win a preliminary hearing.[642] Depending on jurisdiction, the percentage of dismissal ranges from 2 to 30 %. A number of explanations have been advanced to justify the different rates of preliminary hearing dismissals. For example, the higher percentage of dismissal occurs in such jurisdictions where the prosecutors do little screening before the case is brought to such a hearing.[643] Therefore, the legal standards governing the preliminary hearing in the jurisdictions certainly have an impact on the screening effectiveness. The existing disparities in dismissal rates do not show that preliminary hearing screening is more efficient in one jurisdiction than in others. They reflect the types of cases that reach the preliminary hearing.[644]

In a preliminary hearing, the prosecutor must prove that there is "probable cause to believe that a crime was committed and that the offender committed the crime charged."[645] This threshold is seen as too low.[646] Moreover, in general, a counsel—for strategic reasons—prefers not to disclose any defenses he may have, so that the magistrate may have some difficulties in properly evaluating the case.[647]

[636] Weaver et al. (2008), p. 300.

[637] Halsted (1987), p. 112.

[638] LaFave et al. (2007), Section 14.4 (a).

[639] LaFave et al. (2007), Section 14.4 (c).

[640] LaFave et al. (2007), Section 14.4 (b).

[641] Thies v. State, 178 Wis. 98, 103, 189 N.W. 539 (1922).

[642] Singer (2008), p. 74.

[643] LaFave et al. (2007), Section 14.1 (a); Singer (2008), p. 74.

[644] LaFave et al. (2007), Section 14.1 (a).

[645] Weaver et al. (2008), p. 297; Singer (2008), p. 74.

[646] Singer (2008), p. 74.

[647] Singer (2008), p. 74.

Grand Jury Proceeding

In addition to due process rights, the grand jury system has long been considered an important check against oppressive prosecution.[648] Nevertheless, today it is the subject of considerable controversy.

The grand jury is one of the oldest institutions in the common law. Its origins can be traced back to the Assize of Clarendon, an 1166 act of King Henry II of England.[649] The assize established groups of laymen[650] whose function was to report under oath the names of those in the community accused of crimes.[651] Therefore, at the beginning of its existence, the assize had little to do with safeguarding individual rights since its function was to charge individuals accused of crime. It seems that identifying individuals who had committed crimes was its only investigative function. In reality, the establishment of this instrument provoked an increased number of individuals standing trial and, as a consequence, strengthened the king's power.[652] Over time, the grand jury took over the function of lodging all criminal charges regardless of whether a private accuser came forward.[653] The grand jury also started to hear witnesses in private. The introduction of secrecy had the aim of protecting the grand jurors and their witnesses from oppressive governments.[654] After the grand jury refused to return an indictment in several cases,[655] the grand jury was seen as a protective institution against tyranny.[656] It was then considered a counterweight to executive powers and an "arm of the court".[657] The English colonies in the United States adopted the grand jury as an essential safeguard against arbitrary prosecution.[658] By the time of the American Revolution, the grand jury was incorporated into the American Bill of Rights.[659] The Fifth Amendment of the Constitution provides that "[n]o person shall be held to answer for a capital, or otherwise infamous crime, unless on a presentment or

[648] Halsted (1987), p. 103.

[649] For a review of the history of the grand jury, see Helmholz (1983); see also Kuh (1955), pp. 1103–1109; Schwartz (1972); Toomey (1963); Zwerling (1976), pp. 1263–1269. See also LaFave et al. (2007), Section 8.2.

[650] Originally, these groups were composed of 12 laymen. The switch to 23 laymen has been traced back to the reign of Edward III in 1368 (see Morse 1931, pp. 115–116; Shannon 1972, p. 143). Today in the United States of America, the number of grand jurors varies from 12 to 23 and varies from jurisdiction to jurisdiction (see Spain 1964, pp. 122 and 126–142).

[651] Johnston (1974), p. 157; Kuh (1955), p. 1106.

[652] Kuh (1955), pp. 1106–1107; Schwartz (1972), p. 710.

[653] Kuh (1955), p. 1107.

[654] Calkins (1965), p. 457; LaFave et al. (2007), Section 8.2 (a).

[655] The *Colledge*'s case and the *Earl of Shaftesbury*'s case—both decided in 1681—were the first two cases where the grand jury refused to indict (see Howell 1816, pp. 550–724 and 759–835). For a discussion of both cases, see Schwartz (1972), pp. 710–721.

[656] Johnston (1974), p. 158.

[657] Toomey (1963), p. 959.

[658] Johnston (1974), p. 158; LaFave et al. (2007), Section 8.2 (b).

[659] Zwerling (1976), p. 1266.

indictment of a Grand Jury." However, it remained in the states responsibilities to provide for a similar constitutional guaranty.[660] Today, in addition to the federal system and the District of Columbia, 18 states are indictment jurisdictions.[661] 28 states are information states and hence the prosecutor can decide whether he wants to proceed by indictment or information.[662]

This brief overview of the origin and development of the grand jury shows that this institution fulfills two different functions, namely investigating and screening. For this reason, the grand jury has often been linked to a "sword" when acting as an investigative body and to a "shield" when, by refusing to indict, it protects innocent persons from accusations not supported by probable cause.[663] Concerning the screening function, the Supreme Court in *United States v. Dionisio*[664] stated that the purpose of the grand jury is to stand as the "protective bulwark" between a citizen and an overzealous prosecutor.[665]

The effectiveness of the grand jury as an independent and quasi-judicial body able to screen out unmeritorious charges, however, is questionable since the procedure before the grand jury is largely controlled and dominated by the prosecutor.[666] Indeed, in grand jury proceedings the work is conducted in secrecy and the grand jury relies only on the prosecutor for guidance and instruction. The prosecutor controls the evidence presented before the grand jury. Moreover, rules of evidence do not apply, so that the prosecutor can ask questions that would be considered irrelevant if presented at trial. There is no right to counsel and there is no right to cross-examine witnesses. There is no judge presiding over the proceedings.[667] In contrast to a preliminary hearing, due process rights are totally absent in grand jury proceedings.[668] Normally, the grand jury hears only the prosecution's side of the case and the danger may exist that the prosecutor presents only evidence that demonstrates that a crime has occurred.[669] In *United States v. Williams*,[670] the Supreme Court recognized the central role played by the prosecutor in grand jury

---

660 Johnston (1974), p. 158.

661 LaFave et al. (2007), Section 15.1 (d).

662 LaFave et al. (2007), Section 15.1 (g). It has been held that the fifth amendment provision for indictment by grand jury is not incorporated in the 14th amendment and hence does not apply to the states so that they remain free to prosecute felonies by procedures other than indictment [Hurtado v. California, 110 U.S. 516, 538 (1884)].

663 Bernstein (1994), p. 575.

664 U.S. v. Dionisio, 410 U.S. 1 (1973).

665 U.S. v. Dionisio, 17.

666 For a complete discussion about the effectiveness of the grand jury in the screening, see Leipold (1995).

667 Gilboy (1984), p. 5; Aragon (1981), p. 97; Cassidy (2000), p. 362; Henning (1999b), pp. 3–4; Leipold (1995), p. 267.

668 Halsted (1987), p. 114. For a comparison between preliminary hearing and grand jury, see Singer (2008), p. 76.

669 Brice (1972), p. 765; Johnston (1974), p. 160.

670 U.S. v. Williams, 504 U.S. 36 (1992).

proceedings, stating that the prosecutor does not "require leave of court to seek a grand jury indictment. And in its day-to-day functioning, the grand jury generally operates without the interference of a presiding judge."[671] Today, the grand jury is not longer an "arm of the court" but is one of the executive powers instead. With justification, critics characterize the grand jury as a "rubber stamp"[672] or a "puppet"[673] of the prosecutor's office.

Whereas among scholars the notion that grand juries do not screen out weak cases is commonly accepted, courts have consistently upheld the idea that grand juries are an effective institution for protecting citizens against an overzealous government.[674]

Critics of the grand jury often point to statistics to support their view.[675] They state that in a remarkably high percentage of cases the grand jury follows the recommendation of the prosecutor and decides to indict. Federal grand juries return an indictment in over 99 % of cases.[676] Since grand juries rarely refuse to indict, some critics have drawn the conclusion that the grand jury is an ineffective tool.[677] However, this argument fails to support the assumption that grand juries serve no useful function. In fact, it would be rather critical if grand juries refused to indict in a high percentage of cases.[678] This would mean that the prosecution is not doing its job properly and therefore would fail in evaluating whether a case is strong or weak.[679] It can be assumed that weak cases do not reach the grand jury because the prosecutor decides not to pursue an indictment in those cases.[680] It is problematic to infer worthlessness of grand juries' screening function from high indictment rates since such statistical data do not provide information about whether and how prosecutors are controlling the grand jury.[681]

The inability of the grand jury to screen cases properly may be found in the grand jurors' lack of competence to perform their task. Jurors have the duty to determine if probable cause exists. This means that non-lawyers weigh evidence presented by a prosecutor and are asked to determine if a legal test is satisfied. Under this circumstance, it is obvious that the grand jury will decide to indict.[682]

In England, the grand jury was abolished in 1933. In 1973, the National Advisory Commission on Criminal Justice Standards and Goals recommended

---

[671] U.S. v. Williams, 48.

[672] Leipold (1995), p. 269.

[673] Coates (1962).

[674] For possible explanations between both views, see Leipold (1995), pp. 272–274.

[675] LaFave et al. (2007), Section 15.3 (b).

[676] Scolnic (1999), p. 1; Beall (1998), p. 631.

[677] See e.g. Cassidy (2000), p. 363; Arenella (1980), p. 539; Henning (1999b), p. 5.

[678] Leipold (1995), p. 276; Johnston (1974), p. 168.

[679] Leipold (1995), p. 276.

[680] Leipold (1995), p. 278.

[681] Henning (1999b), p. 6.

[682] Leipold (1995), pp. 294–304. See also LaFave et al. (2007), Section 8.2 (c).

the states to do the same.[683] More than half of the states have abolished the grand jury requirement.[684] Grand juries in the federal system are unlikely to disappear since the provision is part of the Bill of Rights and this has never been amended.[685]

5.5.1.3.3 Review of the Prosecutor's Charging Decision by the Court

The prosecutor's decision not to charge is virtually immune from review.[686] Courts for the most part justify their refusal to review prosecutor's discretion in charging on the grounds that separation of powers prohibits such review. In the case of *United States v. Nixon*,[687] the Supreme Court proclaimed that "the Executive Branch has exclusive authority and absolute discretion to decide whether to prosecute a case."[688] In contrast to Switzerland and Germany, where the prosecutor must charge a crime whenever there is sufficient evidence,[689] the courts have recognized that the U.S. system does not give such a role to the prosecutor.[690] The separation of powers doctrine has prevented courts from forcing a prosecutor to commence criminal proceedings.[691]

5.5.1.3.4 Influence of the Victim on the Prosecutor's Charging Decision

Although crime victims have gained more participatory rights in criminal proceedings,[692] they have no legal means to compel a prosecutor to charge a suspect. In the same way, victims cannot prevent a prosecutor from going forward with a case. As a consequence, victims in the U.S. criminal justice system have absolutely no influence on the prosecutor regarding charging decisions.

---

[683] Singer (2008), p. 67.

[684] LaFave et al. (2007), Section 15.1 (g).

[685] Leipold (1995), pp. 314–323.

[686] Bubany and Skillern (1976), pp. 484–485.

[687] U.S. v. Nixon, 418 U.S. 683 (1974).

[688] U.S. v. Nixon, 693.

[689] For the situation in Switzerland and Germany, see Sects. 6.3, 7.3.2, and 7.3.3.

[690] State v. Johnson, 74 Wis. 2d 169, 172, 246 N.W.2d 503, 506 (1976); Pugach v. Klein, 193 F. Supp. 630, 634–635 (S.D.N.Y. 1961); U.S. v. Brokaw, 60 F. Supp. 100, 101 (S.D. III. 1945); State ex rel. Kurkierewicz v. Cannon, 42 Wis. 2d 368, 373, 166 N.W.2d 255, 260 (1969).

[691] Newman v. U.S., 382 F.2d 479 (D.C. Cir. 1967).

[692] See Sect. 3.1.2.5.

5.5.2 *Accountability of Public Prosecutors*

Previous chapters have shown the enormous discretionary power vested in prosecutors. Prosecutors in turn must exercise this power in the most responsible fashion and be able to show this fact to the public. There are several mechanisms for holding prosecutors accountable. They come from the legislature, judges, state licensing authorities, and especially the electoral process. In this section, I briefly describe the legal sources of accountability. I then discuss whether democratic checks work on prosecutors.

5.5.2.1 Civil and Criminal Liability

Prosecutors do not enjoy any immunity from criminal liability for acts committed in the course of their work as prosecutor or outside the prosecutor's office.[693]

In certain circumstances, prosecutorial misconduct can be the basis for a civil action for damages under the Federal Civil Rights Act of 1871, now codified at 42 USC Section 1983.[694] However, the doctrine of prosecutorial immunity is a serious obstacle to any attempt to enforce civil law claims against a prosecutor. Depending on jurisdiction, a prosecutor enjoys either absolute or qualified immunity. Absolute immunity shields a prosecutor from being sued for official acts without regard to motive. Qualified immunity, on the other hand, shields a prosecutor from any litigation in regards to acts undertaken in good faith.[695] The most difficult task for judges has been to determine the type of immunity to afford a prosecutor for his behavior.[696]

Imbler v. Pachtman[697] was the first case in which the Supreme Court addressed the question of prosecutorial immunity. *Imbler* created a broad rule of absolute immunity. The Supreme Court stated that absolute immunity should be granted to a prosecutor for activities "intimately associated with the judicial phase of the criminal process."[698] The Court did not outline the precise boundaries of the "judicial phase", but explained that it was any action the prosecutor might take in his role as advocate for the state.[699] Thus, prosecutors enjoy absolute immunity from civil liability when initiating and pursuing criminal prosecution. In *Imbler*, the Supreme Court suggested that a prosecutor would only have qualified immunity

[693] Gramckow (2008), p. 401.

[694] This civil action is commonly referred as a § 1983 action.

[695] Gershman (2007–2008), Section 14:13.

[696] Gershman (2007–2008), Section 14:13.

[697] Imbler v. Pachtman, 424 U.S. 409 (1976).

[698] Imbler v. Pachtman, 430.

[699] Imbler v. Pachtman, 431.

with respect to nonadvocative roles.[700] As a consequence, prosecutor's administrative or investigative actions would not be subject to absolute immunity.[701] Under these circumstances, the critical point for the court is to determine whether the prosecutor was acting in a judicial and advocative capacity or rather in a nonjudicial and nonadvocative capacity. However, a clear distinction between the forms of prosecutorial conduct is not possible.

When administrative and investigative activity is directly related to the initiation and preparation of a criminal prosecution, courts are likely to qualify the conduct as advocative. On the contrary, when the activity is more similar to that of an ordinary police investigative official, or involves exclusively administrative conduct, the courts are more likely to see the conduct as not protected by absolute immunity.[702]

Courts have upheld the absolute immunity of prosecutors in connection with presenting evidence to a grand jury,[703] filing of charges,[704] and initiating a prosecution.[705] Immunity has also been granted for obtaining arrest and search warrants from a judge,[706] delay in prosecuting,[707] plea bargaining,[708] and suppression of exculpatory evidence.[709]

Absolute immunity has not been applied to certain instances involving investigation,[710] illegal searches and seizures,[711] use of an illegal wiretap,[712] intimidation of witnesses,[713] arrest and filing charges[714] and in some instances involving statements to the press.[715]

Prosecutors' offices may have professional liability insurance covering the exposure of prosecuting attorneys. If the prosecutor's office is the named insured party, the policy will extend coverage to the individual attorneys. If this insurance does not cover all potential costs of a civil suit or is not available, prosecutors may personally subscribe to such insurance. At the federal level, the Department of

---

700 Imbler v. Pachtman, 430-31, n 33.

701 Gershman (2007–2008), Section 14:14.

702 See e.g. Burns v. Reed, 500 U.S. 478 (1991).

703 See e.g. Moore v. Valder, 65 F.3d 189 (D.C. Cir. 1995).

704 See e.g. Anderson v. Simon, 217 F.3d 472 (7th Cir. 2000).

705 See e.g. Kerr v. Lyford, 171 F.3d 330 (5th Cir. 1999).

706 See e.g. Kalina v. Fletcher, 522 U.S. 118 (1997).

707 See e.g. Ryland v. Shapiro, 586 F. Supp. 1495 (1984).

708 See e.g. Taylor v. Kavanagh, 640 F.2d 450 (2d Cir. 1981).

709 See e.g. Lyles v. Sparks, 79 F.3d 372 (4th Cir. 1996).

710 See e.g. Forsyth v. Kleindienst, 599 F.2d 1203 (3d Cir. 1979).

711 See e.g. McSurely v. McClellan, 697 F.2d 309, 67 A.L.R. Fed. 614 (D.C. Cir. 1982).

712 See e.g. Mitchell v. Forsyth, 472 U.S. 511 (1985).

713 See e.g. Tomko v. Lees, 416 F. Supp. 1137 (W.D. Pa. 1976).

714 See e.g. Mancini v. Lester, 630 F.2d 990 (3d Cir. 1980).

715 See e.g. Buckley v. Fitzsimmons, 509 U.S. 259 (1993).

Justice will partially reimburse law enforcement officers, attorneys, supervisors, and managers for costs incurred for professional liability insurance.[716]

5.5.2.2 Disciplinary Liability

The purpose of discipline is to protect the public from future acts of professional misconduct and to maintain a high ethical standard in the legal profession. It is not to punish the lawyer or to compensate an aggrieved party for a loss caused by an attorney's misconduct. A complaint of professional misconduct against a lawyer is a serious matter. A reasonable disagreement about the way a case should be handled or should have been handled does not constitute misconduct. The same is true for a mistake. Since lawyers are human, they are subject to err just like everyone else. Mistakes or errors in judgment do not constitute unethical conduct.

Prosecutors are members of the bar so that, in theory, rules of professional responsibility are an additional means to limit prosecutorial power. Codes of conduct and disciplinary procedures are established by each state's Bar Association and apply to all lawyers in the specific jurisdiction. A national code of conduct for prosecutors does not exist. NDAA and ABA standards only contain references to professional conduct and ethics. Federal prosecutors have to respect a certain number of ethical regulations ranging from state ethical codes[717] to local rules adopted by federal courts to the internal policies of the Department of Justice.[718]

In light of the fact that federal prosecutors have to comply with a multitude of ethical regulations, it may happen that a prosecutor's conduct is examined by the

[716] Section 636 of the FY 2000 Treasury, Postal Service and General Government Appropriation Act.

[717] Federal prosecutors have to comply with the rules of professional conduct for the state(s) in which they practice [28 USC Section 530B. See also 28 CFR Part 77 (Ethical Standards for Attorneys for the Government), which serves the purpose of implementing 28 USC Section 530B and providing guidance to attorneys concerning the requirements imposed on Department of Justice attorneys by 28 USC Section 530B].

[718] With the Principles of Federal Prosecution, the U.S. Department of Justice has developed its own guidelines to assist federal prosecutors in the performance of their duties and to set uniform policy on certain matters (on the Principles of Federal Prosecution, see Sect. 5.3.4.2.1.1). Furthermore, the Departmental Ethics Office, located in the Justice Management Division, is responsible for administering a Department of Justice-wide ethics program and for implementing Department of Justice-wide policies on ethics issues. The office provides advice and training and supervises the ethics programs of the U.S. attorney's offices. Each U.S. attorney's office has a Deputy Designated Agency Ethics Official (DDAEO) who is responsible for administering the ethics program within the office. The Department of Justice follows the government-wide standards of conduct promulgated by the Office of Government Ethics (OGE) at 5 CFR Chapter XVI, especially Parts 2634, 2635, 2636, and 2637; and Department of Justice Order 1200.1 [see USAM, Section 1-4.010 (1997)]. For a detailed discussion about the bewildering array of ethical regulations federal prosecutors are subject to, see Tennis (2010). See also Green (1995).

court and also referred to a separate disciplinary board, such as a state bar association[719] or the Office of Professional Responsibility (OPR).[720] The Office of Professional Responsibility investigates allegations of misconduct involving Department of Justice attorneys that relate to investigations, litigation, or the provision of legal advice.[721] The Office of the Inspector General (OIG) investigates other allegations of misconduct by Department of Justice employees not related to the practice of law.[722] All U.S. attorney staff are required to report to their supervisors any evidence or non-frivolous allegation of misconduct that may be in violation of any laws, rules, regulations, orders, or professional standards. Supervisors then evaluate whether the misconduct at issue is serious, and if so, report the evidence or non-frivolous allegation to the appropriate investigative office. It is also possible to submit a complaint directly to an investigative office.[723]

Upon receiving an allegation, the Office of Professional Responsibility conducts a preliminary review and only opens an investigation if it concludes that further investigation is warranted. Upon completing an investigation, the Office of Professional Responsibility notifies the subject of the allegation, and the supervisor and complainant of the results.[724]

Disciplinary sanctions against assistant U.S. attorneys are sensitive issues that must be closely coordinated with the Executive Office for U.S. Attorneys General Counsel's Office. The authority to initiate and implement disciplinary sanctions against assistant U.S. attorneys has been delegated to the Director of the Executive Office for U.S. Attorneys. Limited authority to issue adverse actions against assistant U.S. attorneys has been delegated to U.S. attorneys who can issue written reprimands and initiate suspensions of 14 days or less.[725]

Disciplinary sanctions include written reprimands, suspensions, reductions in grade or pay, removals, and furloughs for 30 days or less.[726] An employee who receives a reprimand or a suspension for 14 days or less may file a grievance. If the immediate supervisor lacks the authority to handle the grievance, the grievance must be referred to the next level management official within the district or the Executive Office for U.S. Attorneys.[727] For more serious disciplinary sanctions, an appeal to the Merit Systems Protection Board is possible.

---

[719] On the possibility of state bar associations to discipline federal prosecutors, see Blair (2001).

[720] Tennis (2010), p. 172; Green (1995), pp. 79 and 86–87.

[721] USAM, Section 1-4.100 B.

[722] USAM, Section 1-4.100 A.

[723] USAM, Section 1-4.100.

[724] USAM, Section 1-4.140.

[725] USAM, Section 3-4.752.

[726] USAM, Section 3-4.752. See also Human Resources Order DOJ 1200.1, Chap. 3-1, Discipline and Adverse Actions.

[727] USAM, Section 3-4.771. See also Human Resources Order DOJ 1200.1, Chap. 3-2, Agency Grievance Procedure.

As presidential appointees, U.S. attorneys are not subject to discipline or removal by the Department of Justice without the President's approval. If the deputy attorney general and the attorney general reach the conclusion that removal is justified, they request approval from the White House Counsel to ask for the U.S. attorney's resignation. If the U.S. attorney refuses to resign, the President can dismiss him.[728]

Elected district attorneys are only responsible to the voters and can only be removed from office during their term by a state disciplinary procedure for violating the ethical rules established by the state's attorney licensing authority.[729] Complaints about a prosecutor's conduct violating these rules may be made to the state bar associations and grievance committees.[730] Although the disciplinary process differs from state to state, some common features exist. The attorney grievance committees respectively the state bar associations receive written complaints from the public, judges, and other lawyers about behavior that might violate the ethical rules. The grievance administrator or director may also institute an investigation and take disciplinary action on his own, based on knowledge gained from other sources (i.e. news articles, court opinions, and information received in the course of a disciplinary investigation). Such procedure is justified as long as the director has reasonable belief that professional misconduct may have occurred.[731] This also implies that disciplinary jurisdiction extends to all misconduct, even when it goes beyond the specific incident originally reported to the attorney grievance committee.[732] However, it is not allowed to "unduly expand the scope of investigation to explore matters not reasonably related to the original complaint."[733] Thus, it is not permitted to engage in "fishing expeditions".

Upon receipt of a request for investigation, the grievance commission or the office of bar counsel acts quickly to determine whether an investigation is warranted. The first evaluation of the request is usually done by the intake office, which is composed of well-qualified attorneys with substantial experience in the practice of law and the disciplinary field. This office will determine whether the complaint meets basic threshold criteria, thus warranting investigation. If it concludes that the evidence is not strong enough or that the conduct doesn't fall within the Rules of Professional Conduct, the complaint will be dismissed and the

---

[728] U.S. Department of Justice (2008), p. 23.

[729] Gramckow (2008), p. 395.

[730] For an overview of the competent authority to receive grievances against attorneys in the states, see http://grievanceproject.wordpress.com/state-grievance-procedures/ (accessed June 25, 2012). In the state of Minnesota, the Minnesota Lawyers Professional Responsibility Board & Office of Lawyers Professional Responsibility is responsible for investigating complaints of attorney misconduct and prescribing appropriate discipline.

[731] See e.g. Rule 8(a), Rules on Lawyers Professional Responsibility (RLPR) of the state of Minnesota.

[732] See e.g. *In re Nathanson*, 2012 WL 638014, _ N.W.2d _ (Minn. Sup. Ct. Feb. 29, 2012) (per curiam).

[733] *In re Nathanson*, 11.

complainant notified in writing. A decision by the office to close a file without taking action against an attorney is subject to review.[734] Inversely, when it determines that a complaint may lead to discipline, an investigation will be conducted. The investigation includes a process of notifying the attorney respectively the prosecutor of the complaint and giving him the opportunity to respond.[735]

If a lawyer is found to have violated an ethics rule, different levels of discipline are available. The attorney grievance committee may issue a non-public informal admonition informing the lawyer of the rules he has broken and warning him to see that such conduct does not recur. Although the informal admonition is not announced to the public, the complainant is informed of the disposition of his complaint. The attorney grievance committee may issue a public, formal reprimand to the lawyer. In case of admonition and reprimand, a notation is made on the lawyer's bar record. More serious disciplinary sanctions include censure, suspension from practice, and disbarment.[736]

If it is determined that the prosecutor's behavior does not constitute an issue under the Rules of Professional Conduct, no alternative complaint procedure exists against an act or decision of a district attorney. The only recourse for the aggrieved person is the next election.

Depending on jurisdiction, assistant district attorneys serve under the direction and at pleasure of the district attorney or are civil servants. They mostly serve at the discretion of the elected district attorney and thus may generally only be removed for good cause.[737] When assistant district attorneys are civil servants they enjoy the protection of the civil service system with regard to salary, promotions, and dismissals.[738] Assistant district attorneys have to comply with the district attorney's policies. If individual prosecutors do not follow these policies or the instructions of the district attorney or the supervisory prosecutor, a complaint may be launched. Individual offices often implement processes for internal review. If assistant district attorneys repeatedly break prosecution policies, they risk losing their jobs.[739] This applies irrespective of whether the assistant district attorneys serve at the pleasure of the district attorney or are part of the state's civil service system.[740]

Various studies have revealed that prosecutors are rarely disciplined.[741] Thus, disciplinary procedures have failed to hold prosecutors accountable for misconduct.

---

[734] The appellate authority may differ between the states. The decision may be reviewed by the State Supreme Court (e.g. State of Michigan, State of Missouri), the Bar Counsel (e.g. State of Virginia), a board member of the Grievance Commission (e.g. State of Minnesota) or by a panel (e.g. State of Idaho).

[735] Gramckow (2008), pp. 395–396.

[736] Gramckow (2008), p. 396.

[737] Gramckow (2008), p. 399.

[738] Gramckow (2008), p. 400.

[739] Gramckow (2008), p. 400.

[740] Where assistant district attorneys are part of the state's civil service system, a termination of work is usually not possible. This limitation, however, does not apply if an assistant repeatedly refuses to follow the prosecution policies or to direct orders from the district attorney.

[741] See Sects. 5.4.5.1 and 5.4.5.2.

As discussed later, disciplinary proceedings against prosecutors in Europe are rarely instituted and the imposition of disciplinary sanctions is even rarer.[742]

5.5.2.3 Legislature

5.5.2.3.1 Substantive Criminal Law

In contrast to most civil code systems where criminal codes offer prosecutors a relatively limited set of charge options, criminal codes in the United States do not limit the prosecutors' choices at all.[743] Rather, the legislature passes criminal statutes and as a consequence the prosecutors' power increases.[744] Hence, instead of constraining the power of the prosecutors, the legislature expands the legal tools available to prosecutors.[745] Moreover, frequently incoherent criminal codes and overlapping code sections contribute to increasing the prosecutors' powers.[746]

5.5.2.3.2 Prosecutor Budgets

Prosecutors might be held accountable through state budgets.[747] In 2005, half of the local prosecutors' offices in the U.S. received at least 82 % of their funding from the county government, and 32 % received all their funding from the county. Furthermore, 49 % of the prosecutors' offices received state funds.[748] Local prosecutors' budgets allocated in 2005 ranged from about $5,000 to $285 million.[749] The amount of money allocated reflects the size of the office, the size of the population, and its workload. The fact that budgets for state prosecutors does not come from one source but instead is a mix of county and state funds weakens the local control by the concerned authority.[750] Once the budget is approved, the budget authority has no influence on the way the funds are used,[751] except if specific line items were

[742] For Switzerland, see Sect. 6.6.2.2, para 6, for Germany, see Sect. 7.6.2.2 and for France, see Sect. 8.5.2.2.

[743] Wright and Miller (2010), p. 1595.

[744] "The definition of crimes and defenses...empower[s] prosecutors, who are the criminal justice system's real lawmakers. Anyone who reads criminal codes in search of a picture of what conduct leads to a prison term...will be seriously misled" (Stuntz 2007, pp. 506–507).

[745] Wright (2009), pp. 585–586.

[746] Wright and Miller (2010), p. 1605.

[747] Wright (2009), p. 586; Davis (2007), pp. 169–170; Gramckow (2008), pp. 405–407.

[748] Perry (2006), p. 4.

[749] Perry (2006), p. 4.

[750] Wright and Miller (2010), p. 1608.

[751] Gramckow (2008), p. 407; Wright and Miller (2010), p. 1608.

designated for specific activities or initiatives.[752] Local prosecutors' offices may develop particular law enforcement activity, such as asset forfeiture programs.[753] Initiatives may involve enhanced prosecution of certain crimes, such as child sex offenses[754] or domestic violence.[755] However, since such line items are rather exceptional, their impact on the prosecutors' offices is very limited.[756]

Moreover, in general, the public is not aware of the exceptional amount of money that might be allocated for the prosecution of certain crimes. Hence, when the public does not agree with the prosecutor's office policy, it only has a slight chance of expressing its opinion through the electoral process by not reelecting the prosecutor.[757]

5.5.2.4 Judges

As mentioned under Sect. 5.5.1.3.3, the separation of powers doctrine precludes judicial review of the prosecutors' work. The judge only requires the charges to be supported by probable cause. The decision whether or not to prosecute is not subject to judicial review. Guilty pleas are subject to court's approval. However, the judge only rarely refuses to follow the prosecutor's recommendations.[758] In fact, if judges would start consistently calling the prosecutors' decisions into question, the caseload would become overwhelming.[759] In conclusion, separation of powers concerns, together with overloaded court dockets, prevent judges from obtaining an overview of the prosecutor's work.

5.5.2.5 Electoral Process

In the United States, most prosecutors are directly elected by the people in the jurisdiction they serve.[760] The idea is that prosecutors are held accountable for their discretionary choices through elections. But does this democratic check on prosecutors work effectively? Various concerns call the effectiveness of electoral accountability into question.

In reality, voters have very little information about the prosecutors' exercise of discretion and their daily work, so that they cannot meaningfully check their

---

752 Gramckow (2008), p. 407; Wright (2009), p. 586.

753 See Jacoby et al. (1992).

754 See Levine (2005), pp. 1132–1144.

755 Gramckow (2008), p. 405.

756 Wright (2009), p. 586.

757 Davis (2007), p. 170. More about the electoral process under Sect. 5.5.2.5.

758 On this issue, see Sect. 5.3.7.2.

759 Wright (2009), p. 587.

760 See Sect. 5.1.2.2.1 and Appendix IV.

prosecutors.[761] A survey analyzing claims made during contested incumbent prosecutor election campaigns supports this statement and sheds new light on the importance of conviction rates.[762]

During election campaigns, candidates center their discussions on individual qualifications rather than the performance of the entire office. Hence, priorities and policies that might be used in the prosecutor's office are not sufficiently explained to the public.[763] Candidates focus their talk on past high profile cases. This again prevents voters from assessing the performance of the prosecutor's office as a whole.[764] It seems that conviction rates—contrary to what most scholars assume[765]—are a theme that is relatively infrequently discussed.[766] However, a study that has analyzed the effects of prosecutor elections on criminal case outcomes in North Carolina suggests that defendants have a higher probability of conviction and a lower probability of having all charges dismissed in an election year. These effects are even more pronounced in districts with more electoral competition.[767] This might signify that, although conviction rates are not among the central themes discussed during election campaigns, this would not automatically mean that incumbent prosecutors do not change their prosecution policy prior to elections.

In his study, Wright concludes that "the rhetoric of election campaigns puts too much weight on the wrong criteria and completely ignores some criteria that could help voters make meaningful judgments about the quality of a prosecutor's work."[768]

Another obstacle to checking the prosecutor is the public's lack of information concerning how prosecutors spend public funds. In fact, if voters would see the cost side of prosecution, they would better be able to evaluate whether their tax dollars are spent properly.[769]

The turnover rate of chief prosecutors is low. According to the latest nationwide survey of state prosecutors in 2005, 40 % of the chief prosecutors have served 12 years or more, 72 % have served 5 years or more, and only 28 % are relatively new to the job, having served 4 years or less.[770] In fact, prosecutors rarely face

---

[761] Davis (2007), pp. 166–169; Gold (2011), pp. 78–79. See also Gordon and Huber (2002), pp. 336–338.

[762] Newspapers and magazines covering contested elections involving incumbent prosecutors in selected jurisdictions have been analyzed; for the methodology, see Wright (2009), pp. 597–600.

[763] Wright (2009), pp. 600–602.

[764] Wright (2009), p. 602.

[765] See e.g. Gordon and Huber (2002), p. 335; Medwed (2004), pp. 132–137; Ramseyer et al. (2008).

[766] Wright (2009), pp. 603–604.

[767] Dyke (2007).

[768] Wright (2009), p. 605.

[769] See e.g. Gold (2011), pp. 79–83.

[770] Perry (2006), p. 3.

electoral opposition. Incumbents have a reelection rate of 95 %.[771] About 85 % of chief prosecutors run unopposed.[772] Prosecutors in larger districts are more likely to be opposed by a challenger, but even so they are more likely to win.[773]

Given the fact that incumbents have a high chance of being re-elected and therefore don't really perceive any election risk, they don't have to defend their prosecution policy vigorously. In sum, elections of prosecutors are not as promising as one would think.[774]

5.5.3 Conclusion

American prosecutors enjoy considerable discretion in deciding whether to prosecute, what charges to bring, and what plea bargains to offer. Mechanisms intended to control charging decisions—pretrial hearing and grand jury—are revealed as ineffective in practice. Under the separation of powers doctrine, courts have systematically refused to review charging decisions. The same is true of the several methods available to hold prosecutors accountable. Legislature, judges, state licensing authorities, and electoral process all fall short of effectively controlling prosecutorial power.

References

Abadinsky H (1998) Law and justice. An introduction to the American legal system, 4th edn. Nelson-Hall Publishers, Chicago

Alschuler AW (1968) The prosecutor's role in plea bargaining. Univ Chic Law Rev 36:50–112

Alschuler AW (1972) Courtroom misconduct by prosecutors and trial judges. Tex Law Rev 50:629–735

Alschuler AW (1976) The trial judge's role in plea bargaining. Part I. Columbia Law Rev 76:1059–1154

Alschuler AW (1979) Plea bargaining and its history. Columbia Law Rev 79:1–43

American Bar Association (1983) Model code of professional responsibility. American Bar Association, Washington, DC

American Bar Association (1993) ABA standards for criminal justice. Prosecution function and defense function, 3rd edn. American Bar Association, Washington

American Bar Association (1999) Standards relating to pleas of guilty, 3rd edn. American Bar Association, Washington, DC

American Bar Association (2008) Standards for criminal justice relating to prosecutorial investigations. American Bar Association, Washington, DC

771 Wright (2009), p. 592 and 595, Table 1.

772 Wright (2009), p. 592 and 595, Table 1.

773 Wright (2009), pp. 595–596.

774 For possible responses to these failures of the electoral process, see e.g. Wright (2009), pp. 606–610; Gold (2011), pp. 75–91; Bibas (2009), pp. 983–991.

American Bar Association (2010) Model rules of professional conduct. American Bar Association, Washington, DC
Anoka County Attorney's Office (2007) Criminal division annual report 2006. Anoka County Attorney's Office, Anoka
Anoka County Attorney's Office (2008) Criminal division annual report 2007. Anoka County Attorney's Office, Anoka
Anoka County Attorney's Office (2009) Criminal division annual report 2008. Anoka County Attorney's Office, Anoka
Anoka County Attorney's Office (2010) Criminal division annual report 2009. Anoka County Attorney's Office, Anoka
Aragon LM (1981) The federal and California grand jury systems. Historical function, procedural differences and move to reform. Crim Justice J 5:95–112
Arenella P (1980) Reforming the federal grand jury and the state preliminary hearing to prevent conviction without adjudication. Mich Law Rev 78:463–585
Armstrong K, Possley M (1999) Trial & error: how prosecutors sacrifice justice to win. Chicago Tribune (10 January 1999)
Ashcroft J (2003) Memorandum to all federal prosecutors, Department policy concerning charging criminal offenses, Disposition of charges, and sentencing. Office of the Attorney General, Washington
Barkow RE (2006) Separation of powers and the criminal law. Stanford Law Rev 58:989–1054
Beall JM (1998) What do you do with a runaway grand jury? A discussion of the problems and possibilities opened up by the Rocky Flats grand jury investigation. South Calif Law Rev 71:617–639
Beloof DE, Cassell PG, Twist SJ (2006) Victims in criminal procedure, 2nd edn. Carolina Academic Press, Durham
Bemporad HJ (2011) An introduction to federal sentencing, 13th edn. Office of the Federal Public Defender, Western District of Texas, Texas
Bernstein F (1994) Behind the gray door: Williams, secrecy, and the federal grand jury. N Y Univ Law Rev 69:563–623
Bibas S (2009) Prosecutorial regulation versus prosecutorial accountability. Univ Pa Law Rev 157:959–1016
Blair J (2001) The regulation of federal prosecutorial misconduct by state bar associations: 28 U.S.C. § 530B and the reality of inaction. Univ Calif Law Rev 49:625–650
Bradley GV (1999) Plea bargaining and the criminal defendant's obligation to plead guilty. South Tex Law Rev 40:65–82
Breitel CD (1960) Controls in criminal law enforcement. Univ Chic Law Rev 27:427–435
Brice RT (1972) Grand jury proceedings. The prosecutor, the trial judge, and undue influence. Univ Chic Law Rev 39:761–782
Brosi KB (1979) A cross-city comparison of felony case processing. Institute for Law and Social Research, Washington
Bubany CP, Skillern FF (1976) Taming the dragon: an administrative law for prosecutorial decision making. Am Crim Law Rev 13:473–505
Bureau of Justice Statistics (2010) Sourcebook of criminal justice statistics online 2010: criminal defendants disposed of in U.S. District Courts. http://www.albany.edu/sourcebook/pdf/t5222010.pdf. Accessed 24 July 2012
Calkins RM (1965) Grand jury secrecy. Mich Law Rev 63:455–490
Cassidy MR (2000) Toward a more independent grand jury. Recasting and enforcing the prosecutor's duty to disclose exculpatory evidence. Georgetown J Leg Ethics 13:361–403
Caves MA (2008) The prosecutor's dilemma. Obligatory charging under the Ashcroft memo. J Law Soc Chall 9:1–23
Celebrezze FD (1987) Prosecutorial misconduct. Quelling the tide of improper comment to the jury. Cleve State Law Rev 35:237–247

Chiu E (2008) Fast track to a U.S. Attorney's office. Bernard Koteen Office of Public Interest Advising, Cambridge
Coates W (1962) The grand jury, the prosecutor's puppet: wasteful nonsense of criminal jurisprudence. Pa Bar Assoc Q 33:311–317
Cohen TH, Kyckelhahn T (2010) Felony defendants in large urban counties, 2006. Felony defendants in large urban counties series (NCJ 228944). U.S. Department of Justice, Washington
Cohen TH, Reaves BA (2006) Felony defendants in large urban counties, 2002. Felony defendants in large urban counties series (NCJ 210818). U.S. Department of Justice, Washington
Cooper JO (2002) Searching for harmlessness: method and madness in the Supreme Court's harmless constitutional error doctrine. Univ Kans Law Rev 50:309–345
Davis KC (1969) Discretionary justice. A preliminary inquiry. Louisiana State University Press, Baton Rouge
Davis AJ (1998) Prosecution and race: the power and privilege of discretion. Fordham Law Rev 67:13–67
Davis AJ (2007) Arbitrary justice. The power of the American prosecutor. Oxford University Press, Oxford
Del Carmen RV (2007) Criminal procedure. Law and practice, 7th edn. Thomson/Wadsworth, Belmont
Dickerson Moore SA (2000) Questioning the autonomy of prosecutorial charging decisions: recognizing the need to exercise discretion – knowing there will be consequences for crossing the line. La Law Rev 60:371–404
Diepraam W (2006) Prosecutorial misconduct: it is not the prosecutor's way. South Tex Law Rev 47:773–780
Dyke A (2007) Electoral cycles in the administration of criminal justice. Public Choice 133:417–437
Ely AN (2004) Prosecutorial discretion as an ethical necessity: the Ashcroft memorandum's curtailment of the prosecutor's duty to "Seek Justice". Cornell Law Rev 90:237–278
Executive Office for the United States Attorneys (2000) United States Attorney's annual statistical report fiscal year 1999. U.S. Department of Justice, Washington
Executive Office for the United States Attorneys (2010) United States Attorney's annual statistical report fiscal year 2009. U.S. Department of Justice, Washington
Executive Office for the United States Attorneys (2011) United States Attorney's annual statistical report fiscal year 2010. U.S. Department of Justice, Washington
Federal Bar Council (2004) Department of Justice Charging, plea bargaining and sentencing policies under attorneys general Thornburg, Reno, and Ashcroft. Federal Bar Council, Washington
Feeney F, Forrest D, Adrianne W (1983) Arrests without conviction: how often they occur and why. U.S. Department of Justice, Washington
Felkenes GT (1975) The prosecutor: a look at reality. Southwest Univ Law Rev 7:98–123
Fisher SZ (1988) In search of the virtuous prosecutor: a conceptual framework. Am J Crim Law 15:197–261
Fisher SZ (1989) Zealousness and "Overzealousness": making sense of the prosecutor's duty to seek justice. Prosecutor 22(3):9–28
Fisher G (2004) Plea bargaining's triumph. A history of plea bargaining in America. Stanford University Press, Stanford
Forst B, Lucianovic J, Cox SJ (1977) What happens after arrest? A court perspective of police operations in the District of Columbia. Institute for Law and Social Research, Washington
Forst B, Leahy FF, Shirhall J, Tyson HL, Bartolomeo J (1982) Arrest convictability as a measure of police performance. United States Department of Justice, National Institute of Justice, Washington
Frase RS (1980) The decision to file federal criminal charges: a quantitative study of prosecutorial discretion. Univ Chic Law Rev 47:246–330

Free MD Jr (2002) Race and presentencing decisions in the United States: a summary and critique of the research. Crim Justice Rev 27:203–232
Freedman MH (1975) Lawyers' ethics in an adversary system. Bobbs-Merrill Company, Indianapolis
Freedman MH, Smith A (2004) Understanding lawyers' ethics, 3rd edn. LexisNexis, Newark
Friedman HG (1973) Some jurisprudential considerations in developing an administrative law for the criminal pre-trial process. J Urban Law 51:433–469
Friedman LM (1979) Plea bargaining in historical perspective. Law Soc Rev 13:247–260
Gershman BL (1986) Why prosecutors misbehave. Crim Law Bull 22:131–143
Gershman BL (1995) Prosecutorial misconduct in presenting evidence: "Backdooring" hearsay. Crim Law Bull 31:99–112
Gershman BL (2007a) Trial error and misconduct, 2nd edn. LexisNexis, Newark
Gershman BL (2007b) Litigating Brady v. Maryland: games prosecutors play. Case West Reserve Law Rev 57:531–565
Gershman BL (2007–2008) Prosecutorial misconduct, 2nd edn. Thomson/West, St. Paul
Gershman BL (2011) Prosecutorial decisionmaking and discretion in the charging function. Hastings Law J 62:1259–1284
Gifford DG (1981) Equal protection and the prosecutor's charging decision: enforcing an ideal. George Wash Law Rev 49:659–719
Gilboy JA (1984) Prosecutors' discretionary use of the grand jury to initiate or to reinitiate prosecution. Am Bar Found Res J 9:1–81
Gold RM (2011) Promoting democracy in prosecution. Wash Law Rev 86:69–124
Gordon N (2011a) Actual innocence. Exonerated defendants whose cases involved prosecutorial misconduct. http://www.iwatchnews.org/2003/06/26/5531/actual-innocence. Accessed 25 June 2012
Gordon N (2011b) Misconduct and punishment. State disciplinary authorities investigate prosecutors accused of misconduct. http://www.iwatchnews.org/2003/06/26/5532/misconduct-and-punishment. Accessed 25 June 2012
Gordon SC, Huber GA (2002) Citizen oversight and the electoral incentives of criminal prosecutors. Am J Polit Sci 46:334–351
Gottfredson MR, Gottfredson DM (1989) Decision-making in criminal justice. Toward the rational exercise of discretion, 2nd revised edn. Plenum, New York
Gramckow H (2008) Prosecutor organization and operations in the United States. In: Open Society Institute Sofia (ed) Promoting prosecutorial accountability, independence and effectiveness. Comparative research. Open Society Institute Sofia, Sofia, pp 386–429
Green BA (1988) The ethical prosecutor and the adversary system. Crim Law Bull 24:126–145
Green BA (1995) Policing federal prosecutors: do too many regulators produce too little enforcement? St Tomas Law Rev 8:69–95
Greene Burnett C (1999) Of crime, punishment, community and an accused's responsibility to plead guilty. A response to Gerard Bradley. South Tex Law Rev 40:281–298
Greenwood PW, Wildhorn S, Poggio EC, Strumwasser MJ, de Leon P (1973) Prosecution of adult felony defendants in Los Angeles County: a policy perspective. The Rand Corporation, Santa Monica
Griffin LC (2000) The prudent prosecutor. Georgetown J Leg Ethics 14:259–307
Halsted J (1987) The American grand jury – due process or rights regress? Crim Justice Policy Rev 2:103–117
Harris DA (2011) The interaction and relationship between prosecutors and police officers in the U.S., and how this affects police reform efforts. University of Pittsburgh Legal Studies Research Paper Series (Working Paper No. 2011-19)
Heany G (1991) The reality of guidelines sentencing. No end to disparity. Am Crim Law Rev 28:161–232
Helmholz RH (1983) The early history of the grand jury and canon law. Univ Chic Law Rev 50:613–627

Henning PJ (1999a) Prosecutorial misconduct and constitutional remedies. Wash Univ Law Q 77:713–834
Henning PJ (1999b) Prosecutorial misconduct in grand jury investigations. S C Law Rev 51:1–61
Hobbs SE (1949) Prosecutor's bias, an occupational disease. Al Law Rev 2:40–60
Holder EH Jr (2010) Memorandum to all federal prosecutors, Department policy on charging and sentencing. Office of the Attorney General, Washington
Howell TJ (1816) A complete collection of state trials and proceedings for high treason and other crimes and misdemeanors from the earliest period to the year 1783, vol 8. Printed by T.C. Hansard for Longman, Hurst, Rees, Orme, and Brown; J.M. Richardson; Black, Parbury, and Allen; Baldwin, Cradock, and Joy; E. Jeffery; J. Hatchard; R.H. Evans; J. Booker; E. Lloyd; J. Booth, Budd and Calkin; and T.C. Hansard, London
International Association of Prosecutor (1999) Standards of professional responsibility and statement of the essential duties and rights of prosecutors. International Association of Prosecutor, The Hague
Jacoby JE, Gramckow HP, Ratledge EC (1992) Asset forfeiture programs: impact issues and implications. National Institute of Justice, Washington
James DC (1995) The prosecutor's discretionary screening and charging authority. Prosecutor 29 (2):22–29
Johnston RG (1974) The grand jury – prosecutorial abuse of the indictment process. J Crim Law Criminol 65:157–169
Jonakait RN (1987) The ethical prosecutor's misconduct. Crim Law Bull 23:550–567
Jost K (2007) Prosecutors and the law. CQ Res 17:938–960
Joy PA (2002) Making ethics opinions meaningful: toward more effective regulation of lawyers' conduct. Georgetown J Leg Ethics 15:313–396
Kauder NB, Ostrom BJ (2008) State sentencing guidelines: profiles and continuum. National Center for State Courts, Williamsburg
Kirchmeier JL, Greenwald SR, Reynolds H, Sussman J (2010) Vigilante justice: prosecutor misconduct in capital cases. Wayne Law Rev 55:1327–1385
Krimmel JP (1994) Prosecutorial vindictiveness. University of Tennessee Honors Thesis Projects
Krug P (2002) Prosecutorial discretion and its limits. Am J Comp Law 50:643–664
Kuh RH (1955) The grand jury "Presentment": foul blow or fair play? Columbia Law Rev 55:1103–1136
Kuh RH (1975) Plea bargaining: guidelines for the Manhattan District Attorney's office. Crim Law Bull 11:48–61
LaFave WR (1970) The prosecutor's discretion in the United States. Am J Comp Law 18:532–548
LaFave WR, Israel JH, King NJ, Kerr OS (2007) Criminal procedure, 3rd edn. Criminal practice series, 7 vols. Thomson/West, St. Paul
Landes WM, Posner RA (2001) Harmless error. J Leg Stud 30:161–192
Langbein JH (1978) Torture and plea bargaining. Univ Chic Law Rev 46:3–22
Langbein JH (1979) Understanding the short history of plea bargaining. Law Soc Rev 13:261–272
Lawless JF (2008) Prosecutorial misconduct. Law, procedure, forms, 4th edn. LexisNexis, Newark
Leipold AD (1995) Why grand juries do not (and cannot) protect the accused. Cornell Law Rev 80:260–324
Levine KL (2005) The new prosecution. Wake Forest Law Rev 40:1125–1214
Little RK (2010) It's not my problem? Wrong: prosecutors have an important ethical role to play. Ohio State J Crim Law 7:685–737
Little RK (2011) The ABA's project to revise the criminal justice standards for the prosecution and defense functions. Hastings Law J 62:1111–1158
Lynch GE (1998) Our administrative system of criminal justice. Fordham Law Rev 66:2117–2151
Lynch GE (2003) Screening versus plea bargaining. Exactly what are we trading of? Stanford Law Rev 55:1399–1408
Mayer KB (1996) Applying open records policy to Wisconsin district attorneys: can charging guidelines promote public awareness? Wis Law Rev 1996:295–344

McDonald WF, Rossman HH, Cramer JA (1982) Police–prosecutor relations in the United States. Executive summary. Institute of Criminal Law and Procedure, Georgetown University Law Center, Washington
McIntyre D, Lippmann D (1970) Prosecutors and early disposition of Felony cases. Am Bar Assoc J 56:1154–1159
Medwed DS (2004) The zeal deal: prosecutorial resistance to post-conviction claims of innocence. Boston Univ Law Rev 84:125–184
Medwed DS (2009) The prosecutor as minister of justice: preaching to the unconverted from the post-conviction pulpit. Wash Law Rev 84:35–66
Melilli KJ (1992) Prosecutorial discretion in an adversary system. Brigh Young Univ Law Rev 1992:669–704
Metropolitan Crime Commission (2002) Analysis of the processing of state felony and misdemeanor charges in New Orleans: arrest through billing decision. Metropolitan Crime Commission, New Orleans
Metropolitan Crime Commission (2009) Orleans Parish criminal justice system accountability report – Spring 2009. Metropolitan Crime Commission, New Orleans
Metropolitan Crime Commission (2012a) Orleans Parish criminal justice system accountability report – May 2012. Metropolitan Crime Commission, New Orleans
Metropolitan Crime Commission (2012b) Orleans Parish criminal justice system accountability report May 2012 – supplemental exhibits and statistics. Metropolitan Crime Commission, New Orleans
Miller FW (1970) Prosecution: the decision to charge a suspect with a crime. Little Brown, Boston
Miller M, Wright RF (2007) Criminal procedures. Cases, statutes, and executive materials, 3rd edn. Aspen Publishers, New York
Mills R (1966) The prosecutor: charging and "Bargaining". Univ Ill Law Forum 1966:511–522
Misner RL (1996) Recasting prosecutorial discretion. J Crim Law Criminol 86:717–777
Mitchell G (1994) Against 'Overwhelming' appellate activism: constraining harmless error review. Calif Law Rev 82:1335–1369
Morse WL (1931) A survey of the grand jury system – part I. Oreg Law Rev 10:101–160
Motivans M (2008) Federal Justice Statistics 2005 – statistical table (NCJ 218524). U.S. Department of Justice, Washington
Motivans M (2009) Federal Justice Statistics 2006 – statistical table (NCJ 225711). U.S. Department of Justice, Washington
Motivans M (2010a) Federal Justice Statistics 2007 – statistical table (NCJ 230889). U.S. Department of Justice, Washington
Motivans M (2010b) Federal Justice Statistics 2008 – statistical table (NCJ 231822). U.S. Department of Justice, Washington
Motivans M (2011) Federal Justice Statistics 2009 – statistical table (NCJ 233464). U.S. Department of Justice, Washington
National District Association (2009) National prosecution standards, 3rd edn. National District Attorneys Association, Washington, DC
Note (1959) Prosecutor indiscretion: a result of political influence. Indiana Law J 34:477–492
Note (1977) The prosecutor's duty to present exculpatory evidence to an investigating grand jury. Mich Law Rev 75:1514–1538
Note (2001) Breathing new life into prosecutorial vindictiveness doctrine. Harv Law Rev 114:2074–2097
O'Neill ME (2004) Understanding federal prosecutorial declinations. An empirical analysis of predictive factors. Am Crim Law Rev 41:1439–1498
Osler M (2005) This changes everything. A call for a directive, goal-oriented principle to guide the exercise of discretion by federal prosecutors. Valparaiso Univ Law Rev 39:625–659
Perry SW (2006) Prosecutors in state courts, 2005. U.S. Department of Justice, Washington
Pizzi W (1993) Understanding prosecutorial discretion in the United States. The limits of comparative criminal procedure as an instrument of reform. Ohio State Law J 54:1325–1374

Pollock JM (2010) Ethical dilemmas and decisions in criminal justice, 7th edn. Wadsworth, Belmont
Pope PB (2011) Prosecutorial investigation standards: guidance through the thorny thicket that precedes charging. Crim Justice J 26:4–11
Pound R (1960) Discretion, dispensation and mitigation: the problem of the individual special case. N Y Univ Law Rev 35:925–937
Prakash S (2005) The chief prosecutor. George Wash Law Rev 73:521–597
Rainville GA, Reaves BA (2003) Felony defendants in large urban counties, 2000. Felony defendants in large urban counties series (NCJ 202021). U.S. Department of Justice, Washington
Ramseyer MJ, Rasmusen E, Raghav M (2008) Convictions versus conviction rates: the prosecutor's choice. Harvard Law and Economics (Discussion Paper No. 611)
Reaves BA (2001) Felony defendants in large urban counties, 1998. Felony defendants in large urban counties series (NCJ 187232). U.S. Department of Justice, Washington
Reaves BA (2007) Census of state and local law enforcement agencies, 2004 (NCJ 212749). U.S. Department of Justice, Washington
Reno J (1993) Memorandum to holders of U.S. Attorneys' manual, title 9, Principles of federal prosecution. Office of the Attorney General, Washington
Richman D (2003) Prosecutors and their agents, agents and their prosecutors. Columbia Law Rev 103:749–832
Ridolfi KM, Possley M (2010) Preventable error. A report on prosecutorial misconduct in California 1997–2009. Veritas initiative, Northern California innocence project, Santa Clara University School of Law, Santa Clara
Rosett A (1972) Discretion, severity and legality in criminal justice. South Calif Law Rev 46:12–50
Sarat A, Clarke C (2008) Beyond discretion: prosecution, the logic of sovereignty, and the limits of law. Law Soc Inq 33:387–416
Schulhofer SJ (1992) Plea bargaining as disaster. Yale Law J 101:1979–2009
Schwartz HE (1972) Demythologizing the historic role of the grand jury. Am Crim Law Rev 10:701–770
Schwartz BA (1983) The limits of prosecutorial vindictiveness. Iowa Law Rev 69:127–208
Scolnic S (1999) Grand jury: power shift? Lawmaker's vow to give defendants clout is likely to draw heat. Legal Times (12 April 1999)
Scott KM (2007) U.S. Attorneys who have served less than full four-year terms, 1981–2006. United States Congressional Research Service, Washington
Shannon JP (1972) The grand jury: true tribunal of the people or administrative agency of the prosecutor? N M Law Rev 2:141–170
Singer RG (1968) Forensic misconduct by federal prosecutors – and how it grew. Ala Law Rev 20:227–279
Singer RG (2008) Criminal procedure II. From bail to jail, 2nd edn. Aspen Publishers, Frederick
Smith SK, Litras M (2002) Compendium of Federal Justice Statistics, 2000 (NCJ 194067). U.S. Department of Justice, Washington
Smith SK, Motivans M (2003) Compendium of Federal Justice Statistics, 2001 (NCJ 201627). U.S. Department of Justice, Washington
Smith SK, Motivans M (2004) Compendium of Federal Justice Statistics, 2002 (NCJ 205368). U.S. Department of Justice, Washington
Smith SK, Motivans M (2005) Compendium of Federal Justice Statistics, 2003 (NCJ 210299). U.S. Department of Justice, Washington
Smith SK, Motivans M (2006) Compendium of Federal Justice Statistics, 2004 (NCJ 213476). U.S. Department of Justice, Washington
Smith SK, Scalia J (1998a) Compendium of Federal Justice Statistics, 1994 (NCJ 163063). U.S. Department of Justice, Washington

Smith SK, Scalia J (1998b) Compendium of Federal Justice Statistics, 1995 (NCJ 164259). U.S. Department of Justice, Washington
Smith SK, Scalia J (1998c) Compendium of Federal Justice Statistics, 1996 (NCJ 172849). U.S. Department of Justice, Washington
Smith SK, Scalia J (1999) Compendium of Federal Justice Statistics, 1997 (NCJ 176328). U.S. Department of Justice, Washington
Smith SK, Scalia J (2000) Compendium of Federal Justice Statistics, 1998 (NCJ 180258). U.S. Department of Justice, Washington
Smith SK, Scalia J (2001) Compendium of Federal Justice Statistics, 1999 (NCJ 186179). U.S. Department of Justice, Washington
Spain J (1964) The grand jury, past and present: a survey. Am Crim Law Q 2:119–142
Stuntz WJ (2007) The pathological politics of criminal law. Mich Law Rev 100:505–600
Tennis BT (2010) Uniform ethical regulation of federal prosecutors. Yale Law J 120:144–183
Terzano JF, McGee JA, Holt AD (2009) Improving prosecutorial accountability. A policy review. The Justice Project, Washington
The Center for Public Integrity (2011a) Methodology, the team for harmful error. http://www.iwatchnews.org/2003/06/26/5530/methodology-team-harmful-error. Accessed 25 June 2012
The Center for Public Integrity (2011b) Nationwide numbers. State-by-state data for the harmful error. http://www.iwatchnews.org/2003/06/26/5927/nationwide-numbers. Accessed 2 June 2012
Thomas CW, Fitch AW (1976) Prosecutorial decision making. Am Crim Law Rev 13:507–552
Tobolowsky PM, Gaboury MT, Jackson AL, Blackburn AG (2010) Crime victim rights and remedies, 2nd edn. Carolina Academic Press, Durham
Toomey DC (1963) Discretionary power in the judiciary to organize a special investigating grand jury. Univ Pa Law Rev 111:954–973
U.S. Department of Justice (2008) An investigation into the removal of nine U.S. Attorneys in 2006. U.S. Department of Justice, Washington
Vera Institute of Justice (1977) Felony arrests, their prosecution and disposition in New York City's Courts. The Vera Institute of Justice, New York
Vera Institute of Justice (1981) Felony arrests, their prosecution and disposition in New York City's Courts, Rev. edn. Professional studies. The Institute: Longman, New York
Vorenberg J (1976) Narrowing the discretion of criminal justice officials. Duke Law J 1976:651–697
Vorenberg J (1981) Decent restraint of prosecutorial power. Harv Law Rev 94:1521–1573
Weaver RL, Abramson LW, Burkoff JM, Hancock C (2008) Principles of criminal procedure, 3rd edn. Concise hornbook series. Thomson/West, St. Paul
Weigend T (1978) Anklagepflicht und Ermessen. Die Stellung der Staatsanwalts zwischen Legalitäts- u. Opportunitätsprinzip nach deutschem und amerikanischem Recht. Nomos, Baden-Baden
Weinberg S (2011) Breaking the rules: who suffers when a prosecutor is cited for misconduct. http://www.publicintegrity.org/2003/06/26/5517/breaking-rules. Accessed 25 June 2012
Wright RF (2005) Trial distortion and the end of innocence in federal criminal justice. Univ Pa Law Rev 154:79–156
Wright RF (2009) How prosecutor elections fail us. Ohio State J Crim Law 6:581–610
Wright RF, Miller ML (2003) Honesty and opacity in charge bargains. Stanford Law Rev 55:1409–1417
Wright RF, Miller ML (2010) The worldwide accountability deficit for prosecutors. Wash Lee Law Rev 67:1587–1620
Zacharias FC (2001) The professional discipline of prosecutors. N C Law Rev 79:721–778
Zwerling M (1976) Federal Grand Juries v. Attorney independence and the attorney–client privilege. Hastings Law J 27:1263–1290

Chapter 6
Public Prosecutors in Switzerland: Position, Powers, and Accountability

6.1 Structure and Organization of the Prosecution Service

Switzerland has a federal system like the United States in which the prosecution service is organized on cantonal and federal levels.

6.1.1 *Federal Level*

6.1.1.1 Public Prosecutor of the Confederation

The Office of the Attorney General (OAG; *Bundesanwaltschaft*) is responsible for the prosecution of criminal offenses that are directed against the Confederation or that affect its interest, such as organized crime, white collar crime, money laundering, and corruption. Criminal offenses that fall within the jurisdiction of the Office of the Attorney General are expressly listed in the CCrP[1] as well as in various other Federal laws. By far, the majority of criminal acts are prosecuted by the cantons.[2] Federal criminal cases are prosecuted before the Federal Criminal Court in Bellinzona.

In addition to the prosecution of criminal offenses, the Office of the Attorney General is also entrusted with the execution of requests for mutual legal assistance in legal matters and fulfills administrative tasks in the fields of criminal law and criminal procedure. The Office of the Attorney General has no authority over

[1] Articles 23 and 24 CCrP.

[2] In 2008, the Office of the Attorney General brought charges before the Federal Criminal Court in 16 cases, in 2009 in 12 cases, and finally in 2010 in 20 cases. During 2010, a total of 107 preliminary proceedings were closed and 10 cases were transmitted to the federal examining magistrate (Office of the Attorney General 2011, p. 5).

G. Gilliéron, *Public Prosecutors in the United States and Europe*,

DOI 10.1007/978-3-319-04504-7_6,

cantonal prosecutions. Hence, it has neither supervisory oversight over the cantonal authorities nor does it have the right to issue any directives to them.

With the introduction of the CCrP on January 1, 2011, the law enforcement agency had to be reorganized. Besides the abolishment of the federal examining magistrate, the independence of the Office of the Attorney General has been reinforced. It is not attached to the Federal Department of Justice and Police anymore and thus it is also responsible for its own administration. The Office of the Attorney General is a self-governing institution.

The Office of the Attorney General is a hierarchical institution headed by the attorney general. It is divided into various departments: the Directorate, the Services Division, the Competence Centre for Economics and Finance, and operational units. Operational units include the Competence Centre for Mutual Assistance, the State Security and Specific Federal Offenses Division, the Terrorism and Organized Crime Division, the Economic Crime Division, the Lausanne Branch, the Lugano Branch, and the Zurich Branch.[3]

The attorney general heads the Office of the Attorney General in relation to legal, staffing, and organizational matters in accordance with the statutory terms of reference. The Attorney General's Operational Committee and the Resources Steering Committee are assigned to him.[4] The attorney general is entitled to delegate individual cases or other matters to be dealt with independently by his deputy attorneys general, the chief of staff (head of the Services Division), the heads of section (chief federal attorneys), or the federal attorneys.[5]

The Directorate is composed of the attorney general, the deputy attorneys general, and the chief of staff. It is the attorney general's advisory committee. Meetings take place on a regular basis in order to discuss legal, staffing, and organizational questions, to debate important matters, and to make strategic decisions.[6]

The headquarters of the Office of the Attorney General are located in Berne. In addition, there are branch offices in Zurich, Lausanne, and Lugano. These branch offices deal with those offenses listed under Article 24 CCrP. This includes cases of organized crime (Article 260ter SCC), money laundering (Article 305bis SCC), terrorism financing (Article 260^{quinquies} SCC), and bribery (Article 322ter et seq. SCC) with international or intercantonal aspects.

---

[3] Article 1 of the Regulation concerning the Organization and Administration of the Office of the Attorney General of November 22, 2010 (Status as of January 1, 2011); *Reglement über die Organisation und Verwaltung der Bundesanwaltschaft vom 22. November 2010* (*Stand am 1. Januar 2011*); SR. 173.712.22.

[4] Article 2 para. 1 and 2 of the Regulation concerning the Organization and Administration of the Office of the Attorney General.

[5] Article 2 para. 3 of the Regulation concerning the Organization and Administration of the Office of the Attorney General.

[6] Article 4 para. 1 and 3 of the Regulation concerning the Organization and Administration of the Office of the Attorney General.

Each operational unit is headed by a chief federal attorney. Within these units, chief federal attorneys, deputy federal attorneys, and federal attorneys may exercise all duties conferred to the public prosecutor by the CCrP. However, to file criminal charges and to represent the state at the trial, deputy federal attorneys need special authorization from the attorney general.[7]

The attorney general, attorney general's deputies, and chief federal attorneys have supervisory authority over lower-ranking prosecutors, and they must follow the instructions of their superiors (*Weisungsrecht*). Following the hierarchical structure of the Office of the Attorney General, the instructions issued by higher-ranking prosecutors supersede those issued by lower-ranking prosecutors.[8] Instructions in a single case concerning initiation, carrying out, or completion of a procedure as well as concerning the pleading of charges and the recourse to legal remedies are permitted.[9] Directives discontinuing the proceedings, orders that proceedings are not to be opened, and orders that suspend the investigation require approval either from the chief federal attorney, if they have been issued by a federal prosecutor, or from the attorney general, in case they have been issued by a chief prosecutor.[10]

The attorney general as well as the two deputy attorney generals are elected by the Federal Parliament for 4 year terms.[11] The attorney general elects the other attorneys, namely the heads of section (chief federal attorneys) and the federal attorneys.[12] They all serve a 4-year term.[13]

The Office of the Attorney General is answerable to a supervisory authority elected by the Federal Parliament for a term of 4 years.[14] The supervisory authority is entitled to issue general instructions but not to give orders concerning individual proceedings.[15] Removal from office is possible in case of willful or grossly negligent violation of official duties.[16]

The Office of the Attorney General employs approximately 150 members or staff.[17]

---

[7] Article 11 para. 1 and 2 of the Regulation concerning the Organization and Administration of the Office of the Attorney General.

[8] See Hofer (2011), Margin No. 18.

[9] Article 13 of the Law on the Organization of the Federal Criminal Authorities of March 19, 2010 (Status as of April 1, 2012); *Bundesgesetz vom 19. März 2010 über die Organisation der Strafbehörden des Bundes* (*Strafbehördenorganisationsgesetz, StBOG*) (Stand am 1. April 2012); SR 173.71.

[10] Article 14 of the Law on the Organization of the Federal Criminal Authorities.

[11] Article 20 paras 1 and 3 of the Law on the Organization of the Federal Criminal Authorities.

[12] Article 20 para. 2, Articles 10 and 11 of the Law on the Organization of the Federal Criminal Authorities.

[13] Article 20 para. 3 of the Law on the Organization of the Federal Criminal Authorities.

[14] On the supervisory authority, see Sect. 6.1.1.2, para 1.

[15] Article 29 para. 2 of the Law on the Organization of the Federal Criminal Authorities.

[16] Article 21 of the Law on the Organization of the Federal Criminal Authorities.

[17] Office of the Attorney General (2012), p. 9.

6.1.1.2 Evaluation of the Office of the Attorney General

With the introduction of the CCrP on January 1, 2011, the supervisory authority over the Office of the Attorney General has changed. While the supervision of the activities of the Office of the Attorney General was previously carried out by the Swiss Federal Criminal Court, now the Office of the Attorney General receives supervision from a supervisory authority elected by the Federal Parliament for a term of 4 years. This supervisory authority is composed of seven members, namely one judge from the Swiss Federal Supreme Court, one judge from the Swiss Federal Criminal Court, two attorneys recorded in a cantonal attorneys register, and three specialists not belonging to a Federal Court and not inscribed in a cantonal attorneys register.[18] In the following, the situation until 2011 as well as since 2011 is described.

Situation until 2011: In fulfilling its supervisorial duties, the Swiss Federal Criminal Court visited the Office of the Attorney General annually. On this occasion, federal prosecutors respectively teams of the Office of the Attorney General were inspected. Specific topics were discussed with the concerned persons in one and a half hour interviews. General findings and recommendations were summarized in a report and discussed with the attorney general. The Swiss Federal Criminal Court monitored the implementation of the report's recommendations.[19] The Office of the Attorney General reported annually to the Swiss Federal Criminal Court. Parts of its annual report are public and available online.[20]

Situation since 2011: Exerting his supervising duties, the supervisory authority may ask the Office of the Attorney General to inform him about its activities and may conduct inspections. The supervisory authority has access to the case files as far as is necessary for the fulfillment of the mandate.[21] The supervisory authority reports annually to the Federal Parliament.[22]

---

[18] Articles 23 and 25 of the Law on the Organization of the Federal Criminal Authorities.

[19] The Swiss Federal Criminal Court's annual reports are available at http://www.bstger.ch/rapporti.asp?idL=DE (accessed June 25, 2012).

[20] See http://www.bundesanwaltschaft.ch/dokumentation/00024/index.html?lang=de (accessed June 25, 2012).

[21] Article 30 para. 1 and 2 of the Law on the Organization of the Federal Criminal Authorities.

[22] Article 12 of the Federal Assembly Ordinance on the Organization and Duties of the Supervisory Authority over the Office of the Attorney General of October 1, 2010 (Status as of 1 January 2011); *Verordnung der Bundesversammlung über die Organisation und die Aufgaben der Aufsichtsbehörde über die Bundesanwaltschaft vom 1. Oktober 2010 (Stand am 1. Januar 2011)*; SR 173.712.24.

6.1.1.3 Selection of the Attorney General, Attorney General's Deputies, and Federal Attorneys

6.1.1.3.1 Attorney General and Attorney General's Deputies

While prior to the introduction of the CCrP on January 1, 2011, the attorney general and his deputies were appointed by the Federal Council, this is now the responsibility of the Federal Parliament.

The Judicial Committee (JC; *Gerichtskommission*), which is part of the Federal Parliament, is responsible for preparing the election of the attorney general and his deputies. Tasks of the Judicial Committee is tasked with advertizing vacant positions for the attorney general and his deputies, presenting a list of candidates it has selected for the vacant position to the Federal Parliament, and deciding on the details of employment conditions of the attorney general and his deputies.

Applicants must possess a law degree (Master of Laws). Having an attorney's licence and a doctorate degree are considered advantages. In general, candidates are evaluated with respect to their working experience in the legal field, academic record, language skills, and interviews. Only Swiss citizens may be considered for these positions.[23] After their election they must reside in Switzerland.[24]

Michael Lauber, elected in September 2011, is the first Attorney General appointed by the Federal Parliament. His predecessor Erwin Beyeler was not reelected in June 2011, although the Judicial Committee had recommended him. His tenure ended in December 2011.

Employment is no longer contingent upon satisfactory completion of personal and financial background investigation. With the change of election system, it seems that a legal basis for this requirement has been forgotten.

In Switzerland, unlike the United States, there is no official code of ethics for prosecutors. Nevertheless, the attorney general as well as his deputies swear an oath to fulfill their duties faithfully before accession to office.[25]

6.1.1.3.2 Federal Attorneys

Federal attorneys are appointed by the attorney general for a 4-year term.[26] Candidates must possess a law degree. Applicants are evaluated with respect to their

---

[23] Article 20 para. 1bis of the Law on the Organization of the Federal Criminal Authorities.

[24] Article 13 of the Federal Assembly Ordinance on the Employment Relationship and Remuneration of the Attorney General and Attorney General's Deputies of October 1, 2010 (Status as of January 1, 2011); *Verordnung der Bundesversammlung über das Arbeitsverhältnis und die Besoldung des Bundesanwaltes oder der Bundesanwältin sowie der Stellvertretenden Bundesanwälte oder Bundesanwältinnen vom 1. Oktober 2010* (*Stand am 1. Januar 2011*); SR 173712.23.

[25] Article 3 of the Federal Assembly Ordinance on the Employment Relationship and Remuneration of the Attorney General and Attorney General's Deputies.

[26] Article 20 para. 2 of the Law on the Organization of the Federal Criminal Authorities.

litigation experience, academic record, commitment to public service, and interviews. Furthermore, the advertised job may outline specific requirements needed for the position. The attorney general may restrict the eligibility to Swiss citizenship.[27]

6.1.1.4 Training of the Attorney General, the Attorney General's Deputies, and Federal Attorneys

After being hired, prosecutors have no further training requirements. However, the Federal Government offers internal continuing education courses for prosecutors, especially when important legal changes occur. In 2010, for example, members and staff of the Office of the Attorney General attended various internal and external continuing education courses with special attention to the new Swiss CCrP.

Continuing education courses are proposed by various institutions. Although the attendance of these courses is voluntary, participation is highly recommended. Since the Office of the Attorney General has specialized departments, participation in legal training and continuing legal courses may be encouraged to acquire more competency in a specialized field.

However, overall the lack of mandatory continuing legal education may be considered a weakness in the system.

6.1.2 Cantonal Level

6.1.2.1 Public Prosecutors of the Cantons

Although Switzerland now has a unified criminal procedure, the organization of the public prosecution service—and in a broader sense the criminal justice authorities[28]—remains a matter for the cantons.[29] Thus, it is highly decentralized.[30]

Depending on the canton, the public prosecution service belongs either to the executive branch or the judiciary, or is placed between the executive branch and the

---

[27] Article 20 para. 2 of the Law on the Organization of the Federal Criminal Authorities.

[28] Criminal justice authorities are the police, the prosecution, and the criminal justice authorities responsible for prosecuting minor regulatory offenses (Article 12 CCrP).

[29] Article 14 para. 2 CCrP stipulates that the Federation and the cantons shall regulate the election, composition, organization, and powers of the criminal justice authorities to the extent that this is not exclusively regulated by this Statute or by another federal statute.

[30] For an overview on the organization of the cantonal and federal criminal justice authorities, see Arn et al. (2011b).

judiciary.[31] The assignment to one or the other branch of government often reflects the historic development in the cantons.[32]

The adoption of the "public prosecutor model II" inquiry model provoked a profound reorganization of the public prosecutor's office in numerous cantons. Usually, the former examining magistrates were appointed as public prosecutors. In addition, the CCrP confers extended powers to the prosecution, for instance in the field of mutual agreement procedures (Article 316 CCrP), which in turn had the consequence of increasing staff.[33]

The organization of the cantonal public prosecutor's offices are regulated at cantonal level in cantonal laws.[34]

The size, organization, and composition of the cantonal public prosecutor's offices may vary considerably depending on the size of the jurisdiction served.[35] The public prosecutor's office may be organized as a single, indivisible entity, such as the ones in the cantons Basel-City and Zug.[36] It may also be structured as various, functionally independent public prosecutor's offices with different regional and local jurisdiction. Finally, the office of the public prosecutor may also be divided into several divisions (e.g. universal division, special crime divisions, juvenile division, etc.) and either provide a regional structure or not.[37] In the canton of Zurich, criminal offenses are prosecuted through nine public prosecution offices. These are the five regional prosecution offices and the four special prosecution offices (prosecution office for special investigations, prosecution office for drug offenses/organized crime, prosecution office for economic crimes, and prosecution office for violent crimes).

Cantonal public prosecutor's offices have jurisdiction over misdemeanor and felony cases. In a few cantons, minor regulatory offenses (petty offenses) are prosecuted by administrative authorities (Article 17 CCrP).[38] Administrative authorities appointed to prosecute and judge minor regulatory offenses have the same powers as the prosecution. The proceeding is regulated by analogy, with the provisions regulating penal order proceedings (Article 357 CCrP).[39]

In general, prosecution services are organized hierarchically. Hence, prosecutors have to follow directives and instructions received from their superiors. Each public

---

[31] From the supervisory authority over the prosecution service, it is not always easy to identify the branch of government it belongs to. For a detailed discussion, see Lienhard and Kettiger (2008). On the supervisory authority, see Sect. 6.6.1.1.1.

[32] Lienhard and Kettiger (2008), Margin No. 19.

[33] Arn et al. (2011a), Margin No. 31.

[34] On possible organization models for the public prosecutor's office, see Keller. In: Donatsch et al. (2010) Kommentar StPO, Art. 14, Margin Nos. 17–20.

[35] Table 6.1 gives a simplified overview of the organization of the public prosecutor's offices.

[36] In this context, the senior public prosecutor's office or the attorney general's office is not taken into account. Only the structure of the "lower" public prosecutor's office is considered. See Keller. In: Donatsch et al. (2010) Kommentar StPO, Art. 14, Margin No. 18.

[37] See Keller. In: Donatsch et al. (2010) Kommentar StPO, Art. 14, Margin No. 19.

[38] See Arn et al. (2011a), Margin No. 38.

[39] On the penal order proceedings, see Sect. 6.5.1.

prosecutor's office is headed by a first public prosecutor or a chief public prosecutor (*Erster Staatsanwalt*; *Leitender Staatsanwalt*). He is either elected by the executive power, by the parliament, or directly by citizens for a term of 4 respectively 6 years, with possible renewal upon expiration of the term. In general, larger offices consist of several divisions. In that case, each division is under the guidance of a leading public prosecutor (*Leitender Staatsanwalt*). Some cantonal public prosecutor's offices may provide for a senior public prosecutor respectively a senior public prosecutor's office (*Oberstaatsanwaltschaft*) or an attorney general respectively an attorney general's office (*Generalstaatsanwaltschaft*).[40] At the senior public prosecutor's office the head is called the chief senior prosecutor (*Leitender Oberstaatsanwalt*). Some of these cantons made use of the possibility of introducing a "four-eyes principle" (*Vier-Augen-Prinzip*).[41] According to this principle, orders that proceedings will not be opened, directives discontinuing the proceedings, and suspensions of investigations are to be approved by a senior prosecutor or an attorney general.[42]

On the contrary, there are few cantons that renounced a hierarchically organized system. In these cantons, the power of action is given to a council of public prosecutors. Such a constellation is mostly found in small cantons where a hierarchic system does not seem necessary for good functioning of the public prosecutor's office.

The implementation law regulates the relationship between the senior public prosecutor's office or the attorney general's office and the lower-ranking public prosecutor's offices, defines the powers of the higher-ranking prosecutors and, more specifically, their leadership role and oversight function. For instance, the question whether instructions are permitted for lower-ranking prosecutors must be addressed. In other organizational models (e.g. single public prosecutor's office), the powers attributed in the various hierarchical levels also have to be defined by law. Thus, it is possible to declare directives discontinuing the proceedings and penal orders subject to the chief prosecutor's consent.[43]

In general, the tasks of the head of each hierarchical level are representing his office, supervising the other public prosecutors, and if necessary issuing directives.

[40] Article 14 para. 3 CCrP. The law text between the three official languages differs in the sense that in the German and Italian version the senior public prosecutor and the attorney general are mentioned as institutions (senior public prosecutor's office and attorney general's office), whereas in the French version the individual person is meant. The commentary in the German and French message of the Federal Council suggests that the law allows both possibilities. The cantonal implementation laws have to clarify if institutions or individual persons shall have the corresponding tasks and powers conferred by the CCrP (see Keller. In: Donatsch et al. (2010) Kommentar StPO, Art. 14, Margin No. 21).

[41] For instance, the cantons of AG (Section 35 EG-StPO AG), BE (Article 54 EG-StPO BE); FR (Article 67 para. 4 FR-Courts Act), LU (Section 66 subs. 2 LU-COA), NW (Article 52 NW-Law on Courts), OW (Article 44b OW-COA), UR (Article 39a UR-COA), ZG (Section 46 subs. 7 ZG-COA).

[42] Article 322 para. 1 CCrP.

[43] Keller. In: Donatsch et al. (2010) Kommentar StPO, Art. 14, Margin No. 24.

Usually, the directions given may not only be general but may also concern individual cases. Furthermore, the head provides for a homogenous exercise of substantive criminal and criminal procedure law.

6.1.2.2 Selection of Chief Public Prosecutors and Public Prosecutors

In Switzerland, there is a considerable diversity of variants for the election to respectively appointment as public prosecutor. Nomination of the senior public prosecutor, the attorney general and the chief respectively first public prosecutor occurs either by executive power, parliament, directly by citizenry, or by another authority.[44] In a high majority of cantons, the head of the public prosecutor's office is elected by the parliament. In some of these cantons, nomination by parliament is based on the suggestions submitted by the governing council.[45] With the exceptions of the cantons of Appenzell Inner Rhodes, Appenzell Outer Rhodes, Berne, Grisons, Nidwalden, and Zug, the head of service is elected for a period of 4, 5, or 6 years, with possible renewal upon expiration of the term. It can be assumed that a public prosecutor appointed by the cantonal government will be more subject to political pressure or influence than one who has the status of an independent judge and has been elected by the parliament.

Table 6.1 gives a simplified overview of the organization of the public prosecutor's office in the 26 cantons as well as the appointment methods of their heads of service.[46]

The eligibility for public prosecutor is determined by cantonal law. Generally, the occupation as public prosecutor requires a legal degree, an attorney's licence, and, with the exception of a few cantons, Swiss citizenship. In the exception, legal education may be replaced by equivalent knowledge gained through specialized training.[47] To be elected as head of a public prosecutor's office, working experience within the criminal justice system and leadership experience are essential. Before accession to office, public prosecutors swear an oath to fulfill their duties faithfully.

[44] Other authorities can be the Council of Public Prosecutors (canton of Jura), the cantonal Supreme Court (canton of Zug). In the canton of Berne, chief public prosecutors are elected by the Attorney General. In the canton of Geneva, first public prosecutors are elected by a Council composed of the Attorney General, the Vice-President of the Court of Justice, the President of the Criminal Court, and two public prosecutors elected by the plenary session of the Public Prosecutor's Office.

[45] In the cantons of Aargau (Section 4 subs. 2, Section 5 subs. 3, Section 6 subs 2 EG StPO AG); Basel-Land (Section 10 subs. 1 EG StPO BL); Lucerne for the senior public prosecutor (Section 57 subs. 2 LU-COA); Uri for the senior public prosecutor (Article 38 UR-COA).

[46] A comparison is complicated by the fact that in some cantons the senior public prosecutor is really a chief public prosecutor (i.e. OW). In the following table, the official designation is considered.

[47] For instance in the cantons of Basel-Land (Section 11 subs. 2 EG-StPO BL), Grisons (Article 9 para. 2 EG-StPO GR), and Zug (Section 67 lit. a ZG-COA).

Table 6.1 Simplified overview of the organization of the public prosecutor's office and appointment methods of public prosecutors in the 26 cantons

	Organization				Appointment method: elected/engaged/appointed by			
Canton	Single entity[a]	Hierarchical[b]	AG[c]	SPP[d]	Parliament	Governing council	Other	Term (years)
AG		x		x	SPP CPP			4
AI	x	–[e]				PP		*Indefinite*
AR	x	x				CPP		*Appointed*
BE		x	x		AG		CPP	AG: 6 CPP: *Appointed*[f]
BL		x			FPP			4
BS	x	x			FPP			6
FR	x		x		AG/PP			5
GE	x	x	x[g]		AG		FPP	AG: 6 FPP: 3
GL	x	x			FPP			4
GR		x				FPP		*Appointed*
JU	x		x[g]		PP		AG	AG: 1 PP: 5
LU		x		x	SPP/CPP			4
NE			x[g]		AG/PP			4
NW	x	x		x[g]	SPP/PP			*Appointed*[h]
OW	x	x		x[g]	SPP/PP			4
SG		x				FPP/CPP		4
SH	x	x			FPP/CPP	CPP[i]		4
SO	x	x		x[g]	SPP/CPP	CPP[i]		4
SZ		x		x	SPP	CPP		4
TG		x	x	x[g]	AG	SPP		4
TI	x	x	x		AG/PP			4
UR	x	x		x[g]	SPP			4
VD		x	x		AG	CPP[j]		5

VS		x	x	x	AG/SPP			4
ZG	x	x		x[g]			SPP/CPP	*Appointed*
ZH		x		x		SPP/CPP[k]		*Appointed*

AG attorney general, *SPP* senior public prosecutor, *CPP* chief public prosecutor, *FPP* first public prosecutor, *PP* public prosecutor

[a]The senior public prosecutor's office or the attorney general's office is not taken into account. Only the structure of the "lower" public prosecutor's office is considered. Within a single entity, the existence of different departments is possible. Public prosecutor's offices with branch offices within the canton are not considered a single entity

[b]The organization within the public prosecutor's office can be hierarchical or public prosecutors can appear as a collegiate body

[c]Attorney general respectively attorney general's office

[d]Senior public prosecutor respectively senior public prosecutor's office

[e]One public prosecutor with two investigation officers

[f]Appointed by the attorney generals' office

[g]Attorney general or senior public prosecutor

[h]Appointed by governing council

[i]Chief public prosecutors are designated by the governing council among the public prosecutors who are all elected by the parliament

[j]Nomination is based on the suggestion of the attorney general

[k]Chief public prosecutors are designated by the governing council among the public prosecutors who are all elected by citizens

6.1.2.3 Training of Chief Public Prosecutors and Public Prosecutors

Although training is an important aspect to the practice of public prosecutors, after hiring, public prosecutors have no further training requirements.[48] However, public prosecutors have the option to attend continuing education courses, which are proposed by various institutions. Participation in these courses occurs on a voluntary basis. But, since public prosecutor's offices are more and more divided into various specialized departments (i.e. economic crimes, juvenile crime, drug and traffic crimes), attendance of such continuing education courses is highly recommended.[49] Especially younger prosecutors may be encouraged to seek additional training. Certainly this will have an influence on a prosecutor's chance of promotion.

In general, prosecutors are expected to keep up with important legal changes. For this reason, the public prosecutor's head of service—the senior public prosecutor or the chief public prosecutor—invites periodic or at least annual discussion of recent case law and legal changes.[50] In this context, in 2010, cantonal public prosecutor's offices conducted training programs on the new Swiss CCrP.[51]

However, as already stated above, the lack of mandatory continuing legal education may be considered a weakness in the system. In this sense, in line with Recommendation Rec (2000) 19 of the Council of Europe, training should be a duty and a right for prosecutors not only before but also after their appointment.

6.2 Relationship Between the Prosecution Service and the Police

6.2.1 Independently of Each Other

In Switzerland, the police are divided into the Federal Office of Police (*Bundesamt für Polizei*; fedpol), the cantonal police agencies, and numerous municipal and communal police agencies. Hence, police organization reflects Switzerland's federalistic structure. Each canton is in charge of its own police force and has its own police code.

---

[48] Council of Europe (2012), p. 255.

[49] The canton of Nidwalden, for instance, actively encourages the attendance of continuing education courses (see Section 23 of the Regulation of the Public Prosecutor's Office of December 23, 2010; *Reglement über die Staatsanwaltschaft vom 23. Dezember 2010*).

[50] See for instance, the cantons of Nidwalden (Sections 25 et seq. Regulation of the Public Prosecutor's Office of December 23, 2010), Berne (Article 20 of the Organization Regulation of the Public Prosecutor's Office of October 15, 2010; *Organisationsreglement der Staatsanwaltschaft vom 15. Oktober 2010*).

[51] See the annual reports of each cantonal Public Prosecutor's Office.

Police forces, like prosecution services, belong to the executive branch.[52] In the majority of cantons, both authorities are subordinate to the Ministers of Justice,[53] while in others, police agencies are under the Ministers of the Interior and thus are administratively separate.[54] The Federal Office of Police is incorporated in the Federal Department of Justice and Police.

The main tasks of the Federal Office of Police[55] are to conduct criminal investigations that fall under federal jurisdiction,[56] to perform security duties, and to fulfill administrative functions. In addition, the Federal Office of Police provides support to its national and international partners in fulfilling their police tasks. The Federal Office of Police employs approximately 870 staff members.[57]

Similar to the Federal Office of Police, the other police agencies are responsible for investigating criminal offenses and for maintaining order and security in public places. Whereas police agencies at all levels are independent in fulfilling security duties (*Sicherheitspolizei*), they are functionally subordinate to the public prosecution services when it comes to criminal investigations (*Gerichtspolizei*).[58] In this sense, criminal investigations are carried out by the Federal Office of Police on behalf of the Office of the Attorney General.

When the police act as judicial police and hence fulfill repression tasks, they are bound by the regulations of the CCrP (Article 306 para. 3 CCrP). Conversely, police are bound by police legislation when it comes to prevention work (guarantee public peace and order).[59] However, a clear delimitation of both tasks may sometimes be difficult.[60] For instance, police controls at sport events and at demonstrations are preventively imposed for public safety but also repressively for the detection of committed criminal offenses.[61] Where both activities overlap, these

[52] With the exception of the cantons of Geneva, Jura, Neuchâtel, Nidwalden, Thurgau, Ticino, and Zug where the public prosecution service is incorporated in the judicial branch.

[53] See the cantons of Appenzell Inner Rhodes, Appenzell Outer Rhodes, Basel-Land, Basel-City Glarus, Lucerne, Obwalden, St. Gallen, Schwyz.

[54] See the canton of Solothurn. In the cantons of Zurich and Uri, the police are under the Minister of Security, while the public prosecutor's office is under the Minister of Justice.

[55] For more information about Federal Office of Police, see Federal Office of Police (fedpol) (2011).

[56] Articles 23 and 24 CCrP.

[57] http://www.fedpol.admin.ch/fedpol/en/home/fedpol.html (accessed June 26, 2012).

[58] On both duties of the police, see Albertini. In: Albertini et al. (2008) VSKC-Polizeiliche Ermittlung, pp. 11–13. See also Keller. In: Donatsch et al. (2010) Kommentar StPO, Art. 15, Margin Nos. 3–4.

[59] Albertini. In: Albertini et al. (2008) VSKC-Polizeiliche Ermittlung, pp. 11 and 13; Keller. In: Donatsch et al. (2010) Kommentar StPO, Art. 15, Margin No. 6; Landshut. In: Donatsch et al. (2010) Kommentar StPO, Art. 306, Margin Nos. 1–2; Rhyner. In: Niggli et al. (2011) BSK StPO, Art. 306, Margin No. 5.

[60] Keller. In: Donatsch et al. (2010) Kommentar StPO, Art. 15, Margin No. 4; Uster. In: Niggli et al. (2011) BSK StPO, Art. 15, Margin No. 2; Rhyner. In: Niggli et al. (2011) BSK StPO, Art. 306, Margin No. 6; Albertini and Rüegger (2010), p. 363; Blättler (2007), p. 243; Del Giudice (2010), pp. 121–122.

[61] Del Giudice (2010), p. 121.

may be overseen by a public prosecutor if the aspect of crime investigation is more pronounced.[62]

Depending on the field of action and activity, the police are either subordinate to the executive branch (i.e. the government) or the criminal authorities and hence, may receive instructions from the respective superior. In other words, the police are servants to many masters.[63]

6.2.2 *Subordination of the Police*

As just described, the police are subordinate to the public prosecution services in matters of investigation (Article 15 para. 2 CCrP) and hence, the federal, cantonal, and community police comply with the Code of Criminal Procedure (Article 15 para. 1 CCrP).

6.2.2.1 Cooperation of Police and Prosecution

Preliminary investigations[64] start on the basis of reports by a person (Article 301 CCrP) or an authority (Article 302 CCrP) that a criminal offense has been committed, the assignment of the public prosecution (Article 307 para. 2 CCrP), or the police's own findings (Article 306 para. 1 CCrP). In three out of four cases, preliminary investigations are initiated on the basis of a private complaint.[65]

The CCrP entrusts the police with the authority to conduct an independent preliminary investigations in criminal matters. In this sense, preliminary investigations by the police are not restricted to classical duties such as taking all necessary action immediately following the discovery of an offense (i.e. secure traces). Rather, the police have the right to independently investigate criminal offenses without assignment of the public prosecutor.[66]

---

[62] Keller. In: Donatsch et al. (2010) Kommentar StPO, Art. 15, Margin No. 4; Rhyner. In: Niggli et al. (2011) BSK StPO, Art. 306, Margin No. 7.

[63] Blättler (2007), p. 243.

[64] The preliminary proceedings comprise the inquiries conducted by the police and the investigation carried out by the prosecution (Article 299 para. 1 CCrP). The purpose of the preliminary proceedings—based on the suspicion that an offense has been committed—is to collect evidence in order to establish whether a summary penalty is to be issued in respect to an accused person, a criminal charge should be brought against an accused, the proceedings should be discontinued (Article 299 para. 2 CCrP).

[65] Del Giudice (2010), p. 121. See also Rhyner. In: Niggli et al. (2011) BSK StPO, Art. 306, Margin No. 24.

[66] Del Giudice (2010), p. 118; Keller. In: Donatsch et al. (2010) Kommentar StPO, Art. 15, Margin No. 9; Rhyner. In: Niggli et al. (2011) BSK StPO, Art. 306, Margin Nos. 12–13; Schmid (2009b), Art. 306, Margin No. 1; Schmid (2009a), Margin Nos. 343 and 1218.

With respect to the principle of mandatory prosecution (Article 7 CCrP) that not only binds the public prosecutor but all criminal justice authorities, the police are required to investigate whether they have sufficient grounds to suspect that a criminal offense has been committed. Hence, in theory, the police have no discretionary powers or principle of opportunity in the decision of whether or not to investigate. Rather, according to Article 8 para. 1 CCrP, the decision not to prosecute is reserved for the prosecution and the courts.[67] However, Article 307 para. 4 CCrP allows the police not to make a report to the prosecution if there is obviously no reason for the prosecution to take further procedural steps, for instance due to unknown identity of the offender[68] or missing procedural requirements.[69] Furthermore, the police may refrain from making a report if no coercive measures or other formal investigative activities have been imposed or carried out.[70] As a consequence, in reality, the police have broad discretionary powers to independently decide to refrain from investigation.[71] The fact that the police do not make a report to the prosecution according to Article 307 para. 4 CCrP is to be placed on record.[72]

The investigation proceedings initiated by the police are regulated in Articles 306 and 307 CCrP. The function of the police in preliminary investigations consists of investigation and search. In particular, the police shall secure and evaluate traces and evidence, identify and question aggrieved parties and those suspected of being involved in a criminal offense, and stop or arrest those suspected of being involved in a criminal offense or conduct a search of them (Article 306 para. 2 CCrP). Article 307 CCrP aims to involve the public prosecutor at an early stage in the proceeding so that he can take over control of the criminal procedure.[73] Hence, the police have to report all incidents to the prosecution. This has to occur without delay in case of serious criminal offenses and in other serious matters (Article 307 para. 1 CCrP). In this sense, an information obligation exists in particular for homicides, rapes, hostage takings, serious offenses against property such as robberies, serious traffic accidents, and in the event of accidents with serious bodily injuries.[74] This list is not

---

[67] Keller. In: Donatsch et al. (2010) Kommentar StPO, Art. 15, Margin No. 10.

[68] In Albertini's opinion, a report has still to be made on the numerous cases in which the identity of the offender is unknown (Albertini. In: Albertini et al. (2008) VSKC-Polizeiliche Ermittlung, p. 565).

[69] Landshut. In: Donatsch et al. (2010) Kommentar StPO, Art. 307, Margin Nos. 40–45; Maître. In: Kuhn and Jeanneret (2011) Commentaire Romand CPP, Art. 307, Margin No. 17.

[70] Albertini. In: Albertini et al. (2008) VSKC-Polizeiliche Ermittlung, p. 563; Landshut. In: Donatsch et al. (2010) Kommentar StPO, Art. 307, Margin Nos. 46–49.

[71] Keller. In: Donatsch et al. (2010) Kommentar StPO, Art. 15, Margin No. 10. Pieth criticizes this rule, since the public prosecutor has always to be involved in some form or other (Article 2 para. 2 CCrP). Hence, it is somewhat problematic to completely exclude the prosecution from informal preliminary investigations (Pieth 2009, p. 171).

[72] Schmid (2009b), Art. 307, Margin No. 8.

[73] Albertini. In: Albertini et al. (2008) VSKC-Polizeiliche Ermittlung, pp. 14 and 557.

[74] For a list of serious criminal offenses and other serious matters, see Albertini. In: Albertini et al. (2008) VSKC-Polizeiliche Ermittlung, pp. 557–558; Uster (2010), pp. 355–356.

conclusive. Rather, it is a matter of discretion to determine which serious criminal offenses fall within the information obligation.[75] According to Article 307 para. 1 CCrP, some cantons have issued directives in respect to the duty to provide information. In general, it is a list defining precisely which offenses have to be considered serious.[76] In addition, an immediate orientation of the prosecution has to occur in case of police arrests (Article 219 para. 1 CCrP), searches, and investigations (Article 241 para. 3 CCrP).[77]

In addition to those cases where the police have the duty to inform the prosecutor without delay, there may be cases where the prosecutor wants to have knowledge about them at an early stage in the criminal proceedings because it can be expected that the prosecutor will issue instructions and assignments or will even decide to take control of the proceedings themselves (Article 307 para. 2 CCrP).[78] Various cantons have developed case categories. Such case categories include: criminal proceedings concerning rapes or indecent assaults; criminal proceedings concerning sexual offenses with children, with the exception of cases of minor importance; criminal proceedings against doctors, attorneys, and priests, with the exception of violations of the road traffic act; incidents or criminal offenses with suspicion of a serial offender; suspicion of an attempted criminal offense that falls within information obligation according to Article 307 para. 1 CCrP.[79]

In all other cases where there is no duty to inform the prosecutor, police reporting shall occur upon conclusion of their inquiries.[80] Then the police report together with the report that a criminal offense has been committed, written record of the proceedings, and any other files and items and assets which have been secured, are passed promptly to the prosecution (Article 307 para. 3 CCrP).[81]

It must be kept in mind that, in presence of a concrete suspicion that a crime has been committed, there is no longer room for a preliminary investigation by police. In such cases, according to Article 309 para. 1 lit. 1 CCrP, the prosecution shall

---

[75] Maître. In: Kuhn and Jeanneret (2011) Commentaire Romand CPP, Art. 307, Margin Nos. 6–7; Landshut. In: Donatsch et al. (2010) Kommentar StPO, Art. 307, Margin No. 7.

[76] Uster (2010), p. 355.

[77] Landshut. In: Donatsch et al. (2010) Kommentar StPO, Art. 307, Margin No. 10.

[78] Uster (2010), p. 355.

[79] Uster (2010), p. 355.

[80] It is a matter of debate whether police reports have to be passed after the first inquiries or after their conclusions. The message considers that this has to occur as fast as possible so that the prosecution takes over responsibility for the investigations as early as possible (Landshut. In: Donatsch et al. (2010) Kommentar StPO, Art. 307, Margin No. 18; Maître. In: Kuhn and Jeanneret (2011) Commentaire Romand CPP, Art. 307, Margin No. 13; Federal Council 2006, p. 1262). Albertini rejects an immediate transfer of the files after the first inquiries with the reason that this would hinder a rapid and uniform inquiry (see Albertini. In: Albertini et al. (2008) VSKC-Polizeiliche Ermittlung, p. 558).

[81] On the content of the police report, see Landshut. In: Donatsch et al. (2010) Kommentar StPO, Art. 307, Margin Nos. 33–35; Maître. In: Kuhn and Jeanneret (2011) Commentaire Romand CPP, Art. 307, Margin No. 12.

open an investigation.[82] After the investigation proceedings have been opened, the prosecution may also instruct the police to undertake further inquiries (Article 312 CCrP).

In sum, the great majority of preliminary investigations are conducted completely by the police.[83] The prosecution is then informed by police reports upon conclusion of their preliminary investigations (Article 307 para. 3 CCrP). The public prosecutor's office is only involved from the very beginning in cases of serious criminal offenses and in other serious matters, for instance in homicide and robbery cases. In other matters, the police contact the public prosecutor when coercive measures are required that don't fall within police responsibilities.[84]

6.2.2.2 Supervision and Instructions of the Prosecution

The police are subject to "the supervision and instructions of the prosecution" (Article 15 para. 2 CCrP). According to Article 307 para. 2 CCrP, "the prosecution may at any time issue the police with instructions and assignments or take control of the proceedings itself." Ordinarily, instructions relate to a single case and may contain directives on how the investigations have to be conducted and how the reporting has to occur. The right to issue instructions finds its limits in organizational questions.[85] This means that the prosecution determines the objectives of the investigation and the assignments. However, the way in which these directives are executed is a police duty. Hence, questions related to organization, operational tactics, and prioritization are a matter for the police.[86] An exception to this rule is made in the canton of Basel-City where—in contrast to the other cantons where the criminal police (*Kriminalpolizei*) are a division of the cantonal police—the criminal police are part of the public prosecution service and are called "*Kriminalpolizei der Staatsanwaltschaft*".[87] The supervision of the police by the prosecution does not imply an organizational integration of the police in the prosecution service.[88]

The prosecution is only able to issue instructions and assignments if it is informed by the police about their pending criminal proceedings. Hence, the right of supervision of the public prosecutor implies the right to obtain information. However, this cannot mean that the police have to inform the prosecution about

---

[82] Landshut. In: Donatsch et al. (2010) Kommentar StPO, Art. 307, Margin No. 19.

[83] Rhyner. In: Niggli et al. (2011) BSK StPO, Art. 306, Margin No. 16.

[84] See also Pieth (2009), p. 171.

[85] Landshut. In: Donatsch et al. (2010) Kommentar StPO, Art. 307, Margin No. 21.

[86] Albertini. In: Albertini et al. (2008) VSKC-Polizeiliche Ermittlung, pp. 43–44; Landshut. In: Donatsch et al. (2010) Kommentar StPO, Art. 307, Margin No. 26; Rhyner. In: Niggli et al. (2011) BSK StPO, Art. 306, Margin No. 29; Schmid (2009b), Art. 15, Margin No. 10.

[87] Kamber (2011), Margin No. 2.

[88] Albertini. In: Albertini et al. (2008) VSKC-Polizeiliche Ermittlung, pp. 37 and 43; Keller. In: Donatsch et al. (2010) Kommentar StPO, Art. 15, Margin No. 22; Uster. In: Niggli et al. (2011) BSK StPO, Art. 15, Margin No. 10; Schmid (2009b), Art. 15, Margin No. 10.

every single case they handle. This would generate an extremely large number of reports the prosecutor's office would have to treat.[89] Instead, the police have the obligation to report without delay cases of serious criminal offenses and other serious matters to the prosecution.[90] In these cases, the leadership responsibilities of the prosecution are connected to the duty to carry out the first important examination hearings themselves (Article 307 para. 1 CCrP). Furthermore, the police have to inform the public prosecutor about those cases where it is likely that the prosecutor will issue instructions and assignments or will even decide to take control of the proceedings themselves.[91] At the least, the police have to immediately inform the prosecution of pending criminal proceedings or grant access to the inquiry files if the prosecution asks for them.[92]

The question of whether the prosecution can instruct the police in a single case not to report an incident for opportunity reasons is extremely delicate. There is no single answer to this question. However, in principle, the prosecutor should exercise restraint when using the (de facto) opportunity principle, since its use is not subject to judicial review.[93]

If the prosecution takes control of the proceeding itself, the stage of preliminary investigations by the police is closed and the criminal procedure moves to the next step: the prosecution opens an investigation (Article 309 CCrP). In the investigation, the prosecution has to clarify the factual and legal aspects of the case so that it may conclude the preliminary proceedings (Article 308 para. 1 CCrP).

6.3 Discretion in the Swiss Criminal Justice System?

6.3.1 Rule: Principle of Legality

The Swiss criminal justice system basically adheres to the principle of legality and thus, the prosecutor is required by law to prosecute whenever there is enough evidence to believe that a criminal offense has been committed.[94] In contrast to prosecution systems adhering to the principle of opportunity, the prosecutor cannot exercise any discretion in deciding whether or not to prosecute. While the court may acquit someone of a charge in case of doubt (*in dubio pro reo*), the prosecutor may not.[95]

---

[89] Uster (2010), p. 355; Landshut. In: Donatsch et al. (2010) Kommentar StPO, Art. 307, Margin No. 13.

[90] See Sect. 6.2.2.1, para 4.

[91] See 6.2.2.1, para 5.

[92] Landshut. In: Donatsch et al. (2010) Kommentar StPO, Art. 307, Margin No. 21; Schmid (2009a), Margin No. 346.

[93] Albertini and Rüegger (2010), p. 364.

[94] On the principle of legality, see Sect. 3.2.2.2.

[95] Pieth (2009), p. 175.

6.3.2 Introduction of a Moderate Principle of Opportunity

As mentioned above, the Swiss criminal justice system basically adheres to the principle of legality (Article 7 CCrP) and thus, the prosecutor is required to prosecute whenever there is enough evidence to believe that a criminal offense has been committed. This rule seeks to ensure the equal application of the criminal law. However, a strict adherence to this principle may be problematic. Nowadays, it is commonly assumed that important government interests may, under certain circumstances, justify an abandonment of prosecution. Especially the overloaded criminal justice systems and the principle of proportionality have recently led to a restriction of the principle of legality. Indeed, with regard to the defendant and procedural efforts, a compulsory prosecution may be disproportional in some cases.[96] Prior to the introduction of the CCrP it was a matter for the cantonal procedural laws to determine whether they adhered to the principle of legality, the principle of opportunity, or a moderate principle of opportunity. According to the latter, the prosecutor may refrain from prosecution only under certain conditions defined by law.[97] Hence, the authorities' discretionary powers are ordinarily subject to tight limits.[98] Whereas a large majority of cantons had introduced a moderate principle of opportunity, a minority recognized either an unrestricted principle of opportunity[99] or followed the legality principle.[100]

The CCrP has decided to follow the rule in place in the majority of cantons and hence has introduced a moderate principle of opportunity on a nationwide basis.[101]

6.3.3 Conditions for the Application of the Moderate Principle of Opportunity and Its Legal Consequences: Article 8 CCrP

Art. 8 CCrP defines under which conditions the prosecutor refrains from prosecution.

---

[96] Hauser et al. (2005), Section 48, Margin No. 2; Wohlers. In: Donatsch et al. (2010) Kommentar StPO, Art. 8, Margin No. 1; Schmid (2009a), Margin No. 182; Federal Council (2006), p. 1131.

[97] Wohlers. In: Donatsch et al. (2010) Kommentar StPO, Art. 8, Margin No. 2.

[98] Fiolka and Riedo. In: Niggli et al. (2011) BSK StPO, Art. 8, Margin No. 3.

[99] Vaud, Neuchâtel, Geneva, Jura.

[100] Glarus, Appenzell Inner Rhodes, Grisons, Valais. See Hauser et al. (2005), Section 48, Margin No. 10; Schmid (2009a), Margin Nos. 183–186.

[101] Fiolka and Riedo. In: Niggli et al. (2011) BSK StPO, Art. 8, Margin No. 3; Wohlers. In: Donatsch et al. (2010) Kommentar StPO, Art. 8, Margin No. 3; Pieth (2009), p. 38; Riedo et al. (2010), Margin No. 172.

According to Article 8 para. 1 CCrP, the prosecution and courts[102] should refrain from conducting a prosecution if the federal law so provides,[103] namely in accordance with the conditions set out in Articles 52–54 of the SCC.[104] These rules require the prosecutor to make the decision not to prosecute if the level of culpability and consequences of the offense are negligible,[105] or if the offender has made reparation for the loss, damage, or injury, or made every reasonable effort to right the wrong that he has caused,[106] or if the accused is so stricken by the immediate consequences of the offense that an additional penalty would be inadequate.[107]

The possibility to refrain from prosecution according to Article 52 et seq. SCC has the primary purpose of maintaining the proportionality and hence to avoid the imposition of a sentence that under certain circumstances would appear disproportionate.[108]

Article 8 para. 2 CCrP provides for three situations in which the public prosecutor and the courts are required to waive prosecution, namely if the criminal offense is, in light of the other criminal offenses with which the accused is charged, of negligible importance to the determination of the sentence or measure,[109] or if an additional sentence that is likely to be of little consequence would be imposed in combination with a pre-existing sentence,[110] or if an equivalent sentence imposed by a foreign court would have to be taken into account when imposing a sentence for the offense being prosecuted.[111]

---

[102] The police are not allowed to refrain from prosecution according to Article 8 CCrP (Wohlers. In: Donatsch et al. (2010) Kommentar StPO, Art. 8, Margin No. 6).

[103] For an overview on federal provisions that allow the prosecutor to refrain from prosecution, see Fiolka and Riedo. In: Niggli et al. (2011) BSK StPO, Art. 8, Margin Nos. 9–24.

[104] The peculiarity of these provisions containing the principle of opportunity is that they are regulated in the substantive criminal law (Riklin. In: Niggli and Wiprächtiger (2007) BSK StGB I, Vor Art. 52 et seq. Margin Nos. 15–16). For a detailed discussion of these articles, see Killias and Kurth. In: Roth and Moreillon (2009) Commentaire Romand CP I, Arts. 52–54; Riklin. In: Niggli and Wiprächtiger (2007) BSK StGB I, Arts. 52–54.

[105] Fiolka and Riedo. In: Niggli et al. (2011) BSK StPO, Art. 8, Margin Nos. 27–32; Wohlers. In: Donatsch et al. (2010) Kommentar StPO, Art. 8, Margin Nos. 12–14; Pieth (2009), p. 38; Riedo et al. (2010), Margin Nos. 173–178.

[106] Fiolka and Riedo. In: Niggli et al. (2011) BSK StPO, Art. 8, Margin Nos. 33–43; Wohlers. In: Donatsch et al. (2010) Kommentar StPO, Art. 8, Margin Nos. 15–17; Pieth (2009), p. 38; Riedo et al. (2010), Margin Nos. 179–183.

[107] Fiolka and Riedo. In: Niggli et al. (2011) BSK StPO, Art. 8, Margin Nos. 44–56; Wohlers. In: Donatsch et al. (2010) Kommentar StPO, Art. 8, Margin No. 18.

[108] Fiolka and Riedo. In: Niggli et al. (2011) BSK StPO, Art. 8, Margin No. 8.

[109] Fiolka and Riedo. In: Niggli et al. (2011) BSK StPO, Art. 8, Margin Nos. 65–71; Wohlers. In: Donatsch et al. (2010) Kommentar StPO, Art. 8, Margin No. 21; Riedo et al. (2010), Margin Nos. 188–191; Schmid (2009a), Margin No. 192.

[110] Fiolka and Riedo. In: Niggli et al. (2011) BSK StPO, Art. 8, Margin Nos. 72–74; Wohlers. In: Donatsch et al. (2010) Kommentar StPO, Art. 8, Margin No. 22; Riedo et al. (2010), Margin Nos. 192–193; Schmid (2009a), Margin No. 193.

[111] Fiolka and Riedo. In: Niggli et al. (2011) BSK StPO, Art. 8, Margin Nos. 75–91; Wohlers. In: Donatsch et al. (2010) Kommentar StPO, Art. 8, Margin No. 23; Riedo et al. (2010), Margin Nos. 194–198, Schmid (2009a), Margin No. 194.

In all three scenarios, the prosecution can only refrain from conducting prosecution, unless this does not conflict with overriding interests of the private claimant. In particular, the interest of the private claimant regarding the treatment of his civil claims is to be taken into account. Hence, the prosecutor cannot decide to waive prosecution if the aggrieved party decides to file civil claims.[112]

All three cases in para. 2 CCrP have in common that the accused has already been or is already involved in a criminal investigation and thus, the public interest in prosecution is reduced.[113] The restriction of the principle of legality occurs for reasons of economy of procedure.[114]

Finally, according to Article 8 para. 3 CCrP, the prosecution and the courts may waive prosecution if the criminal offense is already being prosecuted by a foreign authority or if the prosecution was relinquished in favor of such an authority. Such a decision can only be made if it does not conflict with the private claimant's overriding interests.

This provision should be applied restrictively, since it is often difficult to make an accurate and reliable forecast about the outcome of a foreign criminal procedure. Thus, in case, there are some doubts regarding the efficiency of the foreign authorities, the Swiss criminal procedure should be continued.[115]

Article 8 para. 3 CCrP has the aim to avoid unnecessary duplication of procedures. In addition, it helps to improve the coordination of all processes. Hence, this provision has been introduced for reasons of economy of procedure.[116]

When the requirements according to Article 8 paras 1 and 2 CCrP are fulfilled, the prosecution must drop the case and is therefore not allowed to exercise any discretion in deciding whether or not to prosecute.[117] However, criminal authorities will issue an order that proceedings are not to be opened or that a current prosecution is to be discontinued (Article 8 para. 4 CCrP) only if they consider the conditions as fulfilled, whereby in this respect a considerable margin of discretion remains.[118] On the other hand, Article 8 para. 3 CCrP is a provision allowing the prosecution to exercise full discretion.[119] However, the prosecutor is bound by the constitutional right to equality [Article 8 of the Swiss Federal Constitution; see also Article 3 para. 2 (c) CCrP].[120]

---

[112] Schmid (2009a), Margin No. 190.

[113] Federal Council (2006), p. 1131.

[114] Fiolka and Riedo. In: Niggli et al. (2011) BSK StPO, Art. 8, Margin No. 61; Wohlers. In: Donatsch et al. (2010) Kommentar StPO, Art. 8, Margin No. 19.

[115] Fiolka and Riedo. In: Niggli et al. (2011) BSK StPO, Art. 8, Margin No. 96; Riedo et al. (2010), Margin No. 203.

[116] Fiolka and Riedo. In: Niggli et al. (2011) BSK StPO, Art. 8, Margin No. 93.

[117] Fiolka and Riedo. In: Niggli et al. (2011) BSK StPO, Art. 8, Margin Nos. 26 and 64; Wohlers. In: Donatsch et al. (2010) Kommentar StPO, Art. 8, Margin No. 4; Riedo et al. (2010), Margin No. 206; Schmid (2009a), Margin No. 189.

[118] Fiolka and Riedo. In: Niggli et al. (2011) BSK StPO, Art. 8, Margin No. 26; Wohlers. In: Donatsch et al. (2010) Kommentar StPO, Art. 8, Margin No. 4.

[119] Fiolka and Riedo. In: Niggli et al. (2011) BSK StPO, Art. 8, Margin No. 95.

[120] Wohlers. In: Donatsch et al. (2010) Kommentar StPO, Art. 8, Margin No. 5.

The application of Article 8 CCrP does not result in a verdict of acquittal,[121] but in an order that proceedings are not to be opened (Article 310 CCrP) or that a current prosecution is to be discontinued (Article 319 et seq. CCrP). These orders must be substantiated and the parties, the victim, and other parties involved in the proceedings affected by the directive must be notified (Article 321 CCrP).[122] The parties may submit a complaint against both kinds of directives to the Complaints Authority within 10 days (see Article 322 para. 2 CCrP; Article 310 para. 2 CCrP; Article 393 et seq. CCrP).[123]

6.3.4 *Purpose of Article 8 CCrP and Its Application Frequency*

6.3.4.1 Preliminary Remark

The purpose of Article 8 CCrP is to reduce the heavy caseload in the criminal justice system by waiving prosecution at an early stage in the criminal procedure, namely as soon as the reasons for discontinuing a prosecution are fulfilled. Due to the provision's narrow scope of application, this cannot be used to set priorities in criminal prosecution. In the Swiss criminal system, the principle of opportunity is not used to overcome the large number of petty crimes (*Bagatellkriminalität*). This is the function of the penal order proceedings.[124]

Article 8 CCrP has been in force since January 1, 2011 and therefore has a young history. It is too early to draw clear conclusions on a nationwide basis. On the other hand, the legal provisions mentioned in Article 8 para. 1 CCrP have been in force since January 1, 2007 so that statements relating to Articles 52–54 SCC[125] can be made.

---

[121] Wohlers. In: Donatsch et al. (2010) Kommentar StPO, Art. 8, Margin No. 5; Schmid (2009b), Art. 8, Margin No. 13.

[122] Wohlers. In: Donatsch et al. (2010) Kommentar StPO, Art. 8, Margin No. 7.

[123] Fiolka and Riedo. In: Niggli et al. (2011) BSK StPO, Art. 8, Margin No. 101; Wohlers. In: Donatsch et al. (2010) Kommentar StPO, Art. 8, Margin Nos. 26–27; Schmid (2009b), Art. 8, Margin No. 17.

[124] Riklin. In: Niggli and Wiprächtiger (2007) BSK StGB I, Vor Art. 52 et seq., Margin No. 9; Fiolka and Riedo. In: Niggli et al. (2011) BSK StPO, Art. 8, Margin No. 4. On the penal order proceedings, see Sect. 6.5.1.

[125] Article 54 SCC incorporates the substance of the former Article 66bis SCC, in force since January 1, 1990.

6.3.4.2 No Need for a Penalty (Article 52 SCC)

6.3.4.2.1 Conditions for the Application of Article 52 SCC and Its Field of Application

The conditions for the application of Article 52 SCC are that the level of culpability as well as the consequences of the criminal offenses are negligible. The fact that both criteria must be fulfilled cumulatively, seriously restricts the scope of application for the provision.[126]

However, at first glance, the potential scope of the provision seems to be quite broad, since minor sentences are pronounced in the majority of judgments and since Article 52 SCC can be considered in very petty offenses, particularly when the offense is caused by negligent conduct. Nevertheless, this would be contrary to the intentions of the legislature who in some cases has consciously penalized petty offenses as well as their negligent commission, for instance offenses against the Road Traffic Act.[127] Thus, the negligibility of the culpability and the consequences of the criminal offense are measured in comparison to the ordinary case of the category the offense belongs to.[128] The culpability is assessed according to the seriousness of the damage or danger to the legal interest concerned, the reprehensibility of the conduct, the offender's motives and aims, and the extent to which the offender, in view of the personal and external circumstances, could have avoided causing the danger or damage (Article 47 para. 2 SCC). Opinions differ as to whether the provision should be applied only when there is no public interest.[129] If this criterion is considered, it must further be examined if, despite a minor fault of the defendant and minor consequences of the offense, a criminal prosecution is necessary for special or general preventive reasons.[130] The basis for discontinuing a prosecution according to Article 52 SCC is not the establishment of guilt, since this would be in conflict with the presumption of innocence,[131] but that the incriminating facts of the case are sufficiently clarified.[132] In regard to the culpability

[126] Riklin. In: Niggli and Wiprächtiger (2007) BSK StGB I, Art. 52, Margin No. 15.

[127] Riklin. In: Niggli and Wiprächtiger (2007) BSK StGB I, Art. 52, Margin No. 15.

[128] Riklin. In: Niggli and Wiprächtiger (2007) BSK StGB I, Art. 52, Margin No. 16; Wohlers. In: Donatsch et al. (2010) Kommentar StPO, Art. 8, Margin No. 12; Trechsel and Pauen Borer. In: Trechsel et al. (2008) Praxiskommentar StGB, Art. 52, Margin No. 2.

[129] Against considering a public interest, see Riklin. In: Niggli and Wiprächtiger (2007) BSK StGB I, Art. 52, Margin No. 17. In favor of considering a public interest, see Wohlers. In: Donatsch et al. (2010) Kommentar StPO, Art. 8, Margin No. 12; Stratenwerth (2006), Section 7, Margin No. 5; Stratenwerth and Wohlers (2009), Art. 52, Margin No. 1.

[130] Riklin. In: Niggli and Wiprächtiger (2007) BSK StGB I, Art. 52, Margin No. 17; Wohlers. In: Donatsch et al. (2010) Kommentar StPO, Art. 8, Margin No. 12.

[131] On the presumption of innocence, see Sect. 3.2.2.6.3, para 1.

[132] Riklin. In: Niggli and Wiprächtiger (2007) BSK StGB I, Vor Art. 52 et seq., Margin No. 31; Trechsel and Pauen Borer. In: Trechsel et al. (2008) Praxiskommentar StGB, Vor Art. 52, Margin No. 4.

mentioned in the provision, this means that, in that phase of the preliminary proceedings, a suspicion of guilt has to exist.[133]

In sum, petty offenses typically fall within the scope of Article 52 SCC.[134] In order to be applied, the criminal case must be negligible in comparison to criminal offenses falling in the same category.[135] In practice, it may be difficult to differentiate ordinary petty offenses from particularly minor offenses.[136]

6.3.4.2.2 Application Frequency

Statistical data informing on the frequency of application are not available. However, different inquiries show that, in practice, Article 52 SCC is only rarely applied. Furthermore, guidelines are usually nonexistent.[137]

6.3.4.3 Reparation (Article 53 SCC)

6.3.4.3.1 Purpose

Reparation is a form of compensatory or corrective justice. It aims to repair the harm caused by wrong, crime, and violence. Thus, "reparation is the act of making amends for a wrong."[138] The consequences of a criminal act do not only leave traces on victims, but also on the perpetrators. This alternative has the advantage of satisfying both the victim and the offender. Offenders avoid punishment and thus, this may help to prevent recidivism. Victims, on the other hand, often prefer to receive compensation rather than seeing the offender punished. In fact, the need for punishment regularly diminishes, once the offender has compensated the victim for the damage suffered.[139] This is especially true for victims of property crimes.[140] In contrast, compensation is not the primary interest for victims of offenses against the person. The latter want to see the offender punished or prevented from injuring other persons.[141]

---

[133] Riklin. In: Niggli and Wiprächtiger (2007) BSK StGB I, Vor Art. 52 et seq., Margin No. 31.

[134] According to Killias and Kurth, the scope of application of this provision may even include felonies as long as the gravity of the offense is negligible (Killias and Kurth. In: Roth and Moreillon (2009) Commentaire Romand CP I, Art. 52, Margin No. 3).

[135] Fiolka and Riedo. In: Niggli et al. (2011) BSK StPO, Art. 8, Margin No. 32.

[136] Riklin. In: Niggli and Wiprächtiger (2007) BSK StGB I, Art. 52, Margin No. 19.

[137] Riklin. In: Niggli and Wiprächtiger (2007) BSK StGB I, Art. 52, Margin No. 19; Schmid (2009b), Art. 8, Margin No. 4.

[138] Black's Law Dictionary, 8th ed., s.v. "reparation". See also Kanyar (2008), pp. 5–6.

[139] Brunner and Heimgartner (2011), p. 615; Riklin. In: Niggli and Wiprächtiger (2007) BSK StGB I, Art. 53, Margin No. 4.

[140] Killias (1990), p. 238; Killias et al. (2011), Margin Nos. 937–939a.

[141] Killias (1990), pp. 238–239.

6.3.4.3.2 Conditions for the Application of Article 53 SCC

Article 53 SCC provides that the prosecution or the courts have the duty to refrain from prosecution, bringing charges, or punishing if the offender has made reparation for the loss, damage, or injury or made every reasonable effort to right the wrong that he has caused and if the requirements for a suspended sentence (Article 42 SCC)[142] are fulfilled and the interests of the general public and of the persons harmed in prosecution are negligible.[143]

The most common type of reparation is the coverage of the damage by either restituting the lost assets or by making a compensation payment.[144] The alternative possibility to right the wrong by making every reasonable effort allows persons who are not financially in the position to make an indemnity payment to benefit from this provision. The amount of reasonable effort required to compensate the offense is at the discretion of the criminal authorities.[145] This alternative is also used for conduct causing non-material damages. In such cases, it is possible to pay a sum of money in satisfaction or to make reparation in form of gifts, work, or payments in favor of organisms of general interest.[146]

The use of Article 53 SCC does not depend on the approval of the aggrieved person, since he might deny his approval for unacceptable or irrational reasons.[147] Conflicting interests of the victim are only relevant when they are not negligible. Concerning offenses against individual interests, the interest of the general public tends to be estimated lower, while private interests are weighed higher. General and special preventive considerations are to be taken into account when deciding whether there is an overriding public interest in prosecution.[148] In regard to offenses against life and limb and against sexual integrity of some gravity there is usually an overriding public interest in prosecution, since high-level, legally protected interests are often affected.[149] The public prosecutor, in balancing the interests, has to act like a judge and is not allowed to use discretion. Such a task is not completely unfamiliar to the public prosecutor. In the penal order proceedings, he already combines the executive and judicial powers.[150] However, in the present case, such competence seems problematic. In fact, when the decision to refrain

[142] In respect to the gravity of the offense, this means that a custodial sentence of no more than 2 years may be pronounced and that there is a favorable legal prognosis.

[143] For a detailed discussion of the conditions, see Kanyar (2008), pp. 216–220; Riklin. In: Niggli and Wiprächtiger (2007) BSK StGB I, Art. 53, Margin Nos. 7–20.

[144] Riklin. In: Niggli and Wiprächtiger (2007) BSK StGB I, Art. 53, Margin No. 7.

[145] Riklin. In: Niggli and Wiprächtiger (2007) BSK StGB I, Art. 53, Margin No. 8; Stratenwerth (2006), Section 7, Margin No. 11.

[146] Riklin. In: Niggli and Wiprächtiger (2007) BSK StGB I, Art. 53, Margin No. 9.

[147] Killias (1990), p. 241.

[148] Riklin. In: Niggli and Wiprächtiger (2007) BSK StGB I, Art. 53, Margin No. 16; for more details, see Angst and Maurer (2008a); Angst and Maurer (2008b).

[149] Bommer (2008), p. 174; Brunner (2008), p. 65.

[150] On the penal order proceedings, see Sect. 6.5.1.

from prosecution is taken in accordance with the aggrieved person, a judicial review of the decision is not possible, and thus judicial supervision of the balancing of interests is missing. Insofar as internal guidelines do not restrict the use of Article 53 SCC,[151] the public prosecutor may use unrestrained discretion.[152]

Although the marginal note "reparation" implies an awareness of wrongdoing, it is not necessary that the offender confesses to the crime, but this should usually be the rule.[153] Indeed, according to the jurisdiction of the Supreme Court it is necessary that the offender recognizes the norm violation,[154] but the way in which this recognition has to be expressed is unclear.[155]

6.3.4.3.3 Proceedings

As soon as the requirements for refraining from prosecution are fulfilled, the prosecutor is obliged to invite the aggrieved person and the accused to a hearing with the aim of reaching an agreement with regard to restitution (Article 316 para. 2 CCrP). In order to avoid agreements that are not accepted by the justice, strong prosecutor involvement is important. In particular, if there is no individual victim, it should be the prosecutor's duty to make a proposal on the service the offender has to provide.[156] In contrast to the abridged proceedings, the CCrP does not contain formal rules concerning a perpetrator-victim-agreement or a judicial mediation conducted under professional direction (i.e. a mediator).[157] While the Swiss Federal Council's draft provided for mediation, this provision was deleted during the parliamentary debates on the controversial grounds that a mediation process would be too costly.[158] The proposition to leave the decision whether to implement a mediation procedure to the cantons has also been rejected.[159] Thus, mediation in adult criminal proceedings does not exist.[160] Nevertheless, the parties are free to

[151] See for example the Guidelines on the Preliminary Investigation for the public prosecutor in Zurich which provide for a restricted application of Article 53 SCC in mass delinquency [WOSTA, point 12.9.3 (2012)].

[152] Brunner and Heimgartner (2011), p. 618. See also Summers (2010), p. 21.

[153] Riklin. In: Niggli and Wiprächtiger (2007) BSK StGB I, Art. 53, Margin No. 18. See also WOSTA, point 12.9.3.

[154] BGE 135 IV 12, 21–22.

[155] Brunner and Heimgartner (2011), p. 617.

[156] Riklin. In: Niggli and Wiprächtiger (2007) BSK StGB I, Art. 53, Margin No. 22.

[157] For the results of a mediation pilot-project in the canton of Zurich, see Schwarzenegger et al. (2006). For a distinction between mediation and private settlement, see Riedo. In: Niggli et al. (2011) BSK StPO, Art. 316, Margin Nos. 6–7.

[158] AB 2007 N 1392; Riedo. In: Niggli et al. (2011) BSK StPO, Art. 316, Margin No. 3; Riedo et al. (2010), Margin Nos. 2358–2359.

[159] AB S 2006 1039 et seq., 2007 722 et seq., 825 et seq.; AB N 2007 995 et seq., 1391 et seq., 1576 et seq.

[160] Landshut. In: Donatsch et al. (2010) Kommentar StPO, Art. 316, Margin No. 2; Schmid (2009a), Margin No. 1240; Schmid (2009b), Art. 316, Margin No. 1; dissenting Pieth (2009), p. 173.

engage a mediator. The results of these negotiations may then be incorporated in the settlement negotiations according to Article 316 CCrP.[161]

6.3.4.3.4 Field of Application

The rule of reparation is mainly used for minor and less serious crimes, since petty offenses can be dealt with following Article 52 SCC. Furthermore, petty offenses are often only liable to prosecution if a complaint was filed. In the event that the criminal matter is resolved by mutual agreement (Article 316 para. 1 CCrP) and the complaint is withdrawn by the victim, there is no longer any need to apply Article 53 SCC. Article 53 SCC cannot be used in cases where the imposition of an unsuspended custodial sentence seems to be appropriate.[162] In constellations in which the imposition of a custodial sentence of up to 5 years appear to be appropriate and the need for a punishment is diminished based on a confession and the intention of making reparation, it is possible to reach a milder punishment by way of abridged proceedings (Article 358 et seq. CCrP). Hence, there are certain similarities between both provisions. Both follow the idea that offenders ready to make concessions should benefit from a reduced sentence. The main difference is that the abridged proceedings do not lead to impunity.[163]

6.3.4.3.5 Application Frequency

In practice, Article 53 SCC is only used with restraint (see Table 6.2). This is mainly due to some concerns that arose in connection with this provision. In the last years, virtually no other provision from the SCC has generated so much negative reaction in the media. Critics argue that this rule only benefits the rich who can buy themselves out of criminal proceedings and hence, this would create a two-class system.[164] Cases in which Article 53 SCC has been applied so far[165] demonstrate

[161] Landshut. In: Donatsch et al. (2010) Kommentar StPO, Art. 316, Margin No. 2; Schmid (2009a), Margin No. 1240; Schmid (2009b), Art. 316, Margin No. 1.

[162] Brunner and Heimgartner (2011), pp. 615–616.

[163] Brunner and Heimgartner (2011), p. 616.

[164] Brunner and Heimgartner (2011), pp. 613–614; Summers (2010), p. 3.

[165] The case "Roland Nef" is the most well-known case in which the use of Article 53 SCC has been criticized. In 2007, the public prosecution service of Zurich conducted criminal proceedings against the then army chief Roland Nef for coercion (Article 181 SCC), sexual harassment (Article 198 SCC), and pornography (Article 197 SCC). After having reached a mutual agreement, which contained an apology and a damage settlement, the public prosecutor, based on Article 53 SCC, decided to refrain from prosecuting all offenses, those prosecuted on complaint (sexual harassment), and also those prosecuted *ex officio* (coercion and pornography). The decision of the prosecutor is publicly available at http://www.weltwoche.ch/uploads/media/Einstellungs verfuegung.pdf (accessed June 26, 2012). Other cases are briefly described in Brunner and Heimgartner (2011), p. 620.

Table 6.2 Total number of proceedings discontinued and number of criminal proceedings discontinued according to Article 53 SCC in the canton of Zurich (2007–2010)

Year	Number of criminal proceedings discontinued on the basis of Article 53 SCC	Total number of criminal proceedings discontinued
2007	8[a]	9,210
2008	13	9,198
2009	13	9,064
2010	9	8,927

Source: Internal statistics of the Senior Public Prosecutor's Office of Zurich
[a]Six cases concerned property offenses where the damage was fully covered and where the victim manifested a lack of interest in prosecution. In two cases, proceedings concerning coercion (Article 181 SCC) were discontinued (Brunner 2008, p. 66)

that this provision was mainly reserved for wealthy persons. Thus, it is completely unrealistic to believe that Article 53 SCC has a chance to be used in mass delinquency perpetrated by poor people.[166] Furthermore, according to the guidelines of the Senior Public Prosecutor's Office of the canton of Zurich, Article 53 SCC should be used with restraint in "victimless" crimes and it should usually not be applied in mass delinquency. In the same canton, the senior public prosecutor's office has to be informed of the criminal proceedings that are discontinued on the basis of Article 53 SCC.[167]

The numbers given in the table do not fully reflect the actual situation, since it may be assumed that not all orders for discontinuation are reported to the senior public prosecutor's office. Thus, the numbers should be higher. It can be expected that approximately 20 criminal proceedings are ended in this way per year in the canton of Zurich.[168] Compared to the total number of criminal proceedings discontinued, proceedings are rather infrequently dropped on the basis of Article 53 SCC.

6.3.4.4 Effect of the Act on the Offender (Article 54 SCC)

6.3.4.4.1 Conditions for the Application of Article 54 SCC and Its Field of Application

According to Article 54 SCC, the prosecutor or the courts should refrain from prosecuting, bringing charges, or punishing if the offender is so seriously affected by the immediate consequences of his act that a penalty would be inadequate. Thus,

[166] Brunner and Heimgartner (2011), p. 621.

[167] WOSTA, point 12.9.3.

[168] Senior Public Prosecutor Dr. Andreas Brunner, e-mail message to author, January 23, 2012.

the purpose of Article 54 SCC is to avoid criminal prosecutions in cases in which a prosecution or punishment would be inappropriate.[169]

The use of Article 54 SCC is not restricted to offenses committed with negligence. It may also be applied in premeditated acts.[170] However, according to the prevailing opinion, in case of intention, it should be applied restrictively.[171]

Immediate consequences are only those consequences directly resulting from the offense in question. They can affect the perpetrator in a direct or indirect way.[172] Hence, consequences resulting from criminal proceedings (i.e. damage to the reputation, detriment to the career, or pretrial detention) cannot justify the use of Article 54 SCC.[173]

Perpetrators who have suffered bodily injury or impairment of health as a consequence of their act are typically affected. Other cases include the death of a close relative/friend or asset damage.[174]

The immediate consequences of the offense must be grave enough to justify a discontinuance of a criminal procedure according to Article 54 SCC. This is the case when the perpetrator has suffered enough from the consequences of his act.[175] A good example of this would be a burglar falling from the roof.

Whether a punishment is inadequate depends, on the one hand, on the degree the offender is affected by the criminal act and, on the other hand, on the culpability, respectively in the preliminary proceedings on the suspicion of guilt, since the establishment of guilt at this stage of the proceedings would be in conflict with the presumption of innocence.[176] In addition, general and special preventive aspects should also be considered.[177]

Article 54 SCC is typically applied in cases in which the offender has committed a minor offense that resulted in serious consequences. For example, if a minor

---

[169] Riklin. In: Niggli and Wiprächtiger (2007) BSK StGB I, Art. 54, Margin No. 6.

[170] Stratenwerth and Wohlers (2009), Art. 54, Margin No. 3.

[171] Riklin. In: Niggli and Wiprächtiger (2007) BSK StGB I, Art. 54, Margin Nos. 36–37; Trechsel and Pauen Borer. In: Trechsel et al. (2008) Praxiskommentar StGB, Art. 54, Margin No. 1.

[172] Fiolka and Riedo. In: Niggli et al. (2011) BSK StPO, Art. 8, Margin No. 47; Stratenwerth (2006), Section 7, Margin No. 19.

[173] Fiolka and Riedo. In: Niggli et al. (2011) BSK StPO, Art. 8, Margin No. 47; Trechsel and Pauen Borer. In: Trechsel et al. (2008) Praxiskommentar StGB, Art. 54, Margin No. 2; Stratenwerth and Wohlers (2009), Art. 54, Margin No. 4.

[174] Fiolka and Riedo. In: Niggli et al. (2011) BSK StPO, Art. 8, Margin No. 46; for a detailed discussion see Riklin. In: Niggli and Wiprächtiger (2007) BSK StGB I, Art. 54, Margin Nos. 12–32; Flückiger (2006), pp. 105–239.

[175] Fiolka and Riedo. In: Niggli et al. (2011) BSK StPO, Art. 8, Margin No. 49.

[176] Riklin. In: Niggli and Wiprächtiger (2007) BSK StGB I, Art. 54, Margin Nos. 34–35; Flückiger (2006), pp. 81–89.

[177] Riklin. In: Niggli and Wiprächtiger (2007) BSK StGB I, Art. 54, Margin No. 38; Flückiger (2006), pp. 83–86; Stratenwerth rejects the fact that general and special preventive aspects should be considered (Stratenwerth 2006, Section 7, Margin No. 20).

traffic offense results in an accident in which the perpetrator is seriously injured.[178] In contrast, this provision is not used in the event of a serious fault that has only lead to a minor dismay.[179] The greater the culpability the more serious the consequences of the offense have to be in order for the punishment to be inadequate.[180]

When applying Article 54 SCC, the criminal authority enjoys wide discretion. It may consider the gravity of culpability and the degree the offender is affected by the criminal act, general and special preventive aspects as well as reasons of equity.[181]

6.3.4.4.2 Application Frequency

Statistical data on the frequency of application are not available. Based on the information received from the first public prosecutor of the canton Basel-City, this provision was rarely applied in 2011.[182] The same is true in the canton of Zurich. Among the Articles 52–54 SCC, Article 54 SCC is probably least applied.[183]

6.4 Prosecutorial Decision-Making

*6.4.1 Order that Proceedings Will Not Be Opened (*Nichtanhandnahmeverfügung*)*

6.4.1.1 Purpose and Reasons for Not Opening Proceedings

The primary purpose of the prosecutor's decision not to take proceedings is protecting persons against unfounded complaints and saving resources.[184]

The prosecution makes the decision not to open an investigation as soon as it is established on the basis of the report that a criminal offense has been committed or the police report that (1) the elements of the offense at hand or the procedural preconditions have clearly not been met, (2) procedural bars exist, or (3) it is necessary for the reasons stated in Article 8 CCrP[185] to refrain from conducting a

[178] Fiolka and Riedo. In: Niggli et al. (2011) BSK StPO, Art. 8, Margin No. 54.

[179] Riklin. In: Niggli and Wiprächtiger (2007) BSK StGB I, Art. 54, Margin No. 40.

[180] Riklin. In: Niggli and Wiprächtiger (2007) BSK StGB I, Art. 54, Margin No. 40.

[181] Riklin. In: Niggli and Wiprächtiger (2007) BSK StGB I, Art. 54, Margin No. 43.

[182] First Public Prosecutor of the canton Basel-City Alberto Fabbri, e-mail message to author, January 5, 2012.

[183] Chief Public Prosecutor of one of the five general public prosecutor's offices of the canton Zurich Ursula Frauenfelder Nohl, e-mail message to author, January 20, 2012.

[184] Landshut. In: Donatsch et al. (2010) Kommentar StPO, Art. 310, Margin No. 1.

[185] On Article 8 CCrP, see Sects. 6.3.3 and 6.3.4.

criminal prosecution (Article 310 para. 1 CCrP). Thus, the complaints in these cases appear to have no prospect of success.

The provision is mandatory, so that the prosecutor is not allowed to exercise any discretion.[186]

As a general rule, a decision not to open an investigation is restricted to those cases where the legal and factual circumstances of the cases are clear.[187] If there are some doubts whether the conditions of Article 310 para. 1 CCrP are fulfilled, the prosecutor has to open an investigation according to Article 309 CCrP. Thus, the principle *in dubio pro duriore* applies.[188] In criminal matters with serious consequences (i.e. serious assaults, fires), the conduct of criminal proceedings should be the rule.[189]

If the prosecution service does not have local or subject-matter jurisdiction, then it has to remit the case to the authority which in its view has competence (Article 39 CCrP). In the event that this authority takes over the case, the prosecution may renounce to issue a directive that proceedings are not to be opened.[190]

Procedural bars include the prohibition of double jeopardy (*ne bis in idem*) or the fact that the limitation of the right to prosecute (*Verjährung*) has already passed.[191] The procedural bars must be irreversible in order for the prosecutor to issue a directive that proceedings are not to be opened.[192]

The decision to refrain from conducting prosecution according to Article 8 CCrP can only be made by the prosecution or the courts, not by the police.[193] In general, the reasons set out in Article 8 CCrP will only come up during a criminal investigation, so that an order that proceedings are not to be opened will only be issued in the exception.[194] Furthermore, the reasons mentioned in Article 8 CCrP allow the prosecutor—despite the imperative character of paras 1 and 2 of the rule—to use relatively wide discretion, which is not unproblematic in regard to the decision

---

[186] Omlin. In: Niggli et al. (2011) BSK StPO, Art. 310, Margin No. 8. On the mandatory respectively voluntary nature of the provision when applied in connection with Article 8 CCrP, see Sect. 6.3.3, para 10.

[187] Omlin. In: Niggli et al. (2011) BSK StPO, Art. 310, Margin No. 9.

[188] Landshut. In: Donatsch et al. (2010) Kommentar StPO, Art. 310, Margin Nos. 4–5; Riedo et al. (2010), Margin No. 2322; Schmid (2009b), Art. 310, Margin No. 2; Albertini. In: Albertini et al. (2008) VSKC-Polizeiliche Ermittlung, p. 549; Federal Council (2006), p. 1265.

[189] Landshut. In: Donatsch et al. (2010) Kommentar StPO, Art. 310, Margin No. 5; Schmid (2009a), Margin No. 1231.

[190] Landshut. In: Donatsch et al. (2010) Kommentar StPO, Art. 310, Margin No. 2; Schmid (2009b), Art. 310, Margin No. 4; Omlin. In: Niggli et al. (2011) BSK StPO, Art. 310, Margin No. 9.

[191] Schmid (2009b), Art. 310, Margin No. 5; Landshut. In: Donatsch et al. (2010) Kommentar StPO, Art. 309, Margin Nos. 19–20; Omlin. In: Niggli et al. (2011) BSK StPO, Art. 310, Margin No. 10.

[192] Landshut. In: Donatsch et al. (2010) Kommentar StPO, Art. 310, Margin No. 7.

[193] Landshut. In: Donatsch et al. (2010) Kommentar StPO, Art. 310, Margin No. 8.

[194] Landshut. In: Donatsch et al. (2010) Kommentar StPO, Art. 310, Margin No. 9.

whether or not to institute criminal proceedings. Hence, these reasons have to be interpreted restrictively.[195]

6.4.1.2 Proceedings

The proceeding conforms to the provisions on the discontinuation of proceedings (art. 310 para. 2 CCrP).[196] The cantons must substantiate the order that proceedings will not be opened[197] and notify the parties, the victim, other parties involved in the proceedings who are affected by the directive,[198] and any other authorities in the event that they have a right to file a complaint[199] (Article 310 para. 2; Article 321 para. 1 CCrP). The order does not need to be published (Article 88 para. 4 CCrP).[200] The prosecutor has no duty to announce his forthcoming decision not to open an investigation to the parties nor, what has been the practice in many cantons until now, to guarantee the right to be heard in any other way.[201] However, the parties have the right to make written objection (Article 393 CCrP) against the prosecutor's decision within 10 days. An objection may contest (1) an infringement of the law, including exceeding and abusing discretionary powers, the denial of justice, and unjustified delay, (2) an incomplete or incorrect assessment of the circumstances of the case, or (3) a decision that is inequitable. If the complaint is approved, then the files are returned to the prosecution with the order to open an investigation. The appeal authority may issue instructions to the prosecution in respect of how the proceedings are to proceed (Article 397 paras 2 and 3 CCrP).

The cantons may stipulate that the directive discontinuing the proceedings is to be authorized by the senior prosecutor or the attorney general (Article 322 para. 1 CCrP). This rule also applies to directives that proceedings are not to be opened.

---

[195] Omlin. In: Niggli et al. (2011) BSK StPO, Art. 310, Margin No. 11.

[196] See Sect. 6.4.4.5.

[197] On the form of the order, see Omlin. In: Niggli et al. (2011) BSK StPO, Art. 310, Margin Nos. 13–18.

[198] E.g. Persons whose objects and assets are the subjects of the procedure (Omlin. In: Niggli et al. (2011) BSK StPO, Art. 310, Margin No. 23). See Article 105 CCrP, which enumerates other people involved in the proceedings (witnesses, persons providing information, experts).

[199] E.g. different supervisory authorities (attorneys, teachers, financial intermediaries). In respect to the federal legislation, various authorities have to be informed of criminal decisions (Regulation concerning the Notification of Cantonal Criminal Decisions of November 10, 2004; *Verordnung über die Mitteilung kantonaler Strafentscheide vom 10. November 2004*; SR 312.3). See Omlin. In: Niggli et al. (2011) BSK StPO, Art. 310, Margin No. 24.

[200] Omlin. In: Niggli et al. (2011) BSK StPO, Art. 310, Margin No. 25.

[201] Landshut. In: Donatsch et al. (2010) Kommentar StPO, Art. 310, Margin No. 11; Omlin. In: Niggli et al. (2011) BSK StPO, Art. 310, Margin Nos. 19–21; Schmid (2009a), Margin No. 1231; Schmid (2009b), Art. 310, Margin No. 7.

The "four-eyes principle"[202] has the purpose of assuring the quality of the prosecutor's decision.[203]

A final and legally binding directive that proceedings are not to be opened is equivalent to a final decision in which the accused person is acquitted (Article 320 para. 4 CCrP). In contrast to an acquittal,[204] a reopening of proceedings is possible under simplified conditions, namely when the prosecution obtains new evidence or information that indicates that the accused is guilty of a criminal offense and that does not result from the previous files (Article 310 para. 2 CCrP; Article 323 CCrP).[205] Although the conditions are the same for orders that proceedings are not to be opened and those discontinuing the proceedings, the requirements for the former are generally lower than for the latter, since the prosecution decided not to institute criminal proceedings without prior investigative acts only on the basis of the complaint or the police report.[206] The prosecution informs those people and authorities who were previously informed of the discontinuation of the proceedings respectively the decision not to open an investigation of the reopening of the proceedings (Article 323 para. 2 CCrP).

6.4.1.3 Application Frequency

As Table 6.3 shows, prosecutors only rarely issue orders that proceedings are not to be opened. In the canton of Zug for instance, prior to the introduction of the CCrP, prosecutors decided not to open an investigation in 1.3 % respectively 2.15 % of the criminal matters handled in 2008 respectively 2010. In 2011, however, the number of cases where the prosecutor decided not to open an investigation reached more than 3 %. In Zurich, until 2010, prosecutors generally decided not to open an investigation in about 3 % of the cases. In 2011, however, this number increased dramatically to 10 %. On the other hand, the number of dropped proceedings decreased from about 38 % per year on average to 33 %.[207] The reason for the increase of orders not to open an investigation in the canton of Zurich can be

[202] See Sect. 6.1.2.1, para 7.

[203] Omlin. In: Niggli et al. (2011) BSK StPO, Art. 310, Margin Nos. 29–30.

[204] In case of an acquittal or a conviction, a revision is possible "if (a) new facts which occurred before the decision was made are, or new evidence is, available which is likely to result in an acquittal, the imposition of a substantially less severe or more severe sentence on a person who was convicted, or the conviction of a person who was acquitted; (b) the decision is irreconcilably at odds with a subsequent criminal decision which involves the same factual circumstances; (c) in the course of other criminal proceedings it transpires that the findings of the proceedings were influenced by criminal activity; a conviction is not necessary; the criminal proceedings cannot be carried out, then the evidence may be brought forth in some other way" (Article 410 para. 1 CCrP).

[205] Omlin. In: Niggli et al. (2011) BSK StPO, Art. 310, Margin Nos. 31–35; Schmid (2009a), Margin No. 1231.

[206] Grädel and Heiniger. In: Niggli et al. (2011) BSK StPO, Art. 323, Margin No. 4; Schmid (2009a), Margin No. 1231; Schmid (2009b), Art. 310, Margin No. 1.

[207] See Table 6.5.

Table 6.3 Number of decisions not to open an investigation in the cantons of Zug and Zurich (2008–2011)

		2008		2009		2010		2011	
		Absolute number	%	Absolute number	%	Absolute number	%	Absolute number	%
Canton of Zug	Total PPS case-ending decision	7,110	100	7,883	100	7,873	100	8,795	100
	Of which: decision not to open an investigation[a]	95	1.3	98	1.24	169	2.15	313	3.56
Canton of Zurich	Total PPS case-ending decision	24,279	100	24,344	100	24,951	100	26,788	100
	Of which: decision not to open an investigation	684	2.8	681	2.8	741	3	2,675	10

Source: Data from Supreme Court of the Canton of Zug (2009, 2010, 2011), Section E III 1.2; Supreme Court of the Canton of Zug (2012), Section E IV 1.2; Data adapted from Senior Public Prosecutor's Office of the Canton of Zurich (2012), p. 27 and from statistical information received from the Senior Public Prosecutor's Office of Zurich on February 2, 2012

[a]The public prosecutor decides not to take proceedings when it is established on the basis of the complaint or the police report that there is obviously no reason for a prosecution (Section 14 of the Code of Criminal Procedure of the canton of Zug of October 3, 1940; *Strafprozessordnung für den Kanton Zug vom 3. Oktober 1940*)

attributed to the introduction of the CCrP. While prior to the introduction of the CCrP, an investigation was usually dropped when a suspect was confronted with charges by the police, the CCrP allows not opening proceedings when the elements of the criminal offense at hand have obviously not been met. Directives that proceedings are not to be opened are the most economic solution for dealing with such cases. Pursuant to Article 309 para. 4 CCrP, the prosecution refrains from opening an investigation if it immediately (i.e. within 90 days in the canton of Zurich) issues a directive that proceedings will not be opened or a penal order. As a result, the prosecution can save a great deal of time and expense by avoiding announcing the conclusion of the proceedings to the parties (Article 318 para. 1 CCrP).[208] Such an announcement must be made after the prosecution has carried out an investigation and considers it to be complete and wants to bring charges or discontinue the proceedings. The aggrieved person remains not without protection,

[208] Article 318 para. 1 CCrP states the following: "If the prosecution considers the investigation to be complete, then it shall issue a penal order to give written notice to the parties whose residence is known of the impending conclusion of the proceedings and shall inform them whether they are going to bring charges or to discontinue the proceedings. They shall, at the same time, provide the parties with a time limit for the submission of a petition that further evidence be taken."

since he has a right to file a complaint against the prosecutor's decision (Article 393 para. 1 lit. a CCrP).[209]

6.4.2 Opening the Investigation

6.4.2.1 Importance

The opening by the prosecutor of an investigation is of fundamental importance. As a result, the prosecutor effectively takes over control of the criminal procedure[210] and the police are no longer allowed to independently investigate in the same case.[211] The role of the parties involved in the criminal process is specified and the legal rights of the parties must be preserved.[212] Furthermore, each decision to open an investigation is connected to the fact that the prosecution is forced to conclude the case in the forms provided by law (abandoning proceedings,[213] issue of a penal order,[214] bringing charges[215]).[216]

The prosecutor, in deciding whether to open an investigation or not, enjoys a certain margin of discretion, whereby he is bound by the principle of *in dubio contra reum*, which means that the investigation process has to be opened even if there are some doubts regarding the conditions necessary for a criminal prosecution.[217]

6.4.2.2 Reasons

In order to open an investigation, the prosecution (1) must have reasonable suspicion[218] that an offense has been committed based on the information and reports from the police, the complaint or its own findings, or (2) intends to order compulsory measures, or (3) has received information from the police in terms of Article

[209] The given reason for the increase of orders not to open an investigation in the canton of Zurich is based on the opinion of the Chief Public Prosecutor of one of the five general public prosecutor's offices of the canton Zurich Jürg Vollenweider, e-mail message to author, February 3, 2012.

[210] The great majority of police enquiries are conducted completely by the police, although it is the prosecutor's duty to conduct the preliminary proceedings (Article 16 CCrP). See 6.2.2.1.

[211] Hürlimann (2006), p. 193.

[212] Hürlimann (2006), pp. 197–210.

[213] Articles 319–323 CCrP.

[214] Articles 352–356 CCrP.

[215] Articles 324–327 CCrP.

[216] Landshut. In: Donatsch et al. (2010) Kommentar StPO, Art. 309, Margin No. 2; Omlin. In: Niggli et al. (2011) BSK StPO, Art. 309, Margin No. 11; Hürlimann (2006), p. 195.

[217] Landshut. In: Donatsch et al. (2010) Kommentar StPO, Art. 309, Margin No. 13.

[218] For a detailed discussion of "suspicion", see Hürlimann (2006), pp. 94–110.

307 para. 1 CCrP, which provides for an information obligation for some serious offenses[219] (Article 309 para. 1 CCrP).

The opening of investigation based on "reasonable suspicion" requires a certain probability of conviction of the offender which goes beyond the general theoretical possibility.[220] There must be serious grounds for believing that a criminal offense has been committed.[221] The question of whether the available evidence suggests a certain probability of conviction is left to the appreciation of the prosecutor.[222]

Reasonable suspicion needs to be distinguished from "initial suspicion" (*Anfangsverdacht*), which is required for the instigation of prosecution (Article 299 para. 2, Article 300 CCrP). An initial suspicion exists when there is a low probability of conviction of the offender.[223] While vague factual indications are enough to institute criminal proceedings, they are not enough for opening an investigation.[224]

Coercive measures are only permitted if, based on the current status of the investigations, there is a substantial likelihood for a guilty verdict (Article 197 para. 1 lit. b CCrP). Such an "urgent suspicion" (*dringender Tatverdacht*) exists, when there is considerable evidence of criminal behavior.[225]

6.4.2.3 Proceedings

The prosecutor opens an investigation by way of a directive that names the accused person and the criminal offense that he is suspected of committing. It is also possible to open an investigation against unknown persons.[226] This order neither requires substantiation[227] nor does it need to be made public.[228] However, the prosecutor is free to inform the parties of the initiation of procedure.[229] Otherwise, the parties are informed of it through procedural acts such as summonses and examination hearings. Furthermore, the prosecutor's decision cannot be challenged

---

[219] See Sect. 6.2.2.1, paras 4 and 5.

[220] Hürlimann (2006), pp. 104–105 and 107–108.

[221] Schmid (2009b), Art. 309, Margin No. 3.

[222] Hürlimann (2006), p. 108.

[223] Hürlimann (2006), p. 104; Omlin. In: Niggli et al. (2011) BSK StPO, Art. 309, Margin No. 31.

[224] Landshut. In: Donatsch et al. (2010) Kommentar StPO, Art. 299, Margin No. 26 and Art. 309, Margin No. 26; Hürlimann (2006), p. 107. But see Omlin. In: Niggli et al. (2011) BSK StPO, Art. 309, Margin No. 26 who equates "reasonable suspicion" with "initial suspicion".

[225] Hürlimann (2006), pp. 105–106; Landshut. In: Donatsch et al. (2010) Kommentar StPO, Art. 299, Margin No. 26 and Art. 309, Margin No. 27.

[226] Schmid (2009b), Art. 309, Margin No. 8; Omlin. In: Niggli et al. (2011) BSK StPO, Art. 309, Margin No. 41; Landshut. In: Donatsch et al. (2010) Kommentar StPO, Art. 309, Margin No. 43.

[227] For more details, Omlin. In: Niggli et al. (2011) BSK StPO, Art. 309, Margin Nos. 41–43.

[228] For more details, Omlin. In: Niggli et al. (2011) BSK StPO, Art. 309, Margin Nos. 44–46.

[229] Schmid (2009b), Art. 309, Margin No. 9.

(Article 309 para. 3 CCrP) unless the accused claims it constitutes a violation of the rule against double jeopardy (Article 300 para. 2 CCrP). The decision is taken without the parties being heard.[230]

The prosecution, before deciding whether to open an investigation, may return police reports and criminal complaints that do not contain clear indications that an offense has been committed to the police so that they may carry out additional enquiries (Article 309 para. 2 CCrP). According to Schmid, this provision should be used with restraint, firstly for reasons of economy of procedure and secondly because the prosecutor may still instruct the police to carry out additional enquiries after the investigation has been opened (Article 312 CCrP).[231] Furthermore, by delaying the formal opening of the investigation, there would be a danger of affecting the legal rights of the parties.[232]

A precise determination of the moment when the prosecutor has to decide about the opening of an investigation is not possible since the decision depends on various factors and each case has its peculiarities.[233] Usually, the prosecutor makes the decision to open an investigation after the police enquiries or at least after the first investigative measures.[234] The principle of procedural efficiency (*Gebot der Verfahrensbeschleunigung*) requires the prosecutor to decide within a reasonable period.[235]

The prosecution has the option of refraining from opening an investigation if it immediately issues a directive that proceedings will not be opened or a penal order (Article 309 para. 4 CCrP). The prosecution should not have carried out any investigations if it wants make use of this possibility.[236]

6.4.3 Suspension of Investigations

6.4.3.1 Reasons

The prosecutor may be confronted with the fact that, for various reasons, he is temporarily not able to pursue and terminate the criminal proceedings. In such situations, he has the option to suspend the investigation and to resume it *ex officio* if the reason for the suspension no longer applies (Article 315 CCrP). The decision

---

[230] Landshut. In: Donatsch et al. (2010) Kommentar StPO, Art. 309, Margin No. 45; Omlin. In: Niggli et al. (2011) BSK StPO, Art. 309, Margin No. 40; Schmid (2009b), Art. 309, Margin No. 2.

[231] Schmid (2009b), Art. 309, Margin No. 8; Federal Council (2006), p. 1263.

[232] Pieth (2009), pp. 61–62.

[233] Hürlimann (2006), pp. 172–173.

[234] Albertini. In: Albertini et al. (2008) VSKC-Polizeiliche Ermittlung, p. 547.

[235] E.g. within 90 days after receipt of the criminal procedure in the canton of Zurich [WOSTA, point 12.6.1 (2012)].

[236] Landshut. In: Donatsch et al. (2010) Kommentar StPO, Art. 309, Margin Nos. 46–48; Omlin. In: Niggli et al. (2011) BSK StPO, Art. 309, Margin Nos. 47–50.

to suspend the investigation is purely optional. The prosecutor is the sole responsible party for deciding about a suspension. Hence, there is no possibility to file a complaint against a refusal of suspension.[237] Since a suspension does conflict with the requirement of having the charge determined within a reasonable time (*Beschleunigungsgebot*),[238] this should only be used with restraint and just over a short period.[239]

A decision to suspend the investigation does not have legal authority in the sense of res iudicata effect.[240] The case is still pending and the authority has to close it either by abandoning proceedings, bringing charges, or issuing a penal order.[241]

The suspension of investigations is regulated by Article 314 CCrP. The reasons for suspension are enumerated in para. 1 of Article 314 CCrP, whereby this list is not exhaustive.[242]

The prosecutor may suspend proceedings if the perpetrator is unknown and there is no reason to conduct any investigative actions (Article 314 para. 1 lit. a CCrP). However, in such cases, there is also the possibility for the police to refrain from making a report to the prosecution (Article 307 para. 4 CCrP).[243] Thus, in practice, only those cases that are directly reported to the prosecutor's office or where the police have a duty to report due to the seriousness of the case (Article 307 para. 1 CCrP) fall within the scope of application.

If the perpetrator's residence is unknown, then the proceedings should also be suspended (Article 314 para. 1 lit. a CCrP). In contrast to the case of unknown offenders, the police cannot refrain from making a report.[244] A proceedings *in absentia* does not exist in preliminary proceedings.[245] In the event that the perpetrator or his place of residence is unknown, the prosecution should instigate a search (Article

---

[237] Landshut. In: Donatsch et al. (2010) Kommentar StPO, Art. 314, Margin No. 25; Omlin. In: Niggli et al. (2011) BSK StPO, Art. 314, Margin No. 8; Schmid (2009a), Margin No. 1238; Schmid (2009b), Art. 314, Margin No. 12.

[238] "The criminal justice authorities shall conduct the criminal proceedings as speedily as possible and shall ensure that they are concluded without unreasonably delay" (Article 5 para. 1 CCrP).

[239] Landshut. In: Donatsch et al. (2010) Kommentar StPO, Art. 314, Margin No. 4; Omlin. In: Niggli et al. (2011) BSK StPO, Art. 314, Margin No. 9.

[240] Landshut. In: Donatsch et al. (2010) Kommentar StPO, Art. 314, Margin No. 1; Omlin. In: Niggli et al. (2011) BSK StPO, Art. 314, Margin No. 10; Schmid (2009a), Margin No. 1239.

[241] Landshut. In: Donatsch et al. (2010) Kommentar StPO, Art. 314, Margin No. 1.

[242] Landshut. In: Donatsch et al. (2010) Kommentar StPO, Art. 314, Margin No. 5; Omlin. In: Niggli et al. (2011) BSK StPO, Art. 314, Margin No. 11.

[243] Landshut. In: Donatsch et al. (2010) Kommentar StPO, Art. 314, Margin No. 6; Omlin. In: Niggli et al. (2011) BSK StPO, Art. 314, Margin No. 12; Schmid (2009a), p. 1236; Dissenting Albertini. In: Albertini et al. (2008) VSKC-Polizeiliche Ermittlung, p. 564. See Sect. 6.2.2.1, para 3.

[244] Landshut. In: Donatsch et al. (2010) Kommentar StPO, Art. 314, Margin No. 7.

[245] Landshut. In: Donatsch et al. (2010) Kommentar StPO, Art. 314, Margin No. 7; Omlin. In: Niggli et al. (2011) BSK StPO, Art. 314, Margin No. 13; Schmid (2009a), p. 1236.

314 para. 3 CCrP).[246] Finally, the investigation may also be suspended when other temporary procedural bars exist (Article 314 para. 1 lit. a CCrP), such as in cases of prolonged and serious illness (e.g. lying in coma) or extended stay abroad.[247]

Criminal proceedings may be suspended in the event that the outcome of the criminal proceedings is dependent on other proceedings and it appears reasonable to await the outcome of those proceedings (Article 314 para. 1 lit. b CCrP). The verdict in the other proceedings must be essential to the further course of the criminal proceedings.[248] This is the case if the same matter is pending before a foreign court. A suspension of investigations may also be pronounced when a foreign authority has requested to take over a criminal proceedings.[249] Furthermore, mutual agreement proceedings are explicitly mentioned (Article 314 para. 1 lit. c CCrP). In this case, the suspension is limited to a period of 3 months, whereby it may be renewed once for a further period of 3 months (Article 314 para. 2 CCrP). In this connection, a suspension may be possible, allowing the offender to make reparation according to Article 53 SCC.[250] This time limit aims to favor a successful conclusion of mutual agreement and to hinder an excessive delay in criminal proceedings.[251]

The prosecution may suspend the investigation if a decision on its merits is dependent on the further development of the consequences of the criminal offense (Article 314 para. 1 lit. d CCrP). This is the case when there are uncertainties regarding the seriousness of bodily injury so that the question of whether the offense has to be prosecuted *ex officio* or on complaint remains temporarily open.[252]

6.4.3.2 Proceedings

Proceedings for the suspension is governed by the provisions on the discontinuation of proceedings (Article 314 para. 5 CCrP; Article 320 et seq. CCrP). The prosecutor must substantiate the decision to suspend the investigation[253] and notify the parties,

---

[246] The search is regulated by Articles 210 and 211 CCrP.

[247] Landshut. In: Donatsch et al. (2010) Kommentar StPO, Art. 314, Margin No. 9; Omlin. In: Niggli et al. (2011) BSK StPO, Art. 314, Margin No. 14; Schmid (2009b), Art. 314, Margin No. 5; Riedo et al. (2010), Margin No. 2336.

[248] Landshut. In: Donatsch et al. (2010) Kommentar StPO, Art. 314, Margin No. 12.

[249] Landshut. In: Donatsch et al. (2010) Kommentar StPO, Art. 314, Margin No. 12.

[250] Landshut. In: Donatsch et al. (2010) Kommentar StPO, Art. 314, Margin No. 15; Omlin. In: Niggli et al. (2011) BSK StPO, Art. 314, Margin Nos. 15 and 21–22; Schmid (2009b), Art. 314, Margin No. 7; Flückiger (2006), p. 329. For more information, see Sect. 6.4.4.3, para 3.

[251] Federal Council (2006), p. 1266; Landshut. In: Donatsch et al. (2010) Kommentar StPO, Art. 314, Margin No. 16; Omlin. In: Niggli et al. (2011) BSK StPO, Art. 314, Margin No. 23.

[252] Landshut. In: Donatsch et al. (2010) Kommentar StPO, Art. 314, Margin No. 17; Omlin. In: Niggli et al. (2011) BSK StPO, Art. 314, Margin Nos. 16–18.

[253] On the form of the decision to suspend the investigations, see Omlin. In: Niggli et al. (2011) BSK StPO, Art. 314, Margin Nos. 27–33.

the victim, other parties involved in the proceedings who are affected by the decision,[254] and any other cantonal authorities in the event that they have a right to file a complaint[255] (Article 321 para. 1 CCrP).[256] The order does not need to be published (Article 88 para. 4 CCrP).[257] In contrast to the decision not to open an investigation, the prosecutor has to announce his forthcoming decision to suspend the investigation to the parties. Until the suspension, the investigations may have produced some evidence, so that the right of the parties to be heard has to be respected.[258]

The parties have the right to make written objection (Article 393 CCrP) against the prosecutor's decision within 10 days.[259]

The cantons may stipulate that the directive suspending the investigation is to be authorized by the senior prosecutor or the attorney general (Article 322 para. 1 CCrP).[260] The "four-eyes principle"[261] has the purpose of assuring the quality of the prosecutor's decision.[262]

6.4.3.3 Application Frequency

As stated under Sect. 6.4.3.1, para 1, a suspension does conflict with the principle of procedural efficiency and thus should be used with restraint. For this reason, it is not surprising that proceedings are only very rarely suspended. Table 6.4 shows the frequency of suspension of criminal proceedings in the canton of Zug. In the canton of Zurich, suspended cases are counted with discontinued cases.

---

[254] E.g. Persons whose objects and assets are the subject of the procedure; persons who would be obliged to pay an indemnity by a later penal order respectively verdict or have to bear costs (see Omlin. In: Niggli et al. (2011) BSK StPO, Art. 314, Margin No. 38). See Article 105 CCrP that lists other people involved in the proceedings.

[255] E.g. different supervisory authorities (attorneys, teachers, financial intermediaries). In respect to the federal legislation, various authorities have to be informed of criminal decisions (Regulation concerning the Notification of cantonal Criminal Decisions of November 10, 2004). See Omlin. In: Niggli et al. (2011) BSK StPO, Art. 314, Margin No. 39.

[256] Hence, Article 314 para. 4 CCrP that enumerates the persons who have to be informed about the decision has no independent meaning (Landshut. In: Donatsch et al. (2010) Kommentar StPO, Art. 314, Margin No. 21; Omlin. In: Niggli et al. (2011) BSK StPO, Art. 314, Margin Nos. 35–39; Schmid 2009b, Art. 314, Margin No. 10).

[257] Omlin. In: Niggli et al. (2011) BSK StPO, Art. 314, Margin No. 43.

[258] Omlin. In: Niggli et al. (2011) BSK StPO, Art. 314, Margin No. 34.

[259] Landshut. In: Donatsch et al. (2010) Kommentar StPO, Art. 314, Margin No. 23; Omlin. In: Niggli et al. (2011) BSK StPO, Art. 314, Margin Nos. 44–47. On the reasons that may be invoked, see Sect. 6.4.1.2, para 1.

[260] Landshut. In: Donatsch et al. (2010) Kommentar StPO, Art. 314, Margin No. 22; Omlin. In: Niggli et al. (2011) BSK StPO, Art. 314, Margin No. 48.

[261] See Sect. 6.1.2.1, para 7.

[262] Omlin. In: Niggli et al. (2011) BSK StPO, Art. 314, Margin No. 49.

Table 6.4 Number of criminal proceedings suspended in the canton of Zug (2008–2010)

	2008		2009		2010		2011	
	Absolute number	%	Absolute number	%	Absolute number	%	Absolute number	%
Total PPS case-ending decision	7,110	100	7,883	100	7,873	100	8,759	100
Of which: Suspension	88	1.2	88	1.1	106	1.3	185	2.1

Source: Data from Supreme Court of the Canton of Zug (2009, 2010, 2011), Section E III 1.2.; Supreme Court of the Canton of Zug (2012), Section E IV 1.2

6.4.4 *Discontinuing Proceedings (*Einstellungsverfügung*)*

6.4.4.1 General Remarks

The aim of a criminal proceeding is to find out the factual truth. Thus, all authorities working in the criminal justice system are bound by the principle of legality (Article 7 CCrP). The prosecutor is required by law to prosecute whenever there is enough evidence to believe that a criminal offense has been committed. As a consequence of the principle of separation of powers, the courts (Article 13 CCrP) and not the prosecuting authorities (Article 12 CCrP) decide on the guilt and innocence of the accused. However, in the interests of procedural economy and for the protection of the accused person, it is important that charges are not brought without sufficient grounds. In the event that there isn't enough evidence to convict, the accused or, for other reasons that would make an acquittal highly probable, the prosecutor may discontinue the proceedings.[263]

The responsibility for making the decision to discontinue the proceedings lies with the prosecutor. Usually, it is the prosecutor already involved in the case who will make this decision. The fact that the prosecutor has also conducted the investigation is not a reason for withdrawal according to Article 56 lit. b CCrP.[264] However, directives may, in certain criminal procedures, provide for a review of the prosecutor's decisions to charge or to discontinue the proceedings by a superior (chief public prosecutor or senior public prosecutor).[265] The cantons may also stipulate that directives discontinuing the proceedings are to be authorized by the senior prosecutor or the attorney general (Article 322 para. 1 CCrP). Furthermore, the parties may submit a complaint against the directive discontinuing the

[263] Grädel and Heiniger. In: Niggli et al. (2011) BSK StPO, Art. 319, Margin No. 1; Landshut. In: Donatsch et al. (2010) Kommentar StPO, Art. 319, Margin No. 3; Pieth (2009), p. 174.

[264] Article 56 lit. b CCrP states the following: "A person acting for the criminal justice authorities shall withdraw if he was involved in the case in another capacity, in particular as a member of an authority, as a legal adviser to a party, as an expert, or as a witness." See Schmid (2009a), Margin No. 1248; Schmid (2009b), Vor Art. 319–327, Margin No. 4.

[265] Schmid (2009a), Margin No. 1248.

proceedings to the Complaints Authority (Article 322 para. 2 CCrP) within 10 days. This constitutes a certain corrective action to the dominant position of the prosecutor in the preliminary proceedings.[266] A final and legally binding directive discontinuing the proceedings is equivalent to a final decision in which the accused person is acquitted (Article 320 para. 4 CCrP).

6.4.4.2 Reasons for Discontinuing Criminal Proceedings

The reasons for discontinuing the proceedings are enumerated in Article 319 CCrP, whereby this list is not to be regarded as exhaustive.[267] If the conditions are fulfilled, then the prosecution should completely or partially discontinue the proceedings (Article 319 para. 1 CCrP).

The following reasons lead to the discontinuance of criminal proceedings, whereas, with the exception of the reason mentioned under e), a discontinuance is mandatory if the conditions are fulfilled.[268] Thus, the prosecutor is not allowed to exercise discretion.

6.4.4.2.1 Insufficient Suspicion that a Criminal Offense Has Been Committed (Article 319 Para. 1 Lit. a CCrP)

A criminal procedure should be discontinued if the investigations could not consolidate the initial suspicion in a way that would justify the bringing of charges.[269] In other words, the suspicion surrounding the suspect had not intensified in such a way that a conviction is to be expected.[270] However, the prosecutor should exercise restraint in deciding whether there is such a suspicion, since it is not the prosecutor's duty to decide on guilt and innocence.[271] The prosecutor should press charges when he considers a participation in a crime and a criminal law reaction (a sentence or a measure) probable.[272]

---

[266] Federal Council (2006), p. 1272; Grädel and Heiniger. In: Niggli et al. (2011) BSK StPO, Art. 319, Margin No. 3.

[267] Grädel and Heiniger. In: Niggli et al. (2011) BSK StPO, Art. 319, Margin No. 5; Landshut. In: Donatsch et al. (2010) Kommentar StPO, Art. 319, Margin No. 13; Schmid (2009b), Art. 319, Margin No. 4.

[268] Grädel and Heiniger. In: Niggli et al. (2011) BSK StPO, Art. 319, Margin No. 6; Landshut. In: Donatsch et al. (2010) Kommentar StPO, Art. 319, Margin No. 14; Schmid (2009b), Art. 319, Margin No. 4.

[269] Schmid (2009b), Art. 319, Margin No. 5. On the decision to charge, see Sect. 6.4.5.

[270] Schmid (2009b), Art. 319, Margin No. 5.

[271] Grädel and Heiniger. In: Niggli et al. (2011) BSK StPO, Art. 319, Margin No. 8; Schmid (2009b), Art. 319, Margin No. 5.

[272] Landshut. In: Donatsch et al. (2010) Kommentar StPO, Art. 319, Margin No. 15.

In the event of contradictory evidence,[273] it is not the prosecutor's duty to make an assessment of evidence. If there are doubts, the prosecutor—with respect to the principle *in dubio pro duriore*—has to press charges.[274] The prosecutor should only refrain from bringing charges, if an acquittal is to be expected. The probability of a verdict of guilt respectively the possible outcome of criminal proceedings is left to the proper exercise of the prosecutor's discretion (*pflichtgemässes Ermessen des Staatsanwalts*).[275]

6.4.4.2.2 Elements of a Criminal Offense Have Not Been Fulfilled (Article 319 Para. 1 Lit. b CCrP)

The prosecutor discontinues a criminal proceedings, when it is clear that the elements of a criminal offense have not been fulfilled. This is the case when, for the crime of fraud (Article 146 SCC), the required element of bad faith is clearly missing, or when, in an offense of negligence, a violation of due diligence is absent.[276]

However, vague legal terms such as "bad faith" in the crime of fraud and "unscrupulousness" in the crime of murder may regularly make the distinction between criminal behavior and behavior that is not punishable by law difficult. In such cases, the prosecutor should exercise restraint when deciding whether the elements of a criminal offense have not been fulfilled, and press charges according to the principle *in dubio pro duriore*.[277] Here, a verdict of acquittal is certain or highly probable from the outset only in the rarest cases.[278]

6.4.4.2.3 Existence of a Justificatory Defense (Article 319 Para. 1 Lit. c CCrP)

Besides the grounds of justification, such as legitimate self-defense (Article 15 SCC), legitimate acts in a situation of necessity (Article 17 SCC), acts permitted

---

[273] On the situation of conflicting statements, see Landshut. In: Donatsch et al. (2010) Kommentar StPO, Art. 319, Margin No. 17. On the situation of different testimonies, Landshut. In: Donatsch et al. (2010) Kommentar StPO, Art. 319, Margin No. 18.

[274] Grädel and Heiniger. In: Niggli et al. (2011) BSK StPO, Art. 319, Margin No. 8; Landshut. In: Donatsch et al. (2010) Kommentar StPO, Art. 319, Margin No. 16; Schmid (2009b), Art. 319, Margin No. 5; Federal Council (2006), p. 1273.

[275] Landshut. In: Donatsch et al. (2010) Kommentar StPO, Art. 319, Margin No. 16; Hauser et al. (2005), Section 78, Margin No. 9.

[276] Grädel and Heiniger. In: Niggli et al. (2011) BSK StPO, Art. 319, Margin No. 9; Landshut. In: Donatsch et al. (2010) Kommentar StPO, Art. 319, Margin No. 19.

[277] Grädel and Heiniger. In: Niggli et al. (2011) BSK StPO, Art. 319, Margin No. 9; Landshut. In: Donatsch et al. (2010) Kommentar StPO, Art. 319, Margin No. 20.

[278] Grädel and Heiniger. In: Niggli et al. (2011) BSK StPO, Art. 319, Margin No. 9.

by law (Article 14 SCC), and grounds of justification beyond-the-law, such as the consent of the injured person, grounds of excuse, or exemption of culpability, such as mitigatory self-defense (Article 16 para. 2 SCC), mitigatory acts in a situation of necessity (Article 18 para. 2 SCC), and absence of legal responsibility (Article 19 et seq. SCC) may also lead to the discontinuance of criminal proceedings.[279]

It is important to note that grounds of justification and grounds of excuse or exemption of culpability are exceptions to the norm. Thus, in these cases, the bringing of charges should be the rule and discontinuation of criminal proceedings should only occur if a verdict of acquittal is to be expected with certainty.[280] The principle *in dubio pro duriore* applies.[281]

If an accused is not legally responsible due to a mental disorder and measures are necessary, then the separate measures procedure (*selbständiges Massnahme-verfahren*) has to be initiated without discontinuing the criminal proceedings on the grounds of lack of capacity (Article 374 para. 1 CCrP).[282] In this procedure, the prosecutor makes a written request to the court of first instance for the imposition of a measure in accordance with Articles 59–61, 63, 64, 67 or 67b of the SCC. The public prosecutor has to announce this procedure to the parties (Article 318 CCrP). The prosecutor's decision is non-contestable (Article 318 para. 3 CCrP). Subsequently, during the trial, any private claimant has the opportunity to comment on the application made by the public prosecutor and his civil claim (Article 374 para. 3 CCrP). When a lack of criminal responsibility is doubtful, the prosecutor has to bring charges, whereupon the court decides on the criminal liability and the necessity to impose a measure.[283] A criminal procedure can only be discontinued when the prosecutor on the basis of expert opinions concludes to an absence of legal responsibility (Article 19 para. 1 SCC) and the needlessness of measures.[284]

6.4.4.2.4 Procedural Bars (Article 319 Para. 1 Lit. d CCrP)

Criminal proceedings are to be discontinued when procedural requirements can definitely not be met or procedural bars have arisen that are irreversible.[285] In these

[279] Grädel and Heiniger. In: Niggli et al. (2011) BSK StPO, Art. 319, Margin No. 11; Landshut. In: Donatsch et al. (2010) Kommentar StPO, Art. 319, Margin No. 21; Schmid (2009b), Art. 319, Margin No. 7.

[280] Grädel and Heiniger. In: Niggli et al. (2011) BSK StPO, Art. 319, Margin No. 11; Landshut. In: Donatsch et al. (2010) Kommentar StPO, Art. 319, Margin No. 22; Schmid (2009b), Art. 319, Margin No. 7.

[281] Grädel and Heiniger. In: Niggli et al. (2011) BSK StPO, Art. 319, Margin No. 11; Schmid (2009b), Art. 319, Margin No. 7.

[282] Grädel and Heiniger. In: Niggli et al. (2011) BSK StPO, Art. 319, Margin No. 12; Landshut. In: Donatsch et al. (2010) Kommentar StPO, Art. 319, Margin No. 21.

[283] Schmid (2009b), Art. 374, Margin No. 3.

[284] Schmid (2009b), Art. 374, Margin No. 5.

[285] Schmid (2009b), Art. 319, Margin No. 8.

cases, a procedure can only be dropped if the factual and legal situations are absolutely clear.[286] If the prosecution service does not have local or subject-matter jurisdiction, then it has to remit the case to the authority which in its view has competence (Article 39 CCrP). In the event that this authority takes over the case, the prosecution issues an assignment order (*Abtretungsverfügung*) and thus it may renounce issuing a directive that the proceedings be discontinued.[287]

Offenses prosecuted only on complaint require the filing of a complaint by the person entitled to file a complaint within 3 months after the discovery of the identity of the suspect (Article 31 SCC). The complaint may be withdrawn at any time before notice is given of the judgment of the second cantonal instance (Article 33 para. 1 SCC). The withdrawal of a complaint constitutes a procedural bar which is irreversible (Article 33 para. 2 SCC). Further procedural bars include, for instance, time limits (Article 97 et seq. SCC), the lack of capacity to participate in the proceedings (Article 114 para. 3 CCrP), the death of the suspect, and the prohibition of double jeopardy (Article 11 CCrP).

6.4.4.2.5 Statutory Regulation Provides for Drop of Prosecution (Article 319 Para. 1 Lit. e CCrP)

The proceedings are to be discontinued if, according to a statutory regulation, the prosecution or punishment can be dispensed. The dropping of charges may be provided by substantive criminal law[288] and procedural law provisions.[289] Supplementary penal provisions outside the criminal code[290] may also lead to the discontinuance of criminal proceedings. Whether the substantive requirements for discontinuing the proceedings are met, and thus if a discontinuation is mandatory or voluntary, has to be determined according to the applied provision and not according to Article 319 CCrP.[291]

---

[286] Landshut. In: Donatsch et al. (2010) Kommentar StPO, Art. 319, Margin No. 24.

[287] Landshut. In: Donatsch et al. (2010) Kommentar StPO, Art. 319, Margin No. 24; Schmid (2009a), Margin No. 399.

[288] E.g. Article 3 para. 3, Article 5 para. 2, Article 6 para. 3, Article 7 para. 4, Article 22 para. 2, Article 52–54, Article 55a, Article 171 para. 2, Article 187 no. 3, Article 188 no. 2, Article 192 para. 2, Article 193 para. 2, Article 304 no. 2, Article 305 para. 2 of the SCC.

[289] E.g. Article 8 CCrP, Article 316 para. 3 CCrP.

[290] E.g. Article 100 no. 1 sentence 2 Road Traffic Act.

[291] Grädel and Heiniger. In: Niggli et al. (2011) BSK StPO, Art. 319, Margin Nos. 18–22; Landshut. In: Donatsch et al. (2010) Kommentar StPO, Art. 319, Margin No. 30; Schmid (2009b), Art. 319, Margin No. 9.

6.4.4.3 Discontinuing Criminal Proceedings After Reaching a Mutual Agreement

After reaching a mutual agreement, a criminal proceeding can be discontinued either according to Article 319 para. 1 lit. d CCrP or to Article 319 para. 1 lit. e CCrP.

Mutual agreement proceedings are laid out in Article 316 CCrP. If the proceedings involve criminal offenses, which are only prosecutable if a criminal complaint has been filed, then the prosecution may summon the person who submitted the complaint and the accused to a hearing with the aim of reaching a mutual agreement. If the person who submitted the complaint fails to appear, then the criminal complaint is considered revoked (Article 316 para. 1 CCrP). It is up to the prosecutor to decide whether to initiate a settlement procedure.[292] However, usually, the prosecutor should make use of it, with the exception of those cases where it is clear from the beginning that reconciliation will fail.[293] The prosecutor is not allowed to intimidate or threaten the parties.[294] In the event that an agreement is reached, the prosecutor issues a directive discontinuing the proceedings (Article 316 para. 3 CCrP; Article 319 para. 1 lit. d CCrP).

If an exemption from punishment comes under consideration in accordance with the provisions in Article 53 SCC on restitution,[295] then the prosecutor should invite the aggrieved person and the accused person to a hearing with the aim of reaching an agreement with regard to restitution (Article 316 para. 2 CCrP). If the conditions of Article 53 SCC are fulfilled, the prosecutor has no other choice but to invite the parties to a hearing.[296] In the event that an agreement is reached, the prosecutor issues an order discontinuing the proceedings (Article 316 para. 3 CCrP; Article 319 para. 1 lit. e CCrP). A failure of the aggrieved party to appear is not considered a revocation of a criminal complaint.[297]

If the accused fails to attend the hearings or if no agreement is reached, the prosecutor should resume the investigation without delay (Article 316 para. 4 CCrP).

[292] Riedo et al. (2010), Margin No. 2349.

[293] Federal Council (2006), p. 1268; Landshut. In: Donatsch et al. (2010) Kommentar StPO, Art. 316, Margin No. 5; Riedo. In: Niggli et al. (2011) BSK StPO, Art. 316, Margin No. 8; Schmid (2009a), Margin No. 1241.

[294] Riedo. In: Niggli et al. (2011) BSK StPO, Art. 316, Margin No. 9.

[295] See Sect. 6.3.4.3 for more details.

[296] Landshut. In: Donatsch et al. (2010) Kommentar StPO, Art. 316, Margin No. 11; Riedo. In: Niggli et al. (2011) BSK StPO, Art. 316, Margin No. 11; Schmid (2009a), Margin No. 1242; Schmid (2009b), Art. 316, Margin No. 6; Federal Council (2006), p. 1268.

[297] Landshut. In: Donatsch et al. (2010) Kommentar StPO, Art. 316, Margin No. 15; Riedo. In: Niggli et al. (2011) BSK StPO, Art. 316, Margin No. 12; Schmid (2009b), Art. 316, Margin No. 6; Federal Council (2006), p. 1268.

In the event that no agreement is reached, declarations provided by the parties should in analogue application of Article 362 para. 4 CCrP not be usable in subsequent ordinary proceedings.[298]

6.4.4.4 Discontinuing Criminal Proceedings in Exceptional Cases

Pursuant to Article 319 para. 2 CCrP, the prosecution may also, in exceptional cases, discontinue the proceedings if (1) this is imperative to protect the interests of a victim who was younger than 18 at the time of the commission of the criminal offense and this interest obviously prevails over that of the state in the prosecution; and (2) the victim or, in the event that he lacks full mental capacity, his statutory representative agrees that the proceedings be discontinued.

According to the wording of Article 319 para. 2 CCrP, the possibility to discontinue criminal proceedings in the interests of a victim under 18 years is an exception. Although the provision leaves application to the discretion of the prosecutor, the predominant legal doctrine supports a compulsory application if the conditions are met.[299]

Dropping criminal proceedings in the interest of the victim is only possible if such a drop is considered to be indispensable as well as advisable.[300] The risks associated with criminal proceedings must be of exceptional nature for the victim. Acute suicidal tendency of the victim constitutes such a risk.[301]

The more serious the criminal offense, the higher the interest in prosecution is to be weighted and the stricter the principle of legality has to be observed. In particular, there is a substantial public interest when there is a risk of reoffending against the victim or children.[302]

---

[298] Landshut. In: Donatsch et al. (2010) Kommentar StPO, Art. 316, Margin No. 10; Schmid (2009b), Art. 317, Margin No. 10. For further information, see also Sect. 6.5.2.2, para 7.

[299] Grädel and Heiniger. In: Niggli et al. (2011) BSK StPO, Art. 319, Margin No. 35; Landshut. In: Donatsch et al. (2010) Kommentar StPO, Art. 319, Margin No. 34; Vogt. In: Gomm and Zehntner (2009) OHG-Kommentar, Art. 319, Margin No. 7; Wohlers (2005), p. 159.

[300] Grädel and Heiniger. In: Niggli et al. (2011) BSK StPO, Art. 319, Margin No. 26; Landshut. In: Donatsch et al. (2010) Kommentar StPO, Art. 319, Margin No. 36; Schmid (2009b), Art. 319, Margin No. 10; Weishaupt (2002), p. 246.

[301] Grädel and Heiniger. In: Niggli et al. (2011) BSK StPO, Art. 319, Margin No. 26; Landshut. In: Donatsch et al. (2010) Kommentar StPO, Art. 319, Margin No. 36; Schmid (2009b), Art. 319, Margin No. 10; Vogt. In: Gomm and Zehntner (2009) OHG-Kommentar, Art. 319, Margin No. 4.

[302] Grädel and Heiniger. In: Niggli et al. (2011) BSK StPO, Art. 319, Margin No. 27; Landshut. In: Donatsch et al. (2010) Kommentar StPO, Art. 319, Margin No. 37; Schmid (2009b), Art. 319, Margin No. 10; Vogt. In: Gomm and Zehntner (2009) OHG-Kommentar, Art. 319, Margin No. 5.

The approval of the victim is not restricted to a specific form.[303] However, it has to be expressly stated and it may be withdrawn as long as the order of discontinuance has not become final.[304]

6.4.4.5 Proceedings

6.4.4.5.1 Form and Content of the Directive

The form and general content of the directive discontinuing the proceedings are determined in accordance with Articles 80 and 81 CCrP (Article 320 para. 1 CCrP).[305] The directive discontinuing the proceedings has to be substantiated (see Article 80 para. 2 CCrP). The duty to give reasons obliges the authority to minimal self-control. It gives the prosecutor the opportunity to evaluate the plausibility of his own decision.[306] The obligation to state reasons also fulfills an information function. The addressees of the directive should be able to understand why the authority has decided in this way and not differently.[307]

A final and legally binding directive discontinuing the proceedings is equivalent to a final decision in which the accused person is acquitted (Article 320 para. 4 CCrP).

6.4.4.5.2 Communication

The prosecution has to inform the parties, the victim, other parties involved in the proceedings who are affected by the decision,[308] and any other cantonal authorities

[303] Grädel and Heiniger. In: Niggli et al. (2011) BSK StPO, Art. 319, Margin No. 34; Vogt. In: Gomm and Zehntner (2009) OHG-Kommentar, Art. 319, Margin No. 6; Weishaupt (2002), p. 247. Dissenting Schmid (2009b), Art. 319, Margin No. 11, who requires the consent to be written or to be noted in the protocol if orally made.

[304] Grädel and Heiniger. In: Niggli et al. (2011) BSK StPO, Art. 319, Margin No. 34; Landshut. In: Donatsch et al. (2010) Kommentar StPO, Art. 319, Margin No. 38; Vogt. In: Gomm and Zehntner (2009) OHG-Kommentar, Art. 319, Margin No. 6.

[305] On the form and content of the directive discontinuing the proceedings, see Grädel and Heiniger. In: Niggli et al. (2011) BSK StPO, Art. 320, Margin Nos. 1–8.

[306] Grädel and Heiniger. In: Niggli et al. (2011) BSK StPO, Art. 320, Margin No. 5.

[307] Grädel and Heiniger. In: Niggli et al. (2011) BSK StPO, Art. 320, Margin No. 5.

[308] E.g. Persons whose assets have been confiscated; persons who have to bear costs (see Grädel and Heiniger. In: Niggli et al. (2011) BSK StPO, Art. 321, Margin No. 3; Landshut. In: Donatsch et al. (2010) Kommentar StPO, Art. 321, Margin No. 9; Schmid 2009b, Art. 321, Margin No. 4). See also Article 105 CCrP that defines other people involved in the proceedings: the aggrieved person, the person who reported the criminal offense, a witness, a person with information, an expert, a third party adversely affected by the procedural activities.

in the event that they have a right to file a complaint[309] about the directive discontinuing the proceedings (Article 321 para. 1 CCrP). The decision does not need to be shared with a senior public prosecutor's office or a general attorney's office.[310] However, the cantons may stipulate that the directive discontinuing the proceedings be authorized by the senior prosecutor or the attorney general (art. 322 para. 1 CCrP).[311]

Third parties may have a right to inspect (*Einsichtsrecht*) directives discontinuing the proceedings and directives that proceedings will not be opened if they can prove an information interest worthy of protection and that this does not conflict with overriding public or private interests.[312]

6.4.4.5.3 Legal Remedies

The parties may submit a complaint against the directive discontinuing proceeding to the Complaints Authority (Article 322 para. 2 CCrP) within 10 days. The legitimating of the parties to lodge a complaint is laid out in Article 382 CCrP. According to it, every party that has a legally protected interest in the quashing or amendment of a decision may have recourse to a legal remedy (Article 382 para. 1 CCrP). The aggrieved person or the victim who did not expressly declare that he wished to participate in the criminal proceedings as a criminal claimant (Article 118 CCrP), even though he had the option to do so,[313] is not entitled to lodge a complaint.[314] The senior public prosecutor and the attorney general are not entitled to file a complaint.[315] The suspect is usually not entitled to lodge a complaint, since

309 E.g. different supervisory authorities (attorneys, teachers, financial intermediaries). In respect to the federal legislation, various authorities have to be informed about criminal decisions (Regulation concerning the Notification of Cantonal Criminal Decisions of November 10, 2004). See Grädel and Heiniger. In: Niggli et al. (2011) BSK StPO, Art. 321, Margin No. 4; Landshut. In: Donatsch et al. (2010) Kommentar StPO, Art. 321, Margin No. 10.

310 Grädel and Heiniger. In: Niggli et al. (2011) BSK StPO, Art. 321, Margin No. 4; Schmid (2009b), Art. 321, Margin No. 6.

311 For further details, see Landshut. In: Donatsch et al. (2010) Kommentar StPO, Art. 322, Margin Nos. 1–6; Grädel and Heiniger. In: Niggli et al. (2011) BSK StPO, Art. 322, Margin Nos. 2–4.

312 Grädel and Heiniger. In: Niggli et al. (2011) BSK StPO, Art. 321, Margin No. 7; Landshut. In: Donatsch et al. (2010) Kommentar StPO, Art. 321, Margin No. 12; Schmid (2009b), Art. 69, Margin No. 6.

313 If the prosecution decides not to open an investigation, drops the proceedings, or issues a penal order, the victim or the aggrieved person may not have had the time to make this declaration (Schmid 2009a, Margin No. 1463; Schmid 2009b, Art. 115, Margin No. 4; Federal Council 2006, p. 1308, n 427).

314 Grädel and Heiniger. In: Niggli et al. (2011) BSK StPO, Art. 322, Margin No. 6; Landshut. In: Donatsch et al. (2010) Kommentar StPO, Art. 322, Margin No. 9; Schmid (2009b), Art. 322, Margin No. 6; Schmid (2009a), Margin Nos. 1462–1463; Riedo et al. (2010), Margin Nos. 2398–2399.

315 Grädel and Heiniger. In: Niggli et al. (2011) BSK StPO, Art. 322, Margin No. 4; Landshut. In: Donatsch et al. (2010) Kommentar StPO, Art. 322, Margin No. 12; Schmid (2009a), Margin No. 1261; Schmid (2009b), Art. 322, Margin No. 7.

he is usually not directly affected by the decision. An exception to this may be made if the reasons given in the directive discontinuing the proceedings correspond to an accusation.[316]

A complaint may contest (1) an infringement of the law, including exceeding and abusing discretionary powers, the denial of justice, and unjustified delay, (2) an incomplete or incorrect assessment of the circumstances of the case, or (3) a decision that is inequitable (Article 393 para. 2 CCrP). If the complaint is approved, then the files are returned to the prosecution with the order to open an investigation. The appeal authority may issue instructions to the prosecution in respect of how the proceedings are to continue (Article 397 paras 2 and 3 CCrP).

6.4.4.5.4 Re-opening of Proceedings

The prosecution reopens the proceedings, when it becomes aware of new evidence or facts that (1) indicate that the person is criminally liable and (2) do not stem from the earlier files (Article 323 para. 1 CCrP).

Subsequent doubts as to the accuracy of the reasons for the discontinuance of the proceedings do not authorize a re-opening of proceedings. Rather, it is required that a probability that the new evidence or facts would lead to a different assessment of the relevant circumstances (such as elements of an offense, costs, compensation, confiscation, etc.) than was assumed in the order discontinuing the proceedings.[317] The requirements for this probability should not be set too high.[318]

Pursuant to the principle of legality and public prosecution, the prosecution has to re-open the proceedings *ex officio* when the conditions are fulfilled.[319] In analogy to the provision regulating the opening of an investigation (Article 309 CCrP), the prosecutor's decision is taken without the parties being heard.[320]

The re-opening of proceedings must be notified to those people and authorities who had previously been informed of the discontinuation of the proceedings

[316] Landshut. In: Donatsch et al. (2010) Kommentar StPO, Art. 322, Margin No. 10; Schmid (2009b), Art. 322, Margin No. 7.

[317] In contrast to this, in case of a petition for revision (Article 410 et seq. CCrP) based on the grounds of new facts or new evidence, these must likely result in an acquittal, the imposition of a substantially less severe or more severe sentence on a person who was convicted, or the conviction of a person who was acquitted.

[318] Grädel and Heiniger. In: Niggli et al. (2011) BSK StPO, Art. 323, Margin No. 13; Landshut. In: Donatsch et al. (2010) Kommentar StPO, Art. 323, Margin No. 17; Schmid (2009b), Art. 323, Margin No. 6.

[319] Grädel and Heiniger. In: Niggli et al. (2011) BSK StPO, Art. 323, Margin No. 16; Landshut. In: Donatsch et al. (2010) Kommentar StPO, Art. 323, Margin No. 27; Schmid (2009b), Art. 323, Margin No. 9.

[320] Grädel and Heiniger. In: Niggli et al. (2011) BSK StPO, Art. 323, Margin No. 16; Landshut. In: Donatsch et al. (2010) Kommentar StPO, Art. 232, Margin No. 28; Schmid (2009b), Art. 232, Margin No. 9.

Table 6.5 Number of dropped proceedings in the cantons of Zug and Zurich (2008–2011)

		2008		2009		2010		2011	
		Absolute number	%	Absolute number	%	Absolute number	%	Absolute number	%
Canton of Zug	Total PPS case-ending decision	7,110	100	7,883	100	7,873	100	8,795	100
	Of which: drops of proceedings[a]	1,062	14.9	1,324	16.8	1,426	18.1	1,547	17.6
Canton of Zurich	Total PPS case-ending decision	24,279	100	24,344	100	24,951	100	26,788	100
	Of which: drops of proceedings[b]	9,198	37.9	9,064	37.2	9,684	38.8	8,927	33.3

Source: Data from Supreme Court of the Canton of Zug (2009, 2010, 2011), Section E III 1.2; Supreme Court of the Canton of Zug (2012), Section E IV 1.2.; Data adapted from Senior Public Prosecutor's Office of the Canton of Zurich (2012), p. 27 and from statistical information received from the Senior Public Prosecutor's Office of Zurich on February 2, 2012

[a]The public prosecution service entirely or partially drops the proceedings when there is no reason for further proceedings (Section 34 ZG-StPO; Article 319 CCrP); suspension according to Article 55a SCC

[b]Suspended proceedings are included in this number. Section 39 ZH-StPO constituted the legal basis for discontinuing proceedings prior to the introduction of the CCrP

(Article 323 para. 2 CCrP). The accused person may file a complaint against the prosecutor's order to reopen an investigation within 10 days. The private claimant, other parties involved in the proceedings who are affected by the decision, or authorities, may lodge a complaint against the refusal of the prosecutor to re-open an investigation (Article 393 et seq. CCrP).[321]

6.4.4.6 Application Frequency

Table 6.5 shows the number of proceedings discontinued in the cantons of Zug and Zurich. Whereas in the canton of Zug, criminal proceedings are discontinued in 17 % of the cases per year on average,[322] this occurs in 37 % of the cases per year on average in the canton of Zurich.[323] Coinciding with the introduction of the CCrP in 2011, there is a decrease in the number of dropped proceedings in the canton of Zurich. For more on the reasons for this decrease, see Sect. 6.4.1.3.

[321] Grädel and Heiniger. In: Niggli et al. (2011) BSK StPO, Art. 323, Margin No. 13; Landshut. In: Donatsch et al. (2010) Kommentar StPO, Art. 323, Margin No. 30; Schmid (2009b), Art. 232, Margin No. 9.

[322] This number is based on the average value of 4 years.

[323] This number is based on the average value of 4 years.

6.4.5 *Decision to Charge*

6.4.5.1 Reasons

The prosecutor brings charges before the relevant court if he considers, on the basis of the investigation, that there is sufficient reason to suspect the accused person of committing the criminal offense and he has not issued a penal order (Article 324 para. 1 CCrP).

Thus, if there is no reason for discontinuing criminal proceedings according to Article 319 para. 1 lit. a CCrP and provided that the conditions for issuing a penal order are not met, then the prosecutor has the duty to file charges.[324]

The filing of charges requires "sufficient grounds for suspicion" that the accused person has committed the criminal offense. This is the case when the investigations have consolidated the initial suspicion in a way that a conviction seems highly probable.[325] A high probability of conviction exists basically only after conclusion of the investigations when all factual and legal circumstances of the case have been clarified.[326] The evaluation of the probability of conviction is left to the proper exercise of the prosecutor's discretion.[327] When deciding whether or not to charge, the principle *in dubio pro reo* does not apply.[328]

Although the prosecutor has to investigate incriminating and exculpatory facts with equal care, it should be kept in mind that the prosecutor's activity is primarily oriented toward the filing of charges.[329]

6.4.5.2 Proceedings

The decision to bring charges cannot be challenged (Article 324 para. 2 CCrP). During the creation of the CCrP, this provision was not entirely uncontroversial, but finally appears to be objectively justified. Furthermore, reasons of procedural

---

[324] Heimgartner and Niggli. In: Niggli et al. (2011) BSK StPO, Art. 324, Margin No. 3; Landshut. In: Donatsch et al. (2010) Kommentar StPO, Art. 324, Margin No. 5; Schmid (2009b), Art. 324, Margin No. 1.

[325] Hürlimann (2006), p. 106; Heimgartner and Niggli. In: Niggli et al. (2011) BSK StPO, Art. 324, Margin No. 10. For other commentators, a simple probability of conviction is enough to file criminal charges (see Federal Council 2006, p. 1275; Landshut. In: Donatsch et al. (2010) Kommentar StPO, Art. 324, Margin No. 5, Schmid 2009a, Margin No. 1266, Pieth 2009, p. 175; Hauser et al. 2005, Section 73, Margin No. 2). In the German criminal procedure, the prosecutor has to press charges when there is a probability that the accused has committed a criminal offense and will be convicted (Beulke 2008, Margin Nos. 114 and 357).

[326] Hürlimann (2006), p. 106.

[327] Heimgartner and Niggli. In: Niggli et al. (2011) BSK StPO, Art. 324, Margin No. 12.

[328] Landshut. In: Donatsch et al. (2010) Kommentar StPO, Art. 324, Margin No. 5; Pieth (2009), p. 175.

[329] Landshut. In: Donatsch et al. (2010) Kommentar StPO, Art. 324, Margin No. 6.

economy speak for this solution. In particular, an appeal proceedings would lead to an examination of the files, evidence, and indictment, a task that in reality falls strictly under the competence of the judge of fact.[330]

There is no board of indictment that would independently review the charges brought by the prosecutor. The legislature has deliberately refrained from introducing such a special procedure, although prior to the introduction of the CCrP such a procedure existed in some cantons.[331] Thus, the indictment is directly submitted to the court. However, the judge in charge of conducting the proceedings (*Verfahrensleitung*) has to examine *ex officio* whether the indictment[332] and the files have been properly compiled and whether the procedural requirements have been met and procedural bars exist (Article 329 para. 1 CCrP). This preliminary review is limited to a formal and summary examination of the indictment and the files. Among others, the judge in charge of conducting the proceedings has to examine whether the described behavior constitutes a criminal offense. Neither the accuracy of the conclusion drawn by the prosecutor nor whether the evidence would be enough to justify a guilty verdict have to be examined.[333] However, since sufficient grounds for suspicion is a procedural requirement, it is conceivable that the court[334] may discontinue the proceedings[335] or remit the indictment back to the prosecution[336] in case of manifest lack of sufficient suspicion (see Article 329 para. 2 CCrP). Hence, although the proceedings are pending before the court,[337] the authority in the

[330] Federal Council (2006), p. 1275; Landshut. In: Donatsch et al. (2010) Kommentar StPO, Art. 324, Margin No. 9; Schmid (2009b), Art. 324, Margin No. 4.

[331] Stephenson and Zalunardo-Walser. In: Niggli et al. (2011) BSK StPO, Art. 329, Margin No. 1.

[332] The indictment indicates the following: "(a) the place and date; (b) the prosecution department responsible for bringing the charge; (c) the court responsible for determining the charge; (d) the accused person and his defense counsel; (e) the aggrieved person; (f) as briefly, but precisely as possible: the criminal offenses that the accused person is accused of, with a description of the place, date, time, nature and consequences of the commission of the criminal offense; (g) the criminal offenses, with reference to the applicable statutory provisions, which, in the opinion of the prosecution, have been committed" (Article 325 para. 1 CCrP).

[333] Federal Council (2006), p. 1278; Griesser. In: Donatsch et al. (2010) Kommentar StPO, Art. 329, Margin Nos. 5 and 9–11; Schmid (2009b), Art. 329, Margin No. 2; Stephenson and Zalunardo-Walser. In: Niggli et al. (2011) BSK StPO, Art. 329, Margin No. 1.

[334] The court makes this decision upon request of the judge in charge of conducting the proceedings. An exception to this may be made in case of a single judge court (Griesser. In: Donatsch et al. (2010) Kommentar StPO, Art. 329, Margin No. 17). However, in any case, the verdict cannot be reached by the same authority previously responsible for deciding about the admittance of the indictment (Griesser. In: Donatsch et al. (2010) Kommentar StPO, Art. 329, Margin No. 17; Stephenson and Zalunardo-Walser. In: Niggli et al. (2011) BSK StPO, Art. 329, Margin No. 4).

[335] Griesser. In: Donatsch et al. (2010) Kommentar StPO, Art. 329, Margin No. 11; Schmid (2009b), Art. 320, Margin No. 2.

[336] Federal Council (2006), pp. 1278–1279; Pieth (2009), p. 181.

[337] According to Article 328 para. 1 CCrP, the proceedings before the court shall be considered to be pending upon receipt of the indictment. Furthermore, Article 328 para. 2 CCrP states that once the proceedings are pending, all authority in the proceeding shall become vested in the court.

proceeding may be returned to the prosecution. However, where the court expects an acquittal anyway, it is usually not necessary to return the indictment to the prosecution. Hence, a return of the indictment will generally only occur in those cases where the court believes that a criminal offense has been committed but that the indictment does not meet the legal requirements.[338] Separation of powers precludes the prosecutor from giving instructions to the prosecution that go beyond the correction of the indictment.[339]

This procedure, put in place for the examination of the charge, was inspired by the German criminal procedure, where the court competent for the main hearing decides on the opening of the main proceedings (*Zwischenverfahren*).[340] In the German criminal procedure, the court decides to open main proceedings if, in light of the results of the preparatory proceedings, there appear to be sufficient grounds to suspect that the indicted accused has committed a criminal offense (Article 203 D-CCP). A refusal has limited res iudicata effect since a re-opening of criminal proceedings is only possible based on new evidence or facts (Section 211 D-CCP).[341] This rule has been criticized for the reason that the order to open main proceedings would amount to a pre-condemnation.[342] The same criticism may also apply to the Swiss criminal procedure and may be increased by the fact that, in contrast to the German criminal procedure, in the event of a negative outcome, the court remits the indictment back to the prosecution when necessary in order for additions or corrections to be made (Article 329 para. 2 CCrP).[343] However, despite these criticisms, this procedure is absolutely necessary in order to control the prosecutor's decision and to protect the suspect against unfounded accusations.[344]

[338] Griesser. In: Donatsch et al. (2010) Kommentar StPO, Art. 329, Margin No. 21.

[339] Stephenson and Zalunardo-Walser. In: Niggli et al. (2011) BSK StPO, Art. 329, Margin No. 12.

[340] See Roxin and Schünemann (2012), Section 42.

[341] See Beulke (2008), Margin No. 363; Roxin and Schünemann (2012), Section 42, Margin No. 19.

[342] Beulke (2008), Margin No. 352; Roxin and Schünemann (2012), Section 42, Margin No. 3; Kühne (2010), Margin Nos. 622–622.1.

[343] The possibility of modifications and additions to the charge are laid down in Article 333 CCrP: "The Court shall provide the prosecution with the opportunity to modify the charge if, in its opinion, the circumstances of the case as set out in the indictment indicate that another criminal offense could have been committed but the indictment does not meet the statutory requirements" (para. 1 CCrP). This rule is an exception to the principle governing the charge (Article 9 para. 1 CCrP). In bringing public charges, the public prosecutor defines the procedural act—the factual behavior which, in his view, requires punishment. The main hearing is restricted to this as the procedural subject. Further offenses, other factual occurrences, cannot be easily taken into consideration during the proceedings.

[344] For Germany, see Beulke (2008), Margin No. 352; Roxin and Schünemann (2012), Section 42, Margin No. 3; Kühne (2010), Margin No. 622.2.

6.4.5.3 Application Frequency

For more on the frequency of charges being pressed in comparison to alternative proceedings, see Sect. 6.5.1.1, para 4 et seq.

6.5 Alternative Proceedings in the Swiss Criminal Justice System

6.5.1 Penal Order Proceedings

6.5.1.1 Nature and Importance of the Proceedings

A preliminary investigation does not always lead to charges being brought before the court, even though the prosecutor may feel that there is sufficient reason to suspect the accused person of having committed the criminal offense. If the accused person has, in the preliminary proceedings, accepted responsibility for the factual circumstances of the case, or if the circumstances have been otherwise sufficiently resolved, and provided that the sentence to be imposed does not exceed 6 months imprisonment, the public prosecutor[345] issues a penal order[346] (also known as summary punishment order; *Strafbefehl*). The prosecutor has no discretion in deciding whether he wants to use the ordinary proceedings or the way of summary punishment. As soon as the conditions are fulfilled, the prosecutor is obligated to issue a penal order.[347]

The penal order proceedings are a special procedure regulated by Article 352 et seq. CCrP. It is a simplified written procedure where the prosecutor decides mainly on the basis of the police files. Thus, this procedure may result in a judgment without the parties being heard. In contrast to judgments, penal orders do not contain reasoning. The content of the penal order is limited to the circumstances of the case of which the accused person is accused; the criminal offenses which have been committed; the sentence; the ensuing costs and compensation; a description of the items and assets seized, to be released or confiscated; and a reference to

---

[345] Prior to the introduction of the CCrP, in some cantons it was the examining magistrate or a judge (*Strafbefehlsrichter*) who was responsible for issuing the penal order. For an overview, see Gilliéron (2010), pp. 109–113.

[346] On the content of the penal order, see Article 353 CCrP.

[347] Riklin. In: Niggli et al. (2011) BSK StPO, Art. 352, Margin Nos. 14–15; Schwarzenegger. In: Donatsch et al. (2010) Kommentar StPO, Art. 352, Margin No. 12; Schmid (2009b), Art. 352, Margin No. 4; Piquerez et al. (2011), Margin No. 1722. An exception to this obligation should be made when it is highly probable that the accused will make opposition. In such a case, there would no longer be a benefit of procedural simplification (Gilliéron and Killias. In: Kuhn and Jeanneret (2011) Commentaire Romand CPP, Art. 352, Margin No. 20; see also Jeanneret 2010, pp. 142–143).

Table 6.6 Numbers of penal orders issued in comparison with charges brought before court in the cantons of Zug and Zurich (2008–2011)

		2008		2009		2010		2011	
		Absolute number	%	Absolute number	%	Absolute number	%	Absolute number	%
Canton of Zug	Penal order	4,850	98.5	5,415	98.3	5,120	98.7	5,546	98.6
	Charges	75	1.5	92	1.7	70	1.3	80	1.4
Canton Zurich	Penal order	12,028	83.5	12,317	84.4	12,354	85	13,727	90.4
	Charges	2,369	16.5	2,282	15.6	2,172	15	1,459	9.6

Source: Data from Supreme Court of the Canton of Zug (2009, 2010, 2011), Section E III 1.2; Supreme Court of the Canton of Zug (2012), Section E IV 1.2; Statistical information received from the Senior Public Prosecutor's Office of Zurich on February 2, 2012

the possibility of raising an objection to the order and the consequences of not raising an objection (Article 353 para. 1 CCrP). The prosecutor must only give brief reasons for a revocation of a suspended sentence or a suspended discharge.

The penal order is not a judgment of first instance but an offer to the parties for an out-of-court settlement of the criminal case[348] or a proposed judgment (*Urteilsvorschlag*)[349] respectively a provisional judgment (*provisorisches Urteil*).[350] In this procedure, an over-ordination and a sub-ordination between the prosecution and the accused still exists.[351] In the event of a penal order, the case is exclusively evaluated by the prosecutor and he is the one who imposes the sentence. During this process, the defendant is usually not represented by a lawyer. Since the prosecutor does not have the duty to hear him prior to the decision, the defendant usually does not participate. The defendant may only accept the order or refuse it by raising written objection within 10 days (Article 354 para. 1 CCrP). Bargaining between prosecution and defendant does not take place. If no objection is made, the penal order becomes final and has the same effect as a judgment following a main hearing (Article 354 para. 3 CCrP).

In the Swiss criminal justice system, the majority of convictions do not result from a court trial but are based upon a penal order. Based on estimation, more than 90 % of all cases overall are settled out of court.[352] Nationwide statistical data are not available. Table 6.6 shows the number of penal orders issued in

[348] In German: *Vorschlag zur aussergerichtlichen Erledigung des Straffalles* (Federal Council 2006, p. 1291). See also Schmid (2009b), Vor Art. 352–357, Margin No. 1.

[349] Riklin (2006b), p. 115; Schubarth (2007), p. 527. See also Piquerez et al. (2011), Margin No. 1718; Jeanneret (2010), p. 139.

[350] Riklin (2006b), p. 115; Schwitter (1996), p. 7; Schubarth (2007), p. 527.

[351] Dissenting Donatsch (1994), pp. 324–325. In his opinion, the prosecution and the accused person stand on an equal footing.

[352] Hutzler (2010), p. 125; Riklin (2006a), p. 505; Riklin (2007), p. 763.

comparison with the number of cases brought before court in the cantons Zug and Zurich.[353]

Although the presented data are not directly comparable, they give a picture of the importance this summary proceeding occupies within the criminal justice system.

The introduction of the CCrP in 2011 has provoked an increase in penal orders issued in the canton of Zurich. This is due to the fact that, in the canton of Zurich prior to the introduction of the CCrP, the sanction pronounced in the penal order was limited to 3 months imprisonment. The CCrP allowing a sentence up to 6 months imprisonment has enlarged the prosecutor's power. To the contrary, in the canton of Zug, prosecutors already had the power to impose a sentence up to 6 months imprisonment prior to 2011.

The penal order procedure is a very efficient way to deal with an increasing caseload. Furthermore, it spares the offender a criminal trial, although not a criminal record. However, this simplified procedure raises some concerns. The next section centers its discussion on the problems related to the powerful position of the prosecutor in this procedure and the lack of external control. Furthermore, it discusses the position of the offender respectively the victim.

6.5.1.2 Selected Problems Related to the Proceedings

6.5.1.2.1 Compatibility with Article 6 ECHR

At first sight, the penal order proceeding violates the right to a fair trial laid out in Article 6 ECHR. Among others, this provision guarantees the right to a public hearing in the determination of any criminal charge by an independent and impartial tribunal. When issuing the penal order, the prosecutor does neither enjoy judicial independence nor impartiality. However, according to established Strasbourg case law, this does not in itself mean that the Convention is breached. [354] In such instances, the Court requires that domestic law provides for the possibility to have all aspects (i.e. legal and factual) of the decision reviewed by a judicial

---

[353] The canton of Basel-City is not included in this table. Until 2011, penal orders were not directly issued by the public prosecutor in this canton, but by a penal order judge (*Strafbefehlsrichter*). The situation was quite similar to the one in Germany (see Sect. 7.5.2). The public prosecutor made a written application to the judge. In his application, he requested a specific punishment. Between 2008 and 2010, the judge did not refer one single application back to the prosecutor. Over this time period, over 96 % of the cases were terminated annually by penal order. The annual reports of the Government Council of the Canton Basel-City to the Parliament in its chapter on courts provide detailed figures.

[354] ECHR, February 21, 1984, Öztürk–Germany (Series A, No. 73), para. 58; ECHR, August 25, 1987, Lutz–Germany (Series A, No. 123), para. 57; ECHR, December 16, 1992, Hennings–Germany (Series A, No. 251), para. 50; BGE 114 Ia 143.

Table 6.7 Number of penal orders issued by the public prosecution service of the canton of Zug and objections (2008–2011)

	2008		2009		2010		2011	
	Absolute number	%	Absolute number	%	Absolute number	%	Absolute number	%
Total penal orders	4,850	100	5,415	100	5,120	100	5,546	100
Written objection	261	5.4	360	6.6	304	5.9	231	4.2
- *of which: by senior public prosecutor*	*5*	*1.9*	*7*	*1.9*	*3*	*0.99*	*5*	*2.2*

Source: Data from Supreme Court of the Canton of Zug (2009, 2010, 2011), Section E III 1.2 and 1.7.1; Supreme Court of the Canton of Zug (2012), Section E IV 1.2 and 1.7.1

institution, which does fully comply with the requirements of Article 6 ECHR.[355] In the Swiss penal order proceedings, the defendant has the possibility of raising objection and asking for a full trial.[356] The right to be heard, as well as all other procedural rights guaranteed by the Constitution, the CCrP, and the ECHR are subsequently respected.[357] However, oppositions occur very infrequently,[358] which does not necessarily mean that the defendant agrees with the prosecutor's decision, but may be the manifestation of indifference, fear, and ignorance of law.[359]

Table 6.7 shows the frequency of objections raised against a penal order in the canton of Zug. On average, 6 % of penal orders are contested annually, a very low percentage of which (i.e. 1–2 %) may be attributed to the senior public prosecutor.

In renouncing opposition, it is assumed that the accused person waives the procedural guarantees of the ECHR.[360] Such a waiver is effective provided that it is clear and unequivocal, which implies that the accused makes his decision with knowledge of the legal and factual situation of the case.[361] This may not always be

[355] ECHR, April 29, 1988, Belilos–Switzerland (Series A, No. 132), paras 69–73.

[356] "If an objection is raised, the prosecution takes any further evidence which is necessary to enable the objection to be determined. Following the taking of evidence, the prosecution decides, whether to (a) stand by its decision to issue a penal order; (b) discontinue the proceedings; (c) issue a new penal order; (d) bring charges at the court of first instance" (Article 355 para. 3 CCrP). If the prosecution stands by its decision to issue a penal order, then it transfers the files to the court of first instance so that the principal proceedings can be conducted (Article 356 para. 1 CCrP).

[357] Hauser et al. (2005), Section 86, Margin No. 1; Donatsch (1994), p. 324; Moreillon (2010), pp. 26–28; see also Schwitter (1996), p. 41.

[358] See Table 6.7. According to Dubs, an opposition occurs in less than 10 % of the cases (Dubs 1996, p. 141).

[359] Hauser et al. (2005), Section 86, Margin No. 5.

[360] On the waiver of the right to be judged by an independent and impartial judge, see Zimmerlin (2008), pp. 538–548.

[361] ECHR, February 27, 1980, Deweer–Belgium (Series A, No. 35), para. 49. See also Donatsch (1994), pp. 326–332; Pieth (2009), pp. 194–195; Zimmerlin (2008), pp. 484–520.

the case, since a non-negligible percentage of the population[362] has some difficulties understanding a text of some complexity.[363]

According to Article 6 ECHR and Article 30 para. 3 of the Swiss Federal Constitution, judgments have to be pronounced publicly. The European Court has interpreted this to mean either oral pronouncement of judgments or depositing the judgments in the registry, where they are accessible to the public.[364] The public availability of judgments is very important in building public confidence in the administration of justice. In contrast to the right of an independent and impartial judge or tribunal, the defendant is not entitled to waive public pronouncements of judgments, since this right belongs to the public.[365] To comply with this, Article 69 para. 2 CCrP provides that penal orders are to be open for public inspection. A proof of interest is not required.[366]

6.5.1.2.2 Issuance of a Penal Order Without Prior Hearing of the Parties

The public prosecutor issues a penal order if the accused person has, in the preliminary proceedings, accepted responsibility for the factual circumstances of the case[367] or if the circumstances have been otherwise sufficiently resolved (Article 352 CCrP).[368] Hence, in the second scenario, a hearing of the accused prior to the decision is not a condition. This is rather problematic since this simplified procedure is inclined to produce wrongful convictions that could be avoided through a better clarification of the circumstances of the case. In fact, wrongful convictions in this kind of proceedings are mainly attributable to the fact that no preliminary hearing of the defendant takes place.[369] Furthermore, the scope

[362] According to the Adult Literacy and Lifeskills Survey (ALL) of 2003, which provides information on the skills and attitudes of adults aged 16–65, about 16 % of the Swiss population is unable to understand a text of some complexity (Notter 2006, p. 9). The results of the Pisa survey (2009) which tested students aged 15 show similar results. Literacy competencies across Europe are situated on the same level as in Switzerland (Nidegger et al. 2010).

[363] On this problematic, see Gilliéron and Killias (2007), p. 391; Riklin (2006a), p. 506; Riklin (2006b), pp. 122–127; Riklin (2007), pp. 775–778.

[364] ECHR, December 8, 1983, Pretto and Others—Italy (Series A. No. 71), paras 25–26; BGE 124 IV 234, 240; BGE 115 V 244, 255; see also Donatsch (1994), p. 343.

[365] Hauser et al. (2005), Section 82, Margin No. 24; Riklin (2006b), pp. 117–122; Zimmerlin (2008), pp. 608–619.

[366] Federal Council (2006), p. 1152.

[367] In the event that an accused has confessed, the prosecution has to examine the credibility of this confession (Article 160 CCrP). On the requirement of a confession, see Hutzler (2010), pp. 475–550.

[368] E.g. blood alcohol test proves drunkenness (Federal Council 2006, p. 1289).

[369] On the problem of wrongful convictions in the penal order proceedings, see Gilliéron (2010), pp. 101–146.

of application of the penal order proceedings, at the origin designed for petty offenses punishable with a fine, has been widely expanded over time.[370] Today, the prosecutor has the possibility to impose a prison sentence of up to 6 months (art. 352 para. 1 CCrP). As a consequence, the penal order proceeding is no longer limited to petty offenses but extends into criminal acts of some gravity, such as misdemeanors.[371] A prison sentence is a sanction serious enough that it should not be imposed only by the appreciation of the prosecutor without compulsory preliminary hearing of the accused and without any judicial control.[372] At least, when the prosecutor wants to order community service instead of a prison sentence, he must conduct a hearing with the accused, since such a sanction can only be imposed with the consent of the offender (Article 37 para. 1 SCC).[373] Furthermore, the prosecutor invites the aggrieved person and the accused to a hearing, if an exemption from punishment comes under consideration in accordance with the provisions in Article 53 SCC.[374]

In general, in the event of serious accusations (misdemeanors and felonies), the standard concerning the requirement of sufficient clarification of the circumstances should be set higher. Thus, in most cases, a hearing by the police or prosecutor should become unavoidable.[375]

Internal guidelines of the cantonal prosecution services may provide for constellations in which a preliminary hearing of the offender is the rule. The instructions of the Senior Public Prosecutor's Office of the canton of Zurich for instance requires the prosecutor to hear the offender prior to the decision if: "(1) the prosecutor has the intention to impose an unsuspended custodial sentence of more than three months or if a suspended prison sentence is revoked; (2) the offender has not reached the age of 20 at the time of the crime; (3) internal guidelines provide for a mandatory hearing (i.e. in the guidelines regarding the way of dealing with violent offenses)."[376]

---

[370] Federal Council (2006), p. 1290; Gilliéron and Killias (2007), p. 381; Riklin (2006a), p. 505; Hauser et al. (2005), Section 86, Margin No. 3.

[371] Gilliéron and Killias (2007), p. 381; Gilliéron (2010), p. 45.

[372] Riklin. In: Niggli et al. (2011) BSK StPO, Art. 352, Margin No. 4; Schwarzenegger. In: Donatsch et al. (2010) Kommentar StPO, Art. 352, Margin No. 5; Schmid (2009b), Art. 352, Margin No. 3; Gilliéron (2010), pp. 183–185; Gilliéron and Killias (2007), p. 397; Hutzler (2010), pp. 319–323.

[373] Schmid (2009b), Art. 352, Margin No. 3.

[374] See Sect. 6.3.4.3.

[375] Schmid (2009a), Margin No. 1354, Schmid (2009b), Art. 352, Margin No. 3; Schwarzenegger. In: Donatsch et al. (2010) Kommentar StPO, Art. 352, Margin No. 5. According to Riklin, such an approach would hardly comply with the law (Riklin. In: Niggli et al. (2011) BSK StPO, Art. 352, Margin No. 4).

[376] WOSTA, point 14.1.2 (2012).

6.5.1.2.3 Notification

Service should take place by way of registered post or by some means that enables acknowledgement of receipt, such as by the police (Article 85 para. 2 CCrP). In case the place of residence of the addressee is unknown and cannot be ascertained, despite reasonable inquiries, service should take place by way of publication in the designated official journal of the Federation or the canton. However, in the event of penal orders, they are deemed to be served even if they are not published (Article 88 para. 4 CCrP). This means that the time-limit for an appeal begins even without notification and that the decision may enter into force. From a legal point of view, this rule is questionable, particularly in regard to the fundamental rights of the individual. In particular, pursuant to Article 32 para. 3 of the Swiss Constitution, every convicted person has the right to have their conviction reviewed by a higher court. Thus, a waiver of rights should not be accepted too rapidly.[377] It is questionable if a time-limit to lodge an appeal can begin without the accused person's knowledge at all. The public prosecution service of the canton of Zurich has recognized this problem. Its guidelines provide that penal orders should, whenever possible, be handed over personally to persons living in unstable housing situations.[378]

6.5.1.2.4 Proceedings in Relation to Objections and Before the Court of First Instance

In case of an objection, the prosecutor still has control over the proceedings. He should take any further evidence necessary to enable an objection to be determined (Article 355 para. 1 CCrP).[379] A need for this exists in particular when the investigations prior to the issue of the penal order were superficial. A hearing of the defendant is usually necessary since he does not have to provide reasons for his objection (Article 354 para. 2 CCrP). Pursuant to Article 355 para. 2 CCrP, if the person who raised the objection fails to appear, despite being summoned and not being excused, the objection is treated as if it had been withdrawn. The same consequence is drawn in the event that the person who raised objection fails to appear before the court of first instance (Article 356 para. 4 CCrP). These severe provisions lead to an unjustified difference of treatment between the accused person whose case is dealt with by way of penal order and the "normal" accused. In ordinary proceedings, a person who, without permission, fails to appear or who

[377] Arquint. In: Niggli et al. (2011) BSK StPO, Art. 88, Margin No. 10; Schmid (2009b), Art. 88, Margin No. 9; Brüschweiler. In: Donatsch et al. (2010) Kommentar StPO, Art. 88, Margin No. 8; Gilliéron and Killias. In: Kuhn and Jeanneret (2011) Commentaire Romand CPP, Art. 353, Margin Nos. 11–16.

[378] WOSTA, point 8.2.3.1.

[379] See footnote 356 for the possibilities the prosecutor has following the taking of evidence.

appears too late may be punished by way of a fixed penalty order and may, in addition, be brought before the authority by the police (Article 205 para. 4 CCrP).[380] Furthermore, in an ordinary proceeding, the accused also has a right to have his case determined by a court in the event that he fails to appear without permission. Then, a proceeding *in absentia* may take place.[381] To agree with Jeanneret, the legislature within this rule has given an excessive priority to the economy of procedure to the detriment of the procedural guarantees.[382]

6.5.1.2.5 Control of the Public Prosecutor

The responsibility to issue penal orders lies within the public prosecutor's office. Control mechanisms in this summary proceeding are almost nonexistent.[383] Ordinarily, a check is exclusively made by the concerned person, namely the defendant.[384] However, whether this mechanism is efficient enough to counterbalance the enormous power vested in the prosecution is questionable. Different reasons already mentioned above may hinder the defendant from lodging an appeal.[385] In the cantons where a senior public prosecution service respectively an office of the attorney general has been introduced, the senior public prosecution may have the possibility to raise written objection against the prosecutor's decision if the canton expressly provides for such a competence (see Article 354 para. 1 lit. c CCrP).[386] This would allow a counter-check of the penal order. The cantons of Zug and Zurich for instance have implemented this possibility.[387] Statistical information from the canton of Zug show that contestations by the senior public prosecutor occur very infrequently. On average, less than 2 % of penal orders are annually contested by the senior public prosecutor.[388] This can either signify that the public prosecutor fulfills his task with the required caution. On the other hand, this can also mean that this control mechanism is not very efficient. It could be that the higher ranking authority does not want to discredit the work of the lower ranking officers

---

[380] Schwarzenegger. In: Donatsch et al. (2010) Kommentar StPO, Art. 355, Margin No. 2; Pieth (2009), p. 195; Schubarth (2007), p. 534.

[381] Riklin. In: Niggli et al. (2011) BSK StPO, Art. 355, Margin No. 2; Moreillon (2010), p. 34; According to Jeanneret, this rule violates Article 6 ECHR, since a failure of the accused person to appear may not necessarily mean that he withdraws his opposition (Jeanneret 2010, pp. 161–162).

[382] Jeanneret (2010), p. 162.

[383] Schubarth (2007), p. 535.

[384] Riklin (2007), p. 770.

[385] See Sect. 6.5.1.2.

[386] Riklin. In: Niggli et al. (2011) BSK StPO, Art. 354, Margin No. 7; Schmid (2009b), Art. 354, Margin No. 5.

[387] Section 46 ZG-COA. In the canton of Zurich, the competence to raise objection has been given to the chief public prosecutor and not to the senior public prosecutor (Section 103 ZH-COA).

[388] See Table 6.7.

publicly. If this is the case, the senior public prosecutor will only intervene in the cases where it is absolutely clear that the prosecutor shouldn't have issued a penal order. To counteract this problem, it might be conceivable to oblige the public prosecutor to obtain the approval of the senior public prosecutor or the attorney general prior to the issue of the penal order. Such a provision would derive from the supervision by the higher ranking authority over the lower-ranking one (see Article 14 para. 5 CCrP). In this case, the senior public prosecutor respectively the attorney general would not be allowed to raise objection against the penal order anymore.[389] The cantons of Fribourg,[390] Lucerne,[391] and Zurich[392] for instance provide for such a possibility. Currently, there is no canton that would provide for an approval of the judge.[393]

Besides the accused person and the senior public prosecutor respectively the attorney general, other parties that are affected may raise an objection to the issuing of a penal order. Persons whose items and assets are seized are, for instance, directly affected.[394] What about the aggrieved person respectively the private claimant? The legislature has deliberately refrained from providing an aggrieved person the right to lodge an appeal with the reasons that, in such a proceeding, no decision is made concerning civil claims and that a penal order cannot contain an acquittal.[395] As a consequence, the aggrieved person would not be directly affected. However, this view overlooks the fact that the aggrieved person respectively the private claimant may be otherwise affected by the penal order, namely when the accused person has accepted the civil claims of the private claimant but, contrary to Article 353 para. 2 CCrP, no note has been made of this in the penal order. This recognition becomes legally effective when no opposition is made and is acknowledged as a judicial vitiation of title.[396] Furthermore, the victim may be affected in the event that the prosecutor has considered a qualification of the criminal offense (i.e. act of aggression instead of an assault) that is too lenient or when the decisions regarding the costs or compensation are erroneous.[397] For this reason, the penal

[389] Schmid (2007), p. 704.

[390] Article 67 para. 4 FR-Courts Act.

[391] Section 66 subs. 2 LU-COA.

[392] Section 46 subs. 7 ZH-COA.

[393] Although the CCrP excludes the option of issuing penal orders by a judge, it should be up to the cantons to decide whether they want to implement such an option.

[394] Riklin. In: Niggli et al. (2011) BSK StPO, Art. 352, Margin No. 8; Schwarzenegger. In: Donatsch et al. (2010) Kommentar StPO, Art. 354, Margin No. 4; Schmid (2009b), Art. 354, Margin No. 4.

[395] AB S 2006 1050.

[396] Federal Council (2006), pp. 1290–1291; Riklin. In: Niggli et al. (2011) BSK StPO, Art. 353, Margin No. 6; Schwarzenegger. In: Donatsch et al. (2010) Kommentar StPO, Art. 353, Margin No. 10; Gilliéron and Killias. In: Kuhn and Jeanneret (2011) Commentaire Romand CPP, Art. 352, Margin No. 28.

[397] Riklin. In: Niggli et al. (2011) BSK StPO, Art. 354, Margin Nos. 9–15; Schmid (2009b), Art. 354, Margin No. 6; Gilliéron and Killias. In: Kuhn and Jeanneret (2011) Commentaire Romand CPP, Art. 352, Margin No. 29.

order should also be made available in writing to the victim respectively the civil claimant and a right to make opposition should be conferred on them.[398] For this reason, the guidelines of the Senior Public Prosecution Service of the canton of Zurich provide for the right of the civil claimant to raise objection against the penal order.[399]

The possibility to lodge an appeal against the penal order is currently the only control mechanism towards the prosecutor. However, the written form and the short 10 day time-limit may hinder the accused person and the other parties affected from exercising this right. Furthermore, objections must be accompanied by reasons. An exception to this is made for objections raised by the accused (Article 354 CCrP).

6.5.1.3 Conclusion

In the Swiss criminal justice system, the overwhelming majority of convictions results from a penal order. Thus, the determination of guilt is mainly made by the prosecutor. As in the United States, Switzerland has an administrative criminal justice system where the prosecutor combines executive and judicial powers. The assessment of the defendant's responsibility is made within the executive branch. The prosecutor decides mainly on the basis of the police files. The prosecutor, in deciding whether to punish the defendant, is an inquisitor seeking the correct outcome.[400] In the event that the accused person contests the prosecutor's decision, he can insist on a full trial that serves as a kind of judicial review.

It is highly problematic that the prosecutor faces extremely little oversight of his decisions. Ordinarily, a check is made exclusively by the concerned person, namely the defendant. Although, the cantons may give the competence to raise written objection to the senior public prosecutor or the attorney general against the prosecutor's decisions, it is hardly conceivable that the "same" authority will engage in a self-checking exercise.

It is clear that the legislature has set a high value on the economy of procedure, this largely to the detriment of procedural guarantees. Furthermore, it is highly questionable how a system where the vast majority of cases are settled out of court can fit with the separation of powers.

---

[398] Riklin. In: Niggli et al. (2011) BSK StPO, Art. 354, Margin No. 9; Schmid (2009b), Art. 354, Margin No. 6; Gilliéron and Killias. In: Kuhn and Jeanneret (2011) Commentaire Romand CPP, Art. 352, Margin No. 30.

[399] WOSTA, point 14.1.6.

[400] See Schubarth (2007), pp. 535–536.

6.5.2 *Abridged Proceedings*

6.5.2.1 Nature of the Proceedings

The CCrP has introduced the possibility of ending a case by way of abridged proceedings (*abgekürztes Verfahren*).[401] This procedure is quite similar to the plea bargaining process under the U.S. system and hence brings the Swiss legal system closer to the common law systems. Prior to the introduction of the CCrP, 3 out of 26 cantons[402] already had such an alternative procedure.

The abridged proceedings are alternative proceedings used to handle serious and less serious felonies and misdemeanors that cannot be dealt with by penal order. This proceeding allows the prosecutor to make a deal with the defendant provided that the defendant agrees to plead guilty.

The law does not determine the possible subject of the agreement. In the absence of such a provision, this may lead to the conclusion that sentence bargaining as well as charge bargaining is allowed.[403] Sentence bargaining involves the agreement to enter a guilty plea in exchange for a lighter sentence.[404] Charge bargaining involves a lowering of the charges in return for a guilty plea.[405] Unlike the United States, fact bargaining is prohibited.[406]

Economy of procedure and the principle of procedural efficiency are the foundation of the abridged proceedings.[407] The Federal Council assumes that this alternative proceeding will be particularly significant in the area of economic crimes. With these kinds of offenses, extensive investigations are usually needed, so that this contributes to the overloading of criminal justice system.[408]

---

[401] On the history, see Greiner and Jaggi. In: Niggli et al. (2011) BSK StPO, Vor Art. 358–362, Margin Nos. 19–23.

[402] Basel-Land, Ticino, Zug.

[403] Greiner and Jaggi. In: Niggli et al. (2011) BSK StPO, Vor Art. 358–362, Margin Nos. 26–28 and Art. 358, Margin Nos. 30–53, Schwarzenegger. In: Donatsch et al. (2010) Kommentar StPO, Art. 358, Margin No. 9–14; On the different types of plea bargains, see Kuhn (1998), pp. 80–82; Kuhn (2009), p. 167.

[404] According to the current practice of the Federal Supreme Court, a confession may lead to a reduction of one-fifth to one third of the foreseen penalty (see i.e. BGE 121 IV 202, 205 et seq.). In the abridged proceedings, a further reduction is possible, when additional reasons to mitigate respectively reduce a sentence exist (i.e. sincere repentance, confession of other crimes).

[405] For a detailed discussion, see Schwarzenegger. In: Donatsch et al. (2010) Kommentar StPO, Art. 358, Margin Nos. 9–14; Greiner and Jaggi. In: Niggli et al. (2011) BSK StPO, Art, 358, Margin Nos. 28–57.

[406] Schwarzenegger. In: Donatsch et al. (2010) Kommentar StPO, Art. 358, Margin Nos. 5–8.

[407] Jositsch and Bischoff (2007), pp. 429 and 437; Oberholzer (1993), pp. 159–160; Schwander (2007), p. 142.

[408] Federal Council (2006), p. 1295.

The prevailing legal opinion rejects the abridged proceedings for constitutional reasons.[409] In fact, numerous basic principles of the criminal procedure are affected, such as the principle of legality (Article 7 CCrP) and the principle of instruction (Article 6 CCrP). Those principles require the prosecutor to search *ex officio* for the factual truth and to bring a charge whenever there are sufficient grounds to suspect a person of having committed an offense. To the contrary, in abridged proceedings, all facts of the case must not be entirely clarified nor must all charges be brought, since the facts are based on a deal between the defendant and the prosecution.[410] Thus, the factual truth is replaced by a formal truth. The presumption of innocence and the right against self-incrimination are also undermined. However, as long as the accused person waives his rights in a clear and unequivocal manner, this alternative procedure does not breach the ECHR.[411]

The abridged proceedings face many of the same concerns as the U.S. plea bargaining process. Thus, there might be a risk of increased wrongful convictions. In fact, the accused might admit his guilt to avoid the uncertainties of trial outcomes.[412] The prosecutor, to be in a better position, might accuse the defendant of a more serious crime or of an additional crime of which he is clearly innocent in order to induce a plea to the proper crime. Furthermore, these alternative proceedings might disadvantage socially weaker defendants since they are often not defended with the same diligence.[413]

6.5.2.2 Proceedings

The accused person may submit an application to the prosecution for the case to be conducted by way of abridged proceedings provided that (1) he accepts liability for those circumstances essential to the legal evaluation of the case and that (2) he accepts at least in principle the civil claims (Article 358 para. 1 CCrP). The fact that only the accused person has the possibility to make an application aims to protect him from coercion by the prosecutor.[414] However, this does not mean that the prosecutor should not be allowed to inform the accused person of this alternative proceeding.[415] The application can be made at any time prior to the bringing of

---

[409] Bommer (2009), pp. 113–115; Donatsch and Cavegn (2008), p. 172; Jositsch and Bischoff (2007), pp. 437–438; Kuhn (1998), pp. 73–94; Oberholzer (1993), pp. 157–174; Pieth (2009), pp. 199–201; Pieth (2010), pp. 166–167; Schlauri (1999), p. 482; Schwander (2007), p. 146; Mazou (2011), p. 4.

[410] Bommer (2009), pp. 28–30; Breguet (2009), Margin Nos. 82–85 and 92–98; Greiner (2009), p. 241; Jositsch and Bischoff (2007), pp. 433–434; Kuhn (1998), p. 83; Kuhn (2009), p. 166; Schwander (2007), p. 142.

[411] ECHR, February 27, (1980), Deweer–Belgium (Series A, No. 35), paras 48–56.

[412] Bommer (2009), pp. 31–32; Breguet (2009), Margin Nos. 88–91; Greiner (2009), p. 231; Hausherr (2008), p. 310; Jositsch and Bischoff (2007), p. 435; Kuhn (2009), p. 167.

[413] Greiner (2009), p. 236.

[414] Federal Council (2006), p. 1295.

[415] Bommer (2009), pp. 10–11; Greiner (2009), p. 237; Pieth (2009), p. 197; Schmid (2009a), Margin No. 1376; Schmid (2009b), Art. 358, Margin No. 1; Jositsch and Bischoff (2007), p. 431.

charges. Furthermore, an abridged proceeding is only possible if the prosecution requests the imposition of a prison sentence not exceeding 5 years (Article 358 para. 2 CCrP).

The public prosecutor evaluates the application and definitively decides whether the case is to be conducted by way of abridged proceedings or not (Article 359 para. 1 CCrP). Thus, the accused has no legal remedies against the prosecutor's decision.[416] The prosecutor has complete discretion in making his decision. Hence, he may decline the petition, although the conditions for an application are fulfilled. The defendant has no legal right to having the case proceed by way of abridged proceedings.[417] The prosecutor will usually consider the strength of evidence and the costs and benefits of the investigation when making his decision. Furthermore, he will evaluate whether an acceptable and balanced solution that would satisfy both sides may be reached.[418] The prosecutor is not obliged to mention the reasons for his decision respectively rejection, so that his discretion remains unchecked.[419] In the canton of Zurich, the prosecutor has to obtain oral approval from the chief prosecutor prior to issuing his decision.[420] A rejection of the application does not preclude the possibility to resubmit a new application at a later stage in the preliminary proceedings.[421]

If the case is heard by way of abridged proceedings, the accused must be represented by defense counsel [Article 130 (e) CCrP]. The mandatory assistance of defense counsel intends to protect the accused person during the informal negotiations with the prosecution and stems from the principle of equality of arms.[422] Thus, the appointment of the defense counsel becomes mandatory as soon as informal negotiations start between the defendant and the prosecution, which usually occur prior to the application.[423]

---

[416] Federal Council (2006), p. 1296; Bommer (2009), p. 11; Schmid (2009b), Art. 359, Margin No. 1.

[417] Jeanneret (2010), p. 172; Bommer (2009), p. 12.

[418] Greiner and Jaggi. In: Niggli et al. (2011) BSK StPO, Art. 359, Margin No. 1.

[419] Contrary to the wording of the rule, some legal scholars assume that a brief justification must be given. Legal equality and prohibition of arbitrary decisions would argue in favor of a brief reasoning (see Hausherr 2008, pp. 311, 314; Kaufmann 2009, p. 157; Bommer 2009, p. 110). Other legal scholars argue that an obligation to state reasons would go too far (see Jeanneret 2010, p. 172; Greiner and Jaggi. In: Niggli et al. (2011) BSK StPO, Art. 359, Margin Nos. 4–6).

[420] WOSTA, point 14.3.1 (2012).

[421] Schmid (2009b), Art. 359, Margin No. 2.

[422] Jeanneret (2010), pp. 170–171; Schwarzenegger. In: Donatsch et al. (2010) Kommentar StPO, Art. 359, Margin No. 5; Bommer (2009), pp. 12–13.

[423] Bommer (2009), pp. 12–13; Schwarzenegger. In: Donatsch et al. (2010) Kommentar StPO, Art. 369, Margin No. 5; Pieth (2009), p. 197; Pieth (2010), p. 168; Mazou (2011), p. 10. Jeanneret on the other hand argues that the appointment of defense counsel becomes mandatory at the time the prosecutor accepts to handle the case by way of abridged proceedings (Jeanneret 2010, pp. 170–171).

Informal negotiations are closed by an indictment the prosecution conveys to the parties.[424] In the canton of Zurich, the draft of indictment requires the written authorization of the chief prosecutor before sending it to the parties.[425] The parties have 10 days to accept or reject the indictment (Article 360 para. 2 CCrP). While the acceptance of the accused has to occur expressively, a tacit acceptance of the private claimant suffices. In addition to the points usually found in an indictment (the accused person; the criminal offenses that the accused person is accused of, with a description of the place, date, time, nature, and consequences of the commission of the criminal offense; and a proposal of their legal qualification), this document contains the sentence, the regulation of the civil law claims of the private claimant, and the warning to the parties that by accepting the indictment they waive the right to ordinary proceedings and to initiate legal remedies (Article 360 para. 1 CCrP). The consequence of this last point is that the convicted may file a petition for revision only in a restricted way. In contrast to the ordinary proceedings, in abridged proceedings the court does not conduct an evidentiary hearing. Thus, it is not possible to file a petition for revision based on new evidence. However, the use of this legal remedy should still be possible for eliminating decisions that are unacceptable from a constitutional point of view (e.g. exercise of coercive power by the prosecution on the suspect or abuse of public office).[426] Some legal scholars argue that in case of false confession of the convicted, the possibility to file a petition of revision should still be open in order to correct a wrongful conviction.[427] If the parties reject the indictment, the prosecution will conduct ordinary proceedings (Article 360 para. 5 CCrP). The rejection of a single private claimant provokes the failure of the whole process.[428] Declarations provided by the parties in respect to the abridged proceedings cannot be used in ordinary proceedings.[429] On the other hand, if the indictment is accepted, the prosecution transmits the indictment together with the files to the Court of First Instance (Article 360 para. 4 CCrP).

Instead of conducting an evidentiary proceedings at the principal hearing, the Court of First Instance questions the accused person in order to establish whether he accepts the circumstances of the case on which the charge is based, and whether this assertion corresponds to the position as set out in the files (Article 361 CCrP). The examination will be limited to ascertain that the rights conferred to the parties have

[424] The accused and the private claimant (see Article 104 para. 1 CCrP). In the event that the aggrieved person and the victim have not expressly declared their participation in the criminal proceedings as a criminal or civil claimant, the prosecution has the duty to inform them of this opportunity (see Article 118 para. 4 CCrP; Article 305 para. 1 CCrP).

[425] WOSTA, point 14.3.2.

[426] Donatsch and Cavegn (2008), pp. 162–163; Kaufmann (2009), p. 156; Schmid (2009b), Art. 362, Margin Nos. 15–16.

[427] Kaufmann (2009), pp. 184–185; Kuhn (2009), pp. 169–170. Contra Greiner and Jaggi. In: Niggli et al. (2011) BSK StPO, Art. 362, Margin No. 55.

[428] Pieth (2009), p. 198.

[429] Jositsch and Bischoff (2007), p. 433; Schmid (2009b), Art. 360, Margin No. 15. See Sect. 6.5.2.2, para 7.

been respected and that the confession of the accused is credible.[430] Party pleadings do usually not take place.[431] If necessary, the court may also question the other parties present, namely the private claimant and the prosecution.

Following the principal hearing, the court retires and conducts its deliberation in private. The court has to determine whether the carrying out of abridged proceedings is lawful and appropriate, whether the charge corresponds to the conclusions of the principal hearing and to the files, and whether the sanctions requested are reasonable (Article 362 para. 1 CCrP). Thus, the court does not determine whether the conviction of the accused person is lawful, but whether it is lawful to convict him by way of abridged proceedings.[432] Legal criteria for the evaluation of the appropriateness are missing.[433] It will be up to the courts, based on specific cases, to develop criteria to determine the inappropriateness. They will have to examine in each case whether objective grounds hinder the conduct of abridged proceedings.[434] Legal equality considerations, for instance, may be considered. A judgment that would deviate significantly from judgments pronounced in similar cases in ordinary proceedings should be deemed inappropriate.[435] The prosecutor enjoys vast discretion regarding the sanction requested. Thus, the court should only intervene in cases of manifest abuse.[436]

If the court comes to the conclusion that the requirements for a judgment by way of abridged proceedings are met, it converts the criminal offenses, sentence, and civil claim of the indictment into a judgment (Article 362 para. 2 CCrP). On the other hand, if the court estimates that the requirements are not met, it sends the files back to the prosecution in order to proceed by way of ordinary proceedings (Article 362 para. 3 CCrP). This decision cannot be challenged. Declarations like confessions provided by the parties in respect to the abridged proceedings cannot be used in ordinary proceedings (Article 362 para. 4 CCrP). Records of the evidence that is not to be used have to be removed from the criminal files and kept separately until the final and legally binding completion of the proceedings. Confessions of the accused person given prior to the application to the prosecution to conduct the case by way of abridged proceedings can still be used.[437] In order to guarantee that a confession of an accused or other concessions made between the parties will not have any influence in the further respectively ordinary proceedings, the prosecutor having conducted the abridged proceedings, the judge having rejected the application, as well as the private claimant should not be questioned as witness in ordinary proceedings.[438] The question of

---

430 Schmid (2009a), Margin No. 1385.

431 Schwarzenegger. In: Donatsch et al. (2010) Kommentar StPO, Art. 361, Margin No. 6; Schmid (2009b), Art. 361, Margin No. 10; Schmid (2009a), Margin No. 1384.

432 Bommer (2010), p. 156.

433 Bommer (2009), p. 114.

434 Greiner and Jaggi. In: Niggli et al. (2011) BSK StPO, Art. 362, Margin No. 7.

435 Schwarzenegger. In: Donatsch et al. (2010) Kommentar StPO, Art. 352, Margin No. 3.

436 Schwarzenegger. In: Donatsch et al. (2010) Kommentar StPO, Art. 362, Margin No. 5; Jeanneret (2010), p. 182; Greiner and Jaggi. In: Niggli et al. (2011) BSK StPO, Art. 362, Margin Nos. 14–15.

437 Schmid (2009b), Art. 362, Margin No. 11.

438 Schmid (2009b), Art. 362, Margin No. 11; Schmid (2009a), Margin No. 1388.

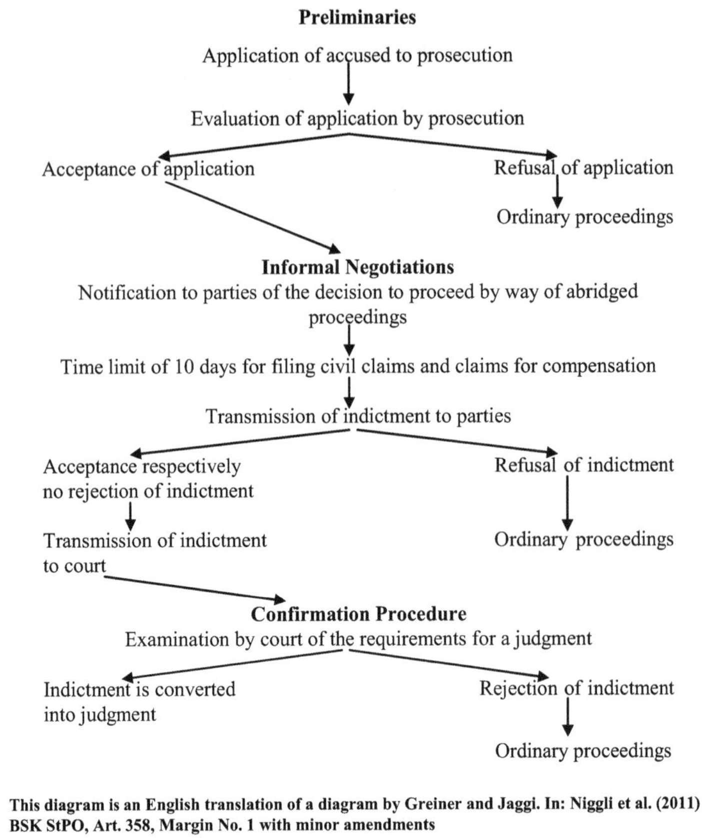

Fig. 6.1 Overview over the abridged proceedings

whether the same prosecutor or one other than the one having conducted the abridged proceedings should be entrusted with the continuation of the investigation is answered in different ways.[439] However, if the defendant withdraws his confession, the case must be assigned to a different prosecutor.[440]

A party may only appeal against a judgment in abridged proceedings on the basis that it did not accept the indictment or that the judgment does not correspond to the indictment (Article 362 para. 5 CCrP).[441]

Figure 6.1 provides an overview over the abridged proceedings.

[439] In favor of a systematic change of prosecutor when the abridged proceeding has failed, see Pieth (2009), p. 199; Pieth (2010), p. 170. According to Schmid, the prosecutor having conducted the abridged proceedings is not automatically biased (Schmid 2009b, Art. 362, Margin No. 10). If, for example, the court refuses the indictment because it concludes that the sanction is not appropriate, then the prosecutor would have no reason for withdrawal (Greiner and Jaggi. In: Niggli et al. (2011) BSK StPO, Art. 362, Margin No. 39).

[440] Greiner and Jaggi. In: Niggli et al. (2011) BSK StPO, Art. 362, Margin No. 39.

[441] On the possibility to file a petition for revision, see Sect. 6.5.2.2, para 4.

6.5.2.3 Area of Application and Application Frequency

6.5.2.3.1 Practical Significance of the Abridged Proceedings Prior to the Introduction of the CCrP in the Cantons of Basel-Land, Zug and Ticino

Basel-Land introduced the possibility to end a case by way of abridged proceedings in 2000. While, with the exception of 2006, the annual number of cases closed by way of abridged proceedings was situated between 11 and 14 from 2002 to 2007, a marked decrease has recently been registered.[442] In 2009 and 2010, the court convicted only one respectively two accused by way of abridged proceedings.[443] After the entry into force of the CCrP, seven persons were convicted by way of abridged proceedings in 2011.[444] From 2002 to 2008, abridged proceedings accounted for 5–10 % of the criminal proceedings subject to the ordinary procedure. The abridged proceedings are mainly used for property offenses, sexual offenses, road traffic offenses, and drug offenses.[445]

The canton of Zug has introduced the possibility to end a case by way of abridged proceedings in 2003. By the end of 2007, Zug had abolished the position of examining magistrate and implemented the "prosecutor model II". As a result, a complete reorganization of the prosecution and the court system occurred, so that the numbers prior to 2008 and thereafter are hardly comparable.[446] In 2008, the public prosecutor applied for abridged proceedings in four cases, in 2009 in six cases, in 2010 in seven cases, and in 2011 in ten cases.[447] From 2008 to 2010, the court did not reject a single application.[448] In 2011, the court did not accept two applications.[449] Similar to Basel-Land, the abridged proceedings accounted for 5–11 % of the criminal proceedings subject to ordinary proceedings. The abridged proceedings are used for property offenses, offenses against life and limb, offenses against liberty, sexual offenses, road traffic offenses, and drug offenses.[450]

The canton of Ticino was the first canton in Switzerland to introduce a kind of abridged proceedings in 1999. However, in reality, this procedure resembled more a modified or extended penal order proceedings. In fact, the prosecution and the

---

[442] The numbers can be found in the annual Official Report of the Canton Basel-Landschaft to the Parliament. The annual numbers are: 2000: 1, 2001: 3, 2002: 11, 2003: 13, 2004: 14, 2005: 13, 2006: 5, 2007: 11, 2008: 8. The numbers refer to *cases* and not to persons convicted.

[443] Cantonal Court of the Canton Basel-Landschaft (2010), p. 92; Cantonal Court of the Canton Basel-Landschaft (2011), p. 95. Since 2009, the numbers refer to convicted *persons*.

[444] Cantonal Court of the Canton Basel-Landschaft (2012), p. 106.

[445] Gilliéron (2010), p. 87.

[446] Supreme Court of the Canton of Zug (2009), pp. 7–8 and 28.

[447] Supreme Court of the Canton of Zug (2009, 2010, 2011), Section E III 1.2; Supreme Court of the Canton of Zug (2012), Section E IV 1.2.

[448] Supreme Court of the Canton of Zug (2009, 2010, 2011), Section E IV 3.2.

[449] Supreme Court of the Canton of Zug (2012), Section E V 3.2.

[450] Gilliéron (2010), p. 89.

defendant could reach an agreement concerning the form of procedure, but not the content. Thus, a deal concerning the charges was excluded.[451] During the years 1999–2008, the annual proportion of criminal proceedings subject to ordinary proceedings handled by way of abridged proceedings was situated between 5 and 10 %.[452]

6.5.2.3.2 First Experiences with the Abridged Proceedings According to the CCrP

Federal Level

According to the 2011 activity report of the Office of the Attorney General, the first experiences with the abridged proceedings have been positive. The introduction of the abridged proceedings allows adjudication of the criminal case more quickly.[453] In 2011, seven applications have been submitted to the Office of the Attorney General for the case to be conducted by way of abridged proceedings.[454]

Cantonal Level

In 2011, the five general prosecution offices of the canton of Zurich handled about 120 cases by way of abridged proceedings, in particular in the following areas: narcotic law, theft, fraud, misappropriation, criminal mismanagement, pornography, indecent assault, sexual acts with children, forgery of a document, and forgery of certificates. The four specific prosecution offices of the canton of Zurich treated 54 cases by way of abridged proceedings. Here, the main emphasis lies on violations of narcotic law (illicit drug trafficking and drug smuggling). Only six procedures in the field of white collar crime were conducted in this way in 2011. So far, the abridged proceedings have no practical importance in cases of serious offenses against life and limb. Thus, a total of approximately 174 procedures ended by way of abridged proceedings in the canton of Zurich in 2011, which represents 12 % of all cases brought before court. However, it is to be expected that there will be an increase in the cases handled by way of abridged proceedings.[455]

In the canton of Basel-City, 15 accused made an application to the prosecution for the case to be conducted by way of abridged proceedings in 2011. The applications were rejected in four cases. In three cases, the rejection occurred for reasons of procedural economy. The prosecution had either already written the accusation and thus, the abridged proceedings would have brought an additional

[451] Schlauri (1999), pp. 486–487.

[452] Bommer (2009), pp. 25–26.

[453] Office of the Attorney General (2012), p. 7.

[454] Office of the Attorney General (2012), p. 28.

[455] Senior Public Prosecutor of the canton Zurich Dr. Andreas Brunner, e-mail message to author, January 23, 2012.

expenditure, or the effort for the prosecution was not lower in the abridged proceedings than in the ordinary proceedings since the evidence was clear. In the fourth case, it was rejected because the expected sentence exceeded 5 years imprisonment. In two other cases, the abridged proceedings failed. In one case, the accused did finally not agree to the indictment and in the other case, no agreement could be reached concerning the sentence. In one case, the prosecution has not yet decided whether to accept or refuse the application. Violations of narcotic law, commercial fraud, theft for financial gain, misappropriation, criminal mismanagement, and forgery of a document are the kind of offenses the accused person was suspected of having committed and where an application was accepted. So far, the court has confirmed three out of eight applications respectively indictments. In the five other cases, the court must still conduct a principal hearing in order to determine whether to accept or reject the application.[456]

6.5.2.4 Conclusion

The introduction of the abridged proceedings has further expanded the power of the prosecutor. The overwhelming majority of procedures are ended by the prosecution alone. Besides the cases that are dropped, a very high percentage of accused is convicted by penal order. Charges are brought in a small percentage of the cases.[457] Thus, today, a court conviction is the exception. The abridged proceedings reinforce this situation. Although, formally the defendant's culpability occurs in court, in practice it is a sanction imposed by the public prosecutor.[458] In numbers, these alternative proceedings are practically negligible for the moment. However, in the abridged proceedings the imposition of prison sentences up to 5 years is possible. Thus, the abridged proceedings are not limited to petty offenses but may extend into serious criminal acts, a field that was previously exclusively reserved for the judge.[459]

In abridged proceedings, in contrast to ordinary proceedings, the court does not evaluate the legal circumstances of the case. In these alternative proceedings, the assessment of the defendant's responsibility is made within the executive branch, in the office of the prosecutor. In this process, the prosecutor acts as quasi-judicial decision-maker. However, the point of view of the prosecutor is naturally different from that of the court. The prosecutor does not sit as neutral fact finder but focuses on the incriminating circumstances. In fact, despite the obligation to objectivity,[460]

[456] Public Prosecutor Christian Triet, e-mail message to author, January 18, 2012. For more information about the cases, see Appendix VI.

[457] See Table 6.6.

[458] Bommer (2010), p. 166.

[459] Bommer (2010), pp. 166–167.

[460] The prosecution is obliged to investigate exculpatory and incriminatory circumstances with equal care (Article 6 para. 2 CCrP).

the prosecutor is not a judge. The submission of the prosecution to the court remains an indictment, even if it is converted into a judgment. The court does not determine whether the conviction of the accused person is lawful, but whether it is lawful to convict him by way of abridged proceedings, which is fundamentally different.[461]

Abridged proceedings were introduced with the idea of reducing the workload within the field of economic crime. However, experience so far shows that, contrary to what has been expected, the abridged proceedings are mainly used for drug offenses, property offenses, sexual offenses, and road traffic offenses.

6.6 Prosecutorial Control and Accountability

6.6.1 Control of Public Prosecutors

This section includes a discussion on the supervisory authorities over public prosecutors as well as their scope of supervision. It will also examine in how far the kind of procedure applied may have an influence on the control of the prosecutor's actions and to what extent the prosecutor's decisions are externally controlled.

6.6.1.1 External Supervisory Structures

Neither the Swiss Federal Constitution nor the CCrP clarifies the position of the prosecution service within the system of division of powers. Rather, this falls within the cantonal organizational autonomy (Article 47 para. 2 and Article 123 para. 2 Federal Constitution; Article 14 para. 5 CCrP). There is no uniform opinion on whether the prosecution service forms part of the executive or judicial power, or on whether it is a body sui generis on the edge of those two powers.[462] It is recognized that some of the prosecution service's competencies have the attributes typical for the executive power, such as representation before the court. At the same time, some of the prosecution service's competencies are more specific to the judicial power, such as deciding criminal cases other than by bringing a criminal action, for example issuing a penal order. Cantons enjoy wide discretion concerning the organizational integration of the prosecution service and concerning the scope of supervision.

This legal fragmentation has the consequence that the issue of the supervision of the prosecution service is not treated uniformly across Switzerland. However, despite this fragmentation two regulatory areas can be identified. Cantonal law

[461] See also Bommer (2010), pp. 167–168.

[462] On the different opinions, see Mettler (2001), pp. 73–82.

designates the competent supervisory body over the prosecution service and regulates the scope of supervision.

6.6.1.1.1 Supervisory Authority

Concerning the competent supervisory authority over the prosecution service, four solutions may be distinguished. The prosecution can either be under the authority of the executive or a judicial authority or the oversight may be split between the government and a judicial authority. A last solution consists of assigning the supervision to an authority sui generis such as a judicial council.

Placing the prosecution service under the control of the executive branch has the advantage for the government of effectively controlling the criminal policy and defining law enforcement priorities. A subordination of the prosecution and police under the same supervisory authority has the further benefit of strengthening control over the criminal justice authorities.[463] However, this model of supervision is connected with the danger of the prosecution service to come under political pressure.[464] The high majority of cantons put the prosecution service under the control of the government.

In cantons where the public prosecution service is completely integrated into the judiciary, an administrative and functional supervision by a court is appropriate. Such a system has the advantage of minimizing the risk of potential political influence.[465] A disadvantage of placing the prosecution service under the control of the judiciary is that it may be difficult for the government to implement a coherent criminal policy.[466] Another concern that arises with such a model of supervision is the loss of impartiality of the court. Such a risk can be lessened by limiting the functional supervision to the issue of general binding directives (i.e. administrative regulation) and by exercising purely administrative supervision.[467]

In principle, it is conceivable to split the control of the prosecution by assigning the functional supervision to the judiciary and the administrative supervision to the executive branch.[468] However, there is a degree of overlap between both types of supervision, in particular concerning the supervision of management within the public prosecution service (i.e. assignment of business and priority-setting) and organizational issues.[469] This may undermine the effectiveness of supervision since the judiciary and the government may pursue different interests. This may even

[463] Lienhard and Kettiger (2008), Margin Nos. 38–40.

[464] Lienhard and Kettiger (2008), Margin Nos. 41–42. On possible measures to reduce this risk, see Sect. 6.6.1.1.2, para 2.

[465] Lienhard and Kettiger (2008), Margin Nos. 43–44.

[466] Lienhard and Kettiger (2008), Margin No. 45.

[467] Lienhard and Kettiger (2008), Margin Nos. 46–52.

[468] On the scope of supervision, see Sect. 6.6.1.1.2.

[469] Lienhard and Kettiger (2008), Margin No. 28.

give rise to conflicts when the judiciary calls for professionally better work (i.e. penal orders more comprehensively justified), while at the same time the government requires a faster and more effective case management without allocating more resources.[470] Consequently, such a model of supervision should be rejected. This is what happened at the federal level. Prior to the introduction of the CCrP,[471] the functional supervision of the Office of the Attorney General was carried out by the Swiss Federal Criminal Court, while administrative supervision was assigned to the Federal Council. This shared supervision inevitably lead to some uncertainty on the part of the authorities responsible for the supervision and thus to time-consuming discussions between them to clarify the responsibilities.[472] Actually, this model is only found in 3 out of 26 cantons.

There is also the possibility to assign the supervision of the public prosecution service to an authority sui generis. Members of such authorities may be elected by the people or the parliament (judicial council). This authority may also be comprised of members of the judiciary (i.e. judges). The cantons of Fribourg, Geneva, Neuchâtel, and Ticino have introduced a judicial council to control the judicial and court authorities. Similarly, since the introduction of the CCrP, the Office of the Attorney General receives supervision from a supervisory authority elected by the Federal Parliament for a term of 4 years.[473] This supervisory authority is composed of seven members, namely one judge from the Swiss Federal Supreme Court, one judge from the Swiss Federal Criminal Court, two attorneys recorded in a cantonal attorneys register, and three specialists not belonging to a Federal Court and not inscribed in a cantonal attorneys register.[474]

6.6.1.1.2 Scope of Supervision

Article 4 para. 1 CCrP states that the prosecuting authorities, in applying the law, are independent and bound only by the law. However, the statutory authority to issue instructions to the prosecution authorities is reserved (Article 4 para. 2 CCrP). The Message of the Federal Council states that the independence and impartiality of the prosecution authorities can only be guaranteed if they are not subject to instructions from other state authorities. Thus, interventions of political authorities in concrete law enforcement activities of the prosecution are excluded.[475] According to this view, external directives are not completely excluded but

[470] Lienhard and Kettiger (2008), Margin No. 34.

[471] On the situation after the introduction of the CCrP, see Sect. 6.1.1.2, para 1.

[472] Mettler and Baumgartner (2010), pp. 63–64.

[473] Since it was recognized that a split supervision of the Office of the Attorney General has failed, the question about the competent authority to fulfill this duty was highly debated. Solutions proposed include: supervision by the government (Federal Council), supervision by an independent panel, supervision by a commission of the Federal Parliament (for an overview about the debates, see Mettler and Baumgartner 2010, pp. 64–69).

[474] Articles 23 and 25 of the Law on the Organization of the Federal Criminal Authorities.

[475] Federal Council (2006), p. 1129.

would typically be limited to an administrative supervision[476] of the prosecution.[477] A functional supervision,[478] however, would be excluded and thus the issuance of general and concrete directives to the prosecution not possible. Nevertheless, a professionally completely independent prosecution is not realized in all cantons. Some cantons, such as Appenzell Outer Rhodes, Basel-City, and Zurich, provide that the government may induce the prosecution to start proceedings but not to stop them.[479] The CCrP does not proscribe such a regulation.[480]

The prosecution service is sometimes regarded as an extended arm of the executive branch. Combating crime is a central task of the state and thus the executive branch will have to determine appropriate criminal policy. The government must therefore be allowed to issue general directives regarding law enforcement priorities to the prosecution.[481] The issue of general guidelines also has the purpose of creating a common practice wherever the law leaves the prosecutor discretion.

The right to issue instructions becomes an issue when the supervisory authority intervenes in individual proceedings. In fact, the danger that the government exploits its right to issue instructions for political reasons may exist.[482] However, the solution to such a danger does not consist of the elimination of the right to issue directives. Rather, measures to protect the prosecution against improper instructions and directives should be strengthened. The means to achieve this goal include the written form of instructions and the possibility in cases of dispute to examine the legality of instructions in an expeditious and binding manner.[483]

In activities where the prosecution is endowed with quasi-judicial authority, such as when it issues penal orders, the requirement to observe instructions from the supervisory authority may be particularly problematic. The legal literature considers that the prosecutor enjoys judicial independence when issuing penal orders,[484] while in recent judgments the federal court has ruled that the prosecutor fulfils a function similar to the one he does when he formulates written accusations (BGE 124 Ia 78 et seq.). However, in view of the fact that, if no objection is lodged in time, a penal order is equivalent to a judgment that has entered into force, instructions from the supervisory authority should be considered inappropriate.[485]

---

[476] Administrative supervision relates to administrative and organizational matters of the public prosecution service. Hence, it relates primarily to the way the available resources are used.

[477] Federal Council (2006), p. 1129.

[478] Functional supervision relates to the substantive work of the prosecution service. It includes an extensive right to information as well as a right of the supervisory authority to issue general directives.

[479] Section 115 subs. 3 ZH-COA, Section 50 subs. 2 BS-COA, Article 41 AR-Courts Act.

[480] Schmid (2007), p. 703.

[481] Schmid (2007), p. 703; Mettler (2001), pp. 257–250.

[482] Mettler (2001), pp. 256–257.

[483] For details, see Mettler (2001), pp. 256–261. See also Wohlers (2006), p. 745.

[484] Wohlers. In: Donatsch et al. (2010) Kommentar StPO, Art. 4, Margin No. 25; Schmid (2009a), Margin No. 121. Dissenting: Mettler (2001), pp. 218–224.

[485] Wohlers. In: Donatsch et al. (2010) Kommentar StPO, Art. 4, Margin No. 25.

In any event, directives find their limits with the principle of legality.[486] Thus, directions from the supervisory authority that are clearly unlawful and unconstitutional have no binding force. On the contrary, such directives must not be observed by the prosecutor. If he decides to carry out such instructions despite this, he can be disciplined and be held liable under civil and/or criminal law.[487] In the event that the prosecutor has some doubts regarding the legality of certain instructions, he has to present this concern to the government. If the supervisory authority maintains the directives, the prosecutor has to follow them with the consequence that, from that moment, the responsibility for the prosecutor's actions lies with the government.[488]

Probably one of the main problems relating to the supervision of the prosecutor arises when the government has not only the right to issue directives but is also responsible for promotion and removal of prosecutors.[489] Such constellations create the risk that prosecutors do not call the potential illegality of directions into question but will simply follow them.[490] In Switzerland, however, such concerns appear to be unfounded. In fact, the burden for a dismissal or transfer of prosecutors is so high that any fears of reprisals seem to be unjustifiable.[491]

6.6.1.1.3 Overview of the Supervisory Authority Over the Prosecution and Its Scope of Supervision

Table 6.8 gives an overview of the supervisory authority over the public prosecutor's office in the different cantons and its scope of supervision. The scope of supervision is not regulated to the same extent in all cantons. While some cantons provide for a precise description of the tasks of the supervisory authority, other cantons treat this question in a summary manner. All cantons have in common that they do not allow the supervisory authority to exert any influence over ongoing prosecutions. In principle, instructions related to individual cases are prohibited. However, a minority of cantons gives the government the right to induce the prosecution to start proceedings but not to stop them. Where the supervision is restricted to administrative supervision, the duty of the supervisory authority is usually limited to receiving the annual report, to controlling the course of business, and to issuing general directions concerning the exercise of the prosecutors' tasks. Functional supervision includes an extensive right to information as well as a right of the supervisory authority to issue general directives. It should be kept in mind that clear delimitation between administrative and functional supervision is hardly

---

[486] Mettler (2001), pp. 250–252.

[487] Mettler (2001), p. 246.

[488] Mettler (2001), p. 246.

[489] In Germany and especially in France this issue is a major concern. See Sect. 7.6.1, para 2 and Sect. 8.5.1, paras 6–8.

[490] Mettler (2001), pp. 260–262.

[491] Mettler (2001), p. 261.

Table 6.8 Simplified overview of the supervisory authority over the prosecution service and its scope of supervision in the 26 cantons

Canton	Supervisory authority	Scope of supervision[a]
AG	Government	Administrative supervision
AI	Government	Administrative supervision
AR	Government	Right to induce the prosecution to start proceedings but not to stop them
BE	Parliament[b]	–
BL	Government	Functional supervision
BS	Government	Right to induce the prosecution to start proceedings but not to stop them
FR	Judicial Council	Administrative supervision
GE	Superior Council of Magistrates	Administrative supervision
GL	Government	Functional supervision
GR	Government	Administrative supervision
JU	Cantonal Court	Administrative supervision
LU	Justice and Security Department High Court	Administrative supervision Functional supervision
NE	Judicial Council	Administrative supervision
NW	High Court	Functional supervision
OW	Justice and Security Department High Court	Administrative supervision Functional supervision
SG	Government	Administrative supervision
SH	Government	Administrative supervision
SO	Government	Administrative supervision
SZ	Government	Functional supervision
TG	Department of Justice	Administrative supervision
TI	Council of Magistrates	Administrative supervision
UR	High Court Government	Functional supervision Administrative supervision
VD	State Council	Administrative supervision
VS	State Council	Administrative supervision
ZG	High Court	Functional supervision
ZH	Justice Department, government	Right to induce the prosecution to start proceedings but not to stop them
Confederation	Judicial Council	Functional supervision

[a]The following constellation is classified under functional supervision: the supervisory authority has the right to ask the prosecution service for additional information and reports about its activities and can have access to their files. The right to induce the prosecution to start proceedings but not to stop them also belongs to this kind of supervision

[b]Ultimate supervision. The supervision of the attorney general is exercised by the Justice Commission of the cantonal parliament. A Judicial Council (joint body for the High Court, the Administrative Court, and the General Public Prosecutor's Office) acts as interlocutor for the legislative branch and the government

possible, since there is a certain overlap. This is especially the case with regard to the supervision of the management within the prosecution office (in particular assignment of business and priority-setting) and regarding organizational issues.[492]

6.6.1.2 Internal Supervisory Structures

The prosecution service is a hierarchical institution[493] and thus, the lower-ranking prosecutors have to carry out the instructions of their superiors. The right to issue instructions has the function of regulating organization, assigning activities and cooperating within the authority. In this way, good functioning, rational, uniform, and lawful exercise of the prosecutors' activities can be guaranteed.[494] Higher-ranking prosecutors have the right to exercise an administrative as well as a functional supervision of lower-ranking prosecutors.[495]

Superiors have the right to issue general as well as concrete directives. Accordingly, they can also intervene in penal orders.[496] The right to direct finds its limit within the principle of legality. Directives are binding as long as they are within the legal order. Illegal instructions are prohibited and thus not binding.[497] In the event that the order is clearly contrary to the law or manifestly invalid, it is in principle not to be followed. In case of doubts regarding the legality of instructions, the prosecutor has to report his concern to his superior.[498]

6.6.1.3 Control of Public Prosecutor's Activities

6.6.1.3.1 Type of Procedure: Normal and Alternative Procedure

In contrast to normal proceedings, where all procedural guarantees are respected, alternative proceedings, such as the penal order and the abridged proceedings, are not surrounded with the same degree of safeguards. That is particularly the case in penal order proceedings where control mechanisms are almost inexistent. If the accused does not make opposition to the prosecutor's decision, a judge is not involved at all in this process.[499] The abridged proceedings are comparable to the U.S. plea bargaining system.[500] Although this procedure still requires a decision by

---

[492] See Sect. 6.6.1.1.1, para 4.

[493] On the structure of the prosecution service in Switzerland, see Sect. 6.1.

[494] Wohlers. In: Donatsch et al. (2010) Kommentar StPO, Art. 4. Margin No. 19; Wohlers (2006), p. 741.

[495] Wohlers. In: Donatsch et al. (2010) Kommentar StPO, Art. 4, Margin No. 19.

[496] On the problem of external directives in penal order proceedings, see Sect. 6.6.1.1.2, para 4.

[497] Hauser et al. (2005), Section 26, Margin No. 13.

[498] Wohlers. In: Donatsch et al. (2010) Kommentar StPO, Art. 4, Margin No. 20.

[499] For a discussion about problems related to the penal order procedure, see Sect. 6.5.1.2.

[500] On the abridged proceedings, see Sect. 6.5.2.

the court, the court hearing provides restriction on prosecutorial power of a much lesser degree. In fact, in contrast to ordinary proceedings, the court does not evaluate the legal circumstances of the case. It determines whether it is lawful to convict the accused person by way of abridged proceedings and not whether the conviction is lawful. In reality, the assessment of the defendant's responsibility is made within the prosecutor's office.

6.6.1.3.2 Complaint as Means of Supervision

Article 393 CCrP regulates the admissibility and the reasons for the complaint. Of interest is that a complaint can be filed against directives and procedural activities of the police, prosecution, and the authorities responsible for prosecuting minor regulatory activities (Article 393 para. 1 lit. a CCrP). This includes, for instance, refusals to open an investigation (Article 309 para. 1 CCrP), orders that proceedings will not be opened (Article 310, Article 357 para. 1 CCrP), suspensions of investigation or their rejections (Article 314 para. 5, Article 322 CCrP), directives discontinuing proceedings (Article 322 para. 2 CCrP), and re-opening of proceedings that were terminated by way of a final and legally binding directive discontinuing the proceedings (Article 323 CCrP).[501] However, a complaint against the decision to open an investigation (Article 309 para. 3 CCrP), the decision to bring charges (Article 324 para. 2 CCrP), and the decision about whether the case is to be conducted by way of abridged proceedings (Article 359 para. 1 CCrP) is excluded.[502]

With this legal remedy, violations of law (including where discretion has been misused or exceeded), denial and delay of justice, incomplete or incorrect establishment of the factual circumstances of the case, and unreasonableness can be contested (Article 393 para. 2 CCrP).

Every party that has a legally protected interest in the quashing or amendment of a decision may have recourse to this legal remedy (Article 382 para. 1 CCrP). The complainant has a legally protected interest when the decision directly affects his rights.[503] Besides the accused and the private claimant, all other persons involved in the proceedings have a right to lodge a complaint, such as witnesses, experts, and third parties adversely affected by the procedural activities (Articles 104 and 105 CCrP).[504]

---

[501] For an overview of directives and procedural activities against which a complaint is possible, see Stephenson and Thiriet. In: Niggli et al. (2011) BSK StPO, Art. 393, Margin No. 10; Keller. In: Donatsch et al. (2010) Kommentar StPO, Art. 393, Margin Nos. 15–16.

[502] For an overview of directives and procedural activities against which a complaint is excluded, see Stephenson and Thiriet. In: Niggli et al. (2011) BSK StPO, Art. 393, Margin No. 11; Keller. In: Donatsch et al. (2010) Kommentar StPO, Art. 393, Margin Nos. 17–18.

[503] Lieber. In: Donatsch et al. (2010) Kommentar StPO, Art. 382, Margin Nos. 7–13; Schmid (2009b), Art. 382, Margin Nos. 1–2.

[504] Lieber. In: Donatsch et al. (2010) Kommentar StPO, Art. 382, Margin Nos. 1–6.

This legal remedy has to be distinguished from the disciplinary complaint with which the conduct of an authority is reviewed by the supervisory authority.[505] The scope of application of disciplinary complaints is very limited since the complaint as legal remedy has priority.[506] Hence, supervisory authorities are only competent in the event of misbehavior of a member of the prosecuting authorities when no complaint can be filed before the court. This may be the case if the member is accused of an offense (i.e. offenses against personal honor, coercion, acts of aggression).[507]

6.6.1.3.3 Review of the Prosecutor's Charging Decision

The decision to charge cannot be challenged. The legislature has deliberately refrained from introducing a board of indictment that would independently review the charges brought by the prosecutor. At least the judge in charge of conducting the proceedings has to examine *ex officio* whether the indictment and the files have been properly compiled and whether all procedural requirements have been met. The scope of this preliminary review is very limited since the judge in charge of conducting the proceedings does not determine whether the described behavior constitutes a criminal offense, nor does he have to examine the accuracy of the conclusion drawn by the prosecutor, nor whether the evidence would be enough to justify a guilty verdict.[508]

6.6.2 Accountability of Public Prosecutors

6.6.2.1 Civil and Criminal Liability

Prosecutors are subject to criminal and civil liability. If civil servants commit crimes that have no connection with their official duties, they are treated as any other citizen. In contrast, for felonies and misdemeanors that prosecutors commit while in office, the situation is different. At the federal level, an authorization of the responsible commission of the confederation's councils[509] is required to prosecute

[505] On the disciplinary complaint, see later Sect. 6.6.2.2, para 5.

[506] According to Lienhard and Kettiger, there is no longer room for disciplinary complaints (Lienhard and Kettiger 2008, Margin Nos. 29–30).

[507] Keller. In: Donatsch et al. (2010) Kommentar StPO, Art. 393, Margin Nos. 3–4; Stephenson and Thiriet. In: Niggli et al. (2011) BSK StPO, Art. 393, Margin Nos. 4–6.

[508] See Sect. 6.4.5.2, paras 2 and 3 for more information.

[509] There is an Immunity Committee appointed for this purpose in the National Council. In the Council of states, applications for the removal of immunity are dealt with by the Legal Affairs Committee.

the attorney general and the deputy attorney generals.[510] For all other federal attorneys, the authorization to prosecute is granted by the attorney general (Article 15 para. 1 Federal Law on the Liability of the Confederation). At the cantonal level, whether an authorization is required to prosecute a prosecutor depends on whether the canton makes use of Article 7 para. 2 lit. b CCrP. According to this provision, the cantons may stipulate that the prosecution of felonies and misdemeanors committed by members of the prosecuting and judicial authorities be dependent on the authorization of a non-judicial authority. A federal court ruling of July 15, 2011 clarifies the possibility to also give this competence to a judicial authority on the grounds that the intention of the legislature was never to exclusively reserve this right to a non-judicial authority.[511] Thus, the canton of Zurich, where the authorization is granted by the High Court, is in conformity with the law.[512] In cantons that provide for an authorization to bring criminal proceedings against prosecutors, this usually falls within the responsibility of the parliament.[513]

The intent and purpose of such an authorization procedure is the protection of civil servants against unfounded and willful accusations and thus to prevent the obstruction of the government's activity.[514] When making the decision to grant or refuse the authorization, the authority will have to determine whether there is considerable evidence suggesting that an offense has been committed. In the event of considerable doubts about the culpability of the accused, authorization will be refused.[515] Furthermore, political considerations may also be taken into account.[516]

Legal remedies against cantonal decisions to grant or refuse the authorization to prosecute are, at most, available under the administrative legislation.[517] Since such decisions are primarily of political nature, cantons remain free to exclude them from the legal guarantee of access to the courts (Article 29a Federal Constitution).[518] Legal remedies according to the CCrP are excluded since a complaint is only possible against directives and procedural activities of the police and prosecution, directives and resolutions and procedural activities of the courts of first

[510] Article 14 para. 1 Federal Law on the Liability of the Confederation; *Bundesgesetz vom 14. März 1958 über die Verantwortlichkeit des Bundes sowie seiner Behördenmitglieder und Beamten*; SR 170.32.

[511] 1B_77/2011. See also Riedo and Fiolka. In: Niggli et al. (2011) BSK StPO, Art. 7, Margin No. 95. According to Schmid, it is problematic to let the decision whether the immunity of civil servants should be waived to a judicial authority since such a decision typically falls within the competences of a non-judicial authority (Schmid 2009b, Art. 7, Margin No. 10).

[512] Section 148 ZH-COA.

[513] This is the case in the cantons of Berne (Article 32 BE-COA), Glarus (Article 27 EG StPO GL), and Zug (Section 103 ZG-COA).

[514] Federal Council (2006), p. 1131; Riedo and Fiolka. In: Niggli et al. (2011) BSK StPO, Art. 7, Margin No. 74; Schmid (2009b), Art. 7, Margin No. 12.

[515] Riedo and Fiolka. In: Niggli et al. (2011) BSK StPO, Art. 7, Margin No. 100.

[516] Riedo and Fiolka. In: Niggli et al. (2011) BSK StPO, Art. 7, Margin No. 101; Schmid (2009b), Art. 7, Margin No. 12; Hauser et al. (2005), Section 18, Margin No. 4.

[517] Schmid (2009b), Art. 7, Margin No. 14.

[518] Riedo and Fiolka. In: Niggli et al. (2011) BSK StPO, Art. 7, Margin No. 107.

instance, and decisions of the Court responsible for Coercive Measures (Article 393 para. 1 CCrP), while an appeal is admissible against judgments of the Courts of First Instance (Article 398 para. 1 CCrP). Appellate procedures to be followed before the Swiss Supreme Court will generally not apply. The appeal in criminal matters [Article 78 et seq. Federal Supreme Court Act (FSCA)][519] is excluded insofar as a violation of cantonal law is raised. A violation of cantonal law can only be raised if it amounts to a violation of a constitutional right, for example in case of arbitrariness or infringement of the right to be heard (Article 95 FSCA).[520] However, since there are usually no cantonal legal remedies against the refusal or the granting of the authorization, a challengeable decision from a previous instance is missing (Article 80 para. 1 FSCA).[521] An appeal in matters of public law is excluded against the refusal to authorize the prosecution (Article 83 lit. e FSCA). This provision applies to prosecutors at the cantonal and federal levels. Furthermore, the granting of the authorization to prosecute cannot be challenged.[522] What remains is the subsidiary constitutional appeal (Article 113 et seq. FSCA) with which violations of fundamental rights can be raised.[523]

If the authorization to prosecute is granted, cantons and the Confederation may provide for the nomination of an extraordinary prosecutor (*ausserordentlicher Staatsanwalt*) who is then responsible for the prosecution of the accused prosecutor.[524] The purpose of such a provision is to ensure the independence of the investigation. The assessment of the case is the task of the ordinary courts.[525]

Some criminal offenses described in the penal code can only be committed by civil servants (e.g. abuse of public office, forgery of a document by a public official).[526] According to the Swiss system of mandatory prosecution, a prosecutor may be held liable for dismissing a case that would have called for prosecution and trial. Prosecutors may also be subject to criminal prosecution whenever they fail to investigate impartially and thus also when they withhold evidence that might be favorable to the defendant. Under these circumstances, prosecutors are charged with "abuse of public authority" according to Article 312 SCC.

Prosecutors at federal and cantonal levels are subject to civil liability for damages resulting from their willful acts or gross negligence.[527] However, the

---

[519] Federal Supreme Court Act as of June 17, 2005 (Status as of April 1, 2012); *Bundesgesetz vom 17. Juni 2005 über das Bundesgericht vom 17. Juni 2005* (*Bundesgerichtsgesetz, BGG*) (*Stand am 1. April 2012*); SR 173.110.

[520] Schmid (2009b), Art. 7, Margin No. 14.

[521] Riedo and Fiolka. In: Niggli et al. (2011) BSK StPO, Art. 7, Margin No. 109.

[522] Riedo and Fiolka. In: Niggli et al. (2011) BSK StPO, Art. 7, Margin No. 110; Schmid (2009b), Art. 7, Margin No. 14.

[523] Riedo and Fiolka. In: Niggli et al. (2011) BSK StPO, Art. 7, Margin Nos. 111–113; Schmid (2009b), Art. 7, Margin No. 14.

[524] See e.g. Article 67 of the Law on the Organization of the Federal Criminal Authorities.

[525] Federal Council (2006), p. 1131.

[526] Offenses against Official or Professional Duty are regulated in title 18 of the SCC.

[527] For a detailed discussion about civil liability at federal and cantonal levels, see Moor and Poltier (2011), pp. 847–872.

administration where the concerned civil servant works is the responsible entity vis-à-vis the aggrieved party.[528] Thus, the administration compensates the victim's damages without regard for culpability of the prosecutor and the administration may enforce civil liability against the individual prosecutor afterwards.[529] One reason for excluding any direct civil action by an aggrieved party against civil servants personally is that such a possibility would lead to paralyzation of the administration.[530] In fact, no civil servant would want to run the risk of making any decision if there was a possibility of it being a wrong decision. Thus, the law favors the obligation of the administration to decide over the possibility of people adopting wrong decisions.[531]

6.6.2.2 Disciplinary Liability

A criminal liability usually also entails an administrative liability. However, not all administrative faults represent a criminal offense. Disciplinary measures have the purpose of maintaining order and preserving the reputation and trustworthiness of the administration. The general legal principle known as *ne bis in idem*, which means that nobody may be punished twice for the same offense, does not necessarily apply in disciplinary law. The imposition of two punishments, one disciplinary and the other criminal, for the same act remains possible.[532] The reason is that, under certain circumstances, an offense should bear legal consequences concerning two different legal orders, administrative and criminal, if the legal system as a whole is to be consistent.

Disciplinary proceedings may include informal warnings issued by superiors and formal proceedings and sanctions. As a consequence of their right to issue directives, superiors can sanction disciplinary infractions of minor importance through a written warning. For more serious prosecutorial misbehaviors, the formal disciplinary proceedings are applicable.

In order for the administration to exercise its punitive powers, a legal basis describing the punishable behavior and the sanctions is required.[533] However, since prosecutors have a wide range of duties, it is not possible to exhaustively enumerate all possible offenses. It is sufficient when they are able to predict what would be a punishable act and what would be the legal consequences. The use of general

[528] Moor and Poltier (2011), p. 852.

[529] See Articles 3, 7, and 8 Federal Law on the Liability of the Confederation.

[530] Häfelin et al. (2010), Margin No. 2225.

[531] Moor and Poltier (2011), p. 850.

[532] Häfelin et al. (2010), Margin No. 1198; Moor and Poltier (2011), p. 144.

[533] For all civil servants, the legal basis for disciplinary measures is to be found in the Human Resources Act of each canton. Some cantons, such as Geneva, Jura, Neuchâtel, and Schaffhausen, provide for a special legal basis for prosecutorial misbehavior in their Courts Act.

formulation is inevitable, but there should be a clear link between punishable behavior and duties or obligations imposed upon prosecutors.[534] A disciplinary breach by a prosecutor may be defined as a breach of his professional duties or failure to preserve his honor, good standing, or dignity. Sanctions include a warning, a reprimand, a fine, a reduction of salary, temporary suspension from office, demotion in rank, and dismissal from office.[535] When imposing a sanction, the administrative authority has to respect the principle of proportionality. Thus, the penalty imposed should be proportionate to the gravity of the offense, taking into account the circumstances. This also means that the administrative authority may refrain from imposing a sentence when it considers that the other sanctions pronounced (i.e. penal sanctions) have been able to restore the public's trust in the criminal justice system respectively in any actions the public prosecutor may take.[536] While a disciplinary procedure is underway, the administrative authority may make the decision to suspend the prosecutor from duty. Such a decision may be appropriate when the prosecutor's continued presence would be harmful to the reputation of the public service or when there is a risk of renewed misbehavior.

Disciplinary proceedings may be opened on the sole initiative of the supervisory authority or following a disciplinary complaint. The supervisory authority[537] in charge of conducting disciplinary procedures and imposing administrative sanctions has to respect the right of the accused civil servant respectively the public prosecutor to be heard.[538] Furthermore, he also has the right to be represented or assisted by a lawyer.[539] The administrative decision has to be substantiated and contain an indication of the right to file an appeal. Administrative courts are competent to review administrative decisions on discipline.

Any person may file a disciplinary complaint (*Aufsichtsbeschwerde*). An applicant's direct concern is not required.[540] The applicant is not party to the procedure. Thus, he has no right to have access to the file or to be heard. Although the administrative authority has no duty to inform the applicant about the kind of sanction imposed, it should at least inform him of the outcome of the application.[541] A legal remedy against a refusal to accept a disciplinary complaint does not exist.[542] At first sight, the scope of application of the disciplinary complaint is fairly broad since it includes the whole spectrum of duties—actions and

[534] Häfelin et al. (2010), Margin No. 1202; Moor and Poltier (2011), p. 142.

[535] Moor and Poltier (2011), pp. 143–144.

[536] Häfelin et al. (2010), Margin No. 1205; Moor and Poltier (2011), p. 144.

[537] On the supervisory authority over prosecutors, see Sect. 6.6.1.1.1. The Human Resources Act of the canton Berne no longer recognizes disciplinary measures. However, the appointing authority, as a consequence of its right to issue directives, can issue informal warnings.

[538] Häfelin et al. (2010), Margin No. 1207. On the right to be heard, see Sect. 3.2.2.6.1.

[539] Moor and Poltier (2011), p. 282.

[540] Häfelin et al. (2010), Margin No. 1845; Moor and Poltier (2011), pp. 616–617.

[541] Häfelin et al. (2010), Margin No. 1836; Moor and Poltier (2011), pp. 617–618.

[542] Häfelin et al. (2010), Margin No. 1836; Moor and Poltier (2011), pp. 618–619.

omissions—of the supervised authority.[543] However, the complaint as formal legal remedy has priority over the disciplinary complaint, which is an informal remedy.[544] This has the consequence of restricting the domain of applicability of disciplinary complaints. Supervisory authorities are only competent in the event of misbehavior of a member of the prosecuting authorities when no complaint can be filed before the court. In criminal proceedings, a complaint can be submitted against directives and procedural activities of the prosecution (Article 393 para. 1 lit. a CCrP). It may be used to contest violations of law, including where discretion has been misused or exceeded and denial and delay of justice (Article 393 para. 2 lit. a CCrP). Room for disciplinary complaints remains where the grounds of complaint concern a prosecutor's behavior that cannot be considered procedural activity. This may be the case if the prosecutor is accused of indecent behavior or an offense (i.e. offenses against personal honor, coercion, acts of aggression).[545]

Compared to other European countries, the number of disciplinary proceedings initiated against prosecutors in Switzerland in 2008 was quite high.[546] In this year, the average number of proceedings initiated against 100 prosecutors in Switzerland was 6.8, while in France the average number was 0.1.[547] In 2008, a total of 29 disciplinary proceedings were initiated against prosecutors in Switzerland, including 21 cases for breach of professional ethics, seven cases of professional inadequacy, and in one case of criminal offense.[548] However, in 2010, only five proceedings were initiated against prosecutors in Switzerland, including four cases of professional inadequacy, and one case for breach of professional ethics.[549] Disciplinary proceedings are rarely successful. In 2008, sanctions were pronounced in only two proceedings. A reprimand was imposed once, temporary reduction of salary and dismissal from the office were pronounced twice each.[550] In 2010, sanctions were pronounced in only one proceedings.[551]

[543] Häfelin et al. (2010), Margin Nos. 1840–1844; Moor and Poltier (2011), p. 617.

[544] Moor and Poltier (2011), p. 617. See also Sect. 6.6.1.3.2, para 4.

[545] Keller. In: Donatsch et al. (2010) Kommentar StPO, Art. 393, Margin Nos. 3–4; Stephenson and Thiriet. In: Niggli et al. (2011) BSK StPO, Art. 393, Margin Nos. 4–6.

[546] These numbers refer to the time period prior to the introduction of the CCrP when the scope of application of disciplinary complaints was broader than today. However, the right to open disciplinary proceedings on the sole initiative of the supervisory authority has always existed so that the introduction of the CCrP shouldn't have a significant impact on the number of conducted disciplinary proceedings.

[547] Council of Europe (2010), Fig. 11.37.

[548] Council of Europe (2010), Table 11.36. Number is based on the information obtained from 19 cantons (Council of Europe 2010, p. 229).

[549] Council of Europe (2012), Table 11.54. Number is based on the information obtained from 16 cantons (Council of Europe 2012, p. 300).

[550] Council of Europe (2010), Table 11.39. Number is based on the information obtained from 19 cantons (Council of Europe 2010, p. 232).

[551] Council of Europe (2012), Table 11.58. Number is based on the information obtained from 16 cantons (Council of Europe 2012, p. 304).

References

Albertini G, Rüegger P (2010) Zur Zusammenarbeit von Polizei und Staatsanwaltschaft. Forumpoenale 3:360–365

Albertini G, Fehr B, Voser B (2008) Polizeiliche Ermittlung. Ein Handbuch der Vereinigung der Schweizerischen Kriminalpolizeichefs zum polizeilichen Ermittlungsverfahren gemäss der Schweizerischen Strafprozessordnung (VSKC-Polizeiliche Ermittlung). Schulthess, Zurich

Angst R, Maurer H (2008a) Das "Interesse der Öffentlichkeit" gemäss Art. 53 lit. b StGB – Versuch einer Konkretisierung (Teil I). Forumpoenale 1:301–308

Angst R, Maurer H (2008b) Das "Interesse der Öffentlichkeit" gemäss Art. 53 lit. b StGB – Versuch einer Konkretisierung (Teil II). Forumpoenale 1:373–378

Arn R, Kuhn A, Saurer N (2011a) Synthese. Inkrafttreten der StPO: Auf dem Weg zu einer Vereinheitlichung der Organisation der Strafbehörden? In: Arn R, Saurer N, Kuhn A (eds) Organisation der kantonalen und eidgenössischen Strafbehörden = Organisation des autorités pénales cantonales et fédérales = Organizzazione delle autorità penali cantonali e federali. Helbing & Lichtenhahn, Basel, pp 39–76

Arn R, Saurer N, Kuhn A (eds) (2011b) Organisation der kantonalen und eidgenössischen Strafbehörden = Organisation des autorités pénales cantonales et fédérales = Organizzazione delle autorità penali cantonali e federali. Helbing & Lichtenhahn, Basel

Beulke W (2008) Strafprozessrecht, 10th edn. Müller, Heidelberg

Blättler S (2007) Die Stellung der Polizei im neuen schweizerischen Strafverfahren. Schweizerische Zeitschrift für Strafrecht 125:242–249

Bommer F (2008) Bemerkungen zur Wiedergutmachung (Art. 53 StGB). Forumpoenale 1:171–177

Bommer F (2009) Abgekürztes Verfahren und Plea Bargaining im Vergleich. Zeitschrift für Schweizerisches Recht 128(II/1):5–124

Bommer F (2010) Kurzer Prozess mit dem abgekürzten Verfahren? In: Heer M (ed) Schweizerische Strafprozessordnung und schweizerische Jugendstrafprozessordnung. Stämpfli, Berne, pp 149–172

Breguet A (2009) La procédure simplifiée dans le CPP: un réel progrès? Jusletter, 16 March 2009, 1–11

Brunner A (2008) Geldstrafe, Busse und Freiheitsstrafe im strafenden Alltag, Wiedergutmachung. In: Tag B, Hauri M (eds) Das revidierte StGB. Allgemeiner Teil: erste Erfahrungen. Dike, Zurich, pp 43–69

Brunner A, Heimgartner S (2011) Es ist gerecht, dass jeder an die Reihe kommt – Gedanken zu Art. 53 StGB. Zeitschrift für Schweizerisches Recht 130:613–626

Cantonal Court of the Canton Basel-Landschaft (2010) Official Report to the Parliament 2009 [Amtsbericht des Kantonsgerichts Basel-Landschaft an den Landrat 2009]. Cantonal Court, Basel-Landschaft

Cantonal Court of the Canton Basel-Landschaft (2011) Official Report to the Parliament 2010 [Amtsbericht des Kantonsgerichts Basel-Landschaft an den Landrat 2010]. Cantonal Court, Basel-Landschaft

Cantonal Court of the Canton Basel-Landschaft (2012) Official Report to the Parliament 2011 [Amtsbericht des Kantonsgerichts Basel-Landschaft an den Landrat 2011]. Cantonal Court, Basel-Landschaft

Council of Europe (2010) European judicial systems. Efficiency and quality of justice (data 2008). Council of Europe Pub., Strasbourg

Council of Europe (2012) European judicial systems. Efficiency and quality of justice (data 2010). Council of Europe Pub., Strasbourg

Del Giudice L (2010) Wann beginnt das polizeiliche Ermittlungsverfahren? Wann beginnt das staatsanwaltschaftliche Untersuchungsverfahren? Schweizerische Zeitschrift für Strafrecht 128:116–131

Donatsch A (1994) Der Strafbefehl sowie ähnliche Verfahrenserledigungen mit Einsprachemöglichkeit, insbesondere aus dem Gesichtswinkel von Art. 6 EMRK. Schweizerische Zeitschrift für Strafrecht 112:317–349

Donatsch A, Cavegn C (2008) Ausgewählte Fragen zum Beweisrecht nach der schweizerischen Strafprozessordnung. Schweizerische Zeitschrift für Strafrecht 126:158–173

Donatsch A, Hansjakob T, Lieber V (eds) (2010) Kommentar zur Schweizerischen Strafprozessordnung (StPO) (Kommentar StPO). Schulthess, Zurich

Dubs H (1996) Strafbefehl – Möglichkeiten und Grenzen eines vereinfachten Strafverfahrens. In: Donatsch A, Schmid N (eds) Strafrecht und Öffentlichkeit. Festschrift für Jörg Rehberg zum 65. Geburtstag. Schulthess, Zurich, pp 139–150

Federal Council (2006) Message from the Federal Council of December 21, 2005 on the unification of criminal procedure [Botschaft des Bundesrates zur Vereinheitlichung des Strafprozessrechts vom 21. Dezember 2005]. Federal Chancellery, Berne

Federal Office of Police (fedpol) (2011) The Federal Office of Police, an overview. Federal Office of Police, Berne

Flückiger S (2006) Art. 66bis StGB, Art. 54 f. StGBneu – Betroffenheit durch Tatfolgen. Straftatfolgen als Einstellungsgrund und Strafersatz? Stämpfli, Berne

Gilliéron G (2010) Strafbefehlsverfahren und plea bargaining als Quelle von Fehlurteilen. Schulthess, Zurich

Gilliéron G, Killias M (2007) Strafbefehl und Justizirrtum: Franz Riklin hatte Recht! In: Niggli MA, Hurtado Pozo J, Queloz N (eds) Festschrift für Franz Riklin. Zur Emeritierung und zugleich dem 67. Geburtstag. Schulthess, Zurich, pp 379–398

Gomm P, Zehntner D (eds) (2009) Kommentar zum Opferhilfegesetz (OHG-Kommentar). Bundesgesetz vom 23. März 2007 über die Hilfe an Opfer von Straftaten, 3rd edn. Stämpfli, Berne

Greiner G (2009) Schuld ohne Sühne? Am Beispiel des "plea bargaining" nach neuer StPO. Forumpoenale 2:234–243

Häfelin U, Müller G, Uhlmann F (2010) Allgemeines Verwaltungsrecht, 6th edn. Dike, Zurich

Hauser R, Schweri E, Hartmann K (2005) Schweizerisches Strafprozessrecht, 6th edn. Helbing & Lichtenhahn, Basel

Hausherr C (2008) Das abgekürzte Verfahren in der schweizerischen Strafprozessordnung – Entlastung der Strafverfolgungsbehörden versus Rechtsstaatlichkeit. Forumpoenale 1:308–314

Hofer T (2011) Bund/Confédération. In: Arn R, Saurer N, Kuhn A (eds) Organisation der kantonalen und eidgenössischen Strafbehörden = Organisation des autorités pénales cantonales et fédérales = Organizzazione delle autorità penali cantonali e federali. Helbing & Lichtenhahn, Basel, pp 77–103

Hürlimann C (2006) Die Eröffnung einer Strafuntersuchung im ordentlichen Verfahren gegen Erwachsene im Kanton Zürich. Unter Berücksichtigung des Entwurfs zu einer Schweizerischen Strafprozessordnung. Schulthess, Zurich

Hutzler D (2010) Ausgleich struktureller Garantiedefizite im Strafbefehlsverfahren. Eine Analyse der zürcherischen, schweizerischen und deutschen Regelungen, unter besonderer Berücksichtigung der Geständnisfunktion. Nomos, Baden-Baden

Jeanneret Y (2010) Les procédures spéciales dans le Code de procédure pénale suisse. In: Pfister-Liechti R (ed) La procédure pénale fédérale. Stämpfli, Berne, pp 137–195

Jositsch D, Bischoff P (2007) Das abgekürzte Verfahren gemäss Art. 365–369 des Entwurfs zu einer Schweizerischen Strafprozessordnung. In: Niggli MA, Hurtado Pozo J, Queloz N (eds) Festschrift für Franz Riklin. Zur Emeritierung und zugleich dem 67. Geburtstag. Schulthess, Zurich, pp 429–440

Kamber UW (2011) Kanton Basel-Stadt. In: Arn R, Saurer N, Kuhn A (eds) Organisation der kantonalen und eidgenössischen Strafbehörden. = Organisation des autorités pénales cantonales et fédérales = Organizzazione delle autorità penali cantonali e federali. Helbing & Lichtenhahn, Basel, pp 211–226

Kanyar A (2008) Wiedergutmachung und Täter-Opfer-Ausgleich im schweizerischen Strafrecht. Entwicklung eines Modells unter Berücksichtigung des deutschen und österreichischen Strafrechts. Helbing & Lichtenhahn, Basel

Kaufmann A (2009) Das abgekürzte Verfahren bei mehreren Tatbeteiligten. Recht 27:152–163

Killias M (1990) "Wiedergutmachung" – Bedürfnis des Opfers oder blaue Blume? Kurze Notizen aus der Sicht der schweizerischen Opferbefragung und ihrer Umsetzung im geplanten Opferhilfegesetz (OHG). In: Eser A, Kaiser G, Madlener K (eds) Neue Wege der Wiedergutmachung im Strafrecht. Internationales strafrechtlich-kriminologisches Kolloquium in Freiburg i. Br. Max-Planck-Institut für Ausländisches und Internationales Strafrecht, Freiburg i. Br, pp 233–245

Killias M, Kuhn A, Aebi MF (2011) Grundriss der Kriminologie. Eine europäische Perspektive, 2nd edn. Stämpfli, Berne

Kuhn A (1998) Le "plea bargaining" américain est-il propre à inspirer le législateur suisse? Schweizerische Zeitschrift für Strafrecht 117:73–94

Kuhn A (2009) La procédure pénale suisse selon le CPP unifié. Zeitschrift für Schweizerisches Recht 128(II/1):125–184

Kuhn A, Jeanneret Y (eds) (2011) Commentaire Romand du Code de Procédure Pénale Suisse (Commentaire Romand CPP). Helbing & Lichtenhahn, Basel

Kühne H (2010) Strafprozessrecht. Eine systematische Darstellung des deutschen und europäischen Strafverfahrensrechts, 8th edn. Müller, Heidelberg

Lienhard A, Kettiger D (2008) Die organisatorische Einordnung der Staatsanwaltschaft in die kantonale Behördenstruktur. Grundlagen im Hinblick auf die Einführung des Staatsanwaltschaftsmodells. Justice-Justiz-Giustizia (2)

Mazou M (2011) La procédure simplifiée dans le nouveau Code de procédure pénale: principes et difficultés. Schweizerische Zeitschrift für Strafrecht 129:1–21

Mettler C (2001) Staatsanwaltschaft. Position innerhalb der Gewaltentrias, Funktion im Strafprozess und aufsichtsrechtliche Situation sowie ein Vorschlag zur Neuordnung. Grundlegendes Recht, vol 1. Helbing & Lichtenhahn, Basel

Mettler C, Baumgartner N (2010) Die Neuregelung der Aufsicht über die Bundesanwaltschaft. In: Fiolka G, Gfeller DR, Riedo C (eds) Liber amicorum für Marcel Alexander Niggli. Von Lemuren, Igeln und anderen strafrechtlichen Themen. Helbing & Lichtenhahn, Basel, pp 59–71

Moor P, Poltier E (2011) Droit administratif II. Les actes administratifs et leur contrôle, 3rd edn. Stämpfli, Berne

Moreillon L (2010) L'ordonnance pénale: simplification ou artifice? Schweizerische Zeitschrift für Strafrecht 128:22–37

Nidegger C, Moser U, Angelone D, Brühwiler C, Buccheri G, Abt N, Mariotta M, Roos E (2010) PISA 2009 – Schülerinnen und Schüler der Schweiz im internationalen Vergleich. Erste Ergebnisse. Neuchâtel, Konsortium PISA.ch

Niggli MA, Wiprächtiger H (eds) (2007) Basler Kommentar zum Strafrecht I (Art. 1-110 StGB) (BSK StGB), 2nd edn. Helbing & Lichtenhahn, Basel

Niggli MA, Heer M, Wiprächtiger H (eds) (2011) Basler Kommentar zur Schweizerischen Strafprozessordnung – Jugendstrafprozessordnung (BSK StPO). Helbing Lichtenhahn, Basel

Notter P (2006) Lesen und Rechnen im Alltag. Grundkompetenzen von Erwachsenen in der Schweiz. Office fédéral de la statistique (OFS), Neuchâtel

Oberholzer N (1993) Absprachen im Strafverfahren – pragmatische Entlastungsstrategie oder Abkehr vom strafprozessualen Modell? Schweizerische Zeitschrift für Strafrecht 111:157–174

Office of the Attorney General (2011) Excerpt from the annual report on the activities of the Office of the Attorney General in 2010 to the board of appeal of the Federal Criminal Court [Auszug aus dem Bericht der Bundesanwaltschaft über ihre Tätigkeit im Jahr 2010 an die I. Beschwerdekammer des Bundesstrafgerichts]. Office of the Attorney General, Berne

Office of the Attorney General (2012) Report of the Office of the Attorney General on the activities in 2011 to the supervisory authority [Bericht der Bundesanwaltschaft über ihre Tätigkeit im Jahr 2011 an die Aufsichtsbehörde]. Office of the Attorney General, Berne

Pieth M (2009) Schweizerisches Strafprozessrecht. Grundriss für Studium und Praxis. Helbing & Lichtenhahn, Basel
Pieth M (2010) Besondere Strafverfahrensarten: das abgekürzte Verfahren. Schweizerische Zeitschrift für Strafrecht 128:161–172
Piquerez G, Macaluso A, Piquerez L (2011) Procédure pénale suisse, 3rd edn. Schulthess, Geneva
Riedo C, Fiolka G, Niggli MA (2010) Schweizerisches Strafprozessrecht. Eine Einführung. Helbing & Lichtenhahn, Basel
Riklin F (2006a) Die Strafprozessrechtsreform in der Schweiz. Goltdammer's Archiv für Strafrecht 153:495–514
Riklin F (2006b) Urteilseröffnung beim Strafbefehl. In: Zen-Ruffinen P (ed) Du monde pénal. Droit pénal, criminologie et politique criminelle, police et exécution des sanctions, procédure pénale; mélanges en l'honneur de Pierre-Henri Bolle. Helbing & Lichtenhahn, Basel, pp 115–127
Riklin F (2007) Der Strafbefehl im deutschen und im schweizerischen Strafprozessrecht – eine rechtsvergleichende Betrachtung. In: Müller-Dietz H et al (eds) Festschrift für Heike Jung. Zum 65. Geburtstag am 23. Nomos, Baden-Baden, pp 761–779
Roth R, Moreillon L (eds) (2009) Commentaire Romand du Code Penal I. Dispositions générales – art. 1-110 (Commentaire Romand CP I). Helbing & Lichtenhahn, Basel
Roxin C, Schünemann B (2012) Strafverfahrensrecht. Ein Studienbuch, 27th edn. C.H. Beck, München
Schlauri R (1999) Die abgekürzten Verfahren in den Strafprozessordnungen der Kantone Baselland und Tessin – eine schweizerische Form des US-amerikanischen plea bargaining? In: Ackermann J, Schmid N (eds) Strafrecht als Herausforderung. Zur Emeritierung von Professor Niklaus Schmid. Schulthess, Zurich, pp 479–506
Schmid N (2007) Möglichkeiten und Grenzen der Kantone bei der Organisation ihrer Strafbehörden nach der künftigen Schweizerischen Strafprozessordnung. Aktuelle juristische Praxis 16:699–707
Schmid N (2009a) Handbuch des schweizerischen Strafprozessrechts. Dike, Zurich
Schmid N (2009b) Schweizerische Strafprozessordnung (StPO): Praxiskommentar. Dike, Zurich
Schubarth M (2007) Zurück zum Grossinquisitor? Zur rechtsstaatlichen Problematik des Strafbefehls. In: Niggli MA, Hurtado Pozo J, Queloz N (eds) Festschrift für Franz Riklin. Zur Emeritierung und zugleich dem 67. Geburtstag. Schulthess, Zurich, pp 527–537
Schwander D (2007) Plea Bargaining als "abgekürztes Verfahren" im Entwurf für eine Schweizerische Strafprozessordnung. Schweizerische Juristenzeitung 103:142–147
Schwarzenegger C, Thalmann U, Zanolini V (2006) Mediation im Strafrecht: Erfahrungen im Kanton Zürich, Schlussbericht der kriminologischen Evaluation des Zürcher Pilotprojekts. Kriminologisches Institut Universität Zürich, Zurich
Schwitter M (1996) Der Strafbefehl im aargauischen Strafprozess. Stellung und Funktion des Strafbefehls des Bezirksamtmanns in der durch Abänderungsgesetz vom 24. Januar 1977 teilrevidierten Strafprozessordnung vom 11. November 1958. Sauerländer, Aarau
Senior Public Prosecutor's Office of the Canton of Zurich (2012) Annual report 2011 [Jahresbericht 2011]. Senior Public Prosecutor's Office, Zurich
Senior Public Prosecutor's Office of Zurich (2012) Guidelines on the preliminary investigation [Weisungen für das Vorverfahren (WOSTA) der Oberstaatsanwaltschaft des Kantons Zürich]. Senior Public Prosecutor's Office, Zurich
Stratenwerth G (2006) Schweizerisches Strafrecht. Allgemeiner Teil. Band II: Strafen und Massnahmen, 2nd edn. Stämpfli, Berne
Stratenwerth G, Wohlers W (2009) Schweizerisches Strafgesetzbuch – Handkommentar, 2nd edn. Stämpfli, Berne
Summers S (2010) Strafbefreiung und Einstellung des Verfahrens. Schweizerische Zeitschrift für Strafrecht 128:1–21
Supreme Court of the Canton of Zug (2009) Accountability report 2008 [Rechenschaftsbericht 2008 des Obergerichts des Kantons Zugs]. Supreme Court of the Canton of Zug, Zug

Supreme Court of the Canton of Zug (2010) Accountability report 2009 [Rechenschaftsbericht 2009 des Obergerichts des Kantons Zugs]. Supreme Court of the Canton of Zug, Zug

Supreme Court of the Canton of Zug (2011) Accountability Report 2010 [Rechenschaftsbericht 2010 des Obergerichts des Kantons Zugs]. Supreme Court of the Canton of Zug, Zug

Supreme Court of the Canton of Zug (2012) Accountability report 2011 [Rechenschaftsbericht 2011 des Obergerichts des Kantons Zugs]. Supreme Court of the Canton of Zug, Zug

Trechsel S et al (eds) (2008) Schweizerisches Strafgesetzbuch. Praxiskommentar (Praxiskommentar StGB). Dike, Zurich

Uster H (2010) Polizei und Staatsanwaltschaft im Vorverfahren – Schnittstelle oder Nahtstelle? Forumpoenale 3:353–359

Weishaupt E (2002) Besonderer Schutz minderjähriger Opfer im Strafverfahren - Teilrevision OHG. Schweizerische Zeitschrift für Strafrecht 120:231–248

Wohlers W (2005) Aktuelle Fragen des Zeugenschutzes - zur Vereinbarkeit der im Strafprozessrecht des Kantons Zürich anwendbaren Zeugenschutznormen mit Art. 6 Abs. 3 lit. d EMRK. Schweizerische Zeitschrift für Strafrecht 123:144–173

Wohlers W (2006) Kritische Anmerkungen zur Konzeption einer weisungsunabhängigen Staatsanwaltschaft. In: Hoyer A (ed) Festschrift für Friedrich-Christian Schroeder zum 70. Geburtstag. Müller, Heidelberg, pp 735–747

Zimmerlin S (2008) Der Verzicht des Beschuldigten auf Verfahrensrechte im Strafprozess. Zugleich ein Beitrag zum Grundrechtsverzicht. Schulthess, Zurich

Chapter 7
Overview of Public Prosecutors in Germany: Position, Powers, and Accountability

7.1 Structure and Organization of the Prosecution Service

7.1.1 Organization of the Public Prosecution Service

Due to the federal structure of Germany, the public prosecution service is organized on federal and state levels.

On the federal level, only one public prosecution office exists, namely the *Bundesanwaltschaft*, which is headed by the federal prosecutor general (*Generalbundesanwalt*). Like in Switzerland, the federal prosecutor general has no authority over state prosecutors.[1] Federal prosecutors deal with certain serious offenses against the state, such as terrorism.[2] They are also responsible for representing the state (*Land*) before the Federal Court of Appeals.[3] On the state level, there is a public prosecution service for each state.

As in France, the organization of public prosecution offices mirrors that of the courts of law. Thus, the Federal Prosecution Office is attached to the Federal Court of Appeal (*Bundesgerichtshof*). On the state level, there is one prosecutor's office attached to every state Supreme Court (*Oberlandesgericht*) and to every regional court (*Landgerichte*), whereby the regional prosecution service also includes district-level courts (*Amtsgerichte*).[4]

---

[1] See Sect. 6.1.1.1, para 2.

[2] See Section 120 and 142(a) of the Court Organization Act (COA) in the version published on May 9, 1975, as most recently amended by Article 4 of the Act of December 7, 2011; *Gerichtsverfassungsgesetz in der Fassung der Bekanntmachung vom 9. Mai 1975, das zuletzt durch Artikel 4 des Gesetzes vom 7. Dezember 2011 geändert worden ist.*

[3] Section 142 subs. 1 COA.

[4] Section 141 COA. On the German institution of the "Amtsanwaltschaft" (*assistant prosecutor office*), see Elsner and Peters (2006), p. 209.

G. Gilliéron, *Public Prosecutors in the United States and Europe*,

DOI 10.1007/978-3-319-04504-7_7,

Prosecution services at federal and at state levels are organized hierarchically with the state or federal Minister of Justice at the top.[5] Thus, higher level offices have supervisory authority over lower offices. This extends to external[6] and internal supervision.[7] Pursuant to Section 146 COA, prosecutors must carry out the instructions of their superiors (*Weisungsrecht*). Instructions may be of a general nature or may relate to an individual case. At any time in the proceedings, higher ranking prosecutors can withdraw cases from the lower ranking prosecutors, taking the case themselves (*Devolutionsrecht*) or reassigning them (*Substitutionsrecht*).[8]

The highest prosecuting officers at the state level are the prosecutors general (*Generalstaatsanwalt*), attached to the state Supreme Courts, who are answerable to the Minister of Justice. Each prosecution office is headed by a chief senior prosecutor (*Leitender Oberstaatsanwalt*) who answers to the prosecutor general. Departments within a prosecution office are headed by senior prosecutors (*Oberstaatsanwalt*).[9]

7.1.2 Selection of Federal and State Prosecutors

The federal prosecutor general and federal prosecutors are appointed by the German President upon proposal of the Minister of Justice and with the consent of the *Bundesrat*, the legislative chamber.[10] State prosecutors are appointed by the State Minister of Justice. In some states, prosecutors are appointed by the State Minister of Justice in collaboration with a judge selection committee (*Richterwahlausschuss*).[11] The Minister of Justice is not obliged to follow the commission's recommendations. However, in practice they are usually followed. Public prosecutors are civil servants.[12] They are appointed for life.[13] This means that their mandate ends at the retirement age.[14] They can only be removed from office for

[5] Section 147 COA.

[6] Supervision of the Prosecution Service as a whole by the Minister of Justice.

[7] Supervision of lower-ranking prosecutors by higher-ranking prosecutors.

[8] Section 145 COA.

[9] On the internal structures of the prosecution service in Germany, see Elsner and Peters (2006), pp. 208–209.

[10] Section 149 COA.

[11] Trendafilova and Róth (2008), p. 221.

[12] Section 148 COA. As civil servants, their work is regulated by the Federal Civil Service Act in the version published on February 5, 2009 as last amended by Article 2 of the Act of March 15, 2012; *Bundesbeamtengesetz vom 5. Februar 2009, das zuletzt durch Artikel 2 des Gesetzes vom 15. März 2012 geändert worden ist.*

[13] Candidates at the beginning of their careers are appointed as junior prosecutor (*Anfänger*) and on a temporary basis for a test period of 3 years (Section 11 Federal Civil Service Act).

[14] Until recently, the retirement age was 65. From 2012 until 2029 the retirement age will be increased stepwise on the age 67. See also Section 51 subs. 1 Federal Civil Service Act.

misconduct after a final verdict. However, in some states, prosecutors general have the status of political appointees (*politische Beamte*) and hence can be moved or removed from office at will of the Minister of Justice. Nevertheless, they will still receive 75 % of their salary.[15]

Public prosecutors in Germany undergo the same training as judges. However, public prosecutors form a separate organization from the judiciary. To be appointed as a public prosecutor, a candidate must be of German nationality, have moral character such as to guarantee that the individual will at all times uphold the free democratic basic order, be qualified to hold judicial office (*Befähigung zum Richteramt*), and have the requisite social skills.[16]

To be qualified to hold judicial office, one must have successfully passed two state examinations.[17] The first state examination concludes the legal studies at the university.[18] A subsequent 2-year period of preparatory training leads to a second state examination.[19]

Before accession to office, public prosecutors swear an oath to fulfill their duties faithfully.[20]

7.1.3 Training of Prosecutors

After accession to office, public prosecutors have no mandatory training requirements.[21] However, numerous continuing legal education courses are proposed by the state and federal governments.

Unlike France, there is no central advanced-training institution offered by the Federal Republic of Germany.[22] However, there is the German Judicial Academy (*Deutsche Richterakademie*). It has the purpose of providing nationwide advanced training of judges and of public prosecutors. The German Judicial Academy is jointly supported by the Federation and the 16 states. It is a national institution but it has a federal character. The German Judicial Academy is not responsible for determining the contents of the conference. This is the responsibility of the Federation and the states.

---

[15] Trendafilova and Róth (2008), p. 220.

[16] Section 9 German Judiciary Act in the version published on April 19, 1972, as last amended by Article 17 of the Act of December 6, 2011; *Deutsches Richtergesetz in der Fassung der Bekanntmachung vom 19. April 1972, das zuletzt durch Artikel 17 des Gesetzes vom 6. Dezember 2011 geändert worden ist.*

[17] Section 5 subs. 1 German Judiciary Act.

[18] Section 5a German Judiciary Act.

[19] Section 5b German Judiciary Act.

[20] Section 64 Federal Civil Service Act.

[21] An exception is made for junior prosecutors. They have the duty to attend courses organized by the prosecutor general on a systematic basis (Trendafilova and Róth 2008, p. 226).

[22] For the situation in France, see Sect. 8.1.3.

Since continuing legal education is not mandatory, the same conclusion as for Switzerland can be drawn, namely that this is a weakness in the system.[23]

7.2 Relationship Between the Prosecution Service and the Police

Germany has no federal police force comparable to the French National Police or the U.S. Bureau of Investigation. The Federal Criminal Police Office of Germany (*Bundeskriminalamt* or BKA) is a national investigative police agency and is subordinate to the Federal Ministry of the Interior. The Federal Criminal Police Office is the central office for cooperation between the federation and the federal states in all criminal police matters. The Federal Criminal Police Office is competent for investigating criminal activities that fall under federal jurisdiction and that are enumerated by statute.[24] In addition, the Federal Criminal Police Office houses the National Central Bureau of the Federal Republic of Germany for the International Criminal Police Organisation (ICPO), known throughout the world as "Interpol".

For the most part, police jurisdiction in Germany falls within the 16 German states.[25] Thus, police forces are organized slightly differently in each state. All state police forces are subordinate to the Ministers of the Interior,[26] while the public prosecution services are under the Ministers of Justice. Usually, the regional police headquarters (called *Polizeipräsidium* in most states) are immediately subordinate to the interior ministries. Under the regional headquarters, there are several district police headquarters (*Polizeidirektion*). Subordinate to each district police headquarters, there are several local stations (*Polizeiinspektion*). Within these police forces, there is a *Schutzpolizei* section and a *Kriminalpolizei* section.

The public prosecutor is the master of criminal investigations. He has the duty to investigate the matter as soon as he obtains knowledge of a suspected criminal offense [Section 160 subs. 1 of the Code of Criminal Procedure (D-CCP)].[27] The prosecutor may make investigations of any kind, either himself or request the police to do so (Section 161 D-CCP). Hence, the public prosecutor may give mandatory

[23] On the situation in Switzerland, see Sects. 6.1.1.4 and 6.1.2.3.

[24] Counterfeiting, terrorism, internationally organized crime (see Section 4 of the Law on the Bundeskriminalamt and the Cooperation between Federal and State Authorities in Criminal Police Matters of July 7, 1997); *Bundesgesetz über das Bundeskriminalamt und die Zusammenarbeit des Bundes und der Länder in kriminalpolizeilichen Angelegenheiten vom 7. Juli 1997.*

[25] Article 30 Basic Law for the Federal Republic of Germany, as last amended by the Act of July 21, 2010; *Grundgesetz für die Bundesrepublik Deutschland, das zuletzt durch Artikel 1 des Gesetzes vom 21. Juli 2010 geändert worden ist.*

[26] Beulke (2008), Margin No. 102; Roxin and Schünemann (2012), Section 9, Margin No. 16.

[27] Code of Criminal Procedure in the version published on April 7, 1987, as most recently amended by Article 2 of the Act of July 21, 2012; *Strafprozessordnung in der Fassung der Bekanntmachung vom 7. April 1987, die zuletzt durch Artikel 2 des Gesetzes vom 21. Juli 2012 geändert worden ist.*

instructions to the police when it comes to the investigation of a criminal offense.[28] Police who are designated "investigative officers" (*Ermittlungspersonen*) of the public prosecution office have more powers and a closer relationship to the public prosecutor's service.[29] However, the majority of police officers are designated "investigative officers", so that this distinction is of little significance.[30] While all police officers can make arrests and carry out identity checks, only investigative officers have the power to investigate further.[31] Administratively, the police remain separate from the public prosecution services. The police are commonly described as "extended arm of the prosecution" (*verlängerter Arm der Staatsanwaltschaft*).[32]

In theory, the police have no power to investigate independently from the public prosecutor's office. The police may proceed on their own initiative only during the initial stages of the investigation when measures that cannot be delayed are needed. Once carried out, the police are obliged to inform the public prosecutor and to transmit their records to him, without delay (Section 163 D-CCP).[33]

In practice, however, the police conduct the great majority of criminal investigations on their own and submit the files to the public prosecutor only at the point at which charges would have to be brought. The public prosecutor is only informed from the very beginning in serious matters. Thus, the involvement of the public prosecutor increases with the gravity and complexity of the criminal matter.[34]

The public prosecutor is not able to effectively control and supervise the police's work as long as he has no knowledge of a case. Since the vast majority of minor cases are independently investigated by the police, this allows them to perform discretionary and unchecked acts.[35]

7.3 Discretion in the German Criminal Justice System?

7.3.1 Preliminary Remarks: Main Features of the German Criminal Justice System

The German criminal procedure is basically governed by the same general principles as the Swiss criminal justice system.

---

[28] Beulke (2008), Margin No. 103.

[29] See also Section 152 subs. 2 COA.

[30] Elsner and Peters (2006), p. 227; Weigend (2005), pp. 209–210.

[31] Trendafilova and Róth (2008), p. 239, n 95; Beulke (2008), Margin Nos. 107–108; Roxin and Schünemann (2012), Section 42, Margin Nos. 17–18.

[32] Trendafilova and Róth (2008), p. 240.

[33] Trendafilova and Róth (2008), p. 240; Elsner and Peters (2006), p. 227; Weigend (2005), pp. 207–208; Roxin and Schünemann (2012), Section 9, Margin No. 19.

[34] Trendafilova and Róth (2008), pp. 240–241; Elsner and Peters (2006), pp. 227–228; Weigend (2005), p. 208; Beulke (2008), Margin No. 106; Roxin and Schünemann (2012), Section 9, Margin No. 21.

[35] Trendafilova and Róth (2008), p. 241.

The state has the monopoly of criminal prosecution. Only with respect to a small number of less serious offenses mentioned in Section 374 D-CCP can the private victim file charges directly with the criminal court if the prosecutor has decided not to prosecute because prosecution would not be in the public interest.[36] In "private prosecution" (*Privatklageverfahren*) the victim takes over the role of the prosecutor, while the prosecutor does not take part.[37] Evidence has to be presented to the judge by the victim. Private prosecutions have become extremely rare. With the exception of certain offenses that can only be prosecuted upon complaint of the victim or on the request of the competent public authority (Sections 77 et seq. DCC),[38] the public prosecutor has the duty to proceed *ex officio*,[39] i.e. even without denunciation and even against the wishes of the victim (Section 152, subs. 1 D-CCP). The German criminal procedure traditionally adheres to the principle of legality, which requires the prosecutor to bring a charge whenever there are sufficient grounds to suspect a person of having committed an offense (Section 152, subs. 2 D-CCP, Section 170, subs. 1 D-CCP). However, in order to diminish the workload of prosecutors and courts, this principle has been limited by a number of exceptions. For less serious crimes, the prosecutor has the power to drop the charge due to a lack of public interest (Section 153 D-CCP) or to dismiss the case in exchange for a payment or other positive activity furnished by the suspect (Section 153a D-CCP).[40] The German criminal justice system is guided by the principle of "instruction" and thus, all authorities involved in criminal proceedings have the duty to search for the material truth.[41] The prosecutor has the duty to collect evidence both against and in the interest of the suspect (Section 160, subs. 2 D-CCP). The right to be heard is constitutionally guaranteed (Article 103 Basic Law) so that the accused must be heard on every decision that the court could make in his case. Several provisions in the D-CCP provide detailed implementations of this principle.[42] Thus, the accused has the right to participate in the proceedings, to appoint a defense counsel, and to be informed about the charge. Furthermore, he has the right to speak and to make comments and motions, to present evidence and to ask questions. The burden of proof rests on the legal authorities. There is a presumption of innocence in favor of the accused. In case

[36] Offenses being dealt with by private prosecution are, e.g. the insult to a person, the damage to property, and the bodily injury.

[37] For more information about this procedure, see Roxin and Schünemann (2012), Section 63.

[38] See Sections 77–77e of the German Criminal Code (DCC) in the version promulgated on November 13, 1998, last amended by Article 1 of the Act of June 25, 2012; *Strafgesetzbuch in der Fassung der Bekanntmachung vom 13. November 1998, das zuletzt durch Artikel 1 des Gesetzes vom 25. Juni 2012 geändert worden ist.*

[39] For more details, see Kühne (2010), Margin Nos. 297–298.

[40] For more details about the principle of legality and opportunity in the German criminal procedure, see Kühne (2010), Margin Nos. 305–310.

[41] Beulke (2008), Margin No. 21; Kühne (2010), Margin Nos. 299–304.

[42] Sections 33 subs. 1 and 3, 136 subs. 1, 201 subs. 1, 243 subs. 4, 257 subs. 1, 258 subs. 1 and 2, 265 D-CCP.

of doubt, he must be acquitted (*in dubio pro reo*).[43] The accused cannot be compelled to testify against himself (*nemo tenetur ipsum accusare*) and hence has a right to remain silent (Section 136 D-CCP).

The victim and close relatives have the possibility to become joint plaintiffs (*Nebenkläger*) in criminal proceedings for serious offenses (Sections 395 et seq. D-CCP). As a joint plaintiff, the victim has participatory rights during the main hearing and has a right to appeal. Under certain circumstances, he may have a right to a lawyer paid by the state.[44] Furthermore, the victim can join his civil suit to the already launched prosecution (Sections 403 et seq. D-CCP).[45] The victim has a number of other rights which are regulated in Sections 406d et seq. D-CCP. The most important are the right of the victim to view case files through his lawyer (Section 406e D-CCP) and, provided that the victim has applied to be informed, must be notified about the dismissals of the case and the outcome of court proceedings. Moreover, the victim can be assisted and represented by a lawyer during the proceedings (Section 406f D-CCP). The law explicitly states that criminal authorities have to inform the victim as early as possible of his rights (Section 406h D-CCP). At every stage of the proceedings the court and the prosecution are obliged to examine whether it is possible to reach a mediated agreement between the accused and the victim and in appropriate cases work towards such mediation (Section 155a D-CCP).[46] If a case has been dropped because of insufficient evidence, the victim may try to force public prosecution with a special proceeding (*Klageerzwingungsverfahren*).[47] Other dismissals are non-appealable, but the victim can make a complaint to a superior prosecutor (*Dienstaufsichtsbeschwerde*).[48]

The German Criminal Code (DCC) classifies criminal actions in *Verbrechen* (felony) and *Vergehen* (misdemeanor). Felonies are punishable by a minimum sentence of 1 year imprisonment (Section 12 subs. 1 DCC). Misdemeanors are punishable by a lesser minimum term of imprisonment or by fine (Section 12 subs. 2 DCC).

7.3.2 *Rule: Principle of Legality*

As just mentioned, the German criminal procedure is governed by the principle of legality. Thus, the prosecution has the legal obligation to take investigative action

[43] Beulke (2008), Margin No. 25.

[44] Beulke (2008), Margin No. 596; Kühne (2010), Margin Nos. 255–257.1; Roxin and Schünemann (2012), Section 64, Margin No. 2.

[45] See Roxin and Schünemann (2012), Section 65, Margin Nos. 1–8 for more information.

[46] Kühne (2010), Margin Nos. 258–259.3.

[47] See Sect. 7.4.2, para 3 for more information.

[48] Beulke (2008), Margin No. 349.

against all criminal offenses that come to its attention (Section 152 subs. 2 D-CCP). Furthermore, it has the duty of bringing these cases to court if there is sufficient evidence that the suspect has committed the crime (Section 170 subs. 1 D-CCP and Section 203 D-CCP). However, with the phenomenon of mass crimes coming up in the 1960s, this leading principle has been tempered more and more with elements of discretion (*Opportunität*).[49]

7.3.3 Introducing Discretionary Non-Prosecution

The German criminal procedure divides dismissals into two categories: unconditional and conditional.

7.3.3.1 Unconditional Dismissals

7.3.3.1.1 Drop Due to Lack of Public Interest

Dismissal without consequences is possible in cases of minor guilt and lack of public interest in prosecution (Section 153 subs. 1 D-CCP).[50] This provision is not applicable with regard to felonies, but is limited to misdemeanors. The court has to affirm the decision of non-prosecution only when the offense concerns a legal norm providing for a mandatory minimum sentence beyond the legal minimum penalty,[51] or the damage is significant. Otherwise, the prosecutor is independent from the judiciary in his decision-making. The suspect's agreement is not required.[52] The decision can even be made without the parties being heard.[53] The prosecutor does not need to give reasons for his decision. Furthermore, his decision is not contestable.[54] The prosecutor's decision does not acquire legal force. Thus, the prosecutor can re-open the case even without new facts and evidence.[55]

---

[49] Albrecht (2000), p. 246.

[50] For details, see Kühne (2010), Margin Nos. 585–588.

[51] For custodial sentences: 1 month (Section 38 DCC), for day fines: 5 day fines (Section 40 DCC).

[52] Beulke (2008), Margin No. 334; Meyer-Gossner (2011), Section 153, Margin No. 13.

[53] Beulke (2008), Margin No. 334; Meyer-Gossner (2011), Section 153, Margin No. 13; Schoreit. In Hannich (2008) KK StPO, Section 153, Margin No. 36. Whether a hearing of the victim is required is a matter of debate (see Schoreit. In Hannich (2008) KK StPO, Section 153, Margin No. 36 with further references).

[54] Meyer-Gossner (2011), Section 153, Margin No. 11.

[55] Beulke (2008), Margin No. 334; Schoreit. In Hannich (2008) KK StPO, Section 153, Margin No. 44.

Table 7.1 Drops due to a lack of public interest in Germany (2008–2011)

	2008		2009		2010		2011	
	Absolute number	%	Absolute number	%	Absolute number	%	Absolute number	%
Total PPS case-ending decision	4,903,552	100	4,710,262	100	4,602,685	100	4,609,786	100
Of which: drops due to a lack of public interest	493,941	10.1	429,394	9.1	413,788	9	414,584	9

Source: Data from Federal Statistical Office (2009b, 2010b, 2011b, 2012b), Table 2.2

The definitions of minor guilt and lack of public interest are imprecise and thus leave the prosecutor wide discretion when deciding whether to apply the norm. Although according to the wording of the provision, the prosecutor may decide to continue with the prosecution even if there is no public interest, the prevailing legal opinion argues that the prosecution has a duty to dismiss the case when there is minor guilt and no public interest.[56] A suspect has no legal remedy against a prosecutor's decision not to dismiss his case.[57]

In making his decision, the prosecutor has the duty to respect the principle of equal treatment.[58] In order to provide for a uniform application of Section 153 subs. 1 D-CCP, the states have issued guidelines. These may allow the use of this legal provision only if the damage caused does not exceed a certain amount. It is also possible to reserve the use of this regulation for certain offenses or to exclude its use for certain types of offenders.[59]

Table 7.1 shows the proportion of drops pursuant to Section 153 subs. 1 D-CCP for the years of 2008–2011. The median value is about 9 %.

Considering the fact that a drop due to a lack of public interest is a real exception to the principle of legality, this proportion is not negligible.

Section 153 subs. 1 D-CCP shows some similarities with Article 52 SCC where the authorities refrain from prosecution when the level of culpability as well as the consequences of the criminal offenses are negligible. However, in the Swiss provision, the requirement of negligible consequences seriously restricts the scope of application and thus it is rarely applied.[60]

---

[56] Beulke (2008), Margin No. 334; Schoreit. In Hannich (2008) KK StPO, Section 153, Margin No. 32.

[57] Meyer-Gossner (2011), Section 153, Margin No. 10; Schoreit. In Hannich (2008) KK StPO, Section 153, Margin No. 30.

[58] Schoreit. In Hannich (2008) KK StPO, Section 153, Margin No. 3.

[59] Elsner and Peters (2006), pp. 220–221.

[60] See Sect. 6.3.4.2.

7.3.3.1.2 Mediation and Restitution

A prosecution may also be dismissed if the defendant has participated in victim offender mediation and/or compensated the victim (Section 46a DCC and Section 153b D-CCP). In contrast to the drop due to lack of public interest, this provision requires positive action from the offender. Thus, he has to demonstrate the required restorative efforts. These efforts may not be imposed by the prosecution.

This option is open to all offenses that would be punishable by no more than 1 year imprisonment or a fine up to 360 daily units. The prosecution needs the consent of the court to dismiss the case (Section 153b D-CCP). Thus, the German rule contains more procedural safeguards since the Swiss provision does not require judicial agreement.

In contrast to the Swiss legal rule (Article 53 SCC), the German provision (Article 46a DCC) belongs to the principles governing the determination of the sentence, which does not necessarily lead to a dismissal of the case when the conditions are fulfilled.

In order to better achieve the objective of Section 46a DCC, the legislature has implemented different rules in the code of criminal procedure. Pursuant to Section 155a D-CCP, the public prosecutor and the court should examine at every stage of the proceedings whether it is possible to reach a mediated agreement between the accused and the aggrieved person. However, an agreement may not be accepted against the express will of the aggrieved person. Furthermore, according to Section 155b D-CCP, the prosecution and the court may transmit the necessary personal data for the purposes of a perpetrator-victim mediation or reparation of damage *proprio motu* or upon application by an agency they have commissioned to carry out the mediation concerned. Finally, Section 153a D-CCP provides for a dismissal combined with conditions. Thus, in a case involving a misdemeanor, the prosecutor may dispense with preferment of public charges and instead impose conditions and instructions upon the accused. The accused may be obliged to make a serious attempt to reach a mediated agreement with the aggrieved person, thereby trying to make reparation for his offense in full or to a predominant extent, or to strive therefore.[61]

Since dismissals according to Section 153b D-CCP are not limited to mediation, but include all provisions where the court may dispense with imposing a penalty, it is not possible to give statistical information concerning the proceedings dismissed according to Section 153b D-CCP as a result of mediation.

[61] On conditional dismissals, see Sect. 7.3.3.2.

7.3.3.1.3 Other Unconditional Dismissals

The criminal procedure provides for further possibilities of unconditional dismissals where a judicial participation is not required, namely:

- Dismissal for policy reasons, including cases of extradition (Section 153c/d D-CCP; Section 154b D-CCP).
- Dismissal for reasons of prosecutorial efficiency (Section 154, 154a D-CCP).
- Dismissal in cases of minor drug offenses if the defendant's guilt is minor and there is a lack of public interest (Section 31a of the Act against the Abuse of Narcotics).
- Dismissal in juvenile cases for minor guilt and lack of public interest (Section 45 subs. 1 of the Juvenile Justice Act).
- Dismissal for juveniles if an educational action has been carried out or if the juvenile has participated in victim offender mediation (Section 45 subs. 2 of the Juvenile Justice Act).
- Dismissal in cases of crimes against the state if the perpetrator has manifested himself "in time" (Section 153e D-CCP).

7.3.3.2 Conditional Dismissals

With Section 153a D-CCP, the prosecution has the possibility to provisionally terminate criminal proceedings in cases involving a misdemeanor and at the same time impose conditions and instructions upon the accused.[62] These conditions and instructions concern in particular:

- Paying a fine to the state or a charitable organization;
- Community service;
- Compensating the victim;
- Maintenance orders;
- Undergo victim offender mediation.

Neither the fine nor the community service that may be imposed by the prosecution have statutory upper limits. However, the prosecutor has to respect the constitutional principle of proportionality.[63] In practice, the fine prevails as a condition.[64] In 2011, a payment of a fine to the state or a charitable organization was ordered in 84.1 % of the cases dismissed with conditions. In the same year, Offender-Victim Mediation was ordered in 5.8 % and compensation in 5.3 % of the cases dismissed with conditions.[65]

---

[62] See Kühne (2010), Margin Nos. 589–591 for details.

[63] Schoreit. In Hannich (2008) KK StPO, Section 153a, Margin No. 17.

[64] Beulke (2008), Margin No. 337c; Schoreit. In Hannich (2008) KK StPO, Section 153a, Margin No. 17.

[65] Federal Statistical Office (2012b), Table 2.2.

Table 7.2 Conditional dismissals in Germany (2008–2011)

	2008		2009		2010		2011	
	Absolute number	%	Absolute number	%	Absolute number	%	Absolute number	%
Total PPS case-ending decision	4,903,552	100	4,710,262	100	4,602,685	100	4,609,786	100
Of which: conditional dismissals	212,652	4.3	199,572	4.2	192,311	4.2	191,166	4.1

Source: Data from Federal Statistical Office (2009b, 2010b, 2011b, 2012b), Table 2.2

The consent of the accused is necessary. The court's approval is required under the same conditions as with Section 153 D-CCP.[66] Furthermore, the application of Section 153a D-CCP necessitates the presence of two substantive requirements: the conditions and instructions imposed upon the accused must be sufficient to eliminate the public interest in criminal prosecution and the degree of guilt must not present an obstacle.

If the accused complies with these conditions and instructions, the disposal is conclusive and, unlike Section 153 subs. 1 D-CCP, it is not longer possible to re-open the case. Prosecution can only be resumed if it appears that the offense was not a misdemeanor but a felony.[67] Conditional dismissals are recorded in a nationwide procedural register (Section 492 subs. 1 no. 5 D-CCP). The prosecutor does not need to give substantive reasons for the dismissal.

Section 153a D-CCP leaves the prosecutor with wide discretion. The states have implemented guidelines in order to avoid disparity in non-prosecution policies. Some states restrict the use of the provision if the damage caused does not exceed a certain amount or they may reserve respectively exclude its use for certain types of offenses.[68]

Table 7.2 shows the number of dismissals with conditions according to Section 153a subs. 1 D-CCP from 2008 to 2011. This provision is applied significantly less often than Section 153 para. 1 D-CCP. This may be due to the fact that the use of this rule requires more work from the prosecutor and thus he may prefer to drop the case due to a lack of public interest. Another explanation is that fewer offenses are committed that would justify the use of Section 153a subs. 1 D-CCP.

In the field of juvenile justice and minor drug offenses, the criminal procedure provides for further possibilities of conditional dismissals. In the field of juvenile justice, a case may be dismissed if the juvenile offender has admitted that he

[66] Beulke (2008), Margin No. 337d; Meyer-Gossner (2011), Section 153a, Margin Nos. 8–9; Schoreit. In Hannich (2008) KK StPO, Section 153a, Margin Nos. 26–29. See Sect. 7.3.3.1.1, para 1.

[67] Beulke (2008), Margin No. 337d; Meyer-Gossner (2011), Section 153a, Margin No. 38; Schoreit. In Hannich (2008) KK StPO, Section 153a, Margin No. 42.

[68] Elsner and Peters (2006), p. 222.

committed the offense and if public prosecution seems unnecessary in light of the conditions fulfilled (Section 45 subs. 3 of the Juvenile Justice Act). In the case of minor drug offenses, dismissal is possible if the penalty expected would not exceed 2 years, the defendant is willing to participate in rehabilitative treatment and successful rehabilitation can be expected (Sections 37 subs. 1 and 38 subs. 2 associated with 37 subs. 1 of the Act against the Abuse of Narcotics).

7.4 Prosecutorial Decision-Making

7.4.1 Opening the Investigation

Criminal proceedings start with an investigation of the facts by the police under the direction of the prosecution, either because an offense has been reported to the police or because the police themselves have discovered something that has given rise to a reasonable suspicion that an offense has been committed (Section 152 subs. 2 D-CCP).[69] Preliminary proceedings have the purpose of ascertaining the facts and thus of deciding whether to bring charges or to drop the case for lack of evidence or lack of violation of criminal law.

7.4.2 Discontinuing Proceedings

In the event that the prosecutor can not substantiate the suspicion, the prosecution drops the proceedings in accordance with Section 170 subs. 2 D-CCP.

As Table 7.3 shows, the prosecution drops about 28 % of proceedings due to inadequate suspicion. Besides these drops, the prosecution may dismiss cases for reasons of opportunity.[70] Taking the conditional and unconditional dismissals together, this accounts for another 26 %.

If a case is dropped, the prosecutor has to notify any claimant and indicate the reasons for his decision. At the same time, if the claimant is also the victim, he must be informed of the possibility of contesting the decision and of the time limit provided therefore (Section 172 subs. 1 D-CCP). This possibility of review is the "proceedings to compel public charges" (*Klageerzwingungsverfahren*).[71] The victim is entitled to lodge a complaint against the notification pursuant to Section 171

---

[69] Beulke (2008), Margin No. 311.

[70] See Sect. 7.3.3 for further information.

[71] See Kühne (2010), Margin Nos. 581–582 and Roxin and Schünemann (2012), Section 41 for more details.

Table 7.3 Drops of proceedings due to lack of suspicion in Germany (2008–2011)

	2008		2009		2010		2011	
	Absolute number	%	Absolute number	%	Absolute number	%	Absolute number	%
Total PPS case-ending decision	4,903,552	100	4,710,262	100	4,602,685	100	4,609,786	100
Of which: drop due to lack of suspicion	1,347,619	27.5	1,325,271	28.1	1,305,090	28.4	1,289,063	28

Source: Data from Federal Statistical Office (2009b, 2010b, 2011b, 2012b), Table 2.2

D-CCP to the general prosecutor within 2 weeks after receipt of such notification. The general prosecutor may either re-open the case or confirm the prosecutor's decision to drop the case. If the latter is the case, the victim may make an appeal to the Higher Regional Court, within 1 month after receipt of notification. Besides these proceedings to compel public charges, the aggrieved person has the possibility to file a disciplinary complaint.

Proceedings can be suspended if the prosecutor is confronted with the fact that, for various reasons, he is temporarily not able to pursue and terminate the criminal proceedings. This is the case when temporary procedural bars exist, such as in cases of serious illness and extended stay abroad.[72] Proceedings are suspended in about 2 % of cases annually.

7.4.3 *Decision to Charge*

Charges must be brought if there is sufficient evidence that a criminal offense has been committed (Section 170 subs. 1 D-CCP).[73] It is obvious that the legal terms "sufficient" and "insufficient" reason leave the prosecution some discretion.

Table 7.4 shows the number respectively the proportion of cases brought to court in relation to the total number of case-ending decisions made by the prosecution, whereby the proceedings in which no offender was identified are not included. Penal order proceedings and accelerated proceedings are excluded from the number of cases brought before court. In general, about 11 % of the cases handled by the prosecution lead to a main hearing.

[72] Section 205 D-CCP, which regulates provisional termination by the court is applicable by analogy in all other phases of the procedure (Beulke 2008, Margin No. 364).

[73] For more details, see Kühne (2010), Margin Nos. 578–579.

Table 7.4 Cases brought before court in Germany (2008–2011)

	2008		2009		2010		2011	
	Absolute number	%	Absolute number	%	Absolute number	%	Absolute number	%
Total PPS case-ending decision	4,903,552	100	4,710,262	100	4,602,685	100	4,609,786	100
Of which: cases brought before court	553,719	11.3	533,247	11.3	512,498	11.1	508,026	11

Source: Data from Federal Statistical Office (2009b, 2010b, 2011b, 2012b), Table 2.2

7.5 Alternative Proceedings

A relatively small number of cases end with charges being brought before court. Instead, the high majority are dealt with by alternative or summary proceedings, namely the accelerated proceedings and the penal order proceedings. In 2009, an amendment of criminal procedural law went into force which formally introduced the possibility of agreements, which had been used in practice since the 1980s.

7.5.1 Accelerated Proceedings

Accelerated proceedings (*beschleunigtes Verfahren*) are a special procedure available for minor offenses where the factual situation or the evidence is simple and thus are suited to immediate hearing[74] and where a single judge or the "Schöffengericht" has jurisdiction (Sections 417 et seq. D-CCP).[75] This kind of proceeding is limited to prison sentences of up to 1 year (Section 419 subs. 1 D-CCP). The prosecution has to make an application to the court for the case to be conducted by accelerated proceedings. The court examines whether the requirements are fulfilled and will only allow an application upon a positive finding.

The accelerated proceedings have different mechanisms that provide for a simplification of the proceedings. In contrast to ordinary proceedings, the main hearing takes place immediately. The intermediary proceedings (*Zwischenverfahren*), where the court decides whether to proceed to main proceedings, are left out (Section 418 subs. 1 D-CCP). Beyond that, the prosecutor has the possibility to bring charges orally at the beginning of the main hearing, so that the main hearing can be initiated without a bill of indictment (Section 418 subs. 3 D-CCP).

[74] The main hearing should take place within 1–2 weeks (Beulke 2008, Margin No. 530).

[75] For details, see e.g. Roxin and Schünemann (2012), Section 61; Beulke (2008), Margin Nos. 530–531; Meyer-Gossner (2011), Vor Section 417 et seq.; Tolksdorf. In Hannich (2008) KK StPO, Section 417 et seq.

Table 7.5 Application for accelerated proceedings in Germany (2008–2011)

	2008		2009		2010		2011	
	Absolute number	%	Absolute number	%	Absolute number	%	Absolute number	%
Total PPS case-ending decision	4,903,552	100	4,710,262	100	4,602,685	100	4,609,786	100
Of which: PPS made an application for accelerated proceeding	24,141	0.5	22,928	0.5	21,064	0.5	19,723	0.4
Court rejection	*1,512*	*6.3*[a]	*1,313*	*5.7*[a]	*1,073*	*5.1*[a]	661	*3.4*[a]

Source: Data from Federal Statistical Office (2009a, 2010a, 2011a, 2012a), Table 2.2; Federal Statistical Office (2009b, 2010b, 2011b, 2012b), Table 2.2

[a]The data for this calculation stem from different data sources. Thus, the proportion given is not an exact value

Furthermore, evidence is gathered in a simplified manner (Section 420 D-CCP). The interrogation of witnesses, experts, or co-accused may be replaced by reading out protocols. The court judge decides as to the extent of evidence to be gathered (Section 420 subs. 4 D-CCP).

Section 418 subs. 4 D-CPP provides for a mandatory appointment of a defense lawyer if the expected sanction is at least 6 months imprisonment.

In general, the accelerated proceedings will mainly be used in cases where the prosecutor has the intention of requesting a suspended or unsuspended prison sentence below 6 months. On the contrary, since the appointment of a defense counsel is mandatory for prison sentences above 6 months, the application of the accelerated proceedings in these cases should not be frequent.[76]

As Table 7.5 shows, the accelerated proceedings are almost never used and the application is rejected in the rarest cases.

7.5.2 *Penal Order Proceedings*

In relation to misdemeanors, the penal order proceedings provide for another procedural simplification (Sections 407 et seq. D-CCP). Given the outcome of the investigation, the prosecutor must consider a main hearing as unnecessary and make a written application to the judge. In the application, the prosecutor requests the imposition of a specific sanction, namely a fine, forfeiture, disqualification from driving, or a suspended prison sentence of up to 1 year combined with probation (Section 407 subs. 2 D-CCP). The judge does not have to hear the accused before making his decision (Section 407 subs. 3 D-CCP) nor does the prosecutor have the

[76] Meyer-Gossner (2011), Section 417, Margin No. 1; Tolksdorf. In Hannich (2008) KK StPO, Section 417 et seq.

Table 7.6 Applications for the issue of a penal order in Germany (2008–2010)

	2008		2009		2010		2011	
	Absolute number	%	Absolute number	%	Absolute number	%	Absolute number	%
Total PPS case-ending decision	4,903,552	100	4,710,262	100	4,602,685	100	4,609,786	100
Of which: PPS applies for the issue of a penal order	562,663	11.5	541,988	11.5	533,732	11.6	538,739	11.7
Court rejection	*7,035*	*1.3*[a]	*6,774*	*1.2*[a]	*7,567*	*1.4*[a]	7,520	*1.4*[a]
Suspect's objection	*163,316*	*29*[a]	*161,229*	*29.7*[a]	*160,069*	*30*[a]	*157,136*	*29.2*[a]

Source: Data from Federal Statistical Office (2009a, 2010a, 2011a, 2012a), Table 2.1; Federal Statistical Office (2009b, 2010b, 2011b, 2012b), Table 2.2

[a]The data for this calculation stem from different data sources. Thus, the proportion given is not an exact value

duty to hear the suspect prior to the submission of the application to the court.[77] The judge will refuse an application if he believes that there are insufficient grounds for suspecting that the accused is guilty of the offense (Section 408 subs. 2 D-CCP). Furthermore, if the judge has reservations about deciding the case without a trial, he will set down a date for the main hearing (Section 408 subs. 3 D-CCP). If the court accepts the application, a penal order is mailed to the suspect who has the possibility to declare opposition to the decision within a period of 2 weeks (Section 410 D-CCP). Where this is admissible, ordinary proceedings take place. If the objection is not lodged in time, the penal order is equivalent to a judgment that has entered into force (Section 410 subs. 3 D-CCP). Thus, the issue of a penal order has the same effect as a judgment following a main hearing.

In the event that the judge is considering granting the prosecutor's application to issue a penal order with the imposition of a suspended sentence, due to the possible impact of the decision, he has to appoint a defense counsel if he does not yet have one (Section 408b D-CCP).[78] The prosecution requests the imposition of a suspended custodial sanction in less than 1 % of cases.

Table 7.6 shows the number of written applications to the court for the issue of a penal order from 2008 to 2011.

[77] Meyer-Gossner (2011), Section 408, Margin No. 24; Fischer. In Hannich (2008) KK StPO, Section 407, Margin No. 20. Pursuant to Section 163a subs. 1 D-CCP, the accused is to be examined at the very latest before the investigation is closed, so that the accused would have received a hearing beforehand either by the police or the prosecution. Only in simple matters it is sufficient to give him the opportunity to respond in writing.

[78] The imposition of custodial sanction by penal order is criticized: the imposition of short custodial sentences (i.e. below 6 months) should be the exception (Section 47 DCC). Without main trial, it is difficult to evaluate whether there is such an exception. Furthermore, it is hard to justify that the evaluation competencies of the prosecutor should be so large in a written proceedings since, according to Section 56 subs. 1 DCC, the decision to suspend the sentence for a probationary period requires the prosecutor to make a prognosis (see Fischer. In Hannich (2008) KK StPO, Section 407, Margin No. 8a).

The court rejects the application in the rarest cases, while objections by the suspect occur more frequently. Thus, the influence of the prosecution in this kind of proceedings is significant. Although the prosecutor is just proposing the penalty to the judge who can either accept or reject it, the sanction is in practice imposed by the prosecutor.[79]

Even though the German penal order is used frequently, Swiss prosecutors makes use of it much more often.[80] To the contrary, prosecutors in Germany will dismiss cases much more often than Swiss prosecutors. The influence of the German prosecutor becomes clearer, when considering only ordinary crimes that may in principle be brought before court. Of these crimes, 54 % are dismissed, another 24 % are dealt with in simplified procedures, and 22 % go to trial.[81] Thus, the high majority of cases are dealt with in an administrative way. As in the U.S. and Swiss criminal justice system, prosecutors have gained a quasi-judicial role.[82]

7.5.3 Agreements

In the 1980s, a discussion emerged around the phenomenon of *Absprachen* (informal agreements or contracting between prosecutor, defense and the court).[83] Although, at this time, there was no legal basis for this type of agreement, informal negotiations between the parties soon played an important role in achieving out of court settlements of criminal cases.[84] During the 1990s, decisions by the Supreme Court and the Federal Constitutional Court dealt with the admissibility of informal agreements. The courts decided that such negotiations should, in principle, be allowed if certain conditions are met.[85]

In 2005, the Supreme Court, in a landmark decision, held that, without a legal basis, it would be difficult to uphold and justify the actual practice of agreements.[86] In fact, by developing a set of rules, the court had created law and thus had interfered with the power of the Parliament. Following this decision, the Parliament

[79] See also Elsner and Peters (2006), p. 218.

[80] On the Swiss penal order, see Sect. 6.5.1.

[81] Federal Statistical Office (2012b), Table 2.2.

[82] For critical considerations, see Weigend (1978), pp. 49–58.

[83] Peters (2011), p. 7.

[84] See Peters (2011), pp. 9–24 which summarizes six studies on informal agreements conducted in Germany in order to identify the extent and the reasons for such agreements.

[85] For an overview and discussion of these decisions, see Peters (2011), pp. 32–42.

[86] BGHSt 50, 40–64; See Peters (2011), pp. 48–49.

drafted a law regulating informal agreements.[87] This law went into force in mid-2009.[88]

The law specifies that discussions about the status of the proceedings are allowed at every stage of the proceedings (Sections 160b, 202a, 212, 257b D-CCP). The central provision of this reform is displayed in Section 257c D-CCP. According to this rule, the court may, in suitable cases, reach an agreement with the participants during the main trial regarding the further course and outcome of the proceedings. Section 244 subs. 2 D-CCP remains unaffected thereby.[89] Subject of such an agreement may only comprise the legal consequences that may be imposed in a judgment, other procedural measures related to trial proceedings, and procedure related acts of the parties. A confession should be an integral part of any negotiated agreement. The verdict of guilt, as well as sentences of rehabilitation and security, may not be part of a negotiated agreement. The court announces what content the agreement can have. The court may also, upon free evaluation of all the circumstances of the case and the general sentencing factors, indicate the minimum and the maximum possible sentence. Subsequently, the parties have the right to comment on this. Furthermore, the defendant and the prosecutor have to agree to the court's proposal in order to conclude the agreement. The court is not longer bound by a negotiated agreement if legal or factually important incidents have been overlooked or have arisen after the agreement was concluded and if the court is of the opinion that, under such new circumstances, the prospective sentencing range is no longer appropriate to the gravity of the offense or the degree of guilt. Furthermore, an agreement is not binding if the further conduct of the defendant at the trial does not match the acts which were assumed to occur by the court. In such cases, the defendant's confession may not be admitted as evidence. If the court concludes that the agreement is no longer binding due to the circumstances mentioned, it has to inform the parties without delay. The parties to proceedings still have the possibility to lodge an appeal respectively a petition of revision in case of negotiated agreements.[90] If a negotiated agreement has preceded the judgment, a waiver of the right to file an appellate remedy is excluded (Section 302 subs. 1 D-CCP).

By obliging the president of the court to announce in public whether talks about agreements have taken place and, if an agreement has been concluded, what content the agreement has, the transparency in negotiated agreements is to a certain extent guaranteed (Section 243 subs. 4 D-CCP). Nevertheless, despite this rule and the

[87] On the necessity of a legal basis, see Peters (2011), pp. 51–58.

[88] Law regulating formal agreements of July 29, 2009, *Gesetz zur Regelung der Verständigung im Strafverfahren vom 29. Juli 2009*.

[89] This provision contains the principle of inquisition by stating that, in order to establish the truth, the court shall extend the taking of evidence to all facts and means of proof relevant to the decision. The fact that this provision must also be considered in the case of agreements contradicts to a certain extent the purpose of agreements, which is economizing. See also Meyer-Gossner (2011), Section 257c, Margin No. 3.

[90] Meyer-Gossner (2011), Section 257c, Margin Nos. 32–34.

principle of a public trial, the essence of agreements will still remain hidden. Only the essential content of the negotiated agreement has to be presented in open court, while negotiations do not have to be carried out in public.

It is not possible to give statistical information about the number of cases ended by way of agreements since this is usually merged with the total number of cases brought before the court. In the event that informal negotiations take place prior to the main hearing, it may happen that the case will either be dismissed pursuant to Sections 153 et seq. D-CCP or will be dealt with by penal order.[91]

7.6 Prosecutorial Control and Accountability

7.6.1 Control of Public Prosecutors

Prosecution services are entirely independent of the police and of the judiciary (see Sections 150 and 151 COA). It is a matter of debate as to which branch the prosecution service should be associated with.[92] The prevailing legal opinion considers the public prosecutor service a judicial organ of the executive branch.[93]

Prosecution services at the federal and at state levels are hierarchically structured with the state or federal Minister of Justice at the top.[94] Thus, higher level offices have supervisory authority over lower offices. In accordance with Section 146 COA, prosecutors are required to follow the orders of their superiors (*Weisungsrecht*). This rule extends to the Minister of Justice and hence, he is entitled to give directions to the prosecution service as to policy and prosecution decisions in individual cases. Although legally the Minister of Justice has unlimited rights to issue instructions to the prosecutors below him, in practice it is very rare for him to interfere with the handling of individual cases. Nevertheless, the Minister of Justice can at any time in the proceedings reassign the case to another prosecutor (*Substitutionsrecht*) and in this way make his wishes clear to the lower-ranking prosecutors (Section 145 COA). There has been criticism of the Minister's power to issue instructions concerning individual proceedings since a danger exists that, in cases of political interest, prosecutors could be impermissibly influenced. Thus, some legal scholars argue that the right of the Ministry to issue instructions should be restricted to guidelines and measures against civil servants.[95] This view seems

---

[91] Peters (2011), pp. 59–60.

[92] See Koller (1997).

[93] On the hybrid judicial-executive role played by German public prosecutors, see Beulke (2008), Margin No. 88; Roxin and Schünemann (2012), Section 9, Margin No. 10; Kühne (2010), Margin No. 133.

[94] See Sect. 7.1.1 for more details about the structure.

[95] Kühne (2010), Margin No. 141.

advisable, especially in view of the fact that in some states prosecutors general have the status of political appointees (*politische Beamte*) and can be removed from office at will.[96] The dangers of political pressures cannot be overlooked.

Within a prosecutor's office, higher-ranking prosecutors not only have the right to reassign proceedings, but also have the authority to withdraw cases from their subordinate, taking the case themselves (*Devolutionsrecht*; Section 145 COA).

Usually, the prosecutor general reports to the Minister of Justice orally. In important cases, the prosecutor general and the prosecutor in charge of the case report to the Minister together. The prosecutor general conducts evaluations of the work of the prosecution office every 3 years. These evaluations are conducted by a team appointed by the prosecutor general and cover all aspects of the prosecutor's work. In addition, cases are randomly selected and reviewed. The report is then submitted to the Minister of Justice and to the head of the prosecutor's service. These reports are not public.[97]

As mentioned above, the prosecution service is a hierarchical institution and thus, the lower-ranking prosecutors have to carry out the instructions of their superiors. However, the right to direct finds its limit in the principle of legality. Hence, the subordination of the individual prosecutor is not absolute. In the event that the prosecutor has some doubts regarding the legality of certain instructions, he has to report this concern to his superior who will then discuss the matter with him.[98] If he cannot persuade his superior of the illegality, the superior has the possibility to reassign the case to another prosecutor. In such cases, individual prosecutors can also exercise their right to withdraw from a specific case without running the risk of being sanctioned.[99]

7.6.2 Accountability of Public Prosecutors

7.6.2.1 Civil and Criminal Liability

Prosecutors are subject to criminal and civil liability. According to the German system of compulsory prosecution, a prosecutor may be held liable either for dismissing a case even though the case would have called for prosecution and trial (Article 339 DCC), or investigating an innocent person (Article 344 DCC).[100] It is not unusual that prosecutors are accused of such offenses by citizens. However,

[96] Kühne (2010), Margin No. 141.

[97] Trendafilova and Róth (2008), p. 220.

[98] Section 63 subs. 2 of the Federal Civil Service Act.

[99] Beulke (2008), Margin No. 85.

[100] Article 331 et seq. DCC enumerates the offenses committed in public office.

in general, such cases do not go beyond the investigative stage, as sufficient evidence of the prosecutor's intent must be shown.[101]

Prosecutors are subject to civil liability for damages resulting from their willful acts or gross negligence. However, the Ministry of Justice is responsible for compensating for such damages, and may then enforce civil liability against the individual prosecutor. Prosecutors are required to have liability insurance for their professional activities.[102]

7.6.2.2 Disciplinary Liability

Prosecutors may be subject to disciplinary proceedings. The same disciplinary rules and procedures (*Disziplinarordnung*) as apply to other civil servants are applicable. Disciplinary proceedings against public prosecutors are initiated by their superiors. Disciplinary proceedings may include informal warnings and formal proceedings and sanctions. The great majority of disciplinary infractions are sanctioned by a superior through a written warning that is not registered in the prosecutor's file. For more serious prosecutorial misbehaviors, prosecutors may be subject to formal disciplinary proceedings before a disciplinary tribunal that belongs to the administrative jurisdiction (*Dienstgericht*).[103] Sanctions include an official reprimand (*Verweis*), which is recorded in the prosecutor's file, reduction in salary, demotion, and dismissal from office.

In 2006, disciplinary proceedings were initiated against prosecutors for breach of professional ethics in about two cases, in about six cases for a criminal offense, in about 17 cases for professional inadequacy, and in one case for another reason.[104] In the same year, disciplinary sanctions were imposed in about four cases. A suspension was pronounced in two cases, a temporary reduction of salary was imposed in one case, and in another case the prosecutor was dismissed from office.[105] In 2010, disciplinary proceedings against prosecutors were initiated in three cases, including two cases for breach of professional ethics, and one case for criminal offense.[106] A reprimand was pronounced in two cases, and in one case the prosecutor was removed from the case.[107]

---

[101] Trendafilova and Róth (2008), p. 225.

[102] Trendafilova and Róth (2008), p. 225.

[103] See Section 122 subs. 4 Judiciary Act.

[104] There are no uniform statistics available at the national level. Thus, the given numbers are only estimates (Heger and Schön 2007, Section 5.2.2).

[105] Council of Europe (2008), Table 101.

[106] Council of Europe (2012), Table 11.54.

[107] Council of Europe (2012), Table 11.58.

References

Albrecht H (2000) Criminal prosecution: developments, trends and open questions in the Federal Republic of Germany. Eur J Crime Crim Law Crim Justice 8:245–256

Beulke W (2008) Strafprozessrecht, 10th edn. Müller, Heidelberg

Council of Europe (2008) European judicial systems. Efficiency and quality of justice (data 2006). Council of Europe Pub., Strasbourg

Council of Europe (2012) European judicial systems. Efficiency and quality of justice (data 2010). Council of Europe Pub., Strasbourg

Elsner B, Peters J (2006) The Prosecution service function within the German criminal justice system. In: Jehle J, Wade M (eds) Coping with overloaded criminal justice systems. The rise of prosecutorial power across Europe. Springer, Berlin, pp 207–236

Federal Statistical Office (2009a) Court statistics 2008 [Strafgerichtsstatistik des Statistischen Bundesamtes 2008]. Federal Statistical Office, Wiesbaden

Federal Statistical Office (2009b) Prosecution statistics 2008 [Staatsanwaltschaftsstatistik des Statistischen Bundesamtes 2008]. Federal Statistical Office, Wiesbaden

Federal Statistical Office (2010a) Court statistics 2009 [Strafgerichtsstatistik des Statistischen Bundesamtes 2009]. Federal Statistical Office, Wiesbaden

Federal Statistical Office (2010b) Prosecution statistics 2009 [Staatsanwaltschaftsstatistik des Statistischen Bundesamtes 2009]. Federal Statistical Office, Wiesbaden

Federal Statistical Office (2011a) Court statistics 2010 [Strafgerichtsstatistik des Statistischen Bundesamtes 2010]. Federal Statistical Office, Wiesbaden

Federal Statistical Office (2011b) Prosecution statistics 2010 [Staatsanwaltschaftsstatistik des Statistischen Bundesamtes 2010]. Federal Statistical Office, Wiesbaden

Federal Statistical Office (2012a) Court statistics 2011 [Strafgerichtsstatistik des Statistischen Bundesamtes 2011]. Federal Statistical Office, Wiesbaden

Federal Statistical Office (2012b) Prosecution statistics 2011 [Staatsanwaltschaftsstatistik des Statistischen Bundesamtes 2011]. Federal Statistical Office, Wiesbaden

Hannich R (ed) (2008) Karlsruher Kommentar zur Strafprozessordnung und zum Gerichtsverfassungsgesetz mit Einführungsgesetz, Rechtsstand: Mai 2008 (KK StPO), 6th edn. C.H. Beck, München

Heger M, Schön H (2007) Evaluation of European judicial systems. Replies to the 2008 questionnaire by Germany. Council of Europe Pub., Strasbourg

Koller C (1997) Die Staatsanwaltschaft – Organ der Judikative oder Exekutivbehörde? Die Stellung der Anklagebehörde und die Gewaltenteilung des Grundgesetzes. P. Lang, Frankfurt am Main

Kühne H (2010) Strafprozessrecht. Eine systematische Darstellung des deutschen und europäischen Strafverfahrensrechts, 8th edn. Müller, Heidelberg

Meyer-Gossner L (2011) Strafprozessordnung. Gerichtsverfassungsgesetz, Nebengesetze und ergänzende Bestimmungen (Beck'scher Kurzkommentar StPO), 54th edn. C.H. Beck, München

Peters J (2011) Urteilsabsprachen im Strafprozess. Die deutsche Regelung im Vergleich mit Entwicklungen in England & Wales, Frankreich und Polen. Universitätsverlag Göttingen, Göttingen

Roxin C, Schünemann B (2012) Strafverfahrensrecht. Ein Studienbuch, 27th edn. C.H. Beck, München

Trendafilova E, Róth W (2008) Report on the public prosecution service in Germany. In: Open Society Institute Sofia (ed) Promoting prosecutorial accountability, independence and effectiveness. Comparative research. Open Society Institute Sofia, Sofia, pp 211–246

Weigend T (1978) Anklagepflicht und Ermessen. Die Stellung der Staatsanwalts zwischen Legalitäts- u. Opportunitätsprinzip nach deutschem und amerikanischem Recht. Nomos, Baden-Baden

Weigend T (2005) The prosecution service in the German administration of criminal justice. In: Tak PJP (ed) Tasks and powers of the prosecution services in the EU member states, vol 1. Wolf Legal Publisher, Nijmegen, pp 203–222

Chapter 8
Overview of Public Prosecutors in France: Position, Powers, and Accountability

8.1 Structure and Organization of the Prosecution Service in France

8.1.1 Organization of the Public Prosecutor's Office

The structure of the public prosecution service (*ministère public or parquet*) largely mirrors that of the courts of law.[1] It is organized in two layers corresponding with the district tribunals and the courts of appeal.[2] Each of the 185 district level prosecution offices (*Parquets du Procureur de la République près le Tribunal de grande instance*) is headed by a chief district prosecutor (*Procureur de la Ré publique*), who assures the investigation and prosecution of criminal offenses in the district of the tribunal.[3] The 35 appellate prosecutors' offices (*Parquets géné raux près la Cour d'appel*) are each directed by a general public prosecutor (*procureur général*), who has authority over public prosecutors acting within the territorial jurisdiction of the court of appeal.[4] Chief district prosecutors and general public prosecutors are assisted by deputies (*premier substituts* and *procureurs adjoints* respectively *avocats généraux* and *substituts généraux*). In addition, there is one general prosecutor's office at the Supreme Court (*Parquet général près la Cour de cassation*), which is headed by a general prosecutor (*Procureur gé néral près la Cour de cassation*). The general prosecutor attached to the Supreme Court does not prosecute criminal offenses but participates in cassation proceedings

[1] See Article 32 para 1 of the French Code of Criminal Procedure (F CCP): "*Il* [*le ministère public*] *est représenté auprès de chaque juridiction repressive.*"

[2] Verrest (2000), pp. 212–213; Smedovska and Falletti (2008), p. 178.

[3] Article 39 et seq. F-CCP. On the powers of the chief district prosecutors, see Marguery (2008), pp. 69–70.

[4] Article 34 et seq. F-CCP. On the powers and functions of the general prosecutors, see Marguery (2008), pp. 68–69.

G. Gilliéron, *Public Prosecutors in the United States and Europe*,

DOI 10.1007/978-3-319-04504-7_8,

before the Supreme Court as a joint party (*partie jointe*). He brings his point of view on the case to the attention of the Supreme Court and ensures the correct application of criminal law.[5]

The French public prosecution service is headed by the Minister of Justice (*Garde des Sceaux*), to whom the general prosecutor at the Supreme Court and the general prosecutors at the court of appeals are answerable.[6] District prosecutors are supervised by general prosecutors.[7] With the exception of the general prosecutor attached at the Supreme Court, public prosecutors in France work in a strong hierarchical structure.[8] The hierarchical structure of the public prosecution service implies that instructions from the higher level are passed to the next lower level. In this sense, the Minister of Justice cannot give instructions to prosecutors at the district court level since this is within the responsibility of the prosecutor general.[9] Within a prosecutor's office, lower-ranking prosecutors must follow instructions issued by their superiors.[10] Instructions may be of general, specific, or individual nature.[11]

The French public prosecution service acts as a single body. The principle of indivisibility (*indivisibilité du Ministère Public*) means that a prosecutor acts in the name of the public prosecution service and not in his own name.[12] As a consequence of this principle, during a proceeding, prosecutors may share responsibility on the same case or be replaced by another magistrate. Opinions differ on the question of whether or not to allow different officers to work on the same case at different stages of the proceedings.[13]

---

[5] On the function of the general prosecutor at the Supreme Court, see Marguery (2008), pp. 67–68.

[6] See Article 5 of the Magistrates Status Act 58-1270 of December 22, 1958; *Ordonnance n 58-1270 du 22.12.1958 portant loi organique relative au statut de la magistrature*. The position of the General Prosecutor's Office at the Supreme Court does not exactly coincide with the parallel structure of the court system since the appellate prosecutors' offices are directly subordinated to the Ministry of Justice and hence do not receive instructions from the General Prosecutor's Office at the Supreme Court (see Dervieux 2006, p. 224; Smedovska and Falletti 2008, p. 179, n 6; Falletti 2005, p. 186; Grebing 1979, p. 26).

[7] The supervisory power is restricted by the right to speak freely about the case before the court ("*La plume est serve, mais la parole est libre*"; "*the pen is a slave, but the spoken word is free*"). On this right, see Grebing (1979), p. 27; Smedovska and Falletti (2008), p. 179; Falletti (2005), pp. 192–193.

[8] Article 3 para. 1, Magistrates Status Act.

[9] Smedovska and Falletti (2008), pp. 179–180.

[10] Smedovska and Falletti (2008), pp. 179–180; Grebing (1979), pp. 27–28.

[11] Dervieux (2006), p. 224.

[12] Stefani et al. (2010), Margin No. 175; Grebing (1979), p. 25; Smedovska and Falletti (2008), p. 180.

[13] Verrest (2000), p. 227.

8.1.2 Selection of General Prosecutors and District Prosecutors

On the suggestion of the Minister of Justice, the general prosecutor at the Supreme Court and the general prosecutors at the Court of Appeals are appointed by the Council of Ministers upon suggestion of the Minister of Justice and nominated by decree by the President of the Republic.[14] All other public prosecutors are appointed at the suggestion of the Minister of Justice by decree by the President.[15] For all nominations,[16] the Minister of Justice has to consult the Superior Council of the Judiciary (SCM; *Conseil Supérieur de la Magistrature*)[17] before submitting his proposal to the President respectively the Council of Ministers. However, the advice of the Superior Council of the Magistracy is not binding and hence the Minister of Justice may decide to waive it.

There are two different methods for recruiting public prosecutors.[18] Traditionally, prosecutors are appointed after having completed a 31-month training program at the National School of Magistrates (*Ecole Nationale de la Magistrature*),[19] which is only accessible to those who have successfully passed a competitive examination.[20] In addition, persons who meet specific requirements provided by law, such as professional experience, which make them particularly suitable for fulfilling judiciary functions, may be directly appointed as magistrates.[21] However, this happens infrequently since only about 5–10 % of the magistrates are recruited in this way.[22]

Article 16 of the Magistrate Status Act sets out the general requirements for a person to become a magistrate. A candidate must possess a recognized university degree requiring 4 years of study,[23] be of French nationality, be of good character,

---

[14] See Article 1 of the Act 58-1136 of November 28, 1958 concerning nominations to civil and military posts (*l'ordonnance n° 58-1136 du 28 novembre 1958 modifiée portant loi organique concernant les nominations aux emplois civils et militaires*) and Article 13 of the Constitution of the French Republic of October 4, 1958 (*Constitution de la République française du 04 octobre 1958*).

[15] See Article 28, Magistrates Status Act.

[16] Prior to the 2008 amendment of the French Constitution, the advice of the Superior Council of the Magistracy was not required for the appointment of the general prosecutor at the Supreme Court and the general prosecutors at the appellate courts.

[17] The Superior Council of the Magistracy comprises magistrates and members outside the Judiciary, whereas magistrates are in the majority.

[18] See Article 15, Magistrates Status Act.

[19] Article 40 of the Decree 72-355 May 4, 1972 on the National School of Magistrates; *Décret n°72-355 du 4 mai 1972 relatif à l'Ecole nationale de la magistrature*.

[20] In France, prosecutors and judges undergo the same formation since they both belong to the same body, namely the "magistrature".

[21] See Articles 22–25-4, Magistrates Status Act.

[22] Smedovska and Falletti (2008), p. 183.

[23] A law degree is not expressly required. However, in order to successfully pass the examination, candidates are supposed to have a high level of legal knowledge.

be entitled to his civic rights, have discharged his obligations under the Code of Military Duty, and meet the health requirements set for exercising the functions of magistrate.

Candidates must reside within the area of the office to which they will be appointed. Exceptionally, the Minister of Justice following consultation with the prosecutor general of the court of appeals may grant derogation to this rule.[24]

Public prosecutors are appointed to permanent terms. However, since 2002, heads of prosecution services are appointed for a term of 7 years without the possibility of reappointment in the same jurisdiction. After expiration of their mandates, they may be appointed elsewhere or to a higher office.[25]

Public prosecutors swear an oath to fulfill their duties faithfully before accession to office.[26] In 2010, the first Compendium of the Judiciary's Ethical Obligations was enacted. It does not constitute a disciplinary code but a guide for prosecutors and judges.[27]

8.1.3 Training of Prosecutors

The National School of Magistrates, established in 1958, has the purpose of improving recruitment and guaranteeing the professional skills of prosecutors and judges.

The initial training period lasts 31 months and comprises various stages and theoretical training. During the training period, judicial auditors (*auditeurs de justice*)[28] are supervised by magistrates and take part in judicial activities. However, they have no delegated power. Judicial auditors can assist examining magistrates, assist prosecutors in various actions in criminal proceedings, participate in judicial deliberations with a consultative vote in civil and correctional courts, and participate in deliberations of the Criminal Court.[29]

Since January 1, 2008, in-service training is compulsory.[30] Each magistrate must receive 5 days' mandatory in-service training per year.[31] In addition to this

---

[24] Article 13, Magistrates Status Act.

[25] Article 28-2, Article 38-1 and Article 38-2, Magistrates Status Act.

[26] Article 6, Magistrates Status Act provides the following: "*I swear to perform my functions rightly and faithfully, to keep with trust the secret of deliberation and to always behave as an honourable and loyal magistrate.*" (*Je jure de bien et fidèlement remplir mes fonctions, de garder religieusement le secret des délibérations et de me conduire en tout comme un digne et loyal magistrat*).

[27] Supreme Judicial Council (2010), p. XI.

[28] Students are called "judicial auditors".

[29] Article 19, Magistrates Status Act.

[30] Article 14, Magistrates Status Act.

[31] Article 50 of the Decree 72-355 May 4, 1972 on the National School of Magistrates.

mandatory in-service training, the National School of Magistrates offers optional ongoing training.[32]

8.2 Relationship Between the Prosecution Service and the Police

There are two distinct police forces in France, namely the National Police (*police nationale*) and the Gendarmerie (*gendarmerie nationale*).[33] The National Police is a police force controlled by the Ministry of the Interior, whereas the Gendarmerie has a military status and hence is part of the Ministry of Defense.[34] The National Police operate mostly in cities and towns, while the Gendarmerie works mainly in smaller towns and rural areas. The judicial police (*police judiciaire*) are administratively part of the police force, but they are functionally separate from the administrative police, whose function is to protect the public, or prevention.[35] The judicial police consist of officers of different ranks. Members of the judicial police include judicial police officers (*officiers de police judiciaire* or OPJ),[36] judicial police agents (*agents de police judiciaire* or APJ),[37] and assistant judicial police agents (*APJ adjoint*),[38] and the civil servants and agents to whom the law assigns certain judicial police functions (Article 15 F-CCP).[39]

[32] For more information, see http://www.enm.justice.fr/formation-continue/accueil.php (accessed June 29, 2012).

[33] See Vlamynck and Perez (2010), pp. 29–40; Stefani et al. (2010), Margin Nos. 370–377; Guinchard and Buisson (2011), Margin Nos. 246–267.

[34] For an analysis of the Gendarmerie, see Matelly (2006).

[35] Smedovska and Falletti (2008), p. 201; Verrest (2000), p. 228; Pradel (1993), p. 108.

[36] The following have the status of judicial police officer: mayors and their deputies; officers and non-commissioned officers of the Gendarmerie, having at least 3 years' service with the Gendarmerie, being designated by name by a decision of the Ministers of Justice and Defense upon receiving the concurring opinion of a commission; inspectors general, active police deputy-directors, general controllers, police superintendents and police officers; Civil servants appointed to the control and application group of the national police who have served for at least 3 years in this body, being designated by name by a decision of the Ministers of Justice and of the Interior upon receiving the concurring opinion of a commission (Article 16 F-CCP). For more details, see Vlamynck and Perez (2010), pp. 15–23; Stefani et al. (2010), Margin Nos. 380–386; Guinchard and Buisson (2011), Margin Nos. 269–275.

[37] The following persons have the status of judicial police agent: gendarmes who do not hold the capacity of judicial police officer; civil servants from active service departments of the national police force; members and trainees who do not hold the capacity of judicial police officer (Article 20 CCP). For more details, see Vlamynck and Perez (2010), pp. 25–28; Stahl (2008), pp. 47–53; Stefani et al. (2010), Margin No. 387; Guinchard and Buisson (2011), Margin Nos. 276–279.

[38] Stefani et al. (2010), Margin No. 388; Guinchard and Buisson (2011), Margin Nos. 280–283.

[39] Stefani et al. (2010), Margin Nos. 389–391; Guinchard and Buisson (2011), Margin No. 284–291.

Judicial police officers and judicial police agents are empowered with different prerogatives during preliminary proceedings. Only judicial police officers have the right to institute an inquiry and have coercive powers, such as to detain a suspect in police custody for up to 24 h (*garde à vue*).[40] Judicial police agents have more limited powers. They do not have the right to take a suspect into custody. The task of judicial police agents is to assist judicial police officers in the performance of their duties. They may draw up official records (*procès verbaux*) in respect to all offenses (felonies, misdemeanors, petty offenses) and also record statements of individuals (Article 20 F-CCP).

Depending on the type of investigation, the judicial police are subject to the authority of the public prosecutor or the examining magistrate. Examining magistrates supervise the work of the judicial police in investigation of serious offenses (*délits graves*),[41] whereas public prosecutors supervise their work in investigations of manifest offenses (*flagrant délit*)[42] and preliminary investigations (*enquête pré liminaire*).[43,44] Depending on the nature of investigation, the powers of the judicial police may vary. In investigations of manifest offenses, the police are empowered with more prerogatives and compulsive powers than in preliminary investigations.[45] In investigations of manifest offenses, judicial police may proceed with the investigation on their own initiative but must immediately notify the public prosecutor (Articles 53 and 54 F-CCP), while in preliminary investigations it may

---

[40] See Vlamynck and Perez (2010), p. 84; Stefani et al. (2010), Margin Nos. 419–420; Guinchard and Buisson (2011), Margin No. 269.

[41] When following an inquiry conducted by the judicial police, a case is referred to an examining magistrate by the public prosecutor a preliminary judicial investigation (*instruction préparatoire*; Article 79 et seq. F-CCP) is opened. The submission of the case to the examining magistrate is compulsory in relation to felonies. It is optional for misdemeanors. It may also be initiated for petty offenses if it is requested by the district prosecutor pursuant to Article 44 (Article 79 F-CCP). For more information, see Vlamynck and Perez (2010), pp. 101–132.

[42] See Vlamynck and Perez (2010), pp. 77–88; Stefani et al. (2010), Margin Nos. 410–428-4; for a detailed discussion see Guinchard and Buisson (2011), Margin Nos. 683–941.

[43] See Vlamynck and Perez (2010), pp. 89–97; Stefani et al. (2010), Margin Nos. 429–440; for a detailed discussion see Guinchard and Buisson (2011), Margin Nos. 942–1024.

[44] The French criminal justice system recognizes two types of investigation, namely the preliminary inquiry (*enquête préliminaire*; Article 75 et seq. F-CCP) and the *flagrante delicto* inquiry (*enquête de flagrance*; Article 53 et seq. F-CCP). The latter is not limited to cases where the offender has been caught while committing the offense, but extends to cases where the suspect is pursued by hue and cry, or is found in the possession of articles, or has on or about him traces or clues that give grounds to believe he has taken part in the felony or misdemeanor (Article 53 F-CCP).

[45] For their powers in investigations of manifest offenses, see Vlamynck and Perez (2010), pp. 84–85. For their powers in preliminary investigations, see Vlamynck and Perez (2010), pp. 92–97. For an overview about the powers of the judicial police officers and the judicial police agents in the different types of inquiries, see Vlamynck and Perez (2010), pp. 141–142.

happen that the prosecutor is unaware of the proceedings until an act needs his approval or until the matter is reported to him.[46]

The judicial police act under the direction of the district prosecutors (Article 12 F-CCP) and within each appeal court's territorial jurisdiction; they act under the supervision of the general public prosecutors and under the control of the investigating chamber (Article 13 F-CCP).[47] As mentioned above, the public prosecutor conducts the preliminary inquiries and the inquiries of flagrancy. Prosecutors and their deputies have the powers of judicial police officers (Article 41 F-CCP). However, they rarely exercise this power since they usually request the assistance of the judicial police (Article 42 F-CCP). As a result, this confers the judicial police with significant power in practice.[48]

The public prosecutor is only able to exercise his supervisory duties when he is informed about the criminal offenses. Thus, the police are obliged to notify the prosecutor of all criminal offenses without delay and to send to him all relevant reports they have recorded as soon as their operations are concluded (Article 19 F-CCP). Furthermore, in case of an arrest and detention, they are obliged to inform the prosecutor at the beginning (Articles 41, 63 and 77 F-CCP).

In practice, on the one hand, the police do not always record all infractions due to capacity and time problems and, on the other hand, for less serious offenses, they may conduct some investigations before reporting them.[49] As a consequence, this leaves considerable discretion to the judicial police to decide on the disposition of less serious offenses.[50]

8.3 Discretion in the French Criminal Justice System?

8.3.1 Preliminary Remarks: Main Features of the French Criminal Justice System

The French describe their criminal justice system as a mix of the inquisitorial and the adversarial models.[51] Traditionally, the police and judicial investigations have

[46] Where the inquiry is being carried out at the police's own initiative, they give the district prosecutor an account of its progress once it has been running for more than 6 months (Article 75-1 F-CCP). The judicial police, carrying out a preliminary inquiry into a felony or misdemeanor, must inform the district prosecutor as soon as a person has been identified against whom there is evidence that he has committed or attempted to commit an offense (Article 75-2 F-CCP). See also Marguery (2008), p. 83.

[47] See Stahl (2008), p. 83; Stefani et al. (2010), Margin No. 379; Guinchard and Buisson (2011), Margin No. 273.

[48] Smedovska and Falletti (2008), p. 202.

[49] See previously Sect. 8.2, para 3.

[50] Smedovska and Falletti (2008), p. 202.

[51] Steiner (2010), pp. 279–281; Pradel (1993), p. 116; For a detailed discussion, Guinchard and Buisson (2011), Margin Nos. 50–121.

taken place in secret (see Article 11 F-CCP). However, in recent years, elements of the adversarial process have been added in order to give greater protection to the rights of the individual.[52] The main trial contains elements of the inquisitorial and the adversarial models. It is public and since the written file prepared during the police and judicial inquiry is central to the hearing, the parties have a limited opportunity to put their case orally.[53]

The public prosecutor has the exclusive right to institute criminal proceedings (*action publique*, Article 1 para. 1 F-CCP). However, where the prosecutor refuses to initiate criminal proceedings, the victim may initiate the prosecution (Article 1 para. 2 F-CCP) and directly summon the suspect before a criminal court (*citation directe*) or before an investigating judge (*plainte avec constitution de partie civile*; Article 85 F-CCP).[54] In the past, this last tool has proved to be efficient in cases with a political dimension where prosecutors have been reluctant to initiate proceedings.[55]

Since the enactment of the Law of June 2000 (*Loi Guigou*), there is a trend emerging towards adversarial procedure. In fact, the 2000 Law has introduced a new preliminary article in the Code of Criminal Procedure, which affirms the following guiding principles: The procedure must be fair and adversarial, and a balance of rights between the parties must be maintained. A separation must be guaranteed between the authorities who conduct the prosecution and those conducting the adjudication. The presumption of innocence must be respected. Prejudgment sanctions must be limited to what is strictly necessary. Reasonable speed in the proceedings must be maintained, and the right to appeal respected. Furthermore, every suspect has the right to be informed of charges brought against him and to be legally defended. The rights of defense guarantee a right of access to the file and a right to request supplementary investigations. Among these principles, the principle of the presumption of innocence, the rights of defense, and the reasonable time standard pervade the entire criminal process. Many of the principles laid out in the preliminary article of the Code of Criminal Procedure mirror those guaranteed by Article 6 ECHR, which was ratified by France in 1974.[56]

The introduction in 2004 of a kind of plea bargaining and the government's proposal in 2009 to abolish the examining magistrate reinforce the trend towards an adversarial procedure.

---

[52] E.g. The Act of December 30, 1996 amended Article 114 CCP and introduced the right of the lawyers to give their clients copies of any documents from the file that they receive, so that the defendant has the possibility to effectively prepare his defense.

[53] Pradel (2008), pp. 142–143.

[54] Stefani et al. (2010), Margin No. 300–309; Steiner (2010), pp. 291–292.

[55] Steiner (2010), p. 292.

[56] For more details concerning the principles governing the criminal proceedings, see Stefani et al. (2010), Margin Nos. 87–130.

Contrary to Switzerland and Germany, the French system follows the principle of opportunity.[57] Thus, the prosecutor[58] enjoys discretion as to whether or not to prosecute the matter beyond the police investigation. The prosecutor needs only to prosecute when there is a general interest in doing so and may dismiss the case if, for instance, it is the first offense committed by the suspect, or if the damages caused by the offense are very small, or if the public safety has suffered virtually no harm, or if the victim withdraws his complaint.[59] The power of the prosecutor not to go forward in a criminal case is limited by the fact that the victim can launch a prosecution by pursuing a civil action.[60]

French law is favorable to the victim in many regards. The preliminary article of the Code of Criminal Procedure contains the duty of the judicial authority to ensure that victims are informed and that their rights are respected throughout any criminal process. Furthermore, the victim may join the criminal proceedings as a civil party (*partie civile*) to seek damages by means of a civil action (*action civile*). He may also rather choose to bring a civil action before a civil court.[61] The right to be included in the proceedings as a civil claimant exists only for those who have personally suffered damage directly caused by the offense (Article 2 F-CCP). As already mentioned, the victim may initiate a prosecution if the prosecutor chooses not to go forward. However, where a crime has caused no harm to an individual, but has simply endangered public order (i.e. possession of drugs or a forbidden weapon), the individual is not entitled to initiate a prosecution. In sum, the victim in the French criminal justice system can launch the criminal process, initiating both a civil action and a prosecution.

The French criminal law distinguishes three categories of offenses. Under Article 111-1 of the French Criminal Code (FCC), these are *crimes* (felony),[62] *dé lits* (misdemeanor),[63] and *contraventions* (petty offenses),[64] which include a large range of regulatory offenses often of strict liability. *Contraventions* are divided into five classes (*contraventions de 1ère, 2ième, 3ième, 4ième et 5ième classe*) and are punishable by a fine.[65] This classification has some influence on the investigation process and procedures. In the first four classes of petty offenses, it is usually a police commissioner instead of a prosecutor who handles the matter. These offenses

[57] Guinchard and Buisson (2011), Margin No. 1438.

[58] The judicial police and the other officers with the power to investigate are required to notify the prosecutor of any crime that comes to their attention without delay (Articles 19, 27, 29 and 40 para. 2 F-CCP).

[59] Marguery (2008), p. 80.

[60] See Sect. 8.3.1, para 2.

[61] For more details concerning civil actions, see Guinchard and Buisson (2011), pp. 1133–1214; Elliott (2001), pp. 32–34.

[62] E.g. murder, rape.

[63] E.g. theft, fraud, assault.

[64] E.g. selling alcohol to someone under age.

[65] The amount of the fine incurred ranges from €38 for the *contraventions* of the first class to €1,500 for the *contraventions* of the fifth class.

are judged by a *juge de proximité* (lay judge).[66] Fifth class petty offenses are judged by the *tribunal de police* (police court).[67] Misdemeanors are tried by *tribunaux correctionels* (Article 381 F-CCP) and felonies are tried by *cours d'assises* (Article 231 F-CCP).

8.3.2 Rule: The Principle of Opportunity

8.3.2.1 Legal Basis

Pursuant to Article 40 F-CCP, the prosecutor receives complaints and denunciations and decides how to deal with them. When he considers that the facts brought to his attention constitute an offense committed by a person whose identity and domicile are known, and for which there is no legal provision blocking further prosecution, he alone decides if it is appropriate:

- to file an indictment with the court (*mise en mouvement de l'action publique*)[68]
- to implement alternative proceedings to a prosecution
- to dismiss the case without taking any further action (*classement sans suite*)

As in the U.S., prosecutors in the French criminal justice system are free to decide whether to prosecute a case or not. Although a crime has been committed, he may for instance decide that it is not in the public interest to bring a prosecution, as it is a minor offense which did not represent a threat to society. The prosecutor can also dismiss a case where popular sentiment in favor of prosecution is weak.[69]

8.3.2.2 Control Over Opportunity

The public prosecution service in France has a centralized, hierarchical structure with the Minister of Justice at the top. This structure is basically designed to guarantee certainty and uniformity in the application of law and to minimize the exercise of discretion.[70]

National criminal policy is promoted through circulars issued by the Minister of Justice and implemented at local levels through the prosecutors (see Article

---

[66] Article 521 para 2 F-CCP. See Stefani et al. (2010), Margin No. 481-1.

[67] Article 521 F-CCP.

[68] In exceptional cases, the decision to prosecute depends on a formal notice or a complaint from a victim or an authority (see Stefani et al. 2010, Margin Nos. 606–616).

[69] Pradel (2008), p. 137.

[70] "The [Penal] Code's provisions are to be applied rigorously by prosecutors and police, both of whom are organized nationally and hierarchically and are subject, in theory, to greater control by superiors than under American practice" (Goldstein and Marcus 1977, p. 247).

30 F-CCP). These circulars may be of a general nature, address specific issues, or they may provide guidance on the interpretation of new legislation. In addition, there are local criminal policies adapted to local circumstances.[71]

In general, prosecutors comply with the Minister's directives for the most part. However, in practice, some disparities in local criminal policies are unavoidable due to resources and local conditions of criminality.[72] A number of prosecutors have criticized the disparity between the local criminal policies of different regions.[73] Furthermore, some scholars have pointed out that these disparities go beyond the limits of acceptable local interpretation of the law and also create the potential risk of undermining the certainty of the law.[74] In recent years, the application of the discretionary principle has been systematized in order to allow transparency. In order to identify the methods used in various situations, statistical forms are filled out by the head of the prosecution service.[75]

The power to decide how to proceed in a given case belongs entirely to the prosecutor.[76] Even if a decision is in opposition to a superior instruction, it remains legal and effective. A superior may only attempt to convince him to change his opinion. Nevertheless, the fact that the lower-ranking prosecutor refuses to act according to the instructions of a superior may lead to disciplinary sanctions.[77]

A decision by the prosecution service to dismiss a case has no legal effect. This means that if new evidence should come to light or if the prosecutor realizes that he can no longer maintain his earlier decision, he can subsequently decide to bring charges as long as the time limit to prosecute has not elapsed.[78]

Since 2004, any plaintiff can lodge an appeal with the prosecutor general against a prosecutor's decision to dismiss a case without taking further action (Article 40-3 F-CCP).[79] If the prosecutor general feels that the appeal is well founded, he may instruct the prosecutor to initiate a prosecution. The instruction is in writing and attached to the case file.

As mentioned several times, the victim has the possibility to initiate proceedings and directly summon the suspect before a criminal court (*citation directe*), in case of misdemeanors and petty offenses, or before an examining magistrate (*plainte avec constitution de partie civile*), optionally in the case of misdemeanors and compulsory in the case of felonies. The victims may be required to deposit a sum of money (*cautionnement*) as surety at the court clerk's office, except in those cases

[71] Hodgson (2005), p. 229. See also Elliott (2001), pp. 25–26.

[72] Hodgson (2005), pp. 230–231.

[73] Hodgson (2005), p. 231.

[74] Hodgson (2005), p. 231.

[75] Smedovska and Falletti (2008), p. 192.

[76] Stefani et al. (2010), Margin No. 601.

[77] See also Sect. 8.5.1, para 5.

[78] Stefani et al. (2010), Margin No. 599; Guinchard and Buisson (2011), Margin No. 1446.

[79] Stefani et al. (2010), Margin No. 599; Guinchard and Buisson (2011), Margin No. 1450.

where they are entitled to legal aid (Article 88 F-CCP). They can be exposed to a claim of damages if the accused is not convicted (Articles 91 and 472 F-CCP).

8.4 Prosecutorial Decision-Making

8.4.1 Preliminary Remarks

Once the police investigation is closed, the prosecution has to decide whether to proceed further with a case. The French prosecutor has a choice between closing a case, prosecuting, or applying intermediary solutions. The latter has become a third option (*troisième voie*) to waive prosecution. Legislation was passed on January 4, 1993 and June 23, 1999 (Article 44-1 F-CCP) that introduced the possibility of closing the prosecution of a misdemeanor on the condition that the offender agrees to make an alternative plea. Thus, mediation between the offender and the victim, reparation, the readiness to enroll in a drug or alcohol treatment program may lead to a dismissal of the case.[80] Germany and Switzerland have similar procedures.[81]

8.4.2 Discontinuing Proceedings

8.4.2.1 Overview

In prosecutable cases,[82] the prosecutor can under certain circumstances decide to dismiss a case. Such dismissals are, for instance, possible if the attempts to find the offender were fruitless, the victim was given compensation immediately, the damage or disorder caused by the offense was slight, the offender is mentally deficient, or the plaintiff is absent. Table 8.1 shows that the number of prosecutable cases dismissed declined from 16.4 % in 2007 to 11.6 % in 2010. Furthermore, the prosecution, instead of bringing the case to prosecution, can choose alternative ways to dispose of the case or offer a transaction (*composition pénale*) for a restricted number of offenses.

---

80 Stefani et al. (2010), Margin No. 595.

81 See Sects. 7.3.3.1.2 and 7.3.3.2 for Germany and Sect. 6.3.4.3 for Switzerland.

82 In order to better evaluate the proportion of dropped cases that really depend on the prosecution, non-prosecutable cases are deducted from the total treated cases. Of the cases annually treated by the prosecution service, around 70 % received are not prosecutable due to an unknown offender and unclear circumstances. Unclear circumstances include the following: The dossier does not bear evidence to the existence of a criminal offense, only contains an insufficiently clear offense or insufficient charges, or cannot be prosecuted on other, purely legal grounds. Cases dropped due to unclear circumstances constitute about 15 % of the non-prosecutable cases annually handled by the prosecution service.

Table 8.1 Number of proceedings discontinued in France (2007–2010)

	2007		2008		2009		2010	
	Absolute number	%	Absolute number	%	Absolute number	%	Absolute number	%
Total prosecutable cases	1,476,535	100	1,500,411	100	1,487,675	100	1,402,671	100
Of which: dismissals[a]	241,597	16.4	219,520	14.6	182,552	12.3	163,039	11.6
Alternative disposals	490,434	33.2	544,715	36.3	558,047	37.5	527,530	37.6
Composition pénale	59,770	4	67,230	4.5	73,392	4.9	72,785	5.2

Source: Data from Ministry of Justice (2012), p. 109

[a]Attempts to find the offender were fruitless (n = 61,674 in 2009), situation was regularized or the victim was given compensation immediately (n = 33,481 in 2009), desisting of the plaintiff (n = 24,636 in 2009), slight damage or disorder caused by the offense (n = 32,383 in 2009). Offender is mentally deficient, absence of the plaintiff, partial responsibility of the victim in the offense suffered (detailed data for 2010 are not available)

8.4.2.2 Alternative Disposals

In the event that prosecution is admissible, the prosecutor may make a number of decisions out of court prior to prosecution, if such a measure is likely to secure reparation for the damage suffered by the victim, or to put an end to the disturbance resulting from the offense, or to contribute to the reintegration of the offender.[83] Pursuant to Article 41-1 F-CCP this include the following:

- Reminder of the Law (*rappel à la loi*)
- Submit the author of the offense to social or medical aid
- Legalize the illegal situation that led to the offense
- Repair the damage caused to the victim of the offense
- Mediation between the offender and the victim

The most frequently used alternative to prosecution is reminder of the law with almost 50 %. The aim of this alternative settlement is to bring to the attention of the offender the duties imposed by the law. Reparation occurs in less than 2 % of the cases, while mediation happens in less than 5 % of the cases ended by way of alternative disposals. Mediation was introduced to French criminal law in 1993. In recent years, the number of cases closed without prosecution following mediation has slightly decreased from 5.4 % in 2007 to 4.2 % in 2009.

Table 8.2 gives an overview about the frequency of the different types of alternatives used. Since no detailed data for 2010 were publicly available, those for the 2007–2009 are presented.

[83] For more details, see Guinchard and Buisson (2011), Margin Nos. 1456–1472.

Table 8.2 Types of alternative disposals in France (2007–2009)[a]

	2007		2008		2009	
	Absolute number	%	Absolute number	%	Absolute number	%
Alternative disposals	490,434	100	544,715	100	558,047	100
Mediation	26,702	5.4	24,471	4.5	23,451	4.2
Reparation	7,824	1.6	9,016	1.7	9,024	1.6
Therapeutic injunction	5,201	1.1	4,727	0.9	4,380	0.8
Submit the offender to social or medical aid	15,154	3.1	16,638	3.1	16,414	2.9
Rappel à la Loi	245,131	50.0	269,202	49.4	273,783	49.1
Desisting of the plaintiff, regularization	81,659	16.7	92,975	17.1	101,205	18.1
Others	108,763	22.2	127,6086	23.4	129,790	23.3

Source: Data from Ministry of Justice (2012), p. 109
[a]The Statistical Yearbook of the Justice System 2011–2012 does not provide data for 2010 concerning alternative disposals

These alternative disposals suspend the limitation period for public prosecution. As a result, a prosecution can always be initiated as long as the statute of limitation has not elapsed. Where these measures are not carried out owing to the offender's behavior, the prosecutor may propose a transaction (*composition pénale*) or initiate a prosecution.

8.4.2.3 Transaction

The legislature by the law of June 23, 1999 introduced the *composition pénale* (transaction). Legislation was passed on March 9, 2004 to expand the field of application and to enhance the kind of offers proposed to the offender.[84] The *composition pénale* is the offer of a transaction presented to the accused which must be approved by the court. Nevertheless, the *composition pénale* is not a simplified trial but is conceived as a disposal arrangement. According to Article 41-2 F-CCP, prior to any prosecution, if the accused admits his guilt to an offense for which the main penalty is a fine or a prison sentence not exceeding 5 years, the public prosecutor may propose a transaction. This alternative to prosecution is not applicable to juveniles. Furthermore, it is excluded in the case of press offenses, involuntary homicide offenses, or political offenses. Of the discontinued proceedings, the percentage of cases ended by way of transaction increased from 4 % in 2007 to 5.2 % in 2010.[85]

[84] Stefani et al. (2010), Margin No. 596; Guinchard and Buisson (2011), Margin No. 1474.

[85] See Table 8.1.

A total of 17 measures are listed in Article 41-2 F-CCP. The prosecution may recommend one or several of those measures. They include, for instance[86]:

- The payment of a mediatory fine to the Public Treasury
- The surrender of his vehicle
- The surrender of the offender's driving license
- Unpaid work for the benefit of the community for a maximum of 60 h over a period that may not exceed 6 months

Once the accused has admitted his guilt, the public prosecutor formulates a written proposal containing the indictment and the nature and quantum of the measures proposed. The offender can request the assistance of a lawyer and has 10 days to respond. If he agrees to the transaction proposal, the prosecutor submits the files to the court for approval. The president of the court may proceed to hear the offender and the victim, assisted, where necessary, by their advocates. If the judge approves the transaction, the measures decided are put into effect. On the other hand, if it is refused, the proposal becomes void. The decision of the judge, of which the offender and the victim are notified, is not open to appeal. If the offender complies with the obligations imposed by the *composition pénale*, no further prosecution will be possible unless new facts are discovered. Thus, the case is not really dismissed but criminal proceedings are waived. If the proceeding fails, the public prosecutor decides on further prosecution.

8.4.3 Decision to Prosecute

8.4.3.1 Overview

If the prosecutor makes the decision to prosecute he has different ways of proceeding. He can refer the case to the examining magistrate, which is mandatory for felonies. He may decide to issue an indictment and summon the offender to appear before court, or he can choose to handle the case by way of penal order or make use of the procedure of *plaider coupable* (guilty plea). Table 8.3 shows which option the prosecutor chooses when he decides to go forward with a case.

8.4.3.2 Preliminary Judicial Investigation or Issuance of an Indictment

If the public prosecutor decides to prosecute the case, he has various options at his disposal. In the case of felonies or complex cases, a preliminary judicial investigation is compulsory (Article 79 F-CCP), so that the public prosecutor has to refer the case to an examining magistrate by issuing an introductory indictment (*réquisitoire introductif*).[87] In 2010, only 3.1 % of cases were referred to the examining magistrate.

---

[86] For more details about those measures, see Guinchard and Buisson (2011), Margin Nos. 1478–1491.

[87] Guinchard and Buisson (2011), Margin Nos. 1512–1523.

Table 8.3 Decision to prosecute in France (2007–2010)

	2007		2008		2009		2010	
	Absolute number	%	Absolute number	%	Absolute number	%	Absolute number	%
Prosecuted cases	684,734	100	668,946	100	673,684	100	639,317	100
Of which:								
Judicial inquiry	*28,063*	*4.1*	*23,409*	*3.5*	*20,899*	*3.1*	*19,640*	*3.1*
Tribunal correctionel	*533,767*	*78*	*530,76*	*79.3*	*540,654*	*80.3*	*514,699*	*80.5*
Citation direct	90,747	17	81,129	15.3	66,968	12.4	61,468	12
Convocation by OPJ[a]/APJ[b]	200,36	37.5	194,301	36.6	189,621	35.1	179,182	34.8
Convocation by PPS	16,801	3.1	17,511	3.3	18,154	3.4	17,403	3.4
Penal order	129,914	24.3	136,124	25.6	144,711	26.8	136,291	26.5
Speeded-up trial proceedings	46,233	8.7	45,369	8.5	43,67	8.1	42,056	8.2
Guilty plea	49,712	9.3	56,326	10.6	77,53	14.3	78,299	15.2
Tribunal de police	*64,937*	*9.5*	*58,272*	*8.7*	*55,857*	*8.3*	*51,009*	*8*
Citation direct	16,4	25.3	12,829	22	10,150	18.2	9,291	18.2
Convocation by OPJ[a]/APJ[b]	13,169	20.3	13,741	23.6	15,341	27.5	14,415	28.3
Penal order	35,368	54.5	31,702	54.4	30,366	54.4	27,303	53.5
Juge des enfants	*57,967*	*8.5*	*56,505*	*8.5*	*56,274*	*8.3*	*53,969*	*8.4*

Source: Data from Ministry of Justice (2012), p. 109
[a]Judicial police officer
[b]Judicial police agent

Once the examining magistrate has completed his investigations, he decides either to dismiss the case (*ordonnance de non-lieu*; Article 177 et seq. F-CCP) or to refer it to the appropriate court (*ordonnance de renvoi*; Article 178 et seq. F-CCP).

When the prosecutor is concerned with relatively simple misdemeanors, the prosecutor will usually refer the case directly to the trial court. In this case, the accused receives a summons by the bailiff requesting his appearance on a specific date and time before the court (*citation directe*; Article 551 F-CCP).[88] The prosecutor can also decide to have the offender brought immediately before the court (*comparution immédiate*; speeded-up trial proceedings; Article 393 et seq. F-CCP). This kind of procedure is mostly used for crimes in which the suspect has been caught red-handed.[89] Charges mainly concern immigration violations, theft, assault, burglary, drug offenses, and fraud. After a brief police investigation, the prosecutor goes through the case record, meets with the suspect, and decides whether or not to apply this rapid proceeding. The condition for the accelerated

[88] Guinchard and Buisson (2011), Margin Nos. 1597–1606.

[89] Stefani et al. (2010), Margin No. 642; Guinchard and Buisson (2011), Margin No. 1532.

criminal procedure of *comparution immédiate* to be used is that the maximum term of imprisonment provided for by law is not less than 6 months in the event of a flagrant misdemeanor or not less than 2 years for offenses where the offender was not caught in the act.[90] This kind of proceedings is not applicable to juveniles. Furthermore, this is excluded in the cases of press offenses, or political offenses, or offenses for which the prosecution procedure is provided for by a special law (Article 397-6 F-CCP). Hearings between the prosecutor and the defendant usually take place after the suspect is arrested, kept in custody, and transferred to the tribunal but before the suspect appears in the court.[91] The prosecutor informs the suspect that he has a right to be assisted by a lawyer. The suspect will generally appear before the court the same day and be judged by three judges in court. At the beginning of the hearing, the judge will ask the accused whether he consents to be judged the same day. If he disagrees, the case will be postponed for a minimum of 2 weeks and a maximum of 6 weeks. The court may send the case file back to the prosecutor if it considers the complexity of the case requires further and more thorough investigation (Article 397-1 F-CCP).[92] Finally, the prosecutor can summon the suspect to appear in court within a period that may run from 10 days to 2 months (*convocation par procès verbal*; Article 393- F-CCP). At the same time, he informs the accused of the facts he is charged with and also of the place, date, and time of the hearing. Furthermore, he informs the defendant that he must appear at the hearing, bringing with him evidence of his income as well as his tax notice or tax exemption documents.[93]

8.4.3.3 Alternative Proceedings

8.4.3.3.1 Penal Order *(Ordonnance Pénale)*

The penal order proceeding is the oldest form of simplified proceeding in French criminal law. It was created by the law of January 3, 1972.[94] This summary proceeding is available for petty offenses (Article 524 et seq. F-CCP)[95] and for a number of misdemeanors explicitly enumerated in the law (Article 495 et seq. F-CCP). Pursuant to Article 495 F-CCP, the prosecutor may choose a proceeding by penal order when the judicial police inquiry has established the matters of which the defendant is accused and has obtained enough information about his income and expenses to allow the penalty to be determined. Furthermore, given the low gravity

---

[90] Guinchard and Buisson (2011), Margin No. 1531.

[91] For a detailed analysis of the structure of this hearing, see Gonzalez Martinez (2006).

[92] Stefani et al. (2010), Margin No. 426; Guinchard and Buisson (2011), Margin Nos. 1547–1548.

[93] Stefani et al. (2010), Margin No. 641; Guinchard and Buisson (2011), Margin No. 1561.

[94] Stefani et al. (2010), Margin No. 831.

[95] For more details about the penal order proceedings for petty offenses, see Guinchard and Buisson (2011), Margin No. 2456.

of the offense it does not seem necessary to impose a prison sentence or a fine exceeding €5,000. Since 1999, fines may be replaced by any complementary measure[96] where the law so provides (Article 495-1 F-CCP; Article 525 F-CCP).[97] Finally, the use of this summary proceeding should not infringe upon the rights of the victim.

The public prosecutor who chooses the penal order proceeding formulates a written recommendation to the judge, using a standard form. Once the judge has signed it, it is communicated to the defendant. In theory, the judge has the possibility to modify the amount of the fine or to acquit the defendant, but in practice the judge systematically accepts the prosecutor's proposal.[98] The decision is issued without hearing the defendant. The defendant has 45 days from the time of notice to lodge an appeal, in which case he is given a public hearing.[99] He is also informed that the court, if it finds him to be guilty of the offense of which he is accused, has the option of imposing a prison sentence where this is applicable to the misdemeanor which was the subject of the order (Article 495-3 F-CCP). When there is no objection, the penal order has the effect of a final decision (Article 495-5 F-CCP, Article 528-1 F-CCP).

From the cases that are brought before the *tribunal correctionel*, 24.3 % were dealt by way of penal order in 2007. In 2009, their proportion increased to 26.8 %. In the same years, before the *tribunal de police*, almost 55 % of the cases ended with a penal order.

8.4.3.3.2 Plea Negotiation (*Plaider-Coupable*)

Since October 2004, the French criminal law gives the prosecutor the possibility to reach an agreement on punishment with the offender (*comparution sur reconnaissance préalable de culpabilité*, or, shorter, *plaider coupable*; Article 495-7 et seq. F-CCP).[100] This procedure is available to defendants charged with a misdemeanor who have admitted their guilt.[101] Its applicability is excluded for

---

[96] Complementary measures are defined in Article 131-10 FCC and include the following: prohibition, forfeiture, incapacity or withdrawal of a right (e.g. suspension of driving licenses), an obligation to seek treatment or a duty to act, the impounding or confiscation of a thing, the compulsory closure of an establishment, the posting a public notice of the decision or the dissemination the decision in the press, or its communication to the public by any means of electronic communication.

[97] Guinchard and Buisson (2011), Margin No. 2456.

[98] Aubusson de Cavarlay (2006), p. 190.

[99] In case of petty offenses, the offender has 30 days to lodge an appeal (Article 527 F-CCP).

[100] A circular of the Ministry of Justice relating to the procedure of *comparution sur reconnaissance préalable de culpabilité* was distributed to the prosecutors and the judges at the time of its implementation (Ministry of Justice 2004).

[101] Until December 2011, its scope of application was restricted to defendants charged with an offense carrying a penalty of a fine or imprisonment of up to 5 years.

certain voluntary and involuntary offenses against the person and against sexual integrity[102] if they are punished with a prison sentence of more than 5 years (Article 495-7 F-CCP). Furthermore, it is excluded in the case of press offenses, political offenses, involuntary homicide offenses. This alternative is not applicable to juveniles (Article 495-16 F-CCP). The prosecutor can propose to the defendant a prison sentence not exceeding either a year or half the prison sentence incurred (Article 495-8 F-CCP). Although not expressly mentioned in the law, this procedure is applicable to cases with clear and simple factual circumstances. Thus, these are cases that would be ready for trial.[103]

The procedure of *plaider coupable* may be initiated by the prosecutor or at the request of the party concerned or his lawyer. The statements in which the person admits his guilt are received and the penalty suggestion is made by the prosecutor in the presence of the lawyer of the party concerned. The person may not waive his right to be assisted by a lawyer. The lawyer has the right to consult the case file immediately. The offender is advised by the prosecutor that he may request to be granted a period of 10 days during which he will decide whether he accepts or refuses the proposed penalty (Article 495-8 F-CCP). It is important to note that the French procedure of guilty plea is not really a plea bargain as known under American law since negotiations are neither conducted on the nature or category of the alleged offense nor on the sentence proposed by the public prosecutor.

In the event that the offender accepts the proposed penalty, his case is brought to court. The judge hears the offender and his lawyer. After checking the truth of the facts and their legal qualification, he may decide to validate the prosecutor's proposal. The judge may decide not to give his approval to the proposed arrangement if in his view the sentence proposed is too low or too high for the alleged offense, or if there is no sufficient evidence to show *prima facie* guilt.[104] The presence of the prosecutor at this public hearing is not mandatory (Article 495-9 F-CCP).[105] The approval given by the court has the effect of a guilty verdict. It may be subject to appeal by the convicted person and the public prosecutor may also lodge an appeal (Article 495-11 F-CCP).

Where the victim of the offense has been identified, he is immediately informed of these proceedings. He is invited to appear before the court at the same time as the offender, accompanied, where appropriate, by his lawyer, in order to constitute himself as a civil party and to request damages for any harm done against him. The civil party may appeal against the order in accordance with the provisions of Articles 498 and 500 F-CCP. If the victim has not been able to exercise his right at the court hearing, the prosecutor has the duty to inform him of his right to summon the offender for a hearing at the correctional court in order to constitute

[102] See Article 222-9 et seq. FCC.

[103] Ministry of Justice (2004), Section 1.2.2.2.

[104] Guinchard and Buisson (2011), Margin No. 1584.

[105] On the non-obligatory character for the prosecutor to assist at the public hearing, see Guinchard and Buisson (2011), Margin No. 1582.

himself as a civil party. The court then rules solely on the civil claim, after consulting the case file, which is attached to the hearing (Article 495-13 F-CCP).

When the person has not accepted the sentence proposed or when the court has not validated the prosecutor's proposal, the official report may not be sent to the court, and neither the parties nor the public prosecutor may make use of any statements made or documents given over the course of the procedure (Article 495-14 F-CCP). The prosecutor will then issue an indictment and summon the accused before the court.[106]

The use of this alternative is steadily increasing. While in 2007, 9.3 % of the cases brought before the *tribunal correctionel* ended with a *plaider coupable*, in 2010 more than 15 % of the cases ended in this way. However, the use of this procedure remains not without criticism. Besides the fact that *plaider-coupable* infringes on almost all fundamental rights guaranteed in the preliminary article of the Code of Criminal Procedure and Article 6 ECHR, it is argued that similar cases are not treated similarly, that there is a risk of wrongful conviction, and that the field of application of this procedure goes beyond the treatment of minor offenses. Thus, a proposal to modify this procedure was submitted to the Senate on March 8, 2011 that provides for restraining its field of application to offenses carrying a penalty of imprisonment of up to 3 years and to exclude its use in case of recidivism. Furthermore, the most notable change proposed would be the elimination of the automatic reduction of the sentence as a reward for self-incrimination. In return, the judge should be allowed to modify the prosecutor's proposal when he estimates the sentence to be too high.[107]

8.5 Prosecutorial Control and Accountability

8.5.1 Control of Public Prosecutors

The French public prosecution service is organized hierarchically with the Minister of Justice standing at the top of the hierarchy. Thus, public prosecutors are responsible to the Minister of Justice, who appoints and may recall them (Article 5, Magistrates Status Act). The 2004 amendment of the F-CCP provided a new Article 30 to the F-CCP[108] and stated that the Minister of Justice, being in charge of carrying out government policies related to the prosecution process, has the responsibility to instruct public prosecutors in these policies. Under the same provision, the Minister may denounce violations of the criminal law of which he has

[106] On the various types of indictment, see Sect. 8.4.3.2.

[107] http://www.senat.fr/dossier-legislatif/ppl10-331.html (accessed June 29, 2012).

[108] Article 30 F-CCP enacts some of the Truche Commission's recommendations. On the Truche Commission, see Sect. 8.5.1, para 7.

knowledge to the prosecutor general and give instructions in writing for the institution of proceedings or for referral to competent bodies.

Article 30 F-CCP does not really provide the Minister of Justice with new rights or powers. Its introduction had the purpose of clarifying current practice and giving legislative support.[109] Under the new system, the Minister of Justice may address general instructions to all prosecutors, while previously such instructions could only be addressed to general prosecutors.[110] The Minister of Justice may issue circulars in order to provide some guidance to the heads of prosecution services. Such circulars have the purpose of clarifying new criminal legislation and providing guidance on its application. They have no binding force because prosecutors should be able to take into account the circumstances of criminality in their own areas.[111]

The Minister of Justice can issue instructions to the prosecutor general on a particular case. Thus, the Minister of Justice cannot give instructions in a specific case to a lower prosecutor. It is the prosecutor general who will then forward the instructions to the competent chief prosecutor. In order to increase the transparency of relations between the prosecution and the Minister of Justice, following the Act of August 24, 1993, such instructions must be in writing and attached to the case file.[112] Instructions on a particular case can relate to the investigation and prosecution of an offense and can also concern the charge and penalty to be requested.[113] In principle, orders not to prosecute or to discontinue a prosecution once opened do not fall within the statutory power of the Minister of Justice. However, the law does not clearly prevent such orders from being issued.[114]

The hierarchical system obliges the lower prosecutors to follow the instructions of their superiors when acting through written submission (Article 5, Magistrates Status Act).[115] Thus, the prosecutor general may, by written instructions attached to the file of the case, direct district prosecutors to initiate prosecutions, or to cause them to be initiated, or to refer to the competent court such written submissions as the prosecutor general considers appropriate (Article 36 F-CCP). The prosecutor general is responsible for the implementation of the criminal policy in his jurisdiction (see Article 35 F-CCP). Another consequence of the hierarchical principle is that prosecutors must inform their superiors of all important cases, in order to ask them for instructions. Without prejudice to any specific reports drafted at the request of the prosecutor general, the chief district prosecutor sends the prosecutor

---

[109] See Warsmann (2003), p. 82.

[110] Marguery (2008), p. 73.

[111] Smedovska and Falletti (2008), p. 199.

[112] Smedovska and Falletti (2008), p. 199.

[113] Marguery (2008), pp. 73–74.

[114] Marguery (2008), p. 74.

[115] The first sentence of Article 33 F-CCP states the following: "The public prosecutor is bound to make written submissions in conformity with the instructions given under the conditions set out in Articles 36, 37 and 44."

general an annual report on the activities and management of his office, as well as on the application of the law (Article 35 F-CCP). In the same way, the Ministry of Justice holds conferences with the public prosecution service on a regular basis. The public prosecution service informs the Ministry of Justice about cases that have attracted the attention of the media.[116]

The supervisory power is limited by Article 40-1 F-CCP, which provides each prosecutor with his own power of prosecution. Thus, in application of this *pouvoir propre*, the prosecutor is the only person within the prosecution service who can initiate the prosecution and no one can force him to do so. This means that, in the event that a prosecutor refuses to prosecute, notwithstanding an order from a superior, no proceedings will take place.[117] However, should the subordinate refuse to act according to an order given by a superior, he may be sanctioned.[118] Furthermore, the supervisory power is restricted by the right to speak freely about the case before the court. The old adage saying *la plume est serve, la parole est libre* (the pen is bound, but the spoken word is free) is restated in Article 33 F-CCP.[119] While the prosecutor is bound to follow written instructions from his superior, when at the hearing, he has the right to express his personal views freely orally.[120]

The accountability of the prosecution service to the Ministry of Justice is seen as a form of democratic accountability, designed to ensure the uniform and impartial application of the law.[121] However, the intervention of the Minister of Justice in the operations of the prosecution service through the use of instructions presents the risk for political interference. There have been strong suspicions that, in ordering no further action in numerous serious cases that otherwise risked causing political embarrassment, prosecutors have been influenced by politicians.[122] Research highlighted the fact that François Mitterrand intervened routinely in matters of justice between 1981 and 1984, including sensitive cases.[123]

The raised suspicions about the relationship between prosecutors and politicians and the independence of the judiciary[124] more widely led to the establishment of the Truche Commission in 1997. This Commission concluded that in a democracy it was the role of the Minister of Justice to determine the judicial policy and thus it was appropriate to maintain a link between the government and the prosecution.

[116] Smedovska and Falletti (2008), p. 199.

[117] Stefani et al. (2010), Margin No. 174; Guinchard and Buisson (2011), Margin No. 1100.

[118] On the sanctions, see Sect. 8.5.2.2.

[119] The second sentence of Article 33 F-CCP states the following: "The public prosecutor is free to make such oral submissions as it believes to be in the interest of justice." Furthermore, Article 5 of the Magistrates Status Act also provides that prosecutors are free to speak at the session.

[120] Stefani et al. (2010), Margin No. 174.

[121] Hodgson (2005), p. 80.

[122] For an overview and summary of the major *affaires*, see Hodgson (2005), pp. 80–81; Elliott (2001), pp. 27–28.

[123] On the influence of François Mitterrand on the prosecution service, see Bancaud (2000).

[124] In France, prosecutors (*magistrats du parquet*) and judges (*magistrat du sièges*) are members of the same professional body. Thus, the independence of the judges was also questioned.

While the development of general guidance on prosecution policy should be strengthened, ordering the initiation of proceedings or giving instructions to prosecutors in specific cases should be abolished.[125] The reform proposed by the Truche Commission aimed to strengthen the independence of the public prosecution service and also to weaken the executive control of the career of the judiciary by recommending that the opinion of the Superior Council of the Magistracy be binding on the Minister of Justice. Not all recommendations of the Truche Commission were legislated. Today, the Minister of Justice remains free to issue orders to public prosecutors, to move, promote, or transfer prosecutors.

According to Dalle and Soulez-Larivière two measures can be taken to remove the objection to hierarchical control: First, prosecutors should not be part of the same professional family as judges and second, prosecutors should not be dependent on the executive branch for their career.[126]

8.5.2 Accountability of Public Prosecutors

8.5.2.1 Civil and Criminal Liability

Prosecutors do not enjoy any criminal immunity and thus they are responsible for any criminal offense that they commit while in office. However, prosecutors have civil and criminal immunity for their statements in court.

Article 11-1 of the Magistrates Status Act provides that prosecutors are subject to civil liability for personal errors committed in their professional capacity. The state may enforce civil liability against individual prosecutors. However, the state is obliged to repair damages caused by the improper functioning of the judicial system. Liability may only be enforced for serious faults or denial of justice.[127] This includes harm committed by individual prosecutors in their professional capacity. The prosecutor's decision not to prosecute does not constitute a denial of justice since he makes this decision pursuant to Article 40 F-CCP.[128]

8.5.2.2 Disciplinary Liability

Pursuant to Article 43 of the Magistrates Status Act, any breach by a magistrate of his professional duties or failure to preserve his honor, good standing, or dignity, is a disciplinary breach. A Compendium of the Judiciary's Ethical Obligations was first published in 2010. The objective of this compendium is to establish ethical

---

[125] Truche (1997), Chap. I, Section I-3.3.

[126] Dalle and Soulez-Larivière (2002), p. 18.

[127] Article L. 141-1 of the Judicial Organization Code; *Code de l'Organisation Judiciaire*.

[128] Stefani et al. (2010), Margin No. 178.

references for the French judiciary. This set of ethical principles is designed to guide the magistrates. It also has the purpose of offering the public a better understanding of the complexity of how the judiciary fulfills its role.[129] This compendium does not constitute a disciplinary code but a guide for prosecutors and judges.[130]

Disciplinary measures may include formal proceedings and sanctions (Article 45, Magistrates Status Act) or informal warnings (Article 44, Magistrates Status Act). The inspector general of the Judicial Services, the president of Courts, the general prosecutors, and the directors in headquarters have the power to issue a warning to any magistrates under their authority. A warning will be deleted automatically from the prosecutor's official file after 3 years provided that no new warnings have been issued or disciplinary sanctions imposed (Article 44, Magistrates Status Act).

Disciplinary sanctions against public prosecutors may be instituted by the Ministry of Justice (Article 48, Magistrates Status Act).[131] However, no disciplinary sanctions may be imposed without first consulting the Superior Council of the Magistracy's prosecutorial panel (Article 59, Magistrates Status Act). The Ministry of Justice approaches the Superior Council of the Magistracy when grounds for the institution of disciplinary proceedings exist (Article 63, Magistrates Status Act).[132] Since 2010, any citizen implicated in a legal proceeding who feels wronged by an action performed by a prosecutor may refer the matter to the Superior Council of the Magistracy. In this case, a commission will first decide on the admission of the complaint. No appeal is possible against a refusal. The Superior Council of the Magistracy's prosecutorial panel will hear the prosecutor and issue an opinion related to the sanction (Articles 64 and 65, Magistrates Status Act). The Ministry of Justice is not bound by the opinion. In the event that the Ministry of Justice intends to impose a stricter sanction than the Council, it must consult the panel for a new opinion (Article 66, Magistrates Status Act). An appeal is possible before the State Council.

Disciplinary sanctions include the following (Article 45, Magistrates Status Act):

- A reprimand recorded in the magistrate's file
- Transfer to a different location
- Withdrawal of functions
- Demotion in rank
- Temporary suspension from office for a maximum of 1 year with total or partial withholding of salary

[129] Supreme Judicial Council (2010), p. X.

[130] Supreme Judicial Council (2010), p. XI.

[131] Judges are disciplined by the Superior Council of the Magistracy (Article 48, Magistrates Status Act).

[132] Until 2010, the Minister of Justice approached the prosecutor general at the Court of Cassation as chairman of the Superior Council of the Magistracy's prosecutorial panel.

- Demotion in position
- Compulsory retirement
- Removal from office with or without a right to a pension.

In the event that the prosecutor is prosecuted for multiple violations, only one of these sanctions may be imposed. However, withdrawal of functions, demotion in rank, temporary suspension from office for a maximum of 1 year with partial or full withholding of salary, and demotion in position may be combined with a transfer to a different location (Article 46, Magistrates Status Act).

Disciplinary proceedings are extremely rare. In 2008, for instance, a total of two disciplinary proceedings were initiated against prosecutors for criminal offense.[133] In the same year, a suspension was pronounced in one case and in another case the prosecutor was transferred to a different location.[134] In 2010, disciplinary proceedings were initiated in two cases.[135] In one case a demotion in position was imposed.[136]

References

Aubusson de Cavarlay B (2006) The prosecution service function within the French criminal justice system. In: Jehle J, Wade M (eds) Coping with overloaded criminal justice systems. The rise of prosecutorial power across Europe. Springer, Berlin, pp 185–205

Bancaud A (2000) Le paradoxe français de la gauche au pouvoir: développement des libertés judiciaires et continuité de la dépendance de la justice. Droit et Société 44/45:61–81

Council of Europe (2010) European judicial systems. Efficiency and quality of justice (data 2008). Council of Europe Pub., Strasbourg

Council of Europe (2012) European judicial systems. Efficiency and quality of justice (data 2010). Council of Europe Pub., Strasbourg

Dalle H, Soulez-Larivière D (2002) Débats, Justice: à la recherche de la bonne coupure. Le Monde, 30 May 2002

Dervieux V (2006) The French system. In: Delmas-Marty M, Spencer JR (eds) European criminal procedures. Cambridge University Press, Cambridge, pp 218–291

Diego O, Dubrocard M (2009) Evaluation of European judicial systems. Replies to the 2010 questionnaire by France. Council of Europe Pub., Strasbourg

Elliott C (2001) French criminal law. Willan Pub, Cullompton

[133] Both proceedings concerned offenses committed outside the professional activity. These misbehaviors have been considered as failures to preserve honor, good standing, and dignity and thus constitute a disciplinary breach (Diego and Dubrocard 2009, Section 5.2.2).

[134] Council of Europe (2010), Tables 11.36 and 11.39. A collection of all disciplinary decisions and disciplinary notices made since 1959 are to be found at http://www.conseil-superieur-magistrature.fr/discipline-des-magistrats (accessed June 29, 2012). According to this collection, disciplinary proceedings were conducted against 63 prosecutors between 1959 and 2010.

[135] Council of Europe (2012), Table 11.54. It must be noted that no data are available concerning breaches of professional ethics and concerning professional inadequacy.

[136] Council of Europe (2012), Table 11.58.

Falletti F (2005) The French prosecution service. In: Tak PJP (ed) Tasks and powers of the prosecution services in the EU Member States, vol 1. Wolf Legal Publishers, Nijmegen, pp 175–201

Goldstein AS, Marcus M (1977) The myth of judicial supervision in three "Inquisitorial" systems: France, Italy, and Germany. Yale Law J 87:240–283

Gonzalez Martinez E (2006) The interweaving of talk and text in a French criminal pretrial hearing. Res Lang Soc Interact 39:229–261

Grebing G (1979) Staatsanwaltschaft und Strafverfolgungspraxis in Frankreich. In: Jescheck H, Leibinger R (eds) Funktion und Tätigkeit der Anklagebehörde im ausländischen Recht. Nomos, Baden-Baden, pp 13–81

Guinchard S, Buisson J (2011) Procédure pénale, 7th edn. LexisNexis, Paris

Hodgson J (2005) French criminal justice. A comparative account of the investigation and prosecution of crime in France. Hart, Oxford

Marguery TP (2008) Unity and diversity of the public prosecution services in Europe. A study of the Czech, Dutch, French and Polish systems. Dissertation, Groningen

Matelly J (2006) Une police judiciaire militaire? La gendarmerie en question. l'Harmattan, Paris

Ministry of Justice (2004) Circular of September 2, 2004 relating to the Procedure of Comparution sur Reconnaissance Préalable de Culpabilité [Circulaire du 2 septembre 2004 relative à la procédure de comparution sur reconnaissance préalable de culpabilité]. http://www.vie-publique.fr/documents-vp/circulaire_plaider_coupable.pdf. Accessed 29 June 2012

Ministry of Justice (2012) Statistical yearbook of the justice system 2011–2012 [Annuaire Statistique de la justice 2011–212]. Ministry of Justice, Paris

Pradel J (1993) France. In: van Wyngaert CD (ed) Criminal procedure systems in the European community. Butterworths, London, pp 105–136

Pradel J (2008) Criminal procedure. In: Bermann GA, Picard E (eds) Introduction to French law. Wolters Kluwer Law & Business, Deventer, pp 127–146

Smedovska R, Falletti F (2008) Report on the prosecution service in France. In: Open Society Institute Sofia (ed) Promoting prosecutorial accountability, independence and effectiveness. Comparative research. Open Society Institute Sofia, Sofia, pp 175–210

Stahl B (2008) Mémento de police judiciaire. Territorial ed., Voiron

Stefani G, Levasseur G, Bouloc B (2010) Procédure pénale, 22nd edn. Dalloz, Paris

Steiner E (2010) French law. A comparative approach. Oxford University Press, New York

Supreme Judicial Council (2010) Compendium of the judiciary's ethical obligations [Recueil des obligations déontologiques des magistrats]. Dalloz, Paris

Truche P (ed) (1997) Report of the commission to consider the justice system [Rapport de la Commission de réflexion sur la justice]. La Documentation française, Paris

Verrest P (2000) The French public prosecution service. Eur J Crime Crim Law Crim Justice 8:210–244

Vlamynck H, Perez É (2010) Droit de la police, 3rd edn. Vuibert, Paris

Warsmann (2003) Report on the bill of law (no. 784) on the adaption of the judicial system to developments in criminality, part I, 2nd part [Rapport sur le projet de loi (no. 784), portant adaptation de la justice aux évolutions de la criminalité, tome I, 2ième partie]. http://www.assemblee-nationale.fr/12/rapports/r0856-t1.asp. Accessed 25 June 2012

Chapter 9
Comparative Overview of Position, Powers, and Accountability of Public Prosecutors

9.1 Structure and Organization of the Public Prosecution Services

It is of high importance that a prosecution service provides neutral, non-political, non-arbitrary decision-making in the application of criminal law and in individual criminal cases. Prosecutorial independence is an essential element that contributes to achieving this goal. On the other hand, a certain amount of control over the prosecutor's activity is desirable to prevent abuse of power. Precedent chapters have shown that a variety of models of prosecution services exist. Their structure is the result of political and historical development.

This section discusses the different structure and organization of the public prosecution institutions surveyed in this research. After examination of the place of the prosecution service within the state, the internal structure of the public prosecution services is presented. In a subsequent section, the appointment methods of public prosecutors are discussed. Furthermore, education and training of prosecutors is outlined. One section sketches the place of the examining magistrate within the prosecution systems. A summary overview concludes this section.

9.1.1 The Place of the Prosecution Service Within the State and Its Independency

The placement of the prosecution service within the branches of the government remains a matter of heated debate in European criminal justice systems. It is not clear whether it is an institution of the executive branch or the judiciary. In the Swiss criminal justice system, neither the Federal Constitution nor the CCrP clarifies the situation. Rather, this falls within the cantonal organizational autonomy. Thus, cantons are completely free to decide on the organizational integration of the prosecution service. With the introduction of the CCrP, the independence of

G. Gilliéron, *Public Prosecutors in the United States and Europe*,
DOI 10.1007/978-3-319-04504-7_9,

the Office of the Attorney has been reinforced. It is no longer part of the Federal Department of Justice and Police or of the federal administration. Since then, the Office of the Attorney General is a self-governing institution and is placed under the supervision of an authority elected by the Parliament. In the vast majority of cantons, prosecutors are subordinated to the government. In a small number, prosecutors are members of the judiciary and supervised either by a judicial council or the court. While the first situation resembles the one found in Germany, the second comes close to the French one. In the German legal system, the public prosecution institution is seen as an adjunct of the executive branch that requires a great deal of independence. Thus, the German doctrine qualifies the prosecution service as a judicial organ of the executive branch. In France, public prosecutors are considered magistrates and thus are members of the judiciary. However, hierarchically they are subordinate to the Minister of Justice. In the United States, prosecutors at the federal and state levels belong to the executive branch. While at the federal level, they are part of the Department of Justice, at the state level, district attorney's offices are completely independent. District attorneys are only responsible to their voters. They occupy a unique position in the world.

Each model has its advantages and disadvantages. Placing the prosecution service under the control of the executive branch has the obvious advantage for the government of effectively controlling the criminal policy and defining law enforcement priorities. A serious drawback is the danger of the prosecution to come under political pressure. When the prosecution service is completely integrated in the judiciary, supervision by the court seems to be the natural solution. Such a system has the advantage of reducing the risk of potential political influence but has the inconvenience that implementation of a coherent criminal policy may be more difficult. Another concern is the loss of impartiality of the court, whereby this risk may be lessened by limiting supervision to administrative matters.

Regardless of the solution chosen, all criminal justice systems agree that public prosecutors should enjoy a high degree of independency in fulfilling their tasks. However, the independence afforded to public prosecutors differs somewhat from that of judges due to their different functions. The prosecutor's duties are the prosecution of crimes, to uphold the laws passed by the parliament, and also to enforce the criminal policy defined by the government.

Independence of public prosecutors implies that they should be independent in applying the law and bound only by the law. Absolute independence of prosecutors can only be achieved when they are not subject to instructions from other state authorities. Thus, in order for the prosecution to be independent from supervisory authority in the conduct of criminal proceedings, a functional supervision would be excluded and only limited to purely administrative supervision. Nevertheless, in the European prosecution systems studied in this research, a professionally completely independent prosecution does not exist.

The Minister of Justice is responsible to the parliament for criminal policy, so that the government, having determined appropriate criminal policy, must be allowed to issue general directives regarding law enforcement priorities to the prosecution. The issue of general guidelines also has the purpose of creating a common practice where the prosecution can exercise discretion. In this context, the difference between criminal justice systems governed by the principle of compulsory prosecution and those based on the principle of opportunity is important.

The principle of compulsory prosecution or legality is in force in Switzerland and Germany. However, in both countries, this principle has been tempered more and more with elements of discretion. According to the principle of legality, the prosecution is obliged to initiate a criminal action if there is good reason to suspect that an offense has been committed. As a consequence, the prosecutor is not allowed to use any discretion in deciding whether or not to prosecute. In this system, the decision not to prosecute does not depend on a prosecutor's personal opinion of whether or not it is opportune to prosecute. The result should be a higher uniformity in prosecution and an intervention from the government should not be necessary.

The French and U.S. criminal justice systems follow the principle of opportunity, where prosecutors are free to choose whether to initiate an action or dismiss a case. The head of the prosecution service or the Minister of Justice will usually issue guidelines in order to provide some guidance. In France, for instance, national criminal policy is promoted through circulars issued by the Minister of Justice that may be of general nature, address specific issues, or provide guidance on the interpretation of new legislation. In the United States, general policies from the U.S. Department of Justice are contained in the U.S. Attorneys' Manual.

The issue of general guidelines is not seen as problematic but, to the contrary, is deemed necessary. On the other hand, the issue of specific directives is very critical. In the Swiss legal system, three cantons provide that the government may induce the prosecution to start proceedings but not to stop them. In the French and German legal system, the Minister of Justice has the power to issue instructions concerning individual proceedings. In the French criminal justice system, in principle, orders not to prosecute or to discontinue a prosecution once opened do not fall within the statutory power of the Minister of Justice. In Germany, the right to issue specific directives has been widely criticized since there is a risk of undue influence of prosecutors in politically sensitive cases. Thus, some German legal scholars argue that the right of the Ministry to issue instruction should be restricted to guidelines. Instead of prohibiting instructions in a particular case, other scholars see a valuable solution to this problem in strengthening the measures protecting the prosecution against improper instructions and directives, which among others include that instructions have to be issued in writing. In the French legal system, such a measure has been introduced following the Act of August 1993, which was in order to increase the transparency of relations between the prosecution and the Minister of Justice.

In those criminal justice systems where the government not only has the right to issue directives but is also responsible for promotion and removal of prosecutors, their independence from other state authorities can be called into question. In fact, there is a risk that prosecutors will not call the potential illegality of directions into question but will follow them. Such concerns are particularly justified in the French criminal justice system where research has highlighted the fact that prosecutors have been influenced by politicians in a number of sensitive cases that otherwise would have caused political embarrassment.

9.1.2 The Internal Structure of Prosecution Services

The prosecution services surveyed vary widely in their internal structure. The public prosecution service in France, having a centralized, hierarchical structure with the Minister of Justice at the top, devolves some autonomy to individual offices and prosecutors. Switzerland, Germany, and the United States are federal states and thus have a system of public prosecution that is extremely decentralized. Prosecution systems are organized on cantonal respectively state and federal levels. On the state level, prosecution services are highly autonomous. In general, however, individual services in these countries are all organized hierarchically.[1] In the German system, the state or federal Minister of Justice stands at the top of the hierarchy. This is also the case in the United States at the federal level, while in Switzerland, the Office of the Attorney General is a self-governed institution.

In the United States, within each state, each district has its own prosecutor's office with its own organization. They are completely independent from one another. In Switzerland, the organization of the public prosecution service falls within the cantonal competence and thus is regulated in cantonal laws. Depending on the size of jurisdiction served, the public prosecutor's office may be organized as a single, indivisible entity or may be structured into various functionally independent public prosecutor's offices with different regional and local jurisdiction.

The organization of prosecution services in Germany and France mirrors that of the courts of law. As a consequence, prosecution offices have the same jurisdiction as their local courts. A prosecutor appointed to a particular office carries out the duties in the same territorial jurisdiction as the court where the office is located.

Public prosecution services, being organized hierarchically, consist of public prosecutors with different ranks, which implies a hierarchical subordination of lower-ranking prosecutors to their superiors. The concept of hierarchy should guarantee certainty and uniformity in the application of law and minimize the exercise of discretion. Uniformity can be reached by issuing general directives. The highest ranking prosecutor may also give case specific instructions. If the lower-ranking prosecutor does not comply with the policy expressed in guidelines or does not follow specific directives by his hierarchical superior, the immediately superior prosecutor can take over the case personally or reassign it to another prosecutor under his supervision.[2] In the Swiss criminal justice system, the powers attributed to the various prosecutors are defined by cantonal law. Depending on the canton, directives discontinuing proceedings and penal orders may be subject to the chief prosecutor's consent.

---

[1] An exception to this is made in some small prosecution services with just a few employees in the Swiss and U.S. system. In fact, in many smaller county prosecution services in the U.S., there is almost no internal structure. In the Swiss system, a few cantons renounced a hierarchically organized system and gave the power of action to a Council of public prosecutors.

[2] For the situation in Germany, see Sect. 7.6.1, paras 2–5; for the situation in France, see Sect. 8.1.1, para 3; Sect. 8.5.1, paras 4–8.

Higher level offices may also have supervisory authority over lower offices and thus have the possibility to intervene in a specific case. This is the case in Germany.[3] In the Swiss legal system, implementing laws regulate the relationship between the senior public prosecutor's office or the attorney general's office and the lower-ranking public prosecutor's offices and define the powers of the higher-ranking prosecutors and in particular their leadership role and oversight function. The question of in how far instructions are permitted to lower-ranking prosecutors is also addressed. Some cantons made use of the possibility of introducing a "four-eyes principle", according to which directives discontinuing proceedings must be approved by a senior prosecutor or an attorney general.[4] In France, the strong hierarchical structure implies that instructions from the higher level are passed to the next lower level. Instructions can thus only arrive from a direct superior. This implies that the Minister of Justice cannot give instructions in a specific case to prosecutors at the district court level since this is within the responsibility of the prosecutor general. This supervisory power is limited by the prosecutor's own power of prosecution, which means that the prosecutor is the only person within the prosecution service who can initiate the prosecution and no one can force him to do so. This means that, in the event that a district prosecutor refuses to prosecute notwithstanding an appellate prosecutor's instructions, no proceedings will take place. Nevertheless, such a behavior can be considered a breach of duty and result in disciplinary measures.

9.1.3 Appointment of Public Prosecutors

The appointment procedure for chief prosecutors differs among the four systems studied. However, they all have in common that chief prosecutors are political appointees of some sort, since they are appointed by the political branches. In Switzerland, the attorney general of the Confederation, as well as his two deputies, are appointed by the Federal Parliament for a 4-year term. Federal attorneys are appointed by the attorney general for a 4-year term. At the cantonal level, a great diversity of variants for the election respectively appointment as chief public prosecutor exists. Chief public prosecutors can either be elected by the government, the parliament, or by another authority such as the cantonal Supreme Court. In the high majority of cantons, the head of service is elected by the parliament. The term of appointment varies between 4 and 6 years, with possible renewal upon expiration of the term. There is a minority of cantons where the head of service is appointed

[3] See Sect. 7.6.1, para 2. The power of the Minister of Justice, however, is limited to a reassignment of the case. In the Swiss criminal justice system, the supervisory authority over the prosecution service has no right to intervene in a particular case. Thus, different levels of offices only exist in cantons that have introduced a senior public prosecutor's office or an attorney general's office.

[4] See Sect. 6.1.2.1, para 7.

by the governing council and not subject to any time limit. In the U.S. system, U.S. attorneys are appointed by the President of the United States with the advice and consent of the senate for a 4-year term. Assistant U.S. attorneys are appointed by the attorney general; although in practice each U.S. attorney has responsibility for hiring new assistant U.S. attorneys. The appointment of district attorneys in the United States is a political process of direct election. The appointment of prosecutors in France and Germany is quite similar. In Germany, the federal prosecutor general and federal prosecutors are appointed by the President of Germany upon proposal of the Minister of Justice and with the consent of the legislative chamber (*Bundesrat*). State prosecutors are appointed by the State Minister of Justice. Public prosecutors are civil servants and thus appointed for life. There are very few states where prosecutors general still have the status of political appointees and thus can be removed from office at will of the Minister of Justice. In France, the general prosecutor at the Supreme Court and the general prosecutors at the court of appeals are appointed by the Council of Ministers upon suggestion of the Minister of Justice and nominated by decree of the President of the Republic. All other public prosecutors are appointed at the suggestion of the Minister of Justice and by decree by the President of Republic. For all nominations, the Minister of Justice will first consult the Superior Council of the Magistracy before submitting his proposal to the Council of Ministers respectively the President of Republic, whereby its opinions are not binding for the Minister of Justice. While, since 2002, heads of prosecution services are appointed for a period of 7 years, other public prosecutors are appointed to permanent terms. After expiration of their mandates, they may be appointed elsewhere or to a higher office. The Minister of Justice is free to move, promote, or transfer prosecutors, or nominate his own political allies.

The direct involvement of the political branches in the career path of the chief prosecutor may be somewhat problematic with regard to the autonomy of the prosecution service, in particular when the internal organization of the service gives the chief prosecutor wide discretion. However, it may be assumed that public prosecutors appointed by the government will be more subject to political pressure than those having been elected by the parliament. Of the four prosecution systems surveyed, the government is always largely involved in the appointment of chief prosecutors. It follows that a completely independent head of prosecution service has not been realized in any system.

9.1.4 Education and Training of Public Prosecutors

In the four systems under review, occupation as public prosecutor usually requires a law degree, being admitted to the bar, and national citizenship. To be elected or appointed as head of service, work experience in the criminal justice system and leadership experience are important factors taken into account. In some cantons, legal education may be replaced by equivalent knowledge gained through specialized training. In the French system, public prosecutors are appointed after having completed a 31-month training program at the National School of Magistrates. In the U.S., district attorneys are elected. Thus, the danger exists that the winner of the election may be more of a politician than a prosecutor.

Ongoing training after appointment is an important aspect of keeping the prosecutor's knowledge up-to-date with changes happening in the criminal justice system. Legal skills can only be maintained through continuing legal education. However, in the Swiss and German criminal systems, public prosecutors, once appointed, have no further mandatory training requirements. Since in both countries continuing legal education courses are proposed by various institutions, public prosecutors have the possibility to attend them on a voluntary basis. However, when important legal changes occur, public prosecutor services generally offer internal training. In the French system, since January 1, 2008 each magistrate must receive 5 days of mandatory in-service training per year. In addition, the National School of Magistrates offers optional ongoing training. In the U.S., continuing legal education is mandatory in 46 states. Continuing legal education for federal prosecutors is proposed at the National Advocacy Center. The courses given at this institute address the special needs of prosecutors.

In line with Recommendation Rec (2000) 19 of the Council of Europe, training should be a duty and a right for prosecutors not only before but also after their appointment. All criminal justice systems must be aware of the fact that continuing legal education of prosecutors can contribute to enhancing the quality of the prosecutor's work.

9.1.5 The Place of the Examining Magistrate Within the Prosecution System

In the nineteenth century, the novelist Honoré de Balzac described the examining magistrate as the "most powerful man in France" in light of his large investigative power. However, the role of the examining magistrate has since seriously decreased in all prosecution systems, having been influenced by the French system, while at the same time, the power of the prosecutor has drastically increased. The German version of the examining magistrate was abolished by the end of 1974. The Swiss prosecution system, having adopted the inquiry model of the "public prosecutor model II", has definitely eliminated the examining magistrate, which was still recognized in some cantons prior to the introduction of the CCrP. Even in the French legal system, the future of this judicial institution was called into question. A judicial reform in 2009 provided for an abolition of the examining magistrate so that all criminal investigations would have been conferred to the public prosecutor. Such a judicial reform has caused concern among French magistrates, who were worried about the political influence that the criminal justice system could be subject to. Due to controversy, the proposal was postponed and, in 2011, the French Government abandoned this idea. However, in the French prosecution system, the role of the examining magistrate has been decreasing since the nineteenth century.

Table 9.1 Structure and organization of public prosecution services in the United States, Switzerland, Germany, and France

	United States	Switzerland	Germany	France
Structure	Federal	Federal	Federal	Unitary
Prosecutors and judges form one group	No	No/yes	No	Yes
Governing principles	Opportunity	Legality and opportunity	Legality and opportunity	Opportunity
Examining magistrate	No	No	No	Yes

Today, only investigations involving serious crimes are referred to the examining magistrate so that a high percentage of cases are disposed of by the public prosecutor without any intervention by the examining magistrate. Furthermore, there is a continuing decrease in the number of examining magistrates, which may also lead to a slow death of this institution.

9.1.6 *Summary Overview*

Table 9.1 summarizes the structure and organization of public prosecution services in the United States, Switzerland, Germany, and France.

9.2 Prosecutorial Discretion

One of the fundamental distinctions among legal systems is the differentiation between criminal justice systems adhering to the principle of legality and those following the principle of opportunity. While Switzerland and Germany employ the principle of legality,[5] France and the United States adhere to the principle of opportunity. Under the latter, the prosecutor's decision not to prosecute cannot be criticized or sanctioned by the court. However, the reality today is that most systems are mixed. The Swiss and German criminal justice systems have progressively introduced elements of opportunity since they have recognized that a strict adherence to the principle of legality may be problematic. In particular, the overloaded criminal justice system has led to a restriction of this principle. Indeed, the prosecution of every alleged crime is practically impossible.

In Switzerland, a moderate principle of opportunity has been implemented on a nationwide basis with the introduction of the CCrP (Article 8 CCrP). Under such a principle, the prosecutor may refrain from prosecution only under certain conditions

[5] In Switzerland, prior to the introduction of the CCrP it was the cantonal procedural laws that determined whether they employed the principle of legality, opportunity, or moderate principle of opportunity. See Sect. 6.3.2.

defined by law. This has the consequence of putting tight limits on the prosecutor's discretionary power, since the prosecutor must drop the case when the requirements are fulfilled and is not allowed to exercise any discretion in deciding whether or not to prosecute. In addition, the aggrieved person has a right to file a complaint against a prosecutor's decision to dismiss a case based on Article 8 CCrP, thus allowing a certain control over the prosecutor's work. In Germany, the principle of compulsory prosecution only remains in effect with respect to most felonies, while the D-CCP provides various grounds for non-prosecution for less serious offenses. The provisions most frequently used are those authorizing dismissal without consequences (Section 153 D-CCP) and conditional dismissals (Section 153a D-CCP).

On the other hand, criminal justice systems adhering to the principle of opportunity make every effort to provide neutral and non-arbitrary decisions. Hence, in reality, both types of criminal justice systems provide similar results. In fact, in a system employing the opportunity principle, it would be difficult to ignore clear evidence of a serious crime or to prosecute in the absence of any conclusive evidence. As one can easily understand, one major concern in criminal justice systems based on opportunity is the risk of disparity. Such a risk can only be diminished by promulgating guidelines. In the United States, a number of guidelines may help the prosecutor decide whether or not to prosecute. Potential guidelines may be found in statements promulgated by prosecutorial offices themselves. Model Standards, such as the NDAA Prosecution Standards and the different ABA Standards, as well as ethical rules may also provide some guiding principles. However, model standards are mostly criticized for the reason that they are based on the "probable cause" standard or "sufficient admissible evidence to support a conviction" and that they therefore offer little guidance. Prosecutor's offices are free to implement a higher standard and to allow a filing of criminal charges in cases where there is a reasonable probability of conviction and that are trial worthy. In opportunity-based systems, prosecutors typically may refrain from prosecution even when evidence of guilt is strong. Reasons for not prosecuting are commonly known as public interest factors, including, e.g., the gravity of the offense and the availability of resources. Guidelines in prosecutor's offices may contribute to guarantee certainty and uniformity in the application of law. In France, the application of the discretionary principle has been systematized in order to allow transparency. In order to identify the methods used in various situations, statistical forms are filled out by the head of the prosecution service.

Prosecutors in both kinds of systems appear to be more similar than at first sight. Prosecutors in inquisitorial and adversarial criminal justice systems have a duty to neutrality and to find out the truth, whereby these obligations are more extensive and explicit in civil law systems than in common law systems. Prosecutors in both systems are principally focused on securing conviction.[6] What makes the real difference between prosecutors in the United States and the prosecutors in other criminal justice systems is the political nature of the office. In the United States, the

[6] See also Waters (2008), p. 55.

position of prosecutor is often viewed as a stepping stone to a higher political office, while in the other prosecution systems surveyed in this research, prosecutors are in the profession for the sake of being prosecutors. Those who become prosecutors will usually remain in this position until the end of their career. The nature of the office is one reason explaining why prosecutors in the United States may more easily be tempted in engaging in prosecutorial misconduct.

Instead of maintaining a pure distinction between legal systems following the principle of legality and those adhering to the principle of opportunity, the focus should be more on how to guarantee transparency of decision-making. In addition to guidelines, transparency may be achieved by requiring prosecutors to give written explanations for their decisions. In addition, regular reporting to political actors as well as court review may prevent abuse of prosecutorial discretion. In Switzerland, every prosecution office has to submit an annual report about its activity to its supervisory authority. In Germany, state prosecutors general regularly give an oral report to the respective state Minister of Justice while in-depth review of the work of each prosecution office occurs every 3 years.[7] In France, in the event that the prosecutor refuses to initiate criminal proceedings, the victim has the possibility to initiate the prosecution and directly summon the suspect before a criminal court or before an investigating judge. Conferring a right to appeal prosecutorial decisions may also ensure that prosecutors do not abuse their discretion.[8] Certainty of disciplinary sanctions if a prosecutor misbehaves may also increase the ethical conduct of prosecutors.

9.3 Alternative Proceedings

In order to cope with growing caseloads, all criminal justice systems display a clear tendency towards providing alternative proceedings. A common trend is the leading role of public prosecutors in such proceedings. Over time, prosecutors have gradually slipped into the role of decision-makers. Today, prosecutors in some instances may act as the sole adjudicator of the criminal case. Another trend is the noticeable emergence of elements of plea bargaining in civil law systems.

9.3.1 Simplified Proceedings

All three European criminal justice systems analyzed in this study recognize penal order proceedings. It is a simplified procedure in writing that allows acquisition of a conviction without trial. Penal orders are usually issued without hearing the

[7] Gramckow (2008), p. 220.

[8] On the control over public prosecutors by victims, see Sect. 9.5.

defendant. This procedure is used when the judicial police inquiry has clearly established the matters of which the defendant is accused of or when the defendant has acknowledged his guilt. These summary proceedings are usually reserved for petty offenses or misdemeanors. In the Swiss legal system, however, felonies may also be handled in this way since there is no restriction concerning the gravity of offenses. The scope of application is instead limited by the length of prison sentence that can be imposed, which is 6 months. While in the German and French criminal procedures, the court is involved in the final stage to impose a sanction, in the Swiss legal system, the prosecutor has sole responsibility to impose a sanction. Because the courts in Germany and France only rarely refuse to follow the prosecutor's advice, the prosecutor's decision really adjudicates the case. The Swiss penal order for its part illustrates the de jure power of the prosecutor to adjudicate criminal cases. Of the three European criminal justice systems surveyed, Switzerland has the highest number of cases settled in this way, with more than 90 % overall. On the contrary, prosecutors in Germany will dismiss cases more often than Swiss prosecutors.

The German legal system provides for accelerated proceedings, which is a simplified procedure available for minor offenses where the factual situation or the evidence are simple and therefore suited to immediate hearing. This procedure is limited to prison sentences of up to 1 year. In contrast to ordinary proceedings, the intermediary proceeding where the court decides whether to proceed to main hearing does not take place. Prosecutors have the possibility to bring charges orally at the beginning of the main hearing. Furthermore, evidence is gathered in a simplified way. The prosecutor who wishes to conduct the case by accelerated proceedings has to submit an application to the court. This proceeding is rarely used.

9.3.2 Plea Agreements

In response to greater efficiency within criminal justice systems, elements of bargaining have emerged in the last few decades. However, no system is completely identical to the U.S. plea bargaining system. Instead, each legal system has adapted the practice to suit their own needs and values.[9] Such proceedings are only available to defendants who have admitted their guilt, so that a confession is an integral part of any negotiated agreement.

Depending on the criminal justice system, judges are not involved to the same extent in the informal negotiation between the prosecutor and the defendant. In Germany, plea bargaining usually involves not only the defendant and the prosecution but also the judge. Such judicial supervision offers the advantage of greater certainty about plea bargaining outcomes. The greater implication of the judge can be explained by the fact that the judge in Germany has very broad discretion in the area of sentencing so that the prosecutor is not able to certify that the court will

[9] See Turner (2009) discussing plea bargaining in various criminal justice systems including Germany. See also Langer (2004).

accept a particular sentence bargaining.[10] In the Swiss legal system, informal negotiations only occur between the defendant and the prosecution. The agreement is then subject to the approval of the court. Negotiations in Switzerland and in Germany may concern the charges, the sentence, or both. In Switzerland, unlike the United States, fact bargaining is prohibited, while in Germany this seems to occur rarely, if at all.[11] While in Germany plea bargaining is not limited to particular offenses, in Switzerland this practice is limited to cases where the prosecution does not request a prison sentence of more than 5 years. In Switzerland, an admission of guilt is commonly rewarded with one-fifth to one-third reduction of the foreseen penalty.[12] In the abridged proceedings, a further reduction is possible when additional reasons to mitigate respectively reduce a sentence exist, such as sincere repentance and confession of other crimes. In Germany, a confession is commonly rewarded with a one-fourth to one-third reduction in the expected sentence. In the U.S. federal courts, a guilty plea may lead to a reduction of two-thirds of the sentence expected. The Swiss and German models of plea bargaining reject the idea of defendants pleading guilty while at the same time contesting their innocence, while in the United States "Alford pleas" are accepted. The participation of the victim in this kind of procedure differs among jurisdictions. In Switzerland, the negotiated agreement is sent to the aggrieved party respectively the private claimant who has 10 days to accept or reject it. In case of rejection, the prosecution is obliged to conduct ordinary proceedings. In Germany, the victim as joint plaintiff can be consulted by the court before an agreement is reached. However, the victim's refusal of the agreement is not binding.[13] In the United States, victims have the possibility to object to a plea agreement at the plea presentation hearing. However, as in Germany, the victim's opinion is not binding upon the court. In Switzerland, a party may only appeal against a judgment in abridged proceedings on the basis that it did not accept the indictment or that the judgment does not correspond to the indictment. Since, in an abridged proceeding, the court has not conducted an evidentiary hearing, a petition of revision based on new evidence cannot be filed. In Germany, the parties to proceedings still have the possibility to lodge an appeal respectively a petition of revision in case of negotiated agreements. A waiver of the right to file an appeal is excluded. On the contrary, in the U.S.-American system, most state and federal courts have concluded that a defendant may explicitly waive the right to appeal as part of the agreement.

In France, the *composition pénale* (transaction) has been considered a homologue of U.S. plea bargaining system because it gives room for negotiations between the prosecution and the defense.[14] Before the beginning of formal proceedings, the prosecutor may offer the defendant the option of diverting his case from the standard criminal trial in exchange for an admission of guilt and the

---

[10] Langer (2004), p. 106.

[11] Turner (2006), p. 229.

[12] BGE 121 IV 202, pp. 205–206.

[13] Meyer-Gossner (2011), Section 257c, Margin No. 24.

[14] Langer (2004), p. 59.

fulfillment of a condition. If the defendant accepts the offer, the prosecutor submits the files to the court for approval. There are major differences between the U.S. plea bargaining system and the *composition pénale*. The application of a plea bargain significantly shortens the trial; in France however, the *composition*, if it's successful, will waive criminal proceedings and the accused will not be convicted. Thus, the *composition* is not a simplified trial but is conceived as a disposal arrangement. In France, when the prosecutor decides to prosecute, he may use the procedure of *plaider coupable*. In this procedure, the prosecutor has the possibility to reach an agreement on punishment with the offender. This procedure is available to defendants charged with a misdemeanor who have admitted their guilt. The French procedure of guilty plea is really an accelerated procedure. It differs greatly from the plea bargaining system as known under U.S. law since negotiations are neither conducted on the nature or category of the alleged offense nor on the sentence proposed by the public prosecutor.

Simplified proceedings inspired by the U.S. plea bargaining system face some concerns. In particular, critics argue that a number of basic principles of the criminal procedure are affected by such proceedings, such as the principle of legality[15] and the principle of instruction. Pursuant to those principles, the prosecutor has the duty to search for the truth and to bring a charge whenever there are sufficient grounds to suspect a person of having committed an offense. On the contrary, in plea bargains, all facts of the case must not be entirely clarified nor must all charges be brought, since the facts are based on a deal between the defendant and the prosecution. As a consequence, the factual truth is replaced by a formal truth. The right to a public trial, the principle of orality, the presumption of innocence, and the right against self-incrimination are also undermined. As long as the accused waives his rights in a clear and unequivocal manner, this alternative procedure does not breach the ECHR.[16]

Proceedings in European criminal justice systems containing elements of bargaining face many of the same concerns as American plea bargaining. It is argued that similar cases are not treated similarly and that there is a risk of wrongful convictions. Furthermore, such proceedings may disadvantage socially weaker defendants since they are not defended with the same diligence.

9.4 Overview Over Out of Court Settlement Procedures

Table 9.2 provides an overview of the various ways of out of court settlements of criminal cases in the prosecution systems surveyed. The proceedings discussed under Sect. 9.2, para 1 et seq. and Sect. 9.3, para 1 et seq. are taken into account.

[15] This criticism does not apply to criminal justice systems adhering to the principle of opportunity, such as France.

[16] ECHR, February 27, 1980, Deweer–Belgium (Series A, No. 35), para. 48–56.

Table 9.2 Overview of out of court settlement procedures (United States, Switzerland, Germany, and France)

Country	Out of court settlements			
Switzerland	**Article 8 CCrP**: **Dismissal** by the prosecutor (no need for a penalty, reparation, effect on the offender of his act)	**Penal order proceedings** *Requirements*: Accused person has accepted responsibility for the factual circumstances of the case or circumstances have been otherwise sufficiently resolved; sentence to be imposed does not exceed 6 months imprisonment; decision issued by public prosecutor	**Abridged proceedings** *Requirements*: Accused person may submit application for abridged proceedings if (1) he accepts liability for circumstances essential to the legal evaluation of the case and (2) he accepts at least in principle the civil claims; prosecution requests imposition of prison sentence not exceeding 5 years *Consequences*: No evidentiary proceedings at the principal hearing; Examination of the court limited to ascertaining that the rights conferred to the parties have been respected and that the confession of the accused is credible; penalty is reduced	
Germany	**Section 153, 153a**: **Conditional or unconditional dismissal** by the prosecutor. Conditions that can be imposed: community service, compensation,	**Penal order proceedings** Given the outcome of the investigation, prosecutor considers main hearing unnecessary; prosecutor	**Accelerated proceedings** *Requirements*: Factual situation or evidence are simple and thus are suited to immediate hearing;	**Agreements**: Informal negotiations between parties; discussions are allowed at every stage of the proceeding;

(continued)

Table 9.2 (continued)

Country	Out of court settlements			
	mediation, transaction fine	makes written application to the judge; decision issued without trial; maximum penalty: fine or suspended prison sentence of up to 1 year if defendant is represented by a lawyer	proceeding limited to prison sentence of up to 1 year *Consequences*: Main hearing takes place immediately; intermediary proceeding is left out; prosecutor has possibility to bring charges orally at beginning of main hearing; evidence is gathered in simplified manner	confession of accused is required *Requirements*: Sentence must remain within what is considered proportional punishment; content of negotiated agreement has to be made public during trial *Consequences*: Penalty is reduced
France	**Transaction** *Requirements*: Confession of the accused; possible for offenses for which the main penalty is a fine or a prison sentence not exceeding 5 years; public prosecutor proposes a transaction; a total of 17 measures are available; proposal must be approved by the court *Consequences* Criminal proceeding is waived	**Penal order proceedings** *Requirements*: Procedure available for petty offenses and a number of misdemeanors; police inquiry must have established the facts; prosecutor makes written application to the judge; decision issued without trial; maximum penalty: fine not exceeding €5,000	**Plea negotiation** *Requirements*: Procedure applicable in cases with clear and simple factual circumstances; available to defendants charged with misdemeanors who have admitted their guilt; excluded for certain voluntary and involuntary offenses against the person and against sexual integrity if they are punished with a prison sentence of more than 5 years; approval by the court is necessary	**Comparution immédiate** Mostly used in crimes where suspect has been caught red-handed *Requirements* Maximum term of imprisonment provided for by law is not less than 6 months in the event of a flagrant misdemeanor or not less than 2 years for offenses where the offender was not caught in the act

(continued)

Table 9.2 (continued)

Country	Out of court settlements		
			Consequences: Prosecutor can propose prison sentence either not exceeding a year or half the prison sentence incurred
United States	**Guilty plea** *Requirements*: Defendant agrees to plead guilty without a trial; in exchange prosecutor can i.e. dismiss charges or make sentence recommendation; negotiated plea is subject to court approval *Consequences* Penalty is reduced	**Restorative justice programs** such as Victim-Offender mediation[a]	

[a]Not discussed in this research

9.5 Potential Control Over Public Prosecutors by Victims

The importance victims can play in the control of public prosecutors is not to be underestimated. Depending on the position and rights conferred to the victim in the criminal procedure, he may contribute to reducing the risk of prosecutorial abuse.

The Swiss and U.S. criminal justice systems give the public prosecution service an exclusive monopoly over charging and prosecution of criminal offenses. On the other hand, Germany and France retain a residual right of private prosecution. In Germany, with respect to a small number of less serious offenses, the victim can file charges directly with the court if the prosecutor has decided not to prosecute because prosecution would not be in the public interest. In France too, the victim may initiate the prosecution if the prosecution has decided not to go forward. However, this tool is limited to individuals who have suffered harm. Private prosecution is, however, rarely employed. In the French system, this tool has proved to be efficient in cases with political dimensions where prosecutors have been reluctant to initiate proceedings.

In the Swiss legal system, victims may file a complaint against directives and procedural activities of the police, the prosecution, and the authorities responsible for prosecuting minor regulatory activities. Regarding the activities of the prosecution, this includes refusals to open an investigation, orders that proceedings will not be opened, suspensions of investigations or their rejections, directives discontinuing proceedings, and finally re-opening of proceedings that were terminated by way of a final and legally binding directive discontinuing the proceedings. Victims have no possibility to lodge a complaint against the decision to open an investigation and to bring charges.

In France, any plaintiff can lodge an appeal with the prosecutor general against a prosecutor's decision to dismiss a case without taking further action. In the event that the prosecutor general feels that the appeal is well founded, he may instruct the prosecutor to initiate a prosecution. In Germany, if a case has been dropped for lack of sufficient evidence, the victim may try to force public prosecution with special proceedings. Pursuant to this procedure, the victim is entitled to lodge a complaint to the general prosecutor who can decide to re-open the case or confirm the prosecutor's decision. If the prosecutor's decision to drop the case is confirmed, the victim has the right to make an appeal to the Higher Regional Court. Other dismissals cannot be appealed but a complaint can be filed with a superior prosecutor.

In the United States, victims have no legal remedies to compel the prosecutor to institute proceedings. Prosecutors have the unreviewed power to decline cases. Prosecutors' decisions are ordinarily immune from judicial review or any other external entity.

9.6 Accountability of Public Prosecutors

9.6.1 Civil and Criminal Liability

Basically, prosecutors are just as subject to civil and criminal liability as any other citizen. In all prosecution systems studied in this research, if public prosecutors commit crimes that have no connection to their official duties, they are treated as any citizen would be. In addition, in the United States, prosecutors do not enjoy any immunity from criminal liability for acts committed in the course of their work as prosecutor. In contrast, European prosecution systems may provide a range of immunities when it comes to alleged criminal offenses committed by prosecutors while in office. In the Swiss system, an authorization of the responsible commission of the confederation's councils is required to prosecute the attorney general and the deputy attorney generals, while for all other federal attorneys, the authorization to prosecute is granted by the attorney general. Cantons may also provide for an authorization to bring criminal proceedings against prosecutors. In this case, it is usually the responsibility of the parliament to decide whether to grant the authorization or not. In France, prosecutors have civil and criminal immunity for their statements in court.

Some criminal offenses described in the penal codes can only be committed by civil servants. According to the Swiss and German systems of compulsory prosecution, a prosecutor may be held liable for dismissing a case that would have called for prosecution and trial. Prosecutors may also be subject to criminal prosecution whenever they fail to investigate impartially and thus also when they withhold evidence that might be favorable to the defendant.

Prosecutors are subject to civil liability for damages resulting from their willful acts or gross negligence. In the European criminal justice systems analyzed, the administration where the concerned civil servant works is the responsible entity vis-à-vis the aggrieved party. Thus, the administration compensates the victim's damages without regard for culpability of the prosecutor and afterwards the administration may enforce civil liability against the individual prosecutor. In the United States, the doctrine of prosecutorial immunity is a serious obstacle to any attempt to enforce civil law claims against a prosecutor. When initiating and pursuing criminal prosecution, prosecutors enjoy absolute immunity from civil liability.

9.6.2 Disciplinary Liability

Public prosecutors may be subject to disciplinary proceedings in all four prosecution systems surveyed. Disciplinary proceedings may include informal warnings issued by superiors and formal proceedings and sanctions. Disciplinary sanctions vary from reprimand to dismissal. Disciplinary infractions of minor importance are usually sanctioned by a superior through a written warning, while more serious prosecutorial misbehaviors are subject to formal disciplinary proceedings. In the Swiss legal system, disciplinary proceedings may be opened on the initiative of the supervisory authority or, following a disciplinary complaint, by citizens. The supervisory authority of the prosecution service is in charge of conducting the proceedings and imposing the sanction. Administrative courts are competent to review administrative decisions on discipline. In Germany, disciplinary proceedings are initiated by the prosecutors' superiors. Formal disciplinary proceedings take place before a disciplinary tribunal that belongs to the administrative jurisdiction. Decisions of state disciplinary courts can be appealed before the Federal Disciplinary Court that is attached to the Federal Supreme Court. In the French legal system, disciplinary proceedings may be instituted by the Ministry of Justice, whereby no disciplinary sanctions may be imposed unless the Superior Council of the Magistracy's prosecutorial panel has issued a non-binding opinion. Since 2010, any citizen implicated in a legal proceedings wronged by an action performed by a prosecutor may refer the matter to the Superior Council of the Magistracy. Administrative sanctions may be appealed before the State Council. In the United States, federal prosecutors have to comply with a multitude of ethical regulations, so that their conduct may be examined by the court or a state bar association or the Office of Professional Responsibility. U.S. attorneys are not subject to discipline without the President's approval. At the state level, elected district attorneys can only be removed from office during their term through a state disciplinary procedure for violating the rules established by the state's attorney licensing authority. Citizens, judges, and other lawyers may submit a written complaint about a prosecutor's conduct violating these rules to the state bar association. The grievance committees may also institute an investigation and take disciplinary action on their own based upon knowledge gained in other ways.

In practice, formal disciplinary proceedings are only rarely used and disciplinary sanctions are applied even less often. In the United States, various studies have revealed that disciplinary procedures have failed to hold prosecutors accountable for misconduct. In the European prosecution systems under review, it is not possible to determine whether disciplinary proceedings are efficient or miss the objective, on the sole basis of the statistical data.

References

Gramckow H (2008) Prosecutor organization and operations in the United States. In: Open Society Institute Sofia (ed) Promoting prosecutorial accountability, independence and effectiveness. Comparative research. Open Society Institute Sofia, Sofia, pp 386–429

Langer M (2004) From legal transplants to legal translations: the globalization of plea bargaining and the Americanization thesis in criminal procedure. Harv Int Law J 45:1–64

Meyer-Gossner L (2011) Strafprozessordnung. Gerichtsverfassungsgesetz, Nebengesetze und ergänzende Bestimmungen (Beck'scher Kurzkommentar StPO), 54th edn. C.H. Beck, München

Turner JI (2006) Judicial participation in plea negotiations: a comparative view. Am J Comp Law 54:199–268

Turner JI (2009) Plea bargaining across borders. Criminal procedure. Aspen Publishers, New York

Waters T (2008) Overview: design and reform of public prosecution services. In: Open Society Institute Sofia (ed) Promoting prosecutorial accountability, independence and effectiveness. Comparative research. Open Society Institute Sofia, Sofia, pp 19–79

Chapter 10
Thematic Problems and the Prospects for Reform

10.1 Public Prosecutors in the United States

This research has highlighted several problems in connection with the position and powers of public prosecutors in the United States. These are the highly political position of state prosecutors, the risk of coercion in the plea bargaining process, and the lack of control over the prosecutors' decisions. Drawing upon the experiences of other nations, the following section proposes solutions to these problems.

10.1.1 The Political Position of District Prosecutors

The benefit of having elected prosecutors is to make them more knowledgeable of and responsible to the people. Various concerns, however, call the effectiveness of electoral accountability into question, among others the fact that voters really have access to very little information concerning the prosecutors' daily work and exercise of discretion. Thus, voters may be unable to effectively check their prosecutors. Having elected prosecutors also brings certain disadvantages. The elective process is costly and time-consuming. Furthermore, the person elected may have little or no criminal justice or management experience. The winner of the election may be more of a politician than a prosecutor. Many prosecutors aspire to be elected to a higher political office. In this context, conviction rates are indicators of success. As a consequence, the prosecutor's emphasis may lie on the achievement of a high conviction rate rather than a high rate of justice. In such circumstances, it is undeniable that the political character of the prosecution service may contribute to enhancing the risk of prosecutorial abuse.

There may be different ways to eliminate or temper the negative aspects of the highly political position of public prosecutors in the United States. A solution proposed by Michael Tonry would consist of the elimination of elected prosecutors and the professionalization of prosecutors as career civil servants, specially trained

G. Gilliéron, *Public Prosecutors in the United States and Europe*,

DOI 10.1007/978-3-319-04504-7_10,

and appointed based on merit.[1] In fact, "career officials are more likely than politically selected officials to decide individual cases on the merits of their distinctive circumstances and to consider policy proposals from long-term perspective of whether they will improve the quality of justice or the effectiveness of administration. Commitment to abstract principles of justice is part of the professionalism and professional self-esteem of career officials, and buffers individual decisions and policy choices from raw emotions and officials' self interest."[2] A further advantage is that career civil servants are largely insulated from political pressure.[3] Promotion would be based on merit rather than public opinion polls.[4] Professionalizing the prosecution and removing them from direct partisan political pressures would, however, not signify that public attitudes and beliefs would not influence prosecutors in their work. Prosecutors are part of the communities in which the live and work and thus it is difficult for them to remain abstract from changes occurring in community norms and values.[5] It is important to note that a shift from elected prosecutors to a legal system in which prosecutors are career civil servants will not eliminate bad decisions and adoption of bad policies, but it will certainly help. Such a reform, however, would change the legal culture and would have the benefit of making people clearly aware of the advantages of prosecutorial decision-making that is insulated as much as possible from political influence and public emotion.[6]

Instead of restructuring the relevant status and experiences of the profession, reform efforts could be made in legal education. Such a solution is extensively discussed by Erik Luna and Marianne Wade.[7] In addition to strengthening clinical legal education, students should also study the criminal justice systems of other nations. Clinical legal education provides the opportunity to learn both the theory and practice of law in context.[8] It also offers the possibility to explore and discuss the ethical rules and special obligations of prosecutors. The benefit of such education is that students will more fully understand the expectations and responsibilities of prosecutors.[9] In fact, by exploring the prosecutor's position and duties, students should be able to fully understand how the exercise of prosecutorial discretion is key to the proper functioning of the criminal justice system.[10] Students should recognize that the prosecutor's obligation is not to seek convictions at all costs. In

[1] Tonry (2004), pp. 206–210.

[2] Tonry (2004), p. 207.

[3] Tonry (2004), pp. 207, 209.

[4] Tonry (2004), p. 209.

[5] Tonry (2004), p. 209.

[6] Tonry (2004), p. 208.

[7] Luna and Wade (2010), pp. 1514–1526.

[8] For more details about clinical legal education and its importance, see e.g. Reno (2005), Caplow (2005), Montoya (2005), and Smith (2005).

[9] Luna and Wade (2010), pp. 1514–1519.

[10] Joy (2005), p. 980.

fact, when winning becomes the primary goal, investigations demonstrate that prosecutors sometimes sacrifice justice to win. This can lead to abuse of prosecutorial power, such as hiding evidence.[11] It is expected that clinical programs can help law students become fair and ethical prosecutors.

Although clinical legal education is a permanent feature in legal education, clinical teaching and clinical education has traditionally remained at the periphery of law curriculum. In 2007, the Carnegie Foundation for the Advancement of Teaching published "Educating Lawyers". Drawing upon extensive field work at 16 law schools, the report is a carefully researched critique of U.S. legal education. One concern expressed in the report is the fact that moral dimensions of legal conflicts and the ethical questions they raise are often left out.[12] Thus, the Carnegie Report's called on legal educators to increase legal education and to pay more attention to the socio-ethical role of law.[13] Many legal educators have acknowledged the Carnegie Report's importance, and some have begun to propose and develop educational programs that implement the Report's recommendations, so that the transformation in American legal education may already be underway.[14]

The incorporation of transnational law into legal education presents some benefits for the profession and American society as a whole.[15] Comparative law perspectives are a valuable way to open the students' minds to the possibility of adopting different approaches to fundamental legal problems. As a matter of fact, the differences between prosecution systems throughout the world shrink gradually, so that the adoption of some approaches into one criminal justice system are easier to fulfill. Furthermore, if practitioners in the United States were familiar with the prosecution functions in other countries, they may have a clearer perspective of their own criminal justice system and the reasons to modify or uphold the current practices.[16] Unfortunately, comparative law remains at the periphery of law school curriculum.[17]

The growing similarity between European and U.S. systems of criminal procedure makes it more likely that Americans can learn something from other nations

---

[11] On the reasons for misconduct, see Sect. 5.4.3.

[12] "Law schools fail to complement the focus on skill in legal analysis with effective support for developing ethical and social skills. Students need opportunities to learn about, reflect on and practice the responsibilities of legal professionals. Despite progress in making legal ethics a part of the curriculum, law schools rarely pay attention to the social and cultural contexts of legal institutions and the varied forms of legal practice" (Sullivan et al. 2007, p. 187).

[13] Sullivan et al. (2007), p. 197.

[14] For an overview, see Coughlin et al. (2011), pp. 283–284.

[15] Luna and Wade (2010), pp. 1519–1526. See also Frase (1998).

[16] Luna and Wade (2010), pp. 1523–1524.

[17] Luna and Wade (2010), p. 1529.

and that some foreign approaches may even be transplanted to the United States.[18] During his career, former Anoka County Attorney Robert Johnson[19] had the opportunity to attend a lot of conferences and to learn about other prosecution systems. He recognizes that the question of how the prosecutor functions could be improved in the states is complex. However, if he were asked to reform the prosecution system in Minnesota, he would propose a centralized system since this would have the advantage of having a continuity of policy throughout the state. Prosecutors should no longer be elected but appointed by an appointing authority constituted of representatives from the court, governor's office, and such other interests as appropriate. It should not be the prerogative of a specific officer as that, in his view, would make the appointment political. The term of appointment should be for at least 5 years with a new appointment process at the end of the term and possible reappointment.[20] Since each state has its own peculiarities, the solution proposed by Robert Johnson in Minnesota is not necessarily applicable to other states. Other states can propose other solutions that better address their needs. The organization of the prosecution services in the 26 cantons in Switzerland offers a wide range of possible solutions. A profound reform in the prosecution system was possible in Switzerland, so why not in the United States?

10.1.2 Coerciveness of Plea Bargaining

One major problem of plea bargaining is that innocent persons might plead guilty. This question has preoccupied many scholars and today, the controversy over the "innocent problem" takes a leading role in the plea bargaining debate.[21] In fact, the prosecutor's enormous power in the plea bargaining process creates a potential risk for abuses and the limited oversight of his decisions by the judge is not sufficient to reduce this risk.

Coercion is a major problem in the plea bargaining process. Prosecutors may force people to waive their rights to jury trial by threatening them with ever greater sanctions if they refuse to plead and instead ask for a jury trial. Since other criminal justice systems, such as Switzerland and Germany, have adopted similar procedures, it can be envisaged to take certain practices from these jurisdictions and to try them in the United States. Coercion may be reduced in different ways. The

[18] "[I]ncreasing similarity means that potential "donor" and "recipient" systems have become more compatible, thus lessening the risk of "rejection" of legal transplants. The fact that foreign systems have already borrowed many practices from the United States, and from each other, shows that such international legal transplants are indeed feasible, even across systems that remain fundamentally different in important respects." (Frase 1998, p. 780).

[19] Robert Johnson was first elected in 1982 and re-elected in 1986, 1990, 1994, 1998, 2002, 2006. In 2010 he retired and thus didn't run for election anymore.

[20] Informal discussion with former Anoka County Attorney Robert M. Johnson on October 4, 2010 and email exchange on November 9, 2010.

[21] See e.g. Gazal-Ayal (2006).

sentencing discount for confessing to a crime is lower in inquisitorial criminal justice systems than in the United States. While in the U.S. federal courts, a guilty plea may lead to a reduction of two-thirds of the sentence expected, in Germany, a confession is commonly rewarded with a one-fourth to one-third reduction in the expected sentence. In Switzerland, an admission of guilt is usually rewarded with one-fifth to one-third reduction in the foreseen penalty. In the European criminal justice systems surveyed, the prosecution is required to fully disclose its evidence to the defendant. In this way, the defendant is aware of the strengths and weaknesses of his case. If the accused decides to confess to a criminal offense, he will act in full knowledge of the prosecutor's file. In addition, this has the advantage that defense lawyers can better evaluate the fairness and accuracy of a proposed plea bargain. Another way to reduce the coerciveness of plea bargaining is to limit the practice to less serious crimes. In the Swiss criminal justice system, for instance, a case can only be conducted by way of abridged proceedings if the prosecution requests the imposition of a prison sentence not exceeding 5 years.[22]

10.1.3 Lack of Control Over Prosecutors

American prosecutors enjoy broad discretion in deciding whether to prosecute, what charges to bring, and what plea bargains to offer. Unfortunately, there are no effective mechanisms able to effectively check prosecutors' decisions. Under the separation of powers doctrine, courts have systematically refused to review charging decisions. Victims thus have no legal remedy against a prosecutor's decision not to prosecute. Disciplinary procedures have also failed to hold prosecutors accountable for misconduct.

As mentioned under Sect. 9.5, para 1 et seq., in prosecution systems where the public prosecution service has broad discretion, the victim's position may be of paramount importance for the control over prosecutors. Giving victims more power in the U.S. criminal justice system would therefore contribute to increasing the control over prosecutors and lessen the risk of prosecutorial abuse. A potential problem with such a solution would lie in the fact that, in criminal justice systems adhering to the principle of opportunity, the judge is not allowed to criticize the prosecutor's decision not to prosecute. However, as discussed under Sect. 9.2, para 5, maintaining a distinction between legal systems following the principle of legality and those employing the principle of opportunity is outdated and the focus should be more on how to guarantee transparency of prosecutorial decision-making. Following this reasoning, appropriate legislation could be passed that would empower judges to review charging decisions.[23]

[22] See also Turner (2009), pp. 274–275.

[23] See also Luna and Wade (2010), p. 1512.

Further measures could be taken by the legislature to adjust the balance of authority in criminal justice. It is, for instance, conceivable that legislators ask that prosecution services issue a comprehensive set of guidelines enforceable by the judiciary.[24]

10.2 Public Prosecutors in Switzerland

Over the years, high case volumes have compromised the principle of legality. As a result, the Swiss legal system now also recognizes a principle of opportunity, which allows the prosecutor to refuse to file charges, even when they are supported by adequate evidence. However, the principle of opportunity has not entirely displaced the principle of legality. Although the principle of legality is no longer strictly applied in the Swiss legal system, it still remains an aspiration with a real impact on prosecutorial culture.[25] An alternative proceeding with elements of plea bargaining has also emerged. In addition, prosecutors can issue penal orders and impose a prison sentence up to 6 months. Nevertheless, although public prosecutors have clearly become more powerful, the context and consequences of prosecutorial adjudication in Switzerland are still different and less serious than in the United States.

The following section outlines the problems related to the increase of prosecutorial power and the lessons the Swiss legal system can draw from the U.S. experiences.

10.2.1 Problems Related to the Increase of Prosecutorial Power

The power of Swiss prosecutors to adjudicate cases is broad. A very high percentage of defendants are convicted by penal order, a decision issued by the prosecutor alone, where the imposition of prison sentences up to 6 months is possible. Hence, in such cases, the prosecutor is the sole "judge". It is true that the defendant can make opposition to the decision and ask for a full trial, however, there are no mechanisms that would guarantee that the recipient of the decision understands the real extent of it. The introduction of the abridged proceedings has further expanded the power of the prosecutor. Although formally the defendant's culpability occurs in court, in practice it is the public prosecutor who imposes the sanction. For the moment, this alternative is practically negligible but, based on the first experiences in the canton of Zurich, this procedure will certainly be applied more often over

[24] Luna and Wade (2010), p. 1512.

[25] See Tonry (2004), p. 276.

time. In the abridged proceedings the imposition of prison sentences up to 5 years is possible. Hence, this alternative procedure is no longer limited to petty offenses but may extend into criminal acts of some gravity. Previously, the adjudication of serious criminal acts was exclusively reserved for the judge.

Alternative and summary proceedings have the advantage of increasing the efficiency of criminal justice systems. A serious drawback of this is the danger of the judicial system becoming marginalized. In addition, prosecutorial adjudication threatens several fundamental principles of the state, such as the separation of powers doctrine and the principle that a party cannot be a judge in his own case.[26] Maintaining a separation between the authority investigating and adjudicating the case is important. The prosecutor, when making a decision, does not have the same perspective as the court. Indeed, the prosecutor does not sit as neutral fact finder but focuses on the incriminating circumstances. Despite the obligation to objectivity requiring the prosecutor to investigate exculpatory and incriminatory circumstances with equal care, the prosecutor is not a judge. In the abridged procedure, the submission of the prosecutor to the court remains an indictment, even if it is converted into a judgment. In the penal order proceedings, the prosecutor is in reality an inquisitor seeking the correct outcome.

It is clear that Swiss prosecutors have accumulated a great deal of power. Now they combine the executive and judicial powers. Setting a high value on the economy of procedure, however, occurred to the detriment of procedural guarantees. The penal order procedure best illustrates this situation. Since a penal order is issued by the prosecutor and usually without previous hearing of the defendant, this should be compensated by the possibility of the defendant to lodge an appeal. The time limit of 10 days and the written form requirement, however, may hinder the defendant in exercising his rights.

A serious concern is the risk of wrongful convictions, which may increase as a consequence of simplification of proceedings at all costs. While this issue is highly discussed in the United States, this point is only rarely addressed in the three assessed European criminal justice systems, despite the fact that wrongful convictions also occur in these systems. A Swiss study on wrongful convictions supports the higher susceptibility to error of the Swiss penal order proceedings.[27] The study concluded that the higher risk of wrongful convictions is related to the procedure as such. Basically, four causes could be identified: careless investigation, issue of the decision by the prosecutor alone, form and time limit to make opposition, and the defendant's behavior. The latter refers to the reasons why defendants miss the deadline to make opposition or renounce to exercise this right and includes

---

[26] See Recommendation Rec (2000) 19 of the Council of Europe stating the following at 17: "States should take appropriate measures to ensure that the legal status, the competencies and the procedural role of public prosecutors are established by law in a way that there can be no legitimate doubt about the independence and impartiality of the court judges. In particular states should guarantee that a person cannot at the same time perform duties as a public prosecutor and as a court judge."

[27] For a complete discussion of this problem, see Gilliéron (2010), pp. 101–146.

functional illiteracy of the defendant so that he is unable to understand the instructions on legal remedies, indifference of the defendant, ignorance of the law, and fear of unfavorable outcome, such as costs of the procedure.

Since the abridged proceedings show great similarity with the U.S. plea bargaining process, this procedure may also increase the risk of wrongful convictions. In order to avoid uncertainties of trial outcomes, the accused might admit his guilt. The abridged proceedings are a recent procedure, so that only the future can tell us if this apprehension proves to be well founded.

There may also be concerns about equal treatment where public prosecutors are entrusted with discretion. To remedy this problem, public prosecutor's offices should implement comprehensive prosecution guidelines. It can be assumed that all larger offices provide for such guidelines. Those in the canton of Zurich are publicly available. On the other hand, other cantons, such as Basel-City, do not give access to these guidelines. In order to provide for uniformity in the penal order proceedings, public prosecutor's offices have sentencing guidelines that are not publicly available.

10.2.2 Lessons Learned from the U.S. Experience

Prosecutors in the United States exercise unfettered discretion in deciding who to charge with a crime, what charges to file, when to drop charges, and whether or not to plea bargain. To limit the risk of abuse, it is absolutely necessary to have some control mechanisms over these officials who enjoy so much power in the criminal justice system. As highlighted in this research all control mechanisms in the United States proved to be inefficient.

When introducing new alternative proceedings, the Swiss legislature should maintain sufficient control mechanisms. Especially the position of the victim is not to be underestimated. Furthermore, proceedings that increase the risk of coerciveness should be avoided. The potential risk of wrongful convictions must be carefully assessed. Although some restrictions on criminal defendant's rights are unavoidable in simplified procedures, such limitations should remain appropriate and not go beyond what is necessary. Mechanisms must ensure that the accused person waives the procedural guarantees of the ECHR in full knowledge of the legal and factual situation of the case.

With respect to the abridged proceedings, it must be ensured that the courts still play their role and refuse to confirm agreements where some doubts of culpability of the defendant remain or where there would be some signs indicating a coerced confession, such as an unusual plea discount.

Broad prosecutorial discretion creates the potential danger of submitting similarly situated individuals to disparate treatment. Therefore, it is important to regulate the exercise of prosecutorial discretion. In the United States, prosecutors' offices have usually implemented guidelines in order to promote consistency and impartiality. These guidelines are generally not public but for internal use only.

Such guidelines have no legal force and thus cannot be enforced by courts. If prosecutors do not comply with such guidelines, victims and accused have no legal remedy. Therefore, internal control is very important. If prosecutors repeatedly fail to follow the guidelines, sanctions should be imposed by the superior, namely the chief public prosecutor.

In the Swiss criminal justice system, prosecutor's offices have also implemented prosecution guidelines but these are not normally available to the public and, as in the United States, have no legal force. Especially with regard to Article 8 CCrP respectively Article 52 et seq. SCC, the transparency of prosecutorial decision-making suffers. This is increased by the fact that annual reports of the prosecutor's offices do not separate statistical data informing about the number of proceedings discontinued based on Article 8 CCrP from those discontinued because of insufficient evidence. As a consequence, it is impossible for the population to evaluate the extent to which prosecutors apply the principle of opportunity. As in the United States, since guidelines cannot be enforced, internal control over prosecutors becomes even more important where prosecutors can exercise discretion. Cantons that provide for a "four-eyes principle", or where such decisions require the approval of the chief prosecutor, are able to guarantee a certain level of control over such decisions. In addition, victims can lodge a complaint, which has the consequence that a court may review the decision.

Not all of the prosecutor's decisions are subject to review. Prosecutors have, for instance, complete discretion to decide whether to accept an application of the defendant to conduct the case by way of abridged proceeding or not. The defendant has no legal remedy if the petition is declined. Furthermore, the prosecutor is not legally obliged to give any reasons for his decision. This can be explained by the fact that the defendant has no legal right to having the case conducted by way of abridged proceedings. However, legal equality and prohibition of arbitrary decisions calls for a brief reasoning. This would also increase the transparency of prosecutorial decision-making.

Actually, the Swiss criminal system ensures a better control over prosecutors than the U.S. system does. There is, for instance, still the possibility to lodge a complaint against a prosecutor's directives, which will lead to a review of the decision by the court. It is essential that continuing case-load pressure not lead to the elimination of control mechanisms that exist today in the Swiss criminal system. What is more critical, however, is the lack of control mechanisms over the implicit agreements of defendants to waive procedural guarantees in penal order proceedings.

To conclude, when proposing reforms to current legislation, legislators should always ask themselves what the aim of the criminal justice system is: If the aim of the criminal justice system is bureaucratic efficiency, alternative proceedings certainly make sense, but if the aim of the justice system is the protection of individual rights, alternative proceedings are certainly harder to justify.

References

Caplow S (2005) "Taking too Close to the Wind": the challenge to prosecution clinics to set our students on a straight course. Miss Law J 74(4):919–953
Coughlin CN, McElroy LT, Gordon DS (2011) The Carnegie Report and legal writing: does the report go far enough? J Leg Writ Inst 17:279–324
Frase RS (1998) Main-streaming comparative criminal justice: how to incorporate comparative and international concepts and materials into basic criminal law and procedure courses. West VA Law Rev 100:773–798
Gazal-Ayal O (2006) Partial ban on plea bargains. Cardozo Law Rev 27:2295–2351
Gilliéron G (2010) Strafbefehlsverfahren und plea bargaining als Quelle von Fehlurteilen. Schulthess, Zurich
Joy PA (2005) Prosecution clinics: dealing with professional role. Miss Law J 74(4):955–981
Luna E, Wade M (2010) Prosecutors as judges. Wash Lee Law Rev 67:1413–1532
Montoya J (2005) The University of San Diego criminal clinic: it's all in the mix. Miss Law J 74 (4):1021–1042
Reno J (2005) The importance of prosecution training in Law School. Miss Law J 74(4):xi–xiv
Smith LF (2005) Benefits of an integrated (prosecution & defense) criminal law clinic. Miss Law J 74(4):1239–1280
Sullivan WM, Colby A, Welch Wegner J, Bond L, Shulman LS (2007) Educating lawyers. Preparation for the profession of law. Jossey-Bass/Wiley, San Francisco
Tonry MH (2004) Thinking about crime. Sense and sensibility in American penal culture. Oxford University Press, New York
Turner JI (2009) Plea bargaining across borders. Criminal procedure. Aspen Publishers, New York

Chapter 11
Conclusion

The structures and organizations of the public prosecution services surveyed in this research differ from each other. They reflect the political and historical development within their respective criminal justice systems. Therefore, each model must be evaluated in context. Each model has advantages and disadvantages. Thus, no prosecution model can claim to be superior to all others.

Prosecutors are the most powerful officials in criminal justice systems. While in the U.S. system prosecutorial discretion has a long tradition, the power of Swiss prosecutors has steadily increased. The same tendency can be noticed everywhere in Europe and is thus not unique to Switzerland. In the criminal justice systems surveyed, prosecutors effectively determine the outcomes of criminal cases. Only a very small percentage of cases are resolved by trial. Depending on the procedure applied, prosecutors enjoy a de jure adjudication, which is the case with the Swiss penal order. In this procedure, prosecutors have the power to impose a prison sentence of up to 6 months without approval of the court. It is up to the defendant to raise objection and ask for a full trial. This, however, occurs only rarely. Generally, the exercise of prosecutorial discretion results in a de facto prosecutorial adjudication. In most alternatives, the prosecutor submits a settlement proposal to the court. Because courts only rarely refuse to reject the prosecutor's proposal, it is the prosecutor who really adjudicates the case. The U.S. plea bargaining system and the German as well as French penal order fall under this category. With respect to the Swiss abridged proceedings, only the future will tell us to what extent the deal between the prosecutor and the defendant will be accepted respectively rejected and the reasons for rejection.

Over time, prosecutors have gradually slipped into the role of decision-makers and conversely the role of judges has been marginalized. This situation seriously threatens the separation of powers doctrine. When determining the defendant's responsibility, the point of view of the prosecutor is obviously different from that of the court. Despite the obligation to objectivity in the Swiss criminal procedure, the prosecutor remains a prosecutor and cannot take the perspective of a judge. In all criminal justice systems, the prosecutor does not sit as a neutral fact finder but focuses on the incriminating circumstances. This in turn may increase the risk of

G. Gilliéron, *Public Prosecutors in the United States and Europe*,

DOI 10.1007/978-3-319-04504-7_11,

wrongful convictions. In view of the fact that defendant's rights are restricted in alternative and summary proceedings, the concern over the risk of wrongful convictions is justified.

The accumulation of too much power in the hands of prosecutors is also problematic. This problem becomes even more pronounced when effective control mechanisms are not available or fail their aim. Although, to a different extent, the U.S. and Swiss criminal justice systems must address this problem. The lack of control over prosecutors in the Swiss criminal justice system is especially found in alternative procedures, while in the U.S. criminal justice system the failure of control mechanisms is a general problem. Although it is acknowledged that public prosecutors must enjoy a high degree of independence in fulfilling their tasks, a certain amount of control over the prosecutor's activity is indispensable in order to prevent abuse of power.

It is clear that prosecutorial adjudication raises serious concerns not only in the United States but also in Switzerland and more generally in Europe. This research has nevertheless shown that, although public prosecutors have gained power, the context and consequences of prosecutorial adjudication in Switzerland respectively Europe are still different and less serious than in the United States. This is in part attributable to the different cultures surrounding Swiss respectively European prosecutors and American prosecutors. European prosecutors make use of alternative and simplified procedures with the aim of relieving caseload pressure while achieving just outcomes. Furthermore, in European criminal justice systems, prosecutors cannot threaten the defendant with drastic sanctions in case he may exercise his right to trial. On the other hand, prosecutors in the United States see plea bargaining as a tool that can be used to secure convictions and at the same time increase conviction rates. Defendants can expect to be threatened with harsher sentences when refusing a plea bargain.

This research has highlighted the fact that the differences between European and U.S. systems of criminal procedure have progressively shrunk. Elements of bargaining emerged in civil law systems. In addition, the traditional distinction between criminal justice systems adhering to the principle of legality and those employing the principle of opportunity is outdated. None of the criminal justice systems studied provides for a strict adherence to the principle of legality anymore, while criminal justice systems following the principle of opportunity make every effort to provide neutral and non-arbitrary decisions. What really matters today is the way transparency of decision-making can best be guaranteed.

The growing similarity between European and U.S. systems of criminal procedure makes it more likely that Americans can learn something from other nations and that some foreign approaches may even be transplanted into the United States. The opposite scenario also holds true. Chapter 10 of this research has demonstrated that such an approach is possible and desirable. The feasibility of such an approach is also supported by the fact that American scholars recognize that possible solutions to the problem of wrongful convictions in the United States may come from other criminal justice systems. This has resulted in an increase in workshops and conferences where international practice on wrongful convictions has been discussed.[1]

Caseload pressure and the call for greater efficiency in criminal justice systems do not predict a decrease of the prosecutor's power. However, prosecutors have actually gained so much power that it is hard to imagine how this power could be further increased. Legal reform is a delicate subject that always threatens to destabilize the equilibrium between legislative, executive, and judicial institutions. Legislators must be aware that every increase in the power of the prosecutor also means a detriment of the defendant's rights. It is up to the government of every criminal justice system to decide where it wants to set its priority: bureaucratic efficiency or the protection of the defendant's rights.

[1] 2011 Innocence Network Conference: An International Exploration of Wrongful Conviction, Cincinnati, Ohio, April 7–10, 2011; International Perspectives on Wrongful Convictions Workshop, U.S. Department of Justice—National Institute of Justice, Washington DC, September 13–14, 2010.

Appendix I: Classification of Criminal Actions

United States

The United States divides crimes into two categories: felonies and misdemeanors.

Felonies (major crime) are considered the most serious types of crimes. The federal system classifies as felonies all offenses punishable by a term of imprisonment of more than 1 year (18 USC Section 3559). About half of the states follow this definition. Defendants convicted of felonies serve their sentences in a state or federal prison rather than a local, city, or county jail. Crimes considered as felonies include: murder, rape, aggravated assault, kidnapping, burglary, grand theft, robbery, and illegal drug use/sales. Beside the sentence, a person convicted of felony will usually face additional consequences, such as the loss of voting rights, exclusion from certain lines of work and difficulty in finding a job in others, exclusion from purchase and possession of firearms, and ineligibility to run for, or be elected to, public office. These losses of privileges are known as collateral consequences of criminal charges.

Misdemeanors (minor crime) are considered less serious in nature than felonies. Misdemeanors are punishable by fines or a jail sentence not exceeding a year (18 USC Section 3559). Depending on the jurisdiction, a fine generally will not exceed $500–1,000. If a jail sentence is imposed, it is typically served in a local jail. Persons convicted of misdemeanors are often punished with probation, community service, short jail term, or part-time imprisonment. Crimes considered as misdemeanors include: petty theft, prostitution, public intoxication, simple assault, disorderly conduct, trespass, vandalism, drug possession, and reckless driving. Misdemeanor convictions usually do not result in the loss of civil rights, but can result in loss of privileges, such as professional licenses, public offices, or public employment.

Administrative Infractions: Administrative infractions are also known as regulatory offenses, petty offenses, minor offenses, minor violation, citations, or ordinance violations. An infraction is a violation of the law less serious than a misdemeanor. The federal system classifies as infraction all offenses punishable by imprisonment of no more than 5 days (18 USC Section 3559). Typically, an infraction is a violation

G. Gilliéron, *Public Prosecutors in the United States and Europe*,
DOI 10.1007/978-3-319-04504-7, © Springer International Publishing Switzerland 2014

of a local ordinance, regulation, or traffic rule. Infractions are, for example, jaywalking, littering, disturbing the peace, or running a red light. Local ordinances are typically prosecuted by the city attorney. For many years, ordinance violations were considered as "quasi-criminal". Today, depending on the jurisdiction, some ordinance violations are procedurally treated in the same way as misdemeanors. However, some states view an ordinance violation punishable only by a fine as non-criminal.

State of Minnesota

The state of Minnesota has the following four types of offenses (Minn.Stat.Ann. § 609.02):

Felony: Felony means a crime for which a sentence of imprisonment for more than 1 year is imposed.
Misdemeanor: Misdemeanor means a crime for which a sentence of not more than 90 days or a fine of not more than $1,000, or both, may be imposed.
Gross misdemeanor: Gross misdemeanor means any crime which is not a felony or misdemeanor. The maximum fine which may be imposed for a gross misdemeanor is $3,000.
Petty misdemeanor: Petty misdemeanor means a petty offense which is prohibited by statute, which does not constitute a crime and for which a sentence of a fine of not more than $300 may be imposed.

Switzerland

The Swiss Criminal Code classifies criminal actions as *Verbrechen* (felony), *Vergehen* (misdemeanor), and *Übertretung* (petty offense).

Verbrechen are actions with a threat of imprisonment of more than 3 years (Article 10 para. 2 SCC, Article 40 SCC). The legal maximum punishment for *Vergehen* is imprisonment of up to 3 years or a fine (Article 10 para. 3, Article 34, Article 40 SCC), *Übertretungen* are subject to a fine (Article 106 SCC).

Appendix II: Comparison of U.S. and Swiss Crime Victims Rights

	United States		
Right to	Crime Victims' Rights Act of 2004	Minnesota Statutes 2010; chapter 611 A	Switzerland[a]
Be treated with fairness and respect	x	x[b]	x
Be informed of rights	x	x	x
Notification of proceedings	x	x	x
Notice of sentence, escape, or release	x	x	x[c]
Be informed of prosecutor's decision to decline prosecution or dismiss case		X (domestic violence, sexual assault, and harassment victims)	x
Protest against decision to dismiss			x
Attend proceedings	x[d]	x	x
Be heard at proceedings	x	x	x
Confer with prosecutor	x	x	x
View file during invest. Stage			x
Speedy disposition	x	x	
Be protected from the accused	x	x	x
Assisted by a lawyer during hearing as a witness			x
Be formally represented during trial alongside Prosecution Service			x
Be notified of appeals filed by the defendant		x	x
Appeal against verdict			x

(continued)

G. Gilliéron, *Public Prosecutors in the United States and Europe*,
DOI 10.1007/978-3-319-04504-7,

Right to	United States		Switzerland[a]
	Crime Victims' Rights Act of 2004	Minnesota Statutes 2010; chapter 611 A	
Restitution/compensation via criminal procedure	x	x	x
Apply for financial assistance		x	x

[a]Rights of the victim as civil claimant are included

[b]The Crime Victim Justice Unit strieves to achieve just, fair, and equitable treatment of crime victims and witnesses

[c]In most cantons there is no obligation to inform the victim about the release of the convicted

[d]The right to not be excluded from any such public court proceeding, unless the court, after receiving clear and convincing evidence, determines that testimony by the victim would be materially altered if the victim heard other testimony at that proceeding (18 USC Section 3771. Crime victims' rights)

Appendix III: Victims' Rights in the Plea Bargaining and Pretrial Diversion

Right to	Crime Victims' Rights Act of 2004	Minnesota Statutes 2010; chapter 611 A
Be notified of any plea agreement		x
Object orally or in writing to a plea agreement at the plea presentation hearing	x	x
Object orally or in writing to a proposed disposition or sentence		x
Provide input in a pretrial diversion decision		x

G. Gilliéron, *Public Prosecutors in the United States and Europe*,
DOI 10.1007/978-3-319-04504-7, © Springer International Publishing Switzerland 2014

Appendix IV: Appointment Methods of Chief Public Prosecutors in the United States

State	Title	Elected	Appointed	Term (years)
Alabama	District Attorney	X		6
Alaska	Attorney General		X	[a]
Arizona	County Attorney	X		4
Arkansas	Prosecuting Attorney	X		4
California	District Attorney	X		4
Colorado	District Attorney	X		4
Connecticut	State's Attorney		X	8[b]
Delaware	Attorney General	X		4/2[c]
District of Columbia	U.S. Attorney		X	4
Florida		X		4
Georgia	State's Attorney	X		4
Hawaii	District Attorney	X		4
Idaho	Prosecuting Attorney	X		4
Illinois	Prosecuting Attorney	X		4
Indiana	State's Attorney	X		4
Iowa	Prosecuting Attorney	X		4
Kansas	County Attorney (District Attorney in five counties)	X		4
Kentucky	County Attorney	X		6
Louisiana	Commonwealth's Attorney	X		6
	District Attorney	X		4
Maine	District Attorney	X		4
Maryland	State's Attorney	X		4
Massachusetts	District Attorney	X		4
Michigan	Prosecuting Attorney	X		4
Minnesota	County Attorney	X		4
Mississippi	District Attorney	X		4
Missouri	Prosecuting Attorney[d] (Circuit Attorney in city of St. Louis)	X		4

(continued)

DOI 10.1007/978-3-319-04504-7,

State	Title	Elected	Appointed	Term (years)
Montana	County Attorney	X		4
Nebraska	County Attorney	X		4
Nevada	District Attorney	X		4
New Hampshire	County Attorney	X		2
New Jersey	County Prosecutor		X	5
New Mexico	District Attorney	X		4
New York	District Attorney	X		4
North Carolina	District Attorney	X		4
North Dakota	State's Attorney	X		4
Ohio	Prosecuting Attorney	X		4
Oklahoma	District Attorney	X		4
Oregon	District Attorney	X		4
Pennsylvania	District Attorney	X		4
Rhode Island	Attorney General	X		4
South Carolina	Solicitors	X		4
South Dakota	State's Attorney	X		4
Tennessee	District Attorneys General	X		8
Texas	District Attorney, Criminal District Attorney, and County and District Attorney	X		4
Utah	County Attorney (District Attorney in Salt Lake County)	X		4
Vermont	State's Attorney	X		4
Virginia	Commonwealth's Attorney	X		4
Washington	Prosecuting Attorney	X		4
West Virginia	Prosecuting Attorney	X		4
Wisconsin	District Attorney	X		2
Wyoming	District Attorney	X		4
Wyoming	Country and Prosecuting Attorney	X		4

[a]The attorney general serves at the pleasure of the governor

[b]The chief state's attorney is appointed for a 5-year term; the deputy chief state's attorneys are appointed for 4-year terms, and the 13 state's attorneys are appointed for 8-years terms

[c]The attorney general is elected to a 4-year term in the "off-year" state election, 2 years before/after the election of the governor

[d]Prosecuting attorney system will be converted to a district attorney system in 2014

Appendix V: Cases Dealt with by the County Attorney's Office of Anoka, Hennepin and Ramsey

Anoka County Attorney's Office

G. Gilliéron, *Public Prosecutors in the United States and Europe*,
DOI 10.1007/978-3-319-04504-7, © Springer International Publishing Switzerland 2014

Case-Ending Decision of the Anoka County Attorney's Office (2003–2009)

	2003		2004		2005		2006		2007		2008		2009	
	Absolute number	%	Absolute number	%	Absolute number	%	Absolute number	%	Absolute number	%	Absolute number	%	Absolute number	%
Adult referrals	1,919	100	1,892	100	2,325	100	2,168	100	2,111	100	1,806	100	1,435	100
Cases charged	1,538	80	1,611	85	1,961	84.5	1,832	84.5	1,662	79	1,414	78	1,054	73.5
Cases denied	381	20	281	15	364	15.5	336	15.5	449	21	392	22	381	26.5

Source: Data from the Criminal division annual reports of the Anoka County Attorney's Office (2003–2009)

Number of Cases Brought Before Court and Guilty Pleas in Anoka County (2003–2009)

	2003		2004		2005		2006		2007		2008		2009	
	Absolute number	%	Absolute number	%	Absolute number	%	Absolute number	%	Absolute number	%	Absolute number	%	Absolute number	%
Adult criminal trials	20	1.7	21	1.6	22	1.5	33	2.1	32	2	31	2.3	10	1.1
Guilty pleas	1,165	98.3	1,257	98.4	1,445	98.5	1,545	97.9	1,571	98	1,301	97.7	924	98.9

Source: Data from the Criminal division annual reports of the Anoka County Attorney's Office (2003–2009)

Complaints Denied Respectively Issued Depending on the Crime Type in Anoka County (2003–2009)

	2007		2008		2009	
	Absolute numbers	%	Absolute numbers	%	Absolute numbers	%
Complaints issued						
Offenses against the person	245	77.3	244	81	189	72
Offenses against property	575	84.2	475	80.5	334	80
Drug offenses	500	85.5	367	86	234	75.5
Sexual offenses	66	36	54	36.5	41	32.5
Complaints denied						
Offenses against the person	72	22.7	58	19	73	28
Offenses against property	108	15.8	115	19.5	84	20
Drug offenses	85	14.5	61	14	76	24.5
Sexual offenses	117	64	93	63.5	85	67.5

Source: Data from the Criminal division annual reports of the Anoka County Attorney's Office (2007–2009)

Hennepin County Attorney's Office

Case-Ending Decisions of the Hennepin County Attorney's Office (2003–2009)

	2003		2004		2005		2006		2007		2008		2009	
	Absolute number	%	Absolute number	%	Absolute number	%	Absolute number	%	Absolute number	%	Absolute number	%	Absolute number	%
Adult referrals[a]	8,193	100	8,370	100	8,752	100	9,140	100	8,597	100	8,293	100	7,868	100
Cases charged	5,906	72	5,868	70	6,072	69.5	6,424	70.3	5,926	69	5,697	68.7	5,293	67.3
Cases declined	2,238	27.3	2,444	29	2,591	29.5	2,663	29	2,637	30.7	2,564	31	2,476	31.5
Pending/other decision[b]	49	0.6	58	1	89	1	53	0.6	34	0.4	32	0.4	99	1.2

Source: Internal statistics of the Hennepin County Attorney's Office

[a]Includes Adult Prosecution cases (Violent Crimes and Gang), Community Prosecution cases (Drug and Property), and Complex Crime cases (white collar crimes including mortgage fraud, identity theft, embezzlement and financial exploitation of vulnerable adults)

[b]Includes cases: awaiting a charging decision, resubmitted by investigating agency, grand jury no bill, diverted to other county, or referred to conflicts prosecutor

Ramsey County Attorney's Office

Case-Ending Decisions of the Ramsey County Attorney's Office (2007–2009)

	2007		2008		2009	
	Absolute number	%	Absolute number	%	Absolute number	%
Adult referrals	5,328	100	5,472	100	5,358	100
Cases charged	3,154	59	2,996	55	2,692	50
Cases declined	2,174	41	2,476	45	2,666	50

Source: Internal statistics of the Ramsey County Attorney's Office

Appendix VI: Abridged Proceedings in the Canton of Basel-City

Application	Failure	Charge	Verdict	Offense	Reason for failure/rejection of application
03/04/2011		04/04/2011	05/19/2011	Commercial fraud (CHF 246,753.00 and EUR 25,000.00)	
03/31/2011	04/04/2011			Narcotic law	Application rejected for reasons of procedural economy and tactical reasons
05/10/2011		07/04/2011	09/23/2011	Theft for financial gain (CHF 222,356.00), attempted coercion	
07/04/2011		08/17/2011	09/29/2011	Narcotic law	
09/12/2011	09/29/2011			Narcotic law, weapons law, robbery, coercion, etc.	Application rejected, because expected sentence exceeds 5 years imprisonment
09/13/2011		11/15/2011		Theft for financial gain, Precious Metals Control Act (CHF 6,500.00)	
09/26/2011		12/05/2011		Theft for financial gain (CHF 22,634.00)	
10/03/2011		11/15/2011		Theft for financial gain, Precious Metals Control Act (CHF 6,500.00)	
10/05/2011		11/15/2011		Theft for financial gain, Precious Metals Control Act (CHF 6,500.00)	

(continued)

DOI 10.1007/978-3-319-04504-7,

Application	Failure	Charge	Verdict	Offense	Reason for failure/rejection of application
10/06/2011	10/21/2011			Narcotic law, theft, attempted theft, attempted robbery, damage to property, handling stolen goods, money laundering, weapons law	Accused person does not agree with the indictment
10/19/2011		11/08/2011		Misappropriation, criminal mismanagement, forgery of a document (CHF 570,069.52)	
10/25/2011				Robbery	
10/27/2011	11/14/2011			Narcotic law	Abridged proceedings failed because no agreement could be reached concerning the sentence
10/31/2011	11/01/2011			Robbery, narcotic law	Application rejected because the prosecution has already written the accusation and the abridged proceedings would have brought an additional expenditure
12/01//2011	12/02/2011			Burglary (theft, unlawful entry, damage to property)	Application rejected because of clear evidence, and, effort for the prosecution is not lower in the abridged proceedings than in the ordinary proceedings

Source: Internal statistics of the Public Prosecutor's Office of the canton of Basel-City

MIX
Papier aus verantwortungsvollen Quellen
Paper from responsible sources
FSC® C105338

If you have any concerns about our products,
you can contact us on
ProductSafety@springernature.com

In case Publisher is established outside the EU,
the EU authorized representative is:
Springer Nature Customer Service Center GmbH
Europaplatz 3, 69115 Heidelberg, Germany

Printed by Libri Plureos GmbH
in Hamburg, Germany